Patagonia Handbook

Janak Jani
& Lucy E Cousins

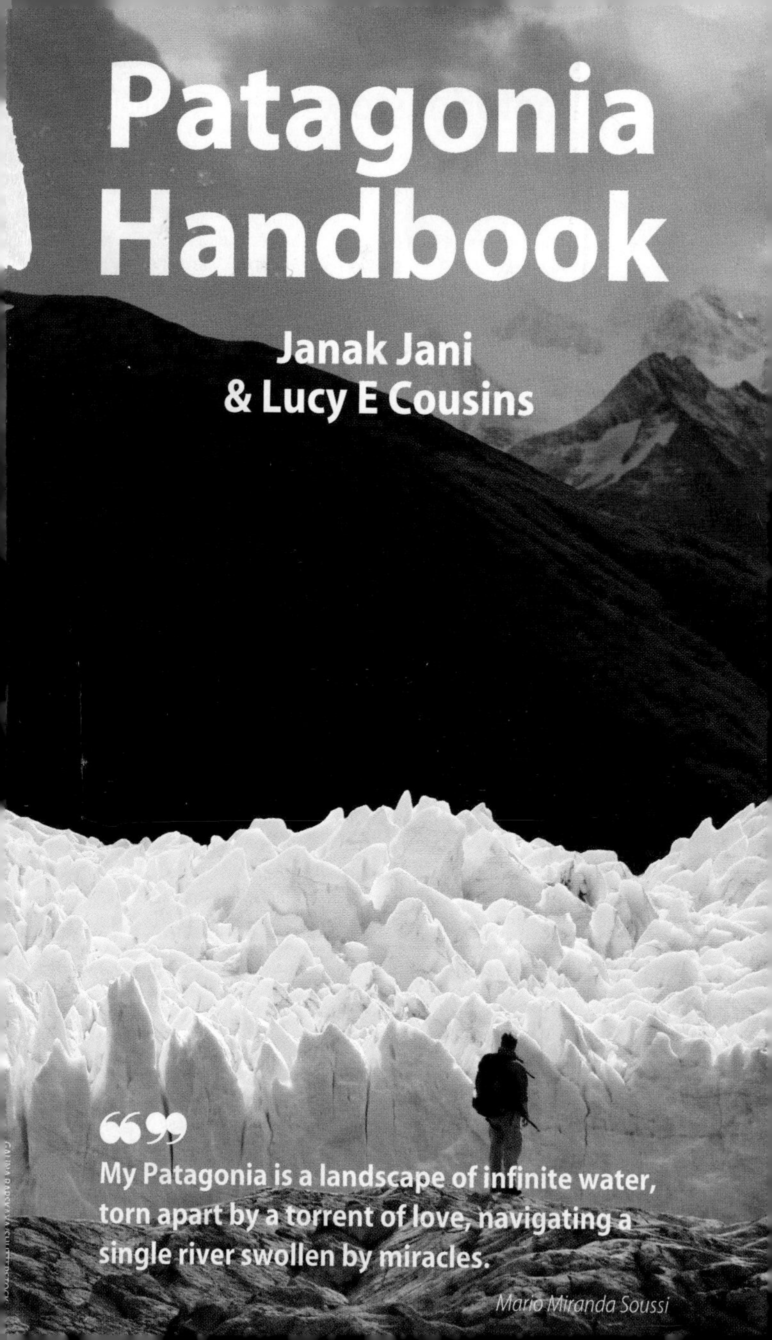

“”

My Patagonia is a landscape of infinite water, torn apart by a torrent of love, navigating a single river swollen by miracles.

Mario Miranda Soussi

Footprint story

It was 1921

Ireland had just been partitioned, the British miners were striking for more pay and the federation of British industry had an idea. Exports were booming in South America – how about a handbook for businessmen trading in that far away continent? The Anglo-South American Handbook was born that year, written by W Koebel, the most prolific writer on Latin America of his day.

1924

Two editions later the book was 'privatized' and in 1924, in the hands of Royal Mail, the steamship company for South America, it became The South American Handbook, subtitled 'South America in a nutshell'. This annual publication became the 'bible' for generations of travellers to South America and remains so to this day. In the early days travel was by sea and the Handbook gave all the details needed for the long voyage from Europe. What to wear for dinner; how to arrange a cricket match with the Cable & Wireless staff on the Cape Verde Islands and a full account of the journey from Liverpool up the Amazon to Manaus: 5898 miles without changing cabin!

1939

As the continent opened up, The South American Handbook reported the new Pan Am flying boat services, and the fortnightly airship service from Rio to Europe on the Graf Zeppelin. For reasons still unclear but with extraordinary determination, the annual editions continued through the Second World War.

1970s

Many more people discovered South America and the backpacking trail started to develop. All the while the Handbook was gathering fans, including literary vagabonds such as Paul Theroux and Graham Greene (who once sent some updates addressed to "The publishers of the best travel guide in the world, Bath, England").

1990s

During the 1990s the company set about developing a new travel guide series using this legendary title as the flagship. By 1997 there were over a dozen guides in the series and the Footprint imprint was launched.

2000s

The series grew quickly and there were soon Footprint travel guides covering more than 150 countries. In 2004, Footprint launched its first thematic guide: *Surfing Europe*, packed with colour photographs, maps and charts. This was followed by further thematic guides such as *Diving the World*, *Snowboarding the World*, *Body and Soul escapes*, *Travel with Kids* and *European City Breaks*.

2009

Today we continue the traditions of the last 87 years that has served legions of travellers so well. We believe that these help to make Footprint guides different. Our policy is to use authors who are genuine experts who write for independent travellers; people possessing a spirit of adventure, looking to get off the beaten track.

JOHNATHAN ESPER/SHUTTERSTOCK

Title page: Up close and personal with Perito Moreno glacier.
Above: Shipwreck on the remote beaches of Tierra del Fuego.

Squeezed between two oceans and split by the tail of the Andes, Patagonia is a land of vast horizons and limitless possibilities. Unvanquished by the conquistadors, it has developed in isolation, attracting brave pioneers, hardy Welsh settlers, Wild West outlaws on the run and Ernesto 'Che' Guevara on a pre-revolutionary jaunt. In northern Patagonia, lakes of emerald surround snow-capped volcanoes and ancient monkey puzzle trees. East of the Andes, sheep roam the Argentine steppe and estancias provide a welcome haven. Head south on the ultimate road trip until, rising up from the flat lands, you see Fitz Roy's spires, or the granite turrets of Torres del Paine. Sculpted glaciers cleave with a roar and the raw power of nature is palpable.
Seals and migrating whales animate the deserted beaches of the Atlantic, while on the Pacific coast, the land splinters into a labyrinth of islets, fjords and looming icebergs. The oceans meet at the tip of Patagonia – the Land of Fire is a final frontier at the end of the world.

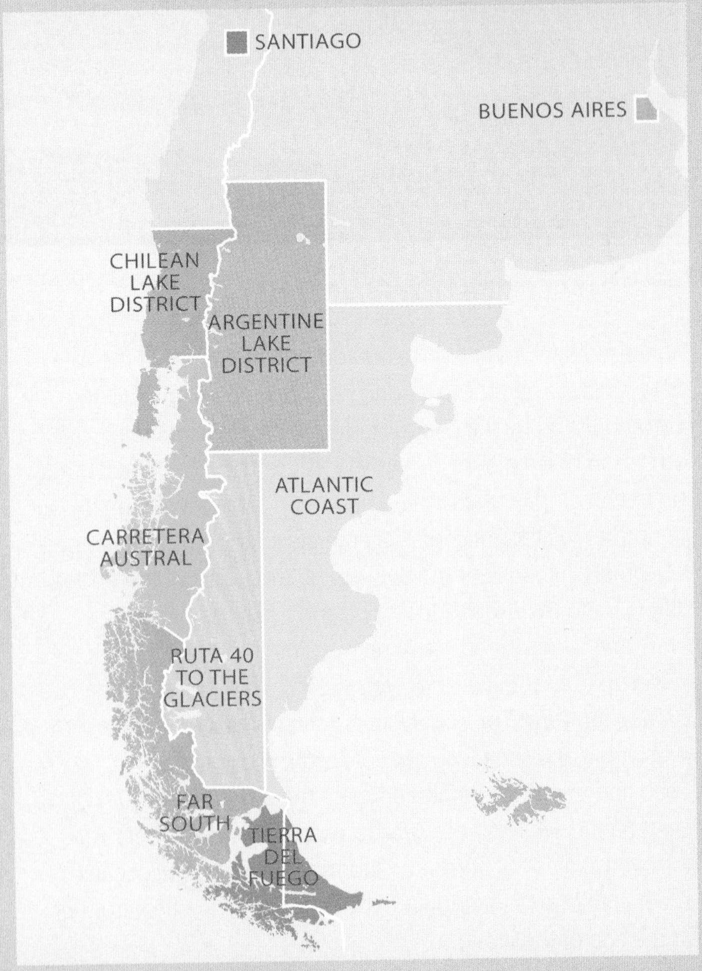

SANTIAGO
BUENOS AIRES
CHILEAN LAKE DISTRICT
ARGENTINE LAKE DISTRICT
ATLANTIC COAST
CARRETERA AUSTRAL
RUTA 40 TO THE GLACIERS
FAR SOUTH
TIERRA DEL FUEGO

Contents

Planning your trip

EDUARDO RIVERO/SHUTTERSTOCK

Cueva de las Manos records one of the earliest human societies; of the more than 800 handprints, all but 31 depict left hands.

Where to go

Possibly the most impressive characteristic of Patagonia is the sense of limitless space and freedom; it takes time to drink in the sheer size of it, the immense skies and the silence. Since it's still a wild and untamed land, allow time for spontaneity – explore a new place mentioned by a local you meet, or take up an offer of hospitality. Also remember that the distances are huge. Pace yourself and don't try and see everything in a short amount of time. Deciding what regions, cities and attractions to visit will be hard as Patagonia offers such diverse geography: snow, mountains, lakes and an endless coastline. Whatever you do, allow more time than you think you'll need. Unless you have unlimited time and money, you'll probably have to accept from the start that you can't see it all. Distances are huge, and it's time consuming to get around. There are daily flights to all the major destinations but most go via Buenos Aires or Santiago. Although there are few trains, there is an efficient and extensive network of long-distance buses which even offer complimentary hot meals.

Buenos Aires is a good start and from there you can head south to the wilds of Argentine Patagonia. Whether escaping like Butch and Sundance, or seeking freedom like the Welsh pioneers, you'll find a liberating expanse of nothing. Head east to Puerto Madryn for amazing marine life or travel the solitary Ruta 40 in Ernesto 'Che' Guevara's tyre tracks. From windy El Calafate, cross an iceberg-strewn lake for breathtaking views of the Southern Ice Field, and later attempt an ice trek on Perito Moreno glacier. Further south, Tierra del Fuego offers the ultimate

PABLO H CARIDAD/SHUTTERSTOCK

BEN BOX/SOUTH AMERICAN PICTURES

Opposite page: A cousin of the llama, the guanaco is indigenous to South America and can be seen roaming wild in Patagonia. **Above**: Punta Arenas, in Chile's Far South.

wilderness and, as you take a boat trip along the Beagle Channel, you'll feel like a true explorer. From there you can follow the Argentine Andes northwards as they stretch along a wonderland of snow-capped mountains, dotted with lakes and lagoons of all shades of blue. Start at picturesque Bariloche: chalet-style hotels, chocolate shops and a backdrop of peaks, where you could hike for a week without getting bored. Along the Seven Lakes visit upmarket San Martín de los Andes or smaller Villa La Angostura or hide out in an estancia to ride the wild lands.

Chilean Patagonia does not have the limitless pampa of its Transandean neighbour. The Pacific side of the Andes is dominated by lush green forests rising up from fractured fjords through fast-flowing rivers and waterfalls, past pristine lakes and smoking snow-capped volcanoes overlooked by the majestic mountain range to the east. In the northern Lake District adventure tourism is easy, with numerous agencies offering a dozen day-long activities in the nearby lakes, rivers, forests and mountains with all the creature comforts of Pucón awaiting you in the evening. For a taste of the real Patagonia head south to the Carretera Austral. The Parque Pumalín is an incredible conservation project with a diverse ecosystem and excellent trails to explore. Towards the Argentine border, Futaleufú has the best whitewater rafting in the southern hemisphere. Further south, the azure waters of Lago General Carrera turn an even more unreal blue as they flow into the broad Río Baker that winds westwards, splitting Patagonia's two enormous ice fields before reaching the sea at Tortel, a unique streetless village where houses are connected by wooden walkways. South of the ice fields is Torres del Paine, whose glaciers and granite towers are the jewel in the crown of Chilean Patagonia.

Itineraries

One week – Argentina

The Argentine Lake District is the most easily accessible region for a short visit. Base yourself near Bariloche and then either go south to the trekking capital, El Bolsón and Parque Nacional Los Alerces, or north to San Martín de los Andes and Pehuenia, to catch a flavour of a different part of the lakes. Alternatively, fly direct from Buenos Aires to El Calafate for access to Parque Nacional Los Glaciares. Visit the famous glacier and if you are game enough, go ice trekking with a qualified guide. From here you can either take a bus to the small town of El Chaltén (four hours) to hike around Cerro Fitz Roy and to breathe in the mountain air, fly on to Ushuaia for the Parque Nacional Tierra del Fuego and the famous Estancia Harberton. Allow time for long bus journeys between each place.

One week – Chile

Take an overnight bus from Santiago to Pucón (there are direct flights in summer) to explore the forests and hills around Lago Villarrica, climbing the famous volcano nearby, doing a day trek in the araucaria forests of Huerquehue or Cañi, braving a day of whitewater rafting and relaxing in natural thermal springs, before flying from Puerto Montt to Puerto Natales, and spending three or four days in Torres del Paine, one of the world's great national parks. If you are up to it,

AGE FOTOSTOCK/SUPERSTOCK

Above: Admiring the view towards Cerro Fitz Roy, Parque Nacional Los Glaciares.
Opposite page: Ancud harbour, Chiloé island.

AGE FOTOSTOCK/SUPERSTOCK

do the W trek, with a backdrop of dark granite peaks and eerie blue glaciers, either camping or staying at the huts along the way.

Two weeks

In two weeks you could fit in both of the above itineraries. Alternatively, use the time to see the extraordinary wildlife at Península Valdés on the Atlantic Coast, including whales in spring (base yourself in Puerto Madryn). Visit the nearby Welsh village of Gaiman and enjoy an afternoon tea. Then fly from Trelew to either Bariloche for the lakes or El Calafate for the glaciers. Two weeks in summer is perfect for exploring the Lake District at length with time for a longer trek, or for visiting two or three different areas. Consider hiring a *cabaña* and hanging out in Butch and Sundance country, or staying at an estancia to try your hand at riding. Or you could cross the border by bus and ferry via Lago Todos Los Santos to explore the area around Lago Llanquihue, where the Osorno volcano provides a spectacular backdrop to the lake. The impressive Petrohué waterfalls are an hour to the east. Activities include horseriding, trekking and sea-kayaking. Another possibility is to head over the Andes via Los Alerces to Futaleufú for a spot of fly-fishing or whitewater rafting and on to the main spine of the Carretera Austral. From Puerto Chacabuco, you may just have time to cruise to the San Rafael glacier in the southern Chilean fjords. If you fly in to Santiago, you could catch a plane south to Puerto Montt or even all the way down to Punta Arenas, in order to hike at Torres del Paine or for access to Tierra del Fuego. For a complete contrast, city lovers should spend 24 hours in Buenos Aires at the end of their trip to enjoy the city life after the wide open spaces.

Three weeks/a month

A month allows you to get a real feel for Patagonia's scale and extraordinary contrasts. You could get off the not-very-beaten track to some remote estancias in Santa Cruz, drive along the isolated Ruta 40 from Los Antiguos to El Calafate or cycle a stretch of the wild Carretera Austral past hanging glaciers, a thousand waterfalls, enchanted forests and fairytale mountains. From Puerto Montt, head north into the lakes, visit the mystical island of Chiloé or take the long ferry south to Puerto Natales. Combine short trips to Península Valdés, the glaciers, Ushuaia and Torres del Paine, ending up in the lake districts to relax, before a short stay in Buenos Aires to finish off the trip.

Patagonia highlights & itineraries

See colour maps at back of book

Parque Pumalín
One of the world's great conservation projects, page 300.

Parque Nacional Los Alerces
Virgin forest, hanging glaciers and perfect hikes, page 143.

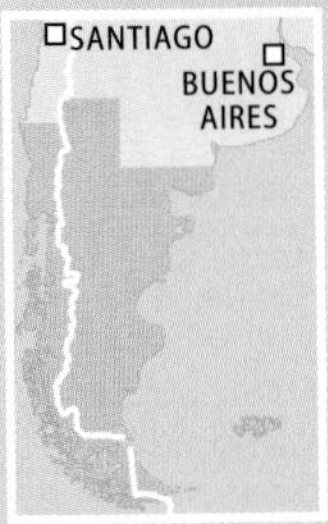

Futaleufú
The southern hemisphere's best white water, page 304.

Carretera Austral
An amazing road trip by jeep or mountain bike, page 295.

Glaciar Perito Moreno
60-m-high walls of ice breaking off into turquoise water, page 195.

Torres del Paine
Trekking between lakes, glaciers and the famous granite towers, page 354.

Pacific Ocean

100 km
100 miles

One week – Argentina
From Bariloche or El Calafate ●→

One week – Chile
From Pucón ●→

Two weeks
From Puerto Madryn or Punta Arenas ●→

Three weeks/a month
From Los Antiguos or Puerto Montt ●→

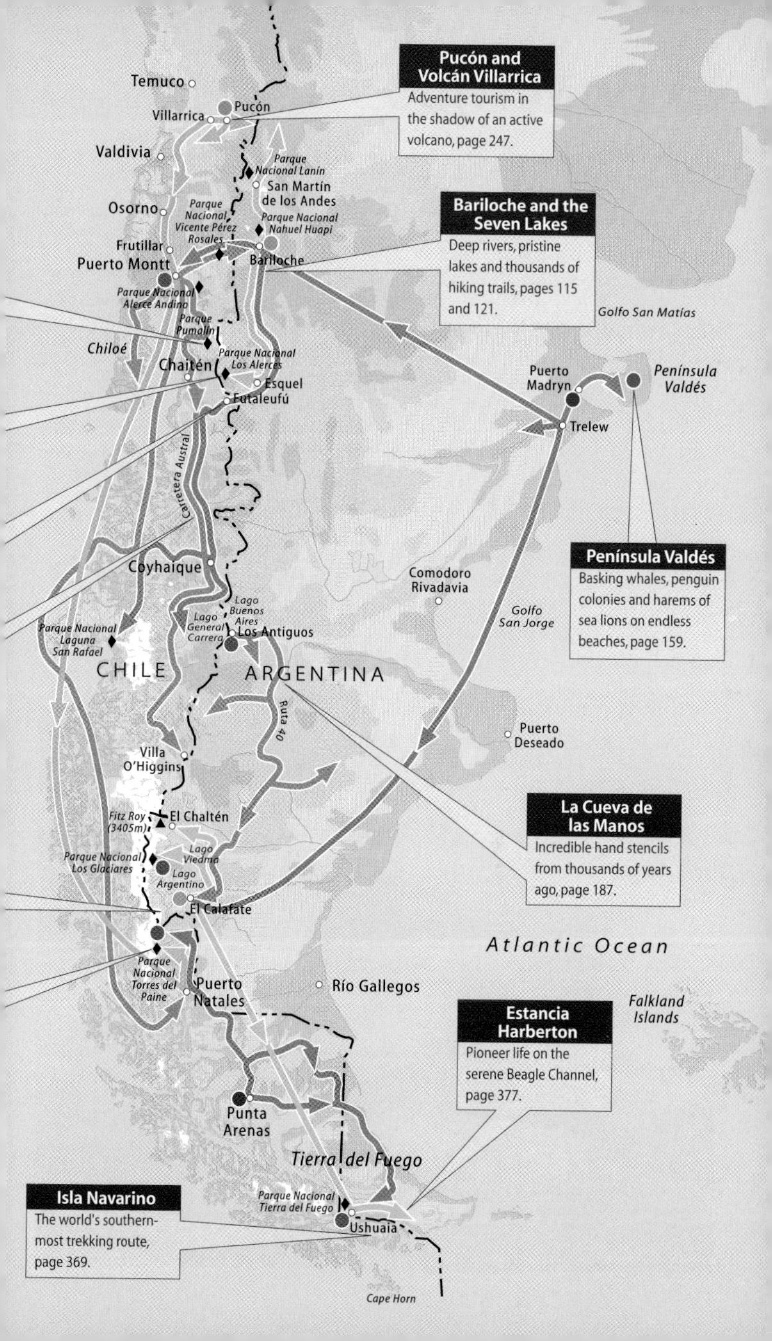

Pucón and Volcán Villarrica
Adventure tourism in the shadow of an active volcano, page 247.
Bariloche and the Seven Lakes
Deep rivers, pristine lakes and thousands of hiking trails, pages 115 and 121.
Península Valdés
Basking whales, penguin colonies and harems of sea lions on endless beaches, page 159.
La Cueva de las Manos
Incredible hand stencils from thousands of years ago, page 187.
Estancia Harberton
Pioneer life on the serene Beagle Channel, page 377.
Isla Navarino
The world's southernmost trekking route, page 369.
Temuco
Pucón
Villarrica
Valdivia
Parque Nacional Lanín
San Martín de los Andes
Osorno
Parque Nacional Vicente Pérez Rosales
Parque Nacional Nahuel Huapi
Frutillar
Puerto Montt
Bariloche
Parque Nacional Alerce Andino
Parque Pumalín
Chiloé
Golfo San Matías
Parque Nacional Los Alerces
Chaitén
Esquel
Futaleufú
Puerto Madryn
Península Valdés
Trelew
Carretera Austral
Coyhaique
Comodoro Rivadavia
Golfo San Jorge
Lago Buenos Aires
Lago General Carrera
Los Antiguos
Parque Nacional Laguna San Rafael
CHILE
ARGENTINA
Ruta 40
Puerto Deseado
Villa O'Higgins
Fitz Roy (3405m)
El Chaltén
Lago Viedma
Parque Nacional Los Glaciares
Lago Argentino
El Calafate
Atlantic Ocean
Parque Nacional Torres del Paine
Puerto Natales
Río Gallegos
Falkland Islands
Punta Arenas
Tierra del Fuego
Parque Nacional Tierra del Fuego
Ushuaia
Cape Horn

six of the best Boat trips

Patagonia is surrounded by two cold-current oceans and its interior is home to myriad lakes, rivers, channels and glaciers. There are hundreds of opportunities to get out on the water whether it be in a large ferry, raft, boat or canoe. Here is a selection of some of the best.

Isla Victoria/Parque Nacional Los Arrayanes

There is no better way to explore Argentina's Lake District than to spend a day on Lago Nahuel Huapi – one of the area's biggest bodies of water. A recommended day trip is to visit Isla Victoria and Parque Nacional Los Arrayanes by boat. Several companies offer this trip and nearly all leave from the pier just outside the famous Llao Llao resort, 20 km from the centre of Bariloche. From there you'll do a 25-km round trip visiting the beautiful Isla Victoria and stopping off for a boardwalk in the Parque Nacional Los Arrayanes. One of Argentina's national trees, the arrayan is characterized by its bright orange bark and even has its own national park named after it.

Perito Moreno glacier

One of the 'don't miss' boat trips of your visit to Patagonia must be the short 30-minute ferry ride to visit the Perito Moreno glacier, near El Calafate. Departing from near the boardwalk viewing area, the two-storey boat will edge you closer and closer to the 60-m-high glacier walls. You'll be able to see the apartment building-sized sheer ice shards crack and fall into the aquamarine slush below. The sound will reverberate in your chest and the splashes may even reach you.

Antarctica

The most famous, most expensive and well-worth-it boat trip of them all. Bobbing away on a huge icebreaker bound for the land of ice has got to be one of the most

DALE MITCHELL/SHUTTERSTOCK

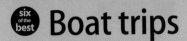

GEN PRODUCTIONS/SHUTTERSTOCK

Opposite page: Perito Moreno, the world's only advancing and retreating glacier.
Above: A ship crossing the rough Drake Passage to Antarctica.

incredible experiences money can buy – and it will cost a lot! If you have the time, bypass the usual routes and arrive in Ushuaia to look for a last-minute berth. Most cruise ships will sell discounted fares to people who can leave straight away. Trawl through the travel agents as you save a huge amount. Then hold on tight while you cross the Drake Passage via Cape Horn. Make sure you bring proper clothes, a decent camera and some rum to warm you up.

Patagonian channels

This four-day journey has long been a backpackers' classic. The Navimag ship is not a cruise liner. The ferry's primary purpose is to transport cargo between the Lake District and southern Patagonia, but accommodation is comfortable enough, from private cabins to 22-berth economy quarters. If you are lucky with the weather you will have amazing views of fjords and jagged coastlines dotted with innumerable tiny islands. Penguins, seals, dolphins and rare blue whales can occasionally be sighted and a detour is usually made to the face of one of two huge glaciers. In poor weather, retreat to the bar, enjoy a game of bingo and meet potential travelling companions for the trek around Torres del Paine.

Lago O'Higgins

While this journey is an attraction in itself – a catamaran trip from the southern point of Chile's Carretera Austral to the face of the imposing O'Higgins glacier, its importance lies in the fact that it also makes a stop at the tiny port of Candelario Mancilla on the southern side of the lake. Thanks to this crossing, the Carretera Austral is no longer a dead end, opening up new horizons for intrepid travellers and extending one of the world's greatest self-contained cycling routes south through Argentina's Parque Nacional Los Glaciares and on to Tierra del Fuego.

Crucero Australis between Punta Arenas and Ushuaia

This is a spectacular four-day luxury cruise around the fjords and islets south of Punta Arenas in the Magellan Straits, Beagle Channel and Southern Ocean. There are two weekly departures from Punta Arenas in season, stopping to explore remote glaciers and wildlife colonies en route to Isla Navarino and Ushuaia. The return cruise from Ushuaia takes a slightly shorter route back to Punta Arenas and is a little cheaper. Both journeys make a stop at the end of the world at Cape Horn.

six of the best Treks

Home to some of the world's most pristine and untouched national parks, Patagonia is a trekker's delight. So why not get out there and experience what the Southern Andes has to offer? Here is a little taste of some of the most rewarding treks in this part of the world.

El Chaltén

Cornered between jagged peaks, and snow-laden valleys, El Chaltén (known as the capital of trekking) is the perfect base for one- and two-day treks in the area. Follow the signs from the edge of town and in less than 30 minutes you'll be completely alone on a mountain pass overlooking deep blue lakes and fertile valleys. Return to your hostel and relax in one of the lively restaurants in town. The treks range from easy to challenging.

Cerro Colorado

The Argentine Lake District links seven large beautiful lakes with camping grounds and trekking trails. Lush green vegetation, unspoilt geography and mirror-perfect lakes attract hoards of trekkers each year. El Bolsón in the south is a mecca for trekkers, but can get very busy. The best thing to do is search out less crowded trekking areas. Located north of San Martín de los Andes, the trail to Cerro Colorado (1774 m), named for its bright red soil, is less travelled and therefore more attractive than some other treks. The trek is intermediate and takes about five to six hours return.

Volcán Lanín

One of the world's most beautiful mountains, Lanín (3776 m), is geologically one of the youngest volcanoes (though now extinct) of the Andes. To reach the summit is a challenging three-day climb, with two *refugios* at 2400 m (both without charge), sleeping 14 to 20 people. The views are spectacular but the climb will keep you out of breath. Because of its relative accessibility, the risks are often underestimated: crampons and ice axe are essential.

GRAHAM S.KLOTZ/SHUTTERSTOCK

AGE FOTOSTOCK/SUPERSTOCK

SEBASTIEN BURE/SHUTTERSTOCK

Opposite page left: Mountains near El Chaltén, including the famous Fitz Roy.
Opposite page right: Spring near Volcán Villarrica.
Above: Hiking the W, Torres del Paine.

Volcán Villarrica

If you have ever wanted to climb an active volcano, the Volcán Villarrica hike is probably the most popular trek in Chile and for good reason. This snow-covered perfect cone of a mountain is a stiff half-day trek with ice axe and crampons to the fore. No previous experience is required but you do need to be reasonably fit. On still days you can peer from the summit into the crater and see molten lava bubbling away, while in the distance half a dozen other volcanoes loom up from lakes and forests. The best part is still to come. Forget walking back down – lie back and slide, toboggan style.

The W – Torres del Paine

Trek for days through some of the most spectacular scenery in Patagonia among iceberg-filled lakes, valleys, waterfalls, glaciers, all the time dominated by the imposing giant granite plugs of the Paine Massif. Experience four seasons in a few hours and have a warm bed and a cooked meal at the end of an arduous day's trekking. If you want to get away from the crowds for a real Patagonian wilderness experience pack up your tent and head off around the north side of the mountains on the week-long circuit trek.

Dientes de Navarino

Named after the teeth-like chain of mountains around which the trail leads, this three- to five-day fully self-contained route is only for hardy, dedicated trekkers. The southernmost trekking route on Earth passes through the Patagonian wilds where trees grow at a 45° angle, sculpted by the shattering westerly winds and where the paths often have a gradient to match. The route will take you past semi-frozen lakes and fast-flowing rivers replete with beaver dams. Views from the passes will leave you speechless with their beauty: the thick forests below and the Beagle Channel to the north with the outline of Tierra del Fuego in the distance, while a solitary condor circles overhead; this really is trekking at the end of the world.

six of the best Wildlife encounters

Península Valdés
Seventeen kilometres from the windy coastal town of Puerto Madryn, Península Valdés is one of the world's most prolific nature reserves and a UNESCO World Heritage Site. The peninsula is home to a startling variety of birds, hundreds of elephant seals, penguins, sea lions and, of course, southern right whales. The best way to visit is by taking a day trip from Puerto Madryn, but those who are a little more adventurous can stay at one of the peninsula's wonderful estancias within the nature reserve itself.

Beagle Channel
Tierra del Fuego is a birdwatcher's paradise and the best way to immerse yourself in it is to visit the Beagle Channel. Take a boat trip to Isla Martillo to see the resident colony of Magellanic penguins and on the way you'll see numerous other sea birds. The variety is endless and includes the black-browed albatross as well as several cormorants and petrels. Visit the Tierra del Fuego national park to see forest-dwelling birds as well.

Punta Tumbo
Located four hours south of Puerto Madryn on Argentina's southeastern coast is the Reserva Provincial Punta Tumbo, home to the largest penguin nesting site on the continent. Over half a million Magellanic penguins come here to breed and raise their young every year. The best time to see them is from September to mid-March. There are so many you will have to try hard not step on one.

Torres del Paine
Although better known for its trekking and awesome landscapes, Torres del Paine national park, also a UNESCO Biosphere Reserve, has a plethora of interesting wildlife. Head away from the well-trodden trekking paths and you may well come across a

SEBASTIEN BUREL/SHUTTERSTOCK

Nesting Magellanic penguins can be seen in both Chilean and Argentine Patagonia.

Above: Spring is the best time to see the southern right whale in Península Valdés on the Atlantic coast.
Right: A rare glimpse of the endangered huemul.

family of spitting guanacos, the ostrich-like Ñandu, chilla and culpeo foxes and, if you are exceptionally lucky, you may catch a glimpse of the elusive puma. Birdlife includes upland geese, pygmy owls, southern lapwings, flamingos and the majestic Andean condor. Specialized wildlife tours are available and accommodation ranges from simple campsites to decent, if expensive, hotels.

In search of the huemul

This shy and beautiful mountain deer has adapted to survive in the rugged terrain of Chilean Patagonia. Pushed by human pressures to the brink of extinction, there are perhaps only 1500 left in the wild. If you are lucky you will catch one peeking at you from behind some foliage along the Carretera Austral, but your best bet is in one of two protected areas: the Reserva Nacional Río Claro, just to the west of Coyhaique, or the Reserva Nacional Tamango, a short distance from Cochrane. Park wardens will accompany you to help make sure you sight one of these elusive creatures.

Parque Marino Fransisco Coloane

This marine conservation area lies off the southeast coast of Isla Carlos III in the Magellan Straits. The area is home to a wide range of birdlife, including penguins, petrels, cormorants and kingfishers, while the sea is home to fur seals, sea lions and sea elephants. Without question, though, the main attraction is the variety of whales in these waters. Killer whales, humpback whales, sei whales and minke whales are all sighted regularly. Tours are available from Punta Arenas and, while expensive, are an unforgettable experience.

When to go

The southern hemisphere summer lasts from December to March. The weather can be positively warm in the Lake District and along the Carretera Austral but the far south suffers from very strong winds at this time. January and February are when Argentine and Chilean schools have their holidays, so the main tourist centres (Bariloche, San Martín, El Calafate, Pucón, Puerto Varas, Puerto Natales and Ushuaia) can get impossibly busy and prices rise significantly. You should book flights, buses and accommodation as far ahead as possible. However, you'll still find plenty of less popular centres offering a good range of accommodation, close to the national parks. December and March are good months for trekking but be aware that transport services may not be running as frequently in rural areas and that the weather will be more unpredictable. April is a spectacular time to visit both the Lake District and further south, as the leaves turn golden and scarlet and days can be clear and windless. Rainfall tends to be higher in these months, but the tourist areas are quieter. Easter week is a major holiday in Argentina, however, so book well ahead. Much of southern Patagonia closes down entirely for winter; accommodation is often shut from May to October, transport services run a reduced schedule and many passes across the Andes are closed by snowfall. However, if you like skiing, then this is the season to visit. The best months are July and August, although many resorts have snow from late June and until September. Ski resort accommodation and transport are generally well organized but bear in mind that July is a school holiday. The rich marine life on the Atlantic Coast is most exciting in the spring, with whale spotting possible from Península Valdés at its best in September and October. Elsewhere, there are fewer tourists and cheaper accommodation than during the summer but still enough daylight hours for trekking. Winds in the far south are less fierce at this time of year.

Activities

	J	F	M	A	M	J	J	A	S	O	N	D
Fish for Patagonian trout and salmon	★	★	★	★							★	★
See southern Patagonia's penguins	★	★	★						★	★	★	★
Go skiing in the Lake District						★	★	★	★	★		
Spot whales in Península Valdés (Argentina)										★	★	
Enjoy the autumn colours of the Argentine Lake District				★	★	★						
Ice trek on the Perito Moreno glacier (Argentina)	★	★	★	★	★	★	★	★	★	★	★	★
Cycle the Carretera Austral (Chile)	★	★	★									★
Trek in Torres del Paine national park (Chile)	★	★	★	★					★	★	★	★
Climb Volcán Villarrica (Chile)	★	★	★	★	★	★	★	★	★	★	★	★
Relax in thermal pools (Chile)	★	★	★	★	★	★	★	★	★	★	★	★

Rainfall and climate charts

Buenos Aires

Month	Average temperature in °C max	min	Average rainfall in mm
Jan	29	17	79
Feb	28	17	71
Mar	26	16	109
Apr	22	12	89
May	18	08	76
Jun	14	05	61
Jul	14	05	56
Aug	16	06	61
Sep	18	08	79
Oct	21	10	86
Nov	24	13	84
Dec	28	16	99

Bariloche

Month	Average temperature in °C max	min	Average rainfall in mm
Jan	22	07	19
Feb	22	07	14
Mar	19	05	39
Apr	14	03	41
May	10	01	90
Jun	07	00	122
Jul	07	-01	106
Aug	08	-01	70
Sep	11	00	51
Oct	14	02	33
Nov	18	04	20
Dec	20	06	17

Puerto Madryn

Month	Average temperature in °C max	min	Average rainfall in mm
Jan	28	14	10
Feb	27	13	16
Mar	25	11	15
Apr	20	07	16
May	15	04	20
Jun	12	01	16
Jul	12	01	09
Aug	15	20	11
Sep	17	04	10
Oct	21	07	12
Nov	24	10	11
Dec	27	12	09

Santiago

Month	Average temperature in °C max	min	Average rainfall in mm
Jan	30	12	00
Feb	30	11	00
Mar	27	10	03
Apr	23	07	09
May	18	05	28
Jun	15	04	43
Jul	15	02	46
Aug	16	04	30
Sep	18	05	15
Oct	22	07	07
Nov	26	09	03
Dec	28	11	01

Pucón

Month	Average temperature in °C max	min	Average rainfall in mm
Jan	24	09	117
Feb	25	09	22
Mar	22	08	43
Apr	18	06	63
May	14	06	112
Jun	12	05	157
Jul	12	04	111
Aug	13	04	91
Sep	15	04	66
Oct	17	06	66
Nov	20	07	49
Dec	22	09	35

Puerto Varas

Month	Average temperature in °C max	min	Average rainfall in mm
Jan	18	08	09
Feb	18	08	93
Mar	17	07	99
Apr	13	05	143
May	12	04	234
Jun	09	03	224
Jul	09	02	229
Aug	10	03	209
Sep	12	03	146
Oct	13	04	121
Nov	14	06	12
Dec	17	07	103

Coyhaique

Month	Average temperature in °C max	min	Average rainfall in mm
Jan	18	07	16
Feb	18	06	13
Mar	16	05	28
Apr	12	02	35
May	08	01	43
Jun	04	-02	56
Jul	04	-02	48
Aug	07	-01	43
Sep	10	00	26
Oct	12	02	23
Nov	14	04	15
Dec	16	06	21

Punta Arenas

Month	Average temperature in °C max	min	Average rainfall in mm
Jan	14	07	36
Feb	14	07	28
Mar	12	06	41
Apr	09	03	41
May	07	02	43
Jun	04	00	33
Jul	03	-01	33
Aug	05	00	33
Sep	08	02	28
Oct	10	03	23
Nov	12	04	28
Dec	13	06	31

Río Grande

Month	Average temperature in °C max	min	Average rainfall in mm
Jan	15	07	20
Feb	14	07	30
Mar	12	05	20
Apr	09	02	30
May	05	00	30
Jun	02	-02	20
Jul	02	-02	20
Aug	04	-01	10
Sep	07	01	20
Oct	10	02	20
Nov	12	04	30
Dec	13	06	30

A.JELLEMA/SHUTTERSTOCK

Sport and activities

PABLO H CARIDAD/SHUTTERSTOCK

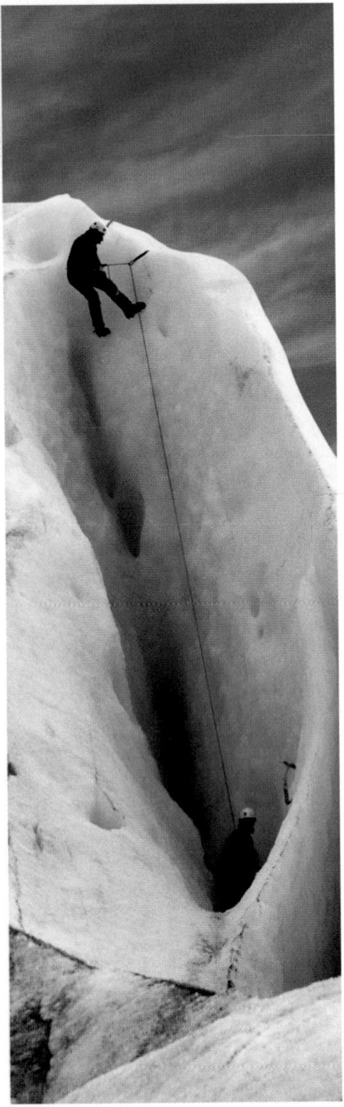

Patagonia might have been designed for adventure tourism. The spectacular geography offers a huge range of outdoor activities, from rafting and skiing to some of the finest trekking and fishing in the world. The infrastructure for 'soft' adventure tourism, such as half-day rafting on a Grade III river or a day spent climbing a volcano, is particularly good in the lake districts of Argentina and Chile. Remote estancias in Argentina are appealing bases for horse riding and wildlife spotting, while further south the terrain promises hardcore self-contained trekking and mountain biking. It is important to check the experience and qualifications of any agency offering excursions to remote areas. In Chile, CATA (Consejo de Autoregulación de Aventura), T02-235 3646, www.catachile.cl, is an association of reputable agencies, which regulates adventure tourism in the country. It works closely with the national park authority, CONAF, T02-236 1416, www.conaf.cl (see page 45).

Canopy

ⓘ www.canopypucon.cl (in Spanish only). Other tour operators are listed in relevant chapters throughout the book.

This activity, imported from Central America, has become all the rage in Chile in recent years. It consists of gliding down zip lines from tree to tree through native forests. Runs are of different lengths and range from easy, child-friendly lines to vertigo-inducing descents from 60 m high. Check your equipment carefully as some operators are more responsible than others. Head for Pucón, Puerto Varas, Ensenada, Volcán Osorno and Cruce Maitén (on the Carretera Austral).

SAM CHADWICK/SHUTTERSTOCK

Opposite page: Ice climbing on the Campo de Hielo Sur.
Above: The long road south ... cycling through Patagonia.

Climbing

ⓘ **Club Andino**, www.caba.org.ar, in Argentina. Also see www.parques nacionales.gov.ar. In Chile, **Federación de Andinismo de Chile**, www.feach.cl. **Dirección de Fronteras y Límites**, 5th floor, Ministerio de Relaciones Exteriores, Bandera 52, Santiago, T02-6714210. For permission to climb some mountains in border areas; apply 3 months in advance. **Federación de Andinismo de Chile**, Almte Simpson 77A, Santiago, T02-2220888, www.feach.cl. Permits, expeditions and equipment hire for members in Chile. At the same address is the **Escuela Nacional de Montaña** (**ENAM**), T02-2220799, www.enamchile.cl. Rock- and ice-climbing courses and the Carnet de la Federación de Chile, required to climb mountains in CONAF-controlled areas.

The Andes offer great climbing opportunities. Popular climbs include Volcán Lanín and Cerro Tronador in the Argentine Lake District, as well as Cerro Fitz Roy and the northern part of Parque Nacional Los Glaciares around El Chaltén, where you can also go ice trekking. One of Argentina's most popular ski resorts, Cerro Catedral, is an excellent base for climbing in summer. In Chile, the sheer walls of the Torres del Paine attract climbers year round. In the northern Chilean Lake District near Pucón is Volcán Villarrica, while in the southern section is Volcán Osorno and Cerro Picada.

For the inexperienced, Vía Ferrata, near Pucón, is an easy introduction to climbing a sheer rock face with the aid of metal hand-holds embedded in the mountainside.

Argentine mountain areas all have a local Club Andino, which sells maps, advises on routes and provides guides. See page 134 for Club Andino Bariloche in the Lake District.

Cycling and mountain biking

ⓘ Two useful websites are www.andes cross.com and www.exchile.com.

Mountain biking is extremely popular in both Argentine and Chilean Patagonia, particularly on descents from peaks around Bariloche. Not only is the area surrounding Bariloche spectacular but the Parque Nacional Los Alerces offers lush, picturesque trails. Longer routes include the Siete Lagos in the Lake

HEMIS.FR/SUPERSTOCK

Above: The best way to enjoy the vast Patagonian pampas.
Opposite page: The famous Ruta 40.

District and south along the iconic Carretera Austral, through the Parque Nacional Los Glaciares and on to Tierra del Fuego. Other notable areas include Parque Nacional Villarrica and Puerto Varas. Most towns will have a bicycle repair shop but don't count on these for more than basic repairs. Take a tool kit and as many spare parts as you can carry.

Fishing

ⓘ **Asociación Argentina de Pesca con Mosca**, T011-4773 0821, www.aapm.org.ar, for fishing licences in Argentina. In Chile, the **Asociación de Pesca y Caza (Sernap)**, San Antonio 427, 8th floor, Santiago, T02-639 1918, www.sernapesca.cl. Also consult the national park authorities. See also www.aapm.org.ar, www.anglerstdf.com.ar, www.argentinachile flyfishing.com, www.flyfishingtravel.com and www.magallanesflyfishing.com.

Patagonia has arguably the finest fly fishing (*pesca con mosca*) in the world, set in unbelievably beautiful surroundings. In the Argentine Lake District watch out for world-class trout (rainbow, brown and brook) from November to April, particularly in Junín de los Andes, called the trout capital of Argentina and with some of the country's best fly fishing. In Chile, Pucón, in the northern Lake District, is also good. Fishing near the Carretera Austral is excellent; including Futaleufú, Coyhaique with the best fishing in Chile and, further south, Río Baker. Look for huge brown trout on both sides of Tierra del Fuego, such as Río Grande in Argentina and Lago Blanco in Chile. Along the Atlantic coast try your hand at shark fishing (bacota and bull shark). All rivers in Argentina are 'catch and release' and to fish anywhere in Argentina you need a permit costing US$5 a day, US$15 a week, US$50 a year. In Chile, a licence is needed and is usually available at the local municipalidad or some tourist offices.

Horse riding

ⓘ See www.estanciasdesantacruz.com, www.horseadventures.com.ar, www.horsebackridingchile.cl.

This is a great way to get to the heart of Patagonia's rural tradition and to see some

Road trips

The sheer size and remoteness of Patagonia means that long-distance road trips are an exhilarating way of exploring the region. What's more, the terrain of endless steppes interrupted by rivers, gorges and gullies is also ideal for off-roading. The two most popular road trips in Argentine Patagonia are the Ruta de los Siete Lagos (Seven Lakes Route) in the Lake District and the endless Ruta 40, a little-used highway running directly south from Bariloche to El Calafate. The Seven Lakes Route is stunning at any time of year. It is a curling, curving road that rings the seven interconnecting lakes of this region. The views are panoramic and breathtaking every step of the way. Visit friendly small towns, stay in wonderful luxury hotels or cheaper wooden cabins and sample local produce (look out for the locally brewed beer, handmade ice creams and delicious jams). Otherwise, if you are looking for something a little more challenging, head south along a part of the lengthy Ruta 40 (which actually starts in La Quiaca on the Bolivian border). For most, the desolate plains south of the Lake District hold immense appeal and they are best accessed by the lonely Ruta 40. Take plenty of food and fuel as houses, let alone towns, are sparse. It is a surreal and unique experience.

In Chilean Patagonia, one road trip stands head and shoulders above the rest: the Carretera Austral, or southern highway. The main spine winds through rough gravel for over 1000 km of dramatic scenery. If the forests of the northern section seem too green to be real the lakes and rivers further south are an even more extraordinary hue. Driving will give you the liberty to stop and marvel at the landscape whenever it takes your fancy, and if you want a different perspective, hitchhike instead and enjoy its beauty from the back of a pickup, a truly exhilarating experience.

Tips Hiring a 4WD vehicle costs from US$1500 for 10 days. Buy road maps from service stations or the Automóvil Club Argentino in Argentina, Copec service stations or the Automóvil Club de Chile. If you are planning to take your vehicle across the border you will need special permission. Arrange this with your car hire company in advance as it can take time to organize. Expect to pay around US$100 for the privilege. For road trips in remote regions, make sure you take extra fuel and food. Also remember that even in summer the temperatures at night can drop severely.

MICHAEL BOYNY/PHOTOLIBRARY

Useful websites

- Automóvil Club Argentino, www.aca.org.ar
- Automóvil Club de Chile, www.automovilclub.cl

MUSHIN44/SHUTTERSTOCK

Glacier treks are an increasingly popular activity.

varied and spectacular scenery. In Argentina expect to pay around US$10 per hour and always check the horses are tame and in good condition. Many estancias in Argentina offer opportunities for riding.

In Chile the scenery is more rugged, such as in Torres del Paine, and options range from gallops across the windswept plains of the south to the breathtaking thick-forested valleys or high up in the Andes around Cochamó.

Day rides are offered in all the major tourist centres but a multi-day trip is one of the best ways of getting off the beaten track. Pucón in the northern Chilean Lake District, Puerto Varas further south, around the Carretera Austral and Puerto Natales in the far south are some of the main trekking areas in Chile.

Skiing

ⓘ www.interpatagonia.com, www.andesweb.com, www.southamericaskiguide.com, www.exchile.com, www.powderquest.com.

The season runs from mid-June to mid-October, but dates vary between resorts. Argentine Lake District resorts such as Cerro Catedral near Bariloche and Cerro Bayo (Villa la Angostura), La Hoya (Esquel) and Cerro Chapelco (San Martín de los Andes) are very well run; facilities in the far south of Chile are basic. However, skiing on an active volcano looking down on three huge lakes (Villarrica/Pucón) or skiing within sight of the sea at the end of the world (Cerro Castor near Ushuaia) or just with a sea view (Cerro Mirador near Punta Arenas) are memories that will truly last a lifetime. Other resorts include Antillanca and Volcán Osorno in the Chilean Lake District and El Fraile (Coyhaique) on the Carretera Austral.

Trekking

ⓘ www.visit-chile.org, www.parquesnacionales.org.ar, www.fitzroyexpediciones.org, www.hieloyaventura.com.

The whole of the Andes region offers superb opportunities for both short and long treks in varied landscapes. The best season for walking is December to April. National parks in both the Argentine and Chilean lake districts offer spectacular hikes on well-marked routes with maps, guides and plenty of information, such as the Parque Nacional Lanín and Parque Nacional Nahuel Huapi in Argentina and the Parque Nacional Huerquehue (Pucón) and Reserva Forestal Cañi in Chile. It's also worth exploring the lesser known lake regions, such as Pehuenia in the north, Parque Nacional Los Alerces and the Seven Lakes in Chile.

The most dramatic trekking is around Cerro Fitz Roy near El Chaltén in the Parque Nacional Los Glaciares where you can walk on the Southern Ice Cap and climb glaciers, as well as in Parque Nacional Torres del Paine and Parque Nacional Tierra del Fuego.

In Chile, over 1000 km of hiking opportunities have been opened up by the building of the Carretera Austral, including the Parque Pumalín and its millennial alerce forests and the four- and five-day circuits around the fairytale castle of Cerro Castillo, though heavy rainfall can be a drawback here outside summer. The Sendero de Chile (www.senderodechile.cl) is a series of walking routes dotted all the way from the Peruvian border to Tierra del Fuego, a long-term project with new stretches opening regularly. Further south still is Isla Navarino with the Dientes de Navarino and the southernmost trekking route on Earth.

You should be reasonably fit before attempting any hikes in Patagonia, especially overnight treks in the far south. Remember that conditions can be harsh at these latitudes and never overestimate your own abilities. Take account of the season, weather and terrain and make sure you are properly equipped. If trekking with a tour operator or guide, check their credentials, equipment and experience. Avoid hiking alone, even in tourist areas, and always register with *guardaparques* or other authorities before you set out. Hikers have little to fear from the animal kingdom – in fact, you are much more of a threat to the environment than vice versa.

Watersports

ⓘ Details of companies offering tuition and equipment hire are listed in relevant chapters throughout the book.

Patagonia has plenty of water and lots to do including canoeing, scuba diving, waterskiing, windsurfing, jet-skiing and sailing. The tourist resorts in both lake districts, such as Bariloche and Río Aluminé in Argentina and Lago Villarrica and Lago Llanquihue in Chile, offer a wide range of watersports.

Whitewater rafting

ⓘ www.politur.com, www.kayakchile.net, www.aguaventura.com, www.exchile.com. Details of companies are listed in relevant chapters throughout the book.

Rafting is generally well organized and equipment is usually of high quality. Access to the headwaters of most rivers is easy. Beginners might be more comfortable in the calmer waters of the Río Petrohué or Río Baker, while adrenalin junkies will want to head for Futaleufú with long stretches of Grade V rapids including the infamous Cañón del Infierno (Hell Canyon). Also check out Río Aluminé and Río Manso (Bariloche) in the Argentine Lake District and Río Trancura (Pucón) in Chile. Tours are operated by several agencies. Choose with care as some of the cut-price operators also cut corners on safety. Rafts should carry no more than six people plus guide.

Sea kayaking

ⓘ www.kokayak.com, www.yakexpediciones.cl. Other tour operators are listed in relevant chapters throughout the book.

This has become a popular activity in the Golfo de Ancud between Chiloé and Hornopirén on the Chilean mainland. Several companies offer day tours but for an unforgettable experience go for a week navigating between fjords and islands, visiting isolated hot springs and swimming with dolphins and sea lions.

Family travel in Patagonia

Argentine Patagonia

Covering almost a third of Argentina, this vast, empty and hauntingly beautiful region is ripe for adventure. If you only have time for visiting one part of Argentinian Patagonia set your sights on Los Glaciares national park, a rugged melange of Andean peaks and giant glaciers that oozes wilderness yet has enough tourist infrastructure to keep families happy. The lakeside resort of El Calafate makes an ideal base for icy escapades to the creaking, groaning snout of the 60-m-tall Perito Moreno glacier. You can also go hiking, horse riding and fishing. Although rather far flung, Tierra del Fuego is also an excellent place to travel with kids. You arrive at the small city of Ushuaia where, each Austral summer, a steady trickle of tourists join cruise ships bound for the Antarctic Peninsula – just two days' voyage across Drake's Passage. But there's plenty to do in and around Ushuaia itself. Excellent museums trace the city's history, from the hardships faced by shipwreck survivors and the indigenous Yámana people to the settlement's early role as a prison. You can also hike in the ancient and mysterious beech forests of Tierra del Fuego national park and take boat trips on the Beagle Channel to spot rare wildlife, such as the flightless steamer duck which propels itself across the surface on stubby wings. Finally, there's Península Valdés, a spectacular wildlife haven jutting from the Patagonian mainland near the town of Puerto Madryn. Southern right whales gather here between June and mid-December to mate and give birth, while Magellanic penguins congregate in one of the largest colonies in South America. The beaches are positively squirming with elephant seals, sea lions and fur seals. Pups born between August and November add to the beach hullabaloo, but things reach fever pitch in March when orca whales surf on to the beach to seize unsuspecting youngsters.

Wild encounters

Where to see penguins if you can't afford an Antarctic cruise?

Rising from the Straits of Magellan, a short boat ride from Punta Arenas, Magdalena Island hosts around 60,000 pairs of Magellanic penguins. Sit quietly and these endearing little creatures will hobble right up to you. Their behaviour is endlessly fascinating – from excavating nesting burrows to braying like donkeys. Few passport stamps evoke that 'ends of the Earth' feeling more than the one you get upon making landfall at Cape Horn. However, the southernmost point of the Americas is surprisingly easy to reach. Departing on four-day voyages between Ushuaia and Punta Arenas, the cruise ship *Mare Australis* (www.australis.com) makes weekly visits throughout the summer. This weatherbeaten outpost, notorious for its ship-swallowing gales and distinctly unfriendly seas, has a permanently manned lighthouse, a chapel and boardwalks.

Chilean Patagonia

The Chilean Lake District has a wide range of activities and attractions and is a popular holiday destination for Chilean and Argentine families alike. There are lots of easy hikes and many of the national parks have special short interpretive trails. On a rainy day, visit the volcanic caves south of Pucón, while if the sun comes out have

EDUARDO RIVERO/SHUTTERSTOCK

The famous narrow-gauge steam train, the Old Patagonian Express, known as La Trochita, leaves from Esquel.

a day relaxing on one of the lakeside beaches. In the southern Lake District a pleasant day tour can be made around Lago Llanquihue visiting the waterfall at Las Cascadas and the German-influenced village of Frutillar and its historical museum. In winter ski down the slopes of Volcán Osorno or, for a glimpse of wildlife in summer, a day trip can be made to see the penguins on Chiloé.

Further south, Torres del Paine is the showcase national park on the Chilean side of Patagonia. The iconic, cloud-snagging towers of Torres del Paine are a magnet for walkers, while there are a range of excursions on offer, from horse riding and boat trips to estancia visits and exploring the Milodon Cave – the object of Bruce Chatwin's quest in his classic travelogue, *In Patagonia*.

Don't miss ...

▸▸ **Wildlife** Península Valdés and Punta Tumbo are a wildlife wonderland for kids. Walking 2 cm away from a Magellanic penguin or feeling the splash from a southern right whale are experiences children will love.

▸▸ **Trains** Although Argentina doesn't have a domestic rail network there are a few train rides that are well worth the effort. Two highlights are the tiny Tren del Fin del Mundo (www.trendelfindelmundo.com.ar), which transports you from Ushuaia to the nearby national park, and the Old Patagonian Express, known as the 'Tronchita', which still carries passengers on a short journey through the leafy Lake District.

▸▸ **Watersports** Depending on the age of your children, the Lake District offers some fun on the water. For the younger ones, try a ferry ride on one of the seven lakes, and for older children, book in canoeing, kayaking and even whitewater rafting.

How big is your footprint?

Travel to the furthest corners of the globe is now commonplace and the mass movement of people for leisure and business is a major source of foreign exchange and economic development in Patagonia. At the same time there is clearly a downside. This is as true in undeveloped and pristine areas (where culture and the natural environment are less 'prepared' for even small numbers of visitors) as in major resort destinations. Resort location and construction can destroy natural habitats and restrict traditional rights and activities.

Travel and tourism can have beneficial effecrs. Patagonia's national parks are part funded by receipts from visitors. Travellers can promote the patronage and protection of important heritage sites through contributions via entrance and performance fees. They can support small-scale enterprises by staying in locally run hotels and hostels, eating in local restaurants and by purchasing local goods, supplies and arts and crafts.

UK organizations such as the Centre for Environmentally Sustainable Tourism (CERT; T01268-795772) and Tourism Concern (T020-7753 3330, www.tourismconcern.org.uk) now offer advice on destinations and sites that have made commitments to conservation and sustainable development. Generally these are larger mainstream destinations and resorts, although efforts are being made to provide information on smaller operations too. Ecotourism has expanded astronomically in Patagonia over the past decade and is probably the fastest-growing sector of the travel industry today, providing access to a vast range of destinations and activities. While the eco-authenticity of some operators needs to be interpreted with care, there is a huge demand and also chances to support worthwhile conservation and social development initiatives.

Organizations such as Tourism Concern (see above), Planeta (www.planeta.com), the International Eco-Tourism Society (T001-802-447 2121, www.ecotourism.org) and Conservation International (T001-202-429 5660, www.conservation.org) have begun to develop ecotourism projects and their websites are an excellent source of information. Additionally, Earthwatch (T01865-311601, www.earth watch.org) and Discovery International (T020-7229 9881, www.discoveryinitiatives.com) offer opportunities to participate directly in scientific and development projects throughout the region.

Go green:

- Although distances are huge in Patagonia, travelling by long-distance buses can be a better option than flying not only for the environment, but also on your pocket. Buses are generally cheaper, offer hot meals and comfortable reclining leather seats and can work out better for your schedule.
- In shops and supermarkets around Patagonia, you will be given a plastic bag even for the smallest of purchases. If you don't need it, just say no.
- Camping and trekking has a major impact on the environment. Before you travel to Patagonia buy some ecological soap and detergent (which can be hard to find in South America) that won't hurt the environment.
- If camping, always use a camping stove to cook on; never use an open fire. Sudden gusts and changes in wind direction can have terrible consequences. In one unfortunate recent incident thousands of hectares of forest were burned down in Torres del Paine by an unwitting backpacker.

Responsible travel

- Where possible choose a destination, tour operator or hotel with a proven ethical and environmental commitment – if in doubt, ask.
- Spend money on locally produced (rather than imported) goods and services, buy directly from the producer or from a 'fair trade' shop, and use common sense when bargaining – the few pounds you save may be a week's salary to others.
- Use water and electricity carefully – travellers may receive preferential supply while the needs of local communities are overlooked.
- Learn about local etiquette and culture – consider local norms and behaviour and dress appropriately for local cultures and situations.
- Protect wildlife and other natural resources – don't buy souvenirs or goods unless they are clearly sustainably produced and are not protected under CITES legislation.
- Always ask before taking photographs or videos of people.
- Consider staying in local accommodation rather than foreign-owned hotels – the economic benefits for host communities are far greater and there are more opportunities to learn about local culture.
- Make a voluntary contribution to Climate Care, www.co2.org, to counteract the pollution caused by tax-free fuel on your flight.

DABOOST/SHUTTERSTOCK

Sea lions in Patagonia

Patagonia on page and screen

Books to read

Viaje a la Patagonia Austral, by Francisco 'Perito' Moreno (Editorial Elefante Blanco, ARG), is the gripping true story of the famous Perito Moreno, a young man who went exploring into the 'unclaimed' areas of Patagonia in the 1800s. He was captured by locals, survived and went on to claim a large portion of Patagonia for Argentina.

In *Travelling with Che: The Making of a Revolutionary* (Newmarket Press, US), Alberto Granado, Ernesto Guevara's travelling partner, tells his version of their journey together. This book will give you an alternative view of the well-worn tale.

Cabo de Hornos, by Fransisco Coloane (Editorial Aguilar, CHI), is a series of evocative short stories detailing the harsh lives of the early European settlers who came to live on the fjords and islands of southern Patagonia.

The Last Cowboys at the End of the World, by Nick Redding (Random House, US), is a quirky and highly readable account of the dying breed of gauchos along the Carretera Austral.

Films to watch

Bombón El Perro (2004) is about a middle-aged Argentine man in Patagonia whose luck changes when he suddenly becomes the owner of a pedigree dog.

Historias mínimas (2002) follows three people (and a baby) who set out on seemingly everyday journeys. Their stories intertwine amid the spectacular backdrop of Patagonian landscapes.

The Take (2004) looks at the struggle of workers all over Argentina who took control of their factories after the owners walked out during Argentina's financial crisis in 2001.

Mi Mejor Enemigo (2005) is a tragicomedy about a platoon of young Chilean conscripts and their encounter with a platoon of Argentinian counterparts in the wilds of Patagonia during the Beagle Channel conflict of 1978.

La Fiebre del Loco (2001) is about the *loco*, a small mollusc in danger of extinction but highly prized by the Japanese who pay handsomely for this Patagonian delicacy. The seasonal ban on its exploitation is lifted for a few days and all hell breaks loose in a small fishing village.

La Frontera (1991) is about a Santiago teacher who is exiled to a desolate coastal village for the crime of protesting against the Chilean military dictatorship.

Essentials

Contents

Footprint features

Border crossings

Getting there

Air

Unless you are arriving from the Falkland Islands, it is not possible to fly directly to Patagonia from outside Argentina or Chile. Instead you must choose to fly into either Buenos Aires' **Ezeiza International Airport** (EZE; see page 60) or Santiago's **Aeropuerto Arturo Merino Benitez** (SCL; see page 214) and pick up onward transport there. There are several flights a day between Santiago and Buenos Aires, operated by **LanChile**, **Aerolíneas Argentinas**, **Air Canada** or the new Brazilian airline, **Gol**.

Fares vary from airline to airline and according to the time of year. Discounted fares are offered through specialist agencies (see page 35) but always check the reservation with the airline concerned to make sure the flight still exists. Note that citizens of Albania (US$30), Australia (US$62), Canada (US$132), Mexico (US$23) and the USA (US$131) are charged a one-off reciprocal entry tax on arrival in Chile, valid for the lifetime of the passport.

Baggage Long-haul flights generally allow one piece of luggage of up to 23 kg, or two pieces of 23 kg for flights from or via the USA. These limits may not strictly enforced if the plane is not full, so if you know you are over the limit, arrive early. However, if you're planning on catching a connecting flight, bear in mind that weight limits for internal services are usually only 20 kg for economy class, and for some flights on small aircraft within Patagonia can be as little as 10 kg.

Flights from Europe

The only direct flight from the UK to **Buenos Aires** is with **British Airways**, www.ba.com, which touches down briefly in São Paulo and takes 14 hours. This is also the fastest way to get to Patagonia from the UK. From Buenos Aires you can fly on to Bariloche, El Calafate or Santiago in Chile. All other carriers stop in a European city, where you have to change planes, and the overall journey takes anything from 18 to 24 hours. Alternatively, there are daily connecting flights on one of the American carriers via New York or Miami. It is impossible to fly directly to **Santiago** from London, so connections have to be made with **British Airways** or **LanChile**, www.lan.com, via Buenos Aires; **Air France**, www.airfrance.com, via Paris; **Iberia**, www.iberia.com, or **Lan-Chile**, via Madrid; **Lufthansa**, www.lufthansa.com, via Frankfurt; **Swiss**, www.swiss.com, or with one of the American carriers via New York, Atlanta or Miami.

Flights from North America

Aerolíneas Argentinas, www.aerolineas.com.ar and other South American and North American airlines fly to **Buenos Aires** from Miami, New York, Washington, Los Angeles, San Francisco, Atlanta, New Orleans, Dallas and Chicago. **Air Canada** www.aircanada.com and LanChile fly from Toronto and Montreal. **LanChile** flies to **Santiago** from Miami (nine hours), New York (12 hours) and Los Angeles (via Mexico City and Lima) and offers connections with sister airlines from Vancouver via Los Angeles, or from Toronto via New York. Other direct flights are provided by **American Airlines**, www.aa.com, and **Delta**, www.delta.com.

Packing for Patagonia

You can buy hiking gear in Buenos Aires or Santiago. However, imported items can be prohibitively expensive. Prices are higher in El Calafate and El Chaltén, so unless you buy before you head south, it's best to bring the essential items with you, including a waterproof jacket, comfortable walking boots and a lightweight fleece top. If you plan to do any outdoor activities, also pack a warm hat, gloves, thermal underwear, windproof and waterproof trousers, wool or fleece jumpers, shorts, and walking socks. In El Chaltén complete hiking gear can be hired for around US$20 a day.

Wear a pouch under your clothes for your money and passport and bring a padlock if you're planning to stay in youth hostels. Carry a photocopy of your passport at all times. You'll need a universal plug adaptor if you're bringing any electrical equipment. A torch can be useful, and a folding knife is handy for camping. You'll need high-factor sun protection cream (particularly in the far south in spring), sunglasses and insect repellent.

Flights from Australia, New Zealand and South Africa

Aerolíneas Argentinas and **Qantas** (www.qantas.com.au) fly to **Buenos Aires** from Sydney (via Auckland). **LanChile/Air New Zealand**, www.airnewzealand.com, or **Aerolíneas Argentinas** (via Buenos Aires) fly from Auckland to Santiago. **South African Airways**, www.flysaa.com, flies to Buenos Aires.

Discount flight agents

UK

Journey Latin America, www.journeylatin america.co.uk, see page 54.

Just the Ticket, Level 2, 28 Margaret St, London W1W 8RZ, T08700275076, www.just theticket.co.uk. Ticket agency, excellent deals.

STA Travel, Priory House, 6 Wrights Lane, London W8 6TA, T08701-600599, www.statravel.co.uk . Specialists in low-cost student/youth flights, tours, insurance.

Trailfinders, 194 Kensington High St, London W8 7RG, T020-7938 3939, www.trailfinders.com. Good deals to Latin America.

North America

Air Brokers International, 685 Market St, Suite 400, San Francisco, CA 94105, T01-800-883 3273, www.airbrokers.com. Consolidator and specialist on RTW and Circle Pacific tickets.

STA Travel, 5900 Wilshire Blvd, Suite 2110, Los Angeles, CA 90036, T1-800-78104040, www.sta-travel.com. Also branches in New York, San Francisco, Boston, Miami, Chicago, Seattle and Washington DC.

Travel CUTS, 187 College St, Toronto, ON, M5T 1P7, T1-800-667 2887, www.travel cuts.com. Student discount fares, IDs and other travel services. Branches in other Canadian cities.

Travelocity, www.travelocity.com. Online consolidator.

Australia and New Zealand

Flight Centre, 82 Elizabeth St, Sydney, T13 3133 www.flightcentre.com.au; 205 Queen St, Auckland, T09-309 6171. Branches in other towns and cities.

STA Travel, T134 782, www.statravel.com.au; 702 Harris St, Ultimo, Sydney, and 256 Flinders St, Melbourne. In New Zealand: 10 High St, Auckland, T09-366 6673. Also in major towns and university campuses.

Getting around

Air

Onward flights to Patagonia

From Buenos Aires All domestic flights from Buenos Aires (as well as some flights to/from neighbouring countries) are handled from Jorge Newbery Airport, known as **Aeroparque**, situated 4 km north of the centre of Buenos Aires (see page 60). **Manuel Tienda León** ⓘ *T0800-888 5366, www.tiendaleon.com*, runs efficient buses between the two airports via the city centre every 30 minutes, 0600-0100, US$13. They have a desk inside the arrivals hall, where you can also book a *remise* taxi, US$40. From Aeroparque, the main air routes to Patagonia are to Bariloche (US$100 one way, 2½ hours), to San Martín de los Andes (US$125, two hours), to Trelew (US$100, two hours), to El Calafate (US$125, 3¼ hours) and to Ushuaia (US$180, three hours 20 minutes).

From Santiago You will go through customs and immigration in international arrivals before transferring to the domestic section of the same terminal. **LanChile** (www.lan.com) flies between Santiago and major cities under the banner **Lan Express. Sky Airline** (www.skyairline.cl) also serves the main destinations but less frequently. Return flights are often cheaper than one-way tickets. The most important routes from Santiago are to Temuco (from US$70 return, 1½ hours), Valdivia (summer only, from US$105, 1½ hours), Osorno (from US$77, 2½ hours), Puerto Montt (from US$87, 1¾ hours, Balmaceda (Coyhaique, from US$146, 2½ hours, can be cheaper with stopover in Puerto Montt) and Punta Arenas (from US$170, 4½ hours).

Air services in Argentina

There are now just two scheduled operators for internal flights: **Aerolíneas Argentinas**, www.aerolineas.com, which has 178 flights to Patagonia each week, and **LanChile**, www.lan.com. This means that there are fewer airline seats than hotel beds available, and you must book well in advance. In addition, Buenos Aires' airports are currently experiencing problems with delays to internal flights; there's nothing you can do about this, but take a book and be patient. All flights to Patagonia start in Buenos Aires, though there are often connections from El Calafate to Bariloche and Ushuaia – ask your airline for details. El Chaltén does not have an airport, but is easily reached in four hours by bus from El Calafate. In addition the army airline **LADE**, T0810-810 5233 in Argentina, T+54 11-5129 9000, www.lade.com.ar, provides a weekly service connecting several towns in Patagonia, which is useful to avoid having to go back to Buenos Aires.

It's wise to leave some flexibility in your schedule to allow for bad weather, which may delay flights in the south. Most provincial airports in Argentina have a tourist information desk, banking facilities and a *confitería* (cafeteria) as well as car hire. There are usually minibus services into the nearest town and taxis are available. Don't lose your baggage ticket; you won't be able to collect your bags without it.

Air services in Chile

Departure tax for domestic flights is US$10.50 each way and is included in the price of the ticket. **LanChile**, www.lan.com, is the main domestic operator. It sells a **South America Airpass**, which can be used on all **LAN** routes throughout South America. This is only recommended if you are planning on doing several long-distance flights; visit the website in order to assess the price implications; domestic air taxes are payable in addition for each flight. The airpass must be purchased abroad at the same time as a transatlantic ticket to South America. It is valid for six months, and must include at least three single flights; there is no maximum. Note that the airpass is more expensive if used in conjunction with an international flight with another carrier. Reservations should be made in advance; flight dates can be altered without penalty but route changes incur a charge of US$30 per change. A refund (minus 10%) can be obtained prior to travel.

Note Flight times may be changed without warning; always double check the time of your flight when reconfirming. The most important Patagonian routes are Puerto Montt to Balmaceda or Punta Arenas; Punta Arenas to Puerto Williams, Ushuaia or Porvenir and Puerto Natales to El Calafate (summer only). **Sky Airline** operate three weekly flights between Balmaceda (Coyhaique) and Punta Arenas. Destinations in the far south are served by **DAP**, www.dap.cl, based in Punta Arenas. **LanChile** also flies from Santiago to Port Stanley on the Falkland (Malvinas) Islands via Punta Arenas and Río Gallegos.

Rail

The only long-distance train within Patagonia runs from **Viedma** on the Atlantic coast to **Bariloche** in the Lake District (see page 136). Patagonia's best-known train, *La Trochita*, www.latrochita.org.ar, made famous by Paul Theroux as the *Old Patagonian Express*, is a purely tourist affair that departs from Esquel in the southern Lake District for the remote Mapuche station at Nahuel Pan (see page 142). Even more touristy is the *Tren del Fin del Mundo*, www.trendelfindelmundo.com.ar, which travels from Ushuaia to the Tierra del Fuego national park (see page 377).

Road

Internal flights are fast, but not green, so consider long-distance buses for some of your journey. Argentina and Chile have very comfortable buses that travel overnight, enabling you to sleep. However, the 24-hour bus ride along the Ruta 40 from Los Antiguos to El Chaltén has fantastic views that you'll want to stay awake for. On long bus journeys, carry small packs of tissues and bottled water, as toilets on buses can be unpleasant. Also take a jumper to combat the fierce air conditioning.

Buses in Argentina

The country is connected by a network of efficient long-distance buses, which is usually the cheapest way of getting around. They run all year, are safe and comfortable, and travel overnight, which saves time on long journeys. The main operators are **Andesmar**, www.andesmar.com, **TAC**, T011-4312-7012 and **Via Bariloche**, www.viabariloche.com.ar. Book seats a day in advance in January. Regional services to tourist destinations within Patagonia tend to be limited after mid-March.

When choosing a bus, bear in mind that *común* buses have lots of stops (*intermedios*), are uncomfortable and not recommended for long journeys. *Semi-cama* have slightly reclining seats, meals and a toilet onboard. *Coche-cama* have fully reclining seats, meals, a toilet, only a few stops and are worth the small extra expense for a good night's sleep.

Bus companies may give discounts to students with ID, and to teachers with proof of employment. Discounts aren't usually available December to March. Make sure your seat number is on your ticket. Luggage is safely stored in a large hold at the back of the bus, and you'll be given a numbered ticket to reclaim it on arrival. *Maleteros* take the bags off the bus, and may expect a small tip – 50 centavos or a peso is fine. For general transport information, consult www.argentinatotal.com.ar.

Buses in Chile

Bus services in Chile are frequent and comfortable. Buses tend to be punctual, arriving and leaving on time. Along the Carretera Austral, however, services are far less reliable, less frequent and usually in minibuses. Services improve again between Punta Arenas and Puerto Natales in the far south. In addition, there are long-distance international services from Santiago to Buenos Aires, from Osorno to Bariloche, from Coyhaique to Comodoro Rivadavia and from Punta Arenas to Río Gallegos and Ushuaia.

When choosing a bus in Chile, remember *clásico/salón-ejecutivo* are comfortable enough for daytime travel but are not ideal for long distances. *Semi-cama* have more leg room and fewer stops but are 50% more expensive. *Salón-cama* are similar to a *coche-cama* in Argentina (see above), and *cama premium* have flat beds. *Salón-cama* are the most spacious, with dinner available on overnight services. They are 50% more expensive than *semi-cama*. The premium service with fully reclining seats runs between Santiago and the lakes (30% more expensive than *salón-cama*).

Apart from at holiday times, there is little problem getting a seat on a long-distance bus and you only need to reserve ahead in high season. Prices are highest from December to March but competition between bus companies means you may be able to bargain for a lower fare, particularly just before departure; discounts are also often available for return journeys. Students may also get discounts out of season. Most bus companies will carry bicycles, but may ask for payment.

Car

Hiring a car is an excellent idea if you want to travel independently and explore the more remote areas of Patagonia, although it can be complicated to take a hire car across the border between Argentina and Chile (see box, page 39). The most important routes in Argentine Patagonia are Ruta 40, which runs along the west side of the Andes and faster Ruta 3, which runs down the Atlantic coast. Santiago is linked to the Chilean Lake district by the paved toll road, the **Pan-American Highway** (or Panamericana), marked on maps as Ruta 5, which runs all the way from the Peruvian frontier south to Puerto Montt. The **Carretera Austral**, a mostly *ripio* (gravel) road marked on maps as Ruta 7, runs south of Puerto Montt, punctuated by three ferry crossings as far as Villa O'Higgins, from where the southbound boat does not carry cars. There is an excellent paved road between Punta Arenas and Puerto Natales from where there are two *ripio* roads to Torres del Paine.

Generally, main roads are in good condition but on some *ripio* roads, particularly south of Puerto Montt, a high-clearance, 4WD vehicle is required, as road surfaces can degenerate to earth (*tierra*). Most roads in Patagonia are single lane in each direction. There's little traffic and service stations for fuel, toilets, water and food are much further apart than in Europe and the US, so always carry water and spare fuel and keep the tank full. Safety belts are supposed to be worn, if fitted.

Car hire Car hire is slightly more expensive in Chile than in Argentina. There are few hire cars available outside the main tourist centres in either country, although small towns will have cheaper deals. Hiring a car from one place and dropping it off in another is rarely

Crossing between Argentine and Chilean Patagonia

The main routes between Argentine and Chilean Patagonia are by boat and bus between Bariloche and Puerto Montt in the Lake District; by road from El Calafate to Puerto Natales and Torres del Paine or by road and ferry from El Calafate via Río Gallegos to Tierra del Fuego. There are many other crossings (some little more than a police post), which are detailed throughout the guide. See also http://www.difrol.cl/html/104a.htm. For some crossings, prior permission must be obtained from the authorities. Note that passes across the Andes may be blocked by snow from April onwards. See also Customs and duty free, page 47, and Visas and immigration, page 56.

→ Crossing the border is not a lengthy procedure unless you're on a bus, when each individual is checked. It is your responsibility to ensure that your passport is stamped in and out when you cross borders. Do not lose your tourist card; replacing one can be inconvenient and costly. Immigration and customs officials are generally friendly, helpful and efficient, however, the police at Chilean control posts a little further into the country can be extremely bureaucratic.

→ Tourist card holders returning across a land border to Argentina will be given a further 90 days in the country. Visa holders should check regulations with the Chilean/Argentine embassies.

→ Fruit, vegetables, meat, flowers and milk products may not be imported into Chile; these will be confiscated at all borders. Searches are thorough.

→ There are often no exchange facilities at the border so make sure you carry small amounts of both currencies. Remember to change your watch if crossing the border between early March and September/October.

practical since very high penalties are charged. The multinational companies (**Hertz**, **Avis**) are represented all over Patagonia but local companies may be cheaper and usually just as reliable. You must be 25 or over in Argentina and 22 or over in Chile to hire a car; a national driver's licence should be sufficient. Vehicles may be rented by the day, the week or the month, with or without unlimited mileage. Rates quoted should include insurance and VAT but ALWAYS check first. Note that the insurance excess, which you'll have to pay if there's an accident, can be extremely expensive. Check the vehicle carefully with the hire company for scratches and cracks in the windscreen before you set off, so that you won't be blamed for them on your return. Hire companies will take a print of your credit card as their guarantee instead of a deposit but are honourable about not using it for extra charges. Ensure that the hire company gives you the vehicle's ownership papers, which have to be shown at police and military checks.

Fuel Petrol (known as *nafta* in Argentina, *petróleo* in Chile) becomes more expensive in Chile the further south you go, but in Argentine Patagonia, fuel prices are a third lower than in the rest of the country. Diesel (*gasoil* in Argentina, *bencina* in Chile) is available in both countries and is much cheaper than petrol. Cars in Argentina are increasingly converting to gas GNC (*gas natural comprimido*), which is about 25% the cost of petrol. However, you will not be able to hire a GNC car outside Buenos Aires and fuel stations offering GNC are very limited in Patagonia. What's more, if you're taking a gas-run vehicle from Argentina into Chile, check that it will run on Chilean gas; there is a difference.

Crossing the border Obtain an authorization form from the hire company. This is exchanged at the outgoing border control for another form, one part of which is surrendered on each side of the border. If you plan to leave more than once you will need to photocopy the authorization. Make sure the number plate is etched on the car windows and ensure that the hire company gives you the vehicle's ownership papers, which have to be shown at police and military checks. At some crossings, you must pay for the car's tyres to be sprayed with pesticides.

Useful contacts

Automóvil Club Argentino (ACA), Av Libertador Gen San Martín 1850, 1425 Buenos Aires, T011-4808 4000, www.aca.org.ar. This motoring association has fuel stations, hotels and *hosterías*, as well as a useful route service. Members of affiliated associations can use ACA facilities and get discounts.

Automóvil Club de Chile, Av Andrés Bello 1863, Santiago, T02-431-1000 (calling from Chile), www.automovilclub.cl. Car-hire agency with discounts for members or affiliates. Also provides road maps.

Touring Club Argentino, Esmeralda 605 and Tucumán 781, 3rd floor, Buenos Aires T011-392-6742. Similar travel services to ACA but no service stations.

Hitchhiking

Hitchhiking is relatively easy and safe (although you should always exercise caution) and often involves an exhilarating ride in the back of a pickup truck. However, traffic is sparse in the south, and roads in places like Tierra del Fuego rarely see more than a few vehicles per day.

Taxis, colectivos and remises

Taxis usually have meters and can either be hailed in the street or booked in advance, although they tend to be more expensive when booked from a hotel. Surcharges are applied late at night and at weekends. Agree fares beforehand for long journeys out of city centre or for special excursions; also compare prices among several drivers.

Collective taxis (*colectivos* in Chile, *remise* in Argentina) operate on fixed routes (identified by numbers and destinations) and are a good way of getting around cities. They are usually flagged down on the street corner, but make sure you have small notes and coins to pay the driver. In Chile, *colectivos* also operate on some inter-urban routes, leaving from a set point when full; they compete favourably with buses for speed but not for comfort.

Sea

Ferries

In the Lake District, ferries on Lago Nahuel Huapi and Lago Frías in Argentina link with bus and ferry services across Lago Todos Los Santos in Chile (see page 124). There are also services across Lago Pirihueico. In the south of Chile, maritime transport is very important. The main transporter/car-ferry operators are Naviera Austral, **Transmarchilay** and **Navimag**. **Puerto Montt** is the hub for boat services south, with regular sailings to Chiloé, Chaitén, Puerto Chacabuco, Puerto Natales (one a week, year round) and the San Rafael glacier. **Punta Arenas** is the departure point for ferry services to Porvenir and Puerto Williams on Tierra del Fuego as well as the Crucero Australis service to Ushuaia. Reservations are essential for the ferries in high summer. Details of all routes are given under the relevant chapters.

Accommodation tips

Hotels

- Sometimes hotels offer cheaper deals through their websites. Always check.
- Before you book check where the hotel is located. Sometimes, such as in El Calafate, there are some fabulous hotels but they are quite a distance out of town and without a car you won't enjoy the stay quite so much.
- Note that most hotels, even the five-star ones in Argentina, do not provide tea- and coffee-making services, nor do they always have minibars.
- Some good websites for hotels are www.tenriverstenlakes.com, www.designsuites.com and www.newage-hotels.com (all in English).

Hostels

- Check hostel descriptions in this guidebook, speak to other travellers or search websites like www.hostelz.com or www.tripadvisor.com; some hostels look much better on their websites than in real life.
- In Patagonia most hostels either don't have cutlery or the take a deposit to use it. Best to buy your own set and guard it.
- In the north, the linen provided by some hostels can be old and thin. If you can, buy a pillowcase and sleeping bag liner that can act as a set of sheets if need be.
- Some good websites for hostels are www.latinbackpackers.com, www.hostels.com and www.hihostels.com (all in English).

Sleeping

Tourist destinations in Patagonia and, especially in the Lake District, have a good range of **hotels** and **hosterías**, although on the Chilean side, there is good-value budget accommodation and some relatively high-end hotels, but not much choice in between. Hosterías have less than 20 rooms; rather than being lower quality, they are often family-run and can be very good value in more remote areas. Residenciales and **hospedajes** tend to provide simpler accommodation, often with full board offered. **Hostales** traditionally offer dorm beds but most also have double rooms for couples and may also offer services geared specifically towards foreign backpackers, such as internet access, tours, bicycle hire, etc. **Cabañas** are more or less well-equipped self-catering cottages, cabins or apartments, often in superb locations. They're very popular among Chilean and Argentine holiday-makers and are a great option if you have your own transport and are travelling in a small group. Camping is popular and there are many superbly situated sites with good facilities, although official Chilean campsites can be surprisingly expensive, with no reductions for single travellers or couples. There are also **refugios** (refuges) for walkers in national parks and reserves; standards of comfort and facilities vary hugely. Camping wild is generally safe, even in remote areas, but always consult *guardaparques* (park rangers) before pitching your tent in a national park.

Accommodation in Argentina is excellent value for visitors from Western countries, while accommodation in Chile is just a little more expensive. Prices also tend to be higher in Santiago and the further south you go from Puerto Montt. However, single travellers do not come off too badly in southern Chile, as many *hospedajes* charge per person (although you may have to share your room). The Chilean government waives the VAT charge (IVA 19%) for

Sleeping price codes

LL over US$200 and **L** US$151-200 Top-quality hotels, mostly offering very well-equipped rooms with dataports, plus a restaurant, bar, pool, health suite, business facilities and excellent service. Also luxurious estancias (see below) and several hotels in Torres del Paine, where you're paying for location not quality.
AL US$101-150 and **A** US$66-100 Comfortable hotels with good facilities, airport transfers, tours, information and buffet breakfasts. Rooms should have TV, minibar, safe and a/c. Estancias in these categories may have simpler accommodation than an ordinary hotel, but activities are usually included.
B US$46-65 and **C** US$31-45 The quality of hotels and *hosterías* in these categories varies widely but most are reliable, with en suite facilities and breakfast.
D US$21-30 and **E** US$12-20 Good quality residenciales and *hospedajes*, especially in rural areas, where a lovely setting makes up for the lack of facilities; breakfast included. Also official Chilean youth hostels www.hostellingcl.achatj.html, which charge rates per person; IYHA or Chilean YHA card required.
F US$7-11 and **G** under US$7 Simple *residenciales* and *hospedajes*, sometimes very basic, with shared bathrooms, but usually supplying a towel and toilet paper. In Chile rates are charged per person (pp). Also beds in Argentine youth hostels (www.argentinahostels.com, www.hostels.org.ar), either in dorms (often mixed), with large communal bathrooms (US$7) or doubles (from US$10). Some have cooking facilities, internet access, lockers and laundry. At the very bottom end are Chilean *albergues*: usually just floor space in a school during the summer. They are very cheap (US$2-4 per person), very noisy and offer no privacy.

bills paid in dollars (cash or traveller's cheques) at designated high-end hotels, but some establishments may get round this apparent discount by offering you a low dollar exchange rate. Prices often rise in high season (*temporada alta*), especially during January and February, but off-season you can often bargain for a discount (*descuento*) if you are staying for two or more days. The ski resorts are more expensive during the winter school holidays. During public holidays or high season you should always book ahead. Few places accept credit cards. In both countries you should establish clearly in advance what is included in the price before booking. For further information on accommodation, see: www.patagonia-chile.com, www.patagoniachile.cl, www.interpatagonia.com, www.backpackerschile.com, www.backpackersbest.cl, and www.i-escape.com.

Estancias

Estancias are the huge sheep and cattle ranches found all over Patagonia, and many of them now welcome paying guests. They offer a marvellous way to see remote landscapes and enjoy horse riding and other activities, as well as providing an authentic experience of rural Argentine life.

You'll need to stay at least two or three nights to make the most of an estancia, as they are often off the beaten track. Hire a car, or arrange with your hosts to be picked up in the nearest town. Estancias can be more expensive than hotels, but they offer a unique experience and, once you add the activities, meals and wine, are often good value. Expect to pay at least US$120 per night.

Eating price codes

¥¥¥	over US$12	¥¥	US$7-12	¥	under US$7

Prices for a two-course meal for one person, excluding drinks or service charge.

Estancias vary enormously in style and activities: **Cristina** offers total isolation and comfort; **Helsingfors** is a giant sheep farm close to glaciers; **Eolo** and **Alta Vista** are luxury estancia-style hotels on the steppe; **Viamonte** and **Harberton** on Tierra del Fuego are infused with history, while on the mainland, **Monte Dinero** has a colony of Magellanic penguins on its doorstep. For more information consult www.estanciasdesantacruz.com, www.tierrabuena.com.ar, www.south trip.com and www.turismo.gov.ar.

Eating and drinking

Buffet-style 'American breakfasts' are served in international hotels but elsewhere, breakfast (*desayuno*) is a very simple affair. Lunch (*almuerzo*) is eaten any time from 1300 to 1530 and is followed, in Argentina (but not Buenos Aires), by a siesta. At around 1700, many Argentines go to a *confitería* for *merienda* (tea, sandwiches and cakes), while Chileans have a snack meal known as *onces* (literally elevenses). Restaurants open for *cena* (dinner) at about 2000 in Chile but rarely before 2100 in Argentina, where most people don't eat until 2230 or later. Many restaurants in Chile serve a cheaper fixed-price meal at lunch time (US$3.50-5), called *la colación* or *el menú*. In Argentina this is known as *el menú fijo*. Those on a tight budget should also try *tenedor libre* (free fork) restaurants, where you can eat all you want for a fixed price. Some hotels, particularly in the Lake District, will offer a packed lunch to take on hikes and to see the glaciers; ask the night before.

Food and drink

In the last few years Argentina has become known for its fresh and sophisticated cuisine; especially salmon and wild game from Patagonia. In general, the meat is legendary. The classic meal is the *asado* – beef or lamb (in Patagonia) cooked over an open fire. In rural areas, a whole lamb is splayed out on a cross-shaped stick at an angle over the fire. Parrilla restaurants, found all over Argentina, grill cuts of meat in much the same way; they can be ordered as individual dishes or as *parrillada* (basically a mixed grill). Other meat to try includes salmon in Patagonia, wild boar in Bariloche and even guanaco. Italian immigration has left a legacy of pizza, *pasta casera* (home-made pasta) and *ñoquis* (gnocchi). Perhaps the most outstanding ingredient in Chilean cuisine is the seafood. Some of the best is to be had at Angelmo (Puerto Montt). The most popular fish are *merluza* (a species of hake, better the further south it is fished), *congrio* (ling), *corvina* (bass – often served marinated in lemon juice as *ceviche*), *reineta* (a type of bream), *lenguado* (sole), *salmon* and *albacora* (sword fish). There is an almost bewildering array of unique shellfish, particularly *erizos*, *machas*, *picorocos* and *locos*. The local *centolla* (king crab) is also exquisite.

Both Argentine and Chilean wines are excellent, and even the cheapest varieties are very drinkable. Also try the home-brewed beer around El Bolsón in Argentina. Cider (*chicha de manzana*) is popular in southern Chile. The most famous spirit in Chile is *pisco*,

The *mate* ritual

Mate (pronounced *mattay*) is the essential Argentine drink. All over the country, whenever groups of Argentines get together, they share a *mate*. Try it, at least once. It's a stimulating but bitter green tea made from the leaves of the yerba mate plant, *Ilex paraguaiensis*, encouraged by the Jesuits as an alternative to alcohol, and grown in their plantations in the northeast of Argentina. The *mate* container is traditionally made of a hollowed gourd, but can also be wood or tin, and there are ornate varieties made to traditional gaucho patterns by the best silversmiths.

Dried yerba leaves are placed in the *mate* to just over half full, and then the whole container is shaken upside down using your hand to prevent spillage. This makes sure that any excess powder is removed from the leaves before drinking. Hot water is added to create the infusion, which is then sipped through a *bombilla*, a perforated metal straw. One person in the group acts as *cebador*, trickling fresh hot water into the *mate* and passing it to each person in turn to sip. The water must be at 80-82°C (just as the kettle starts to 'sing') and generally *mate* is drunk *amargo* – without sugar (but add a little if it's your first time, as the drink is slightly bitter). It is mildly stimulating, less so than caffeine, and effective at ridding the body of toxins as well as being mildly laxative and diuretic. When you've had enough, simply say *gracias* as you hand the *mate* back to the *cebador*, and you'll be missed out on the next round.

If you're invited to drink *mate*, always accept, and then keep trying it: it might take a few attempts before you actually like the stuff. To share a *mate* is to be part of a very special Argentine custom, and you'll delight your hosts by giving it a go.

made with grapes and usually drunk with lemon or lime juice as *pisco sour*, or mixed with Coca Cola or Sprite. The great Argentine drink (also widely drunk in Chilean Patagonia) is *mate* (pronounced mattay), an important social convention. Dried yerba leaves, similar to tea, are placed in a hollowed-out gourd into which hot water (not boiling) is poured, and the resulting infusion is drunk through a metal straw with a filter at the bottom. The cup is filled with water for each person in the group, who then drinks in turn. If offered, give it a go, but be prepared for the bitter taste; you can add a little sugar to make it more palatable. The experience of sharing a *mate* is a great way to make friends and transcends social boundaries (see box, above).

National parks and natural phenomena

The snow-capped mountains, sheer cliffs and deep valleys of Patagonia are home to stunning national parks and incredible natural wonders. There is an extensive network of reserves and protected areas, the most important of which are designated national parks (additional areas are designated as natural monuments and natural reserves). From glaciers and waterfalls to fjords and ancient land marks, Patagonia is a great place to enjoy nature in all its fabulous forms.

Patagonian national parks

Patagonia has an extensive network of reserves and protected areas, the most important of which are designated national parks (PN). Additional areas have been designated as natural monuments (MN) and natural reserves (RN).

Argentina The main office of the Administración de Parques Nacionales is at Santa Fe 680, near the Plaza San Martín in central Buenos Aires, T011-4311 0303, www.parquesnacionales.gov.ar. Most parks have *guardaparque* (ranger) offices at the main entrance, where you can get advice and basic maps. They are usually knowledgeable about wildlife and walks. Parks in the Lake District are particularly well set up for trekking, with signed trails, *refugios* and campsites.

Chile All reserves and national parks in Chile are managed by CONAF (Corporación Nacional Forestal), Avenida Bulnes 285, 1st floor, Santiago, T/F02-697-2273, www.conaf.cl. It maintains an office in each region of the country and kiosks in some natural areas. Most of the parks have public access; details are given in the text. Camping areas are usually clearly designated, wild camping is discouraged and frequently banned.

Petrified forests

Some 130 million years ago during the Jurassic period, parts of southern Patagonia were covered in forests of giant araucarias (a version of today's monkey puzzle trees), and the climate was moist and stable. Then, at the beginning of the Cretaceous period, intense volcanic activity resulted in these forests being buried in ash – a natural preservative. The remains of these petrified forests can be seen today in two areas of Argentine Patagonia: Monumento Nacional Bosques Petrificados (halfway between Caleta Olivia in the north and San Julián in the south, see page 175) and Bosque Petrificado José Ormachea (Saramiento, see page 174). Lying, strewn along the ground are large tree trunks which look like wood, but are actually stone.

Southern Patagonian Ice Field

With an area of over 16,800 km (of which 14,200 km belongs to Chile and 2600 km to Argentina) and extending 350 km, the Southern Patagonian Ice Field is the third biggest extension of continental ice after Antarctica and Greenland. The ice field feeds many of Patagonia's glaciers such as Upsala, Viedma, Bruggen, Grey and the famous Perito Moreno (the world's only advancing and receding glacier), and is home to several volcanoes that lie undisturbed under the ice. Spread over three national parks, this enormous ice field is one of two remnants of the Patagonian Ice Sheet, which was a narrow sheet of ice that covered southern Chile during the last ice age. The other remnant is the much smaller Northern Patagonian Ice Field found within the borders of Laguna San Rafael National Park.

3000-year-old living trees

Just south of Bariloche are the clear blue mountain streams and lush forests of Parque Nacional Los Alerces. Named after a species of slow-growing trees that are found in the area, the park is a great place to enjoy fly-fishing and trekking and it is easily accessible from nearby Esquel. Deep inside the park is an alerce tree that has been growing in the same place for more than 3000 years, and several others which are slightly younger.

Growing only 1 mm per year, the alerce trees in this region attract so much attention that scientists have kept the location of one of the oldest trees a secret from prying eyes. So, for now you'll have to be happy with visiting a 2000-year-old alerce tree.

Volcanoes

Patagonia marks the end of the so-called Pacific ring of fire and is home to over two dozen active volcanoes running in a chain along the west of the Andes. The perfect cones of Villarrica, Osorno and Choshuenco have a history of relatively gentle erruption with lava rising and spilling over the crater's edge. In Volcán Villarrica, for example, lava rises and falls cyclically, and when particularly active the crater rim can be seen from afar glowing red in the night. When in a benign state, though, these volcanoes are perfect for hiking up and skiing down.

Other volcanoes have shattered cones, evidence of more violent erruptions that can have far-flung consequences. In 1991 Volcán Hudson spewed a thick layer of ash over the area around Lago General Carrera – you can still see the evidence today in the Valle del Bosque Muerto (Valley of the Dead Forest). More recently Volcán Chaitén, little known and generally thought to be extinct, roared into life in 2008 and again in 2009, drowning the nearby village of Chaitén under a muddy mix of ash and water (see page 301).

Hot springs

The western edge of South America is geologically very active. The same tectonic forces that created the Andes and gave Chile so many volcanoes and the occasional destructive earthquake, is also responsible for the abundance of natural hot springs.

Today, these come in many different guises, from the indoor swimming pools near Pucón to the beach at Lago Rupanco where digging a hole in the sand will create a hot thermal bath fed from underground! If you want something rustic, head to Ralún where two natural rock pools lie by the side of the icy river, or for a bit of luxury head for the Termas de Puyuhuapi resort.

Many people swear by the medicinal properties of the springs due to their temperature and high mineral content and every year Chileans flock from the capital to 'take the waters'. They may or may not be a cure for rheumatism, but what is certain is that there is nothing better after an arduous day's Patagonian trekking than a long soak in a thermal bath.

Parque Pumalín

The Parque Pumalín is quite simply one of the world's great conservation projects. Stretching from the Gulf of Ancud in the west to the Argentinian border in the east, the park began as the private intiative of US multi-millionaire Douglas Tompkins who bought up some three-quarters of a million acres of private land covered in temperate rainforest to save it from exploitation by the timber industry. The result is a national park (its official status is Nature Sanctuary) run along a strict policy of conservation, with sustainable small organic farms within the park that double as information centres. The park is home to a vibrant ecosystem, with a wide variety of trees and plants, including coigue, lenga, ulmo and ancient alerces, all easily accessible from the main road. The park is also home to the endangered pudú and huemul as well as the Andean puma and a rich variety of birdlife. For hikers there are a dozen well-marked and well-maintained trails and a series of neat campsites. The Parque Pumalín seems to have set an example, as land has been bought privately in both Chiloé and Argentina for similar conservation projects.

Essentials A-Z

Accident and emergency

Argentina: Ambulance T107, Coastguard T101, Fire service T100, Police T101, Air Rescue Service T101.
Chile: Ambulance T131, Coastguard T138, Fire service T132, Police T133, Air Rescue Service T138.

Contact the relevant emergency service and your embassy (see pages 85 and 238). Make sure you obtain police/medical reports required for insurance claims.

Children

Chileans and Argentines will go out of their way to make childeres welcome. More expensive hotels provide a babysitting service; children's meals are offered in many restaurants and most have high chairs. Self-catering *cabañas* may be the best sleeping option for families as they are good value and usually well equipped.

Most tourist attractions charge less for children; on sightseeing tours try to bargain for a family rate. Chilean domestic airlines charge around 66% for children under 12 but long-distance bus fares in Argentina and Chile are calculated per seat, so you'll have to seat small children on your knee to save money. Distances are long; consider flying if possible. Adventure tourism in Patagonia is not really suitable for young children and the climate is often too cold, wet and windy for them.

→ Be very careful about sunburn, especially in the south, due to the lack of ozone.
→ If your child has special dietary needs, learn the appropriate Spanish phrases.
→ Order mineral water rather than tap water.
→ Take water, fruit, biscuits, tissues, games and books on long bus journeys; the videos shown on board are generally action movies, not suitable for under 12s.

Customs and duty free

Argentina

Visitors coming from countries not bordering Argentina are exempt from taxes on articles brought into the country, including new articles up to US$300, and an additional US$300 if goods are purchased at duty free shops within Argentina. You can claim back tax (IVA) at the airport when you leave the country if you've bought goods over the value of US$23 and have the receipts. Ask for the necessary form when you buy goods, and take it to the IVA desk at check-in. Some products give you the option to get the tax back on them. Look for the 'TAX FREE SHOPPING' sign and ask for a form to be filled out. Then go to the designated booth at the airport and port to reclaim your money. The IVA is usually 13.70% of the product's cost. For further information see Global Refund Argentina, Paraguay 755, floor 8, T011-52381976, taxfree@ar.globalrefund.com.ar.

Chile

The following may be brought into Chile duty free: 500 cigarettes or 100 cigars or 500 g of tobacco, plus 3 bottles of liquor, and all articles for personal use, including vehicles, radios, CD/MP3 players, cameras, personal computers, and similar items. Fruit, vegetables, meat, flowers, seeds and milk products may not be imported into Chile; these will be confiscated at all borders, where there are thorough searches.

Disabled travellers

Facilities for the disabled in Argentina and Chile are improving. Many buses and some metro stations are now wheelchair-friendly, however you won't find many ramps or even lowered kerbsides; pavements tend to be shoddy and broken even in big cities. Many upmarket hotels have been fully adapted for wheelchair use. Tourist sights, particularly in national parks, generally only have limited access for disabled visitors. However, the best museums have ramps or lifts and some may offer special guided tours for the visually or hearing impaired: the superb dinosaur museum in Trelew is setting the standard here. Boat trips to some of the glaciers should also be possible with prior arrangement. Airlines are extremely helpful, especially if you let them know your needs in advance; some long-distance buses are still unable to accommodate wheelchairs but drivers will help those with some mobility. Argentines and Chileans generally go out of their way to help you, making up for any lack of facilities with kindness and generosity. Speaking Spanish is obviously a great help, and travelling with a companion is advisable.

Useful organizations

Directions Unlimited, 123 Green Lane, Bedford Hills, NY 10507, T1-800-533-5343, T914-241 1700. A tour operator specializing in tours for disabled US travellers.
Disability Action Group, 2 Annadale Av, Belfast BT7 3JH, T01232-491011, www.disabilityaction.org. Information about access for British disabled travellers.
Disabled Persons' Assembly, PO Box 27-524, Wellington 6035, New Zealand, T04-801-9100, www.dpa.org.nz. Has lists of tour operators and travel agencies catering for the disabled.

Drugs

Using drugs, even soft ones, without medical prescription is illegal and penalties are severe (up to 10 years in prison) even for possession. The planting of drugs on travellers by traffickers or the police is not unknown. If offered drugs on the street, make no response and keep walking. People who roll their own cigarettes are often suspected of carrying drugs and may be subjected to intensive searches.

Electricity

220 volts AC. Chile has 2- or 3-round-pin European-style plugs. Argentina has European-style plugs in old buildings, Australian 3-pin flat-type in the new. Bring a universal adapter, as these are not readily available.

Embassies and consulates

Argentine

Australia, 20/44 Market St, Sydney NSW 2000, T02 9262 2933
Canada, 81 Metcalfe St, Suite 700 Ottawa, Ontario, K1P 6K7 T613-2362351.
Chile, Miraflores 285, Casilla 9867, Santiago de Chile, T02-639 8617/638 0890/633 1076.
New Zealand, 11th floor, Harbour View Building, 52 Quay St, PO Box 2320, Auckland, T09-309757.
United Kingdom, 65 Brook St, London W1K 4AH, T0207-3181300.
United States, 12 West 56th St, New York 10019, T1-212-603 0400.

Chilean

Find Chilean embassies and consulates around the world at www.chileabroad.gov.cl.
Argentina, Tagle 2762, Buenos Aires 1425, T011-4808 8601, data@embajadadechile.com.ar. Also consulates up and down the country.
Australia, 10 Culgoa Circuit, O'Malley Act 2606, PO Box 69, Canberra, T02-6286 2430, chilemb@embachileaustralia.com. Also in Melbourne and Sydney.
Canada, 50 O'Connor St, Suite 1413, Ottawa, Ontario K1P 6L2, T1-613-235 4402, www.chile.ca. Also in Montreal, Toronto and Vancouver.
Ireland, 44 Wellington Rd, Ballsbridge, Dublin 4, T 01-667-5094, www.embachileirlanda.ie.
New Zealand, 19 Bolton St, Wellington, T04-471 6270, www.embchile.co.nz.
UK, 12 Devonshire St, London, W1G 7DS, T020-7580 6392, embachile@embachile.co.uk.

USA, 1732 Massachusetts Av NW, Washington DC 20036, T1-202-785 1746, F1-202-887 5579, embassy@embassy ofchile.org.

Gay and lesbian travellers

Argentina is fast becoming one of the most popular gay destinations in the world and there is enough happening in the capital to keep you busy for a few weeks. New gay-specific hotels are opening, gay clubs are booming and there is a range of gay-orientated travel agencies to help you plan your stay. However, in the interior of the country, away from Buenos Aires, you might encounter homophobia and being openly demonstrative in public will certainly raise eyebrows everywhere apart from the hipper places in Buenos Aires. The tourist office produces a handy leaflet with a map showing gay-friendly bars, pubs, saunas, health centres and wine bars. There is quite a lot of homophobia in Chile and Argentina. Away from the bigger cities, gay men and lesbian women are not encouraged to be open about their sexuality, and there are few places where you can go to meet other gay/lesbian friends.

Useful contacts

www.pride-travel.com, a helpful Argentine agency, organizing tours, nights out in Buenos Aires and travel advice for the rest of the country. Also try **BueGay**, www.buegay.com.ar, **StepGay** (www.stepgay.com) and **Free Attitude** (www.freeattitude.com.ar) for help planning your trip. **www.thegayguide.com.ar** has tips on the Buenos Aires gay scene.

Health

No vaccinations are demanded by immigration officials in Chile or Argentina, but you would do well to be vaccinated against typhoid, polio, hepatitis A and tetanus. Children should, of course, also be up-to-date with any immunization programmes in their country of origin. See your GP or travel clinic at least 6 weeks before departure for general advice on travel risks and vaccinations. Try contacting a specialist travel clinic if your own doctor is unfamiliar with health in the region. Make sure you have sufficient medical travel insurance, get a dental check, know your blood group and, if you suffer a long-term condition such as diabetes or epilepsy, obtain a Medic Alert bracelet/ necklace (www.mediband.com.au).

Health risks

Temperate regions of South America, like Patagonia, present far fewer health risks than tropical areas to the north. However, travellers should take precautions against: **diarrhoea/ intestinal upset**; **hanta virus** (carried by rodents and causing a flu-like illness); **hepatitis** A; **hypothermia**; **marea roja** (see Fishy business, page 340); **rabies**; **sexually transmitted diseases**; **sun burn** (a real risk in the far south due to depleted ozone); and **ticks**.

Further information

www.btha.org British Travel Health Association.
www.cdc.gov US government site that gives excellent advice on travel health and details of disease outbreaks.
www.fco.gov.uk British Foreign and Commonwealth Office travel site has useful information on the country, people, climate and a list of UK embassies/consulates.
www.fitfortravel.scot.nhs.uk A-Z of vaccine/health advice for each country.
www.travelscreening.co.uk Travel Screening Services gives vaccine and travel health advice, email/SMS text vaccine reminders and screens returned travellers for tropical diseases.

Insurance

Always take out comprehensive insurance before you travel, including full medical cover and extra cover for any activities (hiking, rafting, skiing, riding, etc) that you may undertake. Check exactly what's being offered, the maximum cover for each element and also the excess you will have to pay in the case of a claim. Keep details of your policy and the insurance company's telephone number with you at all times and get a police report (*constancia*) for any lost or stolen items.

Internet

The best way to keep in touch is undoubtedly by email. Broadband is widely available in Argentina and Chile, even in remote areas. Dedicated centres/internet cafés are widespread, particularly in towns and tourist centres and most *locutorios* (phone centres, known as *centros de llamadas* in Chile) also have an internet connection. Prices are US$1-2 per hr in both countries.

To access the @ (*arroba*) symbol, you usually press the Ctrl and Alt keys together with 'q'.

Language

Although English is understood in many major hotels, tour agencies and airline offices (especially in Buenos Aires and Santiago), travellers are advised to learn some Spanish before setting out. Argentines and Chileans are welcoming, and are very likely to strike up conversation on a bus, in a shop or a queue for the cinema. They're also incredibly hospitable (even more so away from the capital cities), and may invite you for dinner, to stay or to travel with them, and your attempts to speak Spanish will be enormously appreciated. Spanish classes are available at low cost in a number of centres in Chile and Argentina.

Large cities all offer Spanish classes, see individual chapters for recommendations. If you would like to arrange classes before you arrive as well as your accommodation try one of the following organizations:

Amerispan, 1334 Walnut St, floor 6, Philadelphia PA 19107, USA, T0800-8796640, www.amerispan.com. North American company offering Spanish immersion programmes, educational tours, volunteer and internship positions in Buenos Aires, Córdoba and Mendoza. Also programmes for younger people.

Expanish, Viamonte 927, floor 1, T011-4322 0011, www.expanish.com. Buenos Aires-based agency which can organize packages including accommodation, excursions and classes in Buenos Aires and Patagonia, as well as in Peru, Ecuador and Chile. Highly recommended.

Spanish Abroad, 5112 N, 40th St, Suite 101, Phoenix, AZ 85018, T1-888-722 7623, www.spanishabroad.com. Spanish classes in Buenos Aires and Córdoba.

Argentina

The distinctive pronunciation of Argentine Spanish is Italian-influenced – in Buenos Aires, you might even hear the odd word of *lunfardo*, Italian-orientated slang. It varies from standard Spanish chiefly in the replacement of the 'll' and 'y' sounds by a soft 'j' sound, as in 'beige'. The big change, grammatically, is in the conjungation of verbs: the Spanish 'tú' is replaced by 'vos', which is used both formally and informally.

Chile

Chilean pronunciation, which is very quick and lilting, with final syllables cut off, can present difficulties to the foreigner, even those that speak good standard Spanish. Chileans also have a wide range of unique idioms that even other Latin Americans find difficult to understand. In rural areas of Región IX, travellers may encounter Mapudungún, the Mapuche language.

Media

Newspapers and magazines

The *Buenos Aires Herald* (www.buenosaires herald.com) is a daily English-language paper, with domestic news and a brief digest of world news. *Santiago Times* (www.santiagotimes.cl) and *Patagonia Times* (www.patagoniatimes.cl)

are 2 on-line English-language newspapers. Few foreign-language newspapers are available outside Buenos Aires and Santiago but Spanish speakers may want to check out the national dailies, especially *La Nación* (www.la nacion.com.ar), *Clarín* (www.clarin.com.ar), *El Mercurio* (www.emol.com) and *La Tercera* (www.latercera.cl) all of which have good websites and excellent Sun travel sections. Visitors should also look at *Lugares*, an informative monthly travel magazine with superb photography and a section in English.

Radio and television

The *BBC World Service* broadcasts at 97.1 Mhz from 1200 to 0500 in Argentina, but no longer transmits to Chile. Many hotels have cable TV in the rooms which often have English news channels.

Money

Argentina

→ *£1 = Arg $6.25; €1 = Arg $5.37; US$1 = Arg $3.81; Chilean $1000 = Arg $7.05 (Jul 2009).*

The unit of currency is the peso ($) = 100 centavos. Peso notes in circulation are 2, 5, 10, 20, 50 and 100. Coins in circulation are 1, 5, 10, 25 and 50 centavos and 1 peso.

Chile

→ *£1 = Ch $886; €1 = Ch $761; US$1 = Ch $540; Arg $1 = Ch $142 (Jul 2009).*

US dollar bills are also widely accepted. The unit is also the peso ($). Peso notes in circulation are 1000, 2000, 5000, 10,000 and 20,000; coins come in denominations of 1, 5, 10, 50, 100 and 500.

ATMs and credit cards

In general, the easiest way to get cash while in Patagonia is to use an international credit or debit card at an ATM (*cajero automático*). These can be found in every town or city (with the notable exceptions of El Chaltén in Argentina and along the Carretera Austral, where the only ATM is in Coyhaique), with instructions available in English. Maestro, MasterCard, Plus/Visa and Cirrus are all widely accepted except at the Banco Estado in Chile which does not accept Visa. In Chile, ATMs operate under the sign Redbanc and will accept daily transactions of up to US$400. For a full list of Redbanc machines in Chile, see www.redbanc.cl. Commission is usually 2-3%, but check with your card company before leaving home. You may also be charged a cash handling fee.

Credit cards are generally accepted for payment only in large hotels, city shops and restaurants and for expensive tours. In shops, ID is usually necessary. Credit card use may incur a commission in smaller establishments in Chile, and places accepting Visa and MasterCard usually display a 'Redcompra' sticker in the window. In parts of Argentina commission of 10% is often charged.

Changing money

Most major towns in both countries have **bureaux de change** (*casas de cambio*). They are often quicker to use than banks but may not have the best rates, so shop around. US dollars (US$) and euro (€) are easier to change than other currencies but will only be accepted if in good condition. Travellers to rural areas of Chile should carry supplies of small denomination notes, as 10,000 and 20,000 peso notes are difficult to change. **Traveller's cheques** (TCs) are not very convenient for travel in Patagonia. The exchange rate for TCs is often lower than for cash and the commission can be very high (usually 10% in Argentina).

Cost of travelling

Argentina became relatively cheap for tourists after the peso was devalued in 2002, but smart hotels in tourist centres are creeping up. Comfortable en suite rooms can be found for US$60 in most places, and for US$100 you can stay somewhere very good. Dinner in a local restaurant can be found for under US$8. Touristy areas such as El Calafate and Ushuaia have inflated prices but plenty of choice. Long distance bus travel on major routes is very cheap (see Getting around, page 37).

Chile is a little more expensive than Argentina and southern Chile is even more expensive from 15 Dec to 28 Feb. A budget of US$300 per person per week will allow for basic lodgings, food, overland transport and an occasional tour. With a budget of US$600 a week, you will be able to stay in nice hotels, eat in smart restaurants and not stint on excursions.

Police and the law

The police in Chile and Argentina are usually courteous and will be helpful to tourists. However, always be wary of anyone who claims to be a plain-clothes policeman. If you get into trouble, the worst thing that you can do is offer a bribe, as this will be seen as both an insult and an admission of guilt.

Legal penalties for most offences are similar to what you might expect in a Western European or North American country, although the attitude towards possession of soft drugs, such as cannabis, is very strict. If you get into trouble, your first call should be to your consulate, which should be able to put you in touch with a lawyer who speaks English.

Post

Argentina

The post service is usually reliable, but for assured delivery, register everything. Letters take 10-14 days to get to Europe and the USA. Post (including parcels up to 2 kg) can be sent from the *correo* (post office) or through the private postal service **Oca** from any shop displaying the purple sign. Larger parcels must be sent from the town's main post office, where they are examined by customs and then taken to 'Encomiendas Internacionales' for posting. All incoming packages are also opened by customs. Poste restante (*lista de correo*) is available in every town's main post office.

Chile

The Chilean postal system is usually efficient and cheaper than in Argentina. Letters to Europe/North America cost US$0.75 (add US$0.90 to register them). Surface mail rates for parcels to Europe cost US$18 for less than 1 kg; US$22 for 1-3 kg. The *lista de correos* (poste restante) service holds mail for 30 days, then returns it to sender. The central post office in Santiago is good and efficiently organized, but letters are kept separately for men and women so poste restante envelopes should be marked Señor (Sr), Señora (Sra), Señorita (Srta).

Public holidays

The main holiday period are Jan and Feb, Easter and Jul, when school children are on holiday and most families go away for a few weeks. All popular tourist destinations become extremely busy at this time and you should book transport and accommodation in advance. Banks, offices and most shops close on public holidays although transport should run as normal, except on 25 and 31 Dec and 1 Jan.

Argentina

1 Jan, Good Friday, 2 Apr (Veteran's Day), 1 May, 25 May, 10 Jun, 20 Jun, 9 Jul, 17 Aug, 12 Oct (Columbus Day), 8 Dec (Immaculate Conception Day), 25 Dec.

Chile

1 Jan, Good Friday, 1 May, 21 May, 29 Jun, 16 Jul, 15 Aug, 18-19 Sep (Independence), 12 Oct, 31 Oct, 1 Nov, 8 Dec, 25 Dec.

Safety

Buenos Aires is much safer than most Latin American cities, but petty crime can be a problem in busy tourist areas in Buenos Aires, especially La Boca and Retiro. Travelling in Patagonia itself is very safe indeed. Chile is generally a safe country to visit but, like all major cities, Santiago does have crime problems. Elsewhere, the main threats to your safety are most likely to come from natural hazards and adventure activities than from crime. Don't hike alone in remote areas and always register with *guardaparques* (rangers) before you set off.

General advice

→ Keep valuables out of sight.
→ Keep all documents and money secure.
→ Split up your main cash supply and hide it in different places.
→ Lock your luggage together with a chain/cable at bus or train stations.
→ At night, take a taxi between transport terminals and your hotel.
→ Use the hotel safe deposit box and keep an inventory of what you have deposited. Notify the police of any losses and get a written report for insurance.
→ Look out for tricks used to distract your attention and steal your belongings.
→ Don't fight back – it is better to hand over your valuables rather than risk injury.

Student travellers

If you're in full-time education you are entitled to an **International Student Identity Card** (ISIC), www.isic.org, which is distributed by student travel offices and travel agencies in 77 countries. The **ISIC** gives you special prices on all forms of transport and access to a variety of other concessions and services, including an emergency helpline (T+44-20-8762 8110). In Chile, alternative student ID cards can be obtained from Hernando de Aguirre 201, oficina 602, Providencia, Santiago, and cost US$16 (photo and proof of status required).

Tax

Airport tax

International departure tax (US$18 in Argentina; US$30 in Chile) may be pre-paid; check if it's included in your ticket when you book.

Telephone

In both countries, avoid calling from hotels, which charge very inflated prices. *Locutorios* and *centros de llamadas* (phone centres) are the easiest way to make a call. They have private booths where you can talk for as long as you like and pay afterwards, the price appearing on a small screen in your booth. They often have internet, photocopying and fax services too.

Mobile phones

International roaming is becoming more common, although buying a cheap local pay-as-you-go may be a cheaper option. Major airports and hotels often have rental desks, or can advise on local outlets.

Argentina

→ *Country code: +54. International access code (IDD) 00; operator T19; international operator T000; directory enquiries T110; international directory enquiries T110. Mobile phone prefix (within the country): area code +15.*

For local calls, if you can't find a *locutorio*, use a public payphone, minimum 25 centavos. For long-distance and international calls, use phone scratch cards, available from *kioskos* and *locutorios* for 5 or 10 pesos; 2 good brands are **Argentina Global** and **Hable Más**. Dial the free 0800 number on the card, followed by the code on the card (scratch the silver panel to reveal it) and then the international number. These cards can usually be used in *locutorios* too, but the rates are more expensive.

If calling to Argentina from abroad, dial the country code (+54) and then the area code of the place you want to call. Once in Argentina, dial 0 before each area code. For international calls from Argentina, dial 00, the country code and city code. Note that tariffs are reduced from 2200 to 0800.

Chile

→ *Country code: +56. International access code (IDD) 00; operator T130; international operator T107; directory enquiries T103. Mobile phone prefix (within the country): 08 or 09.*

From public phone boxes, local calls cost US$0.20 for 3 mins and national calls around US$0.20 per min. A call to a mobile costs US$0.35 per min. For international calls it is cheaper to use a *centro de llamadas* or pre-paid phone scratch cards, available from *kioskos*.

Time

Argentina is 3 hrs behind GMT. Chile is 4 hrs behind early Mar to Sep/Oct and 3 hrs behind mid-Sep/Oct to early Mar.

Tour operators

In Europe

See **Latin America Travel Association (LATA)**, www.lata.org, for a full list.

Audley Travel, 6 Willows Gate, Stratton Audley, Oxfordshire OX27 9AU, T01869-276210, www.audleytravel.com. Tailor-made tours to Patagonia and elsewhere.

Austral Tours, 20 Upper Tachbrook St, London SW1V 1SH, T020-72335384, www.latinamerica.co.uk. Interesting and imaginative tours of Chile and Argentina.

Condor Journeys and Adventures, 2 Ferry Bank, Colintraive, Argyll PA22 3AR, UK, T01700-841318, www.condorjourneys-adventures.com. Adventure and ecological tour specialist including expeditions, Magellan Strait cruises and estancia visits.

Encounter Overland, 2002 Camp Green, Debenham, Stowmarket, Suffolk IP14 6LA, UK, T0870-499 4478, www.encounter overland.co.uk. Adventurous expeditions in groups across wild terrain.

Exodus, Grange Mills, Weir Rd, London SW12 0NE, T870-240 5550, www.exodus.co.uk. Excellent, well-run tours of Patagonia, with trekking and climbing included.

Experience Chile, T07977-223 326, www.experiencechile.org. Itineraries and accommodation in Torres del Paine.

Explore, 1 Frederick St, Aldershot GU11 1LQ, T0870-333 4002, www.explore.co.uk. Highly experienced and well-respected tour operator. Small groups. Well executed.

Fidibus Tours, Postfach 178, CH-3033 Wohlen, Switzerland, T+41 79 4325904, www.fidibustours.de. Private tours organized in off-road campers for up to 4. Tents provided.

Galapagos Classic Cruises, 6 Keyes Rd, London NW2 3XA, T020-8933 0613, www.galapagos cruises.co.uk. Good tailor-made tours.

Journey Latin America, 12-13 Heathfield Terrace, Chiswick, London W4 4JE, T020-8622 8464, www.journeylatinamerica.co.uk. Deservedly well regarded, this long-established company runs adventure tours, escorted groups and tailor-made tours to Patagonia and other destinations in South America. Also cheap flights and expert advice.

Last Frontiers, Fleet Marston Farm, Aylesbury, Bucks HP18 0QT, T01296-653000, www.last frontiers.com. Wide range of tours in Argentina and Chile including great estancias and remote expeditions from Carretera Austral to Torres del Paine. Also fishing, skiing and birdwatching.

Latin America Travel, 103 Gainsborough Rd, Richmond TW9 2ET, T0870-4424241, www.latinamericatravel.co.uk. Offers a tour taking in Península Valdés and the glaciers.

Select Latin America, 79 Maltings Pl, 169 Tower Bridge Rd, London SE1 3LJ, UK, T020-7407 1478, www.selectlatinamerica.com. Quality tailor-made holidays and small group tours.

South American Experience, 47 Causton St, Pimlico, London SW1P 4AT, T020-7976 5511, www.southamericanexperience.co.uk. Will book flights and accommodation, also offers tailor-made trips.

Steppes Latin America, 51 Castle St, Cirencester, Glos GL7 1QD, T01285-885333, www.steppeslatinamerica.co.uk. Tailor-made escorted tours to Patagonia, including riding trips and birdwatching.

Trips Worldwide, 14 Frederick Pl, Bristol BS8 1AS, T0117-311 4400, www.tripsworld wide.co.uk. Specialists in tailor-made holidays.

The Travel Company, 15 Turk St, Alton, Hants GU34 1AG, T0870-7941009, www.adventure company.co.uk. For trips exploring Patagonia.

In North America

4StarSouthAmerica.com T1-800-747-4540 (US), T0871-711 5370 (UK), T+49 700 4444-7827 (rest of the world). Tour operator and flight consolidator based in Washington DC, Stuttgart, Germany and Rio de Janeiro, offering tours in Patagonia and South America. For flights, www.4starflights.com.
Argentina for Less, 7201 Wood Hollow Dr, Austin, TX 78731, USA, T1-877-269 0309, www.argentinaforless.com. Progressive tourism company with a focus solely on Latin America. US-based but with local offices and operations.
International Expeditions, 1 Environs Park, Helena, AL 35080, USA, T1-800-6334734 (toll free), T205-428 1700, www.internationalexpeditions.com. Travel company specializing in nature tours.
Ladatco Tours, 2200 S Dixie Highway, Suite 704, Coconut Grove, FL 33133, T1-800-3276162 (toll free), www.ladatco.com. Specialist operator based in Miami, runs explorer tours themed around mysticism, wine, etc.
Lost World Adventures, 337 Shadowmoor Drive, Decatur, GA 30030, T800 999 0558, www.lostworld.com. Long-time tour operator in the region. Interesting itineraries for all budgets.
Mila Tours, T1-800-3677378 (toll free), www.milatours.com. Wide range of tours from rafting to photography.
Myths and Mountains, 976 Tee Court, Incline Village, NV 89451, T1-800-670-6984 (toll free), T775-832 5454, www.mythsandmountains.com. Cultural, wildlife and environmental trips.
Wilderness Travel, 1102 Ninth St, Berkeley, CA 94710-1211, T510-5582488, T1-800-3682794 (toll free), www.wildernesstravel.com. Organizes trips worldwide, including very good tours of Patagonia.

In Australia and New Zealand

Australian Andean Adventures, Suite 601, Level 6, 32 York St, Sydney, NSW 2000, T02-9299 9973, www.andean adventures.com. Specialists in trekking in South America.
South America Travel Centre, 104 Hardware St, Melbourne, T03-96425353, www.satc.com.au. Good, individual tailor-made trips to Chile.

Tourist information

Argentina

Tourism authorities in Argentina are generally better equipped than their Chilean counterparts. You might have to be patient in some parts of the country, even when requesting the most basic information, but the major centres of Bariloche, San Martín de los Andes, Villa la Angostura, Puerto Madryn, El Calafate and Ushuaia all offer good tourist resources. Staff in these popular tourist areas usually speak at least some English and opening hours are long – typically 0800-2000 in summer although they may close at weekends or during low season. Provincial websites, with information on sights and accommodation, can be accessed via the excellent government tourist website: www.turismo.gov.ar. Also consult www.patagonia.com.ar, www.interpatagonia.com and www.revistapatagonia.com.ar. For free information within Argentina call T0800-555 0016 (daily 0800-2000).

Chile

The national secretariat of tourism, **Sernatur** (www.sernatur.cl), has provincial offices in Temuco, Osorno, Puerto Montt, Ancud, Coyhaique, Punta Arenas and Puerto Natales (addresses are given under the relevant destination). These can provide town maps, leaflets and other useful information, otherwise contact head office in Santiago. Other towns have municipal tourist offices. Useful region-specific websites are www.patagoniachile.cl and www.patagonia-chile.com.

Visas and immigration

Visa and immigration regulations change frequently so always check with the Argentine and Chilean embassies before you travel. Keep photocopies of essential documents and some additional passport-sized photographs, and always have a photocopy of your passport with you.

Argentina

Visitors from neighbouring countries only need to provide their ID card to enter Argentina. Citizens of the UK, Western Europe, USA, Australia, New Zealand and South Africa (among other countries) require a **passport**, valid for at least 6 months, and a **tourist card**, which is given to you on the plane before you land. This allows you to stay for a period of 90 days, and can be renewed for another 90 days (US$40), either by leaving the country at a border (see page 39) and immediately re-entering, or by paying US$40 at the **National Directorate of Migration**, Antártida Argentina 1365, Buenos Aires, T011-4312 8663. No renewals are given after the expiry date.

Other foreign nationals should consult with the Argentine embassy in their home country about visa requirements.

Chile

For the latest information: www.minrel.cl.

Carry your passport (or at least a photocopy) at all times; it is illegal not to have ID handy and thorough searches are not unknown. Citizens of the UK, Western Europe, USA, Canada, Australia, New Zealand and South Africa require only a **passport**, valid for at least 6 months, and a **tourist card**, which is handed out at major border crossings and at Chilean airports. This allows visitors to stay for 90 days and must be surrendered on departure from Chile.

Other foreign nationals should consult with the Chilean embassy in their home country about visa requirements. After 90 days the tourist card must either be renewed by leaving and re-entering the country or extended (US$100) at the **Ministerio del Interior** (*Extranjería*) in Santiago or (preferably) from any local government office (*Gobernación*), where the procedure is slightly less time-consuming.

Women travellers

Argentine and Chilean men are generally respectful of a woman travelling alone, although you may hear the traditional *piropo* as you walk past: it's an inoffensive compliment that you can ignore. You can discourage unwanted attention by wearing a wedding ring and, when accepting a social invitation, ask if you can bring a friend, to check the intentions of whoever's inviting you. In other respects, women travellers should follow the safety tips given on page 52 and never go hiking alone. Women travelling in Argentina and Chile should be aware that tampons and towels must never be flushed down the toilet, since the water pressure is too low to cope.

Buenos Aires

Contents

Footprint features

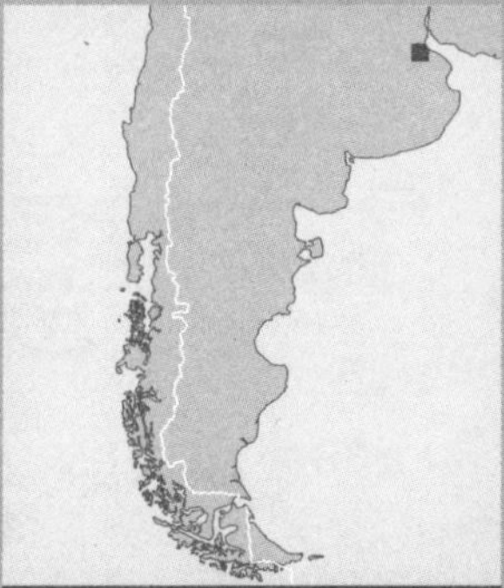

At a glance

Getting around Cheap and frequent buses, trains and relatively affordable taxis. Some areas like Palermo, Recoleta and San Telmo are best on foot.

Time required At least a week to see the sites, enjoy a tango show and go on a day trip.

Weather Summers (Dec-Mar) can be quite hot and humid, and winter (May-Aug) can be windy, cold and rainy.

When not to go Winter, when the winds can be ferocious, or Mar, when the torrential rain can wash the streets away.

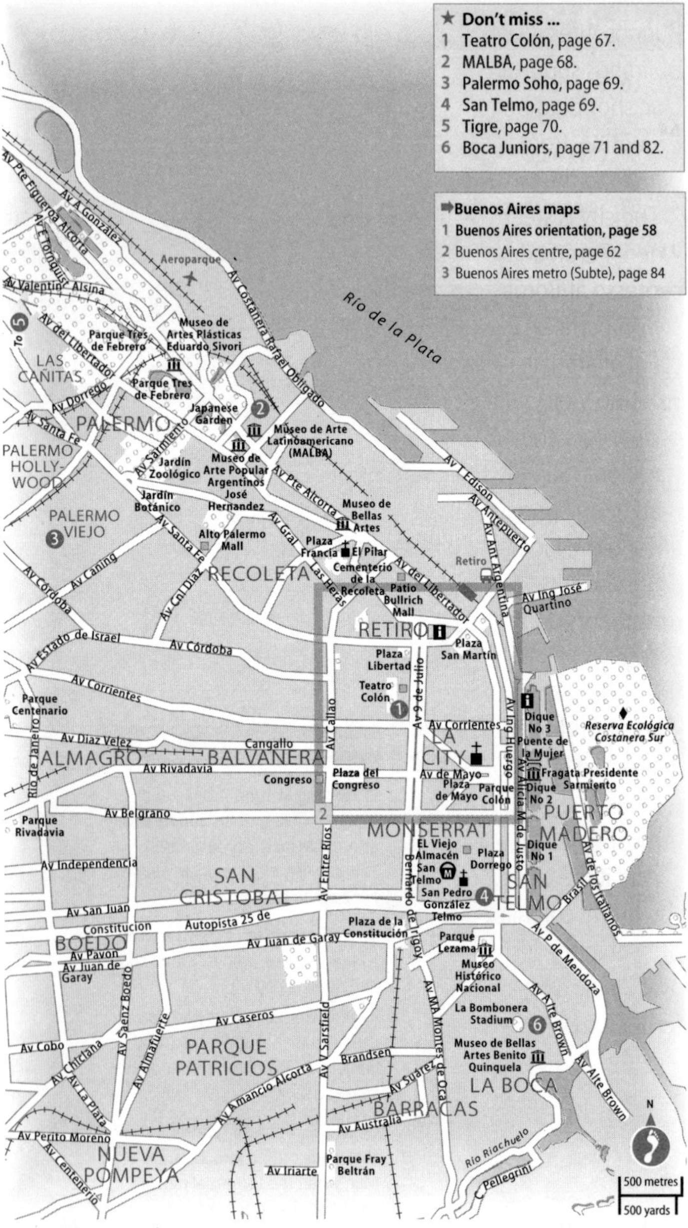
★ Don't miss ...
1 Teatro Colón, page 67.
2 MALBA, page 68.
3 Palermo Soho, page 69.
4 San Telmo, page 69.
5 Tigre, page 70.
6 Boca Juniors, page 71 and 82.
Buenos Aires maps
1 Buenos Aires orientation, page 58
2 Buenos Aires centre, page 62
3 Buenos Aires metro (Subte), page 84
Río de la Plata
Aeroparque
Av Costanera Rafael Obligado
Av Pte Figueroa Alcorta
Av A Gonzalez
Av E Tornquist
Av Valentín Alsina
To 5
Av del Libertador
Parque Tres de Febrero
Museo de Artes Plásticas Eduardo Sivori
LAS CAÑITAS
Parque Tres de Febrero
Av Dorrego
Japanese Garden
PALERMO
Av Santa Fe
Av Sarmiento
Museo de Arte Latinoamericano (MALBA)
PALERMO HOLLYWOOD
Jardín Zoológico
Museo de Arte Popular Argentinos José Hernandez
Av Pte Alcorta
Jardín Botánico
PALERMO VIEJO
Av Santa Fe
Alto Palermo Mall
Av Gral Las Heras
Museo de Bellas Artes
Plaza Francia
El Pilar
Cementerio de la Recoleta
Av Canning
RECOLETA
Av Cnl Díaz
Av Córdoba
Patio Bullrich Mall
Av del Libertador
Av T Edison
Av Antepuerto
Av Ant Argentina
Retiro
Av Ing José Quartino
RETIRO
Av Estado de Israel
Av Córdoba
Plaza San Martín
Plaza Libertad
Av Corrientes
Teatro Colón
Parque Centenario
Av Callao
Av 9 de Julio
Av Ing Huergo
Dique No 3
Reserva Ecológica Costanera Sur
Av Corrientes
LA CITY
Puente de la Mujer
Av Diaz Velez
Cangallo
ALMAGRO
BALVANERA
Av Rivadavia
Río de Janeiro
Plaza del Congreso
Congreso
Av de Mayo
Plaza de Mayo
Parque Colón
Fragata Presidente Sarmiento
Dique No 2
Av Alicia M de Justo
Parque Rivadavia
Av Belgrano
PUERTO MADERO
MONSERRAT
El Viejo Almacén
Plaza Dorrego
Dique No 1
Av Independencia
SAN CRISTOBAL
Av Entre Ríos
Bernardo de Irigoy
San Telmo
San Pedro González Telmo
SAN TELMO
Brasil
Av de los Italianos
Av San Juan
Constitucion
Autopista 25 de
Plaza de la Constitución
Av P de Mendoza
BOEDO
Av Pavon
Av Juan de Garay
Av Juan de Garay
Parque Lezama
Museo Histórico Nacional
Av MA Montes de Oca
Av Alte Brown
La Bombonera Stadium
Av Caseros
Av Saenz Boedo
Av Almafuerte
Av V Sarsfield
Av Cobo
Av Chiclana
PARQUE PATRICIOS
Brandsen
Museo de Bellas Artes Benito Quinquela
Av Alte Brown
Av La Plata
Av Amancio Alcorta
Av Suárez
LA BOCA
BARRACAS
Av Australia
Av Perito Moreno
Av Centenerio
NUEVA POMPEYA
Río Riachuelo
Parque Fray Beltrán
Av Iriarte
C Pellegrini
N
500 metres
500 yards

Buenos Aires is one of the world's great cities. Grand baroque buildings suggest Paris, theatres and cinemas to rival London, chic shopping better than New York. But the feel is uniquely Argentine, from the steak sizzling on your plate in a crowded *parrilla* to the tango danced in the streets.

The city is steeped in history. Marvel at the grand Casa Rosada where Perón addressed his supporters in Plaza de Mayo, then sip espresso at Borges' old haunt, Café Tortoni, and head north to the stylish barrio of Recoleta cemetery where Evita is buried, which is full of art galleries and buzzing cafés. Take a stroll in upmarket Palermo Viejo, with its parks and enticing cobbled streets full of chic bars and little designer shops. Or explore wonderfully traditional San Telmo, the oldest part of the city, with its antique market on Sundays, where tango dancers passionately entwine among the fading crystal and 1920s tea sets.

Buenos Aires' nightlife is legendary and requires stamina, as restaurants don't get busy until 2300 and dancing starts at 0300. Before you fill up on piquant *empanadas*, juicy steak and a glass of fine Argentine Malbec, try a spot of tango in a *milonga* or take in some world-class opera at Teatro Colón. Then stroll around the renovated docks of Puerto Madero, the trendy restaurants of Las Cañitas or the hip hangouts of Palermo Hollywood and lap up the atmosphere in Buenos Aires' elegant nightlife.

And if the city's pleasures become too intense, take a train to the pretty colonial suburb of San Isidro or board a wooden boat upriver in the lush jungle of the Tigre Delta, where you can hide away in a cabin, or retreat to a luxury lodge until you're ready for your next round of shopping, eating and dancing.

Ins and outs

Getting there

Air Buenos Aires has two airports: **Ezeiza**, for international flights, 35 km southwest of the centre, T011-5480 6111, and **Aeroparque Jorge Newberry** for domestic flights, just to the north of Palermo, Avenida Costanera R Obligado, T011-4514 1515. To get from Ezeiza, there's an efficient bus service run by **Manuel Tienda León**, www.tiendaleon.com.ar, linking Ezeiza Airport with the centre, and hotels (leaving every 30 minutes, charging US$11 for the 50-minute journey and US$1 more for transfers to central hotels). Alternatively, take a reliable radio taxi (such as **Onda Verde** – T011-4867 0000), 45 minutes, US$32 – make sure you pay for your taxi inside or just outside the airport and wait in the queue. Don't be tempted to just jump in the closest taxis for security sake. Alternatively you can take a *remise* taxi – these have a fixed fare, and can be booked from a desk at the airport, and charge US$33. There is a local bus which takes 1½ to two hours and costs US$0.60 but it isn't advisable late at night or early morning. Manuel Tienda León is the most reliable company, and has a clearly visible desk by Arrivals. **Aeroparque**, the largely domestic airport, is 4 km north of the city centre, right on the riverside, just 15 minutes drive from anywhere in the centre of town. **Manuel Tienda León** buses charge US$6 for the 20-minute journey to the centre, *remises* US$8 and ordinary taxis US$6. Again, **Manuel Tienda León** is the most reliable company. Their office in town is near Retiro train station and from here you can order a radio taxi. But ask them about their transfer service to hotels in the centre of town. There's a left-luggage office here, phone and banks with ATMs a block away.

Bus Buses connect Buenos Aires with towns all over Argentina and from neighbouring countries, arriving at **Retiro bus terminal** at Ramos Mejía and Antártida Argentina, about five blocks north of Plaza San Martín, T011-4310 0700. Always take a radio taxi to the terminal, and take a *remise* taxi from the terminal into town, since the area is insalubrious, and ordinary taxis here are not reliable. As you get out of the bus look for a *remise* taxi company called **La Terminal**, T011-4312 0711. Go to the kiosk, pay the fixed fare for your journey and your driver will take you down to his car. You can also catch local buses, nearly all of them stop at the train station nearby or you can catch the Subte (underground train) Line C and follow the signs to the bus station. Not recommended late at night or early morning. When leaving Buenos Aires by bus it is best to visit the terminal the day before to buy your ticket, and familiarize yourself with the area as well as where the platforms are so when you return laden with luggage you know exactly where to go.

Getting around ➔ *See metro map, page 84.*

There is a good network of **buses** (*colectivos*), which are frequent, efficient and very fast, plus six **metro** (Subte) lines, labelled 'A' to 'E', and a sixth labelled 'H' – four link the outer parts of the city to the centre; the fifth ('C') links Plaza Constitución with Retiro station and connects with all the other lines, and the newest line, the 'H', cuts across the city from Caseros to Once. The central stations of 9 de Julio ('D'), Diagonal Norte ('C') and Carlos Pellegrini ('B') are linked by pedestrian tunnels. Subte tickets can be bought at each station (try to pay with coins). One journey anywhere on the system costs US$0.30. For maps and more information see www.subte.com.ar. Bus tickets must be bought on board. Tell the driver where you are going, and then use the onboard ticket machine – tickets within the city cost US$0.30 and to the outer suburbs US$0.45. It accepts only coins. **Taxis** are painted yellow and black and carry 'Taxi' flags, but for security reasons always phone a radio taxi (**Onda Verde Taxis**, T011-4867 0000 is a reliable company). Alternatively, *remise* taxis (usually unmarked cars) charge a fixed rate to anywhere in town and are very reliable, although they can work out more expensive for short journeys (**La Terminal Remises**, T011-4312 0711, are recommended, especially from Retiro Train Station).

Tourist information

National Tourist Office ⓘ *Av Santa Fe 883, T011-4312 2232/5550, www.turismo.gov.ar, Mon-Fri 0900-1700*. There are also tourist kiosks at Aeroparque and Ezeiza airports, and city-run tourist kiosks open 1200-2000 on Avenida Florida, junction with Roque Sáenz Peña; at Abasto Shopping Mall (Avenida Corrientes 3200); in Recoleta (on Avenida Quintana, junction with Ortiz); in Puerto Madero, Dock 4, and at Retiro bus station (ground floor). The website www.bue.gov.ar has useful information in English. The **tourist police** can be contacted at Corrientes 436, T011-4346 5748 and T0800-999 5000. For free tourist information or assistance anywhere in the city call T0800-999 2838.

The pocket-size guidebook *Guía T*, which has maps of the federal capital, is available at news-stands, US$2. *Buenos Aires Day & Night* is a free bimonthly magazine with a city map available at tourist offices and newsagents, together with other publications such as the informative *BAInsider* (www.bainsider.com.ar) and, of course, *Time Out BA*. For information about what's on in Buenos Aires see www.buenosairesherald.com (both newspaper and website are in English). Also see www.whatsupbuenosaires.com for a detailed listing (in English) of events, DJs, art exhibitions and basically anything that is going on in the capital. There are countless free publications found in cafés which will also have information, one of the best is *The Argentimes* newspaper (www.theargentimes.com).

South American Explorers ⓘ *Roque Sáenz Peña 1142 (Diagonal Norte), 7th floor, apt A, www.saexplorers.org, Mon-Fri 0930-1700, Sat 0930-1300*, a new clubhouse providing knowledgeable advice and a comfortable meeting place for travellers. Highly recommended.

2 Buenos Aires centre

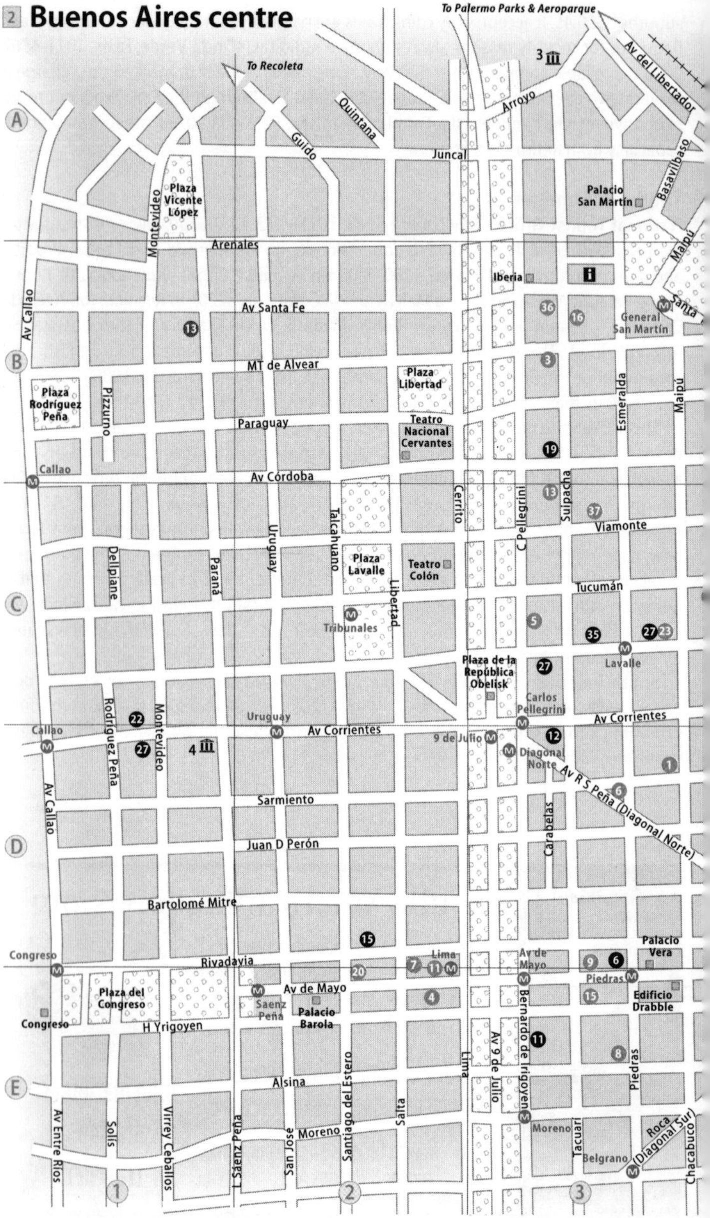

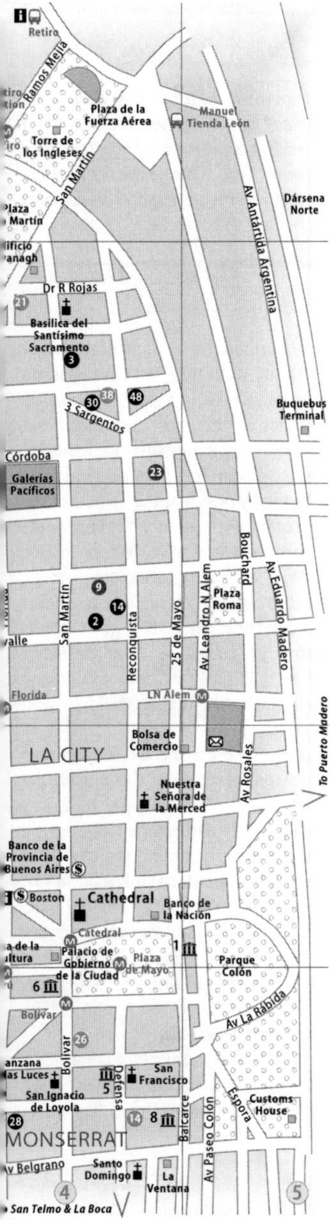

➡ Buenos Aires maps
1 Buenos Aires orientation, page 58
2 Buenos Aires centre, page 62
3 Buenos Aires metro (Subte), page 84

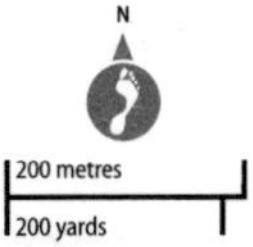

Sleeping

06 Central **1** *D3*
725 Continental **6** *D3*
BA Stop **7** *D2*
Bisonte Palace **3** *B3*
Castelar **4** *E2*
Clan House **8** *E3*
Dolmen **16** *B3*
Frossard **12** *C4*
Goya **13** *C3*
Hispano **9** *D3*
Lime House **11** *D2*
Marbella **20** *E2*
Marriott Plaza **21** *B4*
Moreno **14** *E4*
NH City **26** *E4*
O'Rei **23** *C3*
Panamericano **5** *C3*
Plaza San Martín Suites **36** *B3*
Portal Del Sur **15** *E3*
V&S **37** *C3*
Waldorf **38** *B4*

Eating

Café Tortoni **6** *D3*
California Burrito Company **2** *C4*
Club Español **11** *E3*
Confitería Ideal **12** *D3*
Dadá **3** *B4*
El Gato Negro **22** *C1*
El Palacio de la Papa Frita **27** *C3/D1*
El Querandí **28** *E4*
Empire Bar **30** *B4*
La Casona del Nonno **35** *C3*
La Chacra **19** *B3*
Morizono **48** *B4*
Pura Vida **14** *C4*
Rocket **15** *D2*
Sorrento **25** *C3*

Bars & clubs

La Cigale **23** *B4*
Le Bar **9** *C4*
Milion **13** *B1*

Museums

Casa de Gobierno (Casa Rosada) & Museo de los Presidentes **1** *D5*
Centro Cultural San Martín, Museo de Arte Moderno & Teatro Municipal San Martín **4** *D1*
Museo de Arte Hispanoamericano Isaac Fernández Blanco **3** *A3*
Museo de la Ciudad **5** *E4*
Museo del Cabildo y la Revolución **6** *E4*
Museo Etnográfico JB Ambrosetti **8** *E4*

Sights

The formal centre of the city is around Plaza de Mayo, from where the broad Avenida de Mayo heads west to the congress building. Halfway, it crosses the 22 lanes of Avenida 9 de Julio, which heads north to Avenida del Libertador, the main road leading out of the city to the north and west, via the fashionable suburbs of Recoleta and Palermo. East of the centre are the city's vibrant, renovated docks at Puerto Madero, while to the south are the green spaces of Costanera Sur and the city's most atmospheric barrio, San Telmo. » *For listings, see pages 71-86.*

City centre

Plaza de Mayo

This broad open plaza is the historic heart of the city, surrounded by some of the major public buildings including the famous pink Casa de Gobierno or **Casa Rosada** ① *T011-43443804, tours Mon-Fri 1600 (English on Fri only), book at least 2 hrs earlier at Hipólito Yrigoyen 219, passport required, free,* which lies on the east side, looking out towards the Río Plata, and contains the offices of the president of the Argentine Republic. For more information on the museum see www.museo.gov.ar. The colour derives from President Sarmiento's desire to symbolize national unity by blending the colours of the rival factions, which had fought each other for much of the 19th century: the Federalists (red) and the Unitarians (white). The building has been the site of many historic events: from its balcony, President Perón and his wife, Evita appeared before the masses, and when the economy crumbled in December 2001, angry crowds of *cacerolazas* (middle-class ladies banging their saucepans) rioted outside. Since 1970, the Mothers and Grandmothers of the Plaza de Mayo (*Madres y Abuelas de Plaza de Mayo,* www.madres.org) have marched every Thursday at 1530 anti-clockwise around the central monument in silent remembrance of their children and grandchildren who disappeared during the 'dirty war' (1976-1983).

Opposite the Casa Rosada, on the west side of the plaza is the white-columned **Cabildo**, originally the 18th-century administrative centre. Inside is the **Museo del Cabildo y la Revolución** ① *T011-4334 1782, Tue-Fri 1030-1700, Sat 1400-1800, Sun 1130-1800, US$1,* good for an overview of Argentine history. Of particular interest are the paintings of old Buenos Aires and the documents and maps recording the May 1810 Revolution. On the north side of the plaza, the **Catedral Metropolitana** ① *Rivadavia 437, T011-4331 2845, Mon-Fri 0800-1900, Sat-Sun 0900-1930; guided visits Mon-Fri 1130 (San Martín's mausoleum and crypt), 1315 (religious art) and daily 1530 (temple and crypt), check times for Mass at entrance,* lies on the site of the first church in Buenos Aires, built in 1580. The current structure was built in classical style between 1758 and 1807, and inside, in the right-hand aisle, is the imposing tomb of General José de San Martín (1880), Argentina's greatest hero, who liberated the country from the Spanish.

Just east of the cathedral, the **Banco de la Nación** is regarded as one of the great works of the famous architect Alejandro Bustillo (who designed **Hotel Llao Llao** in Bariloche, see page 129). Built 1940-1955, its central hall is topped by a marble dome 50 m in diameter.

La City

Just north of the Plaza de Mayo lies the main banking district known as La City or simply El Centro, with some handsome buildings to admire. The **Banco de Boston** ① *Florida 99 and*

24 hours in the city

Start with a traditional Buenos Aires breakfast of strong coffee and *media lunas* at **Café Tortoni**, lapping up the atmosphere of leather chairs and art nouveau loved by poets and intellectuals. Then wander down Avenida de Mayo with its splendid buildings to **Plaza de Mayo** where you can admire the bright pink **Casa Rosada**, and pop into the **Cabildo** for a taste of history. If it's a Sunday, take a short stroll along Calle Defensa to pleasingly crumbling **San Telmo**, and see live musicians, tango dancers in the fabulous antiques market. Or take a taxi to **MALBA**, the stunning gallery of Latin American art, and have tea at its chic café before strolling through the airy galleries. From here take a taxi to **Palermo Viejo** for French, Italian, Vietnamese or Armenian food at any of the hip restaurants.

If the sun is shining, take a stroll around the **botanical gardens** in Palermo and cool off with an ice cream at **Persicco**, watching fashionable Porteños wander by. If you'd rather shop for stylish clothes instead, jump into a taxi and head to **Patio Bullrich** or **Alto Palermo**. At around 1700, it's time for *merienda* or tea, nobody does it better than the **Alvear Palace Hotel**. While you're in **Recoleta**, visit the colonial church **El Pilar** and the cemetery next door, where Eva Perón is buried. Just outside on the weekends, there's a huge **craft market**, selling cheap chic jewellery and hand-carved *mate* pots, or you could pop into the **Buenos Aires Design Centre** for some designer Argentine handicrafts.

By now you'll be ready to relax in your hotel for an hour to get ready for the night out. At nine-ish, take a taxi to **Palermo Soho** and find a chic restaurant to sample some modern Argentine cuisine, such as **Dominga**, **Cabernet** or **Cluny**. Hold back from eating too much though, because your **tango** class at the *milonga* starts at 2230. Head for **Confitería Ideal** or **La Viruta**, and let the experts take you in hand. If that's too daunting, sit back and watch the city's best dancers' breathtaking display at **El Viejo Almacén**. If you've caught the infectious Porteño rhythm, have a cosy cocktail at a **Palermo Viejo** bar until the nightclubs open at 0200, perhaps at **El Living**. You'll emerge at dawn, when you can appreciate Buenos Aires' beautiful architecture in the crisp early light before staggering to **Clásica y Moderna** for a laid-back breakfast.

Av R S Pena, dates from 1924 and boasts a lavish ceiling and marble interior. Also worth seeing is the marvellous art deco **Banco de la Provincia de Buenos Aires** at San Martín 137, built in 1940, and the **Bolsa de Comercio**, 25 de Mayo and Sarmiento, which dates from 1916 and houses the stock exchange. The **Basílica Nuestra Señora de La Merced** ⓘ *J D Perón and Reconquista 207, Mon-Fri 0800-1800,* founded in 1604 and rebuilt 1760-1769, has a highly decorated interior and an altar with an 18th-century wooden figure of Christ, the work of indigenous carvers from Misiones. Next door, the **Convento de la Merced**, originally built in 1601, has a peaceful courtyard in its cloisters.

South of Plaza de Mayo

To the southwest of Plaza de Mayo is an entire block of buildings built by the Jesuits between 1622 and 1767, called the **Manzana de las Luces** (Enlightenment Square) – bounded by streets Moreno, Alsina, Perú and Bolívar. The former Jesuit church of **San Ignacio de Loyola** (see below for tours), begun in 1664, is the oldest colonial building in Buenos Aires and the best example of the baroque architecture introduced by the Jesuits. Its splendid golden nave dates from 1710-1734. Worth seeing are the secret **18th-century tunnels** ⓘ *T011-4342 4655, Mon-Fri 1500, Sat-Sun 1500, 1630, 1800 (Mon 1300 free tour) in Spanish (in English by prior arrangement), arrive 15 mins before tour, US$2; weekend tours include San Ignacio*, which are thought to have been used by escaping Jesuits or for smuggling contraband from the port. For centuries the whole block was the centre of intellectual activity, and although little remains today, the history of this area is fascinating.

The **Museo de la Ciudad** ⓘ *Alsina 412, T011-4343 2123, www.museos.buenosaires.gov.ar, Mon-Sun, 1100-1900, US$0.35 (US$1 for non-residents), free on Mon and Wed*, is a historical house with a permanent exhibition covering social history and popular culture, and gives an insight into 19th-century life in Buenos Aires. The **church of San Francisco** ⓘ *Alsina and Defensa, Mon-Fri 0700-1300, 1500-1900, guided visits Tue 1530 and 1630, Sat 1630 and 1730*, was built by the Franciscan Order 1730-1754 and given a new façade in 1911 in German baroque style.

The small, but beautifully designed **Museo Etnográfico J B Ambrosetti** ⓘ *a block south of the San Francisco church at Moreno 350, T011-4345 8196, www.museoetnografico.filo.uba.ar, Tue-Fri 1300-1900, Sat and Sun 1500-1900(closed Jan), US$0.55, guided visits Sat and Sun 1600*, contains fascinating anthropological and ethnographic collections from all over Argentina, charting the development of various indigenous groups. One block further south at Defensa and Belgrano, the **church of Santo Domingo**, founded in 1751, where General Belgrano, a major figure in Argentine independence, is buried.

Avenida de Mayo

From the Plaza de Mayo, take a stroll down this broad leafy avenue which links the presidential palace to the congress building to the west. Constructed between 1889 and 1894 and inspired by the grand design of the city of Paris, it's filled with elaborate French baroque and art nouveau buildings. At Perú and Avenida de Mayo is the **Subte station Perú**, furnished by the Museo de la Ciudad to resemble its original state, with posters and decor of the time. You'll need to buy a US$0.30 ticket to have a look.

Along the avenue west from here, you'll see the splendid French-style **Casa de la Cultura** at No 575, home of the newspaper *La Prensa* and topped with bronze statues. At No 702 is the fine Parisian-style **Edificio Drabble**, and at No 769, the elegant **Palacio Vera**, from 1910. Argentina's most celebrated writer, Jorge Luis Borges, was fond of the many cafés that once lined Avenida de Mayo, of which **Café Tortoni** ⓘ *www.cafetortoni.com.ar*, at No 825, is the most famous. It has been the haunt of illustrious writers, artists and poets since 1858 and its high ceilings and art nouveau stained glass plunge you straight back into another era. It's an atmospheric place for coffee, but particularly wonderful for the poetry recitals, tango and live music, which are still performed here in the evenings (see also Eating, page 77).

Continuing west over Avenida 9 de Julio, look out for the 1928 **Hotel Castelar** at No 1152 (see Sleeping, page 72), the beautiful art nouveau **Hotel Chile** at No 1297 and **Palacio Barola** ⓘ *www.pbarolo.com.ar*, at No 1370. Avenida de Mayo culminates at the Italian academic-style **congress building** ⓘ *T011-4953 3081, guided visits ext 3885, Mon, Tue, Thu, Fri 1100, 1700, 1900, free.*

Plaza San Martín and around

Ten blocks north of the Plaza de Mayo is the splendid **Plaza San Martín**, designed by Argentina's famous landscape architect Charles Thays, and filled with lovely mature palms and plane trees. It's popular with joggers in the early morning and office workers at lunchtimes. At the western corner is an equestrian **statue of San Martín**, 1862, and at the northern end of the plaza is the **Falklands/Malvinas memorial** with an eternal flame to those who fell in the war, 1982. The city's main shopping street, **Avenida Santa Fe**, starts from Plaza San Martín, crosses Avenida 9 de Julio and heads through Retiro and Recoleta to Palermo. Around the plaza are several elegant mansions, among them the **Palacio San Martín**. Most striking, however, is the elegant art deco **Edificio Kavanagh**, east of the plaza, once the tallest building in South America. The **Plaza de la Fuerza Aérea**, northeast of Plaza San Martín was until 1982 (around the time of the Falklands War) called the Plaza Británica in the centre is a clock tower presented by British and Anglo-Argentine residents in 1916, known as the **Torre de los Ingleses**.

Three blocks northwest of Plaza San Martín is one of the city's most delightful museums, the **Museo de Arte Hispanoamericano Isaac Fernández Blanco** ⓘ *Suipacha 1422, www.museofernandezblanco.buenosaires.gov.ar, Tue-Fri 1400-1900, Sat and Sun 1100-1900, US$.30, Thu free, closed Jan, tours in English by prior arrangement T011-4327 0228, tours in Spanish Sat, Sun 1600.* Housed in a beautiful 1920s neo-colonial mansion with tiled Spanish-style gardens, it contains a fascinating collection of colonial art, with fine Cuzqueño school paintings, and dazzling ornate silverware.

Avenida 9 de Julio

This is one of the world's widest thoroughfares, with 11 lanes of traffic in each direction and the city's famous landmark at Plaza de la República: a 67-m-tall **obelisk** commemorating the 400th anniversary of the city's founding, where football fans traditionally congregate to celebrate a victory.

Just a block north of the obelisk on 9 de Julio is **Teatro Colón** ⓘ *main entrance on Libertad between Tucumán and Viamonte, www.teatrocolon.org.ar*. The theatre is characterized by exquisite opulence and an almost perfect acoustic, due to the horseshoe shape and the mix of marble and soft fabrics. Workshops and rehearsal spaces lie underneath the Avenida 9 de Julio itself, and there are stores of costumes, including 22,000 pairs of shoes. The theatre is home to three orchestras, as well as the city's ballet and opera companies (see page 81).The theatre is closed for major renovations until at least 2010.

Four blocks west of Plaza de la República, **Teatro San Martín** ⓘ *Av Corrientes 1530, www.ccgsm.gov.ar, museum US$0.50, Wed free, tango desk daily 1400-2100*, has good photography exhibitions, a theatre and modern art museum. It's a great centre of tango, too (see page 80).

Puerto Madero

East of the city centre at Puerto Madero, the 19th-century docks have been successfully transformed into attractive modern developments of restaurants, shops, expensive housing and even a university campus. Walk along the waterside of the old warehouses lining Avenida Alicia M de Justo from the northern end of Dique 4, where you'll find a helpful tourist information kiosk in a glass construction under one of the permanent cranes.

Walking south, by Dique 3, is the **Fragata Presidente Sarmiento** ⓘ *Av Dávila and Perón, T011-4334 9386, Mon-Fri 0900-2000, Sat and Sun 0900-2200, US$1*, which was the Argentine flagship from 1899 to 1938, and is now an interesting museum. Also over Dique 3 is the striking harp-like construction of the **Puente de la Mujer** (Bridge of the Woman), suspended by cables from a single arm.

Recoleta

Situated north of Plaza San Martín, beyond Avenida 9 de Julio, Recoleta became a fashionable residential area when wealthy families started to move here from the crowded city centre after the yellow fever outbreak of 1871. Its streets, lined with French-style mansions, cafés, art galleries and museums make for a pleasant stroll. At its heart is the **Plaza Francia**, and running down its south eastern side is Calle Ortiz. At weekends, Plaza Francia has an art and craft market from 1100 until 1800, when the whole place is lively, with street artists and performers. There's a helpful **tourist information** ⓘ *T011-4804 5667*, booth at Ayacucho 1958.

The **Cementerio de la Recoleta** ⓘ *entrance at Junín 1790, T011-4804 7040, www.cementeriorecoleta.com.ar, open 0700-1800, free tours in English Tue and Thu 1100*, is a labyrinth of ornate shrines, with a vast congregation of angels on their roofs. Eva Perón is buried here in the Duarte family vault, among other illustrious figures from Argentina's history. The former Jesuit **church of El Pilar**, next to the cemetery dates from 1732 and was restored in 1930. There are stunning 18th-century gold alter pieces made in Alto Perú and an interesting, small museum of religious art downstairs. It is a popular wedding venue, so nearly every weekend you'll see a bride glide up the steps.

Close to the cemetery is **Buenos Aires Design** ⓘ *www.designrecoleta.com.aro*, where you can buy stylish contemporary designer fashion, furniture and handicrafts. There are also lots of good restaurants here, most with chairs out on the huge inviting open terrace. To the north, the **Museo de Bellas Artes** ⓘ *Av del Libertador 1473, T011-4803 0802, www.mnba.org.ar, Tue-Fri 1230-2030, Sat and Sun 0930-2030*, houses a fine collection of Argentine 19th- and 20th-century paintings and examples of European works, particularly post-Impressionist paintings and Rodin sculptures. In nearby **Plaza San Martín de Tours**, you're likely to spot one of Buenos Aires' legendary dog walkers, managing 20 or so dogs without tangling their leads.

The wide and fast avenue **Avenida del Libertador** runs north from Recoleta towards Palermo past parks, squares and several major museums. **Museo de Arte Popular Argentinos José Hernández** ⓘ *Av Libertador 2373, T011-4803 2384, www.museohernandez.org.ar, Wed-Fri 1300-1900, Sat and Sun 1000-2000US$0.40, free Sun, closed in Feb*, has an extensive collection of gaucho artefacts, including ornate silver *mates*, plaited leather *talebartería* and decorated silver stirrups, together with pre-Hispanic artefacts, and paintings from the Cuzco school. The museum not to be missed, however, is the **Museo de Arte Latinoamericano** (**MALBA**) ⓘ *Av Figueroa Alcorta 3415, T011-4808 6500, www.malba.org.ar, daily 1200-2000, Wed free till 2100, Tue closed, US$4.50, US$1.50 for ISIC holders, cinema tickets US$3, book in advance*, which opened in 2001 to house the private art collection of **Eduardo F Costa**, comprising mainly Latin American work. It's a an attractive, modern building, with a wonderful café and a good alternative cinema.

North of the centre

Palermo

Northwest of Recoleta is the attractive sprawling barrio of Palermo, named after Giovanni Domenico Palermo who transformed these lands into productive orchards and vineyards in the 17th century. It has a series of great parks, designed by Charles Thays in the early 20th century. The **Parque Tres de Febrero** ⓘ *winter Mon-Fri 0800-1800, Sat-Sun 0800-2000; summer daily 0800-2000*, is the largest, with lakes, tennis courts, a rose garden and the **Museo de Artes Plásticas Eduardo Sivori** ⓘ *T011-4774 9452,* *www.museosivori.org.ar, Tue-Fri 1200-2000 (winter 1800), US$0.70, Sat and Sun 1000-2000 (winter 1800), US$0.30, Wed free,* where you can immerse yourself in a fine collection of Argentine art. South of here is the beautifully harmonious **Japanese garden** ⓘ *T011-4804 4922, www.jardin japones.org.ar, daily 1000-1800, US$1.50, guided visits Sat 1500, 1600,* a charming place to walk, with koi carp to feed and little bridges over ornate streams. There is also a fantastic sushi restaurant, as well as a cultural centre which runs courses in origami and flower arranging. The **Buenos Aires Zoológico** ⓘ *Las Heras and Sarmiento, www.zoobuenosaires.com.ar, Tue to Sun 1000-1800, US$4.50, guided visits available,* to the west, occupies impressive buildings in spacious grounds, while the **Municipal Botanical Gardens** ⓘ *west of the zoo at Santa Fe 2951, daily 0800-1800, free,* designed by Thays in 1902, has areas planted with characteristic specimens representing the various regions of Argentina. The botanical gardens are home to thousands of stray cats that hide under the bushes during the day and come out at night to hunt. Best to avoid them and don't ever pat them; they're not tame!

Palermo has transformed in recent years into a wonderfully chic place to shop and eat, particularly in the area known now as **Palermo Soho** (also known as **Palermo Viejo**), between the avenues of Córdoba and Santa Fe, south of Juan B Justo and north of Avenida Scalabrini Ortiz. It's a very seductive area, with cobbled streets of tall bohemian houses bedecked with flowers, and leafy plazas and gardens. There are many bars, cafés and chic boutiques lining Calle Honduras, making it a relaxing area for an afternoon stroll. On weekends there is a designer clothes fair from 1400 to 2200, where local designers sell their creations for affordable prices. Best buys include men's and women's T-shirts, skirts, handbags and jewellery.There are plenty of appealing small boutique hotels here, too. On the northwestern edge of Palermo, and separated from the main area by a railway line, is **Las Cañitas**, a popular area of restaurants centred around Calle Báez.

South of the centre

San Telmo

The city's most atmospheric barrio is also its oldest. Formerly one of the wealthiest areas of Buenos Aires, it was abandoned by the rich during the great outbreak of yellow fever in 1871, and it's one of the few areas where buildings remain on the whole un-modernized and crumbling. San Telmo is a delightful place to stroll, with artists' studios, cafés, antique shops and small museums hidden away in its narrow streets. On Sundays a bric-a-brac antique market and free tango demonstrations are held in the central **Plaza Dorrego** and carry on all the way down until Avenida Belgrano (www.feriadesantelmo.com). Plaza Dorrego is a good place to start meandering. Behind the plaza, on Carlos Calvo, there's a wonderful indoor market, **Mercado de San Telmo** built in 1897. In the middle is a food section with butchers, fruit sellers and bakers, then to the sides are antique shops. Walk south along Calle Defensa to the white stuccoed church of **San Pedro González Telmo** ⓘ *Humerto 1, T011-4361 1168, guided tours Sun 1500, 1600, free.* Begun by the Jesuits in 1734, but only finished in 1931, it's a wonderful confection of styles with ornate baroque columns and Spanish-style tiles.

At the end of Defensa (to the south), is **Parque Lezama** ⓘ *Defensa and Brasil,* originally one of the most beautiful parks in the city, but now a little run down and not safe at night. Also on this corner you'll find the famous Bar Británico which, up until 2007, had been open continuously since 1960. It has been featured in films and was an institution in the suburb. It has now been refurbished by new owners, but it is still open 24 hours and is a good place to have a coffee and watch the world pass by. On the west side is the **Museo**

Going further ...

If you have more than a few days to spend in the city, here are three tips for perfect escapes – all possible in a day, or overnight:

→ **Tigre Delta** Take the commuter train from Retiro station (one hour US$1) or the coastal train (*Tren de la Costa*) from Maipú station (reached by commuter train from Retiro) to the little resort of **Tigre** in the jungly overgrown river delta, 29 km north. Popular with families and the jet set in summer, it has lots of hotels and restaurants, a fruit market, excellent fishing, and you could hire a kayak if you're feeling energetic, see www.tigre.gov.ar/turismo, T011-4512 4495. Or take a river bus down the tranquil canals to stay at a luxurious riverside retreat, such as **La Pascuala**, www.lapascuala.com.ar, US$125 per person for 24 hours. A cheaper alternative is to take the local ferry to Tres Bocas (45 minutes, US$4), and have lunch at one of the inexpensive restaurants there.

→ **Colonia de Sacramento** East across the Río de la Plata, on the shores of Uruguay, lies **Colonia del Sacramento**, whose Portuguese colonial centre is beautifully preserved. Hire a bike (US$5 per day) or a scooter (US$10) to see the whole place at your leisure. Boats leave from Puerto Madero three times daily, three hours (US$30 return) or one hour (US$80 return) – see www.buquebus.com, or www.coloniaexpress.com. Take your passport, no visa required, pesos and dollars accepted virtually everywhere.

→ **Estancias in the Pampas** The immense flat lands stretching out from the capital are dotted with grand cattle estancias. Either visit for the day or spend the night to enjoy riding, walking, fishing or just relaxing in complete peace and luxury. **San Antonio de Areco**, 113 km northwest, www.sanantoniodeareco.com, is a good base with a lively gaucho feel, a couple of great museums and three estancias on its doorstep. Alternatively, head 126 km south to the cowboy town of **Chascomús** where **Dos Talas** offers the most exquisite estancia stay in a historic house, www.dostalas.com.ar, from US$160 per person per night, everything included.

Histórico Nacional ⓘ *Defensa 1600, T011-4307 4457, Wed-Sun 1100-1800, US$0.30, tours Sat and Sun 1530*, which presents the history of the city and the country through key figures and events, with some impressive artefacts, portraits and paintings, particularly of San Martín. Among the ever-growing number of lively restaurants in San Telmo, several venues offer tango shows. The best is the historical **El Viejo Almacén** ⓘ *www.viejo-almacen.com.ar*, where the city's finest tango dancers demonstrate their extraordinary skills in a small atmospheric theatre, with excellent live music and singing from some the great names of tango (see page 80).

La Boca

East of the Plaza de Mayo, Paseo Colón, runs south towards the old port district of La Boca, where the Riachuelo river flows into the Río de La Plata. An area of heavy Italian immigration in the early 1900s, La Boca is known for its brightly painted zinc houses, a tradition started by Genoese immigrants who used the leftover paint from ships. It's a much-touted tourist destination, but there's really only one block to see on the pedestrianized street **El Caminito**. Despite the tango demonstrations and tourist souvenirs, take extra care when visiting the area; police are on hand to stop visitors straying from El Caminito as the rest of La Boca can be dangerous for tourists. Always take a radio taxi to and from La Boca.

Vivid paintings of La Boca's ships, docks and workers, painted by Benito Quinquela Martín (1890-1977) can be seen in the **Museo de Bellas Artes 'Benito Quinquela'** ⓘ *Pedro de Mendoza 1835, T011-4301 1080, Tue-Sun 1000-1800, closed Jan, US$0.35*, along with Quinquela Martín's own collection of paintings by Argentine artists. There's a roof terrace with superb panoramic views over the whole port, revealing the marginalized poverty behind the coloured zinc façades.

La Boca is home to one of the country's great football teams, **Boca Juniors** (see page 82), and the area is especially rowdy when they're playing at home. Tour operators can arrange a ticket, and fans will be entertained by the **Museo de la Pasión Boquense** ⓘ *Brandsen 805, T011-4362 1100, www.museoboquense.com, daily 1000-1900, US$5.*

Buenos Aires listings

Hotel and guesthouse prices

LL over US$200	**L** US$151-200	**AL** US$101-150
A US$66-100	**B** US$46-65	**C** US$31-45
D US$21-30	**E** US$12-20	**F** US$7-11
G under US$7		

Restaurant prices

TTT over US$12	TT US$7-12	T under US$7

Sleeping

Hotels in the upper ranges can often be booked more cheaply through Buenos Aires travel agencies. Hotels and guesthouses may display a star rating, but this doesn't necessarily match international standards. Many more expensive hotels charge different prices for *extranjeros* (non-Argentines) in US$, which is unavoidable since a passport is required as proof of residency. If you pay in cash (pesos) you may get a reduction. Room tax (VAT) is 21% and is not always included in the price. All hotels will store luggage for a day, and most have English-speaking staff. For upmarket chain hotels throughout Argentina contact **N/A Town & Country Hotels**, www.newage-hotels.com. For hostels see **Hostelling International Argentina**, www.hostels.org.ar, which offers 20% discounts to card-holders and 10% off long-distance bus journeys. For a complete listing see www.welcomeargentina.com.

City centre and Recoleta *p64, map p62*

LL 725 Continetal, Av Roque Sáenz Peña 725, T011-41316000, www.725continental.com. New, modern, design business hotel in the centre. Wonderful bar, stunning roof-top pool, gym with a view. Very chic.

LL Alvear Palace, Av Alvear 1891, T/F011-4808 2100, www.alvearpalace.com. The height of elegance, an impeccably preserved 1930s Recoleta palace, taking you back in time to Buenos Aires' heyday. A sumptuous marble foyer, with Louis XV-style chairs, and a charming orangery where you can take tea with superb patisseries (US$15). Antique-filled bedrooms. Recommended.

LL Art Hotel, Azcuénaga 1268, T011-4821 4744, www.arthotel.com.ar. Great location on a quiet street in Recoleta and handy for the Subte and shopping in Santa Fe, this is a reliable and comfortable little hotel with small, neat, well-equipped rooms, good breakfasts – though ask for tea pots. It's a pricey option but made worthwhile by the great service from all the multilingual staff who go out of their way to make your stay comfortable. Free internet. Recommended.

LL Four Seasons, Posadas 1086, T011-4321 1200, www.fourseasons.com/buenosaires. An entirely modern palace in traditional style, offering sumptuous luxury in an exclusive atmosphere. Spacious public areas, adorned with paintings and flowers, chic lavishly decorated rooms, and 7 suites in **La Mansión** where Madonna filmed *Evita* and numerous famous guests have enjoyed the residence, pool and health club.

LL Marriott Plaza, Florida 1005, T011-4318 3000, www.marriott.com. With a superb location overlooking Plaza San Martín, this is the city's most historic hotel, built in Parisian style in 1909, and retaining period elegance in the public rooms and bedrooms, which are charming and luxurious. A pool and fitness centre, excellent restaurant, the **Plaza Grill**, and very good service throughout.

LL Palacio Duhau-Park Hyatt, Av Alvear 1661, T011-5171 1234, www.buenosaires.park.hyatt.com. Refurbished aristocratic mansion in the heart of Recoleta, with wonderful gardens and a great terrace for enjoying an evening cocktail.

L-AL Panamericano, Carlos Pellegrini 551, T011-4348 5000, www.panamericanonews.com. Extremely smart and modern city hotel, with luxurious and tasteful rooms, a lovely covered rooftop pool with a million dollar view of Av 9 de Julio, and superb restaurant, **Tomo 1**. Excellent service too.

AL Bisonte Palace, Marcelo T de Alvear 902, T011-4328 4751, www.hotelesbisonte.com. A rather charming place, with calm entrance foyer, which remains gracious thanks to charming courteous staff. The rooms are modern and spacious, breakfast is ample, and this is in a good location.

AL Dolmen, Suipacha 1079, T011-4315 7117, www.hoteldolmen.com.ar. In a good location, this has a smart spacious entrance lobby, with a calm relaxing atmosphere, good professional service, comfortable modern well-designed rooms and a little pool.

AL La Cayetana Historic House, México 1330, T011-4383 2230, This fabulous 1820s restored house only has 11 suites all set off a lovely courtyard. Each room is individually designed, there is Wi-Fi, buffet breakfast and parking. Located a little out of the centre in the quiet suburb of Monserrat. Recommended.

AL Moreno, 376 Moreno, T011-6091 2000, www.morenobuenosaires.com. Decorated in dark, rich tones this hotel is the best value in its category. Large rooms, some with a view over the nearby basilica, and only 150 m to Plaza de Mayo. Jacuzzi, gym and chic bar. Recommended.

AL NH City Hotel, Bolívar 160, T011-4121 6464, www.nh-hoteles.com. Very chic indeed, with perfect minimalist design for a discerning younger clientele, this is 1 of 3 in the Spanish-owned chain in central Buenos Aires, with beautifully designed modern interiors and luxurious rooms in a 1930s building off Plaza de Mayo. Small rooftop pool, good restaurant.

AL Plaza San Martín Suites, Suipacha 1092, T011-4328 4740, www.plazasanmartin.com.ar. Neat modern self-contained apartments, comfortable and attractively decorated, with lounge and little kitchen, so that you can relax in privacy, right in the city centre, with all the services of a hotel. Sauna, gym, room service. Good value.

A Castelar, Av de Mayo 1152, T011-4383 5000, www.castelarhotel.com.ar. A wonderfully elegant 1920s hotel which retains all the original features in the grand entrance and bar. Cosy bedrooms (some a bit too cosy), helpful staff, and excellent value. Ask if there's going to be a fiesta, though, as it can be very noisy. Also a spa with Turkish baths and massage. Recommended.

A Waldorf, Paraguay 450, T011-312 2071, www.waldorf-hotel.com.ar. Welcoming staff and a comfortable mixture of traditional and modern in this centrally located hotel. Good value, with a buffet breakfast, English spoken. Recommended.

B Frossard, Tucumán 686, T011-4322 1811, www.hotelfrossard.com.ar. A lovely old 1940s building with high ceilings and the original doors, attractively modernized and, though the rooms are small, the staff are welcoming. This is good value and near Florida.

B Goya, Suipacha 748, T011-4322 9269, www.goyahotel.com.ar. A range of rooms offered in this friendly welcoming and central place, worth paying **A** for the superior rooms, though all are comfortable and well maintained. Good breakfast, English spoken.

B-C Hispano, Av de Mayo 861, T011-4345 2020, www.hhispano.com.ar. This hotel has been welcoming budget travellers since the 1950s. Rooms are plain but comfortable, set around a light courtyard, with a section of garden to enjoy. Only 3 blocks from the Casa Rosada and 2 from the busy pedestrian Florida.

C The Clan House, Alsina 817, T011-4331 4448, www.bedandbreakfastclan.com.ar. This wonderful B&B has 17 brightly coloured, modern rooms, and offers buffet breakfast, Wi-Fi and a small but lovely terrace.

C Marbella, Av de Mayo 1261, T/F011-4383 3573, www.hotelmarbella.com.ar. Modernized and central, though quiet, breakfast included, English, French, Italian, Portuguese and German spoken. Highly recommended.

D O'Rei, Lavalle 733, T011-4393 7186, www.hotelorei.com.ar. Slightly cheaper without bath, central, simple but comfortable, spotless, laundry facilities, helpful staff.

Hostels

E pp **Portal del Sur**, Hipólito Yrigoyen 855, T011-4342 2821, www.portaldelsurba.com.ar. Lovely dorms, and especially lovely double (**B**) and single rooms (**B**) available. Converted 19th-century building, with 4 storeys of private rooms, and dorms. Recommended for single travellers.

E pp **Trip Recoleta**, Vicente López 2180, T011-4807 8726, www.triprecoletahostel.com.ar. New spotless, dorms and doubles (**B**) decorated in a chic modern style, right next to the Recoleta cemetery, and many popular bars and cafés. Wi-Fi and nice terrace.

E pp **V&S**, Viamonte 887, T011-4322 0994, www.hostelclub.com. **C** in attractive double rooms with bath. This is one of the city's best-loved hostels, central and beautifully run by friendly English-speaking staff, there's a welcoming little café and place to sit, a tiny kitchen, internet access and lots of tours arranged, plus tango nights, etc. Good place to meet people. Highly recommended.

F pp **06Central**, Maipú 306, T011-5219 0052, www.06centralhostel.com. A few metres from the Obelisco and the theatre street of Corrientes, this hostel offers simple, clean spacious dorms, and nicely decorated doubles (**C**). New kitchen, and a small but cosy communal area.

F pp **BA Stop**, Rivadavia 1194, T011-4382 7406, www.bastop.com. Set in a converted corner 1900s corner block, the walls are covered in fun murals, and the communal areas are inviting. Pool table, and buffet breakfast. May be a little noisy as it is right in the middle of the city.

F pp **Lime House**, Lima 11, T011-4383 4561, www.limehouse.com.ar. Fun, lively hostel which organizes bar nights and has a residents-only bar in the reception. Located on busy 9 de Julio, some rooms may be noisy especially the ones close to the reception/bar and pool table, but the staff and the general welcoming atmosphere make this a fun place to stay. Doubles (**E**) available.

Puerto Madero *p67, map p58*

LL Faena Hotel + Universe, Martha Salotti 445, Dique 2, T011-4010 9000, www.faenahotelanduniverse.com. One of the best hotels in the world, this is where the rich and famous stay. Lush, red drapery fills the lobby and the luxury rooms. Stylish swimming pool, extensive gym and glove-wearing men who open doors for you. If you can't afford to stay here, which most of us can't, see a tango show, or have a drink in the bar at least.

LL Hilton, Av Macacha Güemes 351, T011-4891 0000, www.hilton.com. A modern business hotel built on the revamped docks area with views of the Costanera Sur and plenty of restaurants nearby, this has neat functional rooms, the **El Faro** restaurant, a health club and pool.

Palermo *p68, map p58*

LL Legado Mítico, Gurruchaga 1848, T011-4833 1300, www.legadomitico.com. Stylishly designed small hotel with 11 beautiful rooms all subtly thematic. Named after Argentine cultural legends such as Victoria Ocampo, Ernesto Guevara and Jorge Luis Borges, they use local designs, products and art works. Pure luxury. Highly recommended.

LL-AL Bo Bo, Guatemala 4882, Palermo Viejo, T011-4774 0505, www.bobohotel.com. Very chic and one of the most welcoming places to stay in Palermo. Bo Bo has just 7 rooms, designed around different themes, though all are warm, elegant and minimalist, with stylish bathrooms (some with disabled access). There's also an excellent restaurant (🍴) and bar, relaxing places in the evening, with lots of dark wood and smart tables, serving very classy food. Great service from friendly English-speaking staff. Recommended.

AL Five Cool Rooms, Honduras 4742, T011-5235 5555, www.fivebuenosaires.com. Too cool for its own good, perhaps, the style here is brutal concrete with lots of black wood in the spacious rooms, all with king-size beds and bathrooms. There's a living room with DVDs to watch and internet. There's a terrace upstairs too. It's a bit overpriced, but the staff are efficient and speak fluent English.

AL Home, Honduras 5860, T011-4778 1008, www.homebuenosaires.com. Another trendy boutique hotel, this one in Palermo Hollywood, with bold 1950s-inspired textiles and minimalist concrete floors, has a funky vibrant urban chic feel. Just a handful of minimalist rooms around a bar serving light snacks (soup, salads and tapas). Small pool and space to sunbathe at the back. A cool place to hang out in the evenings.

AL Krista, Bonpland 1665, T011-4771 4697, www.kristahotel.com.ar. A delightful surprise, this intimate boutique hotel, hidden behind the plain façade of an elegant townhouse in Palermo Hollywood, was once owned by Perón's doctor, and is well placed for restaurants. It's a very appealing place to stay and good value, with its comfortable, calm, individually designed spacious rooms, all with simple bathrooms and smart bed linen. Wi-Fi, wheelchair access. A real gem. Recommended.

AL Malabia House, Malabia 1555, Palermo Viejo,T011-4833 2410, www.malabiahouse.com.ar. An elegant bed and breakfast in a tastefully converted old house, with 15 light and airy individually designed bedrooms in white and pale green, and lovely calm sitting rooms. Great breakfast. This was the original Palermo boutique hotel, and while it's not the cheapest of the options available, and is always booked ahead, it's recommended as a reliable and welcoming option.

A-B Solar Soler, Soler 5676, T011-4776 3065, www.solarsoler.com.ar. Very homely and extremely welcoming bed and breakfast in a great location in an old town house in Palermo Hollywood and recommended for its excellent service and charming multilingual staff. All rooms have bathrooms, ask for the quiet ones at the back, there's free internet and the breakfasts are good. Recommended.

B Cypress In, Costa Rica 4828, Palermo Viejo, T011-4833 5834, www.cypressin.com. This cosy, compact bed and breakfast offers 8 neat rooms on 2 floors, decorated in pleasing stark modern style, in a centrally located house, where the staff are very friendly. Stylish small sitting and dining area, and outside patio. Charming. Very good value. Recommended.

B Hotel Costa Rica, Costa Rica 4137/39, T011-4864 7390, www.hotelcostarica.com.ar. Small boutique hotel with minimalist design rooms and a bright, welcoming air. Lovely terrace for sunbathing. 3 blocks from Plaza Palermo Viejo's restaurants and boutiques.

B Vida Baires, Gallo 1483, T011-4827 0750, www.vidabaires.com.ar. Located in the residential section of Palermo, close to shops and public transport, this French-style building has been converted into a lovely boutique hotel with 7 clean, light and attractive rooms. Lovely original features, and friendly welcome.

B-C Casa Alfaro, Gurruchaga 2155, T011-4831 0517, www.casaalfaro.com.ar. Homely rustic style in this converted old house, with exposed brick walls, red stone floors, and lots of woven rugs. A variety of rooms, for 2-4, some with bathrooms, and quieter rooms at the back, where there's a lovely little garden. The whole place is clean and neat, and the welcoming owner speaks English.

C Che Lulu, Emilio Zola 5185, T011-4772 0289, www.chelulu.com. Some double rooms and more hostel-style accommodation in this friendly, rambling, laid-back house along a quaint quiet street just a few blocks from Palermo Subte. Not luxurious, but great value and very welcoming. Often recommended.

Hostels

E pp **Zentrum Boutique Hostel**, Costa Rica 4520, T011-4833 9518, www.zentrumhostel.com.ar. More a boutique hotel with some dorm beds, this hostel is located in a renovated townhouse using stylish, modern designs. Double rooms without bathroom (**B**) and with bathroom (**A**) are highly recommended. Enjoy the wonderful wooden terrace to watch the sun go down. Recommended.

F pp **Bait**, El Salvador 5115, T011-4774 3088, www.baitba.com. Small, friendly and located only 3 blocks from the main plaza in Palermo. Rooms are simply decorated, and there is a small private bar upstairs which serves snacks and cold beer.

F pp **Casa Esmeralda**, Honduras 5765, T011-4772 2446, www.casaesmeralda.com.ar. Laid-back, dorms and **D** doubles, neat garden with hammocks and fishpond. Sebastián, owner of trendy bars **La Cigale** and **Zanzibar**, offers basic comfort with great charm.

F pp **Tango Backpackers Hostel**, Thames 2212, T011-4776 6871, www.tangobp.com. Well situated to enjoy Palermo's nightlife, this is a friendly hostel with shared rooms, and **D** doubles, all the usual facilities plus its own restaurant, HI discount.

San Telmo *p69, map p58*

AL Dandi Royal, Piedras 922, T011-4307 7623, www.hotelmansiondandiroyal.com. Perfectly restored 1900s house with stunningly elegant entrance hall and some beautiful rooms all decorated in the original style, with luxurious bathrooms. Interesting location between San Telmo and Congreso, and the added benefit of tango classes downstairs. Charming welcome from English-speaking staff, small pool, and much better value than most of the boutique hotels. Recommended.

AL Ribera Sur, Paseo Colón 1145, between San Juan and Humberto 1, www.riberasurhotel.com.ar. Slightly strange location on a busy 8-lane road on the limit of San Telmo, but inside, this hotel offers a peaceful oasis in shade of grey and white. Chic rooms, with crisp white sheets with earthen-coloured throws. Great bar downstairs, and a tiny pool.

AL Telmho, Defensa 1086, T011-4116 5467, www.telmho-hotel.com.ar. Smartly decorated doubles, with huge beds, and windows that open up onto the famous Plaza Dorrego. See the market from the wonderful roof garden. Flatscreen TVs, new modern bathrooms and helpful staff. Recommended.

AL-A 1890 Hotel, Salta 1074, just outside San Telmo, T011-4304 8798, www.1890hotel.com.ar. This fabulous boutique hotel has 6 rooms all decorated in a modern, attractive way with a/c, heating and wonderful bathrooms. The building itself is a renovated 19th-century residence and there is a tranquil patio to relax in.

A Casa Bolívar, Finochietto 524, T011-4300 3619, www.casabolivar.com. Each room in this wonderful hotel has a different theme, from oriental, to pop to art deco, and they all have a kitchenette and modern bathrooms. Serving breakfast, but no other meals, this is a good longer-term option.

A The Cocker, Av Garay 458, T011-4362 8451, www.thecocker.com. In the heart of the antiques district, this art nouveau house has been cleverly and tastefully restored. It now offers a perfect urban retreat with stylish suites, a cosy, light living room and delightful roof terraces and gardens. Recommended.

A La Casita de San Telmo, Cochabamba 286, T/F011-4307 5073, www.lacasitadesantelmo.com. A restored 1840s house, 7 rooms, most of which open onto a garden with a beautiful fig tree. The owners are tango fans; rooms are rented by the day, week or month.

B The Four, Calvos Calvo 535, T011-4362 1729, www.thefourhotel.com. In the heart of San Telmo this 1930s building has been converted into a lovely bed and breakfast with 6 rooms named after the years of important events in the neighbourhood. Appealing terrace and welcoming staff. Recommended.

C Mi Casa en San Telmo, Chacabuco 764, T011-4300 8583, www.micasaensantelmo.com.ar. Centrally located this small house has 8 large simple rooms and a cosy living area. You will be attended by the welcoming owners.

Hostels

E/F pp **Antico**, Bolívar 893, T011-4363 0123, www.anticohostel.com.ar. On the 1st floor of a wonderful 1900s building, this hostel is slightly more expensive than others but the roof terrace, the bathrooms and the location make up for it. Clean dorms with high ceilings, and doubles upstairs (**C**).

F pp **El Hostal de Granados**, Chile 374, T011-4362 5600, www.hostaldegranados.com.ar. Small well-equipped rooms in an interesting building on a popular street with bars and restaurants, lots of light, for 2 (**C-D**) to 4, with bath, breakfast included, kitchen, free internet, laundry service, reductions for longer stays.

F pp **Hostel-Inn Tango**, Piedras 680, T011-4300 5764, and **Hostel-Inn Buenos Aires**, Humberto Primero 820, T011-43007992, www.hostel-inn.com. Both well-organized hostels in old renovated houses, popular, lively, lots of activities and facilities such as internet, transfers, Spanish lessons. Breakfast included. 20% discount for HI card holders and 10% off long-distance buses.

F pp **Ostinatto**, Chile 680, T011-4362 9639, www.ostinatto.com.ar. The best hostel in the area. Converted 5-level 1920s building, which has a huge open-plan kitchen, spacious dorms, a multi-use dance room where Spanish lessons are held and best of all, a roof terrace where low costs meals are served. Doubles (**C**) with or without a bathroom are also available. In a quiet but central street. Recommended.

F pp **Sandanzas**, Balcarce 1351, T011-4300 7375, www.sandanzas.com.ar. Arty budget hostel run by a group of friends who've created an original and welcoming space, small but with a nice light airy feel, lounge and patio, internet, kitchen, breakfast included. Also (**D**) double rooms with own bath.

Eating

Eating out in Buenos Aires is one of the city's great pleasures, with a huge variety of restaurants from the chic to the cheap. To try some of Argentina's excellent steak, choose from one of the many *parrillas*, where your huge slab of lean meat will be expertly cooked over a wood fire.

Argentines are very sociable and love to eat out, so if a restaurant is full, it's probably a sign that it's a good place. Remember, though, that they'll usually start eating between 2130 and 2230. If in doubt, head for Puerto Madero, where there are lots of good mid-range places. In most restaurants, a *menú fijo* is offered at around US$5-8 for 2 courses. A portion at a *comidas para llevar* (takeaway) costs US$1.50-2.50. Many cheaper restaurants are *tenedor libre*: eat as much as you like for a fixed price. For more information on the gastronomy of Buenos Aires see www.guiaoleo.com.ar, www.vidalbuzzi.com.ar, and 2 fantastic food-orientated blogs (both in English): www.saltshaker.net, written by chef Dan Perlman, and www.foodquests.blogspot.com, by international food writer Layne Molser.

City centre *p64, map p62*

TTT **La Chacra**, Av Córdoba 941 (just off 9 de Julio). A superb traditional *parrilla* with excellent steaks brought sizzling to your table, impeccable old-fashioned service, and a lively buzzing atmosphere.

TTT **Morizono**, Reconquista 899. Japanese sushi and sashimi, as well as other dishes.

TTT **Sorrento** Corrientes 668 (just off Florida). Intimate, elegant atmosphere, with dark wood, nicely lit tables, serving traditional menu with good fish dishes and steak.

TT **Club Español**, Bernardo de Irigoyen 180 (on Av 9 de Julio, near Av de Mayo). Faded splendour in this fine old Spanish social club serving excellent seafood.

TT **Dadá**, San Martín 941. Both a restaurant and bar, and good for gourmet lunches such as prawn salads. Great eclectic decoration.

TT **El Palacio de la Papa Frita**, Lavalle 735 and 954, Av Corrientes 1620. Great traditional place for a filling feed, with a large menu, and quite atmospheric, despite the bright lighting.

TT **El Querandí**, Perú 302 and Moreno. Good food in an intimate atmosphere in this historical place that was opened in the 1920s. Also a popular café, good atmosphere, well known for its gin fizz, and as a tango venue.

Empire Bar, Tres Sargentos 427. Serves slightly expensive but good Thai food in a tasteful atmosphere.

Rocket, Rivadavia 1285. British-style restaurant serving food such as curry and fish pie. Not open weekends.

California Burrito Company, Lavalle 441, www.californiaburritoco.com. Huge Tex-Mex burritos, Corona beers, margaritas, cheap tacos Tue nights. Highly recommended. Not open weekends.

La Casona del Nonno, Lavalle 827. Popular with tourists for its cheap set-price menu, Italian-style food, cheap pastas and *parrilla*.

Pura Vida, Reconquista 516, www.puravidabuenosaires.com. Using all natural ingredients in their salads, juices, sandwiches, wraps and soups. Recommended. Not open weekends. Also in Recoleta.

Tea rooms, cafés and ice cream parlours

Café Tortoni, Av de Mayo 825-9, www.cafetortoni.com.ar. This most famous Buenos Aires café has been the elegant haunt of artists and writers for over 150 years: Carlos Gardel sang here, and Borges was a regular. It's self conscious of its tourist status these days, but still atmospheric, with marble columns, stained-glass ceilings, old leather chairs, and photographs of its famous clientele on the walls. Excellent coffee and cakes, and good tea, all rather pricey, but worth a visit for the interesting *peña* evenings of poetry and music, and jazz and tango.

Clásica y Moderna, Av Callao 892. One of the city's most welcoming cafés, with a bookshop at back, lots of brick and wood, this has a great atmosphere, good for breakfast through to drinks at night, with live music Thu to Sat. Highly recommended.

Como en Casa, Riobamba 1239. Set in a lovely building with a black and white tiled courtyard and a small fountain. Gourmet salads, sandwiches and amazing cakes. Try the brie and sun-dried tomato pizzetta.

Confitería Ideal, Suipacha 384. One of the most atmospheric cafés in the city. Wonderfully old-fashioned 1930s interior, almost untouched, serving good coffee and excellent cakes with good service. Upstairs, tango is taught in the afternoons and there's tango dancing at a *milonga* here afterwards, from 2200. Highly recommended.

El Gato Negro, Av Corrientes 1669. A lovely old traditional café serving a wide choice of coffees and teas, and good cakes. You can also buy a big range of spices here.

Puerto Madero *p67, map p58*

The revamped docks area is an attractive place to eat, and to stroll along the waterfront before dinner. There are good places here, generally in stylish interiors and with good service, if a little overpriced.

Asia de Cuba, Perina Dealessi 750, www.asiadecuba.com.ar. Stunning restaurant serving Asian-influenced dishes, with very attentive staff.

El Bistro + Cava, Martha Salotti 445, in the Faena Hotel + Universe. Expensive but exquisite food with an experienced sommelier to assist in your choices. Highly recommended.

El Clan, Olga Cossettini 1501, www.el-clan.com.ar. Chandeliers, long curtains and shiny cultlery. Try the grilled salmon or the home-made pasta.

i Fresh Market, Azucena Villaflor and Olga Cossettini. Fresh fruits and vegetables served in the most varied ways in this small, trendy restaurant and deli, from breakfasts to dinner.

Recoleta and Barrio Norte *p68, map p58*

Sirop, Pasaje del Correo, Vicente López 1661, T011-48135900. Delightful chic design, delicious French-inspired food, superb patisserie too. Highly recommended.

Tandoor, La Prida1293. Newly opened Indian restaurant with seriously spicy food. Great service but slightly expensive. Recommended.

El Sanjuanino, Posadas 1515. Atmospheric place offering the best of Argentina's typical dishes from the northwest: *humitas*, *tamale*, and *empanadas*, as well as unusual game dishes.

Tea rooms and ice cream parlours

Alvear Palace, Av Alvear 1891, T011-4808 2949. Afternoon tea served in L'Orangerie, with 3-tier cakestands filled with cucumber sandwiches and wonderful cakes. Highly recommended. Book ahead.

Café Victoria, Roberto M Ortiz 1865. A wonderful old-fashioned café, popular with perfectly coiffed ladies sipping tea in a refined atmosphere, great cakes.

Persicco, Salgüero and Cabello, Maure and Migueletes and Av Rivadavia 4933. 'The best ice cream in the world'. You haven't tasted ice cream until you've had Persicco's mascarpone, or their *flan de dulce de leche*. Exquisite chocolate flavours and fruity ice creams and sorbets too. Also delivery: T0810 333 7377. Branches in upmarket areas, but most convenient is **Salgüero** (near Alto Palermo shopping centre) Salgüero 2591 and Cabello. Free Wi-Fi in their shops which also sell coffee. You could sit and eat ice cream all day.

Palermo *p68, map p58*

There are lots of chic restaurants and bars in Palermo Viejo. It's a sprawling area, and lovely to walk around in the evenings. Take a taxi to one of these restaurants, and walk around once you're in the area, before deciding where to eat. Palermo has lots of good cafés opposite the park, including the fabulous ice creams at **Un' Altra Volta**, Av del Libertador 3060, T011-4805 1818.

Palermo Viejo *p69, map p58*

𝛙𝛙𝛙 **Cabernet**, Jorge Luis Borges 1757, T011-4831 3071. The smoked salmon and caviar blinis starter here is unmissable. Sophisticated traditional cuisine, a great wine list and good service. Worth the price for a special dinner.

𝛙𝛙𝛙 **Cluny**, El Salvador 4618, T011-4831 7176. A great place for lunch; the menu is as stylish as the black and cream surroundings, from the excellent home-made bread to the exquisite combinations of flavours of sauces for fish and pasta. One of Palermo's classiest restaurants, whether you dine in the bistro at the back, or chic white armchairs in the middle. Friendly staff, mellow music. Recommended.

𝛙𝛙𝛙 **Dominga**, Honduras 5618, T011-4771 4443, www.domingarestaurant.com. Elegant, excellent food from a short but creative menu, professional service, good wine list, ideal for a romantic meal or treat, open evenings only.

𝛙𝛙 **Bar 6**, Armenia 1676 T011-4833 6807. One of the best chic, modern bars serving food in laid-back spacious surroundings in this large airy space, with bare concrete, bold colours and sofas upstairs for relaxing on. Excellent lunches, friendly atmosphere, good for a drink in the evening. Closed Sun. Recommended.

𝛙𝛙 **Bio**, Humboldt 2199, T011-4774 3880. Delicious gourmet organic food, on a sunny corner where you can sit outside. Fresh lime green decor and a friendly atmosphere. Open daily, but closed Mon for dinner.

𝛙𝛙 **El Diamante**, Malabia 1688 T011-4831 5735. Great loud music in this cosy 1st-floor restaurant and bar with a terrace upstairs for a party atmosphere, gay-friendly. Closed Sun.

𝛙𝛙 **Eterna Cadencia**, Honduras 5574, T011-4774 4100. A real find: this is a fabulous small bookshop with a wonderful selection of English classics and contemporary literature. It has a great little café in beautifully designed high-ceilinged rooms with comfortable sofas at the back, great for a light lunch. Open 0900-2400, closed Mon.

𝛙𝛙 **Krishna**, Malabia 1833. A small, intimate place serving very good Indian-flavoured vegetarian dishes.

𝛙𝛙 **Mark's Deli**, El Salvador 4701. Fabulous café/restaurant serving goodies such as huge salads, overflowing sandwiches and juices. Recommended.

𝛙𝛙 **Omm**, Honduras 5656, T011-4774 4224. Hip, cosy wine and tapas bar with great wines and good food. Open daily from 1800, happy hour from 1800-2100. Sister restaurant **Omm Carnes**, Costa Rica 5198, T011-4773 0954, for steak and meat dishes in a similarly trendy environment. Open daily from 1100 but closed for dinner on Sun.

San Telmo *p69, map p58*

There are plenty of restaurants along Defensa, and in the surrounding streets, and new places are opening all the time.

𝕐𝕐𝕐 **Defensa Al Sur**, Defensa 1338, T011-4300 8017. Converted old shop-front housing one of the smartest restaurants in the area. Wonderful wines and a modern twist on local dishes. Recommended.

𝕐𝕐𝕐 **La Brigada**, Estados Unidos 465, T011-4361 5557. The best choice for *parrilla* in San Telmo, this is a really superb and atmospheric place, serving excellent Argentine cuisine and wines in a cosy buzzing atmosphere. Always reserve.

𝕐𝕐 **Brasserie Petanque**, Defensa and México, T011-4342 7930. Very good French cuisine at affordable prices, and set lunch Mon-Fri. It's an appealing little place, a tasteful combination of Paris and Buenos Aires.

𝕐𝕐 **Café San Juan**, Av San Juan 450, T011-4300 1112. Not a café but a very small *bodegón*, looking just like a typical *restaurant de barrio* (local dive) but with an excellent cook. The short menu includes delicious *tapas de salmón*. It's very popular, book ahead.

𝕐𝕐 **La Vinería de Gualterio Bolívar**, Bolívar 865, T011-4361 4709. Serving tiny portions of tapas-like dishes which are delicious, this small restaurant also boasts efficient staff and an extensive wine list. Recomended.

𝕐𝕐 **Los Lobos**, corner of Estados Unidos and Balcarce. Attractive restaurant, simply designed serving modern fare such as spinach and camembert omelette. Good for lunches.

𝕐 **El Desnivel**, Defensa 855. Popular for cheap and basic food, jam-packed at weekends, good atmosphere.

𝕐 **El Hipopótamo**, Brasil and Defensa (on Parque Lezama). A typical *bodegón*, popular with families, typical Argentine menu, huge portions, though the service is rather slow.

𝕐 **La Trastienda**, Balcarce 460. Theatre café with lots of live events, also serving meals and drinks from breakfast to dinner, great music. Recommended.

𝕐 **Nonna Bianca**, Estados Unidos 425. Great ice cream, as well as an internet café.

𝕐 **Pride Cafe**, corner of Balcarce and Giuffra. Wonderful sandwiches, juices, salads and great brownies. Lots of magazines to read.

Bars and clubs

City centre *p64, map p62*

La Cigale, 25 de Mayo 722. A popular place after office hours that's usually crowded by 2400. Very good music, recommended for Tue evenings with guest DJs.

Le Bar, Tucumán 422. Busy 2-level cocktail bar which attracts the after office crowd, and is a great unpretentious place to chill out.

Milion, Paraná 1048. A French-style residence with lots of sitting areas and tables in the sumptuous halls. It has also a garden and serves very good drinks. A mixed clientele, 25-40 years old, recommended Fri after midnight.

Recoleta *p68, map p58*

Buller Brewing Company, Roberto M Ortiz 1827. Happy hour till 2100.

Locos por el Fútbol, Vicente López 2098. Large brightly coloured cafe/bar filled with TV screens in order to watch local and international football and sometimes rugby.

Palermo *p68, map p58*

878, Thames 878. From the outside this doesn't look like a bar, but knock on the door after midnight and you'll be invited inside to a cosy red room filled with people. Recommended.

Bangalore Pub, Humboldt 1416, y Niceto Vega. Great English pub wonderful mojitos, and wraps. They also serve curries.

Carnal, Niceto Vega 5511 and Humboldt. With a busy roof terrace that is great in summer, good music and a bar downstairs.

Congo, Honduras 5329. Huge bar which extends to a large beer garden at the back.

Interesting crowd and a good range of cocktails. Guys usually have to pay a US$6 cover charge redeemable for drinks.

Mundo Bizarro, Serrano 1222 and Córdoba. This hugely popular bar gets its name from bizarre films shown on a big screen. People usually come here for dinner first, and the food is American style, then they stay all night DJ on Fri and Sat.

Sugar, Costa Rica 4619. Welcoming bar with lots of red and wood to make it feel cosy. Cheapest beer and drinks in Palermo. Happy hour every night. Friendly crowd.

San Telmo *p69, map p58*

Bar Seddon, corner of Defensa and Chile. Wonderful traditional bar open till late with live music on Fri nights. Candles, high ceilings as well as black and white tiles on the floor. Recommended.

Gibralter Peru 895, small British pub, with a tiny beer garden, a pool table and happy hour between 1800-2000 each night. Popular with tourists and locals alike, it is best to go either really early at 1800 or late about 0130. Try the green curry, or the pie.

La Puerta Roja, Chacabuco 733. No sign outside but ring the doorbell and climb the marble stairs. Stylishly designed bar serving pints, great food – wraps and curries – and open till late. Recommended.

La Resistencia, Defensa and Independencia. Local hangout that serves cheap beer and lots of rock music. A fun night out and a chance to speak some Spanish.

Clubs

Generally it is not worth going to clubs before 0230 at weekends. Dress is usually smart, and you can be charged anything from US$10-15, sometimes including a drink.

Club 69 (at Niceto Club), Niceto Vega 5510, T011-4779 9396, www.nicetoclub.com or www.club69.com.ar. On Thu, for a 20-something crowd, good music with live shows, packed after 0200.

El Living, Marcelo T de Alvear 1540, T011-4811 4730. As small, cosy and relaxed as a living room gets, playing 1980s music amongst others.

Mint, Av Costanera Norte and Sarmiento (in Punta Carrasco). On Sat, Latin and electronic music. Mostly 20-somethings. Attractive terrace on the river.

Museum, Perú between Chile and México. Absolutely huge club, which packs out on Wed 'After Office' nights, from 2100 until about 0200.

Pacha, Av Costanera Norte and Pampa, www.pachabuenosaires.com. A big place, upmarket feel, 20- to 30-year-olds, electronic music.

Entertainment

Buenos Aires *p64, maps p58, p62 and p84*

Details of events are given in the 'Espectáculos' section of newspapers, *La Nación* and *Clarín*, and the *Buenos Aires Herald* (English) on Fri, and also in www.whatsupbuenosaires.com.

Cinemas

Films range from new Hollywood releases to Argentine and world cinema; details are listed daily in all main newspapers. Films are shown uncensored and most foreign films are subtitled in Spanish. The cinema will advertise the films which have 'subtítulos'. Tickets are best booked in the early afternoon to ensure good seats (average price US$7-8; discounts on Wed). There are several good cinemas on Lavalle, also in shopping malls, in Puerto Madero (dock 1) and in Belgrano (Av Cabildo and environs). On Fri and Sat nights many central cinemas have *trasnoches*, late shows starting at 0100. Independent foreign and national films are shown during the **Festival de Cine Independiente**, every Apr (www.bafici.gov.ar).

Tango

There are 2 ways to enjoy Buenos Aires' wonderfully passionate dance: watch a show, or learn to dance at a class, and then try your new steps at a *milonga* (tango club). Tango is the key to the Argentine psyche, and you haven't experienced it unless you've tried it on the dance floor. There's a tango information desk at the **Centro Cultural San Martín**, Sarmiento 1551, T011-4373 2829, and a useful website www.tangobuenosaires.gob.ar.

Tango shows See tango at its best. Not cheap, but an unforgettable experience. A show costs around US$70-80, the price includes dinner.

Café Tortoni, see Eating, page 77. Daily tango shows from 2030, US$11.

El Cabaret at Faena Hotel and Universe, Martha Salotti 445, T011-4010 9200. Fabulously choreographed and glamorous, charting tango's evolution. Recommended.

El Viejo Almacén, Independencia and Balcarce, T011-4307 7388, www.viejo-almacen.com.ar. Very impressive dancing from the city's best, excellent live band, and great singing from some of tango's great names. Highly recommended.

La Esquina de Carlos Gardel, Carlos Gardel 3200, T011-4867 6363, www.esquinacarlosgardel.com.ar. A little out of the centre but recommended.

La Ventana, Balcarce 431, T011-4331 0217. Touristy but very good, and the only one to include traditional Argentine folklore music.

Milongas and tango classes Tango has experienced a revival in the last few years and *milongas* are extremely popular among younger Porteños. Classes cost around US$3-4, and complete beginners are welcome. Take a class first, and then stay around to practise when the dancing starts.

La Viruta, Armenia 1366, Palermo Viejo, T011-4774 6357, www.lavirutatango.com. Most popular among a young trendy crowd.

Other recommended places include: **Confitería Ideal**, Suipacha 384, T011-5265 8069; **Central Cultural Torquato Tasso**, Defensa 1575, T011-4307 6506; **Dandi**, Piedras 936, T011-4361 3537, www.mansiondandiroyal.com; and **Porteño and Bailarín**, Riobamba 345, T011-4932 5452, www.porteybailarin.com.ar.

Theatre

Tickets for most popular shows (including rock and pop concerts) are sold through **Ticketek**, T011-5237 7200, www.ticketek.com.ar, **Entrada Plus**, T011-4324 1010, or **Ticketmaster**, T011-4321 9700, www.tm.com.ar.

Teatro Colón, see page 67. Opera and ballet tickets sold 2 days before performance. The best seats cost US$35; 'El Paraíso' tickets are available for standing room in The Gods. Teatro Colón is currently under renovations and is due to open sometime in 2010.

Teatro San Martín, Corrientes 1530, T011-4371 0111/8, www.teatrosanmartin.com.ar. Many cultural activities, often free, including concerts. The **Sala Leopoldo Lugones** shows international classic films, daily, US$2.

O Shopping

Buenos Aires *p64, maps p58, p62 and p84*

Bookshops

Foreign newspapers are available from newsstands on Florida, in Recoleta and the kiosk at Corrientes and Maipú. For English-language books try the friendly **Walrus Books**, Estados Unidos 617, who stock second-hand fiction and non-fiction. The excellent **Yenny-El Ateneo** chain is found in shopping malls and also sells music. Biggest stores are at Florida 340 and Av Santa Fe 1860. The store on Santa Fe is located inside a wonderful old theatre. The café is on the stage. Well worth visiting.

Eterna Cadencia, Honduras 5574, T011-4774 4100, www.eternacadencia.com.ar. Excellent selection of novels in English: classics, translations of Spanish and Argentine authors. Highly recommended for its café too.

Clothes and accessories

Palermo is the best place to find chic boutiques and international designers and you will be spoilt for choice. The 2 main streets are **Honduras** and **El Salvador**.

In the city centre, head to the pedestrianized street of **Florida**, which stretches south from Plaza San Martín, to Av de Mayo, west from Av 9 de Julio to Av Pueyrredón. Along Florida, **Galerías Pacíficos** is a recommended mall with a good range of clothes. Designer clothes shops can be found in exclusive shopping mall **Patio Bullrich** and along Arenales and Santa Fe, between 9 de Julio and Callao. Cheaper clothes can be found in the **Abasto** shopping mall, Subte Carlos Gardel.

Camping equipment

Cacique Camping, Estebán Echeverría 3360, Munro, T011-4762 1668, www.cacique.com.ar. Clothing and equipment.

Ecrin, Av Santa Fe 2723, T011-4792 1935, www.ecrin.com.ar. Imported climbing gear.

Camping Center, Esmeralda 945, www.camping-center.com.ar, T011-4315 0305, and **Montagne**, Florida 719, Paraná 834, www.montagenoutdoors.com.ar, T011-4773 0091, have a good selection of outdoor sports gear and equipment.

Handicrafts

Leather is cheap and of very high quality. **All Horses**, Suipacha 1350, and **Aida**, Galería de la Flor, shop 30, Florida 670, can produce made-to-measure jackets in one day.

Arte y Esperanza, Balcarce 234, and **Artesanías Argentinas**, Montevideo 1386. Excellent little shop with an impressive range of indigenous crafts from all over Argentina. Chaguar bags, masks and weavings. The ethical owners give most of the profits back to the communities. Highly recommended.

Galería del Caminante, Florida 844. A variety of good shops with leather goods, arts and crafts and souvenirs.

Plata Nativa, Galería del Sol, Florida 860, local 41, T011-4312 1398, www.platanativa.com. For Latin American folk handicrafts.

Markets

Many plazas and parks have fairs at weekends, see www.feriademataderos.com.ar for further information.

Feria de Mataderos, 30 mins west of centre by taxi at Av de los Corrales 6436, Sun 1100-2000. Traditional gaucho crafts and games.

Plaza Dorrego, San Telmo. A wonderfully atmospheric market for souvenirs, antiques, some curious bric-a-brac. With free tango performances and live music, Sun 1000-1700.

Plaza Italia, Santa Fe and Uriarte (Palermo). Second-hand books sold daily, handicrafts market on Sat 1200-2000, Sun 1000-2000.

Recoleta, just outside the cemetery. Huge weekend crafts market, with street performers and food. Recommended.

Activities and tours

Buenos Aires *p64, maps p58, p62 and p84*

Football

Soccer fans should go to see the **Boca Juniors** at La Bombonera, Brandsen 805, La Boca, www.bocajuniors.com.ar (see page 71) but it's best to visit with **Tangol** (see Tour operators) as some of the areas are rough. Matches on Sun 1500-1900 and sometimes Fri or Sat. Tour companies will charge around US$40. If you want to go without a tour the cheapest entry is around US$15 but can be hard to buy for popular games and can sometimes be dangerous. Boca's arch-rivals are **River Plate**, www.carp.org.ar. The football season runs Mar-Jun, Aug-Dec.

Polo

Argentina has the top polo players in the world. The high handicap season is Sep-Dec, but it is played all year round (low season: May-Aug). A visit to the national finals at Palermo in Nov and Dec is recommended. For information, **Asociación Argentina de Polo**, T011-4777 6444, www.aapolo.com. To see polo matches and visit stables, you can book tickets through www.ticketec.com.ar.

Tour operators

One way of seeing Buenos Aires is by a 3-hr tour, which can be good for those travelling alone. Longer tours might include dinner and a tango show, or a trip to an estancia. For a cheap tour of the city take the No 29 bus in La Boca – El Caminito – all the way to the posh residential suburb of Belgrano (the bus goes further but this trip will already have taken you at least 1 hr). You will pass colonial houses in San Telmo, the Casa Rosada, the wonderful Tribunales, the bustle of Marcelo T Alvear and Av Santa Fe with its nearby shops, trendy Palermo, and then you can take your leave in Belgrano near Subte stop Juramento and catch the Subte back to the city.

ATI, Esmeralda 567, T011-4329 9000, www.ativiajes.com. Mainly group travel, very efficient, many branches.

BAT (**Buenos Aires Tur**), Lavalle 1444, office 10, T011-4371 2304, www.buenosaires tur.com. City tours twice daily; Tigre and Delta, daily, 6 hrs.

Buenos Aires Visión, Esmeralda 356, p 8, T011-4394 4682, www.buenosaires-vision.com.ar. City tours, Tigre and Delta, Tango (cheaper without dinner) and Fiesta Gaucha.

Cicerones de Buenos Aires, J J Biedma 883, T011-4330 0800, www.cicerones.org.ar. Non-profit organization offering volunteer 'greeting'/guiding service for visitors to the city, free, safe and different.

Class Adventure Travel, Av Presidente Roque Sáenz Peña 615, of 718, www.cat-travel.com. Dutch-owned and run, with 10 years' experience. Excellent for tailor-made travel solutions throughout the continent.

Cultour, www.cultour.com.ar. A highly recommended walking tour of the city. 3-4 hrs led by a group of Argentine history/tourism graduates, US$18. In English and Spanish.

Eternautas, Av Roque Sáenz Peña 1124, p 4B, T011-4384 7874, www.eternautas.com. Historical, cultural and artistic tours of the city and Pampas guided in English, French or Spanish by historians and other social scientists from the University of Buenos Aires, flexible. Highly recommended.

Exprinter, San Martín 170, p 1, office 101, T011-4341 6600, Galería Güemes, www.exprinter viajes.com. Especially their 5-day, 4-night tour to Iguazú and San Ignacio Miní.

Eves Turismo, Tucumán 702, T011-4393 6151, www.eves.com. Helpful and efficient, recommended for flights.

Flyer, Reconquista 617, p 8, T011-4313 8224, www.flyer.com.ar. English, Dutch, German spoken, repeatedly recommended, especially for estancias, fishing, polo, motor-home rental.

La Bicicleta Naranja, Pasaje Giuffra 308, San Telmo, www.labibibletanajanja.com.ar. Bike hire, and bike tours to all parts of the city 4-5 hrs.

Pride Travel, Paraguay 523, p 2, T011-5218 6556, www.pride-travel.com. The best choice for gay and lesbian travellers in Argentina; they also rent apartments.

Say Hueque, Viamonte 749, p 6 of 1, T011-5199 2517/20, www.sayhueque.com. Good-value tours for independent travellers in Argentina.

Smile on Sea, T011-1550188662 (mob), www.smileonsea.com. 2-hr boat trips off Buenos Aires coast in the day and at sunset, leaving from Puerto Madero on 32-ft sailing boats (up to 5 passengers, US$165 for the whole boat). Also 8-hr trips to San Isidro and Delta (US$320 for 5 people) and longer holidays along the Uruguayan coast.

Tangol, Florida 971, p 1, T011-4312 7276, www.tangol.com. Friendly, independent travel agency, specializing in football and tango. Also offers city tours, various sports, such as polo and paragliding, trips to ranches, plane and bus tickets and accommodation. Overland trips to Patagonia Sep-Apr. English spoken. Special deals for students. A reliable and dynamic company. Recommended.

Transport

Buenos Aires *p64, maps p58, p62 and p84*

Air

For flight details, see pages 34-36.
For transport to and from the centre, see page 60.

Airline offices Aerolíneas Argentinas (AR) and **Austral**, Perú 2, Av Leandro N Alem 1134 and Av Cabildo 2900, T0810-2228 6527. **Air France-KLM**, San Martín 344, p 23, T011-43174700. **Alitalia**, Suipacha 1111, T011-4310 9999. **American Airlines**, Av Santa Fe 881, T011-4318 1111, Av Pueyrredón 1997 and branches in Belgrano and Acassuso. **Avianca**, Carlos Pellegrini 1163, p 4, T011-4394 5990. **British Airways**, Viamonte 570, T011-4320 6600. **Copa**, Carlos Pellegrini 989, p 2, T0810-222 2672. **Cubana**, Sarmiento 552, p 11, T011-4325 0691. **Delta**, Reconquista 737, T0800-666 0133. **Iberia**, Carlos Pellegrini, 1163, T011-41311000. **LAB**, Carlos Pellegrini 141, T011-43231900. **Lan Chile**, Cerrito 886 and Paraguay, T0810-999 9526. **Líneas Aéreas del Estado (LADE)**, Perú 710, T011-5129 9000, Aeroparque T011-4514 1524. **Lufthansa**, M T Alvear 590, p 6, T011-4319 0600. **Malaysia Airlines**, Suipacha 1111, p 14, T011-4312 6971. **Mexicana**, Av Córdoba 1131. **puna**, Florida 1, T011-4342 7000. **TAM**, Cerrito 1030, T011-4819 4800. **United Airlnes**, Av Madero 900, T0810-777 8648. **Varig**, Av Córdoba 972, p 4, T011-4329 9211.

3 Buenos Aires metro (Subte)

Buenos Aires maps
1 Buenos Aires orientation, page 58
2 Buenos Aires centre, page 62
3 Buenos Aires metro (Subte), page 84

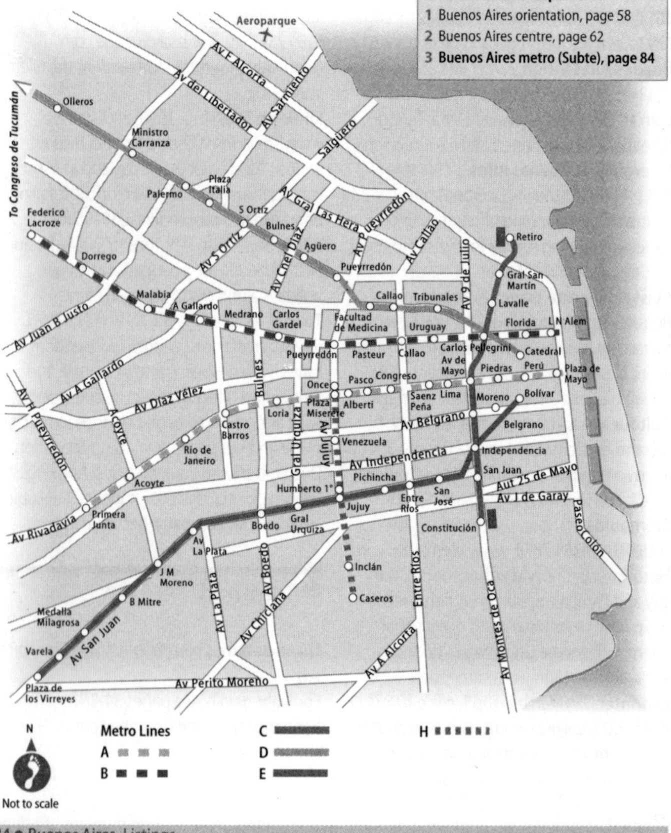

Boat

Connections to the north of Argentina and Uruguay with **Buquebus**, T011-4316 6500, www.buquebus.com.ar. To **Colonia de Sacramento**, 3 daily, 3 hrs, US$20-30 one way (cars US$36-41). **Ferrylíneas Sea Cat** operates a fast service from the same terminal, 1 hr, US$30-34 one-way (cars US$55-61). There is a new company, **Colonia Express**, www.coloniaexpress.com, which also runs trips to Uruguay. They leave from a bit further along the port and offer competitive rates and a much smaller, slightly faster boat. Catch a taxi from town (US$5). Don't forget your passport. Colonia is in Uruguay and you will need to exit Argentina before board the ferry.

Bus

Local *Colectivos* basic fare US$0.30 or US$0.45 to the suburbs, paid with coins into a machine behind the driver. Check that your destination appears on the bus stop, and in the driver's window.

Long distance Boats and buses are heavily booked Dec-Mar, especially at weekends. See also Essentials, page 37. Ticket offices are on the upper floor of **Retiro** bus terminal, Ramos Mejía and Antártida Argentina, and are organized by colour-coded regions of the country.

Car hire

Avis Cerrito 1527 T011-4326 5542, www.avis.com.ar; **Budget**, Santa Fe 869, T011-4311 9870, www.hertz.com, ISIC and GO 25 discount; **Hertz**, Ricardo Rojas 451, T011-4312 1317, www.hertz.com.

Metro

Trains run Mon-Sat 0500-2250, Sun 0800-2200. Free maps are available from Subte stations and the tourist office. Single fare to anywhere US$0.30 payable in pesos only at the ticket booth.

Taxi

For security, phone for a radio taxi: **Onda Verde** T011-4867 0000; **Radio Taxi Sur**, T011-4638 2000; **Radio Taxi 5 Minutos** T011-4523 1200; **Radio Taxi Diez** T011-4585 5007. Fares are shown in pesos, starting at US$0.35, plus US$0.04 for every 200 m or 1-min wait. A charge is sometimes made for hand luggage. *Remise* taxi **La Terminal**, T011-4312 0711, is recommended for journeys from Retiro bus station. About 10% tip is expected.

Directory

Buenos Aires *p64, maps p58, p62 and p84*

Banks and currency exchange

ATMs are widespread. Visa and MasterCard ATMs at branches of **Banco de la Nación Argentina, ABN Amro Bank, BNP, Itaú** and others. MasterCard/Cirrus also at **Argencard** offices. For lost or stolen cards, MasterCard T011-4340 5700, Visa T011-4379 3333. *Casas de cambio* on San Martín and Corrientes. Major credit cards usually accepted but check for surcharges. General **MasterCard** office at Perú 151, T011-4348 7000. **Visa**, Corrientes 1437, 2nd floor, T011-4379 3333.

Embassies and consulates

Open Mon-Fri unless stated otherwise. See also www.paginasblancas.com.ar. **Australia**, Villanueva 1400 and Zabala, T011-4779 3500, www.argentina.embassy.gov.au, 0830-1100. **Canada**, Tagle 2828, T011-4808 1000, www.dfait-maeci .gc.ca/argentina, Mon-Thu 1400-1600, tourist visa Mon-Thu 0845-1130. **Chilean Consulate**, San Martín 439, 9th floor, T011-4394 6582, www.embajadadechile.com.ar, 0900-1300. **New Zealand**, C Pellegrini 1427, 5th floor, T011-4328 0747, www.nzembassy.com/buenosaires, Mon-Thu 0900-1300, 1400-1730, Fri 0900-1300. **UK**, Luis Agote 2412 (near corner Pueyrredón and Guideo), T011-4808 2200 (call T15-5114 1036 for emergencies only out of normal office hours), www.ukinargentina.fco.gov.

uk/es, 0900-1300 (Jan-Feb 0900-1200). **US Embassy and Consulate General**, Colombia 4300, T011-4514 1830, 0900-1800.

Immigration

Migraciones: (Immigration), Antártida Argentina 1335/55, edificios 3 and 4, T011-4317 0200. Visas extended mornings.

Internet

Prices range from US$0.50-1 per hr, shop around. Most *locutorios* (phone centres) have internet access.

Language schools

All-Spanish, T011-4381 3914, www.all-spanish.com.ar; **Argentina ILEE**, T011-4372 0223, www.argentinailee.com; **IBL (Argentina Spanish School)**, Florida 165, 3rd floor, oficina 328, T011-4331 4250, www.ibl.com.ar, group and one-to-one lessons, all levels; **Instituto del Sur**, T011-4334 1487, www.delsur.com.ar; **PLS**, T011-4394 0543, www.pls.com.ar; **Universidad de Buenos Aires**, T011-4334 7512, www.idiomas.filo.uba.ar.

A new school, **Expanish**, T011-4322 0011, www.expanish.com, is quickly becoming the favourite among travellers because they organize lots of activities as well as accommodation. For private lessons and small groups, **Gisela Giunti**, T011-1556 260162, www.gisela giunti.com, is highly recommended.

Medical services

For free ambulance service to an emergency department (day and night) call **Sala de guardia**, T107, or T011-4923 1051/58. **Hospital Argerich**, Almte Brown esq Pi and Margall 750, T011-4124 0700. **Hospital Juan A Fernández**, Cerviño and Bulnes, T011-4808 2600. **British Hospital**, Perdriel 74, T011-4309 6400, www.hospitalbritanico.org.ar, US$26 a visit.

Police

Central Police Station: Moreno 1550, Virrey Cevallos 362, T011-4370 5911/5800.

Post office

Correo Central – Correos Argentinos, Sarmiento and Alem, Mon-Fri 0800-2000, Sat 0900-1300. Poste restante on ground floor (US$1 per letter). **UPS**, Bernardo de Irigoyen 974, T011-4339 2877, www.ups.com.

Safety

If robbed or attacked, call the tourist police, **Comisaría del Turista**, Av Corrientes 436, T011-4346 5748 (24 hrs). English spoken. Street crime is on the rise, especially in La Boca, San Telmo and Recoleta. Be careful when boarding buses and near train and bus stations. Don't change money on the street.

Student travel

Asatej: Argentine Youth and Student Travel Organization, Florida 835, 3rd floor, T011-4114 7600, www.asatej.com. **Asatej Travel Store**, sells travel goods.

Telephone

Locutorios are available on almost every block (see Essentials, page 53). Public telephone boxes use coins (25 centavos minimum). Pre-paid cards are available at *kioskos*), don't accept cards without a wrapper or with a broken seal. International telephone calls from hotels may incur a 40-50% commission.

Argentine Lake District

Contents

Footprint features

Border crossings

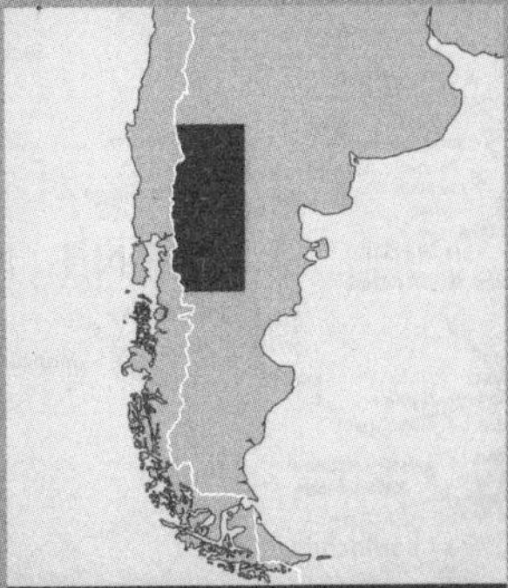

At a glance

Getting around Wonderfully efficient modern minivans run to the main towns, and will drop you off at some camping grounds too. A car or bicycle will give you even more freedom.

Time required At least 4-7 days to visit Bariloche, and a couple of smaller towns/or hikes.

Weather Raining and cold from May-Aug and high temperatures from Nov-Mar.

When not to go Winter (May-Jul) unless you are going skiing, and Aug in Bariloche can be busy with students.

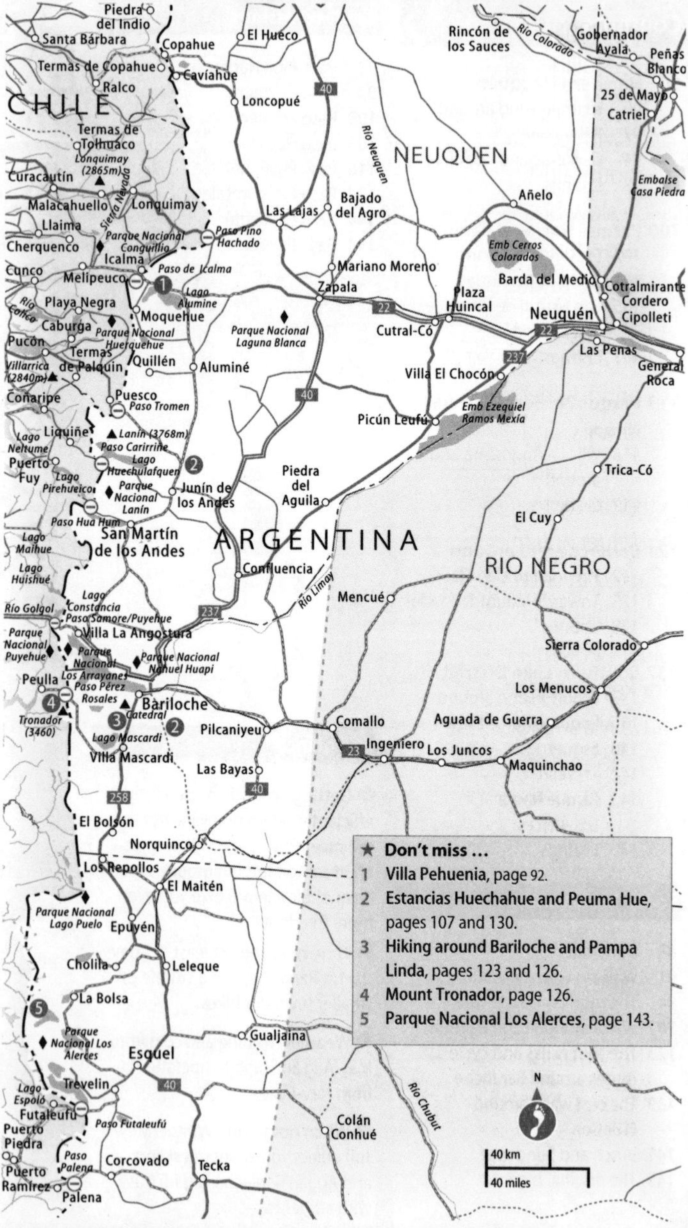

★ **Don't miss ...**

1. **Villa Pehuenia**, page 92.
2. **Estancias Huechahue and Peuma Hue**, pages 107 and 130.
3. **Hiking around Bariloche and Pampa Linda**, pages 123 and 126.
4. **Mount Tronador**, page 126.
5. **Parque Nacional Los Alerces**, page 143.

Trek amongst craggy snow-capped peaks flanked by glaciers, and crystalline rivers running through virgin valdivian rainforest to lakes of peppermint green and Prussian blue. Ski down long pistes with panoramic views of lagoons below, or hike for days in a mountain-top nirvana without seeing any sign of civilization. Take a slow boat across fjords or a hair-raising whitewater rafting trip. Argentina's Lake District stretches over 400 km of spectacular forest-clad Andes mountains, and has four national parks, keeping it pristine.

With a dramatic lakeside setting, Bariloche is the central base for exploring: a friendly town with chocolate shops and chalet-style restaurants, and easy access to a towering range of peaks around Cerro Catedral. From here, a magical road winds past seven lakes to the pretty tourist town of San Martín de los Andes. Retreat to Lago Huechulafquen, where the perfectly conical Volcán Lanín is reflected in cobalt blue waters, try world-class fly fishing, or enjoy breathtaking horse riding at Estancia Huechahue. North of here, wilder Pehuenia is a quiet haven with its forests of prehistoric monkey puzzle trees, broad lagoons, and the rich culture of the native Mapuche people.

At the southern end of the lakes, El Bolsón is a wonderfully relaxed place for a few days' hiking; the mountains are magnificent and the local *cerveza* is excellent . Take the *Old Patagonian Express*, try a Welsh tea in quaint Trevelin, or explore the region's most unspoilt national park, Los Alerces. A jade green river flows between the cinnamon trunks of arrayanes trees and 1000-year-old alerce trees tower above you. And best of all, if you come in March or April, you'll have all this virtually to yourself.

Northern Neuquén

The province of Neuquén contains the northern part of the Lake District, an enormous region stretching from just north of Bariloche to the border with Mendoza province. The gateway to the area is the pleasant city of Neuquén on the province's eastern border. This is an important fruit-growing area, providing most of Argentina's apples, pears and grapes. To the southwest, enormous dinosaur footprints mark the landscape around Villa El Chocón; the skeleton in the museum there is proof that the world's largest known carnivores roamed around this area about 100 million years ago.

The unspoilt wilderness in the northwest of the province has only recently started attracting visitors, although it is just as spectacular as the more popular destinations to the south. The area west of Zapala, known as Pehuenia has large forests of ancient pehuén or monkey puzzle trees. Further north, Caviahue is a good base for walking and skiing in a rugged and unspoilt landscape, while bleaker Copahue is known for its high-quality thermal waters. » *For listings, see pages 95-99.*

Neuquén and around » *pp95-99. Colour map 1, C5.*

The provincial capital is an attractive industrial town, founded in 1904, just after the arrival of the railway. It has no major attractions but is a useful stopping point en route to the lakes and a good base for exploring the dinosaur finds in the area to the southwest.

Ins and outs

Getting there There are daily flights from Buenos Aires to the **airport** ⓘ *7 km west of town, T0299-444 0245*. Take a local bus 10 or 11 to the centre of town for US$0.40 (*tarjeta* bus card needed); taxi US$5. Long-distance buses arrive regularly at the central **bus terminal** ⓘ *Planas and Solalique,T0299-445 2300 left luggage US$1 a day per item*, from Buenos Aires and towns throughout the Lake District as well as from Temuco and Puerto Montt in Chile.

Tourist information ⓘ *Av Argentina and Roca , T0299-442 1200, www.neuquentur.gov.ar, daily Mon-Fri 0700-2000, Sat and Sun 0800-2000.* The office hands out helpful lists of accommodation and a good map.

Sights

At the northern end of Avenida Argentina at the Parque Centenario (not to be confused with the Centenario industrial suburb on the outskirts of town) is the **Mirador Balcón del Valle** with panoramic views over the city and the confluence of the rivers. In the university buildings at the entrance of the park is the **Museo Paleontológico de Ciencias Naturales** ⓘ *Argentina 1400*, which includes exhibitions of dinosaur fossils found in the region. The **former railway station**, at Olascaoga and Pasaje Obligado, has been converted into a cultural centre and exhibition centre. The **Museo de la Ciudad Paraje Confluencia** ⓘ *Independencia and Córdoba, T0299-442 9785*, has a small display on the colonial annihilation of indigenous groups in the Campaign of the Desert (see Background, page 392. South of the centre there is a pleasant walk along the Río Limay.

Facing Neuquén and connected by a bridge is **Cipolletti**, in the Río Negro province, a prosperous fruit-growing centre of the region. All the towns in the valley celebrate the **Fiesta Nacional de la Manzana** (The National Apple Festival – apples are the main local crop) in the

Walking with dinosaurs

Few countries are as important as Argentina for palaeontologists. The relative abundance of fossils near the surface has made the country one of the most important for the study of dinosaur evolution. Patagonia was home to Jurassic dinosaurs (180-135 million years ago) and outstanding examples have been found here. Cerro Cóndor in Chubut is the only site of Middle Jurassic dinosaurs found in the Americas, and has given palaeontologists an important breakthrough in understanding the evolutionary stages of the period. At least five examples of patagosaurus have been found, indicating that these dinosaurs were social creatures, perhaps for purposes of mutual defence. In Santa Cruz traces of dinosaurs from the Upper Jurassic period have been found in rocks which indicate that the climate was arid and desert-like at the time, surprising palaeontologists with the news that dinosaurs could live and breed in such adverse conditions.

The most important discoveries of dinosaurs from the Cretacic period (135-70 million years ago) have been made in Neuquén and Chubut. Dating from the period of separation of the continents of South America and Africa, these provide evidence of the way in which dinosaurs began to evolve in different ways due to geographic isolation. For example, the *Carnotaurus sastrie* had horns and small hands. The Patagonian dinosaurs were relatively huge: the *Argentinosaurus huiculensis* was one of the largest herbivorous dinosaurs found on earth, while the carnivorous *Gigantosaurus carolinii* found near Neuquén city was larger even than the better known *Tyranosaurus rex*, discovered in North America.

The best places for dinosaur spotting in Patagonia are: **Villa El Chocón**, southwest of Neuquén city, boasts huge and perfectly preserved dinosaur footprints next to the lake. Further finds from the site can be seen in Neuquén's palaeontological museum. **Trelew** on the Atlantic coast, has the country's finest dinosaur museum; and as part of the same foundation, there's an excellent site with 40 million years of history near the Welsh village of **Gaiman**.

second half of March. Two lakes nearby, **Lago Pellegrini**, 36 km north, and **Embalse Cerro Colorado**, make a pleasant excursion from the city, with daily buses in summer.

Villa El Chocón and around → *Colour map 1, A5.*

To the southwest of Neuquén lies the huge **Embalse Ezequiel Ramos Mexía** in an area that has become famous in recent years for its wealth of dinosaur fossils. Villa El Chocón lies at the northern end of the lake, 72 km from Neuquén, on the most direct route to Bariloche. It's a neat, rather uninspiring town, but worth a stop for the amazing evidence of **dinosaurs** nearby (take Route 237 towards Piedra del Aguila, and turn left at Barrio Llanquén to the lake shore). Red sedimentary rocks have preserved bones and even footprints of the creatures that lived in this region about 100 million years ago during the Cretaceous period. Some of these can be seen at the **Museo Paleontológico Ernesto Bachmann** ⓘ *Civic Centre, T0299-490 1223, www.interpatagonia.com/paseos/ernestobachmann, daily winter 0900-1900, summer 0800-2100; guided tours, website has information in English.* Exhibits include fossils of the mighty 10-ton, 15-m-long *Gigantosaurus carolinii*, a carnivorous dinosaur larger than the more famous *Tyrannosaurus rex*. There's an interesting display with information on these mind-boggling discoveries.

In the **Valle Cretácico**, 18 km south of Villa El Chocón, near the Dique with its pedestals of eroded pink rock, there are two walks beside the lake to see more dinosaur footprints, amazingly well preserved.

Plaza Huincul → *Colour map 1, A5.*

The town of Plaza Huincul, 107 km west of Neuquén, would be rather dull if it weren't for its impressive dinosaur museum. The **Museo Municipal Carmen Funes** ⓘ *RN22 and RN17, Mon-Fri 0900-1930, Sat and Sun 0900-2100*, includes the vertebrae of *Argentinossaurus huinclulensis*, believed to have weighed over 100 tons and to have been one of the largest herbivorous dinosaurs ever to have lived, as well as a nest of fossilized dinosaur eggs.

Zapala and around → *Colour map 1, A4.*

Zapala (1012 m) lies in a vast dry plain with views of snow-capped mountains to the west. It's a modern and unappealing town, but a useful stopover on Route 40, to cross the border into Chile at the Icalma pass (see page 93), or to explore the less visited northern end of the Lake District. There is a **tourist office** ⓘ *San Martín and Mayor Torres, T02942-424296, summer Mon-Fri 0700-1930, Sat and Sun 0800-1300, 1600-1900; closes earlier off-season, for information and accommodation listings.*

The **Museo Mineralógico Dr Juan Olsacher** ⓘ *Etcheluz 52 (next to the bus terminal), neumin@zapala.com.ar, Mon 0900-1500, Sat and Sun 1600-2000, free*, is one of the best museums of its kind in South America; it contains over 2000 types of mineral and has the finest collection of fossils of marine reptiles and marine fauna in the country. On display is the largest turtle shell from the Jurassic period ever found and an ophthalmosaur, as well as photos of an extensive cave system being excavated nearby.

Southwest of Zapala is the **Parque Nacional Laguna Blanca** ⓘ *entrance 10 km from the junction of RN46 and RN40, www.parquesnacionales.gov.ar, US$4, no public transport*, a reserve covering large areas of high arid steppe and a vast lagoon that is one of the most important nesting areas of the black-necked swan. The landscape is very dry, and rather bleak, so take drinking water and a hat.

Pehuenia ⊖⊖▲⊖ ▸▸ *pp95-99. Colour map 1, A3/A4.*

The magical and unspoilt area of Pehuenia is named after the country's unique forests of pehuén trees, which grow here in vast numbers. Covering a marvellous mountainous landscape, these ancient trees create a mystical atmosphere, especially around the lakes of Aluminé and Moquehue. To make the most of this area, you really need to hire a car in San Martín de los Andes (see page 105), as buses from Zapala and Neuquén are slow and unreliable. Cyclists will love the view, but note that the *ripio* is rough and there is little shade.

Villa Pehuenia and around → *Colour map 1, A3.*

This picturesque sprawling village is prettily situated on the northern shores of Lago Aluminé, 107 km west of Zapala. It makes a lovely base for a few days' relaxation, and there are some wonderful gentle walks in the hills and forests around. The **Mapuche** (see box, page 245), the largest indigenous group in the south of the continent, chose this area for settlement because of its chain of eight volcanoes and its sacred pehuén trees. Villa Pehuenia is well set up for tourism: a whole cluster of upmarket *cabañas* have opened here in recent years, with one exceptionally lovely boutique hotel, **La Escondida** (see Sleeping, page 95). A **tourist kiosk** ⓘ *T02942-498044, www.villapehuenia.gov.ar*, is signposted by the

Border crossings

Paso Pino Hachado

At (1864 m), this pass lies 115 km west of Zapala via Route 22. On the Chilean side the road runs northwest to Lonquimáy, 65 km west and Temuco, 145 km southwest. Buses from Zapala and Neuquén to Temuco use this crossing.

Argentine immigration and customs 9 km east of the border, 0700-1300, 1400-1900.

Chilean immigration and customs Liucura, 22 km west of the border, December-March 0800-2100, April-November 0800-1900. Very thorough searches and two- to three-hour delays reported.

Paso de Icalma

A more tricky route is via Paso de Icalma (1303 m), 132 km west of Zapala, reached by Route 13 (*ripio*). On the Chilean side this road continues to Melipeuco, but is often impassable in winter. Permission to cross must be obtained from the Policía Internacional in Temuco (Prat 19, T045-293890).

Argentine immigration and customs 9 km east of the border, 0800-2000 in summer, 0900-1900 in winter. All paperwork is carried out at the customs office.

Chilean immigration and customs December-March 0800-2100, April-November 0800-1900.

turning for the village. The peninsula stretching out into the lake offers wonderful walks along the araucaria-fringed shore and fabulous views from the **Mirador del Cipres**.

Just a few kilometres further along the main road from Villa Pehuenia, signposted to the right, is the **Batea Mahuida** (*www.interpatagonia.com/bateamahuida*) a reserve created to protect an area of pehuén trees and the majestic volcano, regarded by the Mapuche as sacred. This is a lovely area for walking in summer, with tremendous views of all seven volcanoes. There's also a winter sports centre, **Parque de Nieve**, administrated by the Mapuche people, offering snowmobiles, snowshoe walks and husky rides. Delicious home-cooked food is served.

Lago Moquehue → *Colour map 1, A3.*

Another 10 km on Route 13 brings you to the sprawling village of Moquehue, on the shores of the lake. It's wilder and more remote than Villa Pehuenia with a lovely wide river that's famous for trout fishing. This is a beautiful and utterly peaceful place to relax and walk. A short stroll through araucaria forests brings you to a waterfall, while a longer hike to the top of **Cerro Bandera** (four hours return) provides wonderful views over the area as far as Volcán Llaima. You should also head along Route 13, 11 km to **Lago Norquinco**, past mighty basalt cliffs with pehuén trees all around. There are fine camping spots all around and a couple of comfortable places to stay.

Aluminé and around → *Colour map 1, A3.*

On Route 23 between Pehuenia and Junín lies the area's self-proclaimed rafting capital. There is indeed superb rafting (Grades II-VI) on **Río Aluminé**, but despite the grand setting, the town is a drab little place with *ripio* roads. There's a very friendly **tourist office** ⓘ *C Christian Joubert 321, T0294-496001, www.alumine.gov.ar, 0800-2100 all year*, and a

The monkey puzzle tree

The *Araucaria araucana*, is known in Argentina and Chile as the araucaria or pehuén and elsewhere called variously the Chilean pine, the umbrella tree, the parasol tree and the monkey puzzle tree. The species has flourished on both sides of the Andes at a latitude of 37-39° south for 200 million years, although, it is much more widespread in Chile than in Argentina. Very slow growing, it can reach up to 40 m high and live for 1200 years. The characteristic cones can weigh up to 1 kg. The araucaria was revered by the Mapuche, who ate both its cones and its sharp leathery leaves. Some isolated trees are still seen as sacred by the Mapuche who leave offerings to the tree's spirit.

service station – the first you'll reach driving south from Villa Pehuenia. In March, the harvest of the *piñones* is celebrated in the **Fiesta del Pehuén** with horse riding and live music.

From Aluminé there is access to **Lago Rucachoroi**, 23 km west, in Parque Nacional Lanín. This is the biggest Aigo Mapuche community inside the park and is set in gentle farmland surrounded by ancient pehuén forests. Access is by a rough *ripio* road, spectacular in autumn when the deciduous trees are a splash of orange against the bottle-green araucarias. The *guardería* can advise about a possible trek to Lago Quillén.
⏩ *For information on the rest of Parque Nacional Lanín, see page 100.*

Lago Quillén → *Colour map 1, A3*

At the junction by the small town of **Rahue**, 16 km south of Aluminé, a road leads west to the valley of the Río Quillén and the exquisite Lago Quillén, from where there are fine views of Volcán Lanín peeping above the mountains. The lake itself is one of the region's most lovely, jade green in colour, with beaches along its low-lying northern coast. Further west, where annual rainfall is among the heaviest in the country, the slopes are thickly covered with Andean Patagonian forest. There's no transport, and accommodation only is at the **Camping Pudu Pudu** (with food shop and hot showers) on the lake's northern shore just west of the *guardería*.

Caviahue and Copahue ⏩ *pp95-99. Colour map 1, A3.*

In an attractive lakeside setting 150 km north of Zapala, **Caviahue** is an excellent base for walking and riding in summer and for winter sports from July to September, when it is one of cheaper ski resorts in the Lake District. **Tourist information** ⓘ *8 de Abril, bungalows 5 and 6, T02948-495036, www.caviahue-copahue.com.ar, 0900-1200.*

The arid, dramatic and other-worldly landscape of the **Reserva Provincial Copahue** is formed by a giant volcanic crater, whose walls are the surrounding mountains. The park was created to protect the araucaria trees that grow on its slopes and provides the setting for some wonderful walks through unexpectedly stunning scenery. **Copahue** (1980 m) is a thermal spa resort enclosed in a huge amphitheatre formed by mountain walls. It boasts the best thermal waters in South America, although it's decidedly bleaker than Caviahue Information is available on Route 26, on the approach into town.

Volcán Copahue last erupted, smokily, in 2002 , destroying the bright blue lake in its crater, but the views of the prehistoric landscape are still astounding. Even more highly recommended, however, is an excursion to **El Salto del Agrio**, on Route 27. This is the climax in a series of delightful waterfalls, between ancient araucaria trees poised on basalt cliffs. Other walks will take you to **Las Máquinas**, 4 km south of Copahue, where sulphurous steam puffs through air holes against a panoramic backdrop. And to **El Anfiteatro**, where thermal waters reaching 150°C, are surrounded by a semicircle of rock edged with araucaria trees. Just above Copahue, is **Cascada Escondida**, a torrent of water falling 15 m over a shelf of basalt into a pool surrounded by a forest of araucaria trees; above it is magical **Lago Escondida**.

Northern Neuquén listings

For Sleeping and Eating price codes and other relevant information, see pages 41-44.

Sleeping

Neuquén *p90*

AL Hotel del Comahue, Av Argentina 377, T0299-443 2040, www.hoteldelcomahue.com. The most comfortable by a long way is this international-style, elegant modern 4-star, with spa and pool, excellent restaurant, very good service and business facilities.

B Amucan, Tucumán 115, corner with Rivadavia, T0299-442 5209, www.amucan hotel.com.ar. Smart modern place with nice rooms and good breakfast.

C Alcorta, Alcorta 84, T0299-442 2652. Good value, breakfast, TV in rooms. Also apartments for 4.

C Royal, Av Argentina 143, T0299-448 8902, www.royalhotel.com.ar. A smart modern hotel, but with welcoming rooms, car parking and breakfast included, good value.

Villa El Chocón and around *p91*

B La Posada del Dinosaurio, Costa del Lago, Barrio 1, Villa El Chocón, T0299-490 1200, www.posadadinosaurio.com.ar. Convenient for dinosaur hunting, this has very plain but comfortable rooms, with views over the lake, and a restaurant.

D La Villa, Club Municipal El Chocón, T0299-490 1252. Decent budget choice.

Plaza Huincul *p92*

C Hotel Tortorici, Cutral-Co, 3 km west, Av Olascoaga and Di Paolo, T0299-496 3730, www.hoteltortorici.com.ar. The most comfortable option is this basic hotel with neat rooms and a restaurant.

Zapala *p92*

AL Hostal del Caminante, outside Neuquén 13 km south towards Zapala, T02942-444 0118, www.hostaldelcaminante.com. A popular place in summer, with a pool and garden.

A Hue Melén, Brown 929, T02942-422414, www.hotelhuemelen.com.Good-value 3-star hotel, with decent rooms. The restaurant serves the best food in town, including local specialities.

B Huincul, Av Roca 311, T02942-431422. A spacious place with a cheap restaurant, serving good home-made regional food.

C Pehuén, Elena de Vega y Etcheluz, T02942-423135. Comfortable, 1 block from bus terminal, with an interesting display of maps.

Villa Pehuenia *p92*

There's one superb boutique hotel, and plenty of *cabañas*, many with good views over the lake and set in idyllic woodland. Email or ring first for directions, since there are no road names or numbers here.

AL La Escondida, western shore of the peninsula, T02942-1569 1166, www.posadala escondida.com.ar. By far the best place to stay in the whole area, this really special boutique hotel has just 9 rooms in an imaginatively designed building right on the rocky lakeside. Each room is spacious and beautifully considered, with smart bathrooms (all with jacuzzi), private decks and gorgeous views over the lake. The restaurant is superb and uses fine local produce. Non-residents can dine here with a reservation. Highly recommended.

AL-A Altos de Pehuén, T02942-1566 6849, www.altosdelpehuen.com.ar. Comfortable *cabañas* with lovely views. Also a *hostería*.

A Complejo Patagonia, T02942-1557 9434 , or in Buenos Aires T011-1550114470, www.complejopatagonia.com.ar. Very comfortable indeed, these lovely *cabañas* are traditionally designed and the service is excellent. Recommended.

B Cabañas Bahía Radal, T02942-498057, www.bahiaradal.com.ar. Luxurious *cabañas* in an elevated position with clear lake views.

B-C Las Terrazas, T02942-498036, www.lasterrazaspehuenia.com.ar. The owner is an architect of Mapuche origin, who has retained Mapuche style in his beautiful design of these comfortable *cabañas*: tasteful, warm and with perfect views of the lake, with also **D** B&B. He can take you to visit Mapuche communities. Warmly recommended.

C La Serena, T011-547940319, www.complejo laserena.com.ar. Beautifully equipped and designed *cabañas* for 2-6 people with great uninterrupted views, gardens going down to beach, sheltered from wind, furnished with rustic-style handmade cypress furniture, and wood stoves, all very attractive.

C Puerto Malén Club de Montaña, T02942-498007, T011-4226 8190 (Buenos Aires), www.puertomalen.com. Well-built wooden *cabañas* with lake views from their balconies, and the highest quality interiors. Also a luxurious *hostería*. Recommended.

Camping

Camping Agreste Quechulafquen, at the end of the steep road across La Angostura. Situated among lovely steep hills and dense vegetation, run by Mapuche Puels.

Camping El Puente, La Angostura. US$3 pp, with hot showers; a simpler site, in beautiful surroundings.

Las Lagrimitas, just west of the village, T02942-498003. A lovely secluded lakeside site on the beach, US$3 pp, with food shop, hot showers and fireplaces.

Lago Moquehue *p93*

C-B Hostería Moquehue, T02946-1566 0301, www.hosteriamoquehue.com.ar. Set high above the lake with panoramic views, cosy, stylish, rustic rooms, nicely furnished. Excellent food: try the superb Moquehue trout and local *chivito*. Charming hosts.

D La Bella Durmiente, T0299-496172. In a rustic building with no heating, summer only, the welcoming owner offers good food and also offers trekking, horse riding, diving in the lake, mountain bikes. Call for directions.

Cabañas

A Cabañas Los Maitenes, T02942-421681, T02942-15665621, www.interpatagonia.com/cablosmaitenes. Right by the lake, well-equipped *cabañas*, with breakfast included, and friendly owners. Recommended.

A La Busqueda, T02942-15660377, www.la busquedamoquehue.com.ar. Just north of the lake. Interesting design, well-equipped *cabañas* with TV, including breakfast. Recommended.

B-C Cabañas Melipal, T02948-495056. Very attractive, rustic stone-built *cabañas* in secluded sites right on lake side. Lovely old-fashioned style, well equipped and warm, fabulous views from the balconies, use of boats. Highly recommended.

C Cabañas Huerquen, T0299-4401650, huerquen_patagoni@hotmail.com. Beyond Moquehue on the road to Ñorquinco, these are lovely secluded stone *cabañas* in beautifully tranquil settings.

Camping

Along RN 13, 11 km to Lago Ñorquinco, past mighty basalt cliffs with pehuéns all around, there's idyllic camping. Also idyllic, reached by RN 11 are the smaller campsites of **Lagos Pilhué** and **Ñorquinco Camping**.

Camping Trenel, on the southern shore of Lago Moquehue. Beautiful shady sites in a fabulous elevated position surrounded by ñirre trees; *parrillas* overlooking lake. Hot showers, restaurant and shop Recommended.

Ecocamping Ñorquinco, T02942-496155, www.ecocampingnorquinco.alojar.com.ar.

There's an amazing rustic *cabaña* right on the lakeside, with a café by the roadside, US$6 pp per night US$3 for under 12, Dec-Mar/Apr. Great fishing, hot showers and a *proveduría*. This is a lovely place to eat and drink if it rains.

Aluminé *p93*

AL Estancia Quillén, RN 46 near Rahue, near the bridge crossing Río Aluminé, T02942-496196, www.interpatagonia.com/quillen. A comfortable, traditionally furnished house, with spacious rooms, and a restaurant, where you'll be welcomed by the estancia owners. Open Dec-Apr. Great for fishing and hunting.
AL Piedra Pintada, T02972-429510, www.piedrapintada.com.ar. Only 35 km from town, this is the best option. Only 12 rooms, stylishly fitted out, with a sauna, fantastic views over the lake and an impressive restaurant.
B Pehuenia, just off R23, Crouzeilles 100, T02942-496340, pehuenia2000@yahoo.com.ar. A huge tin chalet-style building, not attractive, but with great views over the hills opposite. The rooms are comfortable and simple, the staff are friendly, and it's good value. Horse riding, bike hire and canoeing at the owner's campsite, **Bahía de los Sueños**, 6 km from the red bridge north of Aluminé.

Camping

La Vieja Balsa, T02942-496001, just outside Aluminé on R23 on the Río Aluminé. A well-equipped site, that offers rafting and fishing, US$2 pp per day to camp, hot showers, food shop, fireplaces, tables, open Dec to Easter.

There are 2 campsites before and after **Lago Rucachoroi**; open all year, but really ideal only Dec-Feb. The first has more facilities, with toilets, but no hot water, some food supplies, including wonderful Mapuche bread and sausages, and offers horse riding.

Caviahue *p94*

B Lago Caviahue, Costanera Quimey-Co, T02948-495110, www.hotellagocaviahue.com. Good value, comfortable lakeside apartments with kitchen, good restaurant, great views, 2 km from the ski centre.
B Nevado Caviahue, 8 de Abril s/n, T02948-495053, www.hotelnevado.com.ar. Plain rooms, but modern, and there's a restaurant, and cosy lounge with wood fire. Also **A-B** for 6 *cabañas*, well equipped but not luxurious.
C Farallon, Caviahue Base, T02948-495085. Neat apartments, some with kitchens.
C La Cabaña de Tito, Puesta del Sol s/n, T02948-495093. *Cabañas* near lake, excellent meals.

Hostels

F pp **Hebe's House**, Mapuche and Puesta del Sol, T02948-495237, www.hebeshouse.com.ar. Lovely chalet-style building with great communal areas and only 2 blocks from the centre of town. Doubles (**D**) available.

Copahue *p94*

A-B Hotel Copahue, Olascoaga y Bercovich, T02948-495117, www.copahuejunin.com.ar. Lovely old place where you'll be warmly welcomed. Recommended. Well-built wood and stone *cabañas*.

Camping

Copahue, T02948-495111; and
Hueney Municipal, T02948-495041.

Eating

Neuquén *p90*

1900 Cuatro, at the **Comahue Hotel**, Av Argentina 377. Posh and a little pricey, but serves superb food.
Anónima, corner of Av Olascoaga y Félix. This supermarket has a good *patio de comidas* (food hall), and games for kids.
El Reencuentro, Alaska 6451. A popular *parrilla* recommended for delicious steaks.
Fatto Dalla Mama, 9 de Julio 56. Fabulous filled pasta.
La Birra, Santa Fe 23. Lots of choice, and is very welcoming, with chic surroundings.
Rincón de Montaña, 9 de Julio 435. Recommended for delicious local specialities and cakes.

Ⴤ **Tutto al Dente**, Alberdi 49. Tasty home-made pasta. Recommended.

Cafés

Café El Buen Pan, Mitre and Corrientes. Open 0600-2300. A bright modern place for snacks and good bakery too.
El Patagonia, Bartolomé Mitre between Corrientes and Río Negro. *Lomitos* and sandwiches, with cheap(ish) deals.
Living Room, Pte Rivadaria. A lovely comfortable bar-café, with armchairs and table outside, a great place to relax.

Zapala *p92*

Ⴤ **El Chancho Rengo**, Av San Martín y Etcheluz, T02942-422795. This is where all the locals hang out.

Villa Pehuenia *p92*

ⴤⴤⴤ **La Escondida**, western shore of peninsula, T02942-1557 0420, www.posadalaescondida.com.ar. By far the best in town. Non-residents only with a reservation. Really special cuisine, all local ingredients, imaginatively prepared and served. Highly recommended.
ⴤⴤ **Anhedonia**, on the lakeside, T02942-1566 9866. Fondue, beef and pasta.
ⴤⴤ **Gnaien Chocolatería and tea room**, on the lakeside, T02942-498082. Good for tea, with lovely views of the lake, chocolate delicacies, *picadas* and range of wines.
ⴤⴤ **La Cantina del Pescador**, on the lakeside, T02942-498086. Fresh trout.
Ⴤ **Costa Azul**, on the lakeside, T02942-498035. Tasty local dishes and pasta; *chivito* (kid) *al asado* is the speciality of the house.

Aluminé *p93*

Ⴤ **La Posta del Rey**, next to the service station, opposite the plaza, Cristian Joubert, T02942-496248. The best place by far, with friendly service, great trout and local kid, delicious pastas, sandwiches. Recommended.

Caviahue *p94*

Ⴤ **Copahue Club Hotel**, Valle del Volcán. Serves good *chivito al asado* and local trout.
Ⴤ **Hotel Lago Caviahue**. The most stylish place to eat with an inspired *chivo a la cerveza* (kid cooked in beer) on the menu, along with more traditional favourites and local specialities.

Activities and tours

Neuquén *p90*

Gondwana Tour, Córdoba 599, T0299-496 3355, geoda@copelnet.com.ar. Excursions to dinosaur sites nearby, and accommodation.

Zapala *p92*

Mali Viajes, Alte Brown 760, T02942-432251.
Monserrat Viajes y Turismo, Etcheluz 101, T02942-422497.

Villa Pehuenia *p92*

Los Pehuenes, T02942-498029, www.lospehuenes.com.ar. Professional, helpful and friendly company offering wide range of activities including trekking, rafting (US$30, for full day, Grade IV), horse riding (US$35 full day with lunch), visits to the local Mapuche communities with fascinating local history and culture, fishing and boat trips. Ask for Fernando. Transfers from San Martín and Neuquén.

Aluminé *p93*

Aluminé Rafting, Ricardo Solano, T02942-496322. US$9-15, depending on difficulty, for 3 hrs rafting, Grades II-VI. All equipment included. **Circuito Abra Ancha** 2½ hrs, Grade II, 6 km, very entertaining, suitable for everyone. **Circuito Aluminé Superior**, 12- to 15-km run, 5-6 hrs, Grade III-IV, very technical river leaving Lago Alumine, for those who like a thrill, passing little woods of araucarias and ñirres, family trips Grades I and II, costs US$20 pp for **Abra Ancha**, US$70 pp for higher level. Trekking US$85 per day, trekking in Cordón de Chachil, US$130 per day, 2 days minimum, but can be up to a week, also kayaking, and biking.

Caviahue *p94*

Caviahue Tours, San Martín 623, Buenos Aires, T02948-4314 1556. Good information.

The ski resort has 3 lifts and excellent areas for cross-country skiing; contact Caviahue Base, T02948-495079.

Transport

Neuquén *p90*

Air

To **Buenos Aires**, daily with AR, Austral, and Aerolíneas Argentinas.

Airline offices Aerolíneas Argentinas/ Austral, Santa Fe 52, T02942-442 2409, Lapa, Argentina 30, T02942-448 8335. Southern Winds, Argentina 237, T02942-442 0124.

Bus

About a dozen companies to **Buenos Aires**, daily, 12-16 hrs, US$28-36. To **Zapala** daily, 3 hrs, US$6. To **San Martín de los Andes**, 6 hrs, US$12. To **Bariloche**, many companies, 5-6 hrs, US$13, best views if you sit on left. To **Mendoza**, Andesmar, and 3 others, daily, 12 hrs, US$21. To **Junín de los Andes**, 5 hrs, US$9.50, many companies.

To **Aluminé**, 6 hrs, US$11, many companies. To **Zapala**, 3 hrs, US$6, Albus, Centenario. To **Plaza Huincul**, 1½ hrs, US$3.50, same companies. To **Caviahue** (6 hrs, US$12) and **Copahue**, 6½ hrs, US$12.50, Centenario.

To Chile Services to **Temuco** stop for a couple of hours at the border, 12-14 hrs, US$23. Some companies offer discount for return, departures Mon-Thu and Sat; 7 companies, some continuing to destinations en route to **Puerto Montt**.

Bus companies Andesmar, T0299-442 2216, Via Bariloche, T0299-442 7054, El Valle, T0299-443 3293.

Zapala *p92*

The bus terminal is at Etcheluz and Uriburu, T02942-423191. To **Neuquén**, 2-3 hrs, US$7, Albus, Centenario, several daily. To **San Martín de los Andes**, 3-4 hrs, US$11. To **Junín de los Andes**, 3hrs, US$9.50 with Albus, Centenario, several daily. To **Aluminé**, 2½ hrs, US$5, several companies, daily. To **Villa Pehuenia**, 2½ hrs, US$8, 4 a week, continue to **Moquehue** 5-6 hrs, US$9. To **Caviahue** (3 hrs, US$8.50) and **Copahue** (3½-4 hrs, US$8.50) daily with Centenario. To **Bariloche**, Albus, TAC, Vía Bariloche via San Martín. To **Buenos Aires**, 18 hrs, US$26-38, many companies. To **Temuco** (Chile), US$17, Mon/Wed/Fri, Centenario (buy Chilean pesos in advance).

Villa Pehuenia *p92*

There are 3 buses weekly to Villa Pehuenia and **Moquehue** from **Neuquén** (less predictable in winter, when the roads are covered in snow) and **Aluminé**, 5½ hrs.

Aluminé *p93*

There are buses daily to and from **Zapala**, with either Aluminé Viajes (T02942-496231), or Albus (T02942-496368), 3 hrs, US$5. Twice a week to **Villa Pehuenia**, 1 hr, US$3. Twice a week to **San Martín de los Andes**, 4 hrs, US$7.50, with Tilleria, T02942-496048.

Caviahue *p94*

To/from **Neuquén**, El Petroleo and El Centenario, T02948-495024. Daily, 6 hrs, US$14, via Zapala (US$8).

Directory

Neuquén *p90*

Banks ATMs along Av Argentina. *Casas de cambio* at Pullman, Alcorta 144, Exterior, San Martín 23. **Consulates** Chile, La Rioja 241, T02942-442 2727. **Internet** Mitre 43, T02942-443 6585, a block from bus station. **Post office** Rivadavia and Santa Fe. **Telephone** Many *locutorios* in the centre, often with internet access. Telecom, 25 de Mayo 20, daily till 0030, and Olascoaga 222, open till 2345. Cheap.

Zapala *p92*

Banks 3 banks including Banco de la Nación Argentina, Etcheluz 465, but difficult to change TCs, Bansud, Etcheluz 108. **Internet** Instituto Moreno, Moreno y López y Planes. CPI, Chanetón and Garayta.

Parque Nacional Lanín

Some of the most beautiful sights in the Lake District are to be found in one of the country's largest national parks, Lanín, which stretches north from Parque Nacional Nahuel Huapi along the border with Chile for 200 km. The park's centrepiece is the magnificent extinct snow-capped Volcán Lanín, a challenging three-day climb, and a dramatic backdrop to the beautiful landscapes all around the park. Lagos Huechulafquen and Paimún, west of Junín de los Andes, offer tranquillity, great hiking, fishing and camping. Southernmost parts of the park can be visited from upmarket San Martín de los Andes, on the shores of picturesque Lago Lacar, with smart hotels, boat trips and beaches. Travel south from here to Bariloche along the famous Seven Lakes Drive, or search out the remote northern areas of the park, where Mapuche communities offer horse riding and run campsites. The park is most rewarding if you hire a bike or car, as bus services are sporadic. ▸▸ *For listings, see pages 107-113.*

Ins and outs

Access There are various points of entry to the park, with *guardaparques* at 3, 4, 7 and 8.

1 Route 18 from Aluminé to Lago Rucachoroi (see page 94).
2 Route 46 from Rahue to Quillén (see page 94).
3 Route 60 to Lago Tromen, for the ascent of Lanín and Paso Tromen.
4 Route 61 from north of Junín de los Andes to Lago Huechulafquen. The easiest entry, with regular buses in summer, fabulous walks and great camping.
5 Route 62 from Junín de los Andes to Lago Curruhué. Good walking and thermal pools.
6 Route 48 from the junction with Route 62 to Puerto Arturo and Lago Lolog.
7 Along Route 48 to Lago Lacar and Paso Hua Hum.
8 Route 234 via San Martín de los Andes.

Park information **Administration** ⓘ *Emilio Frey 749, San Martín de los Andes, T02972-427233, www.parquesnacionales.gov.ar, US$4 paid at point of entry*. There is a helpful **information office** in Junín de los Andes, in the same building as the tourist office, T02972-491160 www.junindelosandes.gov.ar. You're supposed to register at the administration before setting out on major treks, but this not always practical. However, *guardaparques* at Lago Huechulafquen should always be notified before you set off. A good map is essential: pick up the excellent *Parque Nacional* map before you arrive at the park. Fires are a serious hazard: put out campfires with lots of water, not just earth.

Flora and fauna Vegetation is varied due to differences in rainfall and altitude. In the north, between lagos Norquinco and Tromen, araucaria trees dominate, interspersed with lenga and ñirre. Further south, you'll find a combination of southern beech species: roble, rauli and the majestic grey-trunked coihue. Bamboo grows in profusion along Lago Huechulafquen at the centre of the park; this prehistoric species dies en masse every 20 to 30 years, when all the plants simultaneously rot, and new life begins the following year. Wildlife includes wildcats and foxes, the elusive *pudú* (a miniature deer) and some red deer.

Parque Nacional Lanín

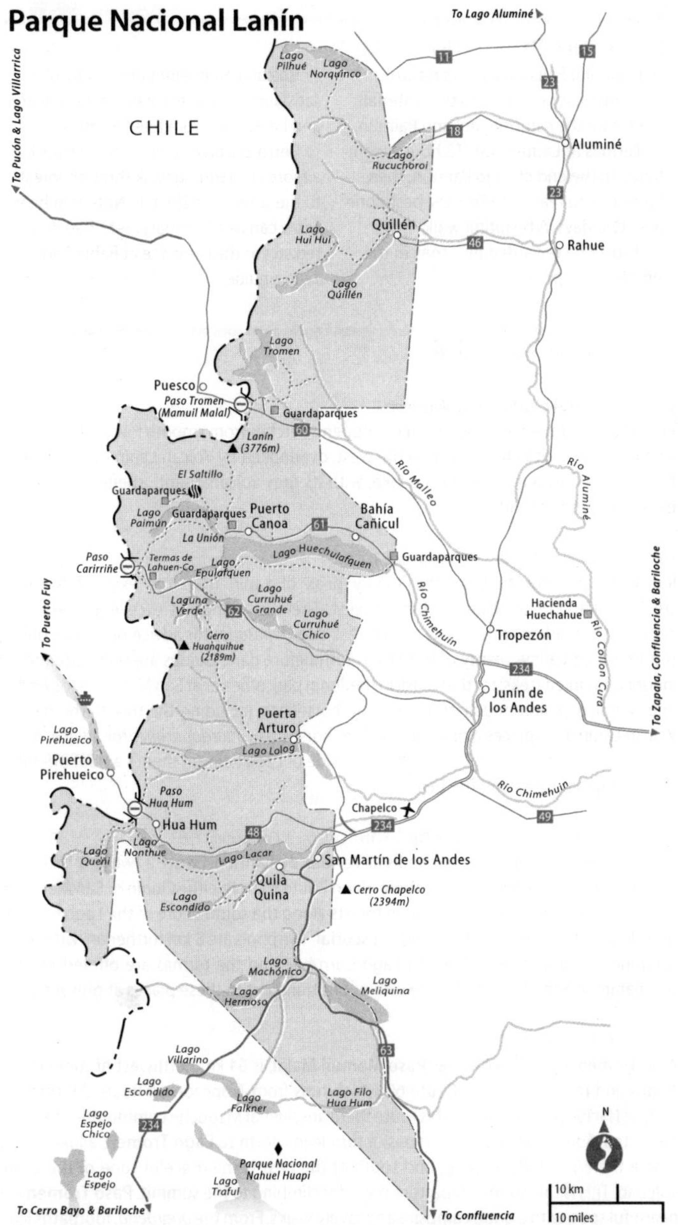

Walks around Lago Paimún

→ **El Saltillo Falls** (two hours return) fabulous views en route to the waterfall. Start from the campsite at Lago Paimún.

→ **Termas at Lahuen-Co** (12 hours) eight hours to the end of Lago Paimún, then four more to reach the Termas, best done over two days. A beautiful walk, and you'll be rewarded by a soak in the simple rustic pools.

→ **Volcán Lanín** (eight hours return) a satisfying walk to the base of the volcano and back. Start from Puerto Canoa.

→ **Cerro El Chivo** (seven hours return), a more challenging walk through forest to the summit at 2064 m. Note that heavy snow can lie till January. Set off early, and register at the campsite at Bahía Cañicul. Take a guide.

Exploring the park » *pp107-113.*

Lago Huechulafquen → *Colour map 1, A3.*

In the centre of the park, Lago Huechulafquen stretches from smooth lowland hills in the east to steep, craggy mountains in the west, overlooked by Volcán Lanín on the Chilean border. The northern shore of the lake, with its grey volcanic sand, shelter beautiful, if basic, camping grounds.

Around Lago Paimún → *Colour map 1, A3.*

It's worth the trek to view the sugary peak of Lanín from the exquisitely pretty crescent-shaped Lake Paimún, further west. There is a range of excellent walks here, along paths marked with yellow arrows. Ask *guardaparques* for advice on routes before setting off and allow plenty of time for return before dark. Guides are only required for longer unmarked treks; for these, ask in the Junín park office or at San Martín de los Andes. You can also explore much of the area on horseback, including the trek to the base of Volcán Lanín. Five places along the lake hire horses: ask *guardaparques* for advice, or ask at Mapuche communities. To cross to other side of Lago Paimún there's a boat operated by the Mapuche: just ring the bell.

Lago Curruhué and Termas de Lahuen-Co → *Colour map 1, B3.*

Lago Curruhué and the thermal pools at **Termas de Lahuen-Co** are a two-day hike from Lago Paimún. Alternatively, drive there along Route 62 from either Junín or San Martín de los Andes. You'll pass ancient pehuén forests along the south shore of the Lago Currhue Grande and the impressive lava field at **Escorial**. The pools are 8 km further on, with rustic camping and a *guardería*. Trips to Lago Curruhué and the termas are offered by tour companies in San Martín but there's no public transport to these places at present.

Paso Tromen and around

Paso Tromen, known in Chile as **Paso Mamuil Malal**, is 64 km northwest of Junín de los Andes and reached by *ripio* Route 60 which runs from Tropezón on Route 23, through Parque Nacional Lanín. Along this route there are several Mapuche communities that can be visited. Some 3 km east of the pass a turn leads north to **Lago Tromen**, a lovely spot where there is good camping, and south of the pass is the graceful cone of the Lanín volcano. This is the normal departure point for climbing to the summit. **Paso Tromen** is a beautiful spot, with a good campsite and lovely walks. From the *guardería*, footpaths lead

Border crossing

Paso Tromen

The Paso Tromen (aka Paso Mamuil Malal) crossing is less developed than the Hua Hum and Puyehue routes further south (see page 106 and 116); although this is the route used by international buses between Junín and Temuco, it is unsuitable for cycles and definitely not usable during heavy rain or snow (June to mid-November), as parts are narrow and steep. For up-to-date information, contact the gendarmería, T02972-491270, or customs, T02972-492163. On the Chilean side the road continues through glorious scenery, with views of the volcanoes of Villarrica and Quetrupillán to the south, to Pucón on Lago Villarrica (see page 247).

Argentine immigration and customs 3 km east of the pass, 0800-2000 all year.

Chilean immigration and customs Puesco, 17 km from the border, December-March 0800-2100; April-November 0800-1900.

to a mirador (a lookout, 1½ hours round trip), or across a grassy prairie with magnificent views of Lanín and other jagged peaks, through ñirre woodland and great araucaria trees to the point where Lago Tromen drains into Río Malleo (4 km).

Climbing Lanín

One of the world's most beautiful mountains, Lanín (3768 m) is geologically one of the youngest volcanoes of the Andes; it is now extinct. It is a three-day, challenging climb to the summit; crampons and ice axe required. The ascent starts from the Argentine customs post at the Tromen pass, where you must register and where all climbers' equipment and experience are checked. A four-hour hike leads from here to two free *refugios* at 2400 m, sleeping 14 to 20 people.

It's vital to get detailed descriptions of the ascent from the *guardaparques*. To climb the north face, follow the path through lenga forest to the base of the volcano, over the stream, arroyo Turbio, and up the *espina de pescado*. From here there are three paths to the *refugios*: **1**) straight ahead, the *espina de pescado* is the shortest but steepest (four to five hours), **2**) to the right, the *camino de mulas* is the easiest but longest (seven hours) and is marked; and **3**) to the left, *canaleta* should be used only for descent. From the *refugios*, it is six to seven hours over ice fields to the summit. Because of Lanín's relative accessibility, the risks of climbing it are often underestimated. An authorized guide is absolutely necessary for anyone other than the very experienced. Crampons and ice-axe are essential, as is protection against strong, cold winds. Climbing equipment and experience is checked by the *guardaparques* at the Tromen pass.

Junín de los Andes

»» *pp107-113. Colour map 1, A3/B3.*

Situated on the beautiful Río Chimehuín, the quiet residential town of Junín de los Andes (773 m) is justifiably known as the trout capital of Argentina. It offers some of the best fly fishing in the country in world-renowned rivers, and the fishing season runs from mid-November to the end of April. Junín is also an excellent base for exploring the wonderful virgin countryside of Parque Nacional Lanín and for climbing the extinct volcano itself.

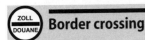

Founded in 1883, Junín is not as picturesque or tourist-orientated as its neighbour, San Martín de los Andes – there are no chalet-style buildings and few chocolate shops here – but it's a quiet neat place with friendly people.

Sights

Most of what you need can be found within a couple of blocks of the central Plaza San Martín with its fine araucaria trees among mature alerces and cedars. The small **Museo Salesiano** ⓘ *Ginés Ponte and Nogueira, Mon-Fri 0900-1230, 1430-1930, Sat 0900-1230*, has a fine collection of Mapuche weavings, instruments and arrowheads, and you can buy a whole range of excellent Mapuche handicrafts in the *galería* behind the tourist office. There's an impressive sculpture park just west of the town, **El Vía Christi** ⓘ *T02972-491684, www.viachristi.com.ar, from the plaza walk up Av Ant Argentina across the main road RN 234, to the end*. Situated among pine forest on a hillside, the stations of the cross are illustrated with sculptures of Mapuche figures, ingeniously depicting scenes from Jesus' life, together

Junín de los Andes

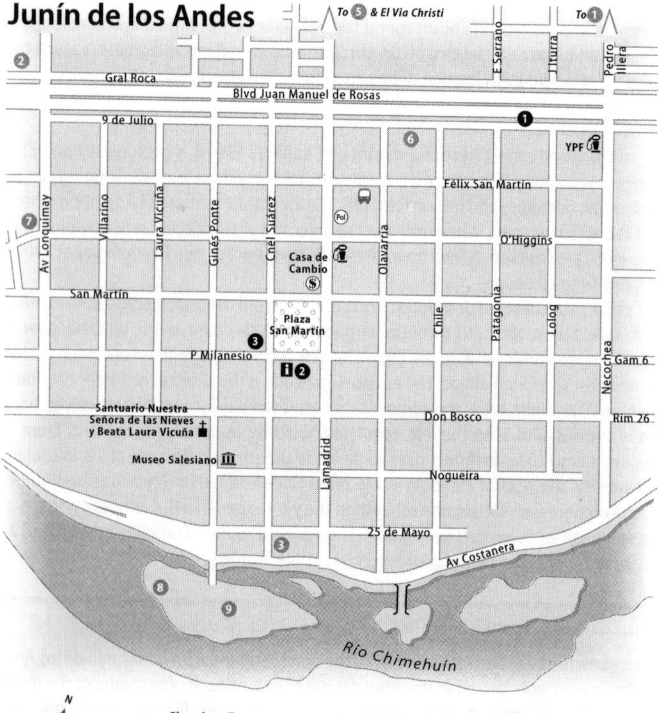

Sleeping
Hostería Chimehuín **3**
La Isla **9**
Mallin Laura Vicuña **8**
Milla Piuke **2**
Residencial Marisa **6**
Río Dorado Lodge & Fly Shop **1**
San Jorge **5**
Tromen **7**

Eating
Centro de Turismo **2**
La Posta de Junín **1**
Ruca Hueney **3**

with a history of the town and the Mapuche community. The sculptures are found along trails through the pine woods. It's a lovely place to walk, and highly recommended. The church, **Santuario Nuestra Señora de las Nieves y Beata Laura Vicuña**, also has fine Mapuche weavings, and is a pleasing calm space. The best fishing is at the mouth of the river Chimehuín on the road to Lago Huechulafquen, although there are many excellent spots around; see guides, below. In the town itself, there are pleasant picnic sites along the river. The fantastic **tourist office** ⓘ *on the main plaza, Domingo/Padre Milanesio and C Suárez, T02972-491160, www.junindelosandes.gov.ar, summer 0800-2200, rest of year 0800-2100*, has friendly staff who can advise on accommodation, and hand out maps.

San Martín de los Andes and around » *pp107-113. Colour map 1, B3.*

San Martín de los Andes is a charming tourist town nestled in a beautiful valley surround by steep mountains on the edge of Lago Lacar, with attractive chalet-style architecture and comfortable but slightly expensive accommodation. It's a good centre for exploring southern parts of the **Parque Nacional Lanín** and lakes **Lolog** and **Lacar**, where there are

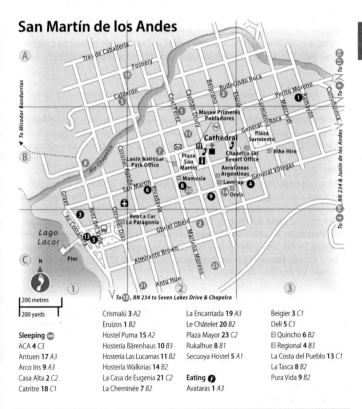

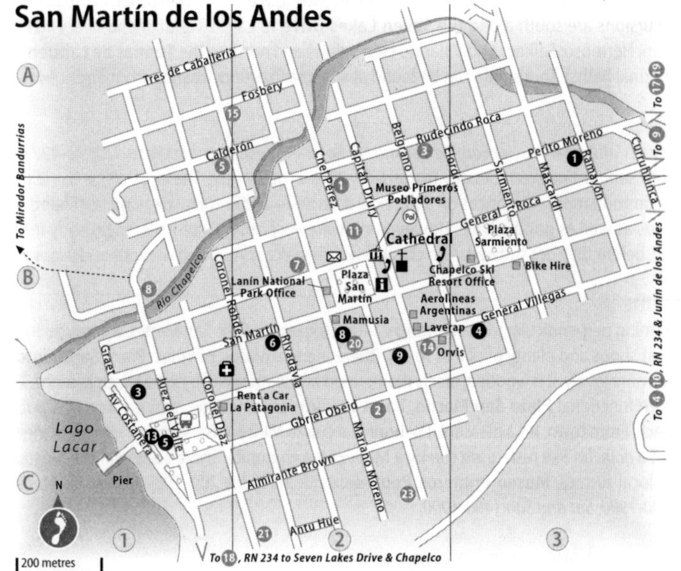

Sleeping
ACA **4** *C3*
Antuen **17** *A3*
Arco Iris **9** *A3*
Casa Alta **2** *C2*
Catritre **18** *C1*
Crismalú **3** *A2*
Eruizos **1** *B2*
Hostel Puma **15** *A2*
Hostería Bärenhaus **10** *B3*
Hostería Las Lucarnas **11** *B2*
Hostería Walkirias **14** *B2*
La Casa de Eugenia **21** *C2*
La Cheminée **7** *B2*
La Encantada **19** *A3*
Le Châtelet **20** *B2*
Plaza Mayor **23** *C2*
Rukalhue **8** *B1*
Secuoya Hostel **5** *A1*

Eating
Avataras **1** *A3*
Beigier **3** *C1*
Deli **5** *C1*
El Quincho **6** *B2*
El Regional **4** *B3*
La Costa del Pueblo **13** *C1*
La Tasca **8** *B2*
Pura Vida **9** *B2*

Border crossing

Paso Hua Hum

Paso Hua Hum (659 m) lies 47 km west of San Martín de los Andes along Route 48 (*ripio*), which runs along the north shore of Lago Lacar. It is usually open all year round and is an alternative to Paso Tromen (see page 102). The road (*ripio*, tough going for cyclists) continues 11 km on the Chilean side to Puerto Pirehueico (see page 254). Buses from San Martín de los Andes, connect with the boat across Lago Pirehueico to Puerto Fuy or there are buses to Panguipulli for onward connections.

Argentine immigration 2 km east of the border, summer 0800-2100, winter 0900-2000.

Chilean immigration Puerto Pirehueico, summer 0800-2100, winter 0900-2000.

beaches for relaxing and good opportunities for water sports, mountain biking and trekking. **Cerro Chapelco** (2394 m), 20 km south of San Martín, offers superb views over Lanín and many Chilean peaks. In summer, this is a good place for trekking, archery, horse riding or cycling (take your bike up on the cable car and cycle down), while in winter it transforms into a well-organized ski resort (see page 111). The other most popular excursions are south along the **Seven Lakes Drive** to Lagos Traful, Meliquina, Filo Hua Hum, Hermoso, Falkner and Villarino (see below) and north to the **Termas de Lahuen-Co** (thermal baths). Tourist info can be found at www.sanmartindelosandes.com (in English).

Ins and outs

Tourist information ⓘ *San Martín and JM Rosas 790, on the main plaza, T02972-427347, www.sanmartindelosandes.gov.ar/turismo, 0800-2100 all year.* The large office has lists of accommodation, with prices on a big board. English- and French-speaking staff hand out maps as well as good advice. However, they are very busy in summer, so go early in the day, before they get stressed. Also check www.chapelco.com.ar and www.smandes.gov.ar.

Sights

Running perpendicular to the *costanera*, along the lake, is Calle San Martín, where you'll find most shops and plenty of places to eat. There are two plazas, of which **Plaza Sarmiento** is the more lovely. It is wooded, nicely maintained and illuminated by little lamps at night. The more functional **Plaza San Martín**, has a sporadic crafts market, and is more of a public space. From town, it's a pleasant 1½-hour walk up to **Mirador Bandurrias** with great views, and a *quincho*-like restaurant run by a Mapuche community. There's a good little museum on local history, **Museo Primeros Pobladores** ⓘ *JM Rosas 700, T02972-428676, Mon-Fri 1000-1900, Sat and Sun 1400-1900.*

Lago Lacar and around → *Colour map 1, B3.*

Lago Lacar can be explored by car along much of its length, as there's a *ripio* road, Route 48, leading to the Chilean border at **Paso Hua Hum**, 41 km. You can cycle or walk all the way around the lake and on to **Lago Escondido** to the south. There are beaches at **Hua Hum**, at the western end of the lake, and rafting on the nearby Río Hua Hum. On the southern shore, 18 km away, there is a quieter beach at **Quila Quina**, where you can walk either to a waterfall, along a guided nature trail, or to a tranquil Mapuche community in the hills above the lake. Both lakeshore villages can be reached by boat from the pier in San Martín de los Andes. » *See also Transport, page 112.*

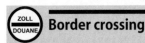

Parque Nacional Lanín listings

For Sleeping and Eating price codes and other relevant information, see pages 41-44.

Sleeping

Lago Huechulafquen *p102*

There are superb campsites and 3 overpriced *hosterías* (**LL**), all rather taking advantage of their lakeside positions. **Hostería Paimún**, RN61, Km 58, T02972-491201, www.interpatagonia.com/hosteriapaimun, is the most luxurious but not the most welcoming. **Huechulafquen**, RN61, Km 55, T02972-427598, has comfortable rooms, peaceful gardens and expert fishing advice. **Refugio del Pescador**, RN61, Km 57, T02972-491319, is the most basic and has a small golf course.

Camping

There are lots of sites along the lake run by local Mapuche communities, often selling delicious *pan casero* or offering horse riding. **Camping Lafquen-co**, just after the sign to Bahía Coihues. Highly recommended for its friendly welcome, with a good spot on the lakeside and lots of room, US$3.50 pp. **Piedra Mala**, beyond **Hostería Paimún**, beautiful wooded site with 2 beaches, hot showers, *parrillas* and a *proveduría*, US$4.

Paso Tromen *p102*

There's a municipal campsite on the Río Curi Leuvú; a free **CONAF** site in Puesco (Chile), with no facilities, and a superb campsite, **Agreste Lanín**, at Puesto Tromen, Dec-Apr US$2 pp, with shaded areas, hot showers, toilets and *parilladas*. Take food.

Junín de los Andes *p103, map p104*

L Rio Dorado Lodge and Fly Shop, Pedro Illera 448, T/F02972-491548, www.riodorado.com.ar. The only 4-star in town. Luxury fishing lodge, with comfortable, spacious rooms in log-cabin style, with huge beds and private bathrooms, lovely gardens and attentive service. Good fly shop.

A San Jorge, at the very end of Antártida Argentina, Chacra 54, T/F02972-491147, www.hotelsanjorge.com.ar. Nov-Apr only. A big, recently modernized 1960s hotel, beautifully located with lovely views and gardens, well furnished rooms with bath and TV. Very good value. Good restaurant and internet. English spoken. Recommended.

C Hostería Chimehuín, Suárez y 25 de Mayo, T02972-491132, www.interpatagonia.com/hosteriachimehuin. A long-established fishing *hostería* with beautiful gardens and friendly owners, quaint decor and comfortable rooms with bath and TV. Ask for the rooms with balconies next to the river. Good breakfasts, open all year. Recommended.

C Milla Piuke, off the RN234, Gral Roca y Av los Pehuenes, T/F02972-492378, www.milla-piuke.com.ar. Delightful and welcoming, with tastefully decorated and stylish rooms all with bath and TV, and apartments for families. Breakfast included. Highly recommended.

E Residencial Marisa, JM Rosas 360, T02972-491175. Simple, good value, with plain clean rooms and cheery family owners. *Confitería* downstairs. It's on the main road, so a little noisy during the day, but handy for the bus terminal and cheap eating places.

Hostels

G pp **Tromen**, Lonquimay 195, T02972-491498. tromen@fronteradigital.net.ar. Small, friendly house which has dorms and rooms for up to 4 people. At night take a taxi from the bus station as the streets in the area have no signs, and there are no street lights.

Estancias

L Estancia Huechahue, north of town, off RN 234 (reached from the Junín–Bariloche bus), T02972-491303, www.huechahue.com. A marvellous self-sufficient, traditional Patagonian estancia, where horses and cattle are bred. Guests stay in comfortable wooden cabins; evenings are spent dining together with delicious food and wine. There's great riding in Parque Nacional Lanín, watching condors, cattle mustering for the adventurous, or longer pack trips over the mountains to Chile. Superb horses, great *asados* in the open air, even a jacuzzi under the stars to rest tired muscles. Highly recommended.

Camping

There are many sites in the area with 2 good ones in town: **La Isla**, T02972-492029, on the river, US$3 pp. **Mallin Laura Vicuña**, Ginés Ponte 861, T02972-491149, campinglv@jandes.com.ar, also on the river, with hot showers, electricity, shop, discounts for stays over 2 days, very good value *cabañas* for 4-7.

San Martín de los Andes *p105, map p105*

Single rooms and rates are scarce. Rates are much higher in Jan/Feb and Jul/Aug.

LL Lois Suites, Route 234, Km 57.5, T02972-410304, www.loisuites.com.ar. Wonderful new 5 star golf resort set on 226 ha just outside of town. Lovely spa and restraurant.

LL Ten Rivers & Ten Lakes, Circuito Arrayanes Km 4, T02972-425571, www.tenriverstenlakes.com. Amazing views from this small lodge with only 4 rooms set on a hill overlooking the lakes. Includes a wonderful breakfast.

AL-L La Casa de Eugenia, Coronel Díaz 1186, T02972-427206, www.lacasadeeugenia.com.ar. Quite the most charming B&B in San Martín, this beautifully renovated 1900s house is more like an exclusive boutique hotel, but completely relaxing and unsnobby. Rooms are beautifully designed, incredibly cosy, and very welcoming. Breakfasts are luxurious. Highly recommended.

AL La Cheminée, Gral Roca y Mariano Moreno, T02972-427617, www.hosterialacheminee.com.ar. One of the most luxurious options, with pretty, cosy cottage-style rooms, spacious bathrooms, and a small pool. Breakfast is included, but no restaurant. Overpriced in high season, but reasonable otherwise.

AL Le Châtelet, Villegas 650, T02972-428294, www.hotellechatelet.com.ar. Really chic and luxurious, everything in this beautiful chalet-style hotel has been thought of to make you feel utterly pampered. Cosy wood lined living room, and gorgeous bedrooms, video library, excellent service, spa and pool with massage and facial treatments. Also some suites.

A Plaza Mayor, Cl Pérez 1199, T02972-427302, www.hosteriaplazamayor.com.ar. A chic and homely *hostería* in a quiet residential area, with traditional touches in the simple elegant rooms, all decorated to a high standard. Pool, *quincho*, parking. Great home-made breakfast is included.

A-B Hostería Walkirias, Villegas 815, T02972-428307, www.laswalkirias.com. A lovely place, homely but smart, with very spacious and well-furnished, tasteful rooms with big bathrooms, breakfast and free transfer from the airport included, sauna and pool room. Great value off season.

B Casa Alta, Obeid 659, T02972-427456. Deservedly popular, this is a welcoming B&B with charming multilingual owners, who will make you feel at home. Comfortable rooms, most with bathrooms, lovely gardens, and delicious breakfast. Closed in low season, book in advance.

C Crismalú, Rudecindo Roca 975, T02972-427283, www.interpatagonia.com/crismalu. Simple rooms in attractive chalet-style place, good value with breakfast included.

C Hostería Las Lucarnas, C Pérez 632, T02972-427085, www.patagoniasuperior.com.ar/hosterialaslucarnas. Really good value, this central, pretty place has simple comfortable rooms and a friendly English-speaking owner.

Hostels

D-E pp **Hostería Bärenhaus**, Los Alamos 156, Barrio Chapelco, T/F02972-422775, www.baerenhaus.com. Welcoming English- and German-speaking young owners have thought of everything to make you feel at home: excellent breakfast, comfortable cosy rooms with bath and heating, or great value shared dorms. Highly recommended. 5 km outside town, free pickup from bus terminal and airport.

E pp **Hostel Puma**, Fosbery 535 (take Rivadavia to the north, 2 blocks after crossing the bridge), T02972-422443, www.puma hostel.com.ar. HI discounts. A lovely hostel, warm, friendly and clean, run by an enthusiastic mountain guide who organizes treks to Lanín, rooms for 4 with private bathroom, also twin and double rooms with bath **D**, and kitchen facilities. Highly recommended.

F pp **Rukalhue**, Juez del Valle 682, T02972-427431, www.rukalhue.com.ar. Large camp-style accommodation with a section of dorm rooms and a section with doubles and triples (**C**). Great new apartments (**B**) with private bathrooms and kitchenette also an option.

F pp **Secuoya Hostel**, Rivadavia 411, T02972-42485, www.hostelsecuoya.com.ar. Charming hostel, 6 blocks from thebus terminal past the river. Small rooms are made up for by welcoming common area. Doubles (**C-D**) also available.

Cabañas

Plentiful *cabañas* are available on the hill to the north of town, and down by the lakeside. Prices increase in high season, but are good value for families or big groups.

Antuen, Perito Moreno 1850, T/F02972-428340, www.antuen.com.ar. Modern well-equipped and luxurious for 2-7, jacuzzi, pool, games room, views from elevated position above valley.

Arco Iris, Los Cipreses 1850, T02972-429450, www.arcoirisar.com. Comfortable and well equipped, spotless *cabañas* in a quiet area of town. Beautifully situated, with their own access to the river. Each has 2 bathrooms, cosy living rooms with TV, and spacious kitchen. The friendly owners are knowledgeable about the area and helpful. Very good value at US$35 for 4 in high season. Highly recommended.

Eruizos, Pérez 428, T02972-425856, www.eruizos.com.ar. Plainer *cabañas* in rustic but comfortable style.

La Encantada, Perito Moreno and Los Enebros, T/F02972-428364, www.laencantada.com. In a spectacular position above town in wooded surroundings, large, beautifully furnished cosy *cabañas* for 2 or more families, pool, games room and fishing.

Camping

ACA, Koessler 2176 (on the access road), T02972-429430. Hot water, laundry facilities.

Catritre, R234, Km 4, southern shore of the lake, T02972-428820. Good facilities in a gorgeous position on the shore.

Quila Quina, T02972-426919. A pretty spot and a peaceful place (out of peak season) with beaches and lovely walks.

Eating

Lago Huechulafquen *p102*

There are places to eat, with *proveduríаs* selling *pan casero* at Bahía, Piedra Mala and Rincón, and meals served at La Valsa, at Población Barriga.

Junín de los Andes *p103, map p104*

TTT Ruca Hueney, on the plaza at Col Suárez y Milanesio, T02972-491113, www.ruca-hueney.com.ar. The best place to eat in town, with a wide menu. Try the famous (enormous) *bife de chorizo Ruca Hueney*, the local wild boar, excellent *parrilla*, and the locally caught trout; all are delicious. Also Middle Eastern dishes US$9 for 2 courses. Great atmosphere, and wonderful service. Highly recommended.

TT-T Centro de Turismo, Domingo Milanesio, on the plaza next to the Tourist Information Centre. Central café serving interesting regional specialities such as the Patagonic sandwich with wild boar and venison.

T La Posta de Junín, Rosas 160 (RN 234), T02972-492303. Good steaks, local trout, tasty home-made pastas and good wine list.

San Martín de los Andes *p105, map p105*

TTT Avataras, Teniente Ramayón 765, T02972-427104, Thu-Sat from 2030. The best in town, this pricey, inspired place is marvellous. The surroundings are elegant, the menu imaginative, US$15 for 3 courses and wine, a treat.

TT El Quincho, Rivadavia y San Martín. A much-recommended traditional *parrilla* for tasty steaks, also offering superb home-made pasta, with good old-fashioned service to match. Great atmosphere. Warmly recommended.

🍴 **El Regional**, Villegas 953, T02972-425326. Hugely popular for regional specialities: smoked trout, pâtés and hams, and El Bolsón's home-made beer, all in cheerful German-style decor.
🍴 **La Costa del Pueblo**, on the *costanera* opposite pier, T02972-429289. Decent value, overlooking the lake. A big family-orientated place with a cheerful atmosphere, offering a huge range of pastas, chicken and trout dishes. Cheap dish of the day (US$4 for 2 courses), good service, recommended.
🍴 **La Tasca**, M Moreno 866, T02972-428663. A great atmospheric family restaurant with superb food and a wonderful wine list. The wood-panelled walls are lined with fascinating paintings and bottles. The food is traditional and includes excellent smoked boar and trout-filled pasta. Recommended.
🍴 **Pura Vida**, Villegas 745, T02972-429302. The only vegetarian restaurant in town, small and welcoming, also fish and chicken dishes.
🍴-🍴 **Deli**, Villegas and Av Costanera, T02972-428631. Great affordable place with views of the bay, and nice salads, pastas and pizzas. Wi-Fi and friendly service.

Teashops

Beigier, Av Costanera 814, T02972-427037. Little hidden cottage with views of the bay serving fantastic afternoon tea with home-made goodies. Friendly staff. Highly recommended.
Casa de Té Arrayán, head up to Mirador Arrayán, and follow signs, T02972-425570, www.tenriverstenlakes.com. Fabulous views from this cosy rustic log cabin with delicious meals, lunch and dinner (reservations essential) and the tea room. A real treat.

Festivals and events

Junín de los Andes *p103, map p104*

Jan Agricultural show and exhibition of flowers and local crafts.
Feb Fiesta Provincial de Puestero, mid-Feb sees the election of the queen, *asados* with local foods and gaucho riding, the most important country fiesta in southern Argentina.
Jul Festival of Indigenous Arts, mid-month.
Dec Inauguration of the church of **Laura Vicuña**, with a special mass on the 8th and singing to celebrate the life of Laura Vicuña (a saint who died very young).

Shopping

Junín de los Andes *p103, map p104*

Crafts stalls behind the tourist office sell good-quality local weavings and woodwork.
Patagonia Rodeo, Padre Milanesio 562, 1st floor, T01972-492839. A traditional shop selling what real gauchos wear in the field, plus quality leather belts, wallets, saddlery.

San Martín de los Andes *p105, map p105*

A great place for shopping, with chic little shops selling clothes and handmade jumpers, and a handicraft market in summer in Plaza San Martín. Lots of outdoor shops on San Martín sell clothes for walking and skiing.
Aquaterra, Villegas 795, T02972-429797. Outdoor equipment and clothing.
La Oveja Negra, San Martín 1025, T02972-428039. Wonderful handmade scarves and jumpers, esoteric crafts to a high standard.
Nomade, San Martín 881. Outdoor gear and camping equipment.

Chocolate

There are 2 recommended places for buying chocolates: **Abuela Goye**, San Martín 807, T02972-429409, also serves excellent ice creams; **Mamusia**, San Martín 601, T02972-427560, also sells home-made jams and a killer hot chocolate.

Activities and tours

Junín de los Andes *p103, map p104*

Fishing

The season runs from 2nd Sat in Nov to Easter. For information, consult. See also **Alquimia Viajes and Turismo**, under Tour operators, below.

Estancia Quillén, Aluminé, T02942-496196, www.interpatagonia.com/quillen/index.html. Fishing on the estancia as well as trips to rivers and lakes in the surrounding area.
Jorge Trucco, based in fly shop **Patagonia Outfitters**, San Martín de los Andes, Pérez 662, T02972-427561. Professional trips, good advice, and many years' experience.
Pesca Patagonia with Alejandro Olmedo, JM Rosas 60, T02972-491632, www.pescapatagonia.com.ar. Guides, tuition, equipment.
Río Dorado Lodge, Pedro Illera 448, T02972-491548, www.riodorado.com.ar. The luxury fishing lodge at the end of town has a good fly shop, and organizes trips, run by experts and passionate fishermen.

Tour operators

Alquimia Viajes and Turismo, Padre Milanesio 840, T02972-491355, www.alquimiaturismo.com.ar. Fishing trips with expert local guides, among a range of adventure tourism expeditions, including climbing Lanín, climbing in rock and ice, rafting and transfers.

San Martín de los Andes *p105, map p105*

Canopy

Canopy, T02944-15596215, www.canopyensmandes.com.ar. 8 km from the city, with 1400 m of course, spread over 10 different resting-stations with a height that varies from 8-20 m off the ground. Recommended.

Cycling

Many places rent mountain and normal bikes along San Martín, all charging similar prices.
Enduro Bikes, Elordi and Pto Moreno, T02972-427093.
HG Rodados, San Martín 1061, T02972-427345, hgrodados@smandes.com.ar. Rents mountain bikes at US$8 per day, also sells spare parts and offers expertise.

Diving

Buceo de los Andes, Club Nautico SMA, Av Costanera and Obeid. T02944-15696838, www.buceodelosandes.com.ar. Diving courses, and excursions throughout the year.

Fishing

The season runs from mid-Nov to May. For guides contact the tourist office or the park office. The following outlets sell equipment and offer fishing excursions: **Fly Shop**, Pedro Illera 378, T02972-491548; **Jorge Cardillo Pesca Fly shop**, Villegas 1061, T02972-428372; **Los Notros**, P Milanesio y Lamadrid, T02972-492157; **Orvis Fly shop**, Gral Villegas 835, T02972-425892; **Patagonian Anglers**, M Moreno 1193, T02972-427376, patagoniananglers@smandes.com.ar. **Rosario Aventura**, Av Koessler 1827, T02972-429233. Also try Martín Castañeda, T02972-422300, equis@smandes.com.ar who runs 1 or more day trips.

Flying

Aeroclub de los Andes, T02972-426254, aeroclubandes@smandes.com.ar. For flights in light aircraft.

Skiing

Chapelco (www.chapelco.com.ar) has 29 km of pistes, many of them challenging, with an overall drop of 730 m. Very good slopes and snow conditions make this a popular resort with foreigners and wealthy Argentines. At the foot of the mountain are a restaurant and base lodge, with 3 more restaurants on the mountain and a small café at the top. To get to the slopes, take the bus from San Martín, US$2.50 return, **Transportes Chapelco**, T02944-1561 8875. Details, passes, equipment hire from office at San Martín and Elordi, T02972-427845, www.sanmartindelosandes.gov.ar.

Tour operators

El Claro, Coronel Díaz 751, T02972-429363, www.interpatagonia.com/elclaro. Trips to the lakes, and also paragliding, horse riding, and other adventure trips.
El Refugio, Access from upstairs on C Pérez 830, just off San Martín, T02972-425140, www.elrefugioturismo.com.ar. Excellent company with friendly bilingual guides. Boat trips to lagos Huechulafquen and Paimún, US$19, Villa la Angustura via Seven Lakes US$19, or to Quila Quina US$13, mountain

bike hire US$24 per day, rafting at Hua Hum US$33, horse riding US$20, and trekking US$20. Lots more on offer. Recommended. **Lucero Viajes**, San Martín 826, 2nd floor, off B, T02972-428453. Rafting at Hua Hum, horse riding, 4WD trips, and tours to Hua Hum and Quila Quina. Also sells ski passes in winter. **Net Sur**, C Pérez 1124, T02972-427929, www.netsurpatagonia.com.ar. Offering rappelling, kayaking, mountain biking, rafting and horse treks.

Transport

Junín de los Andes *p103, map p104*

Bus

The terminal is at Olavarría and Félix San Martín, T02972-492038 (do not confuse with Gral San Martín). To **San Martín de los Andes**, 45 mins, US$3, several a day, **Centenario, Ko Ko, Airén**. To **Neuquén**, 7 hrs, US$24, several companies. To **Tromen**, Mon-Sat 1½ hrs, US$6. To **Caviahue** and **Copahue**, change at Zapala. 3½ hrs, US$13. To **Bariloche**, 3 hrs US$10, Via Bariloche, **Ko Ko**. To **Buenos Aires**, 21 hrs, US$36, several companies.

To Chile To **Temuco** (5 hrs) US$12 via Paso Tromen/Mamuil Malal, daily with either **Empresa San Martín** or **Igi-Llaima.**

San Martín de los Andes *p105, map p105*

Air

Chapelco airport, T02972-428388, is 20 km northeast on the road to Junín de los Andes; taxi US$8. Flights to **Buenos Aires**, Aerolíneas Argentinas, also LADE weekly from **Bahía Blanca**, **Esquel** and **Bariloche**.

Airline offices Aerolíneas Argentinas, Drury 876, T02972-427003. **LADE**, in the bus terminal, Villegas 231, T02972-427672. **Southern Winds**, San Martín 866, T02972-425815.

Boat

Boats from San Martín pier, T02972-428427, depart to **Quila Quina** hourly, 30 mins each way, US$6 return, and to **Hua Hum**, US$16 return, 3 daily in season.

Bus

The bus terminal is reasonably central, at Villegas 251, information T02972-427044.

To **Buenos Aires**, 20 hrs, US$65 *coche cama*, daily, 6 companies. To **Bariloche**, 3½ hrs (not via Seven Lakes Drive), US$9, many daily, **Via Bariloche**, T02972-425325, **Albus**, T02972-428100, minibus along the Seven Lakes Drive via **Traful** and **La Angostura**, 4 hrs, US$6. **Ko Ko**, T02972-427422, daily, fast route via Confluencia. To **Puerto Madryn** (via Neuquén) US$33. To **Neuquén** with **Albus**, 2 daily, takes 6½ hrs, US$15.

To Chile Buses to **Puerto Pirehueico** via Paso Hua Hum leave early morning daily, 2 hrs, US$4; they connect with car and passenger ferries across Lago Pirehueico to **Puerto Fuy**. Bus to **Temuco** with **Empresa San Martín**, T02972-27294, Mon, Wed, Fri, **Igi-Llaima**, T02972-427750, Tue, Thu, Sat, US$12, 6-8 hrs (heavily booked in summer) via Paso Hua Hum.

Car hire

Hansen Rent a Car, San Martín 532, T02972-427997, www.hansenrentacar.com.ar. **Hertz**, San Martín 831, 1st floor, T02972-420820. **Nieves Rent a Car**, Villegas 668, office 2, T02972-428684, **Rent a Car La Patagonia**, Villegas 305, T02972-421807.

Taxi

Eco Taxi, also known as **Lacar**, T02972-428817. Very helpful and efficient. If in town, find them on main street San Martín, or give Abuela Goye as useful meeting point.

Directory

Junín de los Andes *p103, map p104*

Banks TCs can be cashed at **Western Union**, Milanesio 570, 1000-1400, 1600-1930; and money changed at **Banco Provincial Neuquén**, San Martín and Lamadrid, also has ATM. **Internet** In the *galería* behind tourist office. The Parque Nacional Lanín office is in same building as tourist office, T02972-491160, and is very helpful. **Post office** Suárez and Don Bosco. **Telephone** *Locutorio* near tourist office on plaza at Milanesio 540.

San Martín de los Andes *p105, map p105*
Banks Many ATMs along San Martín. *Casa de cambio* at Banco de la Nación, San Martín 687. **Internet** Lots of broadband services, Punto.Com, inside *galería* at San Martín 866, Punto.Net, Galería Azul, Terminal, Vilegas 150. **Laundry** Laverap, Drury 880, daily 0800-2200. Marva, Drury and Villegas, and Perito Moreno 980. Fast, efficient and cheap. **Medical services** Hospital Ramón Carrillo, San Martín and Coronel Rodhe, T02972-427211. **Post office** General Roca and Pérez, Mon-Fri 0800-1300, 1700-2000, Sat 0900-1300. **Telephones** Cooperativa Telefónica, Drury 761, Terminal, Villegas 150.

Parque Nacional Nahuel Huapi

Nahuel Huapi is the park you're most likely to visit, as the tourist centre of Bariloche is right in the middle of it. Covering a spectacular 710,000 ha and stretching along the Andes for over 130 km, this is Argentina's oldest national park, created in 1934. It extends across some of Argentina's most dramatic mountains, with lakes, rivers, glaciers, waterfalls, bare mountains and snow-clad peaks. Among those you can climb are Tronador (3478 m) and Catedral Sur (2388 m). Base yourself either at bustling Bariloche, where there are excellent hotels and restaurants stretching for 25 km along the lakeshore, or on the northern shore, at the quiet upmarket town of Villa La Angostura, where the Parque Nacional Los Arrayanes starts. It contains a rare woodland of exquisite arrayán trees with their distinctive cinnamon-coloured flaky bark.

North of here, a winding road takes you through spectacular landscapes on the famous Seven Lakes Drive to San Martín de los Andes, in Parque Nacional Lanín. Take a diversion east for Lago Traful, with a tranquil village for fishing, camping and walking. West of Bariloche, there are glaciers and waterfalls near Pampa Linda, the base for climbing Tronador, and starting point for the trek through Paso de las Nubes to Lago Frías. Further south, lagos Mascardi, Guillelmoand Gutiérrez have even grander scenery, with horse riding, trekking and rafting along the Río Manso. An excellent base for exploring this area is Estancia Peuma Hue on the southern shore of Lago Gutiérrez, with its beautiful, peaceful setting. » *For listings, see pages 117-121.*

Ins and outs

Park information Bariloche is the main centre for entering the park, where you can find information on transport, walks and maps. The **Parque Nacional Nahuel Huapi Intendencia** ⓘ *San Martín 24, T02944-423111, www.nahuelhuapi.gov.ar, 0900-1400*, is very helpful. Also useful for information on hiking is **Club Andino Bariloche** (**CAB**), see page 134, which sells excellent hand-drawn walking maps, showing average walking times and *refugios*. Note that these are sometimes out of date, so check the paths are open with *guardaparques*. **CAB** can also advise on transport within the park. More detailed maps are available from Buenos Aires, at the **Instituto Geográfico Militar**, www.igm.gov.ar. There are many *refugios* in the park run both privately and by **CAB**, which charge US$6 per night, plus US$2 for cooking, or US$2.50 for breakfast, US$5.50 for dinner. Take a good sleeping bag. Most areas of the park are free to visitors, but you must pay entry, US$4, at Puerto Pañuelo, Villa La Angostura and Pampa Linda.

Parque Nacional Nahuel Huapi

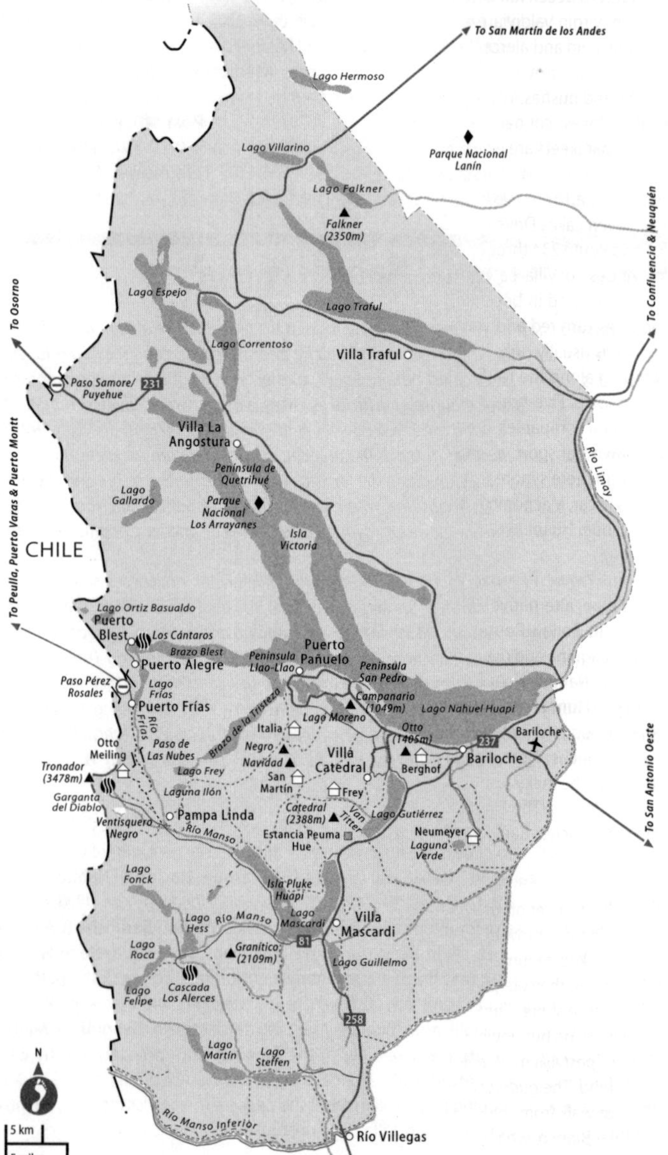

Flora and fauna Vegetation varies with altitude and climate, but includes large expanses of southern beech forest and, near the Chilean border where rainfall is highest; there are areas of virgin valdivian rainforest. Here you will see coihues (evergreen beeches) over 450 years old and alerces over 1500 years old, with the ancient species of bamboo cane, caña colihue, growing everywhere. Eastern parts of the park are more steppe-like with shrubs and bushes. Wildlife includes the small pudú deer, the huemul and river otter, as well as foxes, cougars and guanacos. Among the birds, Magellan woodpeckers and austral parakeets are easily spotted as well as large flocks of swans, geese and ducks.

La Ruta de los Siete Lagos → *Colour map 1, B3.*

The Seven Lakes Drive is the most famous tourist route in the Argentine Lake District. It follows Route 234 through the Lanín and Nahuel Huapi national parks from San Martín de los Andes to Villa La Angostura and passes seven magnificent lakes, all flanked by mountains clad in beech forest. It is particularly attractive in autumn (April/May) when the trees turn red and yellow. Although the road is only partially paved, the hard earth surface is usually only closed after heavy rain or snowfall. There are limited facilities for camping along the route but plenty of perfect picnic spots, especially at Pichi Traful or Lago Espejo. Five-hour round-trip excursions along the Seven Lakes Route are operated by several companies. Buses will stop at campsites on the route, but it's better to have your own transport, as you'll want to be able to explore. The route is good for cycling, although there's more traffic in January and February. The seven lakes are (from north to south) Lácar, Machónico (in Parque Nacional Lanín), Falkner, Villarino, Correntoso, Espejo and Nahuel Huapi.

San Martín de los Andes to Bariloche

There's an alternative direct route south to Bariloche, via **Confluencia**, that's also appealing. Follow Route 234 then take Route 63, unpaved, southeast along the shore of Lago Meliquina and over the **Paso de Córdoba**, Km 77 (1300 m), where you enter Parque Nacional Nahuel Huapi. (You could also turn off along an unpaved track to **Lago Filo-Hua-Hum** at Km 54, before continuing to Confluencia.) From Confluencia, take the paved Neuquén–Bariloche highway, through the astounding **Valle Encantado**, 100 km from Bariloche. Here, the road winds through mountains, whipped into jaggy peaks, alongside the milky turquoise waters of the Río Limay. The weird rock formations include *El Dedo de Dios* (The Finger of God) and *El Centinela del Valle* (The Sentinel of the Valley). The road reaches Bariloche, 157 km from San Martín de los Andes.

Villa Traful and around → *Colour map 1, B3.*

If you want to get off the beaten track, Villa Traful is ideal. The quiet pretty village sprawls alongside the narrow deep-blue sliver of **Lago Traful**, enclosed on both sides by stunning sharp peaked mountains. Approaching from the west, you'll pass forests of lenga and coihue trees, their elegant tall trunks creating a woody cathedral, with idyllic spots to camp all along the shore. There are also some wonderful walks and waterfalls to see here, and little else to do but unwind. Further along the lakeshore, there's a small, but helpful **tourist office** ⓘ *past Aiken cabañas, T02944-479020, www.villatraful.com*, with info on walks, riding and fishing. The *guardería* opposite the pier is open in high season for advice on walks. A 1½-hour walk from the village will bring you to the lovely waterfalls,**Cascadas del Arroyo Coa Có y Blanco**, which thunder down through beech forest and cañas colihues bamboo.

Border crossing

Paso Puyehue

Officially known as Paso Samore, Paso Puyehue (1280 m) lies west of Villa La Angostura via unpaved Route 231 – a spectacular six-hour drive. Some travellers think this route is even more scenic than the ferry journey across Lago Todos Los Santos and Lago Frías (see page 124) and it's certainly far cheaper and more reliable, although it's liable to closure after snow. Heading east to west, the best views are from the southern side of the bus. From Villa La Angostura, Route 231 passes the junction with 'Ruta de Los Siete Lagos' for San Martín at Km 94. The pass itself is at Km 125. On the Chilean side the road continues via Parque Nacional Puyehue and Entre Lagos to Osorno.

Argentine customs and immigration Km 109, 14 km east of the border, winter 0900-2000, summer 0800-2100.

Chilean immigration Pajaritos, Km 146, 22 km west of the border, open 2nd Sat in Oct to 1 May 0800-2100, winter 0900-2000. For vehicles entering Chile, formalities take about 30 minutes and include the spraying of tyres and the wiping of shoes on a mat, for which you pay US$2 to Sanidad (have Chilean pesos ready).

Villa La Angostura and around » *pp117-121.*

This pretty town with a village feel is a popular holiday resort for wealthier Argentines on the shores of Lago Nahuel Huapi and provides access to the wonderful **Parque Nacional Los Arrayanes** (see page 117) at the end of the **Quetrihué peninsula**. The town has two centres: **El Cruce**, where there are countless restaurants, hotels and *cabaña* complexes, and the picturesque port, known as **La Villa**, 3 km away at the neck of the Quetrihué Peninsula. The **tourist office** ⓘ *opposite the bus terminal, Av Siete Lagos 93, T02944-494124, www.villalaangostura.gov.ar, high season 0800-2100, low season 0800-2000*, is opposite the small bus terminal north of town, and is busy and helpful.

Bus company **15 de Mayo** runs buses between El Cruce and La Villa every two hours, but it's also a pleasant walk. About halfway between the two centres is a chapel (1936) designed by Bustillo, the architect who gave this region's buildings their distinctive chalet style. There's also the tiny **Museo Regional** ⓘ *on the road to La Villa, Mon 0800-1400, Tue-Fri 0800-1630, Sat 1430-1700*, with interesting photos of the original indigenous inhabitants. From La Villa, a short walk leads to **Laguna Verde**, an intense emerald green lagoon surrounded by mixed coihue cypress and arrayán forests, where there's a self-guided trail.

Around Villa La Angostura

There are fine views of Lagos Correntoso and Nahuel Huapi from **Mirador Belvedere**, a 3-km drive or walk up the old road, northwest of El Cruce. From the mirador (lookout) a path to your right goes to **Cascada Inacayal**, a waterfall 50 m high, situated in an area rich in native flora and forest. Another delightful walk leads to beautiful 35-m-high **Cascada Río Bonito**, lying 8 km east of El Cruce off Route 66. One of the country's most popular ski resorts is at **Cerro Bayo** (1782 m), see page 120, further along the same path. Alternatively, 1 km further along the road, take the ski lift to a platform at 1500 m, where there's a restaurant with great views. The ski lift functions all year; cyclists can take bikes up and cycle down. For more information see www.cerrobayoweb.com.

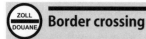

Parque Nacional Los Arrayanes → *Colour map 1, B3.*

ⓘ *Park office: C Inacayal 13, La Villa, T02944-494004, www.bosquelosarrayanes.com.ar. The park entrance is 12 km south of La Villa. See Activities and tours, page 120.*

One of the most magical spots in the Lake District, this park was created to protect a rare forest of arrayán trees. It is one of the few places where the arrayán grows to full size and some of the specimens are 300 years old. Arrayán grow in groves near water and have extraordinary cinnamon-coloured peeling trunks that are cold to the touch. They have no outer bark to protect them, but the surface layer is rich in tannins, which keep the tree free from disease. They have creamy white flowers in January and February, and produce blue-black fruit in March. The most rewarding way to see the park is to take the boat trip across the lake and to stroll along the wooden walkways through the trees, once the guided tour has left. Then walk back to the port through the mixed forest. There's a *confitería* in the park, selling drinks and confectionery.

Parque Nacional Nahuel Huapi listings

For Sleeping and Eating price codes and other relevant information, see pages 41-44.

Sleeping

La Ruta de los Siete Lagos *p115*

B Hostería Lago Villarino, Lago Villarino, T02972-429483, www.hosteriavillarino.com.ar. A lovely setting, fantastic large rooms, attractive 1940s-style lodge. Good food, also camping.

B Lago Espejo Resort, Lago Espejo, T02944-494583, lago_espejo_resort@topmail.com.ar. A beautifully situated hotel and camping area, on the shore of the lake, surrounded by trees.

D Hostería Lago Espejo, Lago Espejo, T02944-494584. Old fashioned and comfortable, with good food in the restaurant, open Jan-Mar only.

Camping

The campsite at **Lago Espejo Resort** (see above) is open all year, US$1 pp. Further along a track is the lovely **Lago Espejo Camping**, open all year, US$2 pp, no showers, but toilets, drinking water, fireplaces and picnic spots, busy Jan.

Villa Traful and around *p115*

A-B Ruca Lico, T02944-479004, www.interpatagonia.com/rucalico. Luxurious *cabañas* in woodland above the lake, lavishly furnished in rustic chic style, with jacuzzi and balcony with splendid views. Good value for 6, a treat for 2. Horse riding trips organized. Recommended.

C Aiken, T02944-479048, www.aiken.com.ar. Rustic and compact, but well-decorated *cabañas* in spacious gardens with open views of the lake below. All have *parrilladas* outside. Cheap for 4 or 5. Recommended.

C Hostería Villa Traful, T02944-479005. A delightful place to stay above the lake, in pretty gardens. Cabins have comfortable furnishings and ample bathrooms. Also *cabañas* for up to 6, US$55. Charming hospitality. Offers fishing and boat trips.

C Marinas Puerto Traful, T02944-475284. Gorgeous uninterrupted views of the lake from this recently modernized place, now bizarrely painted bright blue. Comfortable.

D Cabañas del Montañes, up behind the village, T02944-479035. Accommodation in *cabañas*, offered by the company that makes *alfajores*. Lovely setting.

Hostels

F Vulcanche, T02944-494015, www.vulcanche.com. An attractive chalet-style hostel and 2 *cabañas* (**D**), very comfortable and set in lovely open gardens with good views. Also simple camping in a pleasant open site, US$4.50 pp with hot showers, phone, *parrilladas*.

Camping

Camping Traful Lauquen, on the shore, T02944-479030, www.interpatagonia.com/trafullauquen. With 600 m of beach, this is

among the loveliest of the sites along the lake. Hot showers, fireplaces, restaurant, US$3 pp, Nov-Mar. Calm and beautiful.
Costa de Traful, T02944-479149. If you're under 30 and you've got a guitar, camp at this lively place, US$3 pp, Dec-Apr. 24-hr hot showers, restaurant, fireplaces, *proveduría*, *cabañas*, fishing, horse riding, treks to see cave paintings on the other side of the lake.

Villa La Angostura and around *p116*

See also www.villalaangostura.com.ar.
LL Casa Grande Resort, Blv Quetrihué 338, T02944-494888, www.casagranderesort.com.ar. Spread over 4 ha are 3 4-bedroom lodges. Lovely designs, and spacious living inside and out. Price given for entire lodge, up to 8 people.
LL Correntoso, discreetly hidden off the road, RN 231, and Río Correntoso, T02944-619728, or T011-48030030 in Buenos Aires, www.correntoso.com. Really fabulous setting for this intimate and stylish hotel with a really superb restaurant. Very special. Often recommended.
LL Las Balsas, Bahía Las Balsas (off Av Arrayanes), T02944-494308, www.lasbalsas.com. The most famous and exclusive hotel in the area and one of the best in Argentina. Fabulous cosy rooms, impeccable service, and a wonderfully intimate atmosphere in a great lakeside location with its own secluded beach. The chef, Pablo Campoy, creates really fine cuisine from top local produce. There's a beautiful pool by the lake, and a fantastic spa. Excursions arranged, or transfers to the ski centre in season. Very highly recommended.
LL-L Cabañas La Ruma Andina, Blv Queitrhué 1692, La Villa, T02944-495188, www.rumaandina.com.ar. Top-quality rustic *cabañas* with lots of stone and wood, and cosily furnished, in a lovely setting with pool. Recommended.
AL La Escondida, T02944-475313, www.hosterialaescondida.com.ar. Wonderful setting, right on the lake with only 14 rooms, heated pool and great mid-week and weekend specials. Recommended.
AL-A Casa del Bosque, Los Pinos 160, T02944-475229, www.casadelbosque.com. Luxury and style in wonderfully designed *cabanas*, lots of glass, with jacuzzis and all possible comforts, in secluded in woodland at Puerto Manzana. Recommended.
A Hostería ACA al Sur, Av Arrayanes 8 (behind the petrol station), T02944-494168, www.acavillalaangostura.com.ar. New, modern and very attractive small single-storey hotel with 20 well-designed rooms in the absolute centre of town. Highly recommended.
A Hotel Angostura, T02944-494224, www.hotellaangostura.com.ar. Open all year, beautifully situated on the lakeside at the port, handsome stone and wood chalet was designed by Bustillo in 1938, charming old-fashioned feel, with lovely gardens, and an excellent restaurant.
A La Posada, RN 231, Km 65, west of town, T02944-494450, www.hosterialaposada.com. In a splendid elevated position with clear views over the lake, this is a welcoming, beautifully maintained hotel in lovely gardens, with pool and fine restaurant.
C Verena's Haus, Los Taiques 268, T02944-494467. A quaint and welcoming wooden house for adults and non-smokers only, cosy rooms with a pretty garden, delicious breakfasts. English spoken. Recommended.
D Hostería Del Francés, Lolog 3057, on shore of Lago Correntoso, T02944-488055, www.lodelfrances.com.ar. Excellent value in a lovely chalet-style house, great views (although a little blocked by recent developments in the area) from all the rooms. Recommended.
E pp **Italian Hostel**, Los Marquis 215, T02944-494376, www.italianhostel.com.ar. Closed Apr-Oct, this small central hostel offers dorms in a friendly and cosy oasis. The owners, artists who live next door, can help with local information. Recommended.
F pp **Bajo Cero Hostel**, Av 7 Lagos, T02944-495454, www.bajocerohostel.com. Appealing lodge-style building with cosy dorm rooms and a great games area. Linen and breakfast included. A little out of town, but an easy 5-min walk to a supermarket or 10-15 mins' walk to town. Hire bikes at the hostel. Recommended.
F Hostel La Angostura, Barbagelata 157, 300 m up the road behind the tourist office,

T02944- 494834, www.hostellaangostura.com.ar. A warm, luxurious and cheap hostel. Small dorms with bathroom, trips organized. Doubles (**B-C**) available. Highly recommended.

Camping

There are many sites along the RN 231.

Osa Mayor, signposted off main road, close to town, T02944-494304, www.campingosamayor.com.ar. Highly recommended is this delightful leafy site on a hillside with good, shaded levelled camping spots, all facilities and clean bathrooms, run by a friendly family. US$4.50 pp. Also lovely rustic *cabañas* (**C**) with heating and good views for up to 4 people.

Eating

Villa Traful and around *p115*

Costa Traful, Route 65, T02944-479049. The only restaurant set directly on the lake, also has accommodation (see Hostería Villa Traful, Sleeping). Regional dishes, and sandwiches.

Nancu Lahuen, T02944-479017. A delightful tea room and restaurant serving trout and home-made pastas, cakes and delicious chocolates. Large open fire.

Parrilla La Terraza, T02944-479077. With panoramic lake views. Delicious local lamb and kid on the *asado*. Recommended.

Villa La Angostura *p116*

Cocina Waldhaus, RN 231, Puerto Manzano, T02944-475323, www.saboresdeneuquen.com.ar. Gorgeous local delicacies created by Chef Leo Morsella, served in a charming chalet-style building. Recommended.

Correntoso, Hotel Corentoso, Av 7 Lagos, T02944-1561 9727. A gourmet restaurant, specializing in Mediterranean cuisine, with Patagonian touches, like lamb and trout. Great wine list, gorgeous setting by the lake.

Las Balsas, T02944-494308, www.lasbalsas.com. Possibly the best food in Argentina, created by chef Pablo Campoy. The wines are superb and the atmosphere is a real treat. Book well in advance. Highly recommended.

Gran Nevada, opposite Nativa café. Good for cheap *parrilla*, and *ñoquis* in a cheery friendly atmosphere.

Los Pioneros , Av Arrayanes 263, T02944-495525. Famous for fine local dishes and great Argentine steaks in a chalet-style building. There is a great pizza place next door by the same owners. Try the locally brewed beers.

Nativa Café, Av Arrayanes 198, T02944-495093. A relaxed and welcoming eatery with a high-ceilinged chalet feel, good music and an international menu. Excellent pizzas. Friendly efficient staff. Recommended.

Tasca Placido, Av Siete Lagos 1726, T02944-495763. Spanish-owned, this local hang-out serves great paella and lots of seafood.

El Esquiador, Las Retames 146 (behind the bus terminal), T02944-494331. Best budget meal is the *parrilla*, with fixed-price 3-course menu.

Hora Cero, Av Arrayanes 45. Hugely popular, heaving in summer, with a big range of excellent pizzas, and *pizza libre* (all you can eat US$3.50) on Wed and Sat.

Activities and tours

Villa Traful and around *p115*

Cycling

Del Montanes, T02944-479035, up the road behind the centre of the village, bike hire.

Fishing

The season runs mid-Nov to end Apr.

Andrés Quelin, Hostería Villa Traful (see Sleeping) T02944-479005. A fishing guide who runs trips to see a submerged cypress wood.

Osvaldo A Brandeman, Bahía Mansa, T02944-479048, pescaosvaldo@mail.com. Fishing expert and guide.

Villa La Angostura *p116*

Adventure tours

Club Andino Villa La Angostura, Cerro Bayo 295. Excursions and information.

Lengas Tour, Av Arrayanes 173, T02944-494575, turismo@lengas.com. Horse riding, fishing, hunting, all with bilingual guides.

Rucan Turismo, Av 7 Lagos 90, T02944-495075, www.rucanturismo.com. Skiing, riding, mountain biking and tours.
Terpin Turismo, Los Notros 41, T02944-494551, www.terpinturismo.com.ar. Trips to Chile and surroundings, car hire.
Turismo Cerros y Lagos, Av Arrayanes 21, T02944-495447, www.patagonia adventures.com. Skiing, adventure sports.

Fishing

For permits and a list of fishing guides, ask the tourist office. The following fly shops also arrange fishing trips: Angler's Home Fly Shop, Belvedere 22, T02944-495222; and Class, Av Arrayanes 173, T02944-494411.

Horse riding

Cabalgatas Correntoso, T02944-15552950, www.cabalgatacorrentoso.com.ar. Excursions in the surrounding area and to Villa Traful.

Skiing

Cerro Bayo, T02944-494189, www.cerrobayo web.com. One of Argentina's pricier resorts. 24 pistes covering 20 km in total, and all with excellent views over the lakes below; it's also a great area for snowboarding.

Parque Nacional Los Arrayanes *p117*

Bus company **15 de Mayo** runs buses from El Cruce to **La Villa** every 2 hrs and takes 15 mins. A taxi to La Villa costs US$5. There's a clear path all the way from the tip of the Quetrihué peninsula where the boat arrives, through the prettiest part of the arrayán forest, and then running the length of the peninsula back to La Villa. You can walk or cycle the whole length: 3 hrs one way walking; 2 hrs cycling.

There are 2 companies running catamarans from the pier in La Villa to the end of the peninsula, taking passengers on a guided tour through the forest before heading the boat back to La Villa. Greenleaf Turismo runs *Catamarán Futuleufú*, T02944-494004, angosturaturismo@netpatagon.com; and Catamarán Patagonia Argentina, T02944-494463. Tickets from Hotel Angostura, US$15 return with the catamaran. Boats also run from Bariloche, via Isla Victoria, with **Turisur**, T02944-426109, www.bariloche.com/turisur/.

Transport

Villa Traful and around *p115*

Bus In summer, a daily bus between **Villa la Angostura** and **San Martín** stops here, but in low season, buses run only 3 times a week. Kiosko El Ciervo, by the YPF service station, sells tickets and has the timetable.

Villa La Angostura *p116*

Bus The terminal is at Av 7 Lagos and Av Arrayanes, opposite the ACA service station.

To/from **Bariloche**, 1¼ hrs, US$5, several companies, several daily. Daily buses to **San Martín de los Andes** with Ko Ko and Albus. To **Osorno** (Chile), US$9; arrange for the bus from San Martín to pick you up in **Villa la Angostura**. For other destinations, change at San Martín de los Andes or Bariloche.

Bus companies 15 de Mayo, T02944-495104, Albus, T02944-1561 7578, Andesmar, T02944-495247, Vía Bariloche/ El Valle, T02944-495415.

Car hire Angostura Rent a Car, T02944-424621, www.angosturarentacar.com.ar. Giminez Vidal, Las Muticias 146, T02944-494336. Terpin Turismo, Los Notros 41, T02944- 494551, www.terpinturismo.com.

Directory

Villa La Angostura *p116*

Banks Andina, Arrayanes 256, T02944-495197, Banco de Patagonia, Av Arrayanes 275, Banco Prov de Neuquén, Av Arrayanes 172. Both with ATMs. **Internet** Punta Arrayanes, Av Arrayanes 90, T02944-495288. **Medical services** Hospital Rural Arraiz, Copello 311 (at barrio Pinar), T02944-494170. **Post office** Siete Lagos 26. **Telephone** Several *locutorios* along Av Arrayanes.

Bariloche and around

Beautifully situated on the southern shore of Lago Nahuel Huapi, San Carlos de Bariloche (its full name) is the best base for starting to explore the Lake District. It's right in the middle of Nahuel Huapi national park, and you could easily spend a week here, with plenty of opportunities for hiking in the mountains behind, and adventure sports. The town was founded in 1902, but took off in the 1930s once the national park was created. The chalet-style architecture was established at this time by early German and Swiss settlers. Beautiful Hotel Llao Llao and the Civic Centre, designed by major Argentine architect Bustillo, set the trend for brightly varnished wood and cute carved gable ends.

Bariloche is well set up for tourism, with lots of hotels and restaurants in the town centre, and even more appealing places along the shore of lake Nahuel Huapi, towards Llao Llao, where Argentina's most famous hotel enjoys a spectacular setting. To the immediate south of Bariloche there are tremendous hikes up giant Mount Tronador, reached from Pampa Linda, and two more gorgeous lakes: Gutiérrez, with Estancia Peuma Hue on its shores for excellent horse riding and relaxing, and Mascardi, with access to rafting on the Río Manso. Ski resort Cerro Catedral is arguably the best in South America, and makes a great base for hiking in summer. ▸▸ *For listings, see pages 128-136.*

1 Bariloche

➡ **Bariloche maps**
1 **Bariloche, page 121**
2 Bariloche – the road to Llao Llao, page 124

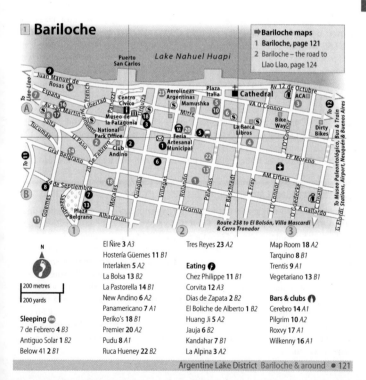

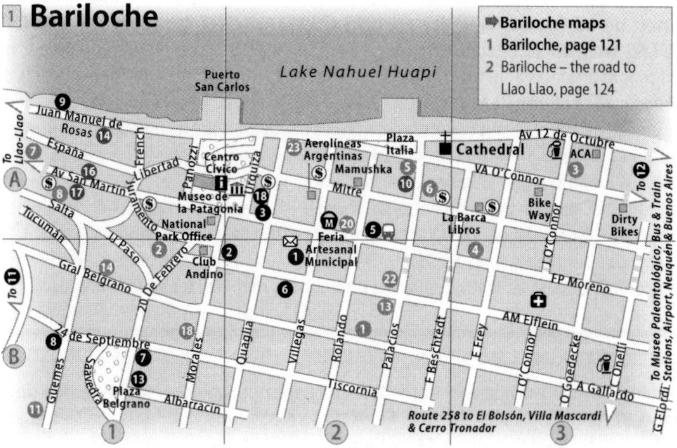

N

200 metres
200 yards

Sleeping
7 de Febrero **4** *B3*
Antiguo Solar **1** *B2*
Below 41 **2** *B1*
El Ñire **3** *A3*
Hostería Güemes **11** *B1*
Interlaken **5** *A2*
La Bolsa **13** *B2*
La Pastorella **14** *B1*
New Andino **6** *A2*
Panamericano **7** *A1*
Periko's **18** *B1*
Premier **20** *A2*
Pudu **8** *A1*
Ruca Hueney **22** *B2*
Tres Reyes **23** *A2*

Eating
Chez Philippe **11** *B1*
Corvita **12** *A3*
Dias de Zapata **2** *B2*
El Boliche de Alberto **1** *B2*
Huang Ji **5** *A2*
Jauja **6** *B2*
Kandahar **7** *B1*
La Alpina **3** *A2*
Map Room **18** *A2*
Tarquino **8** *B1*
Trentis **9** *A1*
Vegetariano **13** *B1*

Bars & clubs
Cerebro **14** *A1*
Pilgrim **10** *A2*
Roxvy **17** *A1*
Wilkenny **16** *A1*

Ins and outs

Getting there There are several flights daily from Buenos Aires. The airport is 15 km east of town; taxi US$6. A bus service run by **Del Lago Turismo**, T02944-430056, meets each flight, US$3. Bikes can be carried. Bus and train stations are both 3 km east of town; taxi US$3, frequent buses Nos 10, 20, 21. If you are staying in one of the hotels on the road to Llao Llao, west of town, expect to pay a little more for transport to your hotel.

Getting around Bariloche is an easy city to walk around and to orient yourself in: the lake lies to the north, and the mountains to the south. The main street is Calle Mitre, running east from the Centro Cívico. More accommodation and many restaurants are spread along Avenida Bustillo, which runs along the southern shore of Lago Nahuel Huapi for some 25 km, as far as **Hotel Llao Llao**, and an area known as Colonia Suiza. Frequent local buses, run by **3 de Mayo**, shuttle along its length.

Tourist information The main **tourist office** ⓘ *Centro Cívico, T02944-429850, www.barilochepatagonia.info, daily 0900-2100*, has helpful multilingual staff, who can provide maps showing city buses, and arrange accommodation and campsites.

Sights

At the heart of the city is the **Centro Cívico**, designed by Bustillo in the 1930s in 'Bariloche Alpine style' and made of local wood and stone. It was inspired by the Swiss and German origins of Bariloche's early settlers. On the attractive plaza above the lake, there's the **Museo de La Patagonia** ⓘ *Tue-Fri 1000-1230, 1400-1900, Mon and Sat 1000-1300, US$1.50, www.bariloche.com.ar/museo*, which, in addition to the stuffed animals, has indigenous artefacts and material from the lives of the first white settlers. Next to it is the **Biblioteca Sarmiento** ⓘ *Mon-Fri 1000-2000*, a library and cultural centre. From the plaza, the chalet style (bordering on kitsch) continues along the tourist-orientated main street, Mitre, in a proliferation of chocolate shops and restaurants serving fondue as well as delicious local trout and wild boar. The **cathedral**, built in 1946, lies six blocks east of the civic centre. Opposite the main entrance, there is a huge rock deposited here by a glacier during the last glacial period. On the lakeshore is the **Museo Paleontológico** ⓘ *12 de Octubre and Sarmiento, Mon-Sat 1600-1900, free*, which has displays of fossils mainly from Patagonia including an ichthyosaur and replicas of a giant spider and shark's jaws.

The road to Llao Llao » *pp128-136.*

Avenida Bustillo runs parallel to the lakeshore west of Bariloche, with **Avenida de los Pioneros** running parallel above it. From these roads, with good bus services, there's access to the mountains above. **Cerro Campanario** (1049 m) ⓘ *chairlift at Km 17.5 on Av Bustillo, T02944-427274, daily 0900-1800, extended opening in summer, 7 mins US$6.50 return*, offers a superb panorama of the lake, edged with mountains. There are more great views from **Cerro Otto** (1405 m) ⓘ *cable car at Km 5 on Av de los Pioneros*, with its revolving restaurant. To climb Cerro Otto on foot (two-three hours) turn off Avenida de los Pioneros at Km 4.6, then follow the trail past **Refugio Berghof**; don't walk this route alone, as the paths can be confusing. For a much longer trek or a good day-long cycle route, tackle **Circuito Chico**, one of the 'classic' Bariloche tours. **Cerro Catedral** ski resort (2388 m), 21 km southwest of Bariloche, is one of the major ski resorts in Argentina (see page 134), and in summer, the **cable car** ⓘ *from Villa Catedral, T02944-423776,*

The best walks and cycle routes around Bariloche

Consult **Club Andino Bariloche** for advice and maps (see page 134).

➔ **Circuito Chico** (trek/cycle route) The classic 60-km circular route begins on Avenida Bustillo at Km 18.3, runs around Lago Moreno Oeste, past Punto Panorámico and through the Parque Municipal Llao Llao and on to Puerto Pañuelo. You could extend this circuit by returning via Colonia Suiza and the Cerro Catedral ski resort or along the Península de San Pedro. Traffic can be a nuisance in summer, but the views are great.

➔ **Around Llao Llao** (walk) Choose from an easy circuit in virgin Valdivian rainforest; an ascent of Cerrito Llao Llao, for wonderful views (three hours), or a 3-km trail to Braza Tristeza, via Lago Escondido.

➔ **To Refugio López** (walk, six hours return) From the southeastern tip of Lago Moreno and climb up Arroyo López (2076 m) for fabulous views, and then along a ridge to **Refugio López**.

➔ **Cerro Catedral to Refugio Frey** (walk, three hours each way) via Río Piedritas. The *refugio* at 1700 m has a beautiful lake setting.

➔ **Cerro Catedral to Bariloche** (walk, six hours/cycle) descend a rocky path to the shores of Lago Gutiérrez and follow the Route 258 back to town. Buses to Catedral will carry bikes.

➔ **Bariloche to Cerro Otto** (cycle) Up a track from Avenida de los Pioneros. From the summit, the hardy could descend to Lago Gutiérrez.

➔ **Around Refugio Neumayer** Cycle to **Refugio Neumayer** southeast of Bariloche then hike to Laguna Verde or through Magellanic forest to a mirador at Valle de los Perdidos.

www.catedralaltapatagonia.com, 0900-1700, US$8, is a useful starting point for walks. ⏩ *See Activities and tours, page 132, and Transport, page 135.*

Llao Llao

Península Llao Llao, 25 km west of town, is a charming area for walking (see box, above) or for just appreciating the gorgeous views. The beautiful **Hotel Llao Llao** (www.llaollao.com) designed by Bustillo, is superbly situated on a hill with chocolate-box views. The hotel opened in 1937 as a wooden construction, but burned down within a few months and was rebuilt using local stone. It overlooks the **Capilla San Eduardo**, also designed by Bustillo, and **Puerto Pañuelo**, where boats leave for Puerto Blest. You can also take a **boat trip** ⓘ *half-day 1300-1830, full-day 0900-1830 or 1300-2000 in season, US$18*, from Puerto Pañuelo across Lago Nahuel Huapi to **Isla Victoria** and the Parque Nacional Los Arrayanes, on the Quetrihué peninsula (see page 117).

Puerto Blest

ⓘ *Tours by Catedral and Turisur (see Activities and tours, page 132). Departure time 0900. US$19, plus US$4 for bus transfer – a cheaper alternative is to take the 3 de Mayo bus at 0730 (US$1.50) to Puerto Pañuelo.*

The all-day boat trip from Puerto Pañuelo to Puerto Blest, at the western end of Lago Nahuel Huapi, is highly recommended. Boats are comfortable but fill up entirely in high season, so are much more pleasant in December and March. There's a good but expensive *cafetería* on board. The boat sails down the fjord-like Brazo Blest, with coihue-clad mountains dropping steeply into the Prussian blue water; it's usually raining, but very atmospheric. When you get to Puerto Blest, walk through beautiful forest to the **Cascada de los Cántaros** (one hour); set off while the rest of the party stops for lunch and you'll have time for your picnic by the falls before the crowd arrives by boat. The *guardaparques* can advise on other walks but the seven-hour 15-km trek to **Lago Ortiz Basualdo** is particularly recommended (summer only). From Puerto Blest, the tour continues by short bus ride to **Puerto Alegre** on Lago Frías and then crosses the peppermint-green lake by launch; for the continuation of the route into Chile, see below.

Three Lakes crossing to Chile

ⓘ *Tickets from Catedral Turismo, Palacios 263, www.crucedelagos.com. Book by 1900 the day before (take passport) and further in advance during high season. Credit cards accepted.*

This popular route to **Puerto Montt** in Chile, involving passenger ferries across Lago Nahuel Huapi, Lago Frías and Lago Todos Los Santos, is outstandingly beautiful whatever the season, though the mountains are often obscured by rain and heavy cloud. It's a long and tiring journey, however, and is not recommended in torrential downpours. The route is from Bariloche to Puerto Pañuelo by road, Puerto Pañuelo to Puerto Blest by boat (1½ hours), Puerto Blest to Puerto Alegre on Lago Frías by bus, Puerto Alegre to Puerto Frías by boat (20 minutes), then 1½ hours by road from Puerto Frías, via **Paso Pérez Rosales**, to Peulla in Chile. Cross Lago Todos Los Santos in the afternoon from Peulla to Petrohué (2½ hours), then continue by bus, via the Petrohué falls, Ensenada and Puerto Varas, to Puerto Montt.

2 Bariloche – the road to Llao Llao

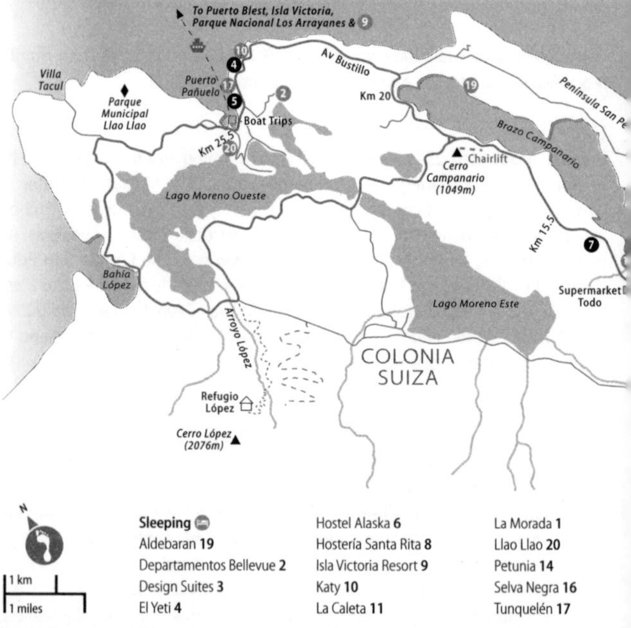

Sleeping
Aldebaran **19**
Departamentos Bellevue **2**
Design Suites **3**
El Yeti **4**
Hostel Alaska **6**
Hostería Santa Rita **8**
Isla Victoria Resort **9**
Katy **10**
La Caleta **11**
La Morada **1**
Llao Llao **20**
Petunia **14**
Selva Negra **16**
Tunquelén **17**

Tickets are available from various operators, but all trips are run by **Catedral Turismo**, who own the exclusive rights, in collaboration with **Andina del Sud** on the Chilean side (see page 292). The journey can be done in one or two days: the one-day crossing (1 September to 30 April) includes a two-hour lunch stop in Peulla during the summer but does not allow you to return to Bariloche the next day. For the two-day crossing (all year round), there is an overnight stop in Peulla. Alternatively, you could do the first section from Puerto Pañuelo to Puerto Blest and Lago Frías, on a regular day trip. Note that the launches (and hence the connecting buses) on the lakes serving the direct route via Puerto Blest to Puerto Montt generally do not operate at weekends. You can't take a bike from Puerto Blest to Lago Frías, 'due to the highest level of eco protection'. ➤ *For details of onward or return transport from Puerto Montt, see page 292.*

Towards Mount Tronador ●● ➤ *pp128-136.*

Lago Gutiérrez → *Colour map 1, B3.*
From Bariloche, Route 258 passes the picturesque **Lago Gutiérrez**, which feels like a fjord, with mountains dropping steeply into its western side and spectacular views all around. There are many ways to access the lake, including hiking/cycling trails from Cerro Catedral or **Refugio Frey**, and it can be explored on foot or bike almost all the way round. Watersports can be practised here in summer. However, by far the best option is to stay at luxurious **Estancia Peuma Hue**, which lies right on the lakeshore and has

⇨ **Bariloche maps**
1 Bariloche, page 121
2 Bariloche – the road to
 Llao Llao, page 124

Lago Nahuel Huapi

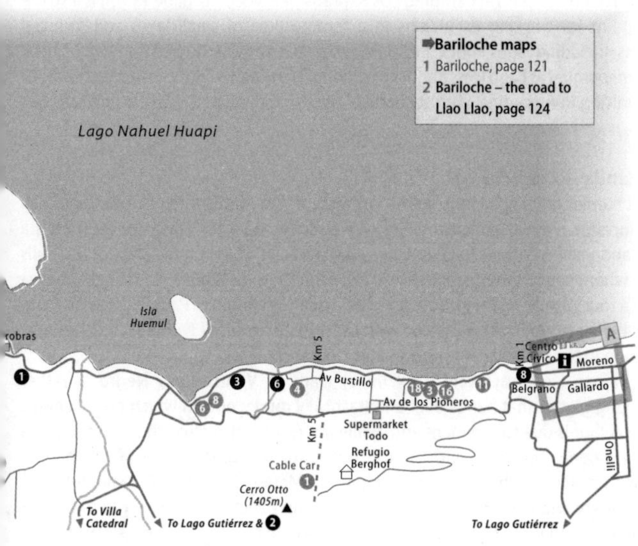

Villa Huinid **18**

Eating 🍴
Cassis **2**
Cervecería Blest **1**

Di Como **8**
El Patacón **3**
Il Gabbiano **4**
MeliHue **5**
Punta Bustillo **6**

Rincón Patagónico **7**

exclusive access to hiking and riding trails, as well as offering boats and kayaks on the lake (see Sleeping, page 130).

Lago Mascardi → *Colour map 1, B3.*

Route 258 continues to Lago Mascardi with its backdrop of grand jagged mountains, around which there are many places to stay and to walk, all easily reached by car (or by bus in summer). There are also boat trips across Lago Mascardi (see Activities and tours, page 132). At the southern end of the lake, **Villa Mascardi** is a small village from where a *ripio* Route 81 with a **one-way system** ⓘ *access going west 1000-1400, going east 1600-1800, 2-way 1900-0900, times may vary, so check with the tourist office, T02944-423022*, runs towards Cerro Tronador and Cascada Los Alerces. A few kilometres west of the Lago Mascardi turn-off is an entrance into the national park, US$5 for foreigners. At Km 10 is the lovely straight beach of **Playa Negro**, handy for launching boats and fishing; opposite is the peaceful **Camping La Querencia** (see Sleeping, page 130). Shortly afterwards, the road forks, with the right-hand branch following a narrow arm of Lago Mascardi towards Tronador. There's a viewpoint in pretty woodland, from where you can see **Isla Piuke Huapi** at the centre of the lake.

Lago Hess and around → *Colour map 1, B3.*

The left-hand fork runs for 18 km through the beautiful valley of the **Río Manso Medio** to **Lago Hess** and on to the nearby **Cascada Los Alerces**. Lago Hess is a beautiful spot for a picnic, with good camping at **Camping Los Rápidos** (see Sleeping, page 130). It is also the starting point for trekking excursions in a remote area of small lakes and forested mountains, including lagos Fonck, Roca, Felipe and Cerros Granito and Fortaleza. Check with *guardaparques* at Lago Hess about conditions on the paths. Río Manso offers some of the best rafting in Argentina, with sections of river suitable for all levels. » *See Activities and tours, page 133.*

Pampa Linda → *Colour map 1, B3.*

The quiet hamlet of Pampa Linda lies 40 km west of Villa Mascardi in the most blissfully isolated location, with spectacular views of Mount Tronador towering above. There's a ranger station with very helpful *guardaparques*, who can advise on the state of the trails and with whom you must register before trekking in the area. A good way to see the area is to take a tour with an agency from Bariloche, and then stay on at Pampa Linda for more trekking, before returning to Bariloche with the minibus service (3½ hours, US$9) run by **Transitando lo Natural** (T02944-423918 and T02944-527926).

From Pampa Linda, a lovely track (*ripio*) leads to **Ventisquero Negro**, a rather filthy-looking glacier that hangs over a fantastically murky pool in which grey icebergs float. The colour is due to sediment and, while not exactly attractive, the whole scene is very atmospheric. The road ends at the **Garganta del Diablo**, one of the natural amphitheatres formed by the lower slopes of Mount Tronador. A beautiful walk (1½ hours there and back) from the car park through beech forest takes you to a more pristine glacier and up to the head of the gorge, where thin torrents of ice water fall in columns from the hanging glacier above.

Mount Tronador → *Colour map 1, B3.*

Mighty Mount Tronador (3478 m) overshadows Pampa Linda, and can be visited in a good day's tour from Bariloche, taking in the beautiful lakes Gutiérrez and Mascardi and

Border crossing

Paso Pérez Rosales
West of Puerto Frías, this crossing is used by buses on the 'Three Lakes' route between Bariloche and Puerto Montt (see page 124). If you plan to make this crossing independently be prepared for some long walks, as cars are not carried on the ferries and it is impossible to buy a separate bus ticket from the border to Peulla, 26 km west.
Argentine immigration and customs Puerto Frías, open all year.
Chilean immigration and customs Peulla, daily summer 0800-2100, winter 0800-2000.
Chilean currency This can be bought at Peulla customs at a reasonable rate.

stopping for lunch at **Hostería Pampa Linda**. From Pampa Linda two paths head up the mountain: the first leads to a *refugio* on the south side, while the other leads to **Refugio Otto Meiling** (15 km, five hours each way), situated at 2000 m on the edge of the eastern glacier. Follow the path for another hour from the *refugio* for a view over Tronador and the lakes and mountains of the national park. Otto Meiling is a good base camp for the ascent, with lots of facilities and activities, including trekking and ice climbing; always ask the *guardaparques* in Pampa Linda if there's space (capacity 60).

Paso de las Nubes → *Colour map 1, B3.*

Pampa Linda is also the starting point for a 22-km walk over Paso de las Nubes (1335 m) to **Laguna Frías** and **Puerto Frías** on the Chilean border. The spectacular glacial landscape was formed relatively recently (11,000 years ago). The pass lies on the continental divide, with water flowing north to the Atlantic and south to the Pacific. Views from the Río Frías valley are tremendous, and from Glacier Frías you enter valdivian rainforest. Allow at least two days for the whole route: camping is available after four hours or after seven hours; then it's another five hours to Puerto Frías. You must register with *guardaparques* at Pampa Linda before setting out and check with them about conditions. The route should only be attempted if there is no snow on the pass (normally December to February only) and when the path is not excessively boggy. For further information, refer to the excellent leaflet produced by Parque Nacional Nahuel Huapi. From Puerto Frías a 30-km road leads to Peulla in Chile on the shore of Lago Todos Los Santos (see page 273), or you can take a boat back across Lago Frías and Lago Nahuel Huapi to Bariloche; three times a day in summer (check this before you leave Bariloche).

Lago Steffen and Lago Martín → *Colour map 1, B3.*

About 20 km south of Villa Mascardi, a one-way dirt road leads to Lago Steffen, where a footpath runs along both northern and southern shores of Lago Steffen to Lago Martín. Both lakes are quite outstandingly lovely, fringed with beech and álamo trees, with far-off mountains in the distance and pretty beaches where you can sit at the waters' edge. There's also great fishing here. Further south, a road leads west along the **Río Manso Inferior** towards Chile. There is excellent rafting on the river (Grade II or III) through lush vegetation towards the Chilean border. **Extremo Sur** and **Aguas Blancas** run full-day trips and three-day expeditions from Bariloche. » *See Activities and tours, page 132.*

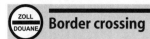

Bariloche and around listings

For Sleeping and Eating price codes and other relevant information, see pages 41-44.

Sleeping

Bariloche *p121, map p121*

Prices rise in Jul-Aug for skiing, and mid-Dec to Mar for summer holidays. Prices given are lake-view high-season prices where applicable. If you arrive in the high season without a reservation, consult the tourist office listing. In Jul and Oct-Dec, avoid the following hotels, which specialize in school trips: **Ayelén**, **Bariloche Ski**, **Interlaken**, **Millaray**, **Montana**, **Piedras** and **Pucón**. For more options see www.barilochepatagonia.info (in English).

LL-L Panamericano, San Martín 536-570, T02944-425846, www.panamericano bariloche.com. Lovely views from these smartly decorated doubles on the lakefront. The building is a little dated but nicely renovated and it includes a spa and casino. Central.

AL-A Hotel Interlaken, VA O'Connor y Palacios, T02944-436011, www.hotel interlaken.com.ar. New central hotel with smart doubles, and a good view of the lake from some rooms.

A La Pastorella, Belgrano 127, T02944-424656, www.lapastorella.com.ar. A cosy, quaint little *hostería*, whose very welcoming owners speak English. Recommended.

A Tres Reyes, 12 de Octubre 135, T02944-426121, hreyes@bariloche.com.ar. Traditional lakeside hotel with spacious rooms and lounge with splendid views, all recently modernized, friendly English-speaking staff.

B-C New Andino Hotel, Palacios 109, T02944-400443, www.newandino,com,ar. Small business hotel with only 21 basic rooms. Wi-Fi in rooms, and a good buffet breakfast.

C Antiguo Solar, T02944-400337, www.antiguosolar.com. Only 2 blocks from the centre of town, this bed and breakfast has nice simple rooms on the upper level of an attractive traditional residential building.

C El Ñire, John O'Connor 94, T02944-423041, www.elnire.com.ar. Comfortable rooms in this wooden alpine building close to the centre. Breakfasts are included though they're nothing special.

C Hotel 7 de Febrero, P Moreno 534, T02944-422244, www.hotel7defebrero.com.ar. Good central budget option with a slightly dated reception but nice clean simple doubles. Small breakfast included.

D Hostería Güemes, Güemes 715, T02944-424785. A lovely quiet B&B in a residential area, with lots of space, very welcoming, all the simple rooms have bath, breakfast is included, and the owner is a fishing expert.

D Premier, Rolando 263, T02944-426168, www.premierhotel.com.ar. Good economical choice in centre of town, with a light spacious entrance and gallery, neat modern rooms with bath and TV, internet, English spoken. Recommended.

Hostels

Bariloche has many good-quality hostels, all charging around US$8 for a bed in a dorm. A lot of hostels are focused on and around the street of Salta.

E pp **Hostel Inn**, Salta 308, T02944-522782, and **Marcopolo Inn**, Salta 422, T02944-400105, www.hostel-inn.com. Mixed and single-sex dorms, discounts for HI members. Breakfast and dinner included in price. Double and twin rooms available (**B**).

E pp **La Bolsa**, Palacios 405 (y Elflein), T02944-423529, www.labolsadel deporte.com.ar. Recommended for its friendly relaxed atmosphere, homely rustic rooms (some with lake views), and a great deck to sit out on. Doubles (**C**) available.

F pp **Below 41**, Juramento 94, T02944-436433, www.hostel41below.com. Extremely cosy, and welcoming hostel, with a great area to chill out filled with travel info. Small but ample kitchen and clean, attractive dorms. A lovely apartment (**B**) also available. Recommended.

F pp **Periko's**, Morales 555, T02944-522326, www.perikos.com. A warm and friendly atmosphere, quiet, with an *asado* every Fri. Towels and sheets included, breakfast extra. Use of kitchen, and laundry, airy rustic rooms for 4, single sex, with bathroom. Also doubles with private bath. Garden, free internet access, can also organize horse riding, rents mountain bikes. Highly recommended.
F pp **Pudu**, Salta 459, T02944-429738, www.hostelpudu.com. An absolute gem in Bariloche. Run by a charming Irish couple, all dorms and doubles (**C**) have a spectacular view of the lake, and downstairs is a small garden, an in-house bar and a huge kitchen. Long-term rates available. Recommended.
F pp **Ruca Hueney**, Elflein 396, T02944-433986, www.rucahueney.com. A lovely calm and welcoming place, with comfortable beds and duvets. Spotless kitchen, and a quiet place to sit and eat. Fabulous double room with bathroom and great view. Also Spanish school. Highly recommended.

The road to Llao Llao *p122, map p124*

There are many *hosterías*, *cabañas* and campsites along Av Bustillo on the shore of Lago Nahuel Huapi. Take buses 10, 11, 20, 21.
LL Llao Llao, Av Bustillo, Km 25, T02944-448530, www.llaollao.com. Deservedly famous, one of the world's most wonderful hotels in a superb location, with panoramic views from its perfect gardens, golf course, gorgeous spa suite, pools, water sports, superb restaurants. Excellent services, but some complaints about tiny rooms. Pay the extra for more space and a view.
LL-L Isla Victoria Resort, www.islavictoria.com. On Isla Victoria just off the coast, this is really something special with spectacular island scenery, a pool, sauna, spacious and cosy places to sit and relax, riding and trekking organized all over the beautiful island, good food. A fabulous and romantic treat.
L Aldebaran, Península San Pedro, reached from Av Bustillo, Km 20.4, T02944-465132, www.aldebaranpatagonia.com. A modern boutique hotel right on the rocky lake shore. Exquisite taste in warm stylish minimalist rooms and superb views across the lake. Chic food in the rustic-style restaurant, wonderful sauna and spa with outdoor pool, so you can bask under the stars.
L Design Suites, 2.5 km from Bariloche centre, Av Bustillo, T02944-457000, www.designsuites.com. Refreshingly modern, with wonderful bold design in glass and wood in the stylish bar and restaurant area. Huge spacious rooms, some with window-side jacuzzis, all very comfortable. Great spa and gym, kids' room, friendly bilingual staff, and excellent food in the bar and restaurant. Warmly recommended. Book ahead.
L Tunquelén, Av Bustillo, Km 24.5, T02944-4444 8233, www.maresur.com. A comfortable 4-star hotel, on the lakeside near Llao Llao, with splendid views and a secluded feel – wilder and closer to nature than **Llao Llao**. Well-decorated cottage-style rooms, attentive service, superb food, warmly recommended. Much cheaper if you stay 4 days.
L Villa Huinid, Av Bustillo Km 2.5, T02944-523523, www.villahuinid.com.ar. Recommended luxurious *cabanas* for 2-8, beautifully furnished, and well equipped.
A Departamentos Bellevue, Av Bustillo, Km 24.6, T02944-448389, www.bellevue.com.ar. The famous tea room with the most beautiful view in Bariloche now has 3 extremely comfortable self-catering *cabañas* with high-quality furnishings. Access to beaches on the lake, gorgeous gardens and native forest. Delicious breakfast included. Highly recommended.
B La Caleta, Av Bustillo, Km 1.9, T02944-15607727, www.bungalows-bariloche.com.ar. *Cabañas* sleep 4, open fire, excellent value.
B-C Hostería Santa Rita, Av Bustillo, Km 7.2, bus 10, 20, 21 to Km 7.5. T/F02944-461028, www.santarita.com.ar. Close to the centre, but with comfortable rooms, peaceful lakeside views, lovely terrace and great service. Warmly recommended.

C Katy, Av Bustillo, Km 24.3, T02944-448023, adikastelic@yahoo.com. A delightful peaceful place in a garden full of flowers, charming family, breakfast included. Also runs adventure tours, www.gringospatagonia.com.

Hostels

E pp **Hostel Alaska**, Av Bustillo, Km 7.5, bus 10, 20, 21, T02944-461564, www.alaska-hostel.com. Well-run, cosy HI chalet-style hostel open all year, doubles and dorms. Kitchen facilities, internet, rafting and riding.

F pp **La Morada**, Cerro Otto, Km 5, T02944-442349, www.lamoradahostel.com. Fantastic views are the focal point of this hostel, located high on a hill behind Bariloche. Huge living area, clean kitchen and comfy rooms, all with a view of the lake and city below. Free transport from sister hotel '1004', San Martín 127, 10th floor, T02944-432228, downtown Bariloche. Recommended.

Camping

A complete list is available from the tourist office www.bariloche.org.

El Yeti, Av Bustillo, Km 5.8, T02944-442073, gerezjc@bariloche.com.ar. Pretty, and there are also *cabañas*.

Petunia, Av Bustillo, Km 13.5, T02944-461969, www.campingpetunia.com. Well protected by trees, a lovely shady lakeside site with beach, all facilities and restaurant, and shop, recommended, also *cabañas*.

Selva Negra, Av Bustillo, Km 2.9, T02944-441013. Very attractive well-equipped site. Highly recommended.

Lago Gutiérrez *p125*

AL El Retorno, Villa Los Coihues, northern shore, T02944-467333, www.hosteriael retorno.com. With a stunning lakeside position, this is a traditional family-run hotel has lovely gardens running down to the beach, tennis courts and comfortable rooms. Also a restaurant. Very relaxing.

AL Estancia Peuma Hue, on the southern shore of Lago Gutiérrez, 3 km off the road, T02944-501030, www.peuma-hue.com. One of the finest places to stay in the area, with a gorgeous rural setting on 2 km of private shoreline at the foot of Cerro Catedral Sur. Luxurious accommodation in 2 beautiful country houses and a mountain cabin. Prices include meals and activities such as trekking into virgin forest, horse riding, exploring the lake in kayaks, and rafting on the Ríos Mansos, massage, yoga. Rooms are decorated with great panache, and have wonderful views from huge windows. Jacuzzi under the stars. Delicious food. Highly recommended.

Camping

Villa los Coihues, by the lake, T02944-467479. Well-equipped and beautifully situated.

Lago Mascardi and around *p126*

A pp **Hotel Tronador**, T02944-441062, www.hoteltronador.com. A lakeside paradise, the lovely rooms have terrific lake views from their balconies, there are beautiful gardens, and a charming owner. It's a really peaceful place. Riding, fishing and excursions on the lake. Only open between Nov and Apr.

B Mascardi, Km 36.8, towards Tronador, T02944-490518, www.mascardi.com. This luxurious place has a delightful setting in lovely gardens on its own beach by the lake. Restaurant and tea room, horse riding, mountain bikes, rafting and fly fishing.

Camping

Camping La Querencia, T02944-426225, RN 258, Km 10. A pretty and peaceful spot on the side of a river, opposite the lovely straight beach of Playa Negro.

Camping Las Carpitas, Km 33, T02944-490527. Set in a great lakeside position, summer only, *cabañas* and restaurant.

Camping Los Rápidos, T/F02944-461861. Attractive site going down to the lake, with *confitería*, food store and all facilities, US$3pp. Also basic *albergue* US$4 pp (sleeping bag needed). Trekking, kayaking, fishing and mountain bikes.

Pampa Linda *p126*

B Hostería Pampa Linda, T02944-490517, www.hosteriapampalinda.com.ar. Comfortable retreat and a good base for trekking. Simple rooms, all with bath and stunning views. The owners are charming; Sebastián de la Cruz is one of the area's most experienced mountaineers. Horse riding, trekking and climbing courses. Full board and packed lunches available.

Camping

Pampa Linda, T02944-424531. Idyllic lakeside site, *confitería* and food shop.

Eating

Bariloche *p121, map p121*

Bariloche is famous for locally smoked trout and salmon, and for wild boar, there are other delicacies to be sampled too, like the berries in season, and the fine chocolate. For details of more options see www.guiasabores.com.ar.

TTT Chez Philippe, Primera Junta 1080, T02944-427291. Delicious local delicacies, really fine French-influenced cuisine, and delicious fondue, in this cosy place with a living-room feel. Book ahead.

TTT Kandahar, 20 de Febrero 698, T02944-424702, www.kandahar.com.ar. Highly recommended for its excellent food and intimate warm atmosphere. Reserve in high season. Dinner only. Argentine dishes, and other imaginative cuisine served in style, in a cosy place, run by ski champion Marta Peirono de Barber, superb wines. The *pisco sours* are recommended.

TTT-TT Jauja, Elflein 148 T02944-422952. Specializes in local delicacies such as trout and wild boar. Friendly and good value. Recommended.

TT Corvita, VA O'Connor, 511, T02944-421708. New vegetarian restaurant (that serves fish too), set in front of the cathedral. Try the curries, masalas and pastas.

TT Días de Zapata, Morales 362, T02944-423128. Great atmosphere. The Mexican food is tasty but not remotely spicy. The staff are welcoming. Recommended.

TT El Boliche de Alberto, Villegas 347, T02944-431433. Very good pasta and live folklore music. So popular that you'll have to queue in summer.

TT Tarquino, 24 de Septiembre y Saavedra, T02944-434774. Warm welcoming design with trees growing through the boldly coloured room, and friendly service, this is great for steak and tasty pasta, with a good wine list.

TT Trentis, JM de Rosas 435, T02944-422350. Great place for pizzas, and sandwiches with a nice outdoor terrace.

TT Vegetariano, 20 de Febrero 730, T02944-421820. Also serves fish in its excellent set menu, beautifully served in a warm friendly atmosphere. Highly recommended.

TT-T Huang Ji, Rolando 268, T02944-428168. Good Chinese food, next door to the bowling.

Cafés

La Alpina, Moreno 98. Charming old-fashioned Alpine-style place, as you'd expect, with delicious cakes, great for tea.

La Esquina, Moreno 10. Another traditional pub with good food and a relaxed atmosphere.

The Map Room, Urquiza 248, T02944-456856. Fantastic café/pub which serves large portions of interesting salads, burgers, and Bariloche's best brunch complete with hash browns and bacon. Recommended.

The road to Llao Llao *p122, map p124*

TTT Cassis, opposite Arelauquen golf club, just off Route 82, call first for directions, T02944-431382, www.cassis-patagonia.com.ar. This is without doubt Bariloche's finest restaurant, with a stunning setting right on the waterfront of Lake Gutiérrez, in secluded gardens, and serving amazing food. Local delicacies, exquisite dishes. Highly recommended. Open evenings only except in high season.

TTT Il Gabbiano, Av Bustillo, Km 24.3, T02944-448346. Excellent Italian food in this intimate restaurant on the lakeside. Delicious trout and sea food and extensive wine list. Booking essential. Closed Tue. Highly recommended.

ΨΨΨ-ΨΨ **Di Como**, Av Bustillo. Km 0.8, T02944-522118. 10-min walk from town. Good pizza/pasta place with a fantastic terrace and great views of the lake. Recommended.

ΨΨΨ-ΨΨ **Punta Bustillo**, Av Bustillo, Km 5.8, T02944-442782, www.puntabustillo.com.ar. Very cutesy chalet-style exterior, but the food is great. Lots of steak, Patagonian lamb, wild boar, smoked delicacies, and locally brewed beer. Cosy, welcoming and a great wine list.

ΨΨ **El Patacón**, Av Bustillo Km 7, T02944-442898. Good *parrilla* and game.

ΨΨ **Rincón Patagónico**, Av Bustillo, Km 14, T02944-463063. Traditional *parrilla*, with tasty Patagonian lamb cooked *al palo* speared over an open fire.

Ψ **Cervecería Blest**, Av Bustillo, Km 11.6, T02944-461026, 1200-2400. Wonderful brewery with delicious beers (try La Trochita stout), imaginative local and German dishes in a rustic atmosphere. Recommended.

Ψ **MeliHue**, Circuito Chico, Av Bustillo, Km 24.7, T02944-448029. Tearoom and B&B, in a lavender garden, selling fragrant produce. Lovely views.

Bars and clubs

Bariloche *p121, map p121*

Antarres, Elflien 47, T02944-431454. Chilled modern bar with a good range of beer.

Cerebro, JM de Rosas 406, T02944-424948, www.cerebro.com.ar. This is where everybody who doesn't go to **Roxvy** goes.

The Map Room (see Cafés). Quiet pub, with good food.

Pilgrim, Palacios 167, between O'Connor and Mitre. One of 2 Irish theme pubs in town, this serves a good range of beers in a lively pub atmosphere, also regional dishes, reasonably priced too.

Roxvy, San Martín 240. Food, and then dancing from 0130. It's where everybody goes.

Wilkenny, San Martín 435, T02944-424444. The other Irish pub, also lively. Expensive food but it really gets busy around midnight.

Shopping

Bariloche *p121, map p121*

The main commercial centre is on Mitre between the Centro Cívico and Beschtedt. The local chocolate is excellent; try **Abuela Goye**, Mitre 258; **Mamushka**, Mitre 216; and **Fenoglio**, Mitre 301 and Rolando.

Arbol, Mitre in the 400 block. Good-quality outdoor gear, clothes and gifts.

La Barca Libros, Quaglia 247, T02944-423170, www.patagonialibros.com. Bookshop with a wonderful range on Patagonia, good selection in English.

Martín Pescador, Rolando 257, T02944-4222275, Also at Cerro Catedral in winter. Fishing, camping and skiing gear.

Patagonia Outdoors, Elflein 27, T02944-426768, www.patagonia-outdoors.com.ar. Maps and loads of equipment, plus adventure tours, trekking and rafting.

Activities and tours

Bariloche *p121, map p121*

Rafting, horse riding, birdwatching, hiking, climbing and skiing can all be arranged through tour operators. There are many along Mitre, but best to use one that's recommended to you, or those below. Excellent trout fishing Nov-Apr; arrange boat hire with tackle shops. Most agencies in Bariloche charge the same. They get very booked up in season, and many trips only run in Jan and Feb.

Tours include: San Martín de los Andes (360 km) US$28, via the Seven Lakes Drive and returning via Paso de Córdoba and the Valle Encantado, a 12-hr minibus excursions. There are also tours around the Circuito

Chico (60 km), US$10, half-day. 'Cerro Tronador' (they mean a view of Tronador, not climbing it) and Cascada Los Alerces full day (255 km) U$23, El Bolsón full day (300 km, including Lago Puelo) US$24. Whole-day excursions to Lagos Gutiérrez, Mascardi, Hess, the Cascada Los Alerces and Cerro Tronador and the Ventisquero Negro, leaving at 0800, US$35, lots of time spent on the bus. Useful as a way to get to walks at Pampa Linda if the bus from CAB isn't running.

Cycling

This is a great area for mountain biking, with some challenging descents. CAB (see under Trekking) has detailed maps and advice on where to go. Also contact Diego Rodríguez, www.atacpatagonia.co.
Cordillera Bike, Av Bustillo, Km 18.6, T02944-524828, arrayanes235@bariloche.com.ar. Great relatively new Zenith bikes for rental at the start of Circuito Chico. Take bus 20, 22 or 10 and save yourself the 60-km ride from town. Recommended.
Dirty Bikes, V O'Connor 681, T02944-425616, www.dirtybikes.com.ar. Very helpful for repairs, if pricey. Also guided excursions on bikes, with bikes for hire. Recommended.
Diversidad, 20 de Junio 728, T02944-428995, www.eco-family.com. Excellent mountain biking around Refugio Neumeyer.
Huala, San Martín 66, T02944-522438, www.huala.com.ar. Superb company offering all kinds of rafting, both Río Manso and also up to the Chilean border. Also cycling, trekking, horse riding, climbing and more challenging rafting offered for the more experienced. Bilingual guides, great value. Recommended.

Fishing

Excellent trout fishing Nov-Mar (permits required); arrange boat hire with tackle shops. For guides, consult AGPP, T02944-421515, www.guiaspatagonicos.com/guias. For more information about fishing in Patagonia see www.interpatagonia.com/pesca/ (in English).
Baruzzi Deportes, Urquiza 250, T02944-424922, baruzzi@barilocher.com.ar. Guided fishing excursions (flycast, trolling, spinning) for experts and newcomers; US$150-300.
Martín Pescador, Rolando 257, T02944-422275, martinpescador@bariloche.com.ar. Great for fishing supplies (also camping and skiing) and excursions with experts.

Horse riding

Bastion del Manso, Mitre 415, 1st floor, T02944-437663, www.bastiondelmanso.com. A relaxed place with tuition and full day's riding offered, including rafting and longer treks.
Estancia Peuma Hue, T02944-501030, www.peuma-hue.com. The best riding in the region, starting at the beautiful estancia on the head of Lago Gutiérrez, with luxurious accommodation, and fine horses, with your own guide and horse whisperer. Day-long rides into the mountains all around, or longer rides to Pampa Linda and across the border into Chile.

Paragliding

Parapente Bariloche, T02944-15413715 , fedemano@ciudad.com.ar. Gliding at Cerro Otto and Cerro Catedral in the winter.

Rafting

Río Manso, south of Bariloche, offers some of the best rafting in Argentina, with sections of river suitable for all levels.
Aguas Blancas, Mitre 515, T02944-429940, www.aguasblancas.com.ar. Rafting on the Manso river with expert guides, equipment and lunch. Also bikes and horse riding.
Extremo Sur, Morales 765, T02944-427301, www.extremosur.com. Rafting and kayaking, all levels, full day all-inclusive packages offered, US$35 to US$55, or a 3-day trip for US$190 including accommodation.

Skiing

Cerro Catedral, T02944-460125. Open mid-Jun to end Aug, ski lifts open 0900-1700, lift pass adults US$28 per day, see also page 122. One of South America's most important ski resorts, with 70 km of slopes of all grades, a total drop of 1010 m and 52 km of cross-country skiing routes. There are also snow-boarding areas and a well-equipped base with hotels, restaurants, equipment hire, ski schools and nursery care. The resort is busiest from mid-Jul to mid-Aug. Bus run by 3 de Mayo 'Catedral', leaves Moreno 480 every 90 mins approximately, T02944-425648, US$1.50. Taxi costs US$6. Cable car for Catedral, T02944-460090, www.catedralaltapatagonia.com. There is also superb cross-country skiing (called Nordic skiing here) around the wonderful **Refugio Neumeyer**, where you can also try out snowshoe walking and stay the night or for dinner. Bilingual guides and equipment for hire. Great fun.

Xtreme Snow Solutions, at the resort, T02944-424659309, www.skipacks.com.ar. Has a ski school and equipment hire.

Tour operators

Active Patagonia, ask in **Club Andino Bariloche**, T02944-527966, www.active patagonia.com.ar. Excellent company with very knowledgeable and well-trained guides. Produce good walking books. Recommended.

Catedral Turismo, Palacios 263, T02944-425444. Tickets for the crossing to Puerto Montt in Chile, www.crucedelagos.com, see page 124 and Transport, below. US$180 for one day; US$250 for 2 days.

Chaltén Travel, Moreno 126, local 3, T02944-456005, www.chaltentravel.com. Well organized and friendly tour company offering trekking, kayaking, and specializing in the Ruta 40 from Bariloche to El Calafate.

Diversidad, 20 de Junio 728, T02944-428995, www.eco-family.com. All kinds of adventures offered by this friendly company with a base in **Refugio Neumeyer**, 12 km south of Bariloche. Treks can be tailor made for you. Highly recommended.

Extremo Sur, Morales 765, T02944-427301, www.extremosur.com. Professional company offering rafting and kayaking, all levels, full day all-inclusive packages, and longer trips including accommodation.

Lagos del Sur, Quaglia 262, T02944-434188, www.lagosdelsurevt.com.ar. Recommended for affordable excursions aroud Bariloche including Circuito Chico, Isla Victoria, Trondador as well as adventure tourism.

Patagonia Road, Chopin 83-8400, T02944-448579, www.patagonia-road.com. Tailor-made trips in Argentina and Chile.

Turisur, Mitre 219, T02944-426109, www.bariloche.com/turisur. Offers trips from Puerto Pañuelo to Isla Victoria and Bosque de Arrayanes full or half-day; to Puerto Blest and Lago Frías full day, including buses. Also offers conventional tours.

Trekking and climbing

There's a good range of peaks around Bariloche, offering walks ranging from 3 hrs to several days (see box, page 123). The season runs Dec-Apr; winter storms can begin as early as Apr making climbing dangerous.

Club Andino Bariloche (**CAB**), 20 de Febrero 30, T02944-422266, www.clubandino.com.ar, Mon-Fri 0900-1300, and 1600-2100 high season only. The club arranges guides; ask for a list. Its booklet *Guía de Sendas y Picadas* gives details of climbs and provides maps (1:150,000) and details of *refugios* and paths. There's also a book *Excursiones, Andinismo y Refugios de Montaña en Bariloche*, by Tonchek Arko, available in local shops, US$2.50.

Recommended trekking guides include: **Andescross.com**, T02944-467502, www.andescross.com; **Angel Fernández**, T02944-524609, T156 09799; and **Daniel Feinstein**, T/F02944-442259.

Transport

Bariloche *p121, map p121*

Air

Airport, 15 km east of town, T02944-405016. Bus service into town meets all flights. US$3 Aerolíneas Argentinas runs several flights a day to **Buenos Aires**, and to **El Calafate** (2 hrs) and **Ushuaia** (2 hrs) in summer. LAN also run flights to **Buenos Aires** and Chilean cities. LADE flies weekly to many destinations in Patagonia, including **Bahía Blanca**, **Comodoro Rivadavia**, **Mar del Plata**, **Puerto Madryn**; book well in advance in peak seasons. There are LanChile flights to/from **Santiago** (2 hrs) and **Puerto Montt** (45 mins).

Airline offices Aerolíneas Argentinas, Mitre 185, T02944-421950, free phone T0810-222 86527, www.aerolineas.com. LADE, Villegas 480, T02944-423562, www.lade.com. LAN, Mitre 534, T02944-431043, T0810-9999-526, www.lan.com.

Bus

The bus terminal, T02944-432860, has toilets, a *confitería*, *kiosko* and phones. Left luggage US$1.50 per day. Frequent buses 10, 20, 21 to centre, US$1, and Av Bustillo, with 3 de Mayo.

Local 3 de Mayo buses leave from the big bus stop on Moreno and Rolando. Useful routes include: bus 20 to **Llao Llao**, for lakeside hotels and restaurants, every 20 mins, journey 45 mins, US$0.70; bus 10 to **Colonia Suiza** and **Bahía López** for trekking; bus 50 to **Lago Gutiérrez**.

Bus marked 'Catedral' for **Cerro Catedral**, leaves from terminal or from Moreno and Palacios, every 90 mins, journey 35 mins, US$1. Bus to **Cerro Otto**, T02944-441031, leaves from hut at the Civic Centre, hourly 1030-1730 to connect with cable car, returning hourly 1115-1915, combined ticket for bus and cable car US$10 pp.

Long distance To **Buenos Aires**, several daily, 22½ hrs, US$62 *coche cama*, Andesmar. To **Bahía Blanca**, 3 companies, US$40. To **Mendoza**, US$40, TAC and Andesmar, 19 hrs, via Piedra de Aguila, Neuquén, Cipolleti and San Rafael. To **Esquel**, via El Bolsón, several companies, 4 hrs, US$10. To **Puerto Madryn**, 14 hrs, US$38 with Mar y Vale and Don Otto. To **San Martín de los Andes**, Ko Ko, 4 hrs, US$10. No direct bus to **Río Gallegos**; you have to spend a night in **Comodoro Rivadavia** en route: Don Otto daily, US$58, 14½ hrs. To **El Calafate**, ask at hostel Alaska, or Periko's about the *Safari Route 40*, a 4-day trip down Ruta 40 to **El Calafate** via the Perito Moreno national park, Cueva de Las Manos and Fitz Roy, staying at Estancia Melike and Río Mayo en route, US$130 plus accommodation at US$10 per day, www.visitbariloche.com/alaska or see www.chaltentravel.com (see Tour operators, above) who also offer this route. For a budget trip that runs all year round see Taqsa, T2944-423081, www.taqsa.com.ar, who run a no-frills services from Bariloche to El Calafate via the Ruta 40 once a week, Long, but interesting.

To Chile To **Osorno** (4-6 hrs) and **Puerto Montt**, 7-8 hrs US$32, daily, Bus Norte, Río de la Plata, TAS Choapa, Cruz del Sur, Andesmar (sit on left side for best views). For **Santiago** or **Valdivia** change at Osorno.

Bus companies 3 de Mayo, for local services, Moreno 480, T02944-425648; Andesmar/Albus, Mitre 385, T02944-430211, bus station T02944-430211; Chevallier/La Estrella/Ko Ko, Moreno 105, T02944-425914; Cruz del Sur, T02944-437699; Don Otto/Río de La Plata, 12 de Octubre T02944-437699; Flechabus, Moreno 107, T02944-423090, www.flechabus.com; TAC, Moreno 138, T02944-434727; Vía Bariloche/El Valle, Mitre 321, T02944-429012, www.viabariloche.com.

Car hire

Let your hire company know if you're planning to drive over the border into Chile, as you need a vehicle which has its registration number engraved on the windows, by law. Give 24 hrs. Rates are around US$40 a day. You can arrange to drop the car at San Martín de los Andes, or Esquel for an extra charge, from US$35. **Budget**, Mitre 106, 1st floor, T02944-422482, www.budget.com.ar. **Travel Rent a Car**, VA O' Connor 602, T02944-435374, www.travelrentacar.com.ar. **Rent a Car Bariloche**, Rolando 258, T02944-426420, www.rentacarbariloche.com.

Taxi

Puerto Remises, T0800-9990885 (freephone), **Radio Taxi Bariloche**, T02944-422103; **Remises Bariloche**, T02944-430222.

Train

Booking office T02944-422450. Closed 1200-1500 weekdays, Sat afternoon and all Sun. Information from the tourist office. Tourist service to **Viedma** (16 hrs, US$12-50 depending if you you want a seat or a bed), also carries cars, www.trenpatagonico.com.ar.

Lago Mascardi *p126*

Buses from Bariloche to **El Bolsón** pass through **Villa Mascardi**. Buses to **Los Rápidos** from the terminal in Bariloche, 0900, 1300, 1800 daily in summer.

Pampa Linda/Mount Tronador *p126*

Bus marked 'Tronador' departs from outside **CAB**, 20 de Febrero 28, daily Jan-Apr, and according to demand in Dec. Run by **Transitando lo Natural**, T02944-423918, T02944-527926, 3½ hrs, US$8.50. From Pampa Linda you can often get a lift with an excursion trip returning to **Bariloche**, US$10.

Directory

Bariloche *p121, map p121*

Banks Usually open from 0900-1300. ATMs at many banks along Mitre. Exchange and TCs, best rates at *casas de cambio*: **Sudamérica**, Mitre 63, T02944-434555. **Consulates** **Chile**, Rosas 180, T02944-422842. **France**, T02944-441960. **Germany**, Ruiz Moreno 65, T02944-425695. **Italy**, Beschtedt 141, T02944-422247. **Switzerland**, Quaglia 342, T02944-426111. **Customs** Bariloche centre T02944-425216, Rincon (Argentina) T02944-425734, Pajarito (Chile) T002944-236284. **Internet** Many along Mitre, and in the first block of Quaglia. **Immigration office** Libertad 191, T02944-423043, Mon-Fri 0900-1300. **Language Schools** **La Montana**, Elflein 251, 1st floor, T02944-524212, www.lamontana.com. Friendly Spanish language school, small classes, activities and accommodation organized, and a fantastic volunteering program which supports the local community. Highly recommended. **Steps**, Morales 764, T02944-422340, www.stepsonline.com.ar. Established school which teaches Spanish, Portuguese and English. **Spanish in the Mountains**, Isla Victoria (street), Villa Los Coihues, T02944-467597, www.spanishinthemountains.com. Unique concept of teaching Spanish whilst exploring the area trekking, kayaking, climbing and skiing. Can organize accommodation. **Medical services** Dial 107 for emergencies, or San Carlos Emergencias, T02944-430000, Clinic: **Hospital Zonal**, Moreno 601, T02944-426100. **Post office** Moreno 175, Mon-Fri 0800-2000, Sat 0830-1300. **Telephone** Many *locutorios* along Mitre, **Telecom** at Mitre and Rolando is helpful.

Southern Lake District

The southern end of the Lake District offers quite different scenery from that further north, with dense forests hugging the Andean foothills and contrasting with the Patagonian steppe further east. At the pretty and easy-going town of El Bolsón, there are beautiful rivers, waterfalls and mountains to explore, and a small national park, Lago Puelo, for fishing and walking. The pioneer town of Esquel is the southernmost centre in the lakes and can be reached via Cholila, a wild small settlement where Butch Cassidy hid out. From Esquel, you can explore the magnificent Parque Nacional Los Alerces, go skiing in winter, take a ride on La Trochita or visit the appealing Welsh pioneer village of Trevelin. ▸▸ *For listings, see pages 146-152.*

El Bolsón and around ▸▸ *pp146-152.*

El Bolsón is situated in a broad fertile valley 130 km south of Bariloche, surrounded by the mountains of the *cordillera* on either side (hence its name: the big bowl), and dominated by the dramatic peak of **Cerro Piltriquitrón** (2284 m). With a river running close by and a warm sunny microclimate, it's a magical setting that inspired thousands of hippies to create an ideological community here in the 1970s. The result is a laid-back town with a welcoming, rather nonchalant atmosphere that still produces the handicrafts, home-brewed beers, fruit and jams for which the town is famous. There are many beautiful mountain walks and waterfalls nearby and swimming and rafting on Río Azul. The small national park of Lago Puelo is within easy reach, with fishing and walking, but if you'd rather just sit and relax, this is a wonderful place to spend a few days. The helpful and friendly **tourist office** ⓘ *San Martín and Roca, opposite the post office, T02944-492604, www.elbolson.gov.ar, daily 0900-2100 all year, till 2400 in summer*, is on the side of the semi-circular plaza and has plenty of English-speaking staff. They provide an excellent map of the town and the area and can suggest places to stay. **Club Andino Piltriquitrón** ⓘ *Sarmiento and Roca, T02944-492600, clubandinopiltriquitron.blogspot.com, summer daily 0800-2200, otherwise closed*, can advise on hikes; all walkers must register here before setting off. For more information, see www.elbolson.com.

Around El Bolsón

There's an impressive long sweep of waterfalls at **Cascada Escondida**, 10 km northwest of town, a good place for a picnic, with a botanical garden and *casa de té* (tea room) nearby, serving delicious home-made beer, cakes and waffles. All along **Río Azul** are lovely places to bathe, camp and picnic. For a pleasant hour-long walk, with views over the town, climb **Cerro Amigo**. There are also good views from **Cabeza del Indio**, so called because the rock's profile resembles a face. It's a good 6-km drive or bike ride from the centre; take Azcuénaga west to cross the bridge over Río Quemquemtreu and follow signs. See also box, page 139.

Parque Nacional Lago Puelo → *Colour map 1, B3.*

This lovely green and wooded national park is centred around the deep turquoise-coloured Lago Puelo, 18 km south of El Bolsón on the Chilean border, surrounded by southern beech forest. With relatively low altitude (200 m) and high rainfall, the forest is rich in tree species, particularly the arrayán and the pitra, coihues (evergreen beech) and cypresses. The lake is glorious in April, when the trees turn a vivid yellow. There's lots of

El Bolsón

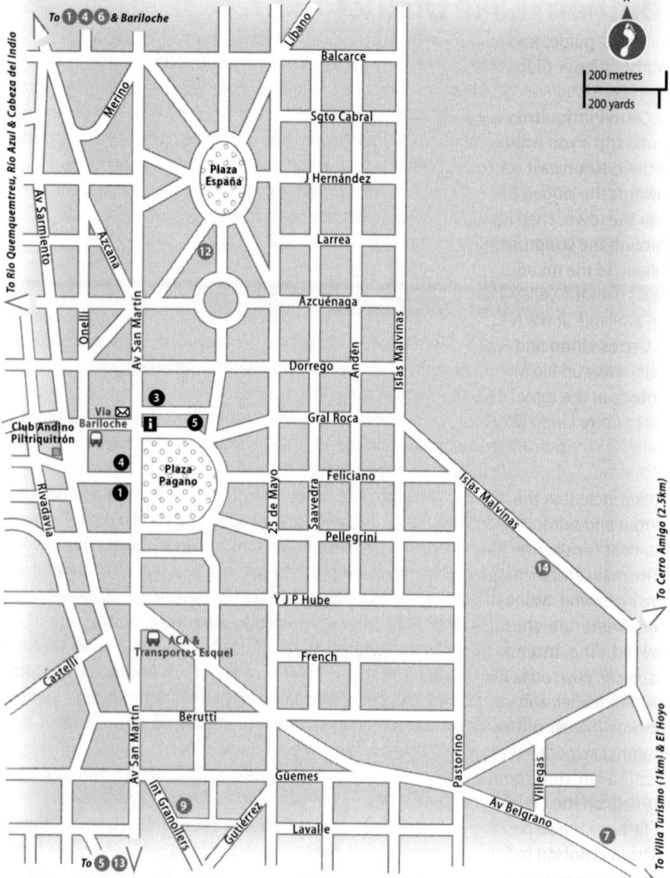

Villa Turismo

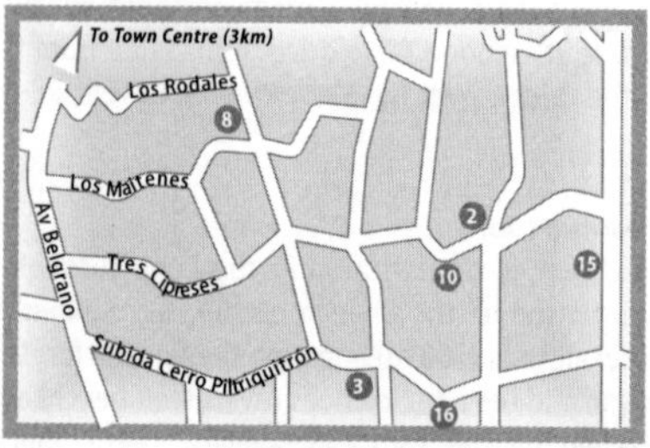

Sleeping
Altos del Sur **2**
Arcos Iris **1**
Cabañas Paraíso **3**
El Pueblito **4**
Hostería Steiner **5**
La Casona de Odile **6**
La Chacra **7**
La Montaña **8**
La Posada de Hamelin **9**
Las Nalcas **16**
Los Teros **10**
Posada de Buscador **12**
Quem Quem **13**
Refugio Patagónico **14**
Sukal **15**

Eating
1915 **5**
Acrimboldo **1**
Jauja **3**
Martin Sheffield **4**

The best walks around El Bolsón

For maps, guides and advice contact the tourist office or **Club Andino Pilquitrón**, see page 137.

➔ **Cerro Piltriquitrón** (six or seven hours round trip if you walk all the way) Walk or drive 10 km east up winding roads towards the jagged peak that looms over the town. Then it's an hour's walk through the sculpture park of the Bosque Tallado to the mirador with fabulous views over the valley. Food and shelter are available at the refugio (1400 m).

➔ **Cerros Lindo and Hielo Azul** (two days) Hike up Río Motoco, with **Refugio Motoco** at the top of the path, up Arroyo Lali to Cerro Lindo (2135 m), with **Refugio Cerro Lindo** at the top, and up to Cerro Hielo Azul (2270 m), also with a *refugio*. Club Andino Piltriquitrón has details of routes and transport.

➔ **Cajón de Azul** (four hours one way) Walk up Río Azul, which flows from a deep canyon to the *refugio* along a well-marked path. It's a bit hairy crossing the two wood and wire bridges, but worth it for a dip in the turquoise water on the way down. Set off early to allow for a leisurely lunch at the top, or spend the night in the *refugio*, with its lovely gardens. To start the walk, take a Nehuén minibus from Belgrano and Perito Moreno to Wharton, leaving El Bolsón at 0900. You'll be collected at 2000.

wildlife, including the huemul, pudú and foxes, and the lake is known for its good fishing for trout and salmon. There are gentle walks on marked paths around the northern shore area, boat trips across the lake and canoes for rent.

The main entrance is along a pretty road south from El Bolsón, through *chacras* (small farms) growing walnuts, hops and fruit, to **Villa Lago Puelo**, 3 km north of the park, where there are shops, plenty of accommodation and fuel. From here the road is unpaved. The **intendencia** ⓘ *500 m north of the lake, T02944-499232, lagopuelo@apn.gov.ar, year round Mon-Fri 0800-1500*, has a booth at the pier in summer. Staff provide a helpful leaflet and can advise on walks. To the left of the entrance, **Bosque de las Sombras** (Forest of the Shadows), is a delightful overgrown forest, which you wander through on wooden walkways, on the way to the shingle beach at 'La Playita'. **Senda a los Hitos** (10-km, three hours each way) is a walk through marvellous woods to the rapids at Río Puelo on the Chilean border (passport required).

Entrance is also possible at **El Desemboque**, on the eastern side of the park: take the bus from El Bolsón to Esquel, alight at El Hoyo, then walk 14 km to El Desemboque. From El Desemboque, you can hike (seven hours) to **El Turbio**, where there's a *guardaparque*, and on to **Cerro Plataforma** (12 hours); allow three days for the whole trip. There's also a three-day trek through magnificent scenery to **Glaciar y Cerro Aguaja Sur**; get advice and directions from the *guardaparques* ▸▸ *For boat trips and fishing, see page 150.*

South towards Esquel ▸▸ *pp 146-152.*

Cholila ➔ *Colour map 1, C3.*

This peaceful scrappy village is sprawled out in a broad open landscape, surrounded by far off mountains. There is good fishing for those with a 4WD and a dedicated guide. Otherwise, your only reason for stopping in Cholila would be to see the wooden cabins where **Butch Cassidy** and the **Sundance Kid** hung out for six years (see box, page 141). The cabins were once rather evocative, falling to pieces, patched up with bits of wood and with a lichen-stained slatted roof. However, they are now being 'renovated' and have lost all their charm. It's not worth the long detour to get there (from Route 258 heading south from El Bolsón, towards Los Alerces National Park's northern entrance; 13 km north of Cholila along Route 71, look out for a sign on the right, park by the little kiosk; US$2); head straight for Parque Nacional Los Alerces instead.

Leleque → *Colour map 1, C3.*

Route 40 (paved) is a faster way to get from El Bolsón to Esquel and is the route that the bus takes. Stop off at Leleque to see the **Museum of Patagonia** ⓘ *off RN 40, Km 1440, Mar-Dec 1100-1700, Jan and Feb 1100-1900, closed Wed and May, Jun and Sep, US$1.50,* located in the vast estate owned by Benetton, the Italian clothes company. There's a beautifully designed exhibition on the lives of indigenous peoples, with dwellings reconstructed of animal skins, using the original construction techniques, a huge collection of delicate arrowheads and the original *boleadoras* for catching cattle. Another moving exhibit highlights the first pioneers in Patagonia, especially the Welsh. And there's an attractive café in a reconstructed *boliche* (provisions shop and bar).

Esquel » *pp146-152.*

Esquel is a pleasant busy town in a fertile valley with a dramatic backdrop of mountains. It was originally an offshoot of the Welsh colony at Chubut, 650 km to the east and still has a pioneer feel to it, thanks to the old-fashioned general stores and architecture from the early 1900s. It's a busy country town, not at all touristy and with few sights, but all the more appealing for that. It's the best base for visiting Parque Nacional Los Alerces and for skiing at La Hoya in winter. Esquel is also famous for the steam train *La Trochita* (www.latrochita.org.ar), immortalized by Paul Theroux as the *Old Patagonian Express*. For more information see www.esquelonline.com (in Spanish).

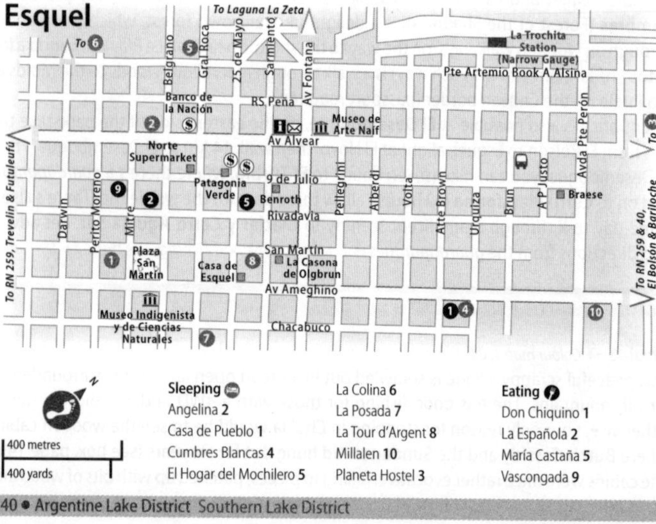

Sleeping
Angelina 2
Casa de Pueblo 1
Cumbres Blancas 4
El Hogar del Mochilero 5
La Colina 6
La Posada 7
La Tour d'Argent 8
Millalen 10
Planeta Hostel 3

Eating
Don Chiquino 1
La Española 2
María Castaña 5
Vascongada 9

Butch and Sundance

Americans Butch Cassidy (real name Robert LeRoy Parker) and the Sundance Kid (Harry Longabaugh) pursued careers in which periods of legal employment were mixed with distinctly illegal activity. In the late 1890s they were part of a gang known variously as the Train Robbers' Syndicate, the Hole in the Wall Gang and the Wild Bunch, which operated out of a high valley on the borders of Utah, Colorado and Wyoming. Gang members specialized in hold-ups on railway payrolls and banks. In 1900 they celebrated the wedding of one of their colleagues by having their photo taken: a big mistake. The photo was recognized and, with their faces on 'Wanted' posters across the land, Cassidy, Sundance and his girlfriend Etta fled for Argentina in February 1901.

Using the names Santiago Ryan and Harry Place, the outlaws settled on government land near Cholila but they were soon tracked down. They lay low, in the house which you can now visit (see page 139); but by 1905 it was time to move on. The gang raided banks in Villa Mercedes and Río Gallegos, posing as ranching company agents. They opened a bank account with US$7000, spent two weeks at the best hotels and socialized with the city's high society, and then entered the bank to close their accounts and empty the safe before escaping to Chile. At this point, Etta returned to the States.

No longer welcome in Argentina, Butch and Sundance moved to Bolivia, finding work at the Concordia tin mine. In 1908 they seized an Aramayo mining company payroll; with military patrols in pursuit and the Argentine and Chilean forces alerted, they rode into the village of San Vicente where they were besieged. The 1969 movie showed Butch and Sundance gunned down by the Bolivian army, but rumours have persisted that, having faked their deaths, they returned to the USA. Butch was said to have become a businessman, a rancher, a trapper and a Hollywood movie extra, while Sundance had run guns in the Mexican Revolution, migrated to Europe, fought for the Arabs against the Turks in the First World War, sold mineral water, founded a religious cult, and still found time to marry Etta. (Adapted from *Digging up Butch and Sundance* by Ann Meadows, London, 1996).

Ins and outs → *Colour map 1, C3.*

Getting there and around There's an airport 20 km east (T02945-451354), reached by bus or taxi, and a smart modern bus terminal on Avenida Alvear 1871, T02945-451584, six blocks from the main commercial centre around Avenida Fontana. Buses arrive here from Comodoro Rivadavia and Bariloche, with connections from those places to other destinations in Patagonia and to the north. Buses also run daily to Los Alerces national park. » *See also Transport, page 151.*

Tourist information The basic **tourist office** ⓘ *Alvear and Sarmiento, T02945-451927, www.esquel.gov.ar, www.esquelonline.com.ar, daily 0800-2000, summer 0730-2200, closed weekends off-season*, is friendly but has little information. It has a useful town map, however, with a plan of Los Alerces National Park. For further information on Los Alerces and the whole area see www.comarcadelosalerces.com.ar.

Sights

The town has two mildly interesting museums: the **Museo Indigenista y de Ciencias Naturales** ⓘ *Belgrano 330 and Chacabuco, Wed-Mon 1600-2000*, which has indigenous artefacts, and the **Museo de Arte Naíf** ⓘ *Av Fontana and Av Alvear*, which displays Argentine 'modern primitive' paintings. It's also the departure point for the famous narrow-gauge steam train, **La Trochita** ⓘ *Estación Viejo Expreso Patagonico, T02945-451403, www.latrochita.org.ar, Jan-Feb daily 0900, 1000, otherwise Sat 1000, 2½ hrs, US$31, tickets from tour operators, or station office*. Although it's a touristy experience, this is a thoroughly enjoyable trip, taking in the lovely valley and mountains of the *precordillera* framed through the windows of the quaint old train, with its wood stoves and little tea room. There's Spanish commentary along the way, and home-made cakes and handicrafts for sale at the Mapuche hamlet **Nahuel Pan**, where the train stops en route to El Maitén at the northern end of the line.

Trevelin ▸▸ *pp146-152.*

The pretty village of Trevelin, 22 km southwest of Esquel, was once an offshoot of the Welsh colony in the Chubut valley (see box, page 162). With a backdrop of snow-capped mountains, it's an appealing place to stay, with fishing and rafting on **Río Futuleufú**, and beautiful waterfalls at **Nant-y-fall**. The enthusiastic **tourist office** ⓘ *central plaza, T02945-480120, www.trevelin.org*, offers maps, accommodation and fishing advice.

Sights

The Welsh chapel of 1910, **La Capilla Bethel**, is now closed but the building can be seen from the outside. There is also a fine old flour mill dating from 1918, which houses the **Museo Histórico Regional** ⓘ *Molino Viejo 488, T02945-480545, daily 1100-1800, US$1.50*, with fascinating artefacts from the Welsh colony. **El Tumbo del Caballo Malacara** ⓘ *200 m from plaza, tours US$2.50*, is a private house and garden that belonged to John Evans, one of the first settlers. The house contains his belongings and outside is the grave of his horse, Malacara, who once saved his life. Eisteddfods are still held in Trevelin every year and *té galés* (Welsh tea), including an excess of delicious cakes, is served at **Nain Maggie** tea rooms.

Around Trevelin

Molino Nant Fach ⓘ *RN 259, 22 km southwest towards the Chilean border, T02945-15465045, US$3*, is a beautiful flour mill built by Merfyn Evans, descendant of the town's founder Thomas Dalar Evans. It's an exact replica of the first mill built in 1899. Merfyn's fascinating tour (English booklets available) recounts a now familiar tale of the government's mismanagement of natural resources and industry, through the suppression of the Welsh prize-winning wheat industry. It's a beautiful spot and Merfyn tells the rather tragic story in a wonderfully entertaining way. The **Nant-y-fall Falls** ⓘ *US$4.50 including guide, 1½-hr walk*, lie 17 km southwest on the road to the border and are reached via an easy trail through the forest. The series of waterfalls is spectacular and the area is great for picnics. Both Molino Nant Fach and Nant-y-fall Falls are only accessible by car or on a tour.

Parque Nacional Los Alerces ⊜▲⊜ » pp146-152.

ⓘ *33 km west of Esquel, via ripio RN17, between Cholila and Trevelin, T02945-471020, www.parquesnacionales.gov.ar, US$4.50, daily bus along RN 71 stops at campsites and hosterías.* One of the most magnificent and untouched expanses of the whole Andes, this park was established to protect the tall and stately alerce trees (*Fitzroya cupressoides*) that grow deep in the valdivian rainforest. Access is possible only at the eastern side of the park, via *ripio* Route 71, which runs along Lagos Futalaufquen, Verde and Rivadavia. The western side of the park, where rainfall is highest can only be accessed by boat or by hiking to Lago

Parque Nacional Los Alerces

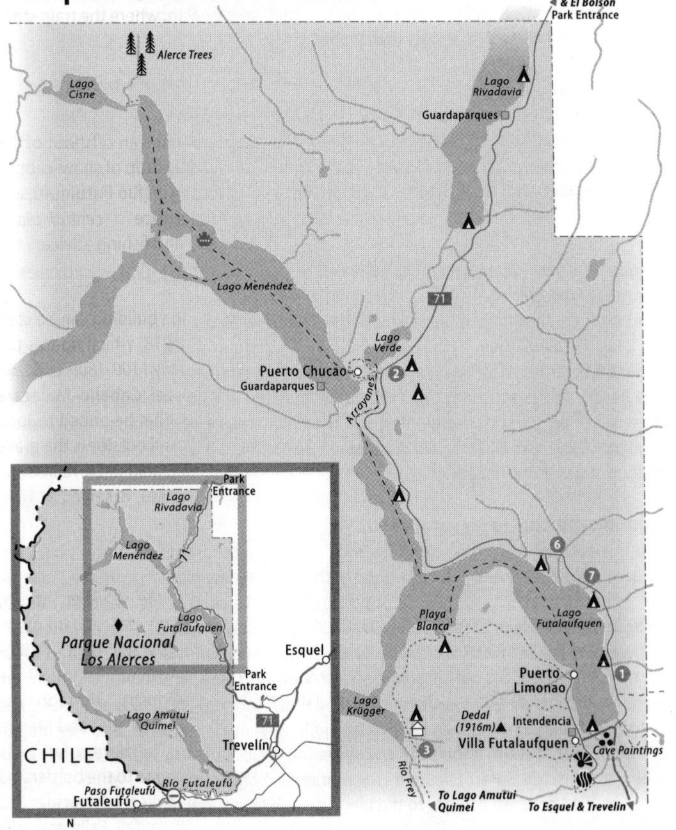

N

4 km

4 miles

Sleeping ⊜
Bahía Rosales **6**
Cabañas Tejas Negras **7**
El Aura: Lago Verde Wilderness Resort **2**
Hostería Quimé Quipan **1**
Krügger Lodge **3**

Border crossing

Paso Futaleufú

There are two border crossings south of Esquel. On the Chilean side, these crossings both link with route 7 north to Chaitén.

Paso Futaleufú lies 70 km southwest of Esquel via Route 259 (*ripio* from Trevelin) towards Futaleufú (see page 304. The border is a bridge over the Río Futaleufú. When entering Chile, change money in Futaleufú and then continue towards Puerto Ramírez; outside Ramírez, take the right turn to Chaitén, or you'll end up at Paso Palena.

Argentine immigration and customs On the Argentine side of the bridge.

Chilean immigration and customs At the border 9 km east of Futaleufú. Formalities should take no longer than an hour.

Paso Palena

This pass lies 120 km southeast of Esquel and is reached by *ripio* Route 17, 26 km west of Corcovado. On the Chilean side, the road continues to Palena.

Argentine immigration and customs At the border, daily 0900-1800.

Chilean immigration and customs Palena, 8 km west of the border.

Krügger. The park offers several good treks, rafting and fishing, plus idyllic lakeside campsites and *hosterías*.

The park contains four major lakes: **Lago Rivadavia** at the northern entrance; vivid blue **Lago Futalaufquen**, with some of the best fishing in the area; **Lago Menéndez**, which can be crossed by boat to visit the ancient *alerce* trees, and the emerald-green **Lago Verde**. At the southern tip of Lago Futalaufquen is **Villa Futalaufquen**, a village with a visitor centre with useful information on the park. Helpful *guardaparques* at the *Intendencia* here give out maps and advise on walks. There is a service station, *locutorio*, two food shops and a restaurant.

Exploring the park → *See map page 143.*

From Puerto Limonao, there are boat trips across Lago Futalaufquen and along the pea-green **Río Arrayanes**, which is lined with extraordinary cinnamon-barked arrayán trees. Even more spectacular, is the trip from **Puerto Chucao** across **Lago Menéndez** (1½ hours) to see the majestic 2600-year-old alerce tree, known as *El Abuelo* at the lake's northwestern tip. From *El Abuelo*, walk to the hidden and silent, jade-green **Lago Cisne** and then back past the rushing white waters of Río Cisne. If walking, register with *guardaparques* before you set off; bear in mind that it takes 10 hours to reach the *refugio* at Lago Krügger. Camping is possible (one night only) at Playa Blanca, but fires are not permitted. Boat trips run frequently in high season (1 December to 31 March) and all can be booked through **Safari Lacustre**, www.brazosur.com.ar, through **Patagonia Verde** (see page 151), or when you get to the piers, though tickets sell out in high season.

Walks

The *Sendas y Bosques* (walks and forests) map and book for El Bolsón, Lago Puelo and Los Alerces is full of great walks, with English summaries and detailed directions in Spanish. Maps are 1:200,000, laminated and easy to read, www.guiasendasybosques.com.ar.

The original big foots

The dry Patagonian plateau was originally inhabited by one principal indigenous group, the **Tehuelches**, who lived along the eastern side of the Andes, as far north as modern-day Bariloche, and were hunters of rheas and guanaco. In the 18th century, they began to domesticate the local wild horses and sailed down the Patagonian rivers to reach the Atlantic coast.

The Tehuelches were very large: it is said that when the Spanish first arrived in this area, they discovered Tehuelche footprints in the sand, exclaiming 'qué patagón' ('what a large foot'), hence the name Patagonia.

In the 18th and early 19th centuries, the Tehuelche interacted with European whalers and were patronizingly described as 'semi-civilized'. The granting by the Chilean government of large land concessions in the late 19th century, combined with Argentine president Julio Roca's wars of extermination | against Patagonian natives in the 1870s, spelled the end for the Tehuelches. They were persecuted by settlers and only a few survived diseases and the change of lifestyle.

Towards the end of the 20th century, a belated sense of moral guilt arose among the colonizers, but it was too late to preserve the Tehuelche way of life. Today only a few isolated groups remain in Patagonia. For details of other indigenous groups, see page 370.

▲ **Cave paintings** There are *pinturas rupestres* to be found just 40 minutes stroll from the park *Intendencia* (Km 1). Also a waterfall, and a mirador with panoramic views over Lago Futalaufquen.

▲ **Lago Verde** The most beautiful walk in the park, and unmissable, is across the suspension bridge over Río Arrayanes (Km 34.3) to heavenly Lago Verde. A self-guided trail leads around a peninsula and to Lago Menéndez, to the pier where boat trips begin, Puerto Chucao. Go in the early evening, to see all kinds of bird life from the beach by Lago Verde, swifts and swallows darting all around you. Signposted off Route 71, Pasarella (walkway) Lago Verde. While you're in the area, take a quick 20-minute stroll up to **Mirador Lago Verde** where you'll be rewarded with gorgeous views up and down the whole valley and can appreciate the string of lakes, running from Lago Futalaufquen in the south, Lago Verde, and Lago Rivadavia in the north.

▲ **Cerro Dedal** For a great day hike, there is a longer trek up Cerro Dedal (1916 m), a circular walk, at least eight hours return, with a steep climb from the *Intendencia*, and wonderful views over the lake and mountains further west. Register with *guardaparques* and get detailed instructions. You're required to start before 1000. Carry plenty of water.

▲ **Lago Krügger** This is a rewarding two- to three-day (12- to 14-hour) hike though coihue forest to the southernmost tip of Lago Krügger, where there is a *refugio* (open only January and February), and campsite, as well as a *guardaparque's* office. Here you can take a boat back to Puerto Limonao; check it's running before you set off, and always register with the *Intendencia*. For information on the boat service, and the *refugio* contact **Hostería Lago Krügger**, T02945-453718, www.krugerlodge.com.ar, a little rustic fishing lodge (US$70 for two, full board).

Southern Lake District listings

For Sleeping and Eating price codes and other relevant information, see pages 41-44.

Sleeping

El Bolsón *p137*

There are *cabañas* and *hosterías* in beautiful settings in the Villa Turismo, 3 km southeast of the centre. Buses run by **Comarca Andina**, opposite Via Bariloche, T02944-455400. For more info see www.elbolson.com.

LL-L Las Nalcas, Villa Turismo, T02944-493054, www.lasnalcas.com. Amazing set of 5 lovely fully equipped lodges for 4-6 people, surrounded by lush forest. Stunning heated pool.

B La Posada de Hamelin, Int Granollers 2179, T02944-492030, www.posadadehamelin.com.ar. Exceptionally welcoming with an outstanding breakfast, including home-made jams and cakes. Lovely chalet-style house with quaint and comfortable rooms all with bathroom, very central. Highly recommended.

C Hostería Steiner, San Martín 670, T02944-492224. Worth going out of the centre to this peaceful place with huge lovely gardens, simple rooms, wood fires. Recommended.

C La Casona de Odile, Barrio Lujan, T02944-492753, www.interpatagonia.com/odile. A really special place to stay, in rustic wooden cabins in this idyllic lavender farm by a stream, with delicious French cooking. Recommended.

C Sukal, Villa Turismo, T02944-492438, www.sukalarteyflores.com.ar. Gorgeous B&B, a haven of peace in a flower-filled garden, with glorious views. Also a *cabaña*. Delightful.

Hostels

E pp **Refugio Patagónico**, Islas Malvinas y Pastorino, T02944-483628, www.refugiopatagonico.com. High-quality hostel, with small dorms all with bathrooms, in a spacious house set in open fields, where you can also camp, with great views of Piltriquitrón, and just 5 blocks from the plaza. Recommended.

F pp **Altos del Sur**, Villa Turismo, T02944-498730, www.altosdelsur.bolsonweb.com. In a lovely setting in Villa Turismo, with beautiful views from the terrace, and nice welcoming sitting areas, this is a peaceful hostel with shared rooms, and 1 double (**D**) with private bath. Dinner available, and breakfast included, lovely welcoming owner Mariela will collect from bus station if you book in advance. Otherwise a US$4 taxi ride. Highly recommended.

F pp **El Pueblito**, Barrio Luján, T02944-493560, www.elpueblitohostel.com.ar. Wonderfully friendly hostel, a US$2.30 taxi ride from the centre, set amongst woodland. Lots of free travel information and huge living room with log fire. Recommended.

F pp **Posada de Buscador**, Diagonal Libano 3015, T02944-492263, posadadelbuscador.blogspot.com. Lovely house in the middle of town, great common areas and friendly hosts.

Cabañas

These cost around US$50 per night for 5 people in the Villa Turismo.

Cabañas Paraíso, T02944-492766, www.cabaniasparaiso.com.ar. Lovely wooden cabins in a gorgeous setting. Pool, good service.

La Montaña, T02944-492776, www.montana.com.ar. Well-equipped smart *cabañas* with pool and play area.

Los Teros, off the road leading up via Los Tres Cipreses, T02944-455 5569, www.cabanaslosteros.com.ar. Lovely cabins, well spaced in park land with good views. Recommended.

Camping

Arco Iris, T02944-15558330. Blissful wooded site near Río Azul, helpful owners.

La Chacra, Belgrano 1128, T02944-492111. 15 mins' walk from town, well shaded, good facilities, lively in season.
Quem Quem, Río Quemquemtreu, T02944-493550, quemquem@elbolson.com. Well-kept with hot showers, pickup from town.

Parque Nacional Lago Puelo *p137*

There are lots of *cabañas*, shops and fuel. Apart from wild camping, there's no accommodation in the park itself, but plenty in Villa Lago Puelo, just outside, with *cabañas*, restaurants and campsites spread out along RN 16 through the little village.

Cabañas

A **Lodge Casa Puelo**, RN 16, T02944-499539, www.casapuelo.com.ar. *Cabañas* for up to 6. Beautifully designed rooms and self-catering cabins in forested mountains. The owner knows the local area intimately. Free internet. Very comfortable. Recommended.
B **Frontera**, off the main road to Esquel, T02944-473092, www.frontera-patagonia.com.ar. *Cabañas* for 4 and a *hostería*, furnished to a very high standard, in a lovely building in isolated woodland. Delicious meals.
B **La Yoica**, just off RN 16, Km 5, T02944-499200, www.layoica.com.ar. Charming Scottish owners make you feel at home in these lovely traditional *cabañas* set in lovely countryside with great views.
B **Río Azul**, RN 16, T02944-499345. Beautifully designed rooms in pretty area next to Río Azul, with gardens, swimming pools, volley ball.
B-C **San Jorge**, a block from the main street, on Plaza Ilia, T02944-491313, www.elbolson.com/sanjorge. Excellent value, these neat little self-catering apartments in a pretty garden have friendly helpful owners.

Cholila *p139*

A-B pp **Hostería La Rinconada**, T02945-498091, www.larinconadaranch.com. Meals and excursions available. Yoga retreat and fly-fishing as well.
C pp **El Trébol**, Lago Los Mosquistos, T02945-498055. Comfortable rooms with stoves, meals available, popular with fishing expeditions, reservations advised.
D **Cabañas Cerro La Momia**, RN71 in Villa Rivadavia, T0297-446 1796, www.cabanascerrolamomia.com.ar. Peaceful setting, basic *cabañas*, but breakfast is included.

Esquel *p140, map p140*

See www.interpatagonia.com/esquel (in English) for more hotel listings.
AL **Canela**, Los Notros, Villa Ayelén, T02945-453890, www.canela-patagonia.com. Helpful, comfortable B&B and tearoom.
A **Cumbres Blancas**, Ameghino 1683, T/F02945-455100, www.cumbresblancas.com.ar. A little out of town, with great views, comfortable traditional rooms and an airy restaurant serving dinner US$10.
B **Angelina**, Alvear 758, T02945-452763, www.hosteriaangelina.com.ar. A warm welcoming place, open high season only, serving good food.
B-C **La Tour D'Argent**, San Martín 1063, T02945-454612, www.cpatagonia.com/esq/latour. The bright modern rooms are very good value in this friendly family-run hotel. Breakfast.
C **La Chacra**, Km 4 on Ruta 259 towards Trevelin, T02945-452471. Tranquil place with spacious modern rooms and huge breakfast, Welsh/English spoken.
C **La Posada**, Chacabuco 905 (cnr Roca), T02945-454095, laposada@art.inter.ar. A real gem. Welcoming tasteful *hostería* in a quiet part of town, with a lovely lounge and good, spacious rooms, breakfast included. Excellent value.

Hostels

E pp **Casa de Pueblo** , San Martín 661, T02945-450581, www.epaadventure.com.ar. A friendly welcoming hostel with smallish rooms, kitchen, laundry. Also run rafting, trekking, climbing and mountain biking.
E pp **La Colina**, Darwin 1400, T02945-455264, www.lacolinaesquel.com.ar. Complex a little

out of the centre offering cramp dorms, but nice doubles (**C**) and camping.
F pp **Planeta Hostel**, Av Alvear 2833, T02945-456845, www.planetahostel.com. Close into town, this small cosy hostel has dorm rooms for 4-6 people, and 1 double (**D**) available.

Camping

El Hogar del Mochilero, Roca 1028, T02945-452166. Jan-Mar only. Hostel and campsite with laundry, 24-hr hot water, friendly owner, internet, free firewood.
La Rural, 1 km on road to Trevelin, T02945-1568 1429. Well-organized and shady site.
Millalen, Ameghino 2063, T02945-456164. Good services.

Trevelin *p142*

AL Challhuaquen, Los Cipreses, T02945-507882, www.challhuaquen.com. Charming place set high up with beautiful views over the river, and high quality accommodation and food, aimed at the fly-fishing market with expert resident fishing guide.
A La Patagonia Lodge, RN 71, Km 1, T02945-480752, www.lapatagonialodge.com. Has been recommended as a great fishing lodge.
D Pezzi, Sarmiento 353, T02945-480146, hpezzi@intramed.com.ar. Jan-Mar only. Attractive small hotel with a garden.

Hostels

E pp **Casa Verde Hostal**, Los Alerces s/n, T/F02945-480091, www.casaverdehostel.com.ar. 'The best hostel in Argentina' is a cosy log cabin, with gardens, and views over Trevelin. Comfortable dorms for 4-6 with bathrooms. Kitchen, laundry, lounge, meals available. Trekking and rafting trips in Los Alerces national park. Also a very comfortable *cabaña*. Highly recommended. HI affiliated.

Cabañas

Ask for a full list at the tourist office.
A-B Casa de Piedra, Brown 244, T02945-480357, casadepiedratrevelin@yahoo.com.ar.
A-B El Tropezón, San Martín and Saavedra, T02945-480016, eltropezon@ciudad.com.ar.

Camping

Many sites on the road to Futuleufú and Chile. **Aikén Leufú**, on the road to Futaleufú dam, T02945-1568 1398. Full facilities and *cabañas*.
Puerto Ciprés, on the banks of Río Futuleufú, T02945-450913. Peaceful place, right on river bank, simple facilities.

Parque Nacional Los Alerces

p143, map p143

The following are on the east side of Lago Futalaufquen. **Hostería Futalaufquen** on the west side of the lake is not nearly as good.
LL El Aura: Lago Verde Wilderness Resort, T011-48165348, www.hosteriaselaura.com. Exquisite taste in these 3 stone cabins and guesthouse by the lake. Luxury, attention to detail, ecologically friendly. Impressive.
A Hostería Quimé Quipan, T02945-471021, www.cpatagonia.com/quimequipan. Delightful, comfortable rooms, impeccably clean, with lake views, dinner included. Very peaceful. Paths lead to a small rocky beach.
B Bahía Rosales, T02945-471044, www.bahiarosales.alojar.com.ar. Welcoming and family-run. Spacious *cabañas* in an elevated position above the lake, also *refugio*-style *cabañas* and camping , fireplaces, hot showers; restaurant and *quincho*.
D Cabañas Tejas Negras, T02945-471046. Comfortable. Good camping. Tea room.

Camping

Several campsites at **Lagos Rivadavia, Verde** and **Río Arrayanes**, ranging from free to US$3. All have marvellous views, lake access and fireplaces; can be busy in high season. **Krügger Lodge** (www.krugerlodge.com.ar) has a *refugio* and campsite, with hot showers, food shop, meals provided, fishing guides, boat trips.

Eating

El Bolsón *p137*

Jauja, San Martín 2867. A great meeting place, welcoming atmosphere, good music and tasty food. Try the trout-filled pasta and the hand-made ice cream.

Martín Sheffield, Av San Martín 2760, T02944-491920. Conveniently central and serving good food, Patagonian specialities, menu of the day, with or without a drink.

Parrilla Patagonia, on the RN 258, 2 km out of town, T02944-492423. Superb *parrilla* for steak, and Patagonian lamb and kid on the *asado* at weekends.

1915, San Martín and Roca. Wonderful café/restaurant with views over the park lake and the markets. Good option to breakfast as it opens at 0800. Recommended.

Acrimboldo, San Martín 2790. Good-value *tenedor libre*, smoked fish and beer, which includes dessert and drinks.

Dulcinea, on the road to El Hoyo. This delightful tea room is not to be missed. Famous for cakes and rose hip tea, and fondue at nights in season.

Parque Nacional Lago Puelo *p137*

Familia von Fürstenberg, RN 16 on the way to the national park, T02944-499392, www.vonfuerstenberg.com.ar. In a delightful perfectly decorated Swiss-style chalet, try the beautifully presented traditional waffles and home-made cakes. Also *cabañas* (**A-B**) to rent.

Sabores de Patagonia, RN 16 on the way to the national park, T02944-499532, www.saboresdelapatagonia.com. Good for lunch or tea, locally caught trout, and smoked salmon. Service is slow, but the food is worth waiting for.

Cholila *p139*

La Casa de Piedra, RN 71 outside village, T02945-498056. Welsh tea room, chocolate cake recommended.

Esquel *p140, map p140*

La Española, Rivadavia 740. Excellent beef, salad bar, and tasty pastas. Recommended.

Vascongada, 9 de Julio y Mitre. Good trout and local specialities.

Don Chiquino, behind Av Ameghino 1649. A fun atmosphere: the walls are lined with number plates, and there are games while you wait for your pasta and pizzas.

La Tour D'Argent, San Martín 1063. Delicious local specialities, good-value set meals and a warm atmosphere.

María Castaña, Rivadavia and 25 de Mayo. Popular for excellent coffee, reading the papers and watching street life.

Trevelin *p142*

Patagonia Celta, 25 de Mayo s/n. The best place to eat by a long way. Delicious local specialities, superb fresh trout, steaks and vegetarian dishes, in elegant stylish surrounds. Very welcoming, and reasonably priced.

Nain Maggie, P Moreno 179, T02945-480232, www.patagoniaexpress.com/nainmaggie.htm. The best tea room with a huge *té galés* and excellent *torta negra*. Recommended.

Parrilla Mirador del Valle, RN 259, Km 46, Excellent *parrilla* and other delicious dishes.

Parrilla Oregón, Av San Martín and Murray Thomas. Large meals (particularly breakfast).

Festivals and events

El Bolsón *p137*

Jan Fiesta de la Fruta Fina (Berry Festival) at the nearby El Hoyo.

Feb Fiesta del Lúpulo (Hops Festival).

Oct The home-brewed beer festival, **Fiesta de la Cerveza Artesanal**, is much more civilized than an Oktoberfest.

Dec The **jazz festival** attracts many famous musicians, for 10 days.

Shopping

El Bolsón *p137*

The handicraft and food market is on Tue, Thu and Sat 1000-1600 in season around the main plaza, for leather and jewellery, carved wood and organic produce.

Centro Artesanal, Av San Martín 1059. Daily 1100-1900. For handicrafts.

Granja Larix, RN 258, Km 118.5, T02944-498018. For fabulous smoked trout, home-made jams.

Mercado Artesanal, Av San Martín 1920. Wonderful Mapuche weavings can be bought here in this co-operative of local weavers, and you can watch women spin and weave beautiful rugs, scarves and bags, in the traditional way. Recommended.

Esquel *p140, map p140*

Braese, at 9 de Julio 1959. Home-made chocolates and regional specialities.

Casa de Esquel, 25 de Mayo 415. Rare books on Patagonia, also souvenirs.

Librería Patagonica, 25 de Mayo 415, T02945-452544. Rare books on Patagonia and recent editions, with friendly service.

Activities and tours

El Bolsón *p137*

Ask at the tourist office for their *Agroturismo* leaflet, with information on the *chacras* (fruit farms) you can visit in summer, for delicious freshly picked soft fruits and berries, jams and other delights. Throughout El Bolsón and El Hoyo, further south.

Grado 42, Av Belgrano 406 y Av San Martín, T02944-493124, www.grado42.com. Excellent company offering a wide range of tours, including *La Trochita*'s lesser-known trip from El Maitén, where there is a superb steam railway workshop and you can learn all about the trains. Also rafting on the Río Manso, horse riding in glorious countryside at Cajón de Azul, fishing in Lago Puelo, paragliding from Plitriquitron, information on buses. Recommended.

Huara, Dorrego 410, T02944-455000, www.huaraviajesyturismo.com.ar. Horse rides, rafting, trekking, and mountain biking. Closed Sun.

Kayak Lago Puelo, T02944-499197, www.kayaklagopuelo.com.ar. Kayaking on the lake with instructor Alberto Boyer.

Puelo Extremo, T02944-499588, www.pueloextremo.com.ar. Trekking and canoeing.

Puelo Trout, T02944-499430. Boat trips and all-inclusive fishing trips with equipment.

Parque Nacional Lago Puelo *p137*

Juana de Arco, San Martín and Juez Fernández T02945-493415, T02945-15-602290, juanadearco@red42.com.ar. Boat trips across Lago Puelo, US$12 for 45 mins, US$10 to the Chilean border, including walk through woodland. Recommended.

Zona Sur, T02945-1561 5989, alemaca@yahoo.com.ar. All-inclusive fishing trips Nov-Apr, US$100 for 3, with equipment.

Esquel *p140, map p140*

Fishing

Lots of guides and equipment for hire. See also **Frontera Sur**, under Tour operators, below.

Jorge Trucco and Patagonia Outfitters, Teniente Coronel Pérez 662 (San Martín de los Andes) T/F02972-427561, www.jorgetrucco.com.

Skiing

La Hoya, 15 km north, 22 km of pistes for beginners and experienced skiers, 7 ski-lifts. Popular and cheap. Ski pass US$10 per day in high season, equipment hire US$5 a day. Contact **Club Andino Esquel**, Volta 649, T02945-453248, www.esquelonline.com.ar.

Tour operators

Frontera Sur, Av Alvear and Sarmiento, T02945-450505, www.fronterasur.net. Good company offering adventure tourism and traditional excursions, ski equipment and trekking.

Patagonia Verde, 9 de Julio 926, T/F02945-454396, www.patagonia-verde.com.ar. Excellent tour to Los Alerces, including the boat across Lago Menéndez. Helpful.

Trevelin *p142*

Adventure tours

Gales al Sur, Patagonia s/n, T/F02945-480427, www.galesalsur.com.ar. Tours to the border, Los Alerces national park and Futaleufú dam; also *La Trochita*. Recommended for rafting, trekking, bike, 4WD and horse riding. Friendly.

Fishing

Fishing is popular in many local rivers and lakes, most commonly in ríos Futuleufú and Corintos and lagos Rosario and Greda. The season runs from mid-Nov to mid-Apr, and the tourist office can advise on guides.

Parque Nacional Los Alerces *p143, map p143*

Boat trips

Boat trips, US$16-27 run frequently in high season, and can be booked through **Safari Lacustre**, T02945-457055, www.brazosur.com.ar, **Patagonia Verde** www.patagonia-verde.com.ar, in Esquel, or **Gales al Sur**, www.galesalsur.com.ar, in Trevelin. US$7 extra for transport from Esquel.

Fishing

Lago Futalaufquen has some of the best fishing in the area; local guides offer trips and boat transport. Ask in the *intendencia* or at **Hostería Cume Hue**, T02945-453639 (am) or T02945-450503 (pm). Fishing licences can be obtained either from the food shops, the *kiosko* or **Hostería Cume Hue**.

Transport

El Bolsón *p137*

Bus

Note there is not a central bus terminal. Different buses companies all stop at their offices. Several buses daily from **Bariloche** and **Esquel**, with **Don Otto**, **Via Bariloche**, **Vía Bariloche/El Valle**, Mitre 321, T02944-429012, www.viabariloche.com. Heavily booked in high season. US$8, 2 hrs. **La Golondrina** runs 3 buses daily Mon-Sat from the plaza to **Mallin Ahogado**, from where you'll have to walk to reach the falls. Buses to **Lago Puelo** with **Vía Bariloche** every 2 hrs, 4 on Sun, 45mins, US$3. To **Parque Nacional Los Alerces** (highly recommended route), with **Transportes Esquel** (from ACA service station), once a day, US$8, 4-5 hrs, via Cholila and Epuyén.

Parque Nacional Lago Puelo *p137*

Buses from **El Bolsón** with **Vía Bariloche** every 2 hrs Mon-Sat, 4 on Sun, 45 mins, US$3. **Transportes Esquel** daily connecting Lago Puelo with **Cholila**, **Parque Nacional Los Alerces** (4-5 hrs) and **Esquel**.

Esquel *p140, map p140*

Air

Airport, 20 km east of town, U$10 by taxi, US$5 by bus. To **Buenos Aires**, 3 per week, **Aerolíneas Argentinas** (agent) Av Fontana 408, T02945-453614. **LADE**, Alvear 1085, T02945-452124, to **Bariloche** and elsewhere.

Bus

The modern terminal at Alvear 1871, T02945-451566, has toilets, kiosko, *locutorio*, left luggage and taxis. 3 daily buses to **La Hoya**, US$6 return.

Long distance To **Bariloche**, 4-5 hrs, US$8, **Don Otto**, **Andesmar**, **Mar y Valle**, T02945-453712, **Vía Bariloche**, T02945-453528. To **El Bolsón**, 2 hrs, US$6, on bus to Bariloche, or via Los Alerces national park, see below. To **Trelew**, 9 hrs, US$16.

Mar y Valle, Emp Chubut, Don Otto, daily. To **Trevelin**, Jacobsen, T02945-453528, Mon-Fri, hourly 0700-2100, every 2 hrs at weekends, US$2. To **Parque Nacional Los Alerces**, Jacobsen, T02945-453528, runs a daily bus through the park from Esquel bus terminal at 0930, arriving at **Futalaufquen** (the entrance and *guardería*) 1100, and on to **Lago Verde** 1215. You can get on or off at any of the campsites or *hosterías* in park. US$5 each way. Returns to Esquel from **Futalaufquen** at 2000, arriving **Esquel** 2115. Ring to check times as they vary from season to season.

To **Buenos Aires** travel via Bariloche: Andesmar, T02945-450143, including change in Bariloche, 24 hrs, *semi cama* US$55. To **Comodoro Rivadavia**, 9 hrs US$15, Don Otto, T02945-453012, 4 times a week (but usually arrives full in season).

To Chile From Esquel to **Paso Futaleufú**, 0800 daily in Jan/Feb, otherwise Mon, Fri, sometimes Wed, with Jacobsen US$4. From the border, Transportes Cordillera T02945-258633, and Ebenezer, to **Futuleufú** and **Chaitén**, 4 times a week (daily Jan/ Feb). From Chaitén there are services to **Coyhaique**.

Trevelin *p142*

Bus

To **Esquel**, with Vía Trevelin, T02945-455222, Mon-Fri, hourly 0700-2100, every 2 hrs weekends, US$3. To the **Chilean border**, Jacobsen bus from Esquel runs through Trevelin, 0830 daily in Jan/Feb, otherwise Mon, Fri, sometimes Wed, US$3, connecting bus at border to **Futuleufú** and on to **Chaitén**.

Parque Nacional Los Alerces

p143, map p143

From Esquel there are 2 services running at the time of writing: Jacobsen, as described above, and Transportes Esquel, T02945-453529, runs daily buses at 0800 from Esquel (returning at 2115) along the east side of **Lago Futalaufquen**, passing **Villa Futalaufquen** 0915 (return 2000), **Lago Verde** 1030 (return 1845), **Lago Rivadavia** 1120 (return 1830), and continuing on to **Cholila**, **El Bolsón** and **Lago Puelo** (return 1500). The driver will drop you at your accommodation, and you can stop the bus at any point on the road. US$5 each way.

❻ Directory

El Bolsón *p137*

Banks Exchange cash and TCs at Banco Patagonia, San Martín and Roca, with ATM outside. **Internet** Ciber Café La Nuez, Av San Martín 2175, T02944-455182. **Post office** San Martín 1940.

Esquel *p140, map p140*

Banks ATMs at Banco de la Nación, Alvear and Roca; Banco Patagonia, 25 de Mayo 739; Bansud, 25 de Mayo 752. **Internet** Lots in the centre. **Post office** Alvear 1192 and Fontana, Mon-Fri 0830-1300, 1600-1930, Sat 0900-1300. **Telephone** many *locutorios* in centre and at bus terminal.

Atlantic coast

Contents

Footprint features

Border crossings

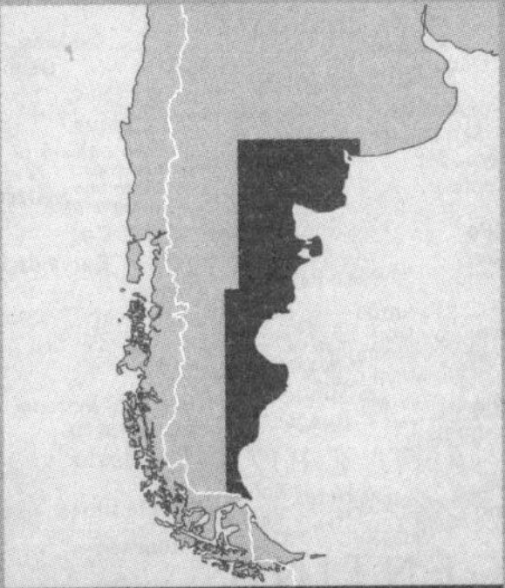

At a glance

Getting around Local buses are expensive but reliable. If you can afford it, a hire car is invaluable.

Time required 3-5 days will allow you to visit the wildlife of Península Valdés, enjoy a Welsh afternoon tea at Gaiman and head south to see the penguin colony at Punta Tumbo.

Weather Dec-Mar is usually pleasantly warm. The rest of the year can be cold and windy.

When not to go May-Jul is really cold and windy, and Dec (around Christmas) and Jan can be really busy.

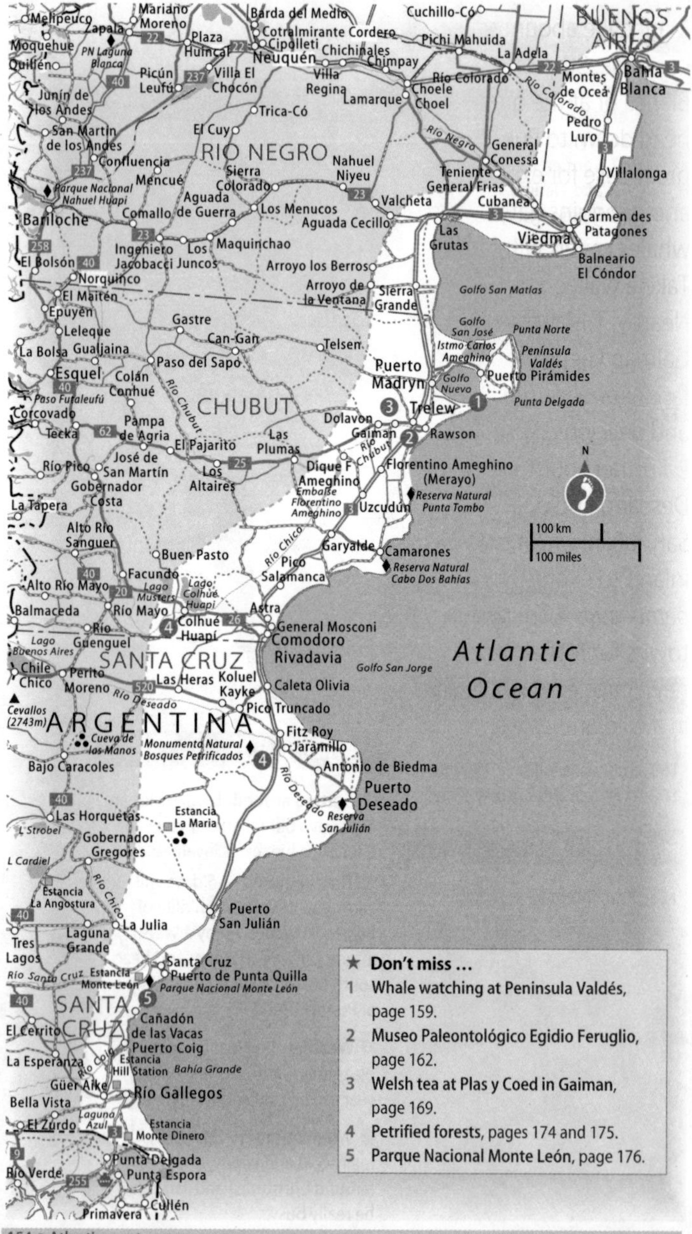

★ **Don't miss …**

1 **Whale watching at Peninsula Valdés**, page 159.

2 **Museo Paleontológico Egidio Feruglio**, page 162.

3 **Welsh tea at Plas y Coed in Gaiman**, page 169.

4 **Petrified forests**, pages 174 and 175.

5 **Parque Nacional Monte León**, page 176.

Marine life abounds along Patagonia's seemingly endless virgin coastline. Stop off on your way south at the friendly city of Bahía Blanca or at the quaint town of Carmen de Patagones and then head down to Puerto Madryn. This pleasant seaside town is a great base for exploring the Península Valdés, where sealions and penguins gather in their thousands, and southern right whales cavort with their young from September to November. Take a walk on the shore and then try the excellent seafood. Nearby, Trelew has a superb dinosaur museum, while pretty Gaiman keeps the Welsh pioneer heritage alive with a fascinating museum, Eisteddfods (Welsh Festival of Arts) and delicious Welsh teas.

Further south, you'll find colonies of cormorants in Ría Deseado and dolphins frolicking in the beautiful bay at Puerto San Julián. Leaving the sublime shorelines behind, venture inland to explore the weird lunar landscapes of the *bosques petrificados* – an unforgettably eerie sight. There are quiet towns for rest at Piedrabuena and Río Gallegos, and the new Parque Nacional Monte León offers superb accommodation in a wild and splendidly isolated setting.

Bahía Blanca to Camarones

Many visitors to Patagonia head for Península Valdés, a splay of land stretching into the Atlantic which hosts an array of wildlife, most famously the southern right whales that come here to breed from September to November. The seaside town of Puerto Madryn makes a good base for exploring the area. Just south, busy Trelew is worth a visit for its superb paleontological museum, and for access to the dainty old Welsh pioneer villages of Gaiman and Dolavon in the Chubut Valley to the west. Halfway from Buenos Aires you could break your journey at the friendly town of Bahía Blanca, spend a night at historic Carmen de Patagones on the Río Negro, or go shark fishing at Bahía San Blas. Viedma has a direct train to Bariloche and Bahía Blanca has excellent transport links to all parts of the country. » *For listings, see pages 164-173.*

Bahía Blanca » *pp 164-173.*

Bahía Blanca is the best stopping point on the route south if you want to make one. It's a busy city, yet relaxed and attractive, with early 20th-century architecture around its large plaza.

Ins and outs → *Colour map 4, A3.*

Getting there and around There are several flights daily from Buenos Aires to **Comandante Espora airport** ⓘ *T0291-486 1456, 11 km northeast of centre*, and weekly flights with **LADE** (www.lade.com.ar) from/to many places in Patagonia. A taxi from the airport to town is US$5. Bahía Blanca is a transport hub, with buses from all over the country to the **terminal** ⓘ *Estados Unidos and Brown, T0291-481 9615*, 2 km east of the centre. From here local buses No 512 and 514 run to the centre; a taxi costs US$3. Trains from Buenos Aires arrive at the **station** ⓘ *6 blocks east of the plaza at Av Gral Cerri 750, T0291-452 9196*. There is a good network of local buses, taking *tarjebus* cards (available from shops and kiosks) rather than cash. Taxis are cheap. » *See also Transport, page 171.*

Sights

At the city's heart is the large **Plaza Rivadavia**, a broad, well-kept leafy space, planted with a wide variety of trees, with a striking sculpture at its centre. On the west side is the Italianate **Municipalidad** (1904), which houses the **tourist office** ⓘ *Alsina 65, T0291-459 4007, www.bahiablanca.gov.ar, Mon-Fri 0800-1900, Sat 0900-1900*. To the south is the impressive French-style **Banco de la Nación** (1927). Three blocks north there's the classical **Teatro Colón** (1922) ⓘ *T0291-456 3973*, which hosts regular theatre, live music and dance. At the side of the theatre, the **Museo Histórico** ⓘ *Dorrego 116, T0291-456 3117, Tue-Sun 1500-2000, www.mhistorico.bahiablanca.gov.ar*, has interesting displays on the city's history. Outside is a statue of Garibaldi, erected by the Italian community in 1928. There are lively, changing exhibitions at the **Museo de Arte Contemporánea** ⓘ *Sarmiento 450, T0291-459 4006, Tue-Fri 1000-1300, 1600-2000, www.mbamac.bahiablanca.gov.ar*. To the northwest of the centre, along the attractive Avenida Além, the **Parque de Mayo** is filled with eucalyptus trees, and there are children's play areas, bars and a fine golf course and sports centre nearby.

Not to be missed is the **Museo del Puerto** ⓘ *Torres and Carrega, Mon-Fri 0830-1230, Sat-Sun 1530-1930, free*, 7 km away at the port area, which is known as **Ingeniero White**. Set in a former customs building, it has entertaining and imaginative displays on immigrant life in the early 20th century, with witty photographs and evocative music and sound. To get there, take bus 500A or 504 from the plaza, running hourly at weekends, or a taxi, US$4.

Carmen de Patagones and Viedma » pp164-173.

These two pleasant towns straddle the broad sweep of the Río Negro, 250 km south of Bahía Blanca. Viedma, on the south bank, was founded in 1779, but destroyed almost immediately by floods, after which Carmen de Patagones was founded on higher ground to the north. The **Fiesta de 7 de Marzo** (for a week around 7 March) is worth a visit, although accommodation is heavily booked. » *See Festivals and events, page 169.*

Ins and outs

Aeropeuerto Gobernador Castelo ⓘ *5 km south of Viedma*, receives flights from Buenos Aires and other Patagonian destinations. There are comfortable buses direct from Buenos Aires several times a day to the **terminal** ⓘ *Av Pte Perón and Guido 1580, T02920-42 6850, 15 blocks from plaza in Viedma, taxi US$2*, and a train three times a week between Viedma and Bariloche in the Lake District. Patagones (as it's known) and Viedma are linked by two bridges and a very small ferry, which takes four minutes and leaves every 15 minutes, US$0.50. Patagones has a very helpful **tourist office** ⓘ *Bynon 186, T02920-461777*. Viedma has a rather impoverished **tourist office** ⓘ *on the costanera, 3 blocks east of Plaza Alsina, T02920-427171, daily 0900-2100.*

Carmen de Patagones → *Colour map 4, A3/B3.*

Carmen de Patagones is by far the most picturesque of the two towns. Its town centre, just east of the river, lies around the Plaza 7 de Mayo, and just west is the **Iglesia del Carmen**, built by the Salesians in 1880. Take a stroll down the pretty adobe streets winding down to the river, to find many early pioneer buildings, including the **Casa de la Tahona**, a disused 18th-century flour mill, that now houses the **Casa de la Cultura**. Nearby is the fascinating **Museo Histórico Regional 'Emma Nozzi'** ⓘ *JJ Biedma 64, T02920-462729, daily 0930-1230, 1900-2100, Sun afternoons only*, which gives a great insight into early pioneer life.

Viedma → *Colour map 4, B3.*

Viedma is the provincial administrative centre and a duller place than Carmen de Patagones. However, it does have better accommodation and a pretty bathing area on the river, with large grassy banks shaded by willow trees where everyone hangs out to swim and drink *mate* on summer afternoons. The river water is pleasantly warm in summer and uncontaminated.

There are two plazas, with the cathedral, built by the Salesians in 1912, on the west of Plaza Alsina. Two blocks east, on the Plaza San Martín, are the French-style **Casa de Gobierno** (1926) and, opposite, the **Museo Antropológico Gobernador Tello** ⓘ *T02920-425900, 0900-1230, 1700-1930*, with fossils, rocks and indigenous *boleadoras*. Along the attractive *costanera*, the **Centro Cultural**, opposite Calle 7 de Marzo, houses a small **Mercado Artesenal** selling beautifully made Mapuche weavings and woodwork.

South and west of Viedma

This whole stretch of coast is great for shore fishing, with pejerrey, variada and even shark among many other species. At **El Cóndor**, 30 km south of Viedma (three buses a day in summer), there is a beautiful beach, with the oldest *faro* (lighthouse) in the country, dating from 1887. **Playa Bonita**, 12 km further south is known as a good fishing spot, with pleasant beaches. The sea lion colony at **Lobería Punta Bermeja** ⓘ *www.puntabermeja.fundacionazara.org.ar*, 60 km south, is visited by some 2500 sealions in summer. You can see the animals at close range and get further information at the impressive visitor centre. There's another stretch of lovely coastline at **Bahía San Blas** ⓘ *www.bahiasanblas.com*, a well-established shark fishing resort 100 km from Patagones.

Puerto Madryn and around

» *pp164-173.*

→ *Colour map 4, B2.*

Puerto Madryn is a pleasant breezy seaside town with a grand setting on the wide bay of Golfo Nuevo, the perfect base for seeing the extraordinary array of wildlife on Península Valdés, just 70 km east. During the breeding season you can see whales, penguins and seals at close range or go diving to explore life underwater. If you want to stay on the peninsula itself, there's the small popular resort town of Puerto Pirámides as well as several estancias to choose from, but Puerto Madryn makes a good place to enjoy the sea for a couple of days. The town was the site of the first Welsh landing in 1865 and is named after the Welsh home of the colonist, Jones Parry. It is a modern, relaxed and friendly place and hasn't been ruined by its popularity as a tourist capital.

Ins and outs

Getting there The **airport** ⓘ *10 km west of centre, taxi US$6*, has regular flights from Buenos Aires and El Calafate plus weekly flights with **LADE** (www.lade.com.ar) to other towns in Patagonia (see Essentials, page 36). There are more frequent services to/from Trelew airport. **Mar y Valle** runs an hourly bus that links Trelew airport with Puerto Madryn's bus terminal (US$10); a taxi will cost US$20. Puerto Madryn is connected to all main tourist destinations by long-distance buses from Buenos Aires, Bahía Blanca and south to Río Gallegos. The **bus terminal** ⓘ *Irigoyen and San Martín, T02965-451789, www.terminalmadryn.com*, is behind the old railway station. Walk three blocks down RS Pena to get into town. » *See also Transport, page 171.*

Puerto Madryn

Sleeping
Bahía Nueva **1**
Casa de Pueblo **15**
El Gualicho **3**
El Muelle Viejo **6**
El Retorno **8**
Gran Palace **14**
La Tosca **13**
Península Valdés **7**
Tolosa **10**

Eating
Caccaros **3**
Centro de Difusión de la Pescada Artesanal **2**
La Casona de Golfo **5**
Los Colonos **7**
Nativo Sur **1**
Plácido **11**
Taska Beltza **12**
Vernardino **13**

Bars & clubs
Margarita **9**

Tourist information This is one of the country's best **tourist information centres** ⓘ *Av Roca 223, off 28 de Julio, T02965-453504, www.madryn.gov.ar/turismo, Mon-Fri 0700-2100, Sat and Sun 0830-2300*, located on the seafront next to the shopping complex; staff are friendly, extremely well organized and speak English and French. They have leaflets on Península Valdés, accommodation lists and can advise on tours.

Around Puerto Madryn

You're most likely to be visiting the town to take an excursion to Península Valdés but there are other worthwhile destinations along the coast nearby. You can stroll along the long stretch of town beach to **El Indio**, a statue marking the gratitude of the Welsh to the native Tehuelche people, whose shared expertise ensured their survival. As the road curves up the cliff here, there's the splendid **EcoCentro** ⓘ *Julio Verne 784, T02965-457470, www.ecocentro.org.ar, daily 1000-1800 (Tue closed in winter, check with tourist office), US$9*, an inspired interactive sealife information centre that combines an art gallery, café and fabulous reading room with comfy sofas at the top of a turret. To get there, take bus line 2 from the corner of 25 de Mayo and Belgrano and it's a five-minute walk from the university. The whole place has fantastic views of the bay; great for an afternoon's relaxation or for finding out about whales.

Less exciting is the **Museo de Ciencias Naturales y Oceanográfico** ⓘ *Domecq García and J Menéndez, T02965-451139, www.hostar.com.ar/museo, Mon-Fri 0900-1200, 1430-1900, Sat 1430-1900, US$1*. It's an old-fashioned museum but the displays on local flora and wildlife are informative and worth a look.

You can spot whales from the *ripio* road at the long **Playa El Doradillo**, 16 km northeast of Puerto Madryn, and sea lions 15 km southeast at the **Punta Loma Reserve** ⓘ *open during daylight hours, US$4, but free with ticket to Península Valdés*. Access is via the coastal road from town and, like the road to the north, makes a great bike ride – allow 1½ hours to get there. The reserve is best visited at low tide in December and January.

Península Valdés » *pp164-173. Colour map 4, B2.*

Whatever time of year you visit Península Valdés, you'll find a wonderful array of marine life, birds and a profusion of Patagonian mammals such as guanacos, rheas, Patagonian hares and armadillos. But in spring (September-November), this treeless splay of land is host to a quite spectacular numbers of whales, penguins and seals, who come to breed in the sheltered waters of the gulf and on beaches at the foot of the peninsula's chalky cliffs. The land is almost flat, though greener than much of Patagonia, and at the heart of the peninsula are large saltflats, one of which, **Salina Grande**, is 42 m below sea level. The peninsula is privately owned – many of its estancias offer grand places to stay in the middle of the wild beauty – but it is also a nature reserve and was declared a World Heritage Site by UNESCO in 1999. The beach along the entire coast is out of bounds and this is strictly enforced. The main centre for accommodation and whale trips is **Puerto Pirámides**, on the southern side of the isthmus.

Ins and outs

Getting there Península Valdés is best visited by taking one of the well-organized full-day excursions from Puerto Madryn but you could also hire a car relatively inexpensively for a group of four, and then take just the boat trip to see the whales (September to

Península Valdés – top tips

→ Take an organized tour rather than hiring a car. The excess charged for turning them over is huge and you'll be too tired after driving on the *ripio* roads to enjoy the wildlife to the full.

→ Whale-watching trips in boats from Puerto Pirámides are not for those who get sea sick. If it's a rough day and you're prone to sickness, bring good binoculars and head for the Playa El Doradillo, 16 km north of Puerto Madryn where you can often spot whales close to the shore in season.

→ Take all your food and drink with you on a day trip as outside Puerto Pirámides cafés are few and far between.

→ To spend more time on the peninsula and see more wildlife, stay at one of several estancias there: **Rincón Chico** and **Faro Punta Delgada** are right in the middle of the land.

November) from Puerto Pirámides. Note that distances are long on the peninsula, and roads beyond Puerto Pirámides are *ripio*, and uneven so take your time. A cheaper option is the daily bus to Puerto Pirámides. ▸▸ *See also Transport, page 171.*

Tourist information The **entrance** ⓘ *US$12, tickets are also valid for Punta Loma,* is 45 km northeast of Puerto Madryn. About 20 km beyond, on the isthmus, there's an interesting **interpretation centre** with stuffed examples of the local fauna, many fossils and a wonderful whale skeleton. Ask for the informative bilingual leaflet on southern right whales. Contact the **tourist office** ⓘ *T02965-495084,* in Puerto Madryn or the small office on the edge of Puerto Pirámides, which has useful information on hikes and driving tours. A useful site is www.enpeninsulavaldes.com.

Whale watching

Puerto Pirámides ⓘ *www.puertopiramides.gov.ar,* 107 km east of Puerto Madryn, is the main centre for visits to the peninsula and whale-watching boat trips leave from its broad sandy beach. Every year between June and December 400-500 **southern right whales** migrate to the Gulfo Nuevo to mate and give birth. It is without doubt one of the best places in the world to watch these beautiful animals, as the whales often come within just a few metres of the coast. Take a boat trip and, with luck, you'll be very close to mother and baby. Sailings are controlled by the Prefectura, according to weather and sea conditions (if you're very prone to sea sickness think twice before setting off on a windy day).

Wildlife colonies

Isla de los Pájaros In the Golfo San José, 5 km from the entrance. Bird Island's seabirds can only be viewed through fixed telescopes (at 400 m distance). Only recognized ornithologists can get permission to visit. Between September and April you can spot wading birds, herons, cormorants and terns.

Punta Norte At the northern end of the peninsula, 97 km from the entrance. Punta Norte is not often visited by tour companies, but it has colonies of Magellanic penguins and sea lions. Killer whales (orca) have also been seen here, feeding on sea lion pups at low tide in March and April. **Estancia San Lorenzo** is nearby (see Sleeping, page 166).

Caleta Valdés About 45 km south of Punta Norte in the middle of the eastern shore, has huge colonies of **elephant seals**, which can be seen at close quarters. During the first half of August the bull-seals arrive to claim their territory, and can be seen at low tide engaging in bloody battles for the females. From September to October, you'll see them hauling their blubbery mass up the beach to breed. Just south of here, at Punta Cantor, you'll find a good café and clean toilets. There are also three marked walks, from 45 minutes to two hours. A short distance inland is **Estancia La Elvira** (see Sleeping, page 166).

Punta Delgada At the southeastern end of the peninsula, 91 km from the entrance, **elephant seals** and **sea lions** can be seen from the high cliffs in such large numbers that they seem to stretch out like a velvety bronze tide line on the beautiful beach below. It's mesmerizing to watch as the young frolic in the shallow water, and the bulls lever themselves around the females. There's an estancia nearby, **Faro Punta Delgada** (see Sleeping, page 166), a good base for exploring this beautiful area further.

Trelew and the Chubut Valley » *pp164-173.*

The Río Chubut flows a massive 820 km from the foothills of the Andes to enter the Atlantic at Rawson. Welsh pioneers came to this part of the world in 1865 and their irrigation of the arid land around the river enabled them to survive and prosper. You can trace their history west along the valley from the pleasant airy town of Trelew, past little brick chapels sitting amidst lush green fields, to the small villages of Gaiman and Dolavon (see box, page 162). If you're keen to investigate much further into the past, there's a marvellous museum full of dinosaurs at Trelew and some ancient fossils in the Parque Palaeontológico Bryn-Gwyn near Gaiman.

Ins and outs

Getting there There are daily flights from Buenos Aires, El Calafate, Ushuaia and Bariloche (in high season) to Trelew's airport, 5 km north of the town. A taxi to the centre costs US$4 and local buses to Puerto Madryn will stop at the airport entrance if asked. The bus terminal is north of the centre on the east side of Plaza Centenario, T02965-420121.

Tourist information A 10-minute walk south is the main plaza, where you'll find the very helpful **tourist office** ⓘ *Mitre 387, T02965-420139, www.trelew.gov.ar, Mon-Fri 0800-2000, Sat and Sun 0900-2100.* It has an excellent map, directing you to the town's older buildings. Visit in mid-October for the Eisteddfod.

Trelew → *Colour map 4, C1.*

Located some 70 km south of Puerto Madryn, Trelew (pronounced *'Trel-Yeah-Oo'*) is the largest town in the Chubut Valley. Founded in 1884, it was named in honour of Lewis Jones, an early settler, and the Welsh colonization is still evident in the remaining chapels in the town's modern centre and in the Welsh language still spoken by some residents.

The lovely, shady Plaza Independencia in the town centre is packed with mature trees and hosts a small handicraft market at weekends. Nearby is the **Capilla Tabernacle** ⓘ *Belgrano between San Martín and 25 de Mayo*, a red-brick Welsh chapel dating from 1889. Heading east, rather more impressive is the **Salón San David**, a Welsh meeting hall first used for the Eisteddfod of 1913 and now, sadly, used for bingo. The most wonderful building in the town, however, is the 1920s **Hotel Touring Club** ⓘ *Fontana 240*. This was

A little Wales beyond Wales

Among the stories of early pioneers to Argentina, the story of the Welsh emigration, in search of religious freedom, is courageous. The first 165 settlers arrived in Patagonia in July 1865. Landing on the bay where Puerto Madryn now stands, they were forced, by lack of water, to walk south across the parched land to the valley of the Chubut river where they found cultivatable land and settled in Gaiman. The first 10 years were harsh, and they were saved by trade with local Tehuelche peoples, who taught them essential survival skills. The British navy also delivered supplies, and there was support from the Argentine government, eager to populate its territory.

The settlement was partly inspired by Michael D Jones, a non-conformist minister who provided much of the early finance and recruited settlers through the Welsh language press and through the chapels. Jones, whose aim was to create a 'little Wales beyond Wales', far from the intruding influence of the English, took particular care to recruit people with useful skills such as farmers and craftsmen. Between 1865 and 1915, the colony was reinforced by another 3000 settlers from Wales and the United States. The early years brought persistent drought, and finding that the land was barren unless irrigated, the pioneers created a network of irrigation channels. Early settlers were allocated 100 ha of land, and when, by 1885, all irrigable land had been allocated, settlement expanded westwards along the valley. The charming town of Trevelin (near Esquel, see page 142), where Welsh is still spoken, was the result of this westward migration.

The success of the Welsh colony was partly due to the creation of their own successful Cooperative Society, which sold their produce and bought necessities in Buenos Aires. Early settlers were organized into chapel-based communities of 200-300 people, which were largely self-governing and organized social and cultural activities. The colony thrived after 1880, growing prize-winning wheat in the valley, and exporting successfully to Buenos Aires and Europe, but was badly weakened by the great depression in the 1930s, and the poor management of the Argentine government. Many of the Welsh survived, however, and most of the owners of Gaiman's extraordinary Welsh tea-rooms are indeed descendants of the original settlers. The Welsh language is kept alive in both Gaiman and Trevelin, and musical Eisteddfods are held every October. So, as you tuck into your seventh slice of Welsh cake, spare a thought for the harsh conditions endured by those brave early pioneers.

the town's grandest hotel in its heyday; politicians and travellers met in its glorious high-ceilinged mirrored bar, which is now full of old photographs and relics. You can eat lunch here and there's simple accommodation; ask the friendly owner to see the elegant meeting room at the back.

The town's best museum – and indeed one of the finest in Argentina – is the **Museo Paleontológico Egidio Feruglio** ⓘ *Fontana 140, T02965-432100, www.mef.org.ar, Sep-Mar daily 0900-2000, Apr-Aug Mon-Fri 1000-1800, Sat and Sun 1000-2000, US$6.50, full disabled access and guides for the blind.* Imaginatively designed and beautifully presented, the museum traces the origins of life through the geological ages, displaying dynamically poised dinosaur skeletons, with plentiful information in Spanish. Tours are free and are available in English, German and Italian. There is also a reasonably cheap café and shop. Ask for information about the Parque Paleontológico Bryn Gwyn near Gaiman.

The **Museo Regional Pueblo de Luis** ⓘ *Fontana and Fontana y Lewis Jones 9100, T02965-424062, Mon-Fri 0800-2000, Sat/Sun 1400-2000, US$1*, is appropriately housed in the old railway station, built in 1889. It was Lewis Jones that founded the town and started the railways that exported Welsh produce so successfully. The museum has displays on indigenous societies, failed Spanish attempts at settlement and on Welsh colonization. Next to the tourist office is the wonderful new **Museo de Artes Visuales** ⓘ *free entry, Mon-Fri 0800-2000, Sat/Sun 1400-2000*, which is located in an attractive wooden building.

Just outside town, on the road to Rawson, you'll find one of the oldest standing Welsh chapels, **Capilla Moriah**. Built in 1880, it has a simple interior and a cemetery with the graves of many original settlers, including the first woman born in the Welsh colony.

Gaiman → *Colour map 4, C1.*

West of Trelew, Route 25 heads through the beautifully green and fertile floodplain of the Río Chubut to Gaiman and Dolavon before continuing through attractive scenery all the way to Esquel (see page 140) and the Welsh colony of Trevelin (see page 142).

Gaiman is a small pretty village with old brick houses, retaining the Welsh pioneer feel, and hosts an annual **Eisteddfod** (Welsh Festival of Arts) in October. The **tourist office** ⓘ *near the old railway on Belgrano between 28 de Julio and Rivadavia, T02965-491571, www.gaiman.gov.ar, Oct-Mar Mon-Sat 0900-2000, Sun 1100-2000, Apr-Sep Mon-Sat 0900-1800, Sun 1100-1800*, is housed in the Casa de Cultura. Around the town plaza are several **tearooms**, many of them run by descendants of the original settlers, serving delicious and 'traditional' Welsh teas (see Eating, page 169). It's hard to imagine their abstemious ancestors tucking into the vast plates filled with seven kinds of cake and scones, so for a reminder of the spartan lives of those idealistic pioneers, visit the wonderful, tiny **Museo Histórico Regional Galés** ⓘ *Sarmiento and 28 de Julio, T02965-491007, Tue-Sun 1500-1900, US$1*. Its impressive collection of Welsh artefacts, objects and photographs is an evocative and moving testimony to extraordinary lives lived in harsh conditions.

Many older buildings remain: the low, stone 'first house' **Primera Casa** (1874) ⓘ *on the corner of the main street, Av Tello and Evans, daily 1400-1900*; the old **railway station** (1909), which now houses the regional museum; the **old hotel** (1899) ⓘ *Tello and 9 de Julio*, and the **Ty Nain tearoom** ⓘ *Plaza at Yrigoyen 283* (1890). On the south side of the river there are two old chapels: **Capilla Bethel** (1913) and the **Capilla Vieja** (1888). A far more recent monument to human energy and inspiration is the extraordinary **El Desafío** ⓘ *2 blocks west of plaza, Brown 52 daily until 1800, US$2, www.eldesafiogaiman.com.ar*, an imaginative sculptural world, made entirely from rubbish by the eccentric Joaquín Alonso – painted plastic bottles, cans and wire form pergolas and dinosaurs, sprinkled liberally with plaques bearing words of wisdom and witty comments. It's beginning to fade now, but still good fun.

Some 8 km south of town, there are fossil beds dating back 40 million years at the **Parque Paleontológico Bryn Gwyn** ⓘ *T02965-420012, for visits consult www.mef.org.ar, Tue-Fri 1000-1700, closed Mon, US$3, taxi from Gaiman US$4*. A mind-boggling expanse of time is brought to life by the guided tour. It takes 1½ hours to do the circuit and see the fossils. There's also a visitor centre where you can experience some fieldwork in palaeontology.

Dolavon and around → *Colour map 4, C1.*

Founded in 1919, the most westerly Welsh settlement in the valley is quiet and not as inviting as Gaiman, although if you stroll around its two intersecting streets, you'll find a few buildings reminiscent of the Welsh past.

If you have your own transport, it's worth driving from Dolavon back towards Gaiman through the neat squared fields of the beautiful irrigated valley, where you'll see Welsh chapels tucked away among poplar trees and silver birches. The **San David chapel** (1917) is a beautifully preserved brick construction, with an elegant bell tower and sturdy oak-studded door, in a quiet spot surrounded by birch trees, an impressive testimony to Welsh pioneer spirit.

South of Trelew » *pp164-173.*

Reserva Natural Punta Tombo → *Colour map 4, C1.*

ⓘ *125 km south of Trelew, access from ripio roads RN 1 towards Camarones. Open Sep-Mar, US$10. Tours from Trelew and Puerto Madryn, US$50, including 45 mins at the site, where there's a café and toilets.*

There is a lovely rock and sand beach with birds and other wildlife at **Playa Isla Escondida**, 70 km south of Trelew, with secluded camping but no facilities. Head south from here to see the penguin colony at the **Reserva Natural Punta Tombo**. This reserve is the largest breeding ground for Magallenic penguins in Patagonia. The birds come here in September, chicks hatch from mid-November and first waddle to the water in January or February. It's fascinating to see these creatures up close, but noisy colonies of tourists dominate the place in the morning; it's quieter in the afternoon. You'll see guanacos, hares and rheas on the way.

Camarones and the Reserva Natural Cabo dos Bahías

Camarones is a quiet fishing port on Bahía Camarones, 275 km south of Trelew, whose main industry is harvesting seaweed. This is prime sheep-rearing land, and Camarones wool is world-renowned for its quality. Aside from the salmon festival that takes place in early February, the only real attraction is the penguin colony at the **Reserva Natural Cabo Dos Bahías** ⓘ *28 km southeast of Camarones at the southern end of the bay via a dirt road, US$8.* It protects around 12,000 pairs of penguins, which you can see close up, but also lots of other marine life. You can see seals and sea lions any time, plus whales from March to November and even killer whales from October to April.

Bahía Blanca to Camarones listings

For Sleeping and Eating price codes and other relevant information, see pages 41-44.

Sleeping

Bahía Blanca *p156*

For more listings see www.bahiablanca.gov.ar.

B Argos, España 149, 3 blocks from the plaza, T0291-455 0404, www.hotelargos.com. The city's finest, a 4-star business hotel with comfortable rooms, restaurant and a good breakfast.

B Austral, Colón 159, T0291-456 1700, www.hoteles-austral.com.ar. A friendlier 4-star with plain spacious rooms, good bathrooms and good views over the city, attentive service, and decent restaurant.

C Bahía Hotel, Chiclana 251, T0291-455 0601, www.bahia-hotel.com.ar. A modern business hotel, good value, with well-equipped rooms, a bright airy bar and *confitería* on street level.

C Italia, Brown 181, T0291-456 2700. Set in a lovely 1920s Italianate building, this is one of the town's oldest, full of character, but some rooms are badly in need of a face lift.

Hostels

F pp **Bahía Blanca Hostel**, Soler 701, www.bahiablancahostel.com. Light, spacious dorms and doubles (**E**), in this old colonial building. Close into town, with lots of travel advice.

Carmen de Patagones and Viedma *p157*

B Austral, 25 de Mayo and Villarino, T02920-422615, www.hoteles-austral.com.ar. Along the *costanera*, this modern hotel has well-equipped, if slightly old-fashioned, rooms with Wi-Fi.

C Nijar, Mitre 490, T02920-422833. Very comfortable, smart modern rooms, a quiet relaxed atmosphere and good attentive service. Recommended.

C Peumayen, on the plaza, Buenos Aires 334, T02920-425222. Old-fashioned and friendly.

D Hotel Iturburu Spa, 25 de Mayo 174, T02920-430459. A real find, this is a great-value hotel in a quiet complex with steam baths, a very relaxing atmosphere and welcoming staff.

Camping

There's a good municipal campsite near the river, T02920-421341, US$2 pp, all facilities including hot showers. Also at the sea lion colony, **La Lobería,** T02920-428883, US$1 pp. **Trenitos**, T02920-497098, US$1 pp, has good facilities.

Puerto Madryn *p158, map p158*

Accommodation often gets full in spring and summer, when prices rise; book in advance. Watch out for the 'international tourist' price in more expensive hotels. For more hotels see www.madryn.gove.ar/turismo.

AL Península Valdés, Av Roca 155, T02965-471292, www.hotelpeninsula.com.ar. Luxurious place on the seafront, great views from many of its spacious rooms. Spa, sauna and gym. International prices here, plus 30% extra for bookings made from outside Argentina.

A Bahía Nueva, Av Roca 67, T/F02965-451677, www.bahianueva.com.ar. One of the best seafront hotels, with a welcoming reception area and high standards in all details. Rooms are on the small side, but comfortable. Breakfasts are generous, and staff are helpful and professional. Cheaper in low season. Recommended.

B Casa de Pueblo, Av Roca 475, T02965-472500, www.madryncasadepueblo.com.ar. Once apparently the first brothel in town, now a charmingly renovated seafront chalet with functional rooms and a homely atmosphere. Good value.

B El Muelle Viejo, H Yrigoyen 38, T02965-471284, www.muelleviejo.com. Ask for the stylish, comfortable modernized rooms in this funny old place. Excellent value large rooms sleep 4 and there are *parrilla* and kitchen facilities if you want to cook.

B Tolosa, Roque Sáenz Peña 253, T02965-471850, www.hoteltolosa.com.ar. An extremely comfortable modern place with faultless service and great breakfasts. The superior rooms are much more spacious and have full wheelchair access. Free use of bicycles and internet. Highly recommended.

D Gran Palace Hotel, 28 de Julio 400, T02965-471009. Attractive entrance to this central place, but rooms are a bit squashed and rather dark, thanks to the mahogany effect wallpaper. But they're clean and have bathroom and TV, making this good value.

E-F pp **El Gualicho**, Marcos A Zar 480, T02965-454163, www.elgualicho hostel.com.ar. By far the best budget place in Puerto Madryn, this hostel is beautifully designed, recently expanded and run by a friendly and enthusiastic owner. Free pickup from bus terminal, *parrilla*, breakfast included, garden, attractive double rooms, and bikes for hire. Book ahead. Discounts to HI members. Highly recommended.

E-F pp **El Retorno**, Mitre 798, T02965-456044, www.elretornohostel.com.ar. Only 3 blocks to the beach, this hostel is clean and friendly. They have an endless supply of hot water, a cosy common area and rent bikes. Double rooms (**C**) available.

E-F pp **La Tosca**, Sarmiento 437, T02965-456133, www.latoscahostel.com. Centrally located. Friendly staff. Dorm rooms have great mattresses and private bathrooms and, if you call them from the bus station, they'll pick up for free. Doubles are small but cosy (**C**).

Península Valdés *p159*

Accommodation is good quality, but can be pricey. The following are all in Puerto Pirámides unless otherwise stated.

LL Las Restingas, T02965-495101, www.lasrestingas.com. The top hotel in town has an exclusive location on the beach, and 8 of its 12 suites have their own balcony for splendid sea views. All very comfortable, with minimalist decoration and there's a small restaurant serving a sophisticated selection of regional food. Great deals in low season.

A Cabañas del Mar, Av Roca s/n, T02965-495049, cabanas@piramides.net. Comfortable *cabañas*, well equipped, but no heating. Sea view.

A The Paradise, far end of the main street, T02965-495030, www.hosteriaparadise.com.ar. Huge, very comfortable light rooms, smart bathrooms. Splendid suites with jacuzzis.

B La Nube del Angel, Segunda Baja, T02965-495070, www.lanubedelangel.com.ar. Open all year, and with lovely owners, these small cabañas built for 2-6 people are located on a quiet street, 5 mins' walk to the beach.

B Motel ACA, Av Roca s/n, T02965-495004, aca@piramides.net. Slightly old fashioned, this has welcoming rooms, handy for the beach. Also a good seafood restaurant, from whose terrace you might even spot whales. Jan and Feb are reserved for ACA members only.

Estancias

To really appreciate the space and natural beauty of the peninsula, staying at an estancia is an appealing (if slightly expensive) option. Ask the tourist office for advice. Day trips to estancias can also be arranged, with access to some of the most beautiful places. For more estancias in Patagonia, see www.interpatagonia.com/estancias.

LL Estancia La Ernestina, T02965-458061, or T02965-15663713, www.laernestina.com. Near Punta Norte, the welcoming owners offer comfortable accommodation in simple rooms, all meals and excursions included. Open mid-Sep to mid-Apr. No credit cards.

LL-L Faro Punta Delgada, T02965-458444, www.puntadelagada.com. Comfortable accommodation right on the cliffs, offering half and full board, excellent food, and horse riding, guided walks, English-speaking guides. Recommended.

L Rincón Chico, south of Puerto Pirámides (office in Puerto Madryn: Blv Brown 1783, T02965-471733), www.rinconchico.com. A working sheep farm, still owned by the original pioneer family who built it. Luxurious, beautifully situated, great for walking. Recommended.

AL Estancia La Elvira, T02965-156-98709 (office in Puerto Madryn: Av Yrigoyen 257, T02965-474248), www.laelvira.com. Traditional Patagonian dishes, and comfortable accommodation in an outstanding location on Caleta Valdés, near Punta Cantor.

AL Estancia San Lorenzo, on RP3, 20 km southwest of Punta Norte T02965-451427 (contact through **Argentina Visión** in Puerto Madryn, see Tour operators). For day trips to a beautiful stretch of coast to see penguins close up in one of the peninsula colonies as well as fossils, birdwatching and horse treks.

Trelew *p161*

Trelew is not touristy, but there are a few decent places to stay and a good campsite. The great tourist office will be able to help.

A Libertador, Rivadavia 31, T/F02965-420220, www.hotellibertadortw.com.ar. Breakfast is included in this large modern place, highly recommended for its friendly service and comfortable rooms – the newer more spacious rooms are slightly pricier but worth it. Book ahead.

A Rayentray, San Martín and Belgrano, T/F02965-434702, www.cadenarayentray.com.ar. Huge modernized 1960s place with comfortable rooms and professional staff –

the spacious 'superior' rooms are worth the extra, with sitting area, good bathrooms and splendid 1970s leather panelling. Swimming pool on top floor is free for guests, but gym, sunbed and sauna are extra.

B Galicia, 9 de Julio 214, T02965-433802, www.hotelgalicia.com.ar. Breakfast included in this recently refurbished and central hotel, whose smallish rooms don't quite live up to the grand entrance, but are extremely comfortable and well decorated, and the staff are friendly.

C Rivadavia, Rivadavia 55, T02965 434 472, www.cpatagonia.com/rivadavia. Simple, comfortable rooms with TV and bath, and some even cheaper rather spartan rooms without, in this well-located place. Breakfast extra.

C Touring Club, Fontana 240, T02965-433997, www.touringpatagonia.com.ar. The best budget option. Gorgeous, faded bar, vast staircase and light corridors. The rooms are on the plain side, but they're quiet and spacious, with big bathrooms, and well kept. Breakfast is extra, but this is still good value.

Camping

Camping Patagonia, 11 km south on RN 7 towards Rawson, T02965-428968. US$4, pretty site with *parrillas*, hot showers, football pitch and *proveduría* (food shop).

Gaiman *p163*

B Posada Los Mimbres, Chacra 211, 6 km west of Gaiman, T02965-491299, www.posadalosmimbres.com.ar. A farmstead in idyllic surroundings with just a few rooms in the charming old house or in a modern one. Gorgeous meals. A wonderful place to unwind.

C Hosteria Ty'r Haul, Sarmiento 121, T02965-491880, Centrally located in a listed historical building, rooms are comfortable and well-lit. Recommended.

C Unelem, Av Tello and 9 de Julio, T02965-491663, www.unelem.com. Very comfortable, this is a restored hotel from 1867. The restaurant serves Welsh cuisine.

D Plas Y Coed, Yrigoyen 320, T02965-491133, www.plasycoed.com.ar. A lovely place run by the charming Marta Rees, descended from a Welsh tea pioneer family, with double and twin rooms with bath and TV including breakfast.

Camping

Los Doce Nogales, Chacra 202, close to **Ty Te Caerdydd** tea room, T02965-155-18030. An attractive site south of the river, with showers.

Camarones *p164*

C Hotel Indalo Inn, Julio A Roca and Sarmiento, T0297-4963004, www.indalo inn.com.ar. A modern complex with hotel rooms, as well as cabins for up to 10 people. Good location, and modern facilities.

Eating

Bahía Blanca *p156*

TT Lola Mora, Av Alem and Sarmiento. The city's most sophisticated restaurant serves delicious Mediterranean-style food, in an elegant colonial-style house. Excellent.

T El Mundo de la Pizza, Dorrego 53. Fabulous pizzas, thin bases loaded with toppings, lots of choice in this big atmospheric place, the city's favourite.

T Micho, Guillermo Torres 3875, Ingeniero White. There are several good fish restaurants in the port area, but this elegant restaurant is the best. Be sure to take a taxi at night.

T Santino, Dorrego 38. Italian-influenced, with a relaxed but sophisticated atmosphere and a welcoming glass of champagne, very good value.

Viedma *p157*

T Camilla's Café, Saavedra and Buenos Aires. A smart and relaxing place for coffee, to watch Viedma trundle by on its errands.

T La Balsa, on the river at Colón and Villarino. By far the best restaurant, inexpensive with a pleasant atmosphere. Delicious seafood, and a bottle of superb Río Negro wine, Humberto Canale Merlot, is highly recommended.

¥ **Parrilla Libre**, Buenos Aires and Colón. Cheap *tenedor libre* steaks in a cheerful atmosphere.

Puerto Madryn *p158, map p158*

An unmissable pleasure of Puerto Madryn is the great seafood served in its beachfront restaurants. While you're here, try at least one plate of *arroz con mariscos* (rice with a whole selection of squid, prawns, mussels and clams). Most restaurants are mid-range and charge similar prices, but quality varies widely.

¥¥¥ **Caccaros**, Av Roca 385, T02965-453767. Stylish simple place on sea front with relaxing atmosphere, good-value seafood menu, and cheap lunch menu.

¥¥¥ **Plácido**, Av Roca 506, T02965-455991, www.placido.com.ar. Overlooking the sea and beautifully designed, with stylish tables and intimate lighting, this is perfect for a romantic dinner. Excellent service and a good range of seafood, with cheaper pasta dishes too, lots of options for vegetarians.

¥¥ **Centro de Difusión de la Pescada Artesanal**, Blv Brown, 7th roundabout, T02965-15-538085. Grandly named, but with no sign outside, this is a basic *cantina* on the coast road east, opposite the municipal campsite, where the fishermen's families cook delicious meals with their catch. Hugely popular with locals, so come early.

¥¥ **Los Colonos**, Av Roca and A Storni, T02965-458486. You can't miss this place as it's partly built into the wooden hull of a boat. A big place but with a cosy atmosphere, the speciality is *parrilla*, very reasonably priced, but there's seafood and pastas too. Great for families, with a big soft play area for kids.

¥¥ **Nativo Sur**, Blv Brown 2000, T02965-457403. Smarter than its more popular sister restaurant **Yoaquina**, this is a good place for a quiet dinner on the beachfront, with an imaginative menu of local Patagonian produce and seafood.

¥¥ **Taska Beltza**, 9 de Julio 345, T02965-15668085. Closed Mon. Chef and owner 'El Negro' cooks superb seafood with great passion and a Basque influence. The *arroz con mariscos* is cheap and superb. Highly recommended. Book ahead.

¥¥ **Vernardino**, Blv Brown 860, T02965-474289, www.vernardinoclubdemar.com.ar. One of the nicest restaurants on the beach, serving great seafood and pastas. Good choice for lunch.

¥ **La Casona de Golfo**, Av Roca 349, T02965-455027. Good-value *tenedor libre* with lots of choices including good *parrilla* and seafood, and '*helados libre*' – as much ice cream as you can eat. Great for families. Kids pay half price.

Península Valdés *p159*

The following are all on the beach in Puerto Pirámides. There are also reasonably priced restaurants at Punta Norte, at Punta Cantor and at **Faro Punta Delgada**.

¥¥¥ **Las Restingas**, 1a Bajada al mar, on the beach, T02965-495101. Perfect for a romantic dinner for the sea views and tranquillity. An imaginative menu combines quality local produce with a touch of sophistication.

¥¥ **Paradise**, Av de las Bellenas and 2a Bajada, T02965-495030. Just off the beach, good atmosphere and seafood.

¥¥ **Quimey Quipan**, by the beach, next to **Tito Bottazzi**, T02965-156 93100. This family-run place specializes in delicious seafood and has a cheap set menu. Open for lunch, ring to reserve for dinner. Recommended.

¥ **Margarita Resto Bar**, Av de las Bellenas, T02965-15202659. Midway along the main street, small and intimate bar serving light meals. Fri/Sat 2100-0500, Sun-Thu 2100-0230.

Trelew *p161*

¥¥ **El Quijote**, 25 de May 90, T02965-434 564. Traditional *parrilla*, popular with locals.

¥¥ **El Viejo Molino**, Galés 250, T02965-428019. Tue-Sun 1130-0030. The best in town, and well worth a visit to see the first flour mill that was built here in 1886. It is now beautifully restored as a fine restaurant and café in relaxed and stylish surroundings. There's an imaginative menu with Patagonian lamb and home-made pastas, good-value set menu and Welsh teas. Recommended.

¥¥ **La Bodequita**, opposite the cinema on Belgrano, T02965-437777. Serves superb home-made pastas in a warm and lively atmosphere. Recommended.

Café Mi Ciudad, Belgrano 294. A smart café serving great coffee; read the papers while watching street life.

Hotel Touring Club, Fontana 240. Open from breakfast to the small hours for sandwiches and drinks, worth a visit to see the splendid 1920s bar.

Gaiman *p163*

There's a stylish small restaurant **El Angel**, Rivadavia 241, serving delicious food in an old-fashioned intimate atmosphere. Also a high-quality *panadería*, **La Colonia**, on the main street. **Siop Bara**, Tello and 9 de Julio, sells cakes and ice creams.

Welsh teas

You're unlikely to be able to resist the Welsh teas for which Gaiman has become famous. Tea is served from 1500, all the tea rooms charge about the same (US$11) and include the best known of the Welsh cakes, *torta negra* – a delicious dense fruit cake.

Plas y Coed, Av Yrigoyen 320. The first house to start serving tea has lovely gardens and the owner Marta Rees is a wonderful raconteur and fabulous cook who can tell you all about her Welsh forebears, married in this very house in 1886. Highly recommended.

Ty Cymraeg, down by the river. In a lovely spot, selling good cakes.

Ty Gwyn, 9 de Julio 111. This large tea house serves a very generous tea in a more modern place with traditional features; the owners are welcoming. Recommended.

Ty Nain, Yrigoyen 283. The prettiest house and full of history. The owner's grandmother was the first woman to be born in Gaiman.

Ty Te Caerdydd, Finca 202, 2 km from the centre, but well signposted. A staggering theme park of its own, with manicured lawns and dressed-up waitresses; its main claim to fame is that Princess Di had tea here. The atmosphere is entirely manufactured.

Bars and clubs

Bahía Blanca *p156*

Lots of discos on Fuerte Argentino (along the stream leading to the park) mainly catering for under 25s: **Bonito**, **Chocolate** and **Toovaks**. The best place for anyone over 25 is **La Barraca**.

Puerto Madryn *p158, map p158*

Margarita, RS Pena, next to Ambigu on RS Pena and Av Roca. Late night bar for drinks and live music.

Festivals and events

Carmen de Patagones *p157*

Mar **Fiesta de 7 de Marzo**, celebrates the victory at the Battle of Patagones with a week of music and handicrafts, fine food, a huge procession, horse-riding displays and lots of meat on *asados*. Great fun. Book accommodation ahead.

Shopping

Bahía Blanca and around *p156*

There's a smart modern shopping mall **Bahía Blanca Plaza Shopping**, 2 km north of town on Sarmiento. Cheap food hall, cinema (T0291-453 5844) and supermarket. Also supermarket **Cooperativa** on Donado. Plenty of clothes and shoe shops on Alsina and San Martín within a couple of blocks of the plaza.

Puerto Madryn *p158, map p158*

The sleek new indoor shopping centre **Portal de Madryn**, 28 de Julio and Av Roca, has all the smart clothes shops, **Café Habana** on the ground floor and a kids games area with a fast, but not cheap, food place, **Mostaza**, on the top floor. **Cardon** is recommended for regional goods and leather bags.

You'll find lots more clothes, T-shirts, high-quality Patagonian crafts, leather goods and artesanal *alfajores* on 28 de Julio and Av Roca.

Trelew *p161*
The main shopping area is around San Martín, and from the plaza to Belgrano. It can't compare with Puerto Madryn for souvenirs, but it has a good little handicrafts market on the plaza.

There's a supermarket, **Norte**, Rivadavia and 9 de Julio, opposite Banco Río.

Activities and tours

Viedma *p157*
Fishing
Fishing equipment is available in Viedma at **Patagonia Out Doors Life**, 25 de Mayo 340, and **Tiburón**, Zatti 250, among others. Ask the tourist office for a leaflet, T02920-427171.

Puerto Madryn *p158, map p158*
Diving
Lobo Larsen, Av Roca 885, T02965-470277, www.lobolarsen.com. Friendly company that specializes in diving with the sea lion colony at Punta Lomas Provincial Widlife Reserve.
Ocean Divers, Blv Brown (between 1st and 2nd roundabout), T02965-472569. Advanced courses (PADI) and courses on video, photography and underwater communication.
Puerto Madryn Buceo, Blv Brown, 3rd roundabout in Balneario Nativo Sur, T02965-1551 3997, www.madrynbuceo.com. All levels from beginners' dives to the week-long PADI course, US$180, US$50 for a day excursion.
Scuba Duba, Blv Brown 893, T02965-452699. Courses, excursions, night dives.

Fishing
Contact **Raul Díaz**, T02965-450812; or **Juan Domínguez**, T02965-1566 4772.

Horse riding
Huellas y Costas, Blv Brown 1900, T02965-15637826. Also hires out kayaks and windsurfs.

Mountain bike hire
El Gualicho, Marcos A Zar 480, T02965-454163. **Vernardino Club Mar**, on beach at Blv Brown 860, T02965-455633.

Tour operators
Lots of agencies in Puerto Madryn do tours to Península Valdés, taking in the same places: the interpretation centre and viewing point for the Isla de los Pájaros (both on the narrow isthmus at the entrance to the peninsula), and then Puerto Pirámides, where the boat trip to see the whales costs US$30 extra. They go on to Punta Delgada and Caleta Valdés, with time to look at wildlife. Trips take 12 hrs. All charge around US$50, plus US$12 entrance to the peninsula. Shop around to find out how long you'll spend at each place, how big the group is, and if your guide speaks English.

Tours are also offered to see the penguins at Punta Tombo or the Welsh village of Gaiman with Ameghino Dam thrown in, but these are 400-km round trips and better from Trelew.
Alora Viaggio, Av Roca 27, T/F02965-455106, www.aloraviaggio.com. A helpful company which also has an office at the bus terminal (T02965-456563).
Argentina Visión, Av Roca 536, T02965-451427, www.argentinavision.com. 4WD adventure trips and can arrange estancias at Punta Delgada. English and French spoken.
Cuyun Co, Av Roca 165, T02965-451845, www.cuyunco.com.ar. Friendly personal service and a huge range of tours: guided walks with biologists, 4WD expeditions, and estancia accommodation. Recommended.
El Gualicho, Marcos A Zar 480, T02965-454163, www.elgualicho.com.ar. Located inside the hostel, the tours on offer cater more for the backpacker market. Great guides and helpful reception staff.
Flamenco Tour, Av Roca 331, T02965-455 505, www.flamencotour.com.ar. For slightly more sedate trips and charming staff.
Golfo Azul, Mitre y H Yrigoyen, T02965-451 181. For windsurf boards, kayaks, jet ski, sailing boats for hire.
Tito Botazzi, Blv Brown and Martín Fierro, T/F02965-474110, www.titobottazzi.com, and at Puerto Pirámides (T02965-495050). Particularly recommended for small groups and well informed bilingual guides; very popular for whale watching.

Península Valdés *p158*

In Puerto Pirámides

Hydrosport, near the ACA, 1a Bajada al Mar, T02965-495065, hysport@infovia.com.ar. Rents scuba equipment and boats, and organizes land and sea tours to see whales and dolphins.

Punta Bellenas, 2a Bajada al Mar, T02965-495012. Offers diving expeditions and provides equipment. Tours do not run after heavy rain in the low season.

Tito Botazzi, see Puerto Madryn, above.

Whales Argentina, 1a Bajada al Mar, T02965-495015. Recommended for whale watching.

Trelew *p161*

Tour operators

Agencies run tours to Punta Tombo, US$35, Chubut Valley (half-day), US$40, both together as a full day US$60. Tours to Península Valdés are best done from Puerto Madryn.

Nieve Mar, Italia 98, T02965-434114, www.nievemartours.com.ar. Punta Tombo and Península Valdés, bilingual guides (reserve ahead). Organized and efficient.

Patagonia Grandes Espacios, Belgrano 338, T02965-435161, infopge@speedy.com.ar. Good excursions to Punta Tombo and Gaiman, and palaeontological trips, staying in *chacras*; also whale watching. Recommended.

Transport

Bahía Blanca *p156*

Air

Several daily flights to **Buenos Aires** with AR/Austral. LADE has weekly flights to various Patagonian destinations (see Air services in Argentina, page 36). Book ahead in summer.

Airline offices Aerolíneas Argentinas, San Martín 198, T0291-426934, www.aerolineas.com.ar. AR/Austral, T0291-456 0561/0810-2228 6527. LADE, Darregueira 21, T0291-437697, www.lade.com.ar.

Bus

Local Buy *tarjetas* (Tarjebus cards) from kiosks for 1 (US$0.50), 2, 4 or 10 journeys.

Long distance To **Buenos Aires** frequent, 8½ hrs, several companies, shop around, US$20; most comfortable by far is **Plusmar** suite bus US$30, with completely flat beds. To **Neuquén**, 6 a day, 8 hrs, US$15. To **Viedma**, Ceferino, Plusmar and Río Paraná (to **Carmen de Patagones**), 4 hrs, US$9. To **Trelew**, Don Otto and others, US$35, 10½ hrs. To **Río Gallegos**, Don Otto US$40.

Bus companies Andesmar www.andesmar.com, T0291-4815462; **Ceferino** www.empresaceferino.com.ar, T0291-481 9566; **Don Otto** www.donotto.com.ar, T0291-481 8585; **Plusmar** www.plusmar.com.ar, T0291-456 0616; **Rápido del Sur** www.el-rapido.com.ar, T0291-481 3118.

Train

To **Buenos Aires**, 3 weekly, 12½ hrs, Pullman US$35, 1st class US$18, tourist class US$15.

Carmen de Patagones and Viedma *p157*

Air

LADE flies to **Buenos Aires** and places in Patagonia. **Airline offices** LADE, Saavedra 403, T/F02920-424420.

Bus

To **Buenos Aires**, 3 daily, 14 hrs, US$25, Don Otto/La Estrella/Cóndor. To **Bahía Blanca**, 4 daily, 4 hrs, US$8, Río Parana.

Train

A comfortable sleeper train, T02944-431777, www.trenpatagonico-sa.com.ar, which also carries cars, goes from Viedma to **Bariloche** overnight once a week, Fri 1800, arriving in the morning. Restaurant and a cinema car showing videos. US$30 for a bed, US$17 for a *semi-cama* seat. Book ahead.

Puerto Madryn *p158, map p158*

Air

Only **LADE** operate from here. Flights, once a week to and from **Buenos Aires**. Also weekly services by **LADE** to other destinations (see Essentials, page 36). More frequent flights serve Trelew airport.

Airline offices Aerolíneas Argentinas, Roca 303, T02920-421257/0800-2228 6527. LADE, Roca 117, T02920-451256.

Bus
To **Buenos Aires**, 19-20 hrs; US$37-68, several companies daily, **Andesmar** recommended. To **Comodoro Rivadavia**, 5 hrs, US$13, many companies. To **Río Gallegos**, 17 hrs; US$42 (from here to **El Calafate**, **Puerto Natales**, **Punta Arenas**), many companies. To **Trelew**, 1 hr, every hr, US$4.50 with **28 de Julio**, **Mar y Valle**. To **Puerto Pirámides**, 1 hr, US$2.50, daily, 28 de Julio. To **Bariloche**, 15 hrs, US$48, daily except Wed, **Mar y Valle**. To **Esquel**, 9-10 hrs; US$28, many companies.

Bus companies 28 de Julio/Mar y Valle, T02965-432429; **Andesmar**, T02965-433535; **El Cóndor**, T02965-431675; **El Ñandú**, T02965-427499; **El Pingüino**, T02965-427400; **Que Bus**, T02965-422760; **Transportadora Patagónica/Don Otto**, T02965-429496; **TUS**, T02965-421343.

Car hire
More expensive than other parts of Argentina, and a large insurance excess. Drive slowly on unpaved *ripio* roads. **Budget**, Roca 353, T02965-451491. Efficient and helpful. **Madryn Rent a Car**, Roca 624, T02965-452355.

Península Valdés *p159*
Join a full day excursion from Puerto Madryn, hire a car or catch the daily bus from Puerto Madryn to **Puerto Pirámides**, departs 1000 daily, **28 de Julio**, 1 hr, returns 1800, US$2.50 each way. Then take the boat trip to see the whales (Sep-Nov) from Puerto Pirámides.

Trelew *p161*
Air
Aerolíneas Argentinas flies to **Buenos Aires**, **Río Gallegos**, **Ushuaia** and **Río Grande**; Lapa (and TAN) fly to **Comodoro Rivadavia**. LADE also flies to several Patagonian airports. Local buses to/from **Puerto Madryn** stop at the airport entrance, turning is 10 mins' walk.

Airline offices Aerolíneas Argentinas, 25 de Mayo 33, T02965-420170. LADE, Terminal de Omnibus, T02965-435925.

Bus
Local Mar y Valle and **28 de Julio** both go frequently to **Rawson**, 30 mins, US$1; to **Gaiman**, 30 mins, US$1; and **Dolavon** 1 hr, US$2; to **Puerto Madryn**, 1hr, US$2.50; to **Puerto Pirámides**, daily, 2½ hrs, US$5.50.

Long distance To **Buenos Aires**, 20 hrs; US$37-68, several companies daily. To **Comodoro Rivadavia**, 5 hrs, US$15, many companies. To **Río Gallegos**, 17 hrs, US$42 (from here to El Calafate, Puerto Natales and Punta Arenas), many companies. To **Esquel**, 9-10 hrs, US$28, many companies.

Bus companies 28 de Julio/Mar y Valle, T02965-432429; **Andesmar**, T02965-433535; **El Cóndor**, T02965-433748; **El Pingüino**, T02965-427400; **El Ñandú**, T02965-427499; **Que Bus**, T02965-422760; **Transportadora Patagónica/Don Otto**, T02965-432434; **TUS**, T02965-421343.

Car hire
Car hire desks at the airport desks are staffed only at flight arrival times. All have offices in town. **AVIS**, Italia 98, T02965-436060; **Hertz**, airport, T02965-1540 5495.

South of Trelew *p164*
Bus
Don Otto from Trelew to **Camarones**, Mon and Fri, 2½ hrs, return 1600. Also **El Nañdu**, Mon, Wed, Fri 0800 to **Reserva Natural Cabo Dos Bahías**, 2½ hrs, return 1600, US$5.

Directory

Bahía Blanca *p156*
Banks Many ATMs on plaza. **Citibank**, Chiclana 232. **Lloyds TSB Bank**, Chiclana 299, T0291-455 3263. **Pullman**, San Martín 171, changes TCs. **Consulates** **Chile**, Güemes 102, T0291-455 0110; **Italy**, Colón 446, T0291-454 5140; **Spain**, Drago 70, T0291-422549.

Migraciones, Brown 963. **Laundry** Laverap, Av Colón 197; Las Heras, Las Heras 86. **Post office** Moreno 34. **Telephone** *Locutorio* at Alsina 108, also internet.

Carmen de Patagones and Viedma *p157*
Banks ATMs at Colon and San Martín in Viedma, and Carmen de Patagones at Bynon and Alsina or Bynon and Paraguay. **Travel agencies** Mona Tour, San Martín 225, Viedma. Sells flights and tickets for the train to Bariloche, www.trenpatagonico-sa.com.ar

Puerto Madryn *p158, map p158*
Banks ATMs at Banco Nación, 9 de Julio 117. Banco del Chubut, 25 de Mayo 154 and Río, 28 de Julio 56. **Medical services** Chemist on 28 de Julio, late night pharmacy on Belgrano y 25 de Mayo. **Post office**, Belgrano and Maíz, 0900-1200, 1500-1900. **Telephone** Many *locutorios* in centre.

Trelew *p161*
Banks Banco de la Nación, 25 de Mayo and Fontana. Banco del Sud, 9 de Julio 320, cash advance on Visa. **Post office** 25 de Mayo and Mitre. **Telephone** Telefónica, Roca and Pje Tucumán, and several *locutorios* in the centre. **Travel agencies** Turismo Sur (aka Patagonia Grandes Espacios), Belgrano 338, also currency exchange.

South to Río Gallegos

Lovers of marine life will want to head south towards Río Gallegos and beyond, where the Atlantic coastline is extraordinarily rich in sea birds, penguins, whales and sealions. The southernmost town, Río Gallegos, is a quiet place, with accommodation and tours offered. Beyond, on the last spit of land before Tierra del Fuego, is Cabo Vírgenes. Inland, Route 26, known as the Bioceanic Corridor, runs west across the steppe amid oil wells, towards Río Mayo, the border and the Chilean towns of Coyhaique and Puerto Aisén and provides access to two petrified forests of ancient araucaria trees. Comodoro Rivadavia is a rather dull base for exploring these forests, but the little town of Sarmiento is far more pleasant. » *For listings, see pages 178-182.*

Comodoro Rivadavia and inland » *pp178-182.*

This is a useful transport hub for all areas of Patagonia – if you have the time to travel by bus. Comodoro Rivadavia is the largest city in the province of Chubut and was established primarily as a sheep-exporting port but flourished when oil was discovered here in 1907. However, since the petrol industry was privatized in the 1990s, there's been increasing unemployment and now the town has a slightly sad, unkempt feel. There's little to make you want to stay, although there's a popular beach at **Rada Tilly**, 12 km south, where you can see sea lions at low tide.

If you're fascinated by oil, you could visit the **Museo Nacional del Petróleo** ⓘ *T0297-455 9558, Tue-Fri 0900-2000, Sat and Sun 1500-2000, taxi US$4, 3 km north of the centre at San Lorenzo 250*, for a history of local oil exploitation, or the **Museo Paleontológico de Astra** ⓘ *20 km north, Sat and Sun 1500-1800*, to look at fossils and reconstructions of dinosaurs. There's a good view of the city from **Cerro Chenque** (212 m), a dun-coloured hill, unattractively adorned with radar masts, whose cliffs give the town its drab backdrop. The **tourist office** ⓘ *Rivadavia 430, T0297-446 2376, www.comodoro.gov.ar, Mon-Fri 0900-2100, Sat and Sun 1500-2100, or in the bus terminal, daily 0800-2100*, is very helpful and the staff speak good English.

Sarmiento and around ➔ *Colour map 2, A4.*

Sarmiento lies on the Río Senguer, 150 km west of Comodoro and just south of two great lakes, **Lago Musters** and **Lago Colhué Huapi**, both of which offer good fishing in summer. Founded in 1897, it's a quiet and relaxed place, sitting in fertile, well-irrigated land, and little-visited by tourists, despite being close to two areas of petrified forest. See www.coloniasarmiento.gov.ar for more details (in English).

Most accessible is the huge park, **Bosque Petrificado de Sarmiento** (**José Ormachea**) ⓘ *32 km south along a ripio road, entry US$3*. Southwest along the same road for a further 40 km (minibus from Sarmiento twice daily December-March, taxi US$18) is the less easy to reach and rather bleaker **Bosque Petrificado Víctor Szlapelis**. These 60-million-year-old forests of fallen araucaria trees, nearly 3 m in circumference and 15-20 m long, are a remarkable sight, best visited in summer (December-February) as the winters here are very cold. **Señor Juan José Valero** ⓘ *Uruguay 43, T0297-4898407*, the *guardaparque*, can give guided tours and provide information on camping. Otherwise contact Sarmiento's helpful **tourist office** ⓘ *Av San Martín, near Alberdi, T0297-489 8220, www.interpatagonia.com/sarmiento*. There is also a small museum – ask the tourist office for directions.

Puerto Deseado and around » *pp178-182.*

Puerto Deseado is a pleasant fishing port on the estuary of the Río Deseado, which drains, into the Lago Buenos Aires in the west. The estuary encompasses a wonderful nature reserve, and provides easy access to more reserves, protecting sea lions and penguins. Outside the former railway station is the **Vagón Histórico** ⓘ *San Martín 1525, T0297-487 0220, www.scruz.gov.ar*, an 1898 carriage, now used as the **tourist office**.

Reserva Natural Ría Deseado ➔ *Colour map 2, B6.*

The submerged estuary (*ría*) of the Río Deseado is an important nature reserve and a stunning area to visit. Among many varieties of seabird, there's a colony of Magellanic penguins, and the crumbling chalky cliffs, mauve and ochre, splattered with guano, are home to four species of cormorant including the unique red-legged cormorant, most appealing with their smart dinner-jacketed appearance. These birds nest from October to April on four offshore islands. The reserve is also the breeding ground for Commerson's dolphins: beautiful creatures, which frolic playfully around the tour boats that run from the town's pier. » *See Activities and tours, page 181.*

Around Puerto Deseado

North of Puerto Deseado, on the shore of the peninsula, is **Cabo Blanco**, the site of the largest fur seal colony in Patagonia. It's another magnificent area, a rocky peninsula bursting out from flat lands, with one of the oldest lighthouses on the coast perched on top, and thousands of seals resting on the rocks below. The breeding season is December to January. A little further west, you should also visit **Reserva Cañadón de Duraznillo** within **Estancia La Madrugada** (see Sleeping, page 179). Here you'll see lots of guanacos, ñandues, foxes and birds, as well as the largest seal colony in the province on spectacular unspoilt beaches.

South of Puerto Deseado are two more reserves: **Isla Pingüino**, an offshore island, with a colony of Magellanic penguins, as well as cormorants and steamer ducks, and the **Reserva Natural Bahía Laura**, an uninhabited bay 155 km south along *ripio* and dirt roads, where black-necked cormorants, ducks and other seabirds can be found in abundance. **Darwin Expediciones** and **Los Vikingos** run tours. » *See Activities and tours, page 181.*

Monumento Natural Bosques Petrificados → *Colour map 2, B5.*

ⓘ *RN 49, 86 km south of Fitz Roy, T0297-4851000, www.parquesnacionales.gov.ar, Oct-Mar 0900-1900, Apr-Sep 1000-1700. Entry by donation. No services or water anywhere close by, and no accommodation.*

Extending over 10,000 hectares in a bizarre, wind-wracked landscape surrounding the **Laguna Grande**, this park contains much older petrified trees than the forests further north around Sarmiento. The trunks, mainly of giant araucaria trees, are up to 35 m long and 150 cm in diameter and were petrified in the Jurassic period 140 million years ago by intense volcanic activity in the Andes *cordillera* which covered the area in ash. The place is more eerie than beautiful, but it does exert a strange fascination, especially when you consider that the fossils of marine animals that you see on the site are a mere 40 million years old, belonging to a sea that covered the land long after the trees had turned to stone. There is a small visitor centre and a well signposted 2-km nature walk. Don't be tempted to take any souvenirs.

Puerto San Julián and around » *pp178-182.*

The quiet port town of Puerto San Julián, on the Bahía San Julian, is the best place for breaking the 834 km run from Comodoro Rivadavia to Río Gallegos. The first Mass in Argentina was held here in 1520 after the Portuguese explorer Ferdinand Magellan had executed a member of his mutinous crew. Then in 1578, Francis Drake also stopped by in order to behead Thomas Doughty. In 1780, Antonio Viedma founded the colony of Florida Blanca here but it failed due to scurvy; you can visit the ruins 10 km west of the present town. Puerto San Julián was finally founded in 1901 to serve as a port for the sheep estancias in this part of Santa Cruz. A small regional museum, **El Museo Regional y Arte Marino** ⓘ *Rivadavia and Vieytes, Mon-Fri 0900-1300, 1400-1700 (open longer hours in peak season)*, houses the amazingly well-preserved dinosaur footprint found in the town. Enquire at the **tourist office** ⓘ *Av Costanera and 9 de Julio, or San Martín 1126, T02962-454396, www.santacruzpatagonia.gob.ar*, about tours to see the wildlife in Reserva San Julian. It's also worth visiting **Estancia La María** (see Sleeping, page 179), 150 km west, which incorporates one of the main archaeological sites in Patagonia: a huge canyon with 87 caves of paintings including human hands and guanacos, 4000-12,000 years old.

Reserva San Julián → *Colour map 2, C5.*

The **Reserva San Julián**, on the shores of Bahía San Julián, includes the islands **Banco Cormorán** and **Banco Justicia** (thought to be the site of the 16th-century executions), where there is a colony of Magellanic penguins and nesting areas for several species of cormorants and other birds. You're also very likely to spot Commerson's dolphins in the bay, particularly if you visit in December. However, there's plenty to see right through until April. It's a lovely location and the concentration of marine life is stunning. **Cabo Curiosa**, 15 km to the north, has 30 km of spectacular coastline and fine beaches.

Piedrabuena → *Colour map 2, C4.*

Known officially as Comandante Luis Piedrabuena, this quiet town is named after the famous Argentine explorer and sailor, Piedra Buena, who built his home on an island in the Río Santa Cruz here, in 1859. On the island is **Casa Histórica Luis Piedra Buena**, a reconstruction of the original building where he carried on a peaceful trade with local indigenous groups. In recent years, **Isla Pavón** ⓘ *T02966-1562 3453*, has become most

Border crossing

Paso Integración Austral

From Río Gallegos, Route 3 continues south to the Chilean border at Paso Integración Austral. On the Chilean side, the road continues as Route 255 via Punta Delgada to Punta Arenas, where ferries cross to Tierra del Fuego. For bus passengers the border crossing is easy, but hire cars will need special documentation.

Argentine immigration and customs 24 hours in summer, April-November 0800-2200.

Chilean immigration and customs Daily 0800-2200.

popular as a weekend resort for those fishing steelhead trout. Accommodation includes a smart four-star *hostería* as well as an attractive campsite. In March there's a national trout festival. Piedrabuena is a good base for exploring the **Parque Nacional Monte León**. The **tourist office** ⓘ *Av Gregorio Ibáñez 388, T02962-497303*, is helpful and informative.

Parque Nacional Monte León → *Colour map 2, C4.*

ⓘ *Access along 23 km of poor* ripio *road that branches off RN 3, 36 km south of Piedrabuena, 210 km north of Río Gallegos, www.parquesnacionales.gov.ar. For more information contact Vida Silvestre in Buenos Aires, T011-4311 6633, www.vidasilvestre.org.ar.*

Monte León incorporates 40 km of coastline, where there are many species of seabirds and an enormous penguin colony. Sea lions occupy the many caves and bays, and the tiny island Monte León is an important breeding area for cormorants and terns. The park is owned by US multi millionaire Douglas Tompkins and looked after by the organization **Vida Silvestre**, but so far access is difficult. However, the effort of getting here is rewarded by wonderful walks along wide isolated beaches, with extraordinary rock formations and cliffs with vast caverns – fabulous at low tide. The old house at the heart of the park has been converted to a *hostería*, which is the best way to enjoy the park in comfort. There are plans to turn the old shearing shed into a visitor centre.

Río Gallegos » *pp178-182. Colour map 3, A4.*

The capital of Santa Cruz province lies on the estuary of the Río Gallegos, the river famous for its excellent brown trout fishing. It's a pleasant airy town, founded in 1885 as a centre for the trade in wool and sheepskins, and is by far the most appealing of the main centres on southern Patagonia's east coast. It was once the main access point for trips to the Parque Nacional Los Glaciares (see page 191) but receives fewer visitors since the airport opened at El Calafate. However, you may well come here to change buses, and could visit the penguin reserve at Cabo Vírgenes some 130 km south, or Monte León 210 km north. The town itself has a couple of museums, and boasts a few smart shops and restaurants.

Ins and outs → *Río Gallegos is pronounced 'rio ga-shay-gos'.*

Getting there Flights arrive at the airport, 10 km from centre, from Buenos Aires, El Calafate and Ushuaia. There are also **LADE** flights connecting all major Patagonian towns, see Essentials, page 36. A taxi into town costs US$5. The crowded **bus terminal** ⓘ *corner of RN 3 and Av Eva Perón*, is inconveniently located 3 km from the centre. Buses 1 and 12 will take you into town, or take a taxi for US$2.

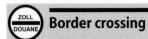

Tourist information There is an excellent and well-organized **tourist office** ⓘ *Av Roca 863, T02966-436920, http://www.santacruzpatagonia.gob.ar/, Mon-Fri 0900-2100, Sat 1000-2000, Sun 1000-1500, 1600-2000*, with information for the whole province. The staff are extremely helpful, speak English and have a list of estancias in Santa Cruz. There's also an office at the airport and a small desk at the bus terminal, T02966-442159.

Sights

The tidy, leafy Plaza San Martín, two blocks south of the main street, Avenida Roca, has an interesting collection of trees (many planted by the early pioneers) and a diminutive corrugated-iron cathedral, with a wood-panelled ceiling in the chancel and stained-glass windows. The best of the town's museums is the small **Museo de los Pioneros** ⓘ *El Cano and Alberdi, T02966-437763, daily 1000-2000, free*, housed in a building that was shipped here from Britain in 1890. The museum has interesting photographs and artefacts telling the story of the first Scottish settlers, who came here in 1884 from the Falkland Islands/Las Malvinas to take up government grants of land.

Río Gallegos

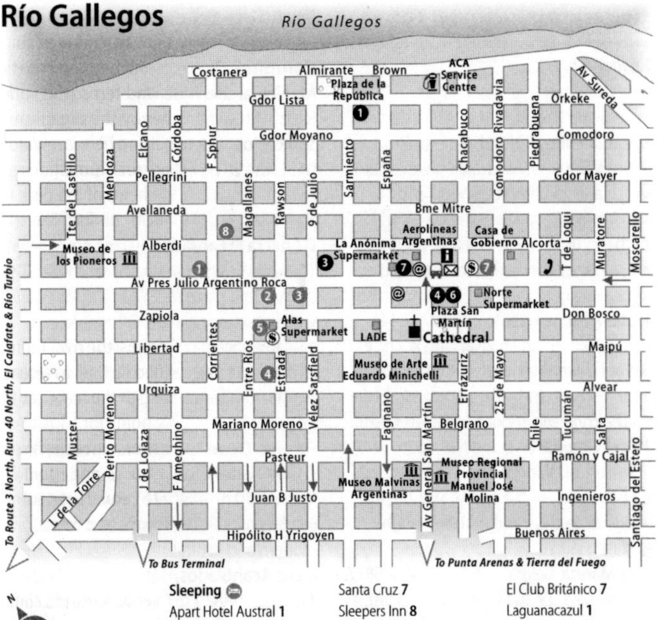

Sleeping
Apart Hotel Austral **1**
Comercio **2**
Covadonga **3**
Croacia **4**
Nevada **5**
Santa Cruz **7**
Sleepers Inn **8**

Eating
Bar Español El Horreo **4**
Chino **3**
El Club Británico **7**
Laguanacazul **1**
Puesto Molino **6**

Around Río Gallegos

Reserva Provincial Cabo Vírgenes

ⓘ *Branch off RN 3, 15 km south of Río Gallegos, onto RN 1 for 119 km, 3½ hrs, US$4.*

This nature reserve protects the second largest colony of Magellanic penguins in Patagonia. There's an informative self-guided walk to see their nests among the calafate and fragrant mata verde bushes. It's good to visit around November, when the chicks are born and there are nests under every bush. You can climb the Cabo Vírgenes **lighthouse** (owned by the Argentine Navy) for wonderful views and there's a *confitería* close by for snacks. **Estancia Monte Dinero** (see Sleeping, page 180), 13 km north of Cabo Vírgenes, is a wonderful base for visiting the reserve.

South of Cabo Vírgenes are the ruins of **Nombre de Jesús**, one of two doomed settlements founded by Pedro Sarmiento de Gamboa in 1584. **Laguna Azul**, near the Monte Aymond border crossing, is a perfect, royal blue lagoon in the crater of an extinct volcano. It's set in an atmospheric and arid lunar landscape and is a good place for a walk. Take a tour, or get off the bus along Route 3, which stops on the main road.

South to Río Gallegos listings

For Sleeping and Eating price codes and other relevant information, see pages 41-44.

Sleeping

Comodoro Rivadavia *p173*

A **Lucania Palazzo Hotel**, Moreno 676, T0297-4499300, www.lucania-palazzo.com. A stylish and luxurious business hotel, with a lovely airy spacious reception, and superb rooms, many with sea views, good value. A huge American breakfast and use of sauna and gym included. Recommended.

D **Hotel Azul**, Sarmiento 724, T0297-446 7539, www.hotelazul.com.ar. This is a nice quiet old place, with lovely bright rooms, friendly owners, and great panoramic views from the *confitería*, though breakfast is extra.

D **Hotel Victoria**, Belgrano 585, T0297-446 0725. An old-fashioned city *hostería*, mostly used by workers in the oil industry, but it's friendly, clean and comfortable enough. Breakfast US$1.20.

D **Rua Marina**, Belgrano 738, T0297-446877. All rooms have TV and bath and breakfast; newer rooms are particularly comfortable.

E **Hospedaje Cari Hue**, Belgrano 563, T0297-472946. Sweet rooms, with separate bathrooms off a central hallway. Very nice owners who like backpackers. Breakfast extra. Best budget choice.

Camping

Municipal site, Rada Tilly, reached by **Expreso** Rada Tilly bus from town. Hot showers.

San Carlos, 37 km north on RN3, T0297-456 0425. The 20 ha are open all year.

Sarmiento *p174*

C **Chacra El Labrador**, 10 km from Sarmiento, T0297-4893329, agna@coopsar.com.ar. This is an excellent place to stay on a small estancia with breakfast included. Other meals are available, including to non-residents. Tours to petrified forests at good prices, will collect guests from Sarmiento (same price as taxi).

Puerto Deseado and around *p174*

C **Isla Chaffers**, San Martín and Mariano Moreno, T0297-487 2246, www.hotelisla chaffers.com.ar. The town's best hotel, modern and central.

C **Los Acantilados**, Pueyrredón and España 116, T0297-487 2167, www.pdeseado.com. ar/acantour. Beautifully located hotel, popular with anglers, comfortable rooms with bath-rooms, good breakfast.

Camping

There is a **municipal campsite** on the seafront, T0297-4872135, or **Camping Cañadón de Giménez**, 4 km away on RN 281.

Estancias

A **Estancia La Madrugada**, on the Atlantic coast, 120 km from Puerto Deseado, reached from the RN281 to Km 79, then RN 68, T0297-47948964, gesino@fibertel.com.ar. Splendid views, plenty of places to spot wildlife, good Patagonian home cooking and comfortable accommodation. The owners also arrange excursions to the sea lion colony and cormorant nesting area. Recommended.

Puerto San Julián and around *p175*

A **Hotel Bahía**, San Martín 1075, T02962-45402, www.hotelbahiasanjulian.com.ar. Modern and comfortable rooms, good value.
B **Hotel Sada**, San Martín 1112, T02962-452 013. www.hotelsada.com.ar. Simple rooms, on a busy road.

Camping

Municipal campsite, Magellanes 650 and M Moreno, T02962-452806. US$3 per site plus US$2 pp, recommended, all facilities.

Estancia

C **Estancia La María**, 150 km west, contact Fernando Behm, Saavedra 1163, T02962-452233. Simple accommodation in a modern house, with amazing cave paintings nearby. Trips to see marine and birdlife organized.

Piedrabuena and around *p175*

A **Hostería El Alamo**, Lavalle 08, T02962-47249. Quiet, breakfast extra. Recommended.
A-B **Hostería Municipal Isla Pavon**, Isla Pavón, T02962-1563 8380. Luxurious 4-star catering to fishermen of steelhead trout.
C **Res Internacional**, Ibáñez 99, T02962-47197. Recommended.

Camping

There are a couple of sites south of town on RN 3; also on Isla Pavón.

Parque Nacional Monte León *p176*

A-B **Estancia Monte León**, on RN3, www.monteleon-patagonia.com. Nov-Apr only. Beautifully modernized but traditional estancia with 4 impeccably tasteful rooms, decorated with Tompkins' considerable style. See also www.vidasilvestre.org.ar.

Río Gallegos *p176, map p177*

Most hotels are within a few blocks of the main street, Av Roca, running northwest–southeast. Do not confuse the street Comodoro Rivadavia with (nearby) Bernardino Rivadavia.
C **Apart Hotel Austral**, Roca 1505, T/F02966-435588, www.apartaustral.com. A smart newly built apart-hotel, with bright rooms, and attractive sunny decor. Very good value, particularly the superior duplexes. Kitchen facilities are basic, but certainly adequate for a couple of nights. Breakfast extra.
C **Comercio**, Roca 1302, T02966-422458, hotelcomercio@informacionrgl.com.ar. Good value, well-designed comfortable en suite rooms, breakfast included. There is an attractive cheap *confitería* on the street.
C **Croacia**, Urquiza 431, T02966-421218. Cheaper, and one of the most reasonably priced places, with comfortable beds, bright spotless rooms with bath, huge breakfasts, and helpful owners. Recommended.
C **Santa Cruz**, Roca 701, T02966-420601, www.advance.com.ar/usuarios/htlscruz. This slightly dated hotel is excellent value. Go for the slightly pricier, spacious new rooms with excellent bathrooms and full buffet breakfast included. Highly recommended.
D **Covadonga**, Roca 1244, T02966-420190 hotelcovadongargl@hotmail.com. Attractive old 1930s building. Rooms are basic but clean and well maintained, with bath and TV. Courtyard. Breakfast included.
D **Nevada**, Zapiola 480, T02966-435790. A good budget option, with clean, simple spacious rooms, nice beds and good bathrooms. Breakfast not included.

Hostel

E Sleepers Inn, F Sphur 78, T02966-444037, www.sleepersinn.blogspot.com. The first and only hostel in town. Simple, clean rooms with shared bath. Note that it can be a little noisy.

Estancias

A-AL Hill Station, 63 km north of Río Gallegos on RN 58, T02966-423897 (in Río Gallegos). An estancia with 120 years of history, run by descendants of the founder, William Halliday. A sheep farm, also breeding criollo horses, this offers wonderful horse riding to see flora and fauna of the coast.

A Monte Dinero, near Cabo Vírgenes, T02966-428922, www.montedinero.com.ar. On this working sheep farm accommodation is comfortable. The house is lined with wood rescued from ships wrecked off the coast, and the food is delicious and home grown. Highly recommended.

Camping

Camping ATSA, RN 3, towards bus terminal, T02966-420310. US$2.50 pp, US$2 for tent.

Chacra Daniel, Paraje Río Chico, 3.5 km from town, T02966-423970, ofaustral@ciudad.com. US$4 pp per day, with *parrilla* and full facilities. Recommended.

Club Pescazaike, Paraje Güer Aike, T02966-423442, www.pescazaike.com.ar. Some 30 km west of town on RN 3. Well equipped, and an attractive place US$2 pp per day, also *quincho* and restaurant.

Eating

Comodoro Rivadavia *p173*

TT Cayo Coco, Rivadavia 102, T0297-4473033. A welcoming little bistro, with very cheery staff and excellent pizzas. Recommended.

TT Dionisius, 9 de Julio and Rivadavia. A smart and elegant *parrilla*, popular with a more sedate clientele. Excellent set menus US$6.

TT La Tradición, Mitre 675. Another popular and recommended *parrilla*.

TT Peperoni, Rivadavia 481. A cheerful modern place serving a good range of home-made pastas, filled with exciting things like king crab, as well as seafood and *parrilla*. US$5-8, for main dish.

T La Barca, Belgrano 935. Welcoming and cheap *tenedor libre*.

Puerto Deseado and around *p174*

T El Pingüino, Piedrabuena 950. Established *parrilla* which serves fabulous rice pudding.

T Puerto Cristal, España 1698. Panoramic views of the port, a great place for Patagonian lamb and *parrilla*.

Puerto San Julián and around *p175*

TT Bar Sportsman, Mitre and 25 de Mayo. Excellent value.

TT El Muelle Viejo, Mitre 1 and 9 de Julio. Good seafood, the *pejerrey* is recommended. Also barsand tearooms. On the seafront.

TT La Rural, Ameghino and Vieytes. Best after 2100.

Río Gallegos *p176, map p177*

There are lots of good places to eat here, many serving excellent seafood, and some smart new inexpensive restaurants.

TT Bar Español El Horreo, Roca 863. Next to Puesto Molino. A more sophisticated option, rather like a bistro in feel, serving delicious lamb dishes and good salads. Recommended.

T Chino, 9 de Julio 29. Cheap and varied *tenedor libre*.

T El Club Británico, Roca 935. Doing its best to look like a London gentlemen's club, though lacking in atmosphere, set lunches.

T Laguanacazul, Sarmiento and Gob Lista, T02966-444114. Chic and not expensive. Near the river, with views across the Plaza de la República. Has an imaginative menu.

T Puesto Molino, Roca 862, opposite tourist office. A relaxed airy place, its design inspired by life on estancias, with bold paintings, wooden tables and excellent pizzas (US$5 for 2) and *parrilla* (US$10 for 2). Recommended.

Activities and tours

Comodoro Rivadavia *p173*

Aonikenk Viajes, Rawson 1190, T02967-446 6768, viajes@aonikenk.com.ar. Tours to the petrified forests, with 2 hrs at the site.

Marco Sur, San Martín 263 Local 9, Galería San Martín, T/F02967-4477490, www.marcosur.com.

Zoyen Turismo, Guemes 2121, Caleta Oliva, 78 km from Comodoro Rivadavia, T0297-4851632, www.zoyenturismo.com.ar. New tour operator, can also help with Ruta 40 connections, and estancia visits. They also have an office in Perito Moreno.

Puerto Deseado and around *p174*

Darwin Expediciones, España 2601, T0297-15-624 7554, www.darwin-expeditions.com, and **Los Vikingos**, Estrada 1275, T0297-487 0020, www.losvikingos.com.ar. Both offer excursions by boat to Río Deseado reserve, and Reserva Provincial Isla Pingüino, as well as trips to see the Monumento Natural Bosques Petrificados.

Monumento Natural Bosques Petrificados *p175*

The site can be visited on a day trip with a tour from San Julián, or from Puerto Deseado with **Los Vikingos**, Estrada 1275, T0297-4870020, www.losvikingos.com.ar.

Puerto San Julián *p175*

Tur Aike Turismo, Av San Martín 446, T02962-452086. Excellent 1½-hr zodiac boat trips.

Río Gallegos *p176, map p177*

Fishing

The southern fishing zone includes the rivers Gallegos, Grande, Fuego, Ewan and San Pablo plus Lago Fagnano, near Ushuaia. It is famous for runs of sea trout. Ask the tourist office for fishing guides and information on permits.

Tours

Macatobiano Turismo, Roca 908, T/F02966-434201, macatobiano@macatobiano.com. Tours to Pingüinero Cabo Vírgenes, also to Laguna Azul, a beautiful lake in a volcanic crater, and to Estancia Monte León. Air tickets to El Calafate and Ushuaia. Recommended.

Transport

Comodoro Rivadavia *p173*

Air

Airport 9 km north. Bus No 6 to airport from bus terminal, hourly (45 mins), US$0.50. Taxi to airport US$4.50. To **Buenos Aires**, with Aerolíneas Argentinas/Austral. Also LADE once a week to **Puerto Madryn**, **Esquel**, **Bariloche**, and **El Calafate**, among others.

Airline offices Aerolíneas Argentinas/Austral, 9 de Julio 870, T0297-444 0050. LADE, Rivadavia 360, T0297-447 6565.

Bus

The terminal, Pellegrini 730, T0297-3367305, has an excellent tourist office 0800-2100. To **Buenos Aires**, 2 daily, 28 hrs, US$55. To **Bariloche**, 14 hrs, US$21 (Don Otto, T0297-447 0450). To **Esquel** (paved road) 8 hrs direct with ETAP and Don Otto, US$19; in summer buses usually arrive full, so book ahead. To **Río Gallegos**, Don Otto, Pingüino and TAC, T0297-444 3376, daily, 11 hrs, US$9.50; **Puerto Madryn**, US$8.50; **Trelew**, Don Otto 3 daily 4 hrs US$7; **Caleta Olivia**, La Unión hourly, US$2; **Sarmiento**, US$4.50, 2½ hrs, 3 daily.

To Chile To **Coyhaique**, US$16, 12 hrs, and **Santiago**, 35 hrs, US$158, Etap Angel Giobbi, twice a week.

Car rental

Avis, 9 de Julio 687, T/F0297-496382.
Patagonia Sur Car, Rawson 1190, T0297-4466768.

Sarmiento *p174*

There are 3 buses daily to **Comodoro** with Etap, T0297-447 4841, and overnight services to **Esquel**, T0297-454756, Sun-Fri.

To Chile Via Río Mayo, Giobbi, 0200, 3 weekly; seats are scarce.

Puerto Deseado and around *p174*

Bus terminal, T0297-155 928598. **Sportman** and **La Unión**, daily to **Caleta Olivia**, US$6, for connections to Comodoro Rivadavia.

Puerto San Julián and around *p175*

Air

LADE, San Martín 1552, T02962-452137, flies each Mon to various Patagonian destinations (see Essentials, page 36).

Bus

To **Buenos Aires**, **Transportadora Patagónica**, T02962-452072, **Pingüino**, T02962-452425. To **Río Gallegos**, **Pingüino**, 6 hrs, US$8.

Río Gallegos *p176, map p177*

Air

Río Gallegos used to be the nearest airport to **El Calafate**, but there are fewer flights now that Lago Viedma airport has opened. Both **Pingüino** and **Interlagos** arrange packages to El Calafate including accommodation and trip to Moreno glacier from offices at the airport.

Regular flights to/from **Buenos Aires**, **Ushuaia** and **Río Grande** direct with Aerolíneas Argentinas. Also LADE to **Río Turbio**, **El Calafate**, **Ushuaia** and **Comodoro Rivadavia** once a week (book as far in advance as possible). The **Ladeco** service from **Punta Arenas** to **Port Stanley** on the **Falkland Islands/Islas Malvinas** stops here once a month in either direction.

Airline offices Aerolíneas Argentinas, San Martín 545, T02966-422020/0810-222 86527, also at airport T02966-442059. **LADE**, Fagnano 53, T02966-422316. **Southern Winds**, San Martín 661, T02966-437171 (closed in low season).

Bus

To **El Calafate**, 4-5 hrs, US$10, Taqsa and Interlagos. To **Los Antiguos**, **Sportman**, daily at 2100, US$21. To **Comodoro Rivadavia**, **Pingüino**, **Don Otto** and **TAC**, 10 hrs, US$11. To **Bariloche**, **Transportadora Patagónica**, daily at 2130. To **Buenos Aires**, 33 hrs, several daily, **Pingüino**, **Don Otto**, **TAC**, US$36. To **Río Grande** and **Ushuaia**, **Tecni Austral**, Tue, Thu, Sat, 1000, US$20-24, 8-10 hrs.

To Chile To **Puerto Natales**, **Pingüino**, Sat, 7 hrs, US$8 or **Bus-Sur**, Tue and Thu 1700. To **Punta Arenas**, **Pingüino** and others, daily, US$12.

Car

Book car rental in advance in high season. Hire companies include: **Cristina**, Libertad 123, T02966-425709; **Localiza**, Sarmiento 237, T02966-424417; **Taxi Centenario**, Maipú 285, T02966-422320.

Taking a car to Chile Make sure your car papers are in order (go first to the tourist office for necessary documents, then to the customs office at the port, at the end of San Martín, very uncomplicated). Let the hire company know, and allow 24 hrs to get the appropriate papers. The car's windows should be etched with the licence plate number.

Directory

Comodoro Rivadavia *p173*

Consulates Belgium, Rivadavia 283. Chile, Sarmiento 936. Italy, Belgrano 1053. **Internet** Rivadavia 201 and along San Martín. **Post office** San Martín and Moreno.

Puerto San Julián and around *p175*

Banks **Banco de la Nación**, Mitre y Belgrano, and **Banco de la Provincia de Santa Cruz**, San Martín y Moreno. **Post office** Belgrano and San Martín.

Río Gallegos *p176, map p177*

Banks Change TCs here if going to El Calafate. 24-hr ATMs are plentiful. **Thaler**, San Martín 484, will change Chilean pesos and US$. **Consulates** Chile, Mariano Moreno 136, Mon-Fri 0900-1300; tourist cards issued at the border. **Internet and telephone** J@va cybercafe (next to British Club on Roca); also various *locutorios* with internet, US$0.80 per hr. **Post office** Roca 893 and San Martín.

Ruta 40 to the glaciers

Contents

Footprint features

Border crossings

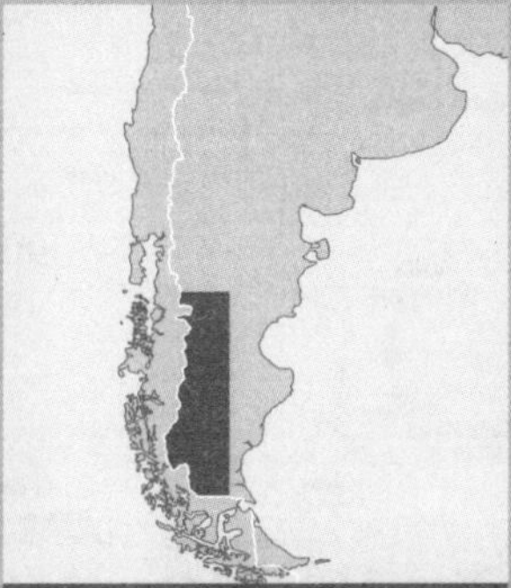

At a glance

Getting around Long distances dictate long hours on buses. Car hire is preferred, as are local flights if your budget allows it.

Time required 7-9 days is enough time to see El Calafate, do a short hike near El Chaltén, and to take a journey along the Ruta 40.

Weather Winter (May-Jul) is extremely cold, and the months either side can bring low temperatures. The nicest weather is from Dec-Mar/Apr when it warms up. But the winds never really stop.

When not to go From May-Oct the weather is cold and windy. Most places close down, and transport is less frequent.

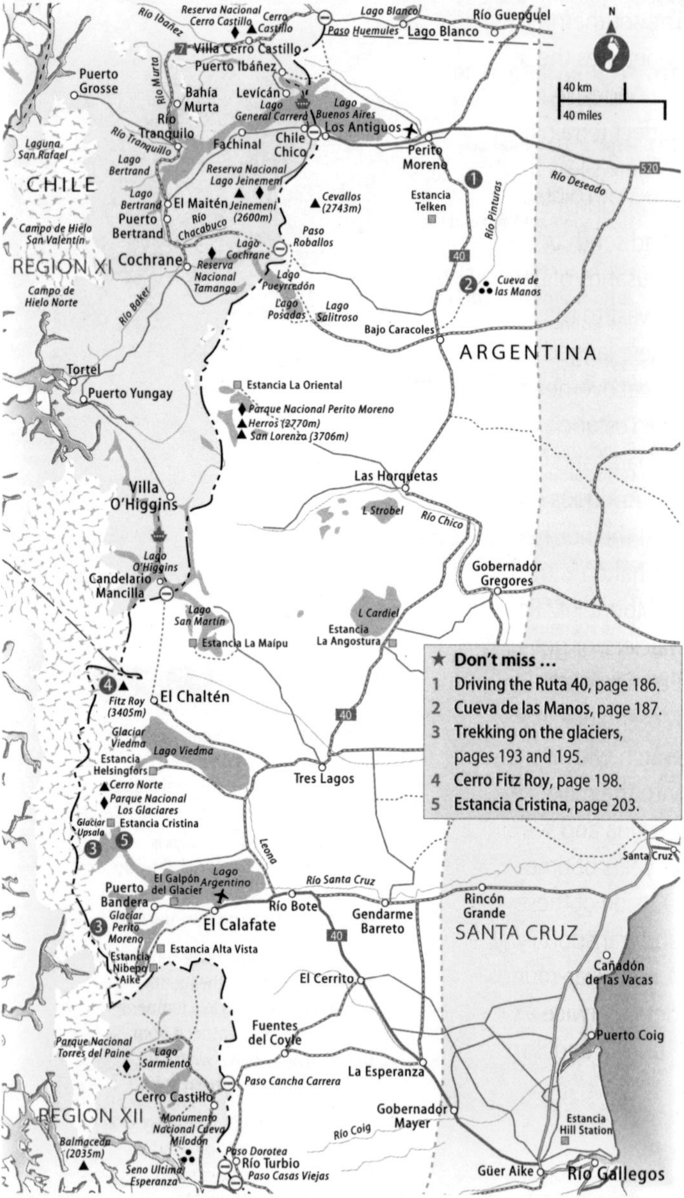
Don't miss …
1 Driving the Ruta 40, page 186.
2 Cueva de las Manos, page 187.
3 Trekking on the glaciers, pages 193 and 195.
4 Cerro Fitz Roy, page 198.
5 Estancia Cristina, page 203.
N
40 km
40 miles
CHILE
ARGENTINA
REGION XI
REGION XII
SANTA CRUZ
Reserva Nacional Cerro Castillo
Cerro Castillo
Río Ibáñez
Villa Cerro Castillo
Paso Huemules
Lago Blanco
Río Guenguel
Puerto Ibáñez
Puerto Grosse
Río Murta
Bahía Murta
Levicán
Lago General Carrera
Lago Buenos Aires
Río Tranquilo
Río Tranquillo
Fachinal
Chile Chico
Los Antiguos
Perito Moreno
Laguna San Rafael
Lago Bertrand
Reserva Nacional Lago Jeinemeni
Jeinemeni (2600m)
Cevallos (2743m)
Estancia Telken
Río Deseado
Río Pinturas
El Maitén
Puerto Bertrand
Río Chacabuco
Campo de Hielo San Valentín
Paso Roballos
Lago Cochrane
Cochrane
Reserva Nacional Tamango
Campo de Hielo Norte
Río Baker
Lago Pueyrredón
Cueva de las Manos
Lago Posadas
Lago Salitroso
Bajo Caracoles
Tortel
Puerto Yungay
Estancia La Oriental
Parque Nacional Perito Moreno
Herros (2770m)
San Lorenzo (3706m)
Las Horquetas
L Strobel
Río Chico
Villa O'Higgins
Lago O'Higgins
Candelario Mancilla
Gobernador Gregores
L Cardiel
Lago San Martín
Estancia La Maipu
Estancia La Angostura
Fitz Roy (3405m)
El Chaltén
Glaciar Viedma
Lago Viedma
Estancia Helsingfors
Tres Lagos
Cerro Norte
Parque Nacional Los Glaciares
Glaciar Upsala
Estancia Cristina
Leona
Santa Cruz
Lago Argentino
El Galpón del Glacier
Río Santa Cruz
Puerto Bandera
Glaciar Perito Moreno
El Calafate
Río Bote
Gendarme Barreto
Rincón Grande
Estancia Alta Vista
Estancia Nibepo Aike
Cañadón de las Vacas
El Cerrito
Fuentes del Coyle
Puerto Coig
Parque Nacional Torres del Paine
Lago Sarmiento
Paso Cancha Carrera
La Esperanza
Cerro Castillo
Monumento Nacional Cueva Milodón
Gobernador Mayer
Río Coig
Estancia Hill Station
Balmaceda (2035m)
Seno Ultima Esperanza
Paso Dorotea
Río Turbio
Paso Casas Viejas
Güer Aike
Río Gallegos
7
40
520

The southernmost part of Argentina's iconic road, the Ruta 40, penetrates the remotest heart of Patagonia, running alongside the Andes, with access to peaks, glaciers and two national parks – perfect terrain for your wildest adventure.

There's less than one person per square kilometre in this part of Patagonia and you'll drive for hours without seeing a soul. Head south to the mysterious Cueva de las Manos, where thousands of handprints were painted by prehistoric people, or west to the Perito Moreno national park, a virgin wilderness, where jagged peaks are reflected in limpid lakes and condors wheel overhead. For a little civilization in your wilderness, stay at an estancia, where you can experience the timeless life on the land and feast on Patagonian lamb or visit the tranquil Los Antiguos on the shores of Lago Buenos Aires.

At the northern end of Parque Nacional Los Glaciares, El Chaltén is the base for trekking around the magnificent peaks of Mount Fitz Roy, where you can hike for days, and even climb glaciers, or get access to expeditions on the Southern Ice Field. Further south, El Calafate is the gateway to the spectacular Perito Moreno glacier. Walk with crampons on the sculpted surface, or watch with wonder as great walls of ice cleave with a mighty roar into the milky lake below. Best of all, take a boat to Estancia Cristina and see Upsala glacier from above: just you and millions of years of time. The best time to go is between October and April. Outside of these months travel is still possible but accommodation and transport is hard to find, and the winter is deadly cold. A new year-round no-frills service run by local bus company Taqsa departs twice a week between El Calafate and Bariloche via the Ruta 40, and is making the route more accessible.

South on the Ruta 40

Route 40 (paved) heads south from Esquel across a deserted landscape that provides a taste for the full experience of Patagonia. The main reason for travelling along this route is to visit the extraordinary Cueva de las Manos, south of Perito Moreno, but the journey itself will also leave a lasting impression; you might not see a soul all day, and passing a car is a major event. However, there are estancias hidden in the emptiness, where a night or two can give you a wonderful flavour of Patagonian life. When at last you arrive at Mount Fitz Roy, you may think you've imagined it. The sight of the great turrets of granite is made all the more spectacular by days spent crossing endless flatlands, with only condors and clouds for company. ▸▸ *For listings, see pages 188-191.*

Ins and outs

Getting there and around **Chalten Travel** and **Itinerarios y Travesías** run a daily bus service between Los Antiguos and El Chaltén; you're unlikely to stop in between, except to see the Cueva de las Manos from Perito Moreno. Various companies organize tours, with estancia stays included (for example www.estanciasdesantacruz.com). For drivers travelling south, the road is paved as far as Perito Moreno, and then good *ripio*, improving greatly after Las Horquetas. Fuel is available in most places but carry extra to avoid a 72-km detour to Gobernador Gregores. If cycling, note that food and water stops are scarce, the wind is fierce and there is no shade.

Perito Moreno and around → *Colour map 2, B3.*

Your most likely stop on the long road south is the little town of Perito Moreno, 25 km west of Lago Buenos Aires and accessible by bus from Esquel or Comodoro Rivadavia. It's the nearest base for exploring the mysterious cave paintings at the Cueva de las Manos to the south (see page 187). The town has no sights as such, but southwest of the town is **Parque Laguna**, where you can see varied bird life, including flamingos and black-necked swans, and go fishing. You could also walk to the crater of **Cerro Volcán**, from a path 12 km outside Perito Moreno: ask at the friendly **tourist office** ⓘ *San Martín 1222, T02963-432222, www.epatagonia.gov.ar, 0700-2300*, for directions. Staff can also advise on tours and estancia stays. You can also ask for information at the small **tourist office** ⓘ *at the bus station, T02963-432732.*

Los Antiguos → *Colour map 2, B3.*

From this part of Argentina, the easiest and most commonly used route to Chile is via the pretty little village of Los Antiguos, which lies just 2 km east of the border, on the southern shore of **Lago Buenos Aires**. This is the second largest lake in South America and extends into Chile as Lago General Carrera (see page 318). The landscape is beautiful and unspoilt and the Río Baker, which flows from the lake, is world-renowned for excellent trout fishing. The main reason to enter Chile here is to take the ferry over the lake to Puerto Ibáñez with bus connections to Coyhaique on the Carretera Austral. (You can also drive to Puerto Ibáñez from Perito Moreno, via the paved road around the northeast side of Lago Buenos Aires.)

Los Antiguos is a sleepy little place, but has a rather pleasant quiet atmosphere, thanks largely to its warm microclimate. It's a rich fruit-growing area with a popular cherry festival in early January that attracts national *folclore* stars. There's a small but willing **tourist office** ⓘ *Av 11 de Julio 446, T02963-491261, www.losantiguos.gov.ar/, summer 0800-2200, at other times 0800-1200 only.* While you're here, you can visit two local

Border crossing

Two roads cross the border into Chile west of Río Mayo to take you to Coyhaique (see page 306). Further south, the road from Perito Moreno to Los Antiguos leads to a border on the shores of Lago Buenos Aires.

Coyhaique Alto

Coyhaique Alto is reached by a 133-km road (87 km *ripio*, then dirt) that branches off Route 40 about 7 km north of Río Mayo, continuing on the Chilean side 50 km west to Coyhaique.

Chilean immigration Coyhaique Alto, 6 km west of the border, May-August 0800-2100, September-April 0700-2300.

Paso Huemules

Paso Huemules is reached by a road that branches off Route 40, some 31 km south of Río Mayo and runs west 105 km via Lago Blanco (fuel), 30 km from the border. This crossing has better roads than Coyhaique Alto. On the Chilean side, this road continues via Balmaceda airport, 61 km to Coyhaique.

Chilean immigration 3 km from the border, winter 0800-2000, summer 0800-2200.

From **Los Antiguos** a bridge crosses the border heading towards Chile Chico (see page 321).

Chilean immigration 20 km from the border, winter 0800-2000, summer 0800-2200.

chacras (small farms). You can walk to **Chacra Don Neno**, where strawberries are grown and good jam is sold, or (if you have transport) head further afield to idyllic **Chacra el Paraíso**, which grows and sells perfect cherries.

Cueva de las Manos → *Colour map 2, B4.*

ⓘ *Access is via an unpaved road east off RN 40, 3 km north of Bajo Caracoles, US$3, 6 hrs return journey by car from Perito Moreno. Estancia Los Toldos (60 km from Perito Moreno, 18 km from the caves) organizes trips, page 189.*

Situated 163 km south of Perito Moreno and 47 km northeast of Bajo Caracoles, the canyon of the **Río Pinturas** contains outstanding examples of handprints and cave paintings, estimated to be up to 9300 years old. In the cave's four galleries are over 800 paintings of human hands (all but 31 of which depict left hands), as well as images of guanacos and rheas, and various geometrical designs painted by the Toldense peoples. The red, orange, black, white and ochre pigments were derived from earth and calafate berries and fixed with a varnish of guanaco fat and urine. The canyon itself is also worth seeing: 270 m deep and 480 m wide, with strata of vivid red and green rock; it's especially beautiful in the early morning or evening light. A *guardaparque* living at the site provides helpful information.

Bajo Caracoles and beyond → *Colour map 2, B3.*

After hours of spectacular emptiness, even tiny Bajo Caracoles is a relief. It's nothing more than a few houses, facing into the wind, with an expensive grocery store and very expensive fuel. From here, Route 41 (unpaved) heads 99 km northwest, past Lago Ghio and Lago Columna, to the **Paso Roballos** border and on to **Cochrane** (see page 322). Although it's passable in summer, the route is often flooded in spring and there's no public transport. **Chilean immigration** ⓘ *11 km from border, winter 0800-2000, summer*

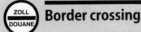

0800-2200. Route 39, meanwhile, heads west for 72 km to **Lago Posadas** and **Lago Pueyrredón**, two beautiful lakes with contrasting blue and turquoise waters, separated by a narrow isthmus, where guanacos and rheas can be seen.

South of Bajo Caracoles, Route 40 crosses the Pampa del Asador and then, near Las Horquetas, swings southeast to follow the Río Chico. There is a turning west to Lago Belgrano and **Parque Nacional Perito Moreno** (see below). South of this junction, Route 40 improves considerably. At Km 464, Route 25 branches off towards **San Julián** on the Atlantic coast, via **Gobernador Gregores** (72 km, fuel), while Route 40 continues southwest towards Tres Lagos. There is no food between Bajo Caracoles and Tres Lagos, although there are estancias roughly every 25 km. See www.ruta40.net for more details.

Parque Nacional Perito Moreno → *Colour map 2, B3.*

ⓘ *Entrance 90 km west of Las Horquetas via RN 37, Nov-Mar, free, no public transport. Infoation from Av San Martín 409, Gobernador Gregores (220 km away), T02962-491477, peritomoreno@apn.gov.ar.*

This is one of the wildest and most remote parks in Argentina. The large, interconnected system of lakes and glaciated peaks offers good trekking and abundant wildlife but much of the park is dedicated to scientific study and is inaccessible.

About 10 km beyond the park entrance, the *guardaparque*'s office has maps and leaflets on walks and wildlife. The most accessible section of the park is a little further on, around turquoise **Lago Belgrano**. Several good hikes are possible from here around the peninsula, with fine views of Cerro Herros; to **Cerro León**, starting from **Estancia La Oriental**, good for spotting condors; and the one- or two-day hike to **Lago Burmeister**, via Cerro Casa de Piedra, 16 km. At the foot of **Cerro Casa de Piedra** is a network of caves containing paintings, accessible only with a guide.

The **Sierra Colorada** dominates the northeast of the park and the erosion of its multicoloured rocks is responsible for the lakes' vibrant colours. Between the lakes are snow-covered peaks, the highest of which is **Cerro Herros** (2770 m), while outside the park itself, but towering over it to the north, is **Cerro San Lorenzo** (3706 m), the highest peak in southern Patagonia. Vegetation changes with altitude: dense coiron grasses and shrubs cling to the windswept steppe, while beech forest, lenga and coihue occupy the higher slopes. Wildlife includes guanacos, foxes and the rare huemul, plus flamingos, ñandus, steamer ducks, grebes, black-necked swans, Patagonian woodpeckers, eagles and condors. The lakes and rivers are unusual for Argentina in that they contain only native species of fish.

South on the Ruta 40 listings

For Sleeping and Eating price codes and other relevant information, see pages 41-44.

Sleeping

Perito Moreno and around *p186*

C Austral, San Martín 1386, T02963-432538. Bath and breakfast, and a decent restaurant. The slightly better of the 2 hotels in town.

D Belgrano, San Martín 1001, T02963-42019. Pleasant, with simple rooms and a restaurant.

E-D Posada del Caminante, Rivadavia 937, T02963-432204. Central new *hosteria* with sparse rooms, but welcoming hosts.

Estancias

L pp **Telken**, 28 km south on RN40, T02963-432079, T011-4797 7216 (Buenos Aires), jarinauta@santacruz.com.ar. Formerly a sheep station, with comfortable wood-lined rooms in the farmhouse and charming simple bed-rooms. All meals shared with the welcoming owners, also horse riding. Highly recommended.

Los Antiguos *p186*

AL-A Hostería La Serena, 29 km east of Los Antiguos, T0297-156250750, www.patagoniasouth.com. Comfortable accommodation, excellent home-grown food, fishing and trips to the Chilean and Argentine lake districts, open Oct-Jun.
A Antigua Patagonia, on the lakeside, signposted from RN43, T02963-491038, www.antiguapatagonia.com.ar. An excellent hotel and worth a detour. Luxurious rooms with beautiful views. There's also a great restaurant. Tours to the Cueva de las Manos and nearby Monte Cevallos can be arranged. Recommended.
C Argentino, 11 de Julio 850, T02963-491132. Comfortable rooms and a decent restaurant.

Hostels

F pp **Albergue Padilla**, San Martín 44 (just off main street), T02963-491140. Big shared rooms for 4-8 with bathrooms, *quincho* and garden, where you can also camp. Very friendly. El Chaltén travel tickets sold.
F pp **Albergue y Bungalows Sol de Mayo**, 11 de Julio 133 A, T02963-491232. Basic rooms, shared bathrooms in a very central location.

Camping

Municipal, T02963-491265. Outstanding site with every facility, lovely grounds 2 km from centre, US$2 pp and cabins (**F**) available for up to 4 people. Linen not provided.

Cueva de las Manos *p187*

L Estancia Los Toldos, 7 km off the RN 40, 60 km south of Perito Moreno, T02963-432856, T011-4901 0436, www.estanciasdesantacruz.com/lostoldos. The closest estancia to the caves. A modest building in a wonderful landscape. The owners run trips by horse or 4WD, as well as to the lakes and PN Perito Moreno. They also have an albergue, the **Hostería Cueva de Las Manos** (**B**), Nov-Easter.

Bajo Caracoles and beyond *p187*

There are some superb estancias around Gobernador Gregores, but they're tricky to get to without your own transport.
L Hostería Lagos del Furioso, Lago Posadas, on the peninsula between the lakes, reached along RN 39, T02963-490253, T011-52374043 in Buenos Aires www.lagosdelfurioso.com. Open Mid Oct-Easter. Extremely comfortable accommodation in cabins in a really incredible setting by the lake shore, offering superb Patagonian cooking with home-produced food and good wines. Also offers horse riding, trekking and excursions in 4WD vehicles. 2 nights minimum – you'll want to stay longer.
D-E Hotel Bajo Caracoles, Bajo Caracoles, T02963-490100. Very old-fashioned 1920s building, with plain spacious rooms and meals, but a rather institutional feel. Given the wilderness, you'll probably be glad of a bed.

Camping

G At the campsite, rooms **E** pp, are also available. A simple and welcoming place, also run excursions to Cueva de las Manos, 10 km by vehicle then 1½- to 2-hrs' walk, and nearby volcanoes by car or horse. Ask for **Señor Sabella**, Av Perón 941, Perito Moreno, T02963-432199.

Estancias

There are some superb estancias in this region, tricky to get to without your own transport.
A pp **La Angostura**, 55 km from Gobernador Gregores is T02962-491501, www.estanciala angostura.com.ar. Horse riding, trekking and fishing. Recommended.

Parque Nacional Perito Moreno *p188*

B Estancia La Oriental, T02962-452196, elada@uvc.com.ar. Open Nov-Apr, full board. In a really splendid setting, rooms are comfortable, and there's superb horse riding.

Camping

Camping is possible and there are 4 free sites inside the park: **Lago Burmeister, Mirador Lago Belgrano, Cerro de Vasco** and **Alberto de Agostini**. No facilities, no fires.

Eating

Perito Moreno and around *p186*

There's good food at **Pipach**, next to Hotel Austral, **Parador Bajo Caracoles**, or pizzas at **Nono's**, 9 de Julio and Saavedra. **Rotisería Chee's I** is cheap and cheery to eat in or take away.

Los Antiguos *p186*

El Negro 'B' Parilla, 11 de Julio 571, T02963-491358. A great *parrilla* restaurant with welcoming staff but looks outdated.

Agua Grande, 11 de Julio 871, T02963-491217. Another great parrilla restaurant, slightly more modern, and busier.

Pizza Uno, 11 de Julio 895, T02963-491471. Pizzeria serving great home-made and affordable dishes. Delivery service.

Activities and tours

Perito Moreno and around *p186*

Guanacondór Viajes Turismo, Perito Moreno 1089, T02963-432117, guanacondor@argentina.com, and **Las Loicas (Transporte Lago Posados)**, T02963-490272, www.las loicas.com. All-day tour collecting from Bajo Caracoles or Estancia Los Toldos, US$40-50. Both do the Circuito Grande Comarca Noroeste, taking in some of Santa Cruz's best scenery. Perito Moreno– Bajo Caracoles, Cueva de las Manos, Lago Posada, Paso Roballos, Monte Cevallos, Los Antiguos.

Zoyen Turismo, San Martín near Saavedra, T02963-432207, www.zoyenturismo.com.ar. The friendly staff can also help with Ruta 40 connections and Estancia visits.

Los Antiguos *p186*

Turismo Toscas Bayas, 11 de Julio 797, T02963-491016, toscasbayas@yahoo.com.ar. Arrange trips to the Cueva de las Manos, Monte Zeballos, Lago Posadas and more. They also run city tours, 4 hrs, US$10. Friendly.

Los Antiguos is a great place to catch rainbow trout; 2 local fishing guides will take you out on the lake: **Mario Rodrigo**, T02966-1551 4923, and **Osvaldo Zeme**, T0297-154137813.

Transport

Perito Moreno and around *p186*

Air

The airport is 7 km east out of town, and the only way to get there is by taxi. **LADE**, Av San Martín 1207, T02963-432055, has flights to/from **Río Gallegos**, **Río Grande**, **Ushuaia**, **El Calafate** and **Gobernador Gregores**.

Bus

The terminal is on the edge of town, T02963-432072. **La Unión**, T02963-432133, to **Comodoro Rivadavia**, 6 hrs US$15, and to **Chile** via Los Antiguos, 2 buses daily in summer, 1hr, US$2. **Co-op Sportman** also daily to **Comodoro Rivadavia**. There are 3 main companies that run to **El Chaltén**, with **Chaltén Travel** even dates, 1000, and **Itinerarios y Travesías** and **Taqsa** other days at 1800, US$40. It's a 14-hr, 582-km journey over bleak emptiness. North- bound buses with **Itinerarios y Travesías** stop at the Cueva de las Manos for a couple of hours at dawn, and while it's a shame to miss the ride in daylight, it's a great way to see the caves. See also page 210.

Los Antiguos *p186*

Bus

Note that there is no real bus terminal in Los Antiguos. Each bus company stops at different spots along the short main street.

Co-op Sportman to **Comodoro Rivadavia**, via Perito Moreno and Caleta Olivia, daily, 7½ hrs, US$10. **Chaltén Travel** and **Itinerarios y Travesías** to **El Chaltén** and **El Calafate**, US$41, see above for details. Tickets from **Albergue Padilla**, San Martín 44 Sur, T02963-491140. **La Unión** across the border to **Chile Chico** (Chile), 45 mins, US$1; also **Transportes VH**, US$2. For the Ruta 40, **Taqsa** have the same schedules as **Itinerarios y Travesías** but run once a week, all year round. Their terminal is 11 de Julio at the end of town, near the bridge, T02963-491174.

Cueva de las Manos *p187*
Northbound buses run by **Itinerarios y Travesías** stop here at dawn for a couple of hours en route between **El Chaltén** and **Los Antiguos**, see above. It's a great way to see the caves. Tickets are available from **Albergue Patagonia** (see page 205). Tickets also available though the Chaltén Travel in Los Antiguos on San Martín 44, T02693-491140, www.chaltentravel.com. The Perito Moreno tourist office can advise on tours, see page 186.

Parque Nacional Perito Moreno *p188*
There is no transport into the park but it may be possible to get a lift with estancia workers. Also consult www.parquesnacionales.gov.ar.

Directory

Perito Moreno and around *p186*
Banks ATMs in the main street, at **Banco de la Provincia de Santa Cruz** and **Banco de la Nación**, but there's nowhere to change TCs.

Parque Nacional Los Glaciares

Of all Argentina's impressive landscapes, the sight of the immense glaciers stretching out infinitely and silently before you, may stay with you longest. This is the second-largest national park in Argentina, extending along the Chilean border for over 170 km. Almost half of it is covered by the Southern Ice Cap; at 370 km long, it's the third largest in the world. From it, 13 major glaciers descend into two great lakes: Lago Argentino in the southeast and Lago Viedma to the northeast.

There are two main areas to explore: the glaciers can be visited by bus and boat trips from El Calafate, while from El Chaltén, 230 km northwest, there is superb trekking around the dramatic Fitz Roy massif and ice climbing near its summit. The central section, between Lago Argentino and Lago Viedma, is the Ice Cap National Reserve, inaccessible to visitors apart from a couple of estancias.

East of the ice fields, there's southern beech forest before the land flattens to the wind-blasted Patagonian steppe. Birdlife is prolific; often spotted are black-necked swans, Magallenic woodpeckers, and, perhaps, even a torrent duck, diving in the rivers. Guanacos, grey foxes, skunks and rheas can be seen on the steppe, and the rare huemul inhabit the forest. ▸▸ *For listings, see pages 201-210.*

Ins and outs

Getting there Access to the park is via **El Calafate**, 50 km from the park's eastern boundary, for the glaciers, or via **El Chaltén**, 230 km northwest, for trekking, near Fitz Roy on the northeastern edge of the park. There are regular flights to El Calafate airport, 20 km east of town, as well as buses from Río Gallegos and Puerto Natales. El Chaltén is three hours' drive north then west, with several buses daily from El Calafate and Río Gallegos. ▸▸ *See also Transport, page 209.*

Best time to visit Although this part of Patagonia is generally cold, there is a milder micro-climate around Lago Viedma and Lago Argentino, which means that summers can be reasonably pleasant, with average temperatures between 5°C and 22°C, though strong winds blow constantly at the foot of the *cordillera*. In the forested area, around 1500 mm of rain falls annually, mainly between March and late May. In winter, the whole area is inhospitably cold and most tourist facilities are closed. The best time to visit, therefore, is between November and April, avoiding January and early February, when Argentines take their holidays, campsites are crowded and accommodation is hard to find. Park entry US$9. For further information contact T02962 491477, peritomoreno@apn.gov.ar. For more information see www.losglaciares.com.

Parque Nacional Los Glaciares

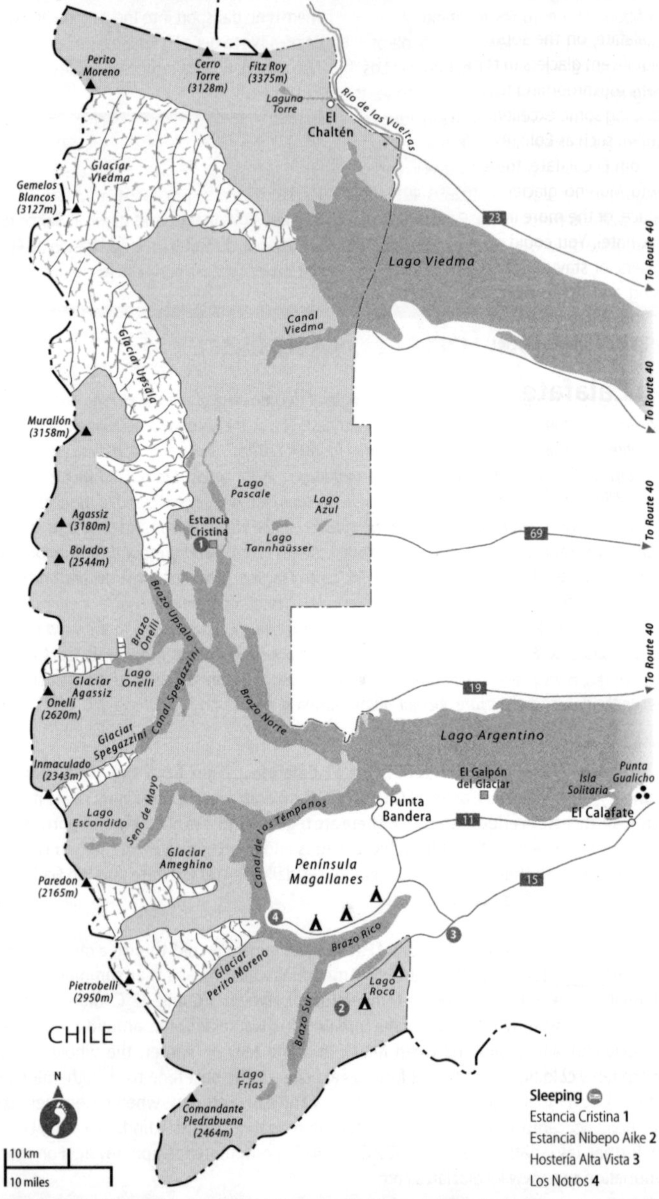

Sleeping

Estancia Cristina **1**

Estancia Nibepo Aike **2**

Hostería Alta Vista **3**

Los Notros **4**

El Calafate » p201-210.

El Calafate, on the southern shore of Lago Argentino, is the only base for exploring the magnificent glaciers to the west. The town has expanded rapidly in the last few years, with hotels mushrooming to exploit tourism. There is accommodation to cater for all budgets, including some excellent hostels, but if you can afford it, stay at an estancia-style hotel out of town such as **Eolo, Alta Vista** or **Los Notros**, where you will feel close to nature.

From El Calafate, tours take you on boat trips and to walkways right beside the wall of Perito Moreno glacier. Highly recommended is the **Minitrekking** walk on the glacier's surface, or the more intrepid six-hour **Big Ice** hike. All these can be booked in town, or by your hotel. You could also head further north by boat to see the Spegazzini and Upsala glaciers, or stay a night at the remote **Estancia Cristina** (page 203), which offers superb hiking and horse riding to see the Upsala glacier from above, and down a fossil-filled canyon. Whatever you do, this is an unmissable part of any trip to Patagonia. You can visit the Perito Moreno glacier year round, but weather close to the glacier can make it unpleasant.

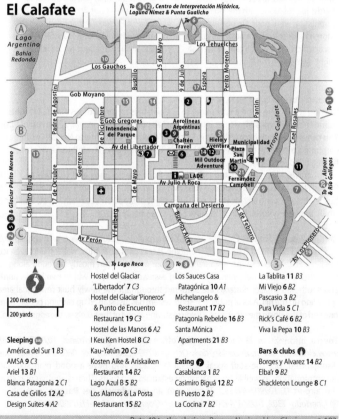

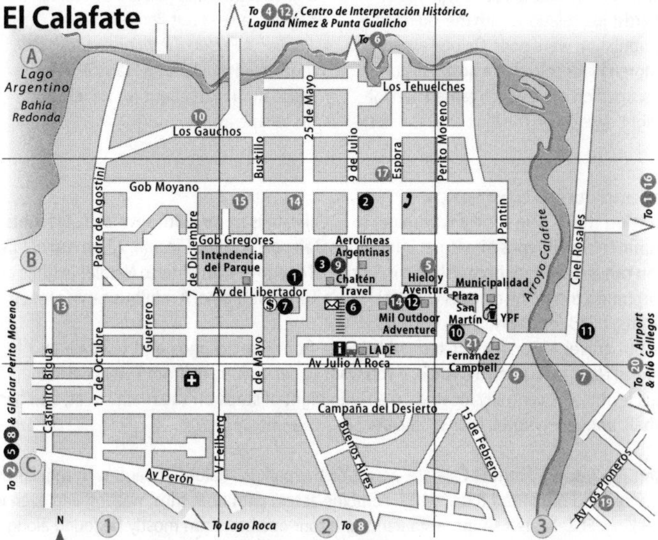

200 metres
200 yards

Sleeping
América del Sur **1** *B3*
AMSA **9** *C3*
Ariel **13** *B1*
Blanca Patagonia **2** *C1*
Casa de Grillos **12** *A2*
Design Suites **4** *A2*
Hostel del Glaciar 'Libertador' **7** *C3*
Hostel del Glaciar 'Pioneros' & Punto de Encuentro Restaurant **19** *C3*
Hostel de las Manos **6** *A2*
I Keu Ken Hostel **8** *C2*
Kau-Yatún **20** *C3*
Kosten Aike & Ariskaiken Restaurant **14** *B2*
Lago Azul B **5** *B2*
Los Alamos & La Posta Restaurant **15** *B2*
Los Sauces Casa Patagónica **10** *A1*
Michelangelo & Restaurant **17** *B2*
Patagonia Rebelde **16** *B3*
Santa Mónica Apartments **21** *B3*

Eating
Casablanca **1** *B2*
Casimiro Biguá **12** *B2*
El Puesto **2** *B2*
La Cocina **7** *B2*
La Tablita **11** *B3*
Mi Viejo **6** *B2*
Pascasio **3** *B2*
Pura Vida **5** *C1*
Rick's Café **6** *B2*
Viva la Pepa **10** *B3*

Bars & clubs
Borges y Alvarez **14** *B2*
Elba'r **9** *B2*
Shackleton Lounge **8** *C1*

Francisco Moreno, El Perito

You can't miss the name of Argentina's favourite son as you travel around Patagonia. Francisco Pascasio Moreno (1852-1919) is commemorated by a national park, a town, countless streets and a world-famous glacier. Moreno, a naturalist and geographer, explored areas previously unknown to the authorities. At the age of 20, he travelled up the Río Negro to Lago Nahuel Huapi, along the Río Chubut, and then up the Río Santa Cruz to reach the giant lake which he named Lago Argentino. Expeditions such as these were dangerous: apart from physical hardships, relations with the indigenous population were poor. On one expedition, Moreno was seized as a hostage, but escaped on a raft which carried him for eight days down the Río Limay to safety.

His fame established, Moreno was elected to congress and became an expert (*perito*) adviser to the Argentine side in the negotiations to draw the border with Chile. His reward was a grant of land near Bariloche, which he handed over to the state to manage, the initial act in creating the national parks system in Argentina, and an inspiring gesture at a time when anyone who could was buying up land as fast as possible. Moreno's remains are buried in a mausoleum on Isla Centinela in Lago Nahuel Huapi. For a good read while you are travelling Argentina seek out *Perito Moreno's Travel Journal: A Personal Reminiscence* (published by Elefante Blanco). It is a fascinating read about his travels, and his escape from capture.

Ins and outs → *Colour map 3, A3.*

Getting there The easiest way to get to El Calafate is by air, with several daily flights in summer from Buenos Aires to its international **airport** ⓘ *Lago Viedma, 22 km east of town*. You can also fly here from Ushuaia in Tierra del Fuego or from Puerto Natales in Chile and combine a trip to the glaciers with trekking in Torres del Paine. A minibus service meets all flights, US$3 (one way, a taxi costs US$10.

Bus travel is convenient too, with buses from Río Gallegos and Ushuaia and from Puerto Natales, via Cerro Castillo, if you want to get directly to/from Torres del Paine. The bus terminal is centrally located up a steep flight of steps off the main street, and has a small, not very helpful, tourist office. » *See Transport, page 209.*

Getting around From El Calafate, access to the park is straightforward, with regular bus services and organized tours, which combine access with boat trips, walking and even ice trekking. El Calafate's shops, restaurants and tour operators can mostly be found along its main street, Avenida del Libertador, running east-west. Hotels lie within two blocks north and south and smaller *hosterías* are scattered throughout the newly built residential area sprawling up the hill. A local public transport system has just started up carrying people from one end of the city to the other; useful if you're staying at one of the hotels on the edge of town.

Tourist information El Calafate **tourist office** ⓘ *in the bus terminal, T02902-491090, www.elcalafate.gov.ar, in English, daily Oct-Apr 0700-2200, May-Sep 0800-2100*, may look disorganized, but the staff speak several languages and have a good map showing accommodation, as well as information on estancias and tours. There's another branch at the **airport** ⓘ *T02902-491230*. There's also an **Intendencia del Parque** (park office) ⓘ *Libertador 1302, T02901-491005, losglaciares@apn.gov.ar, Mon-Fri 0800-1600.*

Around El Calafate

Just west of the town centre is **Bahía Redonda**, a shallow part of Lago Argentino that freezes in winter, when ice-skating and skiing are possible. From the **Intendencia del Parque**, an hour's stroll will take you to **Laguna Nímez** at the eastern edge of the bay, where there's a bird reserve with flamingos, black-necked swans and ducks. To get there, follow Calle Bustillo up the new road among cultivated fields and orchards to cross the bridge. Keep heading north; the laguna is signposted. Hike to the top of the **Cerro Calafate**, behind the town (2½ to three hours), for views of the silhouette of the southern end of the Andes, Bahía Redonda and Isla Solitaria on Lago Argentino. There is also scope for good hill-walking to the south of the town, while **Cerro Elefante**, to the west, on the road to the Perito Moreno glacier, is good for rock climbing.

In addition to the glaciers, El Calafate provides access to some other good places for trekking, horse riding and exploring by 4WD, if you're here for a few days. There are several estancias within reach of the town, which offer a day on a working farm, a lunch of superb Patagonian lamb, cooked *asado al palo*, and outdoor activities. **El Galpón del Glaciar** (formerly **Estancia Alice**) offers displays of sheep shearing, walking and horse-riding trips to the Perito Moreno glacier and Cerro Frías. Overnight accommodation is available in the lovely house with views of Lago Argentino.

Lago Roca, 40 km southwest of El Calafate, is set in beautiful open landscape, with hills above offering panoramic views. The lake is perfect for lots of activities, including trout and salmon fishing, climbing and walking, and there are several estancias, where you can see farm activities, such as the branding of cattle in summer. There is also good camping in a wooded area and a restaurant.

Lago Argentino and the glaciers » *p201-210.*

Perito Moreno glacier → *Colour map 3, A2.*

Perito Moreno is one of the few glaciers in the world that is still advancing. Some 30 km long, it reaches the water at a narrow point on one of the fjords, **Brazo Rico**, opposite **Península Magallanes**. Every few years, the glacier blocks the fjord and, as water pressure builds up behind the ice wall, the ice suddenly breaks, reopening the channel and sending huge icebergs (*témpanos*) rushing down the Canal de los Témpanos. Naturally, there are concerns about the effects of climate change on the glacier, but these are not straightforward, and the glacier's calving has no relationship with increased temperature.

Viewing the glacier There are various ways to approach the glacier. All excursions (and the regular bus service) will take you 85 km from El Calafate direct to the car park on Península Magallanes, where you begin the descent along a series of wooden walkways (*pasarelas*) to see the glacier slightly from above, and then, as you get lower, directly head-on. There are several wide viewing areas, where, in summer, crowds wait expectantly, cameras poised, for another hunk of ice to fall from the vertical blue walls at the glacier's front. There is a large and fairly inexpensive café at the site with clean bathrooms.

Boat trips leave constantly during the day from the tourist pier (well signposted from the car park), to survey the glacier from the water below, giving you a chance to appreciate its magnitude and its varied sculptural forms. To get closer still, there are guided treks on the ice itself, known as *minitrekking*, which allow you to walk along the crevices and frozen crests in crampons. This is not technically demanding and is possible for anyone with a reasonable level of fitness. Highly recommended for the fitter and more intrepid are the longer six-hour

Border crossings

Three crossings provide access to Puerto Natales and Torres del Paine. They are open, subject to weather conditions, 24 hours a day from September to May and 0700-2300 at other times. Most buses use the Río Turbio crossing but Cancha Carrera is quicker if you're driving to the national park from El Calafate. Note that Argentine pesos cannot be exchanged in Torres del Paine.

Paso Cancha Carrera

129 km west of La Esperanza and 42 km north of Río Turbio. The most northerly of the crossings is the most convenient (though desolate) crossing between Argentina and Torres del Paine but it is often closed in winter. On the Chilean side the road continues to Cerro Castillo, where it meets the good *ripio* road that runs between Puerto Natales (65 km south) and the national park.

Argentine customs and immigration Cancha Carrera, 2 km east of the border, is fast and friendly.

Chilean customs and immigration Cerro Castillo, 7 km west of the border, 0800-2200.

Paso Dorotea

14 km south of Río Turbio, 27 km from Puerto Natales. On the Chilean side the road runs south for 11 km to join Route 9 between Puerto Natales and Punta Arenas.

Chilean customs and immigration 2 km from the border, winter 0800-2400, for summer times, check in Puerto Natales.

Paso Casas Viejas 33 km south of Río Turbio via 28 de Noviembre. On the Chilean side, the road continues west to join Route 9 east of Puerto Natales at Km 14.

Argentine customs and immigration Winter 0800-2200, summer 0800-2400.

Chilean customs and immigration 1 km from the border, winter 0800-2200, summer 0800-2400.

hikes on the ice (known as Big Ice); the sight of the glacier from within, with its cobalt blue ice caves and turquoise rivers, is utterly magical. **Hielo y Aventura** offers both and can be booked through any hotel or tour operator. » *See Activities and tours, page 207.*

Upsala glacier → *Colour map 3, A2.*

The fjords at the northwestern end of Lago Argentino are fed by four other glaciers. The largest is the Upsala glacier, named after the Swedish university that commissioned the first survey of this area in 1908. It's a stunning expanse of untouched beauty, covering three times the area of the Perito Moreno glacier, and is the longest glacier flowing off the Southern Patagonian ice fields. Unusually it ends in two separate frontages, each about 4 km wide and 60 m high, although only the western frontage can be seen from the lake excursion. The best way to see the glacier is to stay at **Estancia Cristina** (see page 203) and take the trip up to the viewpoint, where vermillion rocks have been polished smooth by the glacier's approach. The estancia can be reached only by boat from Punta Bandera, 50 km west of El Calafate. Further south, the **Spegazzini** glacier has a frontage 1.5 km wide and 130 m high. In between are **Agassiz** and **Onelli**, both of which feed into **Lago Onelli**, a quiet and very beautiful lake, full of icebergs of every shape and size, surrounded by beech forests on one side and ice-covered mountains on the other.

Around Cerro Fitz Roy » p201-210.

At the northern end of Parque Nacional Los Glaciares, the soaring granite of **Cerro Fitz Roy** (3405 m) rises up from the smooth baize of the steppe, more like a ziggurat than a mountain, surrounded by a consort of jagged snow-clad spires, with a stack of spun-cotton cloud hanging constantly above them. It is one of the most magnificent mountains in the world and it towers above the nearby peaks: **Torre** (3128 m), **Poincenot** (3076 m) and **Saint-Exupery** (2600 m). Its Tehuelche name was El Chaltén ('smoking mountain' or 'volcano'), perhaps because at sunrise the pink towers are occasionally lit up bright red for a few seconds in a phenomenon known as the *amanecer de fuego* ('sunrise of fire'). Perito Moreno named the peak after the captain of the *Beagle*, who saw it from afar in 1833, and it was first climbed by a French expedition in 1952. It stands in the northern end of Parque Nacional Los Glaciares at the western end of Lago Viedma, 230 km north of El Calafate, in an area of lakes and glaciers that makes marvellous trekking country. The base for walking and climbing around Fitz Roy is the modern town of El Chaltén, which has been built right next to the mountains.

Ins and outs

Getting there and around The quickest way to reach El Chaltén is to fly to El Calafate and then catch one of the frequent buses for the 230-km journey north (about four hours). There are also daily buses to El Chaltén from Los Antiguos along Route 40, useful if you've come from the Lake District. Access to the park is free and it is not necessary to register before you set out. Most paths are very clear and well worn but a map is essential, even on short walks: the park information centre has photocopied maps of treks but the best is one published by *Zagier and Urruty*, US$5, and is available in shops in El Calafate and El Chaltén.

Best time to visit Walking here is only really viable mid-October to April, with the best months usually March to April when the weather is generally stable and not very cold, and the autumn colours of the beech forest are stunning. Mid-summer (December and January) and spring (September to October) are generally very windy. And in December and January the campsites can be full to bursting, with many walkers on the paths.

Tourist information The **Intendencia del Parque** ⓘ *T02962-493004*, is in El Chaltén, across the bridge at the entrance to the town. It hands out helpful trekking maps of the area, with paths and campsites marked, giving distances and walking times. El Chaltén's **tourist office** ⓘ *Güemes 21, T02962-493011, www.elchalten.com, Mon-Fri 0900-2000, Sat and Sun 1300-2000*, has an excellent website, with accommodation lists. Most services in El Chaltén and some hotels close out of season.

El Chaltén → *See map, page 198. Colour map 2, C2.*

The small modern town of El Chaltén is set in a wonderful position at the foot of Cerro Fitz Roy and at the mouth of the valley of the Río de las Vueltas but, having been founded in 1985 in order to pre-empt Chilean territorial claims, it has grown with little thought for aesthetics. Now hugely popular as a centre for trekking and climbing in summer, and for cross-country skiing in winter, it's an expensive place and can be unattractive, especially when the harsh wind blows. But the steady stream of visitors creates a cheerful atmosphere and, from the town, you can walk directly into breathtaking landscapes. Tourist infrastructure is still developing in El Chaltén and, so far, there are no ATMs, so take sufficient cash. Accommodation ranges from camping and hostels to not-quite-luxurious *hosterías*. Food can be expensive, though there is increasingly plenty of choice. Credit cards are only accepted in larger establishments. El Chaltén is also the base for two unique expeditions onto the Southern Ice Field; Consult the guides at **Fitz Roy Expediciones**. ▶▶ *See Activities and tours, page 209.*

Hiking around Cerro Fitz Roy

→ *These are the most popular walks from El Chaltén.*

▲▲ **Laguna Torre** (short – two hours each way) Walk west to Mirador Laguna Torre (1½ hours) for views of Cerro Torre then continue to busy **Camping De Agostini** (30 minutes) on the lake shore, where there are fantastic views of the dramatic peaks of Cordón Torre.

▲▲ **Laguna de Los Tres** (four hours each way) Walk up to Laguna Capri (two hours), with great views of Fitz Roy, then continue to **Camping Poincenot** (one hour) and **Camping Río Blanco** (only for climbers, by prior arrangement). From Río Blanco you can head southwest to Laguna de los Tres, where you'll get a spectacular view on a fine day (one hour) but in bad weather, you're better off walking to Piedras Blancas.

▲▲ **Laguna Torre** (long – seven hours each way) A marvellous walk with views of both mountain groups. Climb past Laguna Capri and take the signed path to your left, passing two lakes (Madre and then Hija), to reach the path that leads to Laguna Torre.

▲▲ **Loma del Pliegue Tumbado** (four hours each way) A marked path from the *guardería* (park ranger's office) leads southwest to this viewpoint where you can see both condors and Lago Viedma. This is a good day walk, best in clear weather. More experienced trekkers can continue to the glacial Laguna Toro (six hours from El Chaltén).

▲▲ **Río Blanco to Piedra del Fraile** (seven hours each way) This beautiful walk starts at **Camping Río Blanco** and runs north along the Río Blanco and then west along the Río Eléctrico to **Camping Piedra del Fraile** (four hours), just outside the national park. From here a path leads south, up Cerro Eléctrico Oeste (1882 m)

El Chaltén

Sleeping 🛏
Albergue Patagonia 1
Aylen-Aike 2
Cóndor de los Andes 3
Estancia La Quinta 12
Hospedaje La Base 6
Hostería El Pilar 13
Hostería El Puma
 & Restaurant Terray 5
Hostería Posada
 Lunajuim 7
Inlandsis 4
Los Cerros 10
Mi Rincón 8
Northofagus 9
Pioneros de Valle 14

Eating 🍴
Ahonikenk Chaltén 3
El Muro 7
Estepa 9
Fuegia 6
Josh Aike 1
Pangea 4
Patagonicus 5

Bars & clubs 🍸
Elal Resto-Bar 8
La Cervecería 10

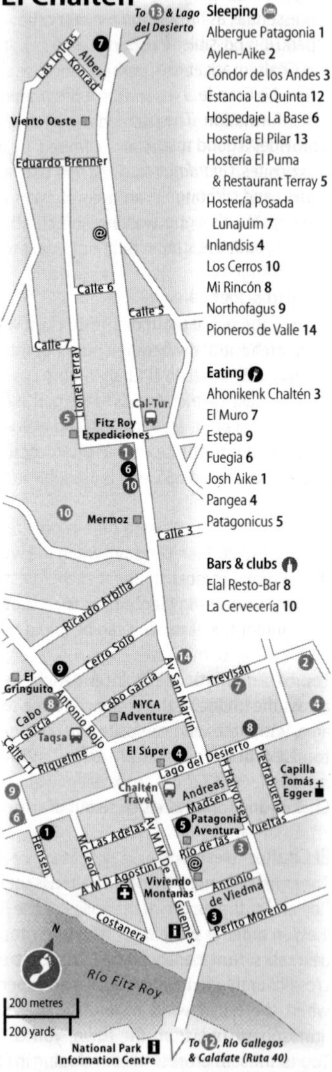

Hiking around El Chaltén and Cerro Fitz Roy

→ **Equipment** A map is essential, even on short walks. Also take plenty of warm clothes and a four-season sleeping bag, if you're camping. A gas or alcohol stove is essential, as fires are prohibited in the park. It is possible to rent equipment in El Chaltén; ask at the park office or Rancho Grande.

→ **Information** The park's *Intendencia* provides a good map, showing walks and campsites. *Guardaparques* can advise on walks and, although you're not required to register, it's a good idea to check with them about the state of the paths. Some speak English.

→ **Paths** Paths are well marked. Stick to the centre of the path so as not to make it any bigger and walk in single file (this means at times that you're walking in a rut).

→ **Rubbish** Take all rubbish back down the mountain with you.

→ **Water** All river water in the national park is drinkable. Don't bathe in rivers and lakes; do not wash or bury waste within 70 m of a water source.
Never go to the toilet near water sources.

→ **Weather** The weather changes hourly, so don't wait for a sunny day to go hiking and be prepared for a sudden deterioration in conditions. Always wear sun screen (factor 30 at least).

→ **Wildlife** As you leave El Chaltén, don't let the dogs follow you, as they frighten the huemules (a rare and endangered species of deer).
For more information see www.elchalten.com.

towards the north face of Fitz Roy (two hours); it's tough going but with spectacular views. You should take a guide for the last bit. Ask at **Hostería El Pilar** and outdoor centre, www.hosteriaelpilar.com.ar.

Climbing Cerro Fitz Roy → *Colour map 2, C2.*

Base camp for ascents of Fitz Roy (3375 m) is **Camping Río Blanco**. Other peaks include Cerro Torre (3128 m), Torre Egger (2900 m), Cerro Solo (2121 m), Poincenot (3002 m), Guillaumet (2579 m), Saint-Exupery (2558 m), Aguja Bífida (2394 m) and Cordón Adela (2938 m): all of these are for very experienced climbers only. However, most climbers can try ice climbing at the foot of Cerro Torre; contact **Fitz Roy Expediciones**, page 209. The best time to climb is mid-February to the end of March; November and December are very windy and the winter (May to July) months are extremely cold. Permits for climbing are available at the national park information office and guides are available in El Chaltén.

Around El Chaltén

The main attraction here is the trekking around Fitz Roy, but there is also stunning virgin landscape to explore outside the park, around **Lago del Desierto**, 37 km north. The long skinny lake is fjord-like and surrounded by forests. It's reached by unpaved Route 23, which leads along the Río de las Vueltas via **Laguna Cóndor**, where flamingos can be seen. A mirador at the end of the road gives fine views over the lake and a path runs along the east side of the lake to its northern tip, from where a trail leads west along the valley of the Río Diablo to **Laguna Diablo**, and north to Lago O'Higgins in Chile, see page 323.

En route to the lake is **Hostería El Pilar**, www.hosteriaelpilar.com.ar, in a stunning position with views of Fitz Roy. Accommodation is available here but you can also visit for tea or use it as an excellent base for trekking up **Río Blanco** or **Río Eléctrico**.

Lago Viedma to the south of El Chaltén can also be explored by boat. The trips usually pass Glaciar Viedma, with the possibility of ice trekking on some excursions.
▶ *See Activities and tours, page 208.*

The Fitz Roy area

To Lago del Desierto

Laguna Cóndor

Laguna Azul

Río de las Vueltas

23

Río del Bosque

Lago Eléctrico

Río Eléctrico

Piedra del Fraile ⛺1

Cerro Eléctrico Oeste (1882m) ▲

Río Blanco

Estancia El Pilar

Guillaumet ▲ (2579m)

Laguna Piedras Blancas

Aguja Bifida ▲ (2394m)

Torre Egger ▲ (2900m)

Cerro Torre ▲ (3128m)

Cerro Fitz Roy ▲ (3375m)

Cerro Poincenot (3002m)

Laguna de los Tres

2 ⛺ ⛺3

Laguna Sucia

Río Blanco

Cerro Saint-Exupery (2558m)

Laguna Madre

Cordón Adela

Glaciar Torre

Cerro Mojón Rojo (2163m)

Loma de las Pizarras (2208m)

Laguna Hija

Laguna Capri 🌴 ⛺4

Laguna Nieta

▲ (2938m)

Mirador Laguna Torre

El Chaltén ☐

Laguna Torre ⛺5

Río de las Vueltas

Glaciar Grande

1000

National Park Office

Cerro Solo (2121m)

Parque Nacional Los Glaciares ◆

Río Fitz Roy

Loma del Pliegue Tumbado (1298m) 🌴 ▲

N

⛺6

Laguna Toro

1 km

1 miles

Camping ⛺
Capri 4
De Agostini 5

Laguna Toro 6
Piedra del Fraile 1
Poincenot 3

Río Blanco
(Climbers only) 2

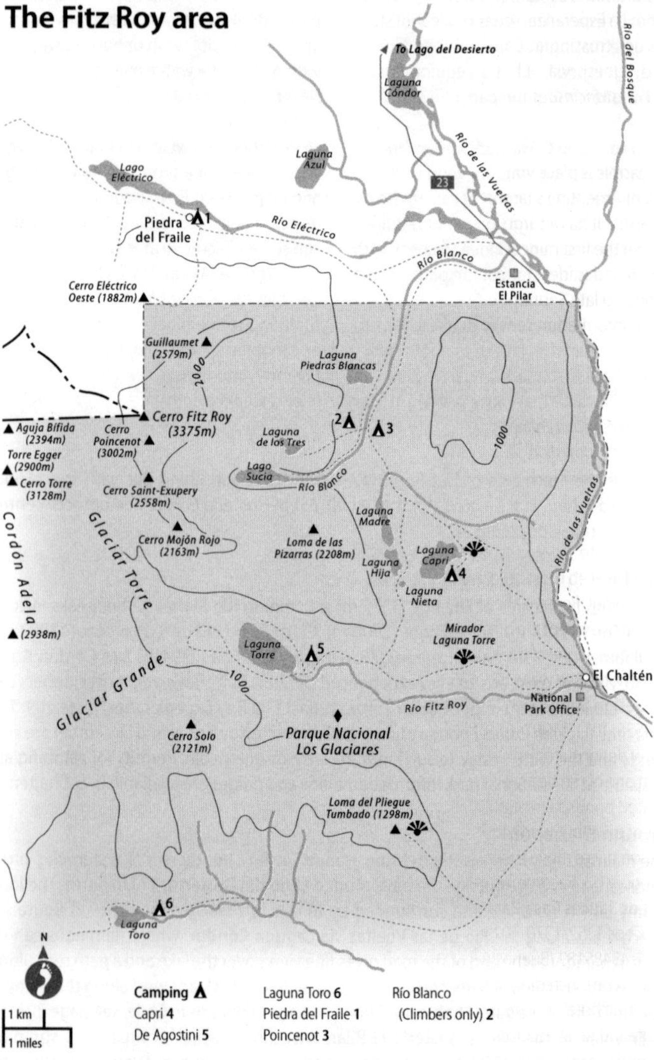

Towards Torres del Paine » p201-210.

From El Calafate

From El Calafate you can take the paved combination of Routes 11, 40 and 5 to **La Esperanza** (165 km), where there's fuel, a campsite and a large but expensive *confitería*. From La Esperanza, *ripio* Route 7 heads west along the valley of the Río Coyle towards the border crossing at Cancha Carrera. A shorter route (closed in winter) misses Esperanza and goes via El Cerrito direct to **Estancia Tapi Aike** ⓘ *T02966-420092, www.estanciasdesantacruz.com/TapiAike/tapiaike.htm.* » *See Transport, page 209.*

Río Turbio → *Colour map 3, A3.*

A charmless place you're most likely to visit en route to or from Torres del Paine in Chile. The site of Argentina's largest coalfield hasn't recovered from the recent depression hitting the industry. It has a cargo railway connecting it with Punta Loyola, and visitors can see Mina 1, where the first mine was opened. There's a small ski centre nearby, **Valdelén**, which has six pistes and is ideal for beginners; there's also scope for cross-country skiing between early June and late September. The **tourist office** is in the municipal building on San Martín. For more information see www.welcomeargentina.com/rioturbio.

Parque Nacional Los Glaciares listings

For Sleeping and Eating price codes and other relevant information, see pages 41-44.

Sleeping

El Calafate *p193, map p193*

From Dec-Feb most hotels are generally booked out. Reserve ahead of time. Low season (May-Sep) is a great time to find a great deal at one of the top hotels. For more hotels see www.todocalafate.com.

LL Design Suites, C 94 No 190, T02902-494525, T011-51997465 (Buenos Aires), www.designsuites.com. Large stylish hotel with one of the best views of Lago Argentino. Heated pool, spa treatments and gym. A little out of town but worth the short drive. Low season prices move this hotel down a category (**L**). Recommended.

LL Los Sauces Casa Patagónica, Los Gauchos 1352/1370, T02902-495854, T011-43485189 (Buenos Aires), www.casalossauces.com. Incredibly stylish and welcoming boutique hotel close to town. Attention to detail and great accommodation packages make this a hotel a must. Member of Small Luxury Hotels. Highly recommended.

L Kosten Aike, Gob Moyano 1243, T02902-492424, www.kostenaike.com.ar. A special place, relaxed and yet stylish with large elegant rooms, king-sized beds throughout, jacuzzi and gym. The restaurant **Ariskaiken** is open to non-residents and has an excellent chef; there's a cosy bar with a wood fire, and a garden. The staff are extremely attentive and speak English.

L Los Alamos, Gobernador Moyano and Bustillo, T02902-491144, www.posadalosalamos.com. Located in 2 separate chalet-style buildings, this is an extremely comfortable large hotel, with charming rooms, beautifully decorated and equipped, good service, lovely gardens, golf course and the best restaurant in town, **La Posta**. Recommended.

AL Blanca Patagonia, Parque Nacional Los Glaciares 149, T02902-493370, www.blancapatagonia.com. With only 13 rooms, this small *hostería* offers cabins for 2 and 4 people, as well as doubles. Fantastic views from the main building, as it is situated within the city heights. Recommended.

AL Patagonia Rebelde, José Haro 442, T02902-494495, www.patagoniarebelde.com. Charming building in traditional Patagonian style, resembling an old inn with its corrugated zinc walls and rustic decor, all looking pretty basic though offering good comfort with well-heated bedrooms and comfy sitting rooms.

A Michelangelo, Espora and Gobernador Moyano 1020, T02902-491045, www.michelangelohotel.com.ar. A lovely, quiet and welcoming place, modern and stylish in design, with a really excellent restaurant. The menu is innovative, and includes hare, steak and squid ink ravioli. All rooms have TV, bath and minibar, breakfast included. Excellent value. Recommended.

A Santa Mónica Apartments, Josefa Freile 42, T02902 491835, www.santamonicaaparts.com.ar. Located in the middle of town, just off the main street, this little collection of wooden cabins is perfect for couples or groups of up to 4 . Very convenient. Open all year.

B Ariel, Av del Libertador 1693, T02902-493131, www.hotelariel.com.ar. A modern functional place west of centre, very clean and well-maintained rooms with bath and TV. Breakfast included.

B Casa de Grillos, Los Condores 1215 corner of Las Bandurrias, T02902-491160, www.casadegrillos.com.ar. Marta and Alejandro are the welcoming hosts at this B&B situated in the calm green area, next to Nímez nature reserve. It has the comfort and charm of a family house.

E pp **Lago Azul 'B'**, Perito Moreno 83, T2902-491419. Cheapest in the area, this pioneer house with a couple of simple and spotless rooms to share is the most welcoming budget choice, with charming Mrs Echeverría and her husband offering traditional Patagonian hospitality. Recommended.

Camping

AMSA, Olavarría 65 (50 m off the main road, turn south at the fire station), T02902-492247, US$5 pp, hot water, security. Summer only.

There are 2 campsites in the park en route to Lago Roca: **El Huala**, 42 km from El Calafate, free with basic facilities, open all year; and **Lago Roca**, 50 km from El Calafate, T02902-499500. Beautifully set, with hot water, public phone, restaurant, bike hire, US$6 pp.

Hostels

E pp **Marcopolo Inn**, Calle 82 No 405, T02902-493899, www.hostel-inn.com. Discounts for HI members. Breakfast included. Double and triple rooms available (**B**).

E-F pp **Hostel del Glaciar 'Libertador'**, Av del Libertador 587 (next to the bridge on the access to town), T02902-491792, www.glaciar.com. Clean, modern and open almost all year (closed in Jun) with functional, well-heated rooms, private doubles or rooms to share among 4, all with own bath. Breakfast is only included in the high season rate for the private rooms; free transfer from bus station. Discounts to HI members. Recommended.

F pp **América del Sur**, Puerto Deseado153, T02902-493525, www.americahostel.com.ar. A short walk from the centre of town on a hilltop, each room in this hostel has uninterrupted lake views. Friendly staff and a no-shoes policy create a relaxed atmosphere.

F pp **Hostel del Glaciar 'Pioneros'**, Los Pioneros 251, T/F02902-491243, www.glaciar.com. Larger, older, a bit further from the centre and cheaper than its sister hostel **Libertador**, this long-established hostel is open only in high season (Oct-Mar), and offers a range of accommodation for all budgets: shared dorms for up to 4 people, **C** standard private doubles (also for 3 and 4) and **B** larger superior doubles, both with bath. They run **Patagonia Backpackers** agency with the **Alternative Glaciar Tour** (see page 208), and organize a booking service for **Navimag**, hotels and transport throughout Patagonia, and run free shuttle service from the bus terminal. Book well in advance.

F pp **I Keu Ken Hostel**, FM Pontoriero 171, T02902-495175, www.patagoniaikeuken.com.ar. Basic dorms, well-equipped kitchen, and fantastic views. 2 cabins (**B**) attractively decorated and great for a couple or group.

G pp **Hostel de las Manos**, Egidio Feruglio 59, T02902-492996, www.hosteldelasmanos.com.ar. Clean, comfortable private rooms and basic dorms (**F**) available at this welcoming hostel 6 blocks from the main street. Take a taxi from the bus station and they will reimburse you. Call first to arrange.

Around El Calafate *p195*

Estancias

LL Estancia Cristina, T02902-491133, www.estanciacristina.com. For many people, a visit to historical Estancia Cristina is the highlight of their trip. A boat leaves Puerto Bandera early in the morning and travels 2 hrs to the northernmost reaches of Lago Argentina, strewn with mighty icebergs, to see the Upsala glacier from the water. Then, having taken in the sheer size and unspoilt beauty, the boat continues to the remote estancia situated in isolation on the shores of the lake under a crown of mountains. Visit for the day to enjoy a real Patagonian *asado*, or better still, stay overnight in comfortable rooms with superb views. An overnight stay allows for a horse-riding trip, or an 4WD excursion to a viewpoint high above the Upsala glacier, with the still milky Prussian blue lake below, and fire-coloured rocks all around. From here hike down the staggering Cañón de los Fósiles, with your own private guide; it's mind-blowingly beautiful. Day trips cost from US$110, all included. Same owners as **Los Notros** and **Los Cerros** in El Chaltén, see below.

LL Hostería Alta Vista, 35 km west of El Calafate (on the way to Lago Roca-Ruta 15), T02902-499902, www.hosteriaaltavista.com.ar. Set within the land of Estancia Anita, the largest estancia in the area (74,000 ha) Alta Vista has all the facilities you could possibly need, and only 15 guests. Favoured by celebrities and politicians, the lovely house was built in the 1930s and mostly retains its original style. Full-board is possible with excellent cuisine and wines included. There are attractive walks and a great range of excursions all within the vast expanse of the ranch. Recommended.

LL Kau-Yatún, Estancia 25 de Mayo (10 blocks from town centre, east of Arroyo Calafate), T02902-491059, T011-47832930 (Buenos Aires), www.kauyatun.com. The easiest way to stay at an estancia, this is a very comfortable renovated main house of an old estancia, now on the outskirts of town, and surrounded by 4 ha of well-kept gardens, where vegetables are grown to serve in its 2 excellent restaurants. The welcoming hosts combine a homely feel with rustic decor, typical of a traditional Patagonian estancia. Either half board or all-inclusive programmes with excursions in the park included.

LL Los Notros (Experience Patagonia), Ruta 11, Km 76, frente al Glaciar Perito Moreno, T011-5277 8200, www.experience patagonia.com. An exclusive retreat by the lake with luxurious accommodation in spacious, well-designed rooms. The only option if you want to wake up to direct views of the Perito Moreno glacier. You can walk, hike, trek and ride horses. Expensive, but there are all-inclusive packages with free transfers to the glacier *pasarelas* included.

AL Estancia Nibepo Aike, in the far south of the park on the shores of Brazo Sur of Lago Argentino, T02966-436010 in Río Gallegos, www.nibepoaike.com.ar. A spectacular setting inside the national park, near the shores of the lake, the house has just 15 simple rooms, decorated with lovely old furniture, and there's a cosy sitting room. Lots of activities are possible in the park or the surrounding 12,800 ha. The premises are open for day visits too. Open Oct-Apr.

Camping

Bahía Escondida, 7 km east of the glacier. Facilities include fireplaces, hot showers and a shop. Crowded in summer, US$3 pp.
Correntoso, 10 km east of the glacier. An unmarked site with no facilities but a great location. No fires. US$3 pp.
Lago Roca, 50 km from El Calafate, T02902-499500. Beautifully set, with hot water, public phone, restaurant, bike hire, US$4 pp.

Cerro Fitz Roy *p197*

There are campsites in the park at **Poincenot**, **Capri** and **Laguna Toro**. **Río Blanco** is for climbers with prior permission. Campsites have no services but all have latrines, apart from Toro. A gas/alcohol stove is essential as fires are prohibited. See box, page 199.
Camping Piedra del Fraile, on Río Eléctrico, just north of the park boundary. Privately owned with *cabañas* and hot showers (**E** pp) as well as camping (US$6 pp).

El Chaltén *p197, map p198*

See www.elchalten.com for a full list. Most hotels close from Apr/May-Sep and Dec-Mar finding accommodation can be challenging. Book ahead.

LL Los Cerros (Experience Patagonia), Av San Martín, T011-5277 8200, www.experiencepatagonia.com. On a hill above the town, this large hotel is by far the most sophisticated choice. Stylish, yet informal, all rooms are very comfortable with impressive attention to detail. Half-board and all-inclusive packages with excursions available.
AL Hostería El Puma, Lionel Terray 212, T02962-493095, www.hosteriaelpuma.com.ar. The most desirable place in town, set a little apart, and with splendid views up the valley, a welcoming lounge with log fire and tasteful furnishings, spacious rooms and plush bathrooms. Transfers and breakfast included. Tours arranged through **Fitz Roy Expediciones**, see Activities and tours, page 209. Recommended.
AL Hostería Posada Lunajuim, Trevisán s/n, T/F02962-493047, www.elchalten.com lunajuim. Stylish, relaxed and welcoming with comfortable rooms (thick duvets on the beds) with bathrooms and a lovely big lounge with wood fire. Full breakfast included. Charming hosts. Recommended.
B-C Northofagus, Hensen s/n T02962-493087, www.elchalten.com/northofagus. A small cosy B&B, with simple double rooms with shared bath, including breakfast. Welcoming and good value.
C Hospedaje La Base, Lago de Desierto 97, T02962-493031. A friendly little place with basic en suite doubles or dorms for 3-4 (**E**). Tiny kitchen for guests to use, self-service breakfast included, and a great video lounge.

C Inlandsis, Lago del Desierto 480, T02962-493276, www.elchalten/inlandsis. This B&B has 8 cosy rooms, some with magnificent views. Quiet, clean and good value. Recommended.
C Mi Rincón, Cabo García 115, T02962-493099, www.mirincon-elchalten.com.ar. Simple, clean and inviting doubles and triples with a view of Fitz Roy. Good value.

Hostels

E pp **Albergue Patagonia**, San Martín 493, T/F02962-493019, www.elchalten.com/patagonia. HI-affiliated. The most appealing hostel. Cosy and friendly with rooms for 4-6, kitchen, video room, bike hire and laundry. Information and excursions available. Next door is their restaurant **Fuegia**.
E pp **Aylen-Aike**, Trevisan 125, T02962-493142, www.elchalten.com. Large, modern yellow building on one of the quieter streets, has friendly staff. 4- or 10-bed dorms. Closed late-Apr to Oct.
E pp **Cóndor de los Andes**, Av Río de las Vueltas y Halvorsen, T02962-493101, www.condordelosandes.com. Friendly, small and modern, with nice little rooms for 4-6 or en suite doubles, sheets included, breakfast extra. Washing service, library, kitchen facilities. Quiet atmosphere. HI-discount. Recommended. Closed mid-Apr to Sep.
E pp **Pioneros de Valle**, San Martín 451, T02962-493079. Central, large new hostel with basic, clean but slightly cramped dorms and a modern kitchen.

Around El Chaltén *p199*

There is a campsite at the southern end of Lago del Desierto and *refugios* at its northern end and at Laguna Diablo.
L Estancia La Quinta, on Ruta 23, 2 km south of El Chaltén, T02962-493012, www.estancialaquinta.com.ar. Oct-Apr. A spacious pioneer house with renovated rooms and beautiful gardens. A superb breakfast is included and the restaurant is open for lunch and dinner. Free transfer to/from El Chaltén bus terminal.
L-AL Hostería El Pilar, on Ruta 23, Km 17, T/F02962-493002, www.hosteriaelpilar.com.ar. A special place to stay a little way out of town on the road to Lago del Desierto. This simple country house, in a spectacular setting with views of Fitz Roy, offers the chance to access less visited parts of the park. Spacious rooms and great food. Tailor-made trekking tours. Recommended.
AL Estancia Lago del Desierto, Punto Sur, southern tip of Lago del Desierto, T02962-493010. Basic place with *cabañas* for 5, camping US$5 pp, hot showers, kitchen. Recommended.

Towards Torres del Paine *p201*

In La Esperanza, **Restaurant La Esperanza** has bunk beds, with bath. There are also 6-person *cabañas* at the YPF service station.
C De La Frontera, 4 km from Río Turbio, Paraje Mina 1, T02962-421979. The most frequently recommended option.
D Hostería Capipe, Dufour, 9 km from town, T02902-482930, www.hosteriacapipe.com.ar. Simple rooms with bath, friendly. Restaurant.

Eating

El Calafate *p193, map p193*

TTT Casimiro Biguá, Av del Libertador 963, T02902-492590. A popular upmarket place with quality food, including the excellent stew *cazuela de cordero*.
TTT El Puesto, Gobernador Moyano y 9 de Julio, T02902-491620. Tasty thin-crust pizzas in a cosy old house. Also pricier regional meals and takeaway service. Recommended
TTT Pascasio, 25 de Mayo 52, T02902-492055. Cosy, exclusive and a very good spot for romantic dinners.
TT La Cocina, Av del Libertador 1245, T02902-491758. Pizzeria, a large variety of pancakes, pasta, salads, in cosy warm atmosphere. Good wine list.
TT La Tablita, Coronel Rosales 28 (near the bridge), T02902-491065. The best place for a *parrilla* with generous portions and quality beef.

Mi Viejo, Av del Libertador 1111, T02902-491691. Popular *parrilla*, try the grilled lamb for US$9.

Punto de Encuentro, Los Pioneros 251 (at **Hostel del Glaciar 'Pioneros'**). Ideal for meeting fellow travellers over creative meals that include veggie options.

Pura Vida, Av del Libertador 1876. Recommended for a relaxed place to eat well, with comfortable sofas, home-made Argentine food, lots of veggie options, and a lovely warm atmosphere with lake view.

Viva la Pepa, Emilio Amado 833, T02902-491880. Mainly vegetarian café with great sandwiches and crêpes with special fillings. Closed Wed.

Casablanca, Av del Libertador and 25 de Mayo, T02902-491402. A welcoming place, serving omelettes, hamburgers and vegetarian food, US$11 for steak and chips.

Rick's Café, Av del Libertador 1091, T02902-492148. A lively, packed place with good atmosphere and cheapish food. *Parrilla tenedor libre* for US$15.

El Chaltén *p197, map p198*

Los Cerros, Hotel Los Cerros T02962-493182. Top cuisine in sophisticated surroundings, where regional meals such as *puchero patagónico* and *carbonada de liebre* sit well next to more international fare. The wine list includes produce from the best *bodegas*.

Ahonikenk Chaltén, Güemes 23, T02962-493070. Centrally located small café with large portions of pizza and pasta.

El Muro, San Martín 948, T02962-493248. Inviting restaurant/bar serving pasta, pizza, and home-made beers. Strangely there is a climbing wall to practice on – before you try the beer.

Estepa, Cerro Solo and Antonio Rojo. Small, intimate place with a varied menu that includes excellent lamb, selected wines and imaginative vegetarian options. Open from 1500. Closed Mon.

Fuegia, San Martín, T02962-493243. The usual international menu in a warm atmosphere, plus some Patagonian dishes as well as curries and veggie food. Great breakfast menu, served until 1430 in high season.

Josh Aike, Lago del Desierto 105. Excellent *confitería*, delicious home-made food, in a beautiful building. Recommended.

Pangea, Lago del Desierto and San Martín, T02962-493084. Open for lunch and dinner, drinks and coffee, in comfortable surroundings with good music, a varied menu, from pastas to steak, trout and pizzas. Recommended.

Patagonicus, Güemes and Madsen, T02962-493025. A lovely, cosy, stylish place with salads, home-made pastas and the best pizzas. Great family photos of mountain climbers on the walls. Open from 1200-2400. Recommended.

Terray, Lionel Terray 212, **Hostería El Puma**, T02962-493095. Climbers, trekkers and other visitors chat about their expeditions, over excellent food in a homely atmosphere.

Bars and nightclubs

El Calafate *p193, map p193*

Borges y Alvarez, Av del Libertador 1015, Galería de los Gnomos. T02902-491464. Cosy wooden, 1st-floor bar with huge windows over the shopping street below. Affordable, and delicious lunch and dinner options, as well as live music, and books for sale. A must.

Elba'r, 9 de Julio 57, T02902-493594. Just off the main street, this café/bar serves hard-to-find waffles, and juices as well as home-made beer and sandwiches.

Shackleton Lounge, Av del Libertador 3287, T02902-493516. On the outskirts of town (US$2.50 in taxi). A great place to relax, lovely views of the lake, old photos of Shackleton, great atmosphere, good music. Highly recommended for a late drink or some good regional dishes. Afternoon tea served.

El Chaltén *p197, map p198*

El Bodegón Cervecería, San Martín 724. Packed-out café/bar serving home-brewed beers from their own microbrewery, as well as great vegetarian pizzas, sandwiches and

soups. The wooden interior creates a homely feel.
Elal Resto-bar, Lago del Desierto 410, T02962-493106. Open every night, live shows attract large crowds in summer, and they follow up a good night by serving a great breakfast. Open 0730-2400.

Festivals

El Calafate *p193, map p193*

15 Feb People flock to the rural show **Lago Argentino Day**, and camp out with live music, dancing and *asados*.
10 Nov Displays of horsemanship and *asados* on **Día de la Tradición**.

Shopping

El Calafate *p193, map p193*

All along Libertador there are souvenir shops selling hats and gloves for those chilly boat rides to the glacier. There are lots of fine-quality handicrafts; look out for Mapuche weavings and woollen items. Handicraft stalls are on Libertador at around 1200.
Abranpampa, Libertador 1341, T02902-491697. Clothing, and camping gear rentals from backpacks, to tents to cookers.
Ferretería Chuar, a block away from the bus terminal. The only place selling white gas for camping and camping supplies.
La Anónima, Av del Libertador and Perito Moreno. Supermarket.

El Chaltén *p197, map p198*

Camping Center, San Martín, T02962-493264. Buy or rent equipment for climbing, trekking and camping.
El Gringuito, Av San Martín. The best of many supermarkets. All are expensive and have little fresh food. Fuel is available.
El Súper, Lago del Desierto and Av Güemes, T02902-493039. A supermarket that also rents and sells camping and climbing equipment, maps, postcards, books and handicrafts.
Eolia Rental & Outdoor Shop, San Martín and Fonruge, T02962-493066. Equipment hire, advice on personalized APN-certified guides. These guys know their stuff when it comes to ice and rock climbing and glacier trekking.
Viento Oeste, Av San Martín s/n (northern end of town), T02962-493021. Equipment hire such as tents and sleeping bags. Also arranges mountain guides and sells handicrafts.

Activities and tours

El Calafate *p193, map p193*

Ballooning

Hotel Kau Yatun, T02902-491059, www.kauyatun.com. Organizes balloon trips over El Calafate and Lago Argentino, weather permitting, US$150 per hr for group of 7.

Birdwatching

Cecilia Scarafoni, T02902-493196, ecowalks@cotecal.com.ar. Expert-led birdwatching walks to Laguna Niménez, lasting 2 hrs, US$6, Mon-Sat.

Boat trips

Boat trips are also run by **Hielo y Aventura**, see Ice trekking, below.
Fernández Campbell, Av del Libertador 867, T02902-491298, www.solopatagonia.com.ar. The main operator for trips on Lago Argentino to the Perito Moreno and Upsala glaciers.
Mar Patag, www.crucerosmarpatag.com or call T02902-492118 or T011-50310756 in Buenos Aires. Run the *Spirit of the Glaciers* luxurious boat trip, a recommendable 2-day exclusive experience for viewing Moreno, Upsala and Spegazzini glaciers (US$365 pp, full board).

Fishing

Calafate Fishing, C Espora 33, T02902-496545, 9 de Julio 29, T02902-493311, www.calafatefishing.com. From half-day excursions to 3-day expeditions.

Ice trekking

Always Glaciers, Gobernador Moyano 1226, T02902-492450, www.alwaysglaciers.com. Prolific agency which offers tours in the area. Their speciality is the packages they offer combining several tours in one. HI card-holders receive a discount.

Hielo y Aventura, Av del Libertador 935, T02902-492205, www.hieloyaventura.com. *Safari Náutico* 1-hr boat trip for viewing Moreno glacier from the south side, leaves from Bajo de las Sombras pier, US$9 (tickets also sold at the pier); *Brazo Sur* boat trip, the same as Safari plus a landing to give you the chance to see more glaciers, US$32; the famous *minitrekking*, with 90 mins on the glacier with crampons, US$88, and *Big Ice*, a much longer walk on ice in the same area of the minitrekking, US$119. Recommended. Note that people under 18 and over 45 are not permitted to attempt the ice trekking.

Horse riding

Cabalgata en Patagonia, Av del Libertador 3600, T02902-493203, www.cabalgata enpatagonia.com . For 2-hr rides (US$25 pp) or 6-hr excursions (US$45 pp, lunch included) to see the Gualicho cave paintings by the lake.

Mountain bikes

On Rent a Car, Av del Libertador 1831, T02902-493788, www.onrentacar.com.ar. US$21 per day.

Offroading

Mil Outdoor Adventure, Av del Libertador 1029, T02902-491437, www.miloutdoor.com. Exciting excursions in 4WD to see wild places with wonderful views, 3-6 hrs, US$42-70.

Rafting

Nonthue Aventura, Libertador 1177, T02902-491179. Rafting on the Río Santa Cruz, 4-5 hrs, US$41 with transport.

Tour operators

Most agencies charge the same rates for excursions: to the Perito Moreno Glacier US$21; to Lago Roca, a full-day including lunch at Estancia Anita, US$30; horse riding to Gualichó caves, 2 hrs, US$21.

Chaltén Travel, Av del Libertador 1174, T2902-492212, www.chaltentravel.com. The most helpful, with a huge range of tours: glaciers, estancias, trekking, and trips to El Chaltén with a visit to Torres del Paine, US$69; also sells tickets along Ruta 40 to Los Antiguos. English spoken. Highly recommended.

Lago San Martín, Av del Libertador 1215, 1st floor, T02902-492858, www.lagosanmartin.com. Specializes in reservations to estancias in Santa Cruz province, very helpful.

Leutz Turismo, Av del Libertador 1341, T02902-492316, www.leutzturismo.com.ar. Daily excursion to Lago Roca 1000-1800, US$36 pp, plus US$18 for optional lunch at Estancia Nibepo Aike, and an interesting tour of the sheep and fruit estancia **Quien Sabe**, with a traditional *cordero asado* for dinner.

Patagonia Backpackers, at Hostels del Glaciar, Los Pioneros 251 or Av del Libertador 587, T/F2902-491243, www.glaciar.com. Offers the 'Alternative Tour to Moreno Glacier'. Highly recommended, it includes lots of information on the landscape and wildlife, followed by the boat trip, to see it up close, US$40. Other trips include 'Supertrekking en Chaltén', a 2-day hiking trip, featuring the best treks in the Fitz Roy massif, including camping and ice trekking; and a 2-day visit to Torres del Paine, including camping and trekking (US$190). They also sell tickets for the Navimag ferries in the Chilean fjords. Highly recommended.

El Chaltén *p197, map p198*

Boat trips

Patagonia Aventura, San Martín 56 , T02962-493110 www.patagonia-aventura. com.ar. Boat trips along Lago Viedma to see the Glaciar Viedma, informative; transfers US$12 extra. Also a good full day's trip along Lago Viedma, with ice trekking on Glaciar Viedma. They also operate Lago del Desierto crossings, US$18 pp.

Tour operators and trekking guides

Fitz Roy Expediciones, Lionel Terray 212 (next to **Hostería El Puma**), T02962-493017, www.fitzroyexpediciones.com.ar. The best and most experienced company with excellent guides. Trekking, rock climbing and ice-climbing courses, adventure expeditions, including 2-day ascents of Cerro Solo (2121 m), 3-day trekking crossing from Lago Viedma to Lago San Martín, and 8-day trekking expeditions on the Campo de Hielo. Also organizes superb kayaking down the Río de las Vueltas from its wonderful adventure camp, the FRAC, on the way to Lago del Desierto. Great *asados*, hiking, biking, and guides on hand too. Highly recommended.

Transport

El Calafate *p193, map p193*

Air

Aerolíneas Argentinas, 9 de Julio 57, T02902-492814, flies daily to/from **Buenos Aires**, with many more flights in summer. LADE, Julio Roca 1004, at the bus station, T02902-491262) flies twice a week to **Río Gallegos**, **Comodoro Rivadavia**, **Esquel** and **Bariloche**. To **Puerto Natales**, Aerovías Dap, www.aeroviasdap.cl, daily, Nov-Mar only. Airport charge for departing passengers US$6.

Bus

The terminal is on Roca, 1 block up steep stairs from Libertador.

Long-distance To **Ushuaia** take a bus to Río Gallegos; (the **Taqsa** 0300 is the best connection). To **Río Gallegos**, daily with **Interlagos**, T02902-491179, **Sportman**, T02902-492680, and **Taqsa**, 4 hrs, US$8-11. To **El Chaltén**, daily with **Cal-Tur**, **Chaltén Travel**, T02902-491833, and **Taqsa**, 4-4½ hrs, US$16-18. To **Perito Moreno glacier**, daily with **Cal-Tur**, T02902-491842, 1½ hrs, US$12. **Taqsa**, T02902-491843, goes only in summer. To **Perito Moreno** and **Los Antiguos**, contact **Chaltén Travel**. To **Bariloche** along Ruta 40 with **Overland Patagonia**, www.overlandpatagonia.com, 4 days via the Perito Moreno national park, Cueva de las Manos, Estancia Melike, Río Mayo and Fitz Roy, US$96 plus accommodation at US$6 per day; bookings in El Calafate from **Patagonia Backpackers** (Hostels del Glaciar), T02902-491243, www.glaciar.com.

To Chile To **Puerto Natales**, daily with either **Cootra** T02902-491444, or **Bus Sur** T02902-491631, US$18, advance booking recommended. **Bus Sur** (Tue, Sat 0800) and **Zaahj** (Wed, Fri, Sun 0800) also run to Puerto Natales via **Cerro Castillo**, where you can pick up a bus to **Torres del Paine** in summer. Take your passport when booking tickets to Chile.

Car hire

Adventure Rent a Car, Av del Libertador 290, T02902-492595, www.adventurerentcar.com **On Rent a Car**, Av del Libertador 1831, T02902-493788, www.onrentacar.com.ar . Average US$55 per day for a small car including insurance.

Taxi

To **Río Gallegos**, 4 hrs, US$110 irrespective of number of passengers, up to 5 people.

Perito Moreno glacier *p195*

The cheapest way to get to the glacier is on the regular daily **bus** services run by **Taqsa** T02902-491843, and **Cal-Tur** T02902-491842, to the car park above the walkways. Many agencies in El Calafate (see Activities and tours) also run minibus **tours** (park entry not included) leaving 0800 and returning 1800, giving you 3 hrs at the glacier; the return ticket is also valid if you come back next day (student discount available). **Patagonia Backpackers** run an extended alternative itinerary. **Boat** trips for up to 60 passengers are run by **Fernández Campbell** (see Activities and tours). 'Safari Náutico' offers the best views, US$12 pp, 1 hr. Boats leave from the tourist pier signposted from the car park in Parque Nacional Los Glaciares, bus travel is included. Out of season, trips to the glacier are difficult to arrange, but you can gather a party and hire a **taxi** (*remise* T02902-491745/ 492005). These will charge US$50 for 4 passengers, round trip.

Upsala glacier *p196*

Tour boats usually run daily. The main operator is **Fernández Campbell** (see Activities and tours) who charges US$25, including transfer bus and park entry fees. The bus departs at 0730 from El Calafate for Punta Bandera, with time allowed for lunch at the restaurant (not included, so take your own food) near the Lago Onelli track. The return bus to El Calafate is at 1930. A more expensive but also more spectacular trip is offered by **Estancia Cristina**, see page 203.

El Chaltén *p197, map p198*

Bus

In summer, buses fill quickly, so book ahead. The following are high-season services; they are less frequent in winter. Daily buses to **El Calafate**, 4-4½ hrs, US$16-18 one way: run by **Chaltén Travel**, San Martín 635 (at Albergue Rancho Grande), T02902-493005, www.chaltentravel.com, **Cal-Tur**, San Martín 520 (at Fitz Roy Inn), T02902-493062, and **Taqsa**, Av Güemes 68, T02902-493068. To **Los Antiguos** along the RN 40, **Itinerarios y Travesías**, T002902-493088 overnight, even dates (ie 2nd, 4th, 6th), includes trip to Cueva de las Manos in the early morning. **Chaltén Travel** runs a service Nov-Mar, leaving on odd dates to go along RN 40 up to Bariloche, with a stopover at the small town of Perito Moreno, US$114 transport only.

Overland Patagonia does trips to **Bariloche** in 4 days, staying at estancias and visiting Cueva de las Manos.

Río Turbio *p201*

Bus

To **Puerto Natales**, 1 hr, US$3.50, several daily with: **Cootra**, Tte del Castillo 01, T02902-421448. **Bus Sur**, Baquedano 534, Pto Natales, T+56(0)61-411859, www.turismozaahj.co.cl. **Lagoper**, Av de Los Mineros 262, T02902-411831, **El Pingüino**. To El Calafate, Cootra, Taqsa, daily, US$14, 4½ hrs. To **Río Gallegos**, Taqsa, www.taqsa.com.ar, daily, 4 hrs, US$11. **Taqsa** also run a year-round service from El Calafate, via El Chaltén (weather permitting) to **Bariloche** stopping at **Perito Moreno**, **Los Antiguos**, **Esquel** and **El Bolsón**. It is long, and the bus is basic, but it is a great way to see the famous Ruta 40. Bring your own food. US$90, 28 hrs. An alternative route to **Bariloche** via the coast which is cheaper and takes less time is offered by **Las Lengas**, Viedma 95, T02962-493023, laslengasel chalten@yahoo.com.ar. Unlike most companies, instead of transiting through El Calafate and then Río Gallegos on the way to Bariloche, the bus travels directly through **Piedra Buena** to the north (5 hrs, US$30) with connections to Bariloche and **Puerto Madryn**. Only in high season.

Directory

El Calafate *p193, map p193*

Banks Best to take cash as high commission is charged on exchange. Plenty of ATMs. Change money at **Thaler**, 9 de Julio 57, www.cambio-thaler.com. **Post office** Av del Libertador 1133. **Telephone** Open Calafate, Libertador 996, huge *locutorio* for phones and internet. **Centro Integral de Comunicaciones**, Av del Libertador 1486, is cheaper.

El Chaltén *p197, map p198*

Banks There are no banks or ATMs in El Chaltén, and you will have a hard time trying to change a TC or paying with credit card. So bring ready cash. **Internet** There is internet available at **Rancho Grande**, San Martín 724. Open late. **Telephone** There are also 3 *locutorios* with phones, and internet on Av Güemes at the entrance to the town. There is no cellular phone coverage here, and you will find the internet excruciatingly slow.

Santiago

Contents

Footprint features

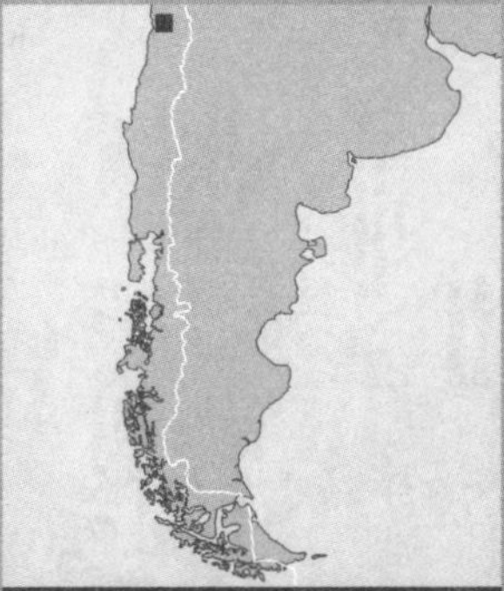

At a glance

Getting around The efficient metro system is easier to use than the local bus network. Otherwise take taxis and provincial buses.

Time required 2 days to acclimatize. The highlights of your trip lie further south!

Weather Warm days and cool nights. Dry season Oct-Apr.

When not to go Jan can be on the hot side, while smog can be a problem in winter (Jun-Aug).

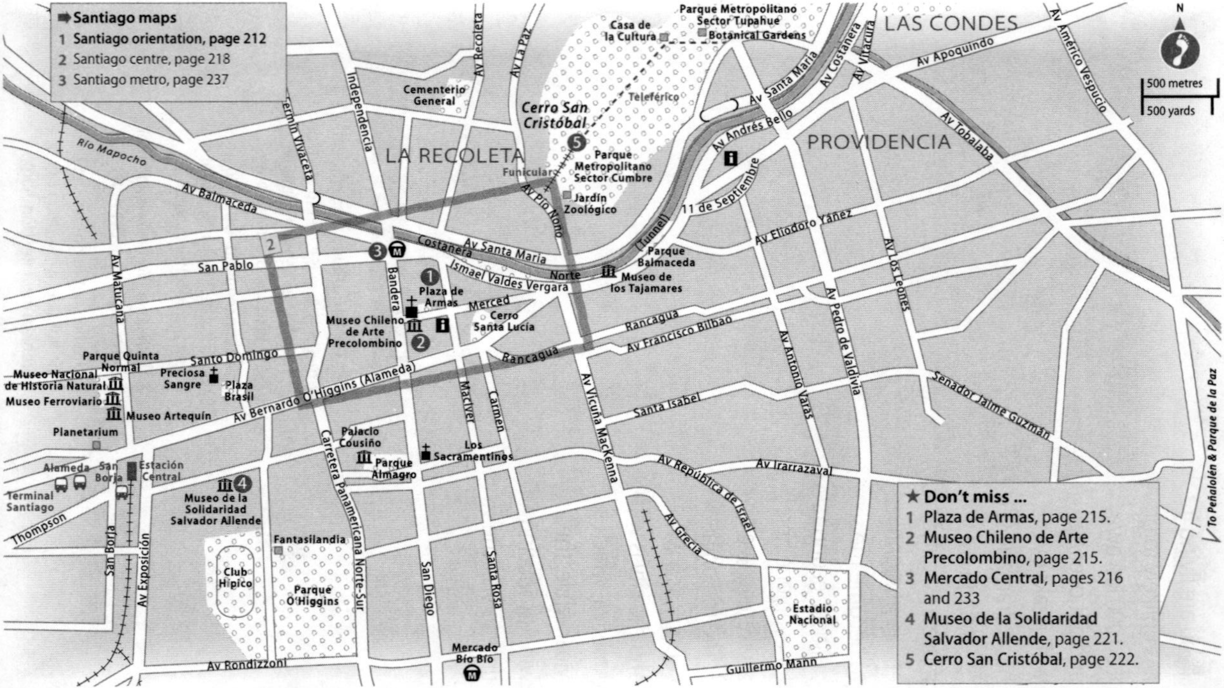
Santiago maps
1 Santiago orientation, page 212
2 Santiago centre, page 218
3 Santiago metro, page 237
LAS CONDES
PROVIDENCIA
LA RECOLETA
Cerro San Cristóbal
Parque Metropolitano Sector Tupahue
Casa de la Cultura
Botanical Gardens
Teleférico
Funicular
Parque Metropolitano Sector Cumbre
Jardín Zoológico
Cementerio General
Parque Balmaceda
Museo de los Tajamares
Plaza de Armas
Museo Chileno de Arte Precolombino
Cerro Santa Lucía
Parque Quinta Normal
Museo Nacional de Historia Natural
Museo Ferroviario
Museo Artequín
Planetarium
Preciosa Sangre
Plaza Brasil
Palacio Cousiño
Parque Almagro
Los Sacramentinos
Alameda
San Borja
Estación Central
Terminal Santiago
Museo de la Solidaridad Salvador Allende
Fantasilandia
Club Hípico
Parque O'Higgins
Mercado Bío Bío
Estadio Nacional
Río Mapocho
Av Balmaceda
Fermín Vivaceta
Independencia
Av Recoleta
Av La Paz
Av Pío Nono
Av Santa María
Costanera
Av Andrés Bello
Av Costanera
Av Vitacura
Av Apoquindo
Av Américo Vespucio
Av Tobalaba
11 de Septiembre
(Tunnel)
Av Eliodoro Yáñez
Av Los Leones
Av Pedro de Valdivia
Av Antonio Varas
Senador Jaime Guzmán
Av Irarrazaval
Av República de Israel
Av Grecia
Guillermo Mann
Av Vicuña MacKenna
Santa Isabel
Rancagua
Av Francisco Bilbao
Norte
Ismael Valdes Vergara
Merced
San Pablo
Santo Domingo
Av Bernardo O'Higgins (Alameda)
Bandera
MacIver
Carmen
Santa Rosa
San Diego
Carretera Panamericana Norte-Sur
Av Matucana
Av Exposición
San Borja
Thompson
Av Rondizzoni
To Peñalolén & Parque de la Paz
N
500 metres
500 yards
Don't miss ...
1 Plaza de Armas, page 215.
2 Museo Chileno de Arte Precolombino, page 215.
3 Mercado Central, pages 216 and 233
4 Museo de la Solidaridad Salvador Allende, page 221.
5 Cerro San Cristóbal, page 222.

If you are flying into Chile, you will probably arrive in Santiago. It is unlikely to prove a highlight of your Patagonian adventures – it's 1000 km away for a start – but it's a good place to acclimatize and get over any jet lag. In a hollow surrounded by mountains with peaks over 5000 m, no one can deny that the Chilean capital has a dramatic setting.

Santiago is a vibrant, progressive city. Its many parks, excellent museums, glittering high-rises and boutiques, not to mention ebullient nightlife, burst with possibilities. Santiago has grown to become the sixth largest city in South America, as well as the political, economic and cultural capital of Chile. But life isn't easy for everyone here. Many people, particularly those originally from rural areas, live in appalling *villas miserias* on the city's outskirts.

The region near the capital can be seen as a microcosm of the country as a whole. Coastal resorts are less than two hours away, and the city is within easy reach of the best ski resorts in South America, which are great spots for weekend hikes in summer. Meanwhile, the area south of Santiago is perhaps the best wine-producing area in Chile. Autumn is a particularly good time to visit the vineyards.

Ins and outs

Getting there

Air International and domestic flights use **Aeropuerto Arturo Merino Benítez** ⓘ *Pudahuel, 26 km northwest of centre, T02-6901900, flight information T02-6763149, www.aeropeurtosantiago.cl.* It is a modern, safe and efficient terminal, with banks and ATMs, fast-food outlets, tourist information with an accommodation booking service, a *casa de cambio* and car hire offices. Left luggage is US$8 per item per day. Frequent bus services between the airport and the city centre are operated by **TurBus** ⓘ *every 30 mins, US$3*, and **Centropuerto** ⓘ *T02-6019883, every 15 mins, 0600-2230, US$2.50.* All airport buses stop at the new terminal at Metro Pajaritos, where buses also leave for the coast. En route to the airport, buses also pick up at Estación Central and Terminal Santiago. Minibus services between the airport and hotels or other addresses in the city (US$10 per person to/from the city centre, US$12 to/from Las Condes) are operated by **Transfer** ⓘ *T02-7777707*, **Delfos** ⓘ *T02-6010590, www.transferdelfos.cl*, and **Trans Vip**, ⓘ *T02-677 3000, www.transvip.cl*, and should be booked the previous day. Taxis to/from centre cost around US$20, to/from Providencia US$25; agree the fare beforehand. There is a taxi office inside the international terminal. » *For flights, see Essentials, pages 34 and 36.*

Bus and train Intercity buses arrive at one of four terminals, all located close to each other, just west of the centre and not far from the train station, along Avenida Libertador Bernardo O'Higgins. This is the main east-west avenue through the city and within easy reach of line 1 of the metro. » *For information on long-distance services, see Essentials, page 37.*

Getting around

The city's main avenue, O'Higgins, is almost always referred to as the Alameda, and Plaza Baquedano is known as Plaza Italia (this book follows suit). Although parts of the centre can be explored on foot, you will need to master the city's fast but crowded metro system. Buses, known as micros, also ply the city's streets but these can be confusing for foreign visitors and are slow during peak periods. It is not advisable to hail taxis on the street for night-time journeys. There is a new east-west motorway running under the city cutting travelling times by car enormously. An automatic toll is charged (cars must have a radio receiver fitted) but these are generally included in the hire price of a car. » *See metro map, page 237.*

Tourist information

Municipal Tourist Board ⓘ *Casa Colorada, Merced 860, metro Plaza de Armas, T02-6327783, www.munistgo.cl/colorada, also at Cerro Santa Lucía, T02-6644216, santalucia@munistgo.cl.* **Sernatur (Servicio Nacional de Turismo)** ⓘ *Av Providencia 1550, metro Manuel Montt, T02-7318336, www.sernatur.cl, Mon-Fri 0845-1830, Sat 0900-1400.* The national tourist board has maps, brochures and posters. English, German and some French are spoken. Many tourist offices in small towns in Patagonia are closed in winter, so stock up on information here. **Sernatur** also have a basic **information office at the airport** ⓘ *daily 0900-2100.*

Background

Santiago was founded by Pedro de Valdivia in 1541 on the site of a small indigenous settlement between the southern bank of the Río Mapocho and the Cerro Santa Lucía. During the colonial period, it was one of several Spanish administrative and cultural centres. Much of the fledgling city was destroyed by two earthquakes in 1647 and 1730

Playing it safe

Like all large cities, Santiago has problems of theft. Pickpockets and bag snatchers operate in the central area, mostly on the metro, around the Plaza de Armas, in Barrio Brasil, near Cerro Santa Lucía and around the restaurants in Bellavista, and can easily be avoided with common sense. The biggest risk is in unwittingly entering a dangerous *barrio* away from the centre; avoid Pudahuel in the west, Conchalí in the north and Macul and La Pintana in the south. At night, take a public bus (*micro*) for safety in numbers or call for a radio taxi.

but following Independence, Santiago became more significant. In the 1870s, under Benjamín Vicuña MacKenna, an urban plan was drafted, the Cerro Santa Lucía was made into a public park and the first trams were introduced. As the city grew at the end of the 19th century, the Chilean elite built their mansions west of the centre around Calle Dieciocho. The spread of the city east towards Providencia began in 1895. In the latter part of the 20th century, Santiago grew rapidly as affluent residents moved east into new neighbourhoods in the foothills of the Andes and poorer neighbourhoods were established to the west of the centre.

Sights

The centre of the old city lies between the Río Mapocho and the city's main avenue, Alameda. From Plaza Italia, in the east of the city's central area, the river flows to the northwest and the Alameda runs to the southwest. From Plaza Italia, Calle Merced runs due west to the Plaza de Armas, the heart of the city, which lies five blocks south of the Río Mapocho. ▸▸ *For listings, see pages 224-238.*

Plaza de Armas and around

On the eastern and southern sides of the Plaza de Armas, there are arcades with shops and cheap restaurants; on the northern side is the post office and the Municipalidad; and on the western side the cathedral and the archbishop's palace. The **cathedral**, much rebuilt, contains a recumbent statue in wood of San Francisco Javier and the chandelier that lit the first meetings of Congress after Independence; it also houses a museum of religious art and historical pieces. In the Palacio de la Real Audiencia is the **Museo Histórico Nacional** ⓘ *Plaza de Armas 951, T02-4117000, www.museohistoriconacional.cl, Tue-Sun 1000-1730, US$1, free on Sun*, which covers the period from the Conquest until 1925 and contains a model of colonial Santiago.

Around the plaza

Southwest of the cathedral are the courts and **Museo Chileno de Arte Precolombino** ⓘ *Bandera 361, www.precolombino.cl, Tue-Sun 1000-1800, US$6*. Housed in the former Real Aduana, this is one of the best museums in Chile with an excellent representative exhibition of objects from the pre-Columbian cultures of Central America and the Andean region. Displays are well labelled in English. Two blocks west is **Palacio de la Alhambra** ⓘ *Compañía 1340, T02-6890875, www.snba.cl, Mon-Fri 1100-1300, 1700-1930*, a national monument, with art exhibitions and a permanent display.

Just east of the Plaza de Armas is the Casa Colorada. Built in 1769, it was the home of the governor in colonial days and then of Mateo de Toro, first president of Chile. It now holds the **Museo de Santiago** ⓘ *Merced 860, T02-6330723, Tue-Sat 1000-1800, Sun and holidays 1100-1400, US$3, students free*, which covers the history of Santiago from the Conquest to modern times with excellent displays, models and guided tours.

From the Plaza de Armas, Paseo Ahumada runs south to the Alameda, four blocks away. **Ahumada** is a pedestrianized street and the commercial heart of the centre. Ahumada and nearby **Calle Huérfanos** are always interesting places to come for a stroll, especially at night, when those selling pirated CDs or playing the three-card trick mix with evangelist preachers and satanists.

Four blocks north of the Plaza de Armas is the interesting **Mercado Central** ⓘ *Av 21 de Mayo y San Pablo*. This is the best place to come for seafood in Santiago and is so prominent in the Chilean psyche that it was the setting for a recent national soap opera, *Amores del Mercado*. The building faces the **Parque Venezuela**, on which is the Cal y Canto metro station on Line 2; at its western end, the former Mapocho railway station is now a cultural centre and concert venue, www.estacionmapocho.cl. If you head east from Mapocho station, along the river, you arrive at the **Parque Forestal**. The **Museo Nacional de Bellas Artes** ⓘ *www.mnba.cl, Tue-Sun 1000-1900, US$1.20*, is located in the wooded grounds and is an extraordinary example of neoclassical architecture, inspired by the Petit Palais in Paris. Inside is a large display of Chilean and foreign painting and sculpture; contemporary art exhibitions are held several times a year. In the west wing is the **Museo de Arte Contemporáneo** ⓘ *www.mac.uchile.cl, US$1.20, Bellas Artes metro.*

Alameda and around

The Alameda runs through the heart of the city for over 3 km. It is 100 m wide, choked full of *micros*, taxis and cars day and night and ornamented with gardens and statuary.

At the eastern end of the Alameda is **Plaza Italia**, where there is a statue of General Baquedano and the Tomb of the Unknown Soldier. Four blocks south is the **Museo Nacional Benjamín Vicuña MacKenna** ⓘ *Av V MacKenna 94, www.dibam.cl/subdirec_museos/mbm_mackenna, Mon-Sat 0930-1300, 1400-1750, US$1.20*, which records the life and works of the 19th-century Chilean historian and biographer who became one of Santiago's most important mayors. It also has occasional exhibitions.

Between the Parque Forestal, Plaza Italia and the Alameda is the **Lastarria** neighbourhood (Universidad Católica metro). For those interested in antique furniture, pieces of art and old books, the area is worth a visit, especially the **Plaza Mulato Gil de Castro** (Calle Lastarria 305). Occasional shows are put on in the plaza, and surrounding it are restaurants, bookshops, handicraft and antique shops, an art gallery, the **Instituto de Arte Contemporáneo** and the **Museo de Artes Visuales** ⓘ *Lastarria 307, T02-6383502, www.mavi.cl, Tue-Sun 1030-1830, US$2, free on Sun*. The museum also houses the the **Museo Arqueológico de Santiago** with temporary exhibitions of Chilean archaeology, anthropology and pre-Columbian art.

Heading west from here, the Alameda skirts **Cerro Santa Lucía**, a cone of rock rising steeply to a height of 70 m. It can be scaled from the Caupolicán esplanade, but the ascent from the northern side of the hill – wit h its statue of Diego de Almagro – is easier. On clear days you can see across to the Andes from the top and even when it is smoggy the sunset is good. There is a fortress, the **Batería Hidalgo** (closed to visitors) on the summit. The hill closes at 2100; visitors must sign a register at the entrance, giving their ID card number. It

24 hours in the city

First, try to make sure you are here on a Saturday. If you're staying in the centre, get up early and walk down to Calle San Diego for a cheap and cheerful breakfast. Afterwards, continue down San Diego to the **Iglesia de los Sacramentinos** – Santiago's answer to Sacré Coeur – and then west through gardens until you reach the **Palacio Cousiño** in time for the first tour at 0930. This extraordinary building gives a real insight into the Chilean aristocracy and the opulence to which the upper classes became accustomed. After the tour, stroll to Toesca metro and head south to Franklin. Here you will find swarms of people all making their way to the **Mercado Bío Bío**. This market will show you how most of Santiago lives and it provides a striking contrast to Palacio Cousiño.

When you start feeling hungry, head back to Franklin metro and take the train north to Cal y Canto, where you will find the **Mercado Central**, with some of the best seafood restaurants in Santiago – don't be put off by all the choice.

After lunch, it's time to remind yourself that Santiago has one of the most dramatic settings of any of the world's major cities. Cross over the Río Mapocho and stroll east towards the conical hill of **Cerro San Cristóbal**. If it's summer, the heat may be making you feel a little tired by now, in which case you could go up the hill on the **funicular railway**. If you are lucky and it is a clear day, you will have an unforgettable view of the Andes. Stroll through tree-lined lanes and discover a world away from the clutter of the city. There are even swimming pools to cool off in and the chance to do some wine tasting. Towards dusk, have a drink in the café near the funicular railway station and watch the sun go down over the coastal mountain range, lighting up the snows of the Andes.

After dark, go back down the hill by funicular railway (it's not advisable to walk here in the evening) in time to sample Santiago's nightlife. At the foot of Cerro San Cristóbal is **Barrio Bellavista**. Here you can take your pick of any one of dozens of excellent (and expensive) restaurants, before going out to one of the area's buzzing *salsotecas*. These don't really get going until midnight and you'll usually find that you don't leave much before 0500, so perhaps head back to your hotel room for some sleep after dinner and then go out dancing later on.

is best to descend the eastern side, to see the small **Plaza Pedro Valdivia** with its waterfalls and **statue of Valdivia**. The area is known to be dangerous after dark and you should beware of thieves.

Past the hill, on the right, the Alameda goes past the **Biblioteca Nacional** ⓘ *Av Libertador Bernardo O'Higgins 651, Santa Lucía metro, www.dibam.cl/biblioteca_nacional, Mon-Fri 0900-1900, Sat 0910-1400, free*. Beyond, on the left, between Calle San Francisco and Calle Londres, is the oldest church in Santiago: the red-walled church and monastery of **San Francisco** (1618). Inside is the small statue of the Virgin that Valdivia carried on his saddlebow when he rode from Peru to Chile. Free classical concerts are sometimes given in the church in summer; arrive early for a seat. Annexed to the church, near the cloisters, is the **Museo Colonial** ⓘ *Londres 4, T02-6398737, www.museosanfransisco.cl, Tue-Sat 1000-1300, 1500-1800, Sun1000-1400, US$1.50*, containing displays of religious art and Gabriela Mistral's Nobel Prize medal.

2 Santiago centre

➡ **Santiago maps**
1 Santiago orientation, page 212
2 Santiago centre, page 218
3 Santiago metro, page 237

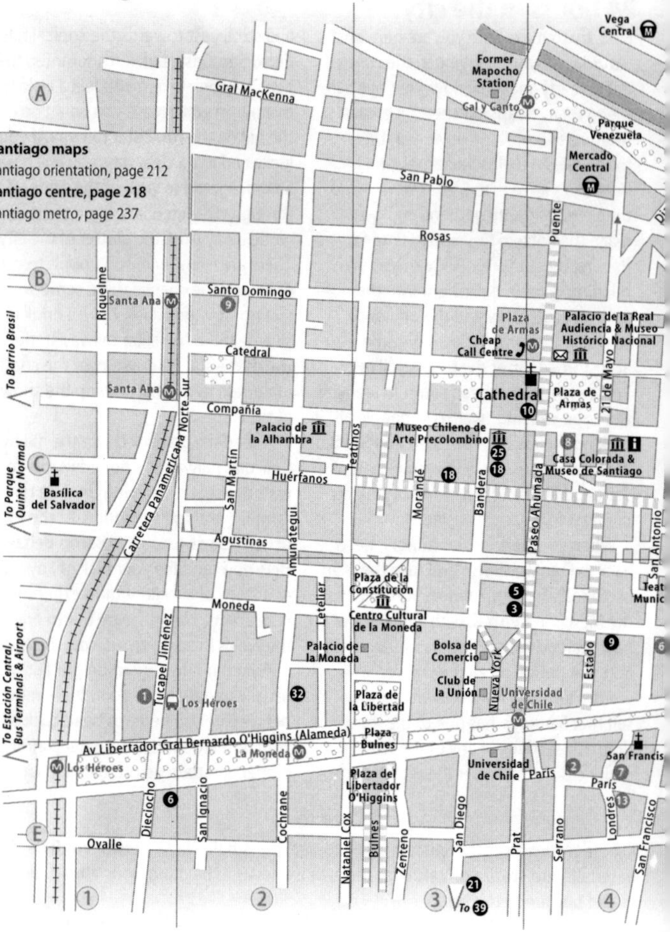

N
300 metres
300 yards

Sleeping
Andes Hostel **10** *C5*
Bellavista Hostel **5** *B8*
Del Patio **16** *B8*
El Marqués del Forestal **12** *B5*
Fundador **2** *E4*
Galerías **6** *D4*
Hostal Casa Grande **4** *D8*
Hostal Che Lagarto **1** *D1*
Hostal Forestal **17** *C7*
Hostal Santa Lucía **11** *D5*
Kapital **14** *C6*
Majestic **9** *B2*
Montecarlo **3** *C6*
París **7** *E4*
Plaza de Armas Hostel **8** *C4*
Residencial Londres **13** *E4*
Tulip Inn Presidente **15** *D8*

Eating
Azul Profundo **22** *B8*
Bar Nacional **18** *C3*
Bombón Oriental **24** *C6*
Café Caribe **3** *D3*
Café Colonia **4** *D5*
Café de la Dulcería Las Palmas **23** *B8*
Café Haiti **5** *D3*
Café Universitario **11** *D6*

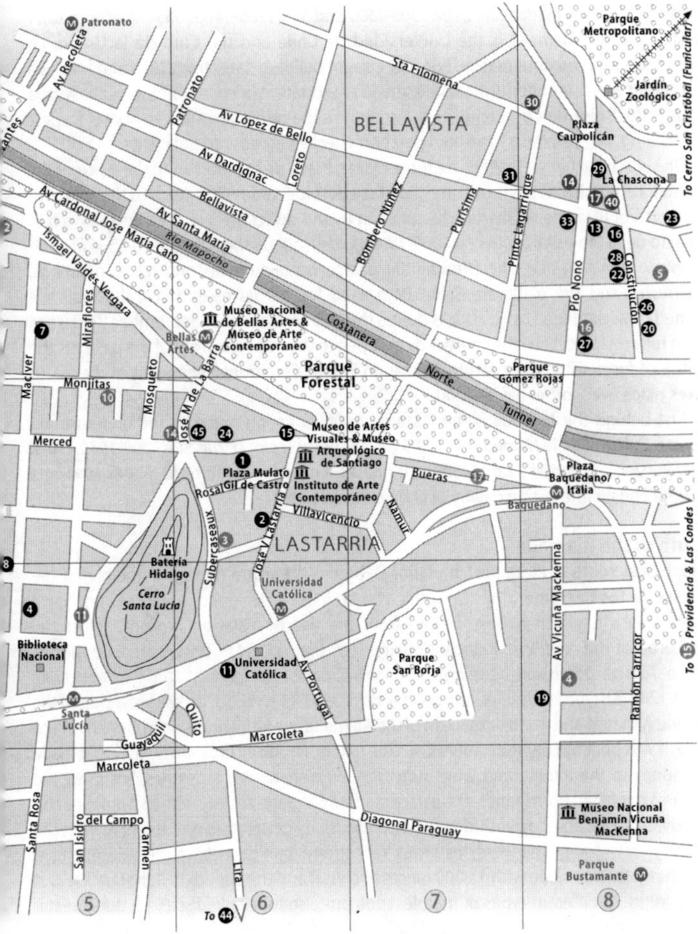

Cienfuegos **20** *B8*
Círculo de Periodistas **32** *D2*
Como Agua Para Chocolate **26** *B8*
Confitería Torres **6** *E1*
Da Carla **7** *B5*
Eladio **29** *A8*
El Antojo de Gaugin **27** *B8*
El Diablito **1** *C6*
El Naturista **9** *D4*
El Otro Sitio **31** *A7*
El Rápido **25** *C3*
El Tablao **28** *B8*
Empanatodos **13** *B8*
Etniko **16** *B8*
Faisan d'Or **10** *C4*
Gatopardo **2** *C6*
Las Tejas **39** *E3*
Les Assassins **15** *C6*
Los Adobes del Argomedo **44** *E6*
Lung Fung **12** *D4*
Masticón **21** *E3*
Nuria **8** *D5*
Opera Catedral **45** *C6*
Tercera Compañía de Bomberos **19** *D8*
Venezia **33** *B8*

Bars & clubs
Club 4-40 **30** *A8*
Disco Salsa **17** *B8*
La Bodega de Julio **40** *B8*
La Otra Puerta **14** *A8*

Two blocks north of the Alameda is the **Teatro Municipal** ⓘ *C Agustinas, www.municipal.cl, guided tours Tue 1300-1500 and Sun 1100-1400, US$4*. A little further west along the Alameda is the **Universidad de Chile** and the **Club de la Unión**, an exclusive social club founded in 1864. The current building dates from 1925 and houses a restaurant where wonderful meals are served at exorbitant prices. Nearby, on Calle Nueva York, is the **Bolsa de Comercio** (stock exchange). The public are allowed access to view the trading, but you must have your passport checked in order to get inside.

One block further west there are three plazas: **Plaza de la Libertad** to the north of the Alameda, **Plaza Bulnes** in the centre and **Plaza del Libertador O'Higgins** to the south. To the north of Plaza de la Libertad, hemmed in by the skyscrapers of the Centro Cívico, is **Palacio de la Moneda** ⓘ *Mon-Fri 1000-1800, guided tours of the palace 0900-1300 last Sun of every month* (1805), the presidential palace containing historic relics, paintings, sculptures and the elaborate Salón Rojo used for official receptions. Although the Moneda was damaged by air attacks during the military coup of 11 September 1973 it has been fully restored. Only the courtyards are open to the public. In front of the palace is the statue of former President Arturo Alessandri Palma. Ceremonial changing of the guard takes place every other day at 1000.

Just behind the Moneda is the Plaza de la Constitución home to the underground **Centro Cultural de la Moneda** ⓘ *T02-3556500, www.ccplm.cl, Tue-Sun 1000-1930*. Like a mini version of London's Tate Modern, it houses temporary exhibitions as well as an arts cinema and an interesting gallery of Chilean handicrafts.

South of the Alameda

Four blocks south of Plaza del Libertador O'Higgins is **Parque Almagro**, notable for the **Iglesia de los Sacramentinos**, a Gothic church loosely designed in imitation of Sacré Coeur in Paris, which is best viewed from the nearby Palacio Cousiño against the backdrop of the *cordillera*. **Palacio Cousiño** ⓘ *C Dieciocho 438, www.palaciocousino.cl, metro Toesca, admission by guided tour only (Spanish or English), Tue-Fri 0930-1330, 1430-1700 (last tour 1600), Sat, Sun and holidays 0930-1330, US$3*, on the west side of the Parque Almagro and five blocks south of the Alameda, is a large mansion in French rococo style. It was built by Luis and Isadora Cousiño, part of a wealthy Chilean dynasty that made its money in the mining and wine industries. Furnished with tapestries, antiques and pictures imported from France, the palace startled Santiago society with its opulence and its advanced technology, including its own electricity generators and the first lift in the country. Even today, the word 'luxurious' falls short when describing the palace: one of the chandeliers is made with 13,000 pieces of crystal and the superb Italian staircase was built using 20 different types of marble. Look out also for the '*indiscretos*', three-seater armchairs designed for courting couples and a chaperone. Now owned by the Municipalidad, the palace is used for official receptions but is also open as a museum. Unfortunately part of the upper floor was recently damaged by fire. It has been restored to some extent but not to its original state, however, a visit is still highly recommended.

Parque O'Higgins lies about 10 blocks south of the Alameda, just to the west of the Panamericana. It has a small lake and various entertainment including the **Club Hípico** racecourse, and an amusement park, **Fantasilandia** ⓘ *daily in summer, Sat and Sun only in winter, US$10, children US$7.50*. There are kite-flying contests on Sundays and, during the Independence celebrations around 18 September, there are many good *peñas*. There are also three small museums. The park can be reached by metro Line 2 to Parque O'Higgins station or by bus from Parque Baquedano via Avenida MacKenna and Avenida Matta.

Moving mountains

While Santiago's smog is not too bad in spring, summer and autumn, those who arrive here during winter could be in for an unpleasant shock. It might not take more than half an hour for your throat to begin to itch and your eyes to water due to one of Santiago's biggest problems – pollution. In 2001, it was rated the eighth most polluted city in the world. When Pedro de Valdivia founded the city in 1541, between the coastal mountains and the Andes, it must have seemed like a perfect site; he could never have imagined that the city would one day engulf the whole valley, and that the mountains would become a serious problem.

The principal reason for Santiago's high levels of pollution is that it lies in a bowl, encircled by mountains, which means that the smog is trapped. This, combined with the centralization of Chilean industry in Santiago and the sheer volume of cars, trucks and buses that choke the city's highways, conspires to create a problem that cannot easily be resolved. It is a serious issue: asthma rates are high and older people sometimes die during the winter *emergencias*, when the pollution gets particularly bad.

Over the years, all sorts of solutions have been proposed. A team of Japanese scientists once even suggested blowing up the part of the Andes nearest the city, so that the pollution could disperse more easily. Each weekday, cars that have number plates ending in one of two digits are prohibited from circulating. But, until the government finds a means of dispersing the population more widely throughout the country, the problem is likely to remain.

Further west, four blocks south of the Alameda, is the **Museo de la Solidaridad Salvador Allende** ⓘ *República 475, T02-6898761, www.mssa.cl, Tue-Sun 1000-1900, US$1.20, Sun free.* Located in former military police station used as a detention centre under the military regime, it houses a collection of over 400 art works produced by Chilean and foreign artists in support of the Unidad Popular government and in opposition to the Pinochet dictatorship. Artists include Alexander Calder, Joan Miró, Frank Stella, Oswaldo Guayasamín and Roberto Matta. There are also videos of interviews (in Spanish) with survivors of the 1973 coup and an information sheet in English.

Barrio Brasil

On the northern side of the Alameda, immediately to the west of the Panamericana, is the Barrio Brasil, a bohemian neighbourhood in which many of the houses are brightly painted. This historic part of the city was the first area to be colonized by Santiaguinos away from the centre, at the end of the 18th century. It is now a more bohemian, studenty neighbourhood than the surrounding areas and has rich colonial architecture, inexpensive hotels and good restaurants. It is also a centre for nightlife with underground bars, clubs and restaurants.

The heart of the barrio is **Plaza Brasil**, easily reached by walking straight up Calle Concha y Toro from the República metro stop. This is a narrow, winding cobblestone street that passes elegant old stone homes in rococo and German Gothic styles, before reaching the plaza, which is shaded by palms, lime trees and silk cottons. Just east of the plaza (Plaza Brasil), on Huérfanos, is the **Basílica del Salvador**, a striking yellow- and rose-coloured church built between 1870 and 1872, with stained glass and a statue of the

Virgen del Carmen. A little further along Compañía is the **Iglesia Preciosa Sangre**, a bright red church of neoclassical design, with impressive reliefs and twin towers.

Around Estación Central

The Alameda continues westwards across the Pan-American Highway towards the impressive railway station, **Estación Central**, which is surrounded by several blocks of market stalls. Opposite Estacíon Central is the **Planetarium** ⓘ *Alameda 3349, T02-7182910, www.planetariochile.cl, US$6*, while to the north, on Avenida Matucana y Diego Portales, is **Parque Quinta Normal**. The park was founded as a botanical garden in 1830, and is a pleasant, popular spot, which gets very crowded on Sundays with families and the street entertainers who vie with one another to get their pesos.

The park contains several museums. **Museo Ferroviario** ⓘ *www.corpdicyt.cl, Tue-Fri 1000-1800, Sat and Sun 1100-1900, US$2*, contains the former presidential stagecoach and 13 steam engines built between 1884 and 1953, including a rare surviving Kitson-Meyer. The **Museo Nacional de Historia Natural** ⓘ *www.mnhn.cl, Tue-Sat 1000-1730, Sun and holidays 1100-1830, US$1.20, Sun free, students free*, was founded in 1830 and is one of Latin America's oldest museums. Housed in a neoclassical building, it has exhibitions on zoology, botany, mineralogy, anthropology, ethnography and archaeology. **Museo Artequín** ⓘ *Av Portales 3530, T02-6825367, www.artequin.cl, Tue-Fri 0900-1700, Sat, Sun and holidays 1100-1800, US$1.60*, is housed in the Chilean pavilion built for the 1889 Paris International Exhibition. It contains prints of famous paintings and explanations of the techniques of the great masters. Recommended.

Bellavista and Cerro San Cristóbal

Santiago's bohemian face is most obvious in the **Bellavista** district, east of the centre on the north bank of the Río Mapocho at the foot of **Cerro San Cristóbal**. This is the main focus of nightlife in the old city; the area around Pío Nono and López de Bello buzzes, especially at weekends. In the bars you can see everything from live Cuban music to local imitations of Georges Brassens, while eating options range from classic Italian to sushi and West African palm-nut stew. There are also theatres, art galleries and craft shops specializing in lapis lazuli, and the recently remodelled Patio Bellavista with several boutiques, bars and restaurants.

La Chascona ⓘ *Márquez de la Plata 192, www.fundacionneruda.org, Tue-Sun 1000-1300, 1500-1800, guided visits only, US$4 in Spanish, US$6 in English*, was the Santiago residence of the poet Pablo Neruda. The house is in three parts, built on a steep hillside and separated by gardens and, apart from numerous objets d'art, it contains works by Diego Rivera, Fernand Léger and Roberto Matta as well as Neruda's Nobel Prize, Order of Lenin and Order of the French Legion of Honour. La Chascona was completed in 1955 and thereafter Neruda lived here whenever he was in the capital. It is basically in the same condition as when he lived here (it was restored after being damaged by the military in the aftermath of the 1973 coup) and is also now the headquarters of the **Fundación Pablo Neruda**.

Parque Metropolitano

Bellavista lies at the foot of the **Cerro San Cristóbal**, which forms the **Parque Metropolitano** ⓘ *daily 0900-2100, cars US$4*, the largest and most interesting of the city's parks. On a clear day it provides excellent views over the city and across to the Andes. More usually, however, the views provide a graphic demonstration of Santiago's continuing smog problem. From the top, the **Cementerio General** can also be seen, situated in the barrio of La Recoleta to the north. This cemetery contains the mausoleums of most of the great figures in Chilean history, including Violeta Parra, Victor Jara and Salvador Allende. There is also an impressive monument to the victims of the 1973-1990 military government. There are two entrances: on Pío Nono in Bellavista, on Pedro de Valdivia Norte, further to the east. To get to the summit you can go by **funicular** ⓘ *every few mins from Plaza Caupolicán at the northern end of C Pío Nono, daily 1000-2000, US$3 return;* or by **teleférico** ⓘ *from Estación Oasis, Av Pedro de Valdivia Norte via Tupahue, to San Cristóbal, the funicular's upper station, summer only, Mon 1430-1830, Tue-Fri 1030-1830, Sat-Sun 1030-1900, US$4 combined funicular/teleférico ticket.* Halfway between the Bellavista entrance and the *cumbre* (on the funicular) is the **Jardín Zoológico** ⓘ *www.zoologico.cl, Tue-Sun 1000-1800, US$4,* which has a well cared for collection of animals. On **Cerro Cumbre** (300 m), there is a colossal statue of the Virgin, which is floodlit at night and now blighted by a giant antenna; beside it is an astronomical observatory.

When the teleférico is closed, the Tupahue sector is reached by taxi either from the Bellavista entrance or on foot from the Pedro de Valdivia metro. This section of the park contains terraces, gardens and paths. One building houses the **Camino Real** ⓘ *T02-2321758, www.eventoscaminoreal.cl,* a good restaurant with a splendid view from the terrace, especially at night, and an **Enoteca** of Chilean wines from a range of vineyards, which you can taste (US$3 per glass), or buy, although prices are higher than in shops. Nearby is the **Casa de la Cultura**, which has art exhibitions and free concerts at midday on Sunday. There are also two good **swimming pools** in the park. East of Tupahue are the **botanical gardens** ⓘ *daily 0900-1800, tours available,* with a collection of native plants.

East to Providencia and Las Condes

East of Plaza Italia, the main east-west axis of the city is known as **Avenida Providencia**, as it heads towards the affluent areas of Providencia and Las Condes. On the south bank of the Mapocho is **Parque Balmaceda**, also known as Parque Gran Bretaña. It is one of the more attractive parks in Santiago and houses the **Museo de los Tajamares** ⓘ *Av Providencia 222, T02-340 7329, Mon-Fri 0900-1400 and 1500-2100,* an exhibition of the 17th- and 18th-century walls built to protect the city from flooding by the river. There is also an exhibition of photographs.

South of Las Condes

Parque de la Paz ⓘ *Av Arrieta 8401, www.villagrimaldicorp.cl,* the new peace park in the southeastern suburb of Peñalolén, stands on the site of **Villa Grimaldi**, the most notorious torture centre during the Pinochet regime. The Irish missionary, Sheila Cassidy, has documented the abuses that she underwent when imprisoned without trial in this place. The walls are daubed with human rights' graffiti and the park makes a moving and unusual introduction to the conflict that has eaten away at the heart of Chilean society for the past 30 years. To reach the park, take a metro to Tobalaba and then any bus marked Peñalolén heading south down Tobalaba. Get off at the junction of Tobalaba y José Arrieta and then walk five minutes up Arrieta towards the mountains.

Hotel and guesthouse prices

LL over US$200	**L** US$151-200	**AL** US$101-150
A US$66-100	**B** US$46-65	**C** US$31-45
D US$21-30	**E** US$12-20	**F** US$7-11
G under US$7		

Restaurant prices

¥¥¥ over US$12	¥¥ US$7-12	¥ under US$7

Sleeping

Expensive hotels in the city centre, Providencia and Las Condes tend to be slightly characterless but with good service. Most budget accommodation is located in the city centre or further west around the bus terminals. Decent *hostales* are also starting to appear in Barrio Brasil and around Providencia. Accommodation in Santiago tends to be more expensive than the rest of the country (see Essentials, page 41).

Plaza de Armas and around *p215, maps p218 and p237*

AL-A Majestic, Santo Domingo 1526, T02-6958366, www.hotelmajestic.cl. With breakfast, pool, US-chain standard. The rooms, while spacious, retain their 1970s decor and are rather careworn. 1st-class Indian restaurant. English spoken.

B El Marqués del Forestal, Ismael Valdés Vergara 740, T02-6394157, www.hotelmarques.cl. Good-value apartments.

B Kapital, Merced 433, T02-6381624. Small, understated hotel. Rooms are clean and of decent size. Less street noise from upper floors. Some rooms have full jacuzzis. Great value although somewhat lacking in character.

B-C Andes Hostel, Monjitas 506, T02-6329990, www.andeshostel.com. **E** pp in dorms. Some rooms with bath. In one of Santiago's more interesting neighbourhoods. Bar downstairs with pool table. Barbeque nights on the roof terrace. Kitchen facilities. Well run if slightly formulaic.

B-C Plaza de Armas Hostel, Compañía 960, Apt 607, T02-6714562, www.plazadearmashostel.com. **F** pp in dorms. Some rooms with bath. Bright with fantastic views over the plaza. High enough for noise from the street not to be an issue. Pleasant terrace. Kitchen facilities. Also quieter rooms in an annex. A decent choice.

Alameda and around *p216, maps p212, p218 and p237*

Along the Alameda

LL-AL Fundador, Paseo Serrano 34, T02-3871200, www.hotelfundador.cl. In a nice area, central, with helpful staff, conference rooms and banqueting halls. Pool, bar, restaurant, internet connections. Some rooms on the small side. Look for special internet rates. Universidad de Chile metro, south exit.

LL-AL Galerías, San Antonio 65, T02-4707400, www.hotelgalerias.cl. Large rooms, good location, generous breakfast. Good value if booked over the internet.

A-B Conde de Anzúrez, Av República 25, T02-6960807, www.ansurez.cl. República metro. Convenient for airport, central station and bus terminals, spacious rooms, clean, helpful, safe, luggage stored, good car hire deals and occasional special offers.

A-B Montecarlo, Victoria Subercaseaux 209, T02-6392945, www.hotelmontecarlo.cl. At foot of Cerro Santa Lucía, interior design is like some sort of art deco gone wrong, common areas showing their age. Small singles charged at the same rate as much bigger doubles.

B-C Hostal Che Lagarto, Tucapel Jiménez 24, T02-6991493, www.chelagarto.com. **E** pp in dorms. Some rooms with bath. South American chain hostel, HI affiliated. Comfortable common areas, kitchen facilities, internet.

B-C Hostal Santa Lucía, Santa Lucía 168, T02-6648478, www.hostalsantalucia.cl. **D** singles, **E-F** pp in dorms. With breakfast. Some rooms with bath. Friendly hostel opposite Cerro Santa Lucía. Fine views from upstairs rooms and the roof terrace. Wi-Fi, friendly staff, some English spoken.

B-C Residencial Mery, Pasaje República 36, off 0-100 block of República, T02-6968883, www.residencialmery.virtuabyte.cl. Art deco building down an alley, some rooms with bath, breakfast extra, friendly owners, quiet, Wi-Fi.

C Hostal Forestal, Santiago Bueras 122, T02-6381347, www.hostalforestal.cl. **D** singles, **F** pp in dorms. With breakfast. Some rooms with bath. Lively hostel, recently improved and expanded. Good location. Comfy lounge with internet and big-screen TV, kitchen facilities, barbeque nights. English spoken, a decent option.

C París, París 813, T02-6640921, carbott@latinmail.com. **D** singles. With bath, quiet, clean, no frills but good value, breakfast extra, luggage store. Book in advance in summer. Recommended.

C Residencial Londres, Londres 54, T02-6382215, www.londres.cl. **E** singles. Near San Francisco Church, former mansion, large old-fashioned rooms and furniture, some rooms with bath, few singles, no heating so cold in winter, some English spoken, book exchange, good value. Recommended.

South of the Alameda

C Hostal de Sammy, Toesca 2335, T02-6898772, www.hostaldesammy.com. **E** singles, **F** pp in dorms. Good-value US-run hostel. Decent common areas. Table tennis and good-sized pool table. Big-screen TV with hundreds of films on demand. Hearty breakfast included. Good info. Fast internet, Wi-Fi, kitchen facilities. Staff generally helpful. Recommended.

Barrio Brasil

A-B Happy House Hostel, Catedral 2207, metro Cumming or República, T02-6884849, www.happyhousehostel.cl. **D-E** pp in dorms. In a completely refurbished mansion, this high-end hostel is one of Santiago's best. High-ceilinged spacious rooms, fully equipped kitchen, comfy lounge, internet, bar, pool room. One room with en suite sauna. Friendly English speaking staff. On the downside, some rooms facing the main street can be noisy. Expensive for a hostel, but still highly recommended.

C Hostal Americano, Compañía 1906, T02-6981025, www.hostalamericano.cl. Nondescript brick and concrete building. Clean, comfortable rooms, some with private bathroom. Friendly atmosphere, some English spoken. There is a pleasant garden at the back. Better value if paying in US dollars. Recommended.

C Hostal Río Amazonas, Rosas 2234, T02-6719013, www.hostalrioamazonas.cl. **D** singles. With breakfast and bath, internet, good value if paying in US dollars or euros. Also have a branch near the Plaza Italia. Recommended.

C La Casa Roja, Agustinas 2113, T02-6964241, www.lacasaroja.cl. **F** pp in dorms. 7 years of restoration have borne fruit in this huge mansion. Fantastic kitchen, 2 bars, swimming pool, cricket net, lots of activities and tours, Spanish classes. Sets the standard for 'lively' hostels in the capital. Highly recommended, but remember to pack earplugs if you want a good night's sleep.

Around Estación Central

Only think of staying near Estación Central if you are on a lightning visit or have an early or late start.

A Tur Hotel Express, Av Libertador Bernardo O'Higgins 3750, piso 3, in the Turbus Terminal, T02-6850100, www.turbus.com/turismo/TurHotel/tur-Hotel-Santiago.html. Comfortable business standard with breakfast, cable TV, a/c, free internet. Particularly useful if you need to take an early flight as buses leave for the airport from here.

C-D Residencial Sur, Ruiz Tagle 055, T02-7765533. **E-F** singles. Pretty grim, but an option of last resort if you arrive in the middle of the night at the bus terminal.

Bellavista and Cerro San Cristóbal *p222, maps p212, p218 and p237*

AL Del Patio, Pío Nono 61, Bellavista, T02-7327571, www.hoteldelpatio.cl. New boutique hotel in a refurbished old wooden building overlooking the lively Patio Bellavista. The location is great for bars, restaurants and nightlife, but at weekends it can be seriously noisy until late at night.

C Bellavista Hostel, Dardignac 0184, T02-7328737, www.bellavistahostel.com. **E-F** pp in dorms. Fun hostel in the heart of this lively area. European-style hostel, sheets provided but you make your own bed. With breakfast. Kitchen facilities, free internet, satelite TV in common area, bicycles lent to guests. Good meeting place.

Providencia *p223, maps p212 and p237*

LL-L Santiago Park Plaza, Av Ricardo Lyon 207, T02-3724000, www.parkplaza.cl. 5-star, another typical luxury hotel geared towards business travellers. Occasional online special deals.

AL Orly, Pedro de Valdivia 027, T02-2318947, www.orlyhotel.com. Pedro de Valdivia metro. Small, comfortable, excellent location. Also more expensive suites, small café attached with reasonable food. Highly recommended.

A Tulip Inn Presidente, Eliodoro Yáñez 867, almost at Providencia, T02-2358015, www.presidente.cl. Salvador metro. Slightly soulless, medium-sized chain hotel. Good location. Rooms vary enourmously in size. The larger rooms with a desk are good value, while the smaller rooms are overpriced.

A Vilafranca Petit Hotel, Pérez Valenzuela 1650, T02-2351413, www.vilafranca.cl. Manuel Montt metro. Homely, high-end B&B. Small but impeccable rooms. Quiet neighbourhood. Pleasant garden. Friendly service. English spoken. Wi-Fi. Recommended.

B Marilú's Bed and Breakfast, Rafael Cañas 246 C, T02-2355302, www.bedandbreakfast.cl. Salvador metro. Comfortable B&B, all rooms with shared bathroom, very friendly owner, good beds, English and French spoken. A little overpriced.

B-C Casa Condell, Condell 114, T02-2092343 Salvador metro, www.casacondell.cl. **D** singles. Pleasant old house, central, quiet, nice roof terrace. Kitchen facilities, free local phone calls, friendly, English spoken. Recommended, but only 2 bathrooms shared between 7 rooms can be an issue in high season.

B-C Patio Suizo, Condell 847, Bustamante metro (line 5), T02-4740634, www.patiosuizo.com. Comfortable and pleasant Swiss-run B&B in a quiet area. Some rooms with bath. Patio with vines and a hammock. Breakfast included, English, German spoken, Spanish classes. Friendly owner with lots of tips. Wine tours offered. Wi-Fi. Highly recommended.

C Hostal Casa Grande, Vicuña MacKenna 90, T02-2227347, www.hostalcasagrande.cl. Baquedano metro. **D-E** singles. Laberinthine *hostal* on the 2nd floor of an old high-ceilinged building. Some rooms with bath and TV, quiet, good value.

Las Condes *p223, maps p212 and p237*

LL-L Radisson Plaza, Av Vitacura 2610, T02-2036000, www.radisson.cl. Metro Tobalaba. 5-star, excellent, disabled access, attentive staff. Recommended.

AL Manquehue, Esteban Dell'Orto 6615, T02-4301100, www.hotelmanquehue.com. Small 4-star with pool. Rack rates overpriced but occasional very good internet deals.

B Urania's Bed and Breakfast, Boccaccio 60, T02-9515307, www.uraniabalut.tripod.com. **C** singles. Comfortable, friendly, good beds, English and French spoken. Recommended, though not particularly convenient for public transport.

Eating

El Mercurio's website has an excellent restaurant guide: www.emol.com. For excellent cheap seafood lunches make for the Mercado Central (Cal y Canto metro), or the Vega Central market on the opposite bank of the Mapocho. For cheap meals in the evening try the *fuentes de soda* and *schoperías* scattered around the centre.

Plaza de Armas and around *p215, maps p218 and p237*

ΨΨΨ-ΨΨ **Da Carla**, MacIver 577, T02-6333739. Intimate old-time Italian trattoria, elegant yet informal atmosphere. Good service and has maintained it quality over the years.

ΨΨΨ-ΨΨ **Majestic**, Santo Domingo 1526. This hotel has one of few excellent Indian restaurants in South America, good range of vegetarian dishes.

ΨΨ **Faisan d'Or**, Plaza de Armas. Good *pastel de choclo*, pleasant place to have a drink and watch the world go by. There are also many cheap eateries on the south side of the plaza.

Ψ **Bar Nacional**, Huérfanos 1151. Good restaurants, popular, local specialities, very traditional. There is another branch at Bandera 317.

Ψ **El Rápido**, C Bandera, next door to **Bar Nacional**. Famed for its *empanadas* and *completos*, cheap, quick service, popular.

Café Caribe and **Café Haití**, Paseo Ahumada, institutions among Santiago's business community and good places to see the people who make Chile tick; also branches throughout the centre and in Providencia.

Alameda and around *p216, maps p212, p218 and p237*

Along the Alameda

ΨΨΨ-ΨΨ **Les Assassins**, Merced 297, Lastarria, T02-6384280. Small family-run French bistro. Excellent food with friendly service and a decent wine list. Good-value set lunches. Recommended.

ΨΨΨ-ΨΨ **Opera Catedral**, José Miguel de la Barra 407, Lastarria, Bellas Artes metro, line 5, T02-6645491, www.operacatedral.cl. Very good, if expensive, French restaurant on the ground floor. Upstairs there is a minimalist pub-restaurant, usually packed at night, serving fusion food at reasonable prices.

ΨΨ **El Naturista**, Moneda 846. Excellent vegetarian, serving quiches, tortillas, a wide range of soups and wholemeal sandwiches. Also serves organic coffee, fruit and vegetable juice as well as beer and wine. Always full at lunchtime. Closes 2100.

ΨΨ **Gatopardo**, Lastarria 192, opposite the plaza Mulato Gil de Castro, T02-6336420. A mixture of Bolivian and Mediterranean cuisine. Good-value lunch buffet. Recommended.

ΨΨ **Lung Fung**, Agustinas 715. The oldest Chinese restaurant in Santiago. Pricey but serves decent food. There is a large cage in the centre with noisy parrots.

ΨΨ-Ψ **El Diablito**, Merced 336, Local 2, Lastarria, Bellas Artes metro, line 5. Fashionable somewhat Bohemian bar-restaurant serving sandwiches and a wide range of beer.

ΨΨ-Ψ **Nuria**, Agustinas y MacIver. This was a well-known Bohemian hang-out in the 1960s. Now past its heyday, it still serves a wide variety of decent food and generous sandwiches.

Ψ **Círculo de Periodistas**, Amunátegui 31, piso 2. Unwelcoming entrance, good-value lunches. Recommended.

Ψ **Confitería Torres**, Av Libertador Bernardo O'Higgins 1570. One of Chile's oldest bar/restaurants dating from 1879, good atmosphere, live tango music at weekends. Cheap lunches are served in a large underground *comedor*.

Bombón Oriental, Merced 345, Lastarria, T02-6391069, www.bombonoriental.cl. Superb Turkish coffee, Arabic snacks and sweets.

Café Colonia, MacIver 133. Splendid variety of cakes, pastries and pies, efficient if somewhat brusque service by staff who haven't changed for decades. Recommended.

Café Universitario, Alameda 395 y Subercaseaux (near Santa Lucía), Lastarria. Good, cheap *almuerzos*, lively at night, separate room for lovers of rock videos, very pleasant.

Tip-Top Galletas, for freshly baked biscuits, there are 2 branches on the Alameda just east of the Moneda, takeaway only.

South of the Alameda

¥¥¥-¥¥ Los Adobes del Argomedo, Argomedo 411 y Lira, 10 blocks south of the Alameda, T02-2222104, www.losadobesdeargomedo.cl. Long-established traditional restaurant. Good Chilean food, floor show (Mon-Sat) includes *cueca* dancing, salsa and folk.

¥ Las Tejas, San Diego 234. Old-time southern *chichería*. Lively, rowdy crowd, very cheap cocktails and drinks such as *pisco sour* and *pipeño*, excellent *cazuelas* and other typical dishes.

¥ Masticón, San Diego 152. Good service, excellent value, popular, wide range of fast food and traditional Chilean food.

Barrio Brasil

¥¥¥-¥¥ Las Vacas Gordas, Cienfuegos 280, T02-6971066. Excellent *parrillada*. Very popular, so book in advance.

¥¥¥-¥¥ Ocean Pacific's, Cumming 221, T02-6972413. Extremely kitsch seafood restaurant with ship and submarine themed rooms. You can find better food elsewhere, but for over the top exuberance this is hard to beat.

¥¥ Los Buenos Muchachos, Cumming 1031, T02-6980112, www.losbuenosmuchachos.cl. Cavernous hall seating over 400 and serving traditional Chilean food in abundant portions. Very popular, especially at night when shows of traditional Chilean dances are held.

¥¥ Los Chinos Ricos, Brasil 373, T02-6963778, www.chinosricos.cl, on the plaza. Famed Chinese. The restaurant used to be called Los Chinos Pobres, but was so popular it had to change its name. Fills up with noisy families on Sun lunchtimes.

¥¥ Ostras Azócar, Bulnes 37, T02-6816109. Long-established traditional restaurant specializing in seafood and oysters in particular.

Around Estación Central

¥¥ El Hoyo, San Vicente 375, T02-6890339. Closed Sun, 100-year-old Chichería serving hearty Chilean fare such as *arrollado* and *prietas*, recently described by celebrity chef Anthony Bourdain as "f****** awesome".

Bellavista and Cerro San Cristóbal *p222, maps p212, p218 and p237*

Most restaurants in Bellavista close on Sun and public holidays, but this is one of the liveliest places to come out and eat at night, with many excellent and costly restaurants. There are dozens more restaurants than those listed below, with a new place seeming to open every few weeks.

¥¥¥ Azul Profundo, Constitución 111, Bellavista. Fish and seafood with a touch of invention. Good range of cocktails.

¥¥¥ Cienfuegos, Constitución 67, Bellavista. T02-2489080. Tue-Sat evenings. Reputedly one of the best restaurants in town serving a Chilean/European fusion. The food is always excellent, though portions are tiny for the hefty pricetag and service can be slow, especially at weekends.

¥¥¥ Como Agua Para Chocolate, Constitución 88, Bellavista. Mexican and Mediterranean. Slightly pretentious presentations but excellent service.

¥¥¥ El Otro Sitio, Antonia López de Bello 053, Bellavista. Upmarket Peruvian. Good service, elegant surroundings, excellent range of starters. If you are feeling brave try the *rocoto relleno*. Recommended.

¥¥¥-¥¥ Etniko, Constitición 172, Bellavista, T02-7320119. Sushi and Thai restaurant that also fuctions as a lively bar later in the night. No sign. Just knock.

¥¥ Eladio, Pío Nono 251, Bellavista. Argentine cuisine, good steaks, bingo.

¥¥ El Antojo de Gaugin, Pío Nono 69 inside the Patio Bellavista. Arabic. Good *brochetas a la plancha*.

¥¥ El Tablao, Constitución 110, Bellavista, T02-7378648. Traditional Spanish restaurant. The food is reasonable, but the main attraction is the live flamenco show on Fri-Sat nights.

¥¥ Venezia, Pío Nono y Antonia López de Bello, Bellavista. Traditional Chilean home-cooked fare. Large servings, good value. One of Neruda's favourite haunts.

Café de la Dulcería Las Palmas, Antonia López de Bello 190, Bellavista. Good pastries and lunches.
Empanatodos, Pío Nono 153, Bellavista. Serves 32 different types of *empanadas*.

Providencia *p223, maps p212 and p237*
¥¥¥ **Carousel**, Los Conquistadores 1972, T02-2321728. Fine French cuisine, exceptionally smart, nice garden, very expensive.
¥¥¥ **Centre Catalá**, Av Suecia 428 near Lota. Elegant Catalan restaurant, quiet street, nice decor, cheaper set lunch.
¥¥¥ **El Giratorio**, 11 de Septiembre 2250, piso 16, T02-2321827. Good French food eaten while the whole city rotates outside your window. Recommended for the view.
¥¥¥-¥¥ **A Pinch of Pancho**, Gral del Canto 45, T02-2351700. Seafood and fish specialities, very good.
¥¥¥-¥¥ **Baco**, Nueva de Lyon 113, T02-2314444. Metro Los Leones. Sophisticated French restaurant. The food is good but what stands out is the extensive winelist and the amount of quality wines available by the glass.
¥¥¥-¥¥ **De Cangrejo a Conejo**, Italia 805 y Bilbao, Providencia, T 02-6344041, www.decangrejoaconejo.cl. Metro Parque Bustamante or Salvador. Small but varied menu, ranging as the restaurants name suggests, from crab to rabbit. The food is invariably excellent. Lovely garden. Deservedly popular. No sign outside.
¥¥¥-¥¥ **Oriental**, M Montt 584, T02-352389. One of the best Chinese restaurants in Santiago. Excellent service.
¥¥ **Café El Patio**, Providencia 1652, next to **Phone Box Pub**. Tofu and pasta as well as fish dishes, nice sandwiches, popular. Turns into more of a pub at night. Wide range of cocktails.
¥¥ **Eladio**, 11 de Septiembre 2250, piso 5. Reasonably priced, good meat dishes. There is often karaoke on Fri and Sat nights.
¥¥ **El Huerto**, Orrego Luco 054, T02-2332690. Santiago's oldest vegetarian restaurant. Varied dishes from around the world, athough slightly on the bland side. Vegan options available. Good juices. Local artwork on display.
¥¥-¥ **Olan**, Seminario 96A-B, Providencia. Incredibly good-value tasty Peruvian food in unpretentious surroundings. Another branch opposite at No 67, slightly higher prices.
¥ **Mercado de Providencia**, Santa Beatriz, off Av Providencia. This small market has a couple of good cheap lunchtime eateries.
¥ **Tercera Compañía de Bomberos**, Vicuña Mackenna 097, Providencia, near the junction with Diagonal Paraguay. Good food, very cheap. Recommended.

Cafetto, Pedro de Valdivia 030, by **Hotel Orly**. Upmarket café with a variety of sandwiches.

There are several good places for snacks and ice cream on Av Providencia including: **Copelia**, No 2211; **Bravissimo**, No 1406; **El Toldo Azul**, No 1936. Also, **Salón de Té Tavelli**, Drugstore precinct, No 2124. However, the best is probably **Sebastián** Fuenzalida 26, Los Leones Metro.

Las Condes *p223, maps p212 and p237*
This area has many 1st-class restaurants, including grills, serving Chilean (often with music), French and Chinese cuisine. They tend to be more expensive than central restaurants. Lots of expensive eateries are located on El Bosque Norte, near the Tobalaba metro stop.
¥¥¥ **Coco Loco**, El Bosque Norte 0215, T02-2313082. Fish, seafood, good.
¥¥¥ **Isla Negra**, next door to **Coco Loco**, El Bosque Norte. Seafood a speciality.
¥¥¥ **Pinpilinpausha**, Isidora Goyenechea 2900, T02-2325800. Basque specialities, good.
¥¥-¥¥ **Miguel Torres**, Isidora Goyenechea 2874, T02-2429360. Tapas bar owned by the well-known Spanish winery.
¥¥¥-¥¥ **Puerto Marisko**, Isidora Goyenechea 2918, T02-2519542. Renowned for seafood but also serves pasta and meat dishes. Has maintained its quality over 20 years.
¥¥ **Le Fournil**, Vitacura 3841, opposite Cuerovaca, T02-2280219. Excellent French bakery and restaurant. Particularly popular at lunchtime. Good soups. Service can be poor.

Bars and clubs

As in most of South America, a night out in Santiago begins late. Arrive in a restaurant before 2100 and you may be eating alone, while bars and clubs are often empty before 2400. There is a good selection of bars, discos and *salsotecas* from the reasonably priced in **Bellavista** (Baquedano metro) to the smarter along Av Suecia and G Holley in **Providencia** (Los Leones metro). El Bosque Norte in **Las Condes** (Tobalaba metro) is lined with chic bars and expensive restaurants for the Chilean jetset, while **Barrio Brasil (República metro)** is popular with Chilean students. Most clubs and bars playing live music charge around US$2 (for student-orientated places), usually with a drink included, although some clubs in Las Condes and Providencia may charge US$20 or more.

Bellavista *p222, maps p218 and p237*
Back Stage, Patio Bellavista. Good quality live jazz and blues.
Club 4-40, Santa Filomena 81. Named after popular singer Juan Luis Guerra's backing group from the Dominican Republic, live Cuban music, packed at weekends.
Disco Salsa, Pío Nono 223. Good atmosphere, salsa dance classes downstairs.
La Bodega de Julio, Constitución 256. Cuban staff and Cuban cocktails, excellent live music and dancing, very popular, free entry before 2300, good value.
La Casa en el Aire, Patio Bellavista. Pleasant atmosphere, live music. Recommended.
La Otra Puerta, Pío Nono 348. Lively *salsoteca* with live music. Recommended.

Providencia *p223, maps p212 and p237*
Brannigan's Pub, Suecia 35, T02-232 7869. Good beer, live jazz, lively.
Golden Bell Inn, Hernando de Aguirre 27. Popular with expats.
Ilé Habana, Bucaré just off Suecia. Bar with salsa music, often live, and a good dance floor.
Phone Box Pub, Providencia 1670, T02-2350303. Very popular with expats, serves numerous European beers, including Pilsener Urquell, and canned British beers, including Newcastle Brown Ale, Beamish Stout and Old Speckled Hen. A good place to go if you are missing home.

Las Condes *p223, maps p212 and p237*
Country Village, Av Las Condes 10680. Mon-Sat from 2000, Sun from lunch onwards, live music Fri and Sat.
Flannery's Irish Geo Pub, Encomenderos 83, T02-2336675, www.flannerys.cl. Irish pub, serving Guinness on draft, good lunches including vegetarian options, popular among gringos and Chileans alike.
Las Urracas, Vitacura 9254. US$20 but free before 2300 if you eat there. Huge variety of cocktails.
Morena Pizza and Dance Bar, Av Las Condes 10120. Good sound system, live music at weekends, happy hour before 2200.
Tequila, Av Las Condes at Paseo San Damián. One of a few popular bar-restaurants nearby.

Entertainment

Santiago *p215, maps p212, p218 and p237*
For all entertainment, clubs, cinemas, restaurants, concerts, *El Mercurio Online* website has listings and a good search feature. Look under the *tiempo libre* section: www.emol.com. There are also listings in weekend newspapers, including *Santiago What's On* (in English).

Cinemas

A good guide to daily cinema listings can be found in the 2 free newspapers, *La Hora* and *tmg*, handed out at metro stations early on weekday mornings. Tickets cost US$4-7 with reductions on Mon, Tue and Wed.

There are many mainstream cinemas showing international films, usually in original English with Spanish subtitles. 'CineArte' (art-house cinemas that show quality foreign films) are also very popular and include the following:

Casa de Extensión Universidad Católica, Av B O'Higgins 390, T02-6351994. Universidad Católica metro, south exit, line 1.
Centro Arte Alameda, Av Bernado O'Higgins 139, Baquedano metro, line 1, T02-6648821, www.centroartealameda.cl.
Cine Arte Normandie, Tarapacá 1181, T02-6972979. Varied programme, altered frequently, films at 1530, 1830 and 2130 daily, students half price. Moneda metro, south exit.
El Biógrafo, Lastarria 181, T02-6334435. Universidad Católica metro, north exit.
Tobalaba, Av Providencia 2563, T02-2316630. Tobalaba metro.

Performing arts

Teatro Municipal, Agustinas y San Antonio, www.municipal.cl. Stages international opera, concerts by the Orquesta Filarmónica de Santiago and performances by the Ballet de Santiago, throughout the year. On Tue at 2100 there are free operatic concerts in the Salón Claudio Arrau. Tickets range from US$10 for a very large choral group with a symphony orchestra, and US$12 for the cheapest seats at the ballet, to US$100 for the most expensive opera seats. Some cheap seats are often sold on the day of concerts.
Teatro Municipal de Ñuñoa, Av Irarrázaval 1564, www.ccn.cl, T02-2777903. Dance, art exhibitions, cinema, children's theatre.
Teatro Universidad de Chile, Plaza Baquedano, www.teatro.uchile.cl, T02-9782203. Home of the Orquesta y Coro Sinfónica de Chile and the Ballet Nacional de Chile.

A great number of more minor theatres around the city stage plays, including **Abril**, Huérfanos 786; **Camilo Henríquez**, Amunátegui 31; **Centro Arrayán**, Las Condes 14891; **El Galpón de los Leones**, Av Los Leones 238; **El Conventillo**, Bellavista 173 and **La Comedia**, Merced 349. Events are listed in *El Mercurio* and *La Tercera*.

❁ Festivals and events

Santiago *p215, maps p212, p218 and p237*
Mar/Apr Religious festivals and ceremonies continue throughout **Holy Week**, when a priest ritually washes the feet of 12 men.
End of May A food festival called **Expo Gourmand**. Its location changes every year.
16 Jul The image of the **Virgen del Carmen** (patron saint of the armed forces) is carried through the streets by cadets.
18 Sep Chile's **Independence Day** when many families get together or celebrate in *fondas* (small temporary constructions made of wood and straw where people eat traditional dishes, drink *chicha* and dance *cueca*).
19 Sep **Armed Forces Day** is celebrated with an enormous military procession through the Parque O'Higgins. It takes 4 hrs.
Nov A free **art fair** lasting a fortnight is held in the Parque Forestal on the banks of the Río Mapocho.

O Shopping

Santiago *p215, maps p212, p218 and p237*
The shops in the centre and to the north of the Plaza de Armas are cheaper and more downmarket than the countless arcades and boutiques strung along Providencia, especially near Av Ricardo Lyon. Specialist shops tend to be grouped together, eg bikes and second-hand books on San Diego, new bookshops on Providencia, opticians on Mac Iver, lapis lazuli in Bellavista. Many stalls on Paseo Ahumada/ Huérfanos sell overseas newspapers.

Bookshops

Book prices are very high compared with Europe, even for second-hand books. There are many bookshops in the Pedro de Valdivia area on Av Providencia. Much better value but with a smaller selection are the bookshops in the shopping mall at Av Providencia 1114-1120. For cheap English-

language books try the second-hand book kiosks on San Diego, 4 blocks south of Plaza Bulnes, next to Iglesia de los Sacramentinos.
Books, Providencia 1652, Local 5, in a courtyard beside the Phone Box Pub and Café El Patio. Wide selection of English-language books for sale or exchange, English spoken. On the expensive side.
Books & Bits, Av Apoquindo 6856, Las Condes, T02-2109100. Sells books in English.
Feria Chilena del Libro, Huérfanos 623. Largest bookstore in Santiago, good for travel books and maps; also at Nueva York 3, Agustinas 859, Mall Parque Arauco and Providencia 2124.
Librería Inglesa, Huérfanos 669, local 11, Pedro de Valdivia 47, Vitacura 5950, Providencia 2653, T02-2319970, www.libreriainglesa.cl. Sells only books in English, good selection.
LOM Ediciones, Estación Mapocho. Mon-Fri 1000-2000, Sat 1000-1400. Sells a stock of literature, history, sociology, art and politics from its own publishing house. Also a bar and a reading room with recent Chilean newspapers and magazines.

Camping and outdoors equipment

There are a number of 'hunting' shops on Bulnes 1-2 blocks south of the Alameda which have a basic range of outdoor equip ment. Also try the Mall Sport, Av Las Condes 13451.
Andes Gear, Helvecia 210, Las Condes, T02-2457076, www.andesgear.cl. Wide range of good-quality clothes and equipment.
Club Andino and **Federación de Andinismo** (see page 234). Expensive products as most articles are imported.
La Cumbre, Apoquindo 5258, Las Condes, T02-2209907, www.lacumbreonline.cl. Climbing equipment.
Lippi, Av Italia 1586, Ñuñoa, Santa Isabel Metro, T02-2256803, www.lippi.cl. Chile's premier outdoor equipment maker. Excellent quality clothes, boots, tents, etc.
Parafernalia, Huérfanos 1973 y Brasil. Second-hand gear. Recommended.
Peregrin, del Arzobispo 0607, Bellavista, Salvador Metro, T02-7351587. Decent quality locally made outdoor clothes.

Handicrafts

The gemstone, lapis lazuli, can be found in a few expensive shops in Bellavista but is cheaper in the arcades on the south side of the Plaza de Armas. Antique stores can be found in Plaza Mulato Gil de Castro and elsewhere on Lastarria (Merced end). Other craft stalls can be found: in an alleyway, 1 block south of Av O'Higgins between A Prat and San Diego; on the 600-800 blocks of Santo Domingo; and at Pío Nono y Av Santa María in Bellavista.
Centro Artesanal Santa Lucía, Santa Lucía metro, south exit. This is the best place to buy generic *artesanía* in the centre of Santiago. Lapis lazuli can be bought here cheaply. Also has a variety of woollen goods, jewellery, etc.
Dauvin Artesanía Fina, Providencia 2169, local 69, www.artesaniasvdauvin.cl. Los Leones metro. Recommended.
Pueblito Artesanal Los Domínicos, Apoquindo 9805, Las Condes, www.pueblitolosdominicos.com. Metro Los Domínicos. The best upmarket craft fair in Chile. A good range of modern and traditional Chilean crafts from ceramics to textiles, a pleasant central plaza, and places where the artisans can be seen working on wood, silver, glass and so on. Although more expensive than, for instance, the market in Santa Lucía, this is a good and attractive option.

Maps

Automóvil Club de Chile, Av Andrés Bello 1863, Pedro de Valdivia metro, T02-4311000, www.automovilclub.cl). Mon-Thu 0900-1815, Fri 0900-1700. Route maps of Chile, US$6 each, free to members of affiliated motoring organizations; very helpful.
CONAF, see page 45. Maps of national parks.
Instituto Geográfico Militar, Dieciocho 369, near Toesca metro, T02-4109463. Detailed geophysical and topographical maps of the whole of Chile, very useful for climbing.

Expensive (about US$15 each), but **Biblioteca Nacional**, Av Libertador Bernardo O'Higgins 651, T02-360 5200, stocks them and will allow you to photocopy parts of each map.
Librería Australis, Av Providencia 1670, local 5. All sorts of local, regional and trekking maps.

Markets

For craft markets, see Handicrafts, above.
Bío Bío flea market, C Bío Bío. Every Sat and Sun morning. This is the largest and cheapest flea market in the city and sells everything from spare parts for cars and motorbikes to second-hand furniture. Those trying to do up a new flat on the cheap, a car on the hoof, or who are simply interested in sharing a street with tens of thousands of others, should find their way here; just go to Franklin metro, line 2 and follow the crowds. Beware of rip-offs.
Mercado Central, Puente y 21 de Mayo by the Río Mapocho. Cal y Canto metro. Brilliant for seafood, with many places to eat cheaply, **Donde Augusto** is recommended. Otherwise an excellent range of goods, but quite expensive.
Vega Central, on the opposite bank of the river, is cheaper than Mercado Central, with lots of fruit and veg stalls, butchers and dozens of very cheap eateries.

Wine

There's a good selection of wines at **Jumbo**, **Líder** and **Santa Isabel** supermarkets.
El Mundo del Vino, Isidora Goyenechea 2929www.elmundodelvino.cl. Also in Patio Bellavista as well as the Alto Las Condes and Parque Arauco malls.
Vinopolis, Pedro de Valdivia 036, Pedro de Valdivia metro, line 1. Mon-Fri 0900-2300, Sat 1000-2300, Sun 1000-2200. Also at the airport. Exclusively Chilean wines. Good selection.

Activities and tours

Santiago *p215, maps p212, p218 and p237*

Boat operators

Antarctic Expeditions, Ebro 2740, oficina 602, Las Condes, T02-481 6910, www.antarctica.cl. Expeditions in Patagonia and Antarctica on board their *Antarctic Dream*, www.antarcticdream.com.
Cruceros Australis, El Bosque Norte 0440, T02-442 3115, www.australis.com. Punta Arenas to Puerto Williams, Cape Horn and Ushuaia.
M/N Skorpios, Augusto Leguía Norte 118, Las Condes, T02-231 1030, www.skorpios.cl, for Puerto Montt–Laguna San Rafael.
Naviera Austral, Agustinas 715, oficina 403, T02-633 5959, www.navieraustral.cl. For Chiloé and the Carretera Austral. **Navimag**, Av El Bosque Norte 0440, 11th floor, Las Condes, T02-442 3120, www.navimag.com. For Puerto Montt-Puerto Natales.
Patagonia Connection SA, Fidel Oteíza 1921, oficina 1006, Providencia (metro Pedro de Valdivia, T02-225 6489, www.patagonia-connection.com. For Puerto Montt– Coyhaique/ Puerto Chacabuco–Laguna San Rafael.

Soccer nation

Football arrived in Chile towards the end of the 19th century, courtesy of the British. The role of British workers – most of whom were employed in the construction of the railway system – is reflected in the names of several of the leading teams, notably Santiago Wanderers (based in Valparaíso), Everton (based in Viña) and Rangers (based in Talca). The game's popularity grew rapidly and by the 1940s most large towns boasted their own team and stadium. In 1962, Chile's importance as a soccer nation was recognized internationally when it hosted the World Cup and the national side finished third.

The season is split into two tournaments, the *apertura* running from March to June and the *clausura* from August to December. Most of the support (and money) goes to the big three clubs, all based in Santiago: **Universidad de Chile** (known as 'La U'), **Colo-Colo** (known as 'Los Indios', as their strip carries an image of the great Mapuche leader) and **Universidad Católica.**

A visit to a match is an unforgettable experience as the supporters dance, sing and wave their team colours beneath a rain of confetti, fireworks and coloured smoke. Cheap tickets cost around US$5.

Climbing

Federación de Andinismo de Chile, Almte Simpson 77A, T02-222 0888, www.feach.cl. It has the addresses of all the mountaineering clubs in Chile. Runs a mountaineering school.
La Cumbre Ltda, Av Apoquindo 5258, T02-220 9907, www.lacumbreonline.cl. Mon-Fri 1100-2000, Sat 1100-1600. Dutch owners very helpful, good climbing and trekking equipment.
Mountain Service, Santa Magdalena 75, T02-234 3439, Providencia, www.mountain service.cl. English spoken, tents, stoves, clothing, equipment rental. Recommended.

Football

If you decide to visit the **Estadio Nacional**, where international matches are played, find a space high up on the terraces and you will be able to watch the sun set over the mountains behind Santiago. See box, above.
Colo Colo, play at the Estadio Monumental, reached by any bus to Puente Alto or Pedrero metro, line 5; tickets from Av Marathon 5300, Macul, T02-294 7300.
Universidad Católica, play at San Carlos de Apoquindo, reached by bus from Escuela Militar metro; tickets from Andrés Bello 2782, Providencia, T02-231 2777.
Universidad de Chile, play at Estadio Nacional, Av Grecia 2001 Ñuñoa, Ñuble metro, line 5. Tickets from Av General Miranda 2094, Ñuñoa.

Skiing

Farellones, 1½ hrs from the city, has good accommodation and facilities but can get very busy at weekends. Expect to pay US$40-50 for a combined ticket for the 4 resorts in the area. Buses operated by **Ski Total**, T02-246 6881, www.skitotal.cl, also rents equipment.
Portillo, www.skiportillo.cl. Widely regarded as one of the best resorts in Chile. Only 1 hotel but extra activities are available, such as a visit to the Laguna del Inca. All buses from Santiago to Mendoza pass through Portillo.

Ski clubs Club Andino de Chile, Av Libertador Bernardo O'Higgins 108, local 215, T02-274 9252, www.skilagunillas.cl. **Skitotal**, Av Apoquindo 4900, oficina 40-42, T02-246 0156. Rents equipment, organizes accommodation and lessons. Also provides transport.

Tour operators

Altue Expediciones, General Salvo 159, Providencia, T02-2351519, www.altue.com. For wilderness trips including tour of Patagonia and sea-kayaking in Chiloé.

Azimut 360, General Salvo 159, Providencia, T02-235 1519, www.azimut.cl. Salvador metro. Reasonable prices. Adventure and ecotourism throughout Chile, including tours to the Atacama Desert. Aconcagua base camp services and mountaineering expeditions to Parinacota and Sajama. Recommended.
Cascada Expediciones, Camino al Volcán 17710, T02-861 1777, www.cascada-expediciones.cl. Activity tours in remote areas.
Mountain Service, Paseo Las Palmas 2209, T02-233 0913, www.mountainservice.cl, Los Leones metro. Climbing trips.
Patagonia Connection SA, Fidel Oteíza 1921, oficina 1006, Providencia, T02-2256489, www.patagonia-connection.com, Pedro de Valdivia metro. For cruises to Patagonia.
Sertur, Hernando de Aguirre 201, oficina 401, T02-411 2000, www.sertur.cl. Cheap flights, tours, car rental, ISIC cards, insurance, hotels.
Sportstours, Moneda 970, piso 18, T02-549 5200, www.sportstour.cl. Helpful, 5-day trips to Antarctica. Another branch at **San Cristóbal Tower**, Av Santa María 1742.
Turismo Cabo de Hornos, www.turismocabodehornos.cl. Agustinas 814, oficina 706, T02-664 3458. For **DAP** flights and Tierra del Fuego/Antarctica tours.

Transport

Santiago *p215, maps p212, p218 and p237*

Air

For details of the Aeropuerto Arturo Merino Benítez, see page 214. For flights see Essentials, pages 34-36.

Airline offices Aerolíneas Argentinas, Roger de Flor 2921 y 2907, Las Condes, Tobalaba metro, T02-2109300, www.aerolineas.com; **AeroMéxico**, Isidora Goyenechea 2939, oficina 602, Las Condes, Tobalaba metro, T02-3901000, www.aeromexico.com; **Air France**, Nueva Costanera 3420, Vitacura, T02-2909330, www.airfrance.cl; **American**, Huérfanos 1199, Universidad de Chile metro, www.american airlines.cl, T02-6790000; **Continental** (Chilean agents are Copa Airlines) Fidel Oteíza 1921, oficina 703, Pedro de Valdivia metro, south exit, T02-2002100, www.continental.com; **Delta**, Isidora Goyenechea 2939, oficina 601, Las Condes, Tobalaba metro, T02-2801600, www.delta.com; **Iberia**, Bandera 206, piso 8, Universidad de Chile metro, north exit, T02-8701050, reservations T02-8701060, www.iberia.com; **LACSA**, Dr Barros Borgoño 105, piso 2, Providencia, Manuel Montt metro, south exit, T02-2355189, www.grupotaca.com; **LanChile**, Huérfanos 926, Universidad de Chile metro, north exit. Also at Av Providencia 2006, Providencia, Los Leones or Pedro de Valdivia metro and Isidora Goyenechea 2888, Las Condes, Tobalaba metro, T02-6005262000, www.lan.com; **Lufthansa**, Av El Bosque Norte 500, piso 16, Las Condes, Tobalaba metro, T02-6301655, airport 6901112, www.lufthansa.cl; **Sky Airline**, Andrés de Fuenzalida 55, Providencia, Los Leones metro, north exit, T02-600-6002828, www.skyair line.cl; **United**, Av Andrés Bello 2687, piso 16, Las Condes, Tobalaba metro, www.united.com, T02-3370000; **Varig**, El Bosque Norte 0177, oficina 903, piso 9, Las Condes, Tobalaba metro, T02-7078020, www.varig.com.

Bus

Local

The capital's integrated public transport system is known as transantiago (www.transantiago.cl). The city is divided into 10 zones lettered A to J. Within each zone, buses (known as *micros*) are the same colour as that given to the zone (eg white for zone A – central Santiago); Zones are linked by trunk lines, run by white *micros* with a green stripe. The system integrates with the metro. Buses display the number and direction of the route within the system. Payment is by prepaid Bip card only. A card costs US$3, to which you add however much you want to pay in advance. They are most conveniently bought at metro stations. You can travel as much as you want by bus (with 1 metro journey also allowed) in a 2-hr period for a fixed rate of US$0.70 ($0.80 at peak times).

Long distance There are frequent, good inter-urban buses to all parts of Chile (see Essentials, page 37). Fares from/to the capital are given in the text. Bear in mind that on Fri in summer, when the night buses depart, the terminals are nightmarishly chaotic and busy.

Terminal Alameda, O'Higgins 3712, T02-2707 1500, has the best left-luggage facilities in the city, and 2 of the best companies, **TurBus**, www.turbus.com, and **Pullman Bus**, www.pullman.cl, leave from here.

Terminal Santiago, O'Higgins 3878, T02-376 1755, 1 block west of Terminal Alameda. Sometimes referred to as 'Terminal Sur', this terminal is used by services to and from the south, as well as buses to the central coast. It is the only terminal with services to **Punta Arenas** (48 hrs), and is also the centre for most international services.

Terminal San Borja, O'Higgins y San Borja, T02-7760645, 1 block west of Estación Central, 3 blocks east of Terminal Alameda. Estación Central metro. Buses to destinations in the **Santiago area**.

Terminal Los Héroes, Tucapel Jiménez, just north of the Alameda, T02-420 0099. Los Héroes metro. A smaller terminal for 8 companies to some useful destinations.

Terminal Pajaritos, at the entrance of Pajaritos metro station (line 1). Another small terminal. All buses between Santiango and Valparaíso and Viña del Mar stop here. It is generally quicker and more convenient to take a bus from here than from the terminals in central Santiago. Shuttle buses to the airport also stop here.

International Almost all international buses leave from the Terminal Santiago. There are frequent services via **Mendoza** to **Buenos Aires** and **Bahía Blanca**, but if you're going to destinations such as **Bariloche** or **Neuquén** in Argentine Patagonia, it is better to travel south to Temuco or Osorno and connect there. There are also services to destinations throughout the rest of South America; consult bus companies at the terminal.

Car

Driving in the city is restricted according to licence plate numbers; each day, certain plates are prohibited from circulating (numbers are given in the press).

Hertz, Avis, Budget and others are available from the airport; **Alameda**, Av Bernado O'Higgins 4332, T02-779 0609, www.alame darentacar.cl, San Alberto Hurtado metro, line 1, also in the airport, good value; **ANSA**, Av Eleodoro Yáñez 1198, Providencia, T02-2510256; **Automóvil Club de Chile**, Av Vitacura 9511, Providencia, T02-4311106, 25% discount for members of associated motoring organizations; **Avis**, San Pablo 9900, T02-3310121, www.avischile.cl, also in Vitacura, poor service reported; **Hertz**, Costanera Andrés Bello 1469, T02-3608600, www.autorentas.cl, has a good network in Chile and cars are in good condition; **Rosselot**, Francisco Bilbao 2032, Providencia, T02-3813690, www.rosselot.cl, and airport, T02-6901374, reputable Chilean firm with national coverage; **Seelmann**, Monseñor Edwards 1279, La Reina, T02-2779259, www.seelmann.cl, mixed reports; **Trekker Ltd**, www.trekkerchile.com, has camper vans, trucks and 4WD vehicles available; **Verschae**, Manquehue Sur 660, T02-202 7266, www.verschae.cl, reasonable value, branches throughout the country.

Colectivo/taxi

Collective taxis operate on fixed routes between the centre and the suburbs. They display destinations and route numbers. Fares vary, depending on the length of the journey, but are usually US$1.50-2.50. Higher fares at night.

Regular taxis (black with yellow roofs) are abundant, minimum charge US$0.35, plus US$0.15 per 200 m, more at night. Avoid taxis with more than 1 person in them, especially at night. For journeys outside the city arrange the charge beforehand. **Radio Taxis Andes Pacífico**, T02-9126000, www.andespacifico.cl.

Metro
The metro, www.metrosantiago.cl, is modern, fast, quiet and very full during rush hour. At the busiest times of day it will be all but impossible to board a train with any luggage. 1st train Mon-Sat 0600, Sun and holidays 0800; last train 2300. Fares vary according to time of journey; there are 3 charging periods: high 0715-0900 and 1800-2000, US$0.80; mid 0630-0700, 0900-1800 and 2000-2045, US$0.70, low all other times, US$0.65. The simplest solution is to buy a **Tarjeta Bíp**, which costs US$3 (and can be topped up subsequently).

Train
For the **Temuco** service, see page 264. Booking office at Estación Central, T02-689 5718/689 1682, www.efe.cl, till 2230.

Santiago metro

Santiago maps
1 Santiago orientation, page 212
2 Santiago centre, page 218
3 **Santiago metro, page 237**

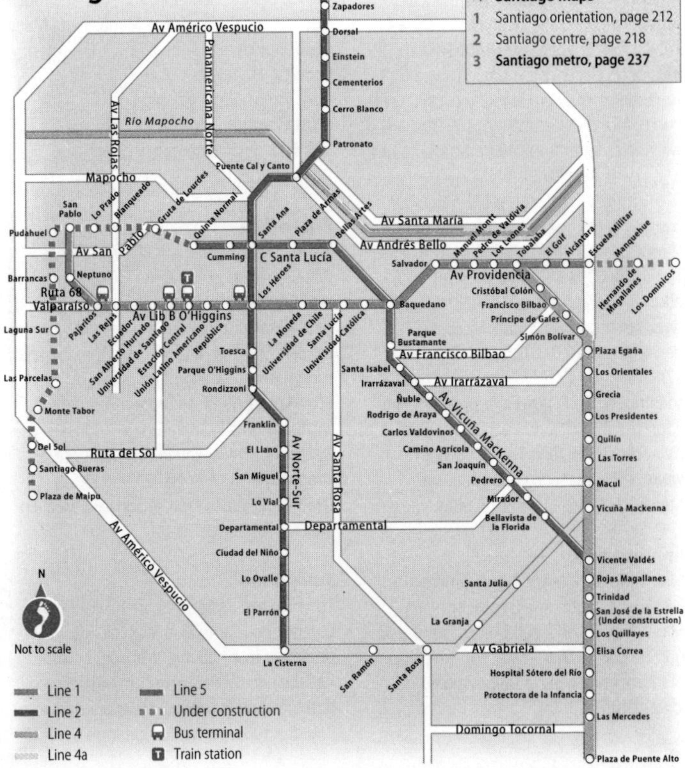

Directory

Santiago *p215, maps p212, p218 and p237*

Banks and currency exchange

Redbanc ATMs (for Cirrus) are everywhere. Official exchange rates are published in *El Mercurio*, *La Nación*, and on www.xe.com. The best rates are offered by *casas de cambio* around Paso Ahumada and Huérfanos (metro Universidad de Chile or Plaza de Armas). There is also a good selection on Pedro de Valdivia near the Alameda in Providencia. Most charge 3% commission to change TCs into dollars. Avoid street money changers (common on Ahumada and Agustinas).

Embassies and consulates

Argentina, Miraflores 285, T02-5822500. Also Argentine consulate, Vicuña MacKenna 41, T02-582 2608, open 0900-1400 (visa US$25, free for US citizens), if you need a visa for Argentina, get it here or in the consulates in Puerto Montt or Punta Arenas. Australians will need a letter from their embassy to get a visa here. **Australia**, Isidora Goyenechea 3261, Torre B, Las Condes, T02-5503500, consular.santiago@dfat.gov.au; **Canada**, Nueva Tajamar 481, Torre Norte, 12th floor, T02-3629660; **New Zealand**, El Golf 99, oficina 703, Las Condes, T02-290 9802, www.nzembassy.cl; **South Africa**, Av 11 de Septiembre 2353, Torre San Román, 17th floor, T02-2312862, www.embajada-sudafrica.cl; **UK**, El Bosque Norte 0125, 6th floor, T02-370 4100, www.britemb.cl; **USA**, Av Andrés Bello 2800, T02-3303000, www.embajadaeeuu.cl, consulate at Merced 230, T02-710 133, for visas.

Immigration

Ministerio del Interior, Departamento de Extranjería, Teatinos 950 (near Estación Mapocho), T02-674 4000, www.extranjeria.gob.cl, Mon-Fri 0900-1200. For extension of tourist visa or any enquiries regarding legal status.

Internet

Internet cafés are ubiquitous. Prices vary from US$0.60-1 per hr.

Language schools

Tandem Santiago, Ernesto Pinto Lagarrigue 362A, Recoleta-Barrio Bellavista, T02-735 8240, www.tandemsantiago.cl; **Natalislang Language Centre**, Vicuña Mackenna 06, piso 7, of 4, T02-222 8721, www.natalislang.com; **Pacifíca**, Guillermo Acuña 2884, Providencia, T02-205 5129, pacifica@netline.cl.

Medical services

If you need to get to a hospital, take a taxi rather than waiting for an ambulance. **Clínica Central**, San Isidro 231, T02-4631400, open 24 hrs; **Clínica Santa María**, Santa María 0500, Providencia, T02-4612000; **Emergency hospital**, Marcoleta 377, US$60, for vaccinations (not cholera); **Hospital de Urgencia (Posta Central)**, Portugal 125, cheapest public hospital; **Emergency pharmacy**, Portugal 155, T02-382 439.

Post office

The main post office is at Plaza de Armas (0800-1900), poste restante (30 days max) is well organized with a list of post received on display (one list for men, another for women, indicate Sr or Sra/Srita on envelope), passport essential for collection. Sub offices in Providencia, Av 11 de Septiembre 2092, Manuel Montt 1517, Pedro de Valdivia 1781, Providencia 1466, and in **Estación Central** shopping mall, Mon-Fri 0900-1800, Sat 0900-1230. Paper, tape, etc on sale, Mon-Fri 0800-1900, Sat 0800-1400.

Telephone

The cheapest call centres are on Bandera, Catedral and Santo Domingo, all near Plaza de Armas. International calls from here are half the price of the main company offices: to the US and Europe, US$0.20 per min, eg at Catedral 1033 and Santo Domingo 1091.

Going further ... Valparaíso

On the shores of the Pacific, 120 km west of Santiago, lies Valparaíso, from where dozens of cruise ships set off on the journey south to Patagonia every summer. Once the south Pacific's most important port and now the most beguiling city in Chile, part of Valparaíso has been declared a UNESCO World Heritage Site. It's really two cities: the flat, vaguely ordered area between the bus terminal and the port known as 'El Plan', and the chaotic crescent of 42 hills sprawling up from the sea, where packs of dogs lie sunning themselves, brightly painted houses pile on top of one another and half-forgotten passageways head up and down the hills, offering fantastic views of the Pacific, the city and – on a clear day – right over to the snow-capped cordillera. A city of contradictions and bohemia, Valparaíso has attracted a steady stream of poets and artists throughout its history.

Getting there Buses leave every 10 minutes from Pajaritos bus terminal in Santiago, 1½ hrs, US$7. Taxis can be caught directly from Santiago's international airport, 1¼ hrs, US$95. In summer there are direct bus services south as far as Pucón and Puerto Montt.

Don't miss ...

→ The World Heritage area around Cerros Alegre and Concepción built by rich British and German merchants now full of boutiques, cafés and artists.

→ Pablo Neruda's houses at La Sebastiana, and further down the coast at Isla Negra, with architecture and objets d'art as eccentric as their owner.

→ The resort city of Viña del Mar, just 9 km up the coast.

→ Cerro La Campana with some of Chile's finest views from its summit.

→ The Casablanca valley – Chile's premier white wine producing area

Sleeping B-C **Luna Sonrisa,** Templeman 833, Cerro Alegre, T032-2734117, www.lunasonrisa.cl. C-E singles, E per person in shared rooms. Some rooms with bath. Newly restored, bright, comfortable, large kitchen, lots of information and travel tips, excellent breakfast including wholemeal bread and real coffee, tours arranged, English and French spoken, friendly and helpful, and run by one of the authors of this guide. Highly recommended – of course! Also stylish appartment on upper floor with all mod cons A.

Chilean Lake District

Contents

Footprint features

Border crossing

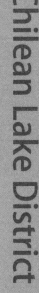

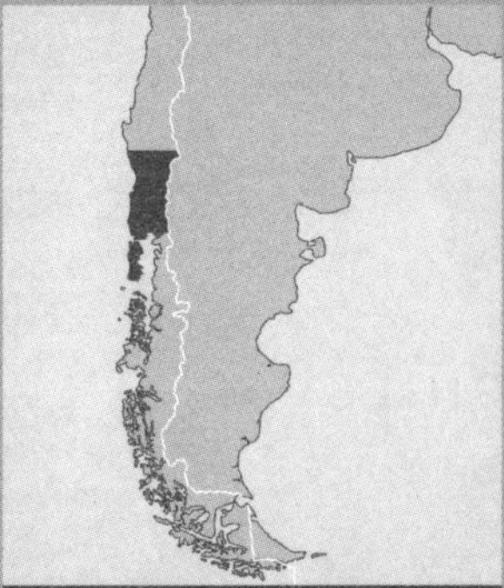

At a glance

Getting around There is an extensive bus network as well as numerous local tour operators to take you to sites of interest. Hiring a car will make things easier.

Time required You could do a different activity every day for a week and still have tons left to see.

Weather Pleasant during the day in summer and autumn. It can be a bit nippy at night and can rain at any time of the year.

When not to go Winter is seriously wet. More popular destinations are crowded in Feb.

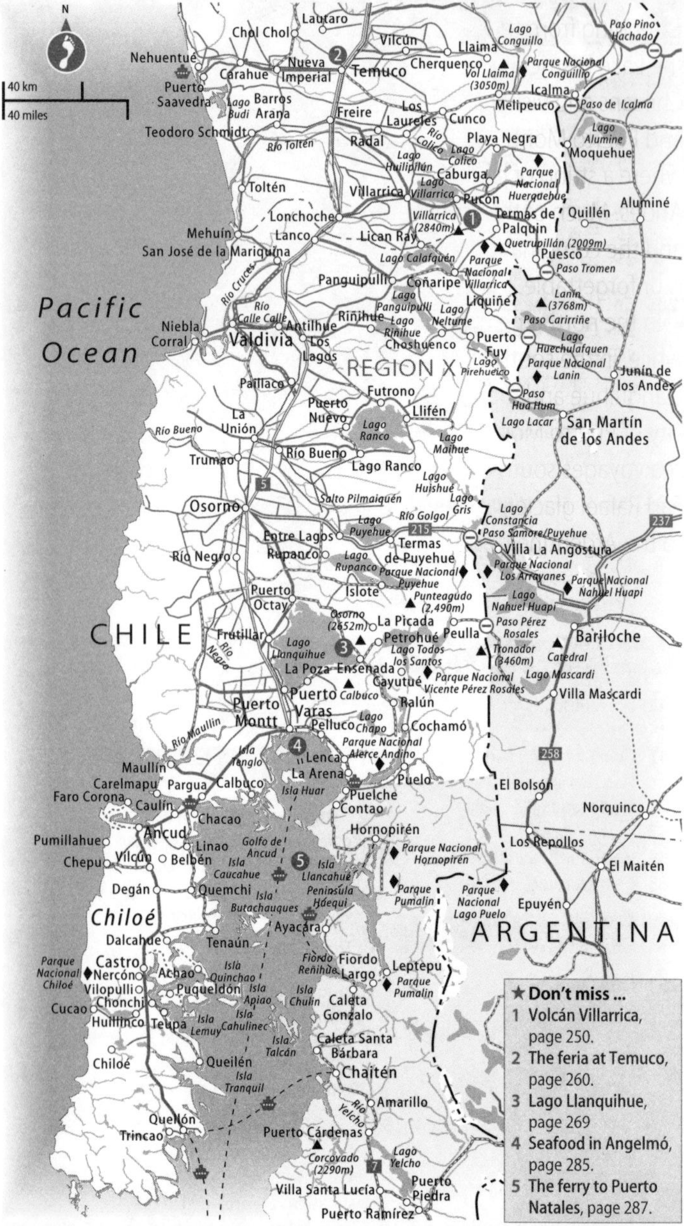

★ Don't miss ...

1. Volcán Villarrica, page 250.
2. The feria at Temuco, page 260.
3. Lago Llanquihue, page 269
4. Seafood in Angelmó, page 285.
5. The ferry to Puerto Natales, page 287.

Extending from the Río Biobío south to the city of Puerto Montt, the Lake District is one of the most popular destinations for both Chileans and visitors. The main cities are Temuco, Valdivia, Osorno and Puerto Montt, but the most attractive scenery lies further east, where a string of lakes stretches down the western side of the Andes. Much of this region has been turned into national parks and the combination of forests, lakes and snow-capped volcanoes is unforgettable.

In the north, the major resort is Pucón on Lago Villarrica, while, in the south, Volcán Osorno keeps watch over Lago Llanquihue and the Argentine border. Puerto Varas or the nearby city of Puerto Montt can both be used as the starting point for sea voyages south to Puerto Natales, Puerto Chacabuco and the San Rafael glacier, as well as east across the lakes and mountains to the Argentine resort of Bariloche.

Northern lakes

Patagonia really starts with the southern lakes but there's plenty to see further north, including Volcán Villarrica, which has erupted 10 times in the last century. The popular resort of Pucón around Lago Villarrica provide access to the volcano and the opportunity for a wealth of outdoor activities. Access is via Temuco, a good starting point for any exploration of the region, providing a gateway to some of the most beautiful spots in the Chilean Lake District. » *For listings, see pages 254-265.*

Ins and outs

Getting there 6 km southwest of Temuco is **Manquehue Airport**, with several daily flights north to Santiago and south to Puerto Montt. Taxis from airport to Temuco city centre cost US$8; there is no airport bus service. The **airport** 2 km east of Pucón on the Caburga road also has several flights a week to/from Santiago in summer. There is a new long-distance **bus terminal** on the outskirts of Temuco, with many daily connections to/from Santiago and other large Chilean towns, including Valdivia and Puerto Montt, plus Neuquén and Bariloche in Argentina. Pucón is served by four daily buses from Puerto Montt, several daily from Santiago, as well as regular services from Temuco and Villarrica. **Train** connections to Santiago and south as far as Puerto Montt are currently suspended. » *For further details, see Transport page 263.*

Getting around Temuco is the transport hub for the Lake District and its municipal bus station serves much of the region, as well as the communities towards the coast. Pucón is the main tourist centre on Lago Villarrica, offering tours and transport to nearby lakes and national parks.

Tourist information In Temuco, **Sernatur** ⓘ *Bulnes 586, T045-211969, infoaraucania @sernatur.cl, summer daily 0830-2030, winter Mon-Fri 0900-1200, 1500-1700*, has good leaflets in English. There is also a tourist kiosk in the market and an office of **CONAF** ⓘ *Bilbao 931, T045-234420.* Pucón's **tourist office** ⓘ *Municipalidad, O'Higgins 483, T045-293002, ofturismo@municipalidadpucon.cl*, provides information and sells licences for fishing on the lake. The **CONAF** office is at Lincoyan 336, with leaflets and information on the national parks. Villarrica's **tourist office** ⓘ *Valdivia 1070, T045-411162, daily in summer, Mon-Fri off season*, has information and maps.

Temuco » *pp254-265.*

At first sight, Temuco may appear a grey, forbidding place. However, in reality, it is a lively industrial and university town. For visitors, it is perhaps most interesting as a contrast to the more European cities in other parts of Chile. Temuco is proud of its Mapuche heritage, and it is this that gives it a distinctive character, especially around the *feria* (outdoor market). North and east of the city are national parks and reserves, and several hot springs.

Sights → *See map page 246. Colour map 1, A2.*

The city is centred on the newly redesigned **Plaza Aníbal Pinto**, around which are the main public buildings including the cathedral and the municipalidad. The cathedral was destroyed by the 1960 earthquake, when most of the old wooden buildings in the city were also burnt down. On the plaza itself is a monument to 'La Araucanía' featuring

The Mapuche

The largest indigenous group in southern South America take their name from the words for 'land' (*mapu*) and 'people' (*che*). They were known as Araucanians by the Spanish.

Never subdued by the Incas, the Mapuche resisted Spanish attempts at conquest. At the time of the great Mapuche uprising of 1598 they numbered 500,000, concentrated in the area between the Río Biobío and the Reloncaví estuary. The 1641 Treaty of Quilín recognized Mapuche autonomy south of the Biobío.

Although tools and equipment were privately owned, the Mapuche held land in common, abandoning it when it became exhausted. This relatively nomadic lifestyle helped them to resist the Spanish. They became formidable guerrilla fighters and pioneered the use of horses by two men. Horses also enabled the Mapuche to extend their territory to the eastern side of the Andes and the Argentine pampas.

The conquest of the Mapuche was made possible by the building of railways and the invention of new weapons. The settlement of border disputes between Chile and Argentina allowed Argentine troops to occupy border crossings, while the Chileans subjugated the Mapuche.

Under the 1881 treaty, the Mapuche received 500,000 ha from the government. They were confined to reservations, most of which were situated near large estates for which they provided a labour force. By the 1930s, the surviving Mapuche, living in more than 3000 separate reservations, had become steadily more impoverished and dependent on government money. Today Mapuche communities remain among the poorest in Chile and occupy only 1.5 % of the lands they inhabited at the time of the conquest.

Between Temuco and the Pacific coast is the indigenous heartland of Chile, home to the largest Mapuche communities. Here you will find traditional thatched houses (*rucas*) and villages still fiercely proud of their traditions, hinting at the sort of country that the first conquistadors might have found. It is well worth making a trip to the dusty, friendly town of Chol Chol. Buses (Huincabus, four daily 1100-1800, one hour, US$1), laden with people and produce, make the 30-km journey from Temuco across rolling countryside. You will see people travelling by ox cart on the tracks nearby, and a few traditional round *rucas*. The town has a small museum dedicated to Mapuche culture.

figures from local history. Nearby are fountains and a small **Sala de Exposiciones**, which stages exhibitions. More compelling, though, is the huge produce **market** (*feria*) at Lautaro y Aníbal Pinto, which is always crammed with people (many of them Mapuche), who have come from the countryside to sell their produce (see page 260).

West of the centre, the **Museo de la Araucanía** ⓘ *Alemania 084, Mon-Fri 0900-1700, Sat 1100-1700, Sun 1100-13001400, US$1.50 (free Sun)*, houses a well arranged collection devoted to the history and traditions of the Mapuche nation; there's also a section on German settlement.

A couple of kilometres northeast of the centre is the **Museo Nacional Ferroviario Pablo Neruda** ⓘ *Barros Arana 0565, T045-973940, www.museoferroviariotemuco.cl, Tue-Sun 0900-1800, US$2, concessions US$0.50, bus 1 variante or taxi (US$3 from the centre)*. Exhibits include over 20 engines and carriages (including the former presidential carriage) dating from 1908 to 1953. The grounds contain rusting hulks and machinery, while the annex houses temporary exhibitions.

On the northern edge of the city is the **Monumento Natural Cerro Ñielol** offering views of the city and surrounding countryside. The final peace treaty between the Chilean army and the Mapuche was signed on Cerro Nielol in 1881, under 'La Patagua', a tree that can still be seen. It is a good spot for a picnic. There is an excellent **visitor centre** ⓘ *0830-2030, US$1.50*, run by **CONAF** and a fine collection of native plants, including the *copihue rojo*, the national flower. Note that the hill has a one-way system for drivers (entry by Prat, exit by Lynch) and that bicycles are only allowed in before 1100.

Southeast of the centre is the predominantly Mapuche suburb of **Padre las Casas**. Here you will find the **Casa de la Mujer Mapuche** ⓘ *Corvalín y Almte Barroso, T045-233886, Mon-Fri 0930-1300, 1500-1830, bus 8a/10, colectivo 13a*, which sells crafts and textiles made by a co-operative of 135 Mapuche weavers. The items are very good quality, but expensive.

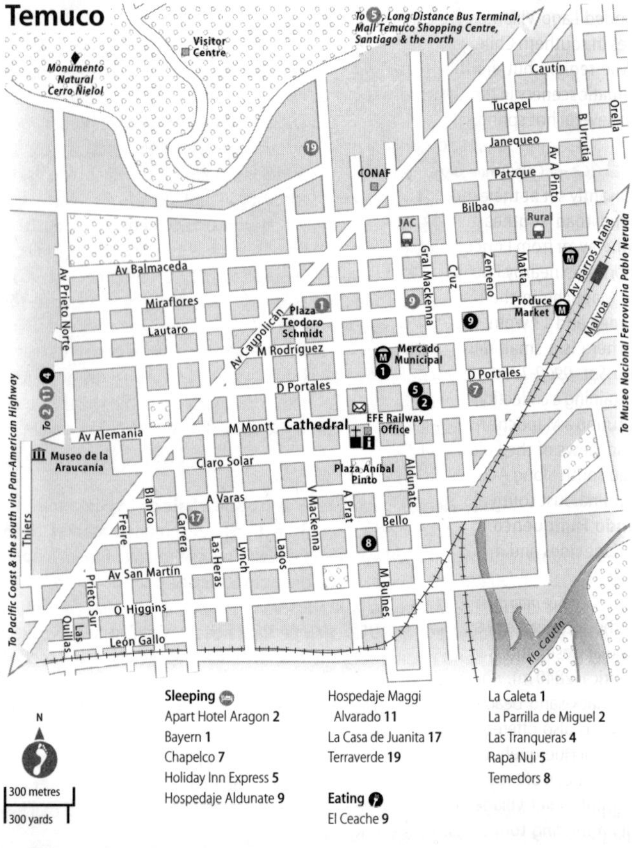

Sleeping
Apart Hotel Aragon **2**
Bayern **1**
Chapelco **7**
Holiday Inn Express **5**
Hospedaje Aldunate **9**
Hospedaje Maggi Alvarado **11**
La Casa de Juanita **17**
Terraverde **19**

Eating
El Ceache **9**
La Caleta **1**
La Parrilla de Miguel **2**
Las Tranqueras **4**
Rapa Nui **5**
Temedors **8**

Going further ... Parque Nacional Conguillio

One of the most popular national parks in Chile lies 80 km east of Temuco and is a good stopping point en route to the Argentine border at Paso Pino Hachado (see page 103). At the centre of the park is the still-active Volcán Llaima. It is possible to climb the volcano, hike through the forests of ancient araucaria and also ski. The best means of visiting is with a hired 4WD or as part of a tour. The three park entrances are accessible from Curacautín, Melipeuco and Cherquenco, respectively. There is a visitor centre at the entrance by Lago Conguillio. Open December to March, US$7.

Lago Villarrica » pp254-265.

Backed to the southeast by the active and snow-capped Villarrica volcano (2840 m), wooded Lago Villarrica, 21 km long and about 7 km wide, is one of the most beautiful lakes in southern Chile. Its resorts – Villarrica and Pucón – are among the more expensive in the region, but are definitely worth a visit. Within easy reach is some of the most dramatic scenery in the Chilean Lake District, encompassing two lakes, two national parks and several hot spring resorts, perfect for relaxation after a hard day's trekking.

Villarrica → *Colour map 1, A3.*

Pleasantly set at the extreme southwest corner of the lake, Villarrica can be reached by a paved road southeast from **Freire**, 24 km south of Temuco on the Pan-American Highway, or from **Loncoche**, 54 km south of Freire, also paved. Less significant as a tourist resort than nearby Pucón, it is also cheaper. Founded in 1552, the town was besieged by the Mapuche in the uprising of 1599: after three years the surviving Spanish settlers, 11 men and 13 women, surrendered. The town was refounded in 1882.

There is a small museum, the **Museo Histórico** ⓘ *Pedro de Valdivia 1050 y Zegers, Mon-Sat 0900-1730, 1800-2200, Sun 1800-2200, reduced hours in winter, US$0.650,* containing a collection of Mapuche artefacts. Next to it is the **Muestra Cultural Mapuche**, featuring a Mapuche *ruca* and stalls selling good-quality handicrafts in summer. There are good views of the volcano from the *costanera*; for a different perspective over the lake, head south along Aviador Acevedo and then take Poniente Ríos towards the **Hostería de la Colina**. Just south of town (500 m along Avenida Matta), there is a large working farm, **Fundo Huifquenco** ⓘ *T045-412200, www.fundohuifquenco.cl*, with trails, horse riding, carriage rides and meals (book in advance).

Pucón → *See map page 248. Colour map 1, A3.*

On the southeastern corner of the lake, 26 km east of Villarrica, Pucón is one of the most popular destinations in the Lake District, famous above all as a centre for visiting Volcán Villarrica (2840 m), which lies to the south. Built across the neck of a peninsula, the town has two black-sand beaches, which are popular for swimming and watersports. Whitewater rafting is also offered on the nearby rivers and excursions can be made into the Parque Nacional Huerquehue and Parque Nacional Villarrica, which both lie east of the town.

The Pucón of today is very different from the town of 30 years ago, when it was a small, pleasant, quiet village with seasonal Chilean tourism, but no foreign backpackers. It is now a thriving tourist centre, full of Chileans in summer and gringos in the spring and autumn. Neon signs are forbidden and road signs and telephone kiosks are made of wood, but the streets are full of bars, restaurants and *artesanía*. The commercial centre lies between **Avenida O'Higgins**, the main thoroughfare, and the **Gran Hotel Pucón**. Private land (ask for permission at the entrance) leads west from the centre to **La Península**, where there are views of the lake and volcano, as well as a golf course. There is also a nice walk along the **Costanera Otto Gudenschwager**, starting at the northern end of Calle Ansorena and following the lakeside to the north.

Boat trips ⓘ *daily 1500 and 1900, summer only, 2 hrs, US$8*, on the lake leave from the landing stage at La Poza at the western end of O'Higgins. Walk a couple of kilometres

Sleeping
Antumalal **2** *C1*
Donde Germán **6** *C3*
Gran Pucón **8** *A2*
Gudenschwager **4** *A1*
Hospedaje Graciela **13** *C2*
Hospedaje Lucía **17** *C2*
Hospedaje M@yra **10** *B3*
Hospedaje Sonia **18** *B2*
Hospedaje Victor **11** *C2*
Hostal Backpackers **3** *C2*
Hostal Gerónimo **26** *B3*
Hostal Willy **5** *C3*
Hostería École **21** *B3*
La Posada Plaza-Pucón **28** *B1*
La Poza **9** *C1*
La Tetera **29** *B2*
Malalhue **7** *C3*
Tree House Hostel **14** *B3*

Eating
Arabian **1** *B2*
il Baretto **5** *B2*
La Maga **7** *B2*
Puerto Pucón **10** *B2*
Rap Hamburguesa **9** *B3*
Senzo **11** *B2*

north along the beach from here to the mouth of the Río Trancura for views of volcanoes. Or take a **boat** ⓘ *summer only, US$15*, to the mouth of the river from near the Gran Hotel.

From the road to the Villarrica volcano, a *ripio* road branches off for 5 km to some privately managed *cuevas volcánicas* (**volcanic caves**) ⓘ *US$18*, surrounded by a small attractive park with tunnels and a museum, as well as paths through the forest. Entry to the site is expensive, but it's recommended as a bad-weather option. Snowmobile tours are also offered.

Lago Caburga and around » *pp254-265. Colour map 1, A3.*

Lago Caburga (spelt locally Caburgua) is a very pretty lake in a wild setting 25 km northeast of Pucón. It is unusual for its beautiful white-sand beach (other beaches in the area have black volcanic sand), and is supposedly the warmest lake in the Lake District. The western and much of the eastern shores are inaccessible to vehicles, but the village of **Caburga**, at the southern end of the lake, is reached by a turning off the main road to Argentina, 8 km east of Pucón.

If walking or cycling, there is a very pleasant alternative route: turn left 3 km east of Pucón, cross the Río Trancura via Puente Quelhue, then turn right and follow the track for 18 km through beautiful scenery. (From the bridge, there are also pleasant walks along the north shore of Lago Villarrica to the Mapuche settlement of **Quelhue** and the beach at **Río Plata**.) Just off the main road from Pucón, Km 15, are the **Ojos de Caburga** ⓘ *US$1*, beautiful pools fed from underground, particularly attractive after rain.

The northern tip of Lago Caburga can be reached by a road from Cunco, which runs east along the northern shore of **Lago Colico**. This is one of the less accessible lakes, and lies north of Lago Villarrica in a remote setting.

Parque Nacional Huerquehue → *Colour map 1, A3.*

ⓘ *Open all year but often closed in winter after heavy snowfall, US$6, parking 1.5 km along the track.*

Located a short distance east of Lago Caburga, Parque Nacional Huerquehue covers 12,500 ha at altitudes rising to 1952 m at Cerro San Sebastián in the **Nevados del Caburgua**. It also encompasses about 20 lakes, some of them very small, and many araucaria (monkey puzzle) trees. The entrance and administration is on the western edge, near **Lago Tinquilco**, the largest lake in the park. From the entrance there is a well-signed track north up a steep hill to **Lago Chico**, where the track divides left to **Lago Verde** and right to **Laguna Toro**. Both paths eventually meet up, making a circuit. The lakes are surrounded by trees and are very beautiful. At **Lago Huerquehue**, a further 20 km of trails begin. None of the routes is particularly taxing, making the park a good warm-up for the Volcán Villarrica hike. An adequate map is available at the entrance and the warden is very helpful. People in the park rent horses and boats, and there is a restaurant.

Reserva Forestal Cañi

ⓘ *Information from Fundación Lahuén, Urrutia 477, Pucón, T045-441660, lahuen@interaccess.cl. Park entrance is US$5 per person; tours arranged by Hostería École, Urrutia, Pucón, see under accommodation below.*

Situated south of Parque Nacional Huerquehue and covering 500 ha, this is a private nature reserve owned by the **Fundación Lahuén**, and only accessible on a guided tour – it is definitely worth a visit. The reserve contains 17 small lakes and is covered by ancient native forests of coigue and lenga; it also has hundreds of millennial araucaria trees. From its highest peak, **El Mirador** (1550 m), there are panoramic views over neighbouring parts of Argentina and Chile, including four volcanoes: Lanín, Villarrica, Quetrupillán and Llaima. As the reserve is above the winter snowline, tours are normally restricted to summer, though visits in winter are sometimes possible.

Parque Nacional Villarrica ⏵⏵ *pp254-265. Colour map 1, A3.*

This park, which covers 61,000 ha, stretches from Pucón to the Argentine border near Puesco. There are three sectors: around Volcán Villarrica; around Volcán Quetrupillán and the Puesco sector, which includes the slopes of the Lanín volcano on the Argentine border. Each sector has its own entrance and ranger station. Between July and October it is possible to ski at the **Pucón resort**, which is situated on the eastern slopes of Villarrica and reached by a badly maintained track (see page 262).

Climbing Villarrica → *Colour map 1, A3.*

The Villarrica volcano, 2840 m high and still active, lies 8 km south of Pucón. Access to the volcano, US$5, is in theory restricted only to groups with a guide and to individuals who can show proof of membership of a mountaineering club in their own country. Entry is refused if the weather is poor. There is no public transport, although several agencies offer excursions (see Activities and tours, page 263). Tours from Pucón cost US$70-85, including park entry, guide, transport to park entrance and equipment (no reduction for those with their own equipment). Bargain for group rates. You should also take sunglasses, sun block, plenty of water and chocolate or some other snack. For those wanting to climb the volcano independently, good boots, crampons and ice picks are essential; these can be rented for US$12 per day from tour operators. Equipment is checked at the park entrance.

Lagos Villarrica, Caburga & Colico

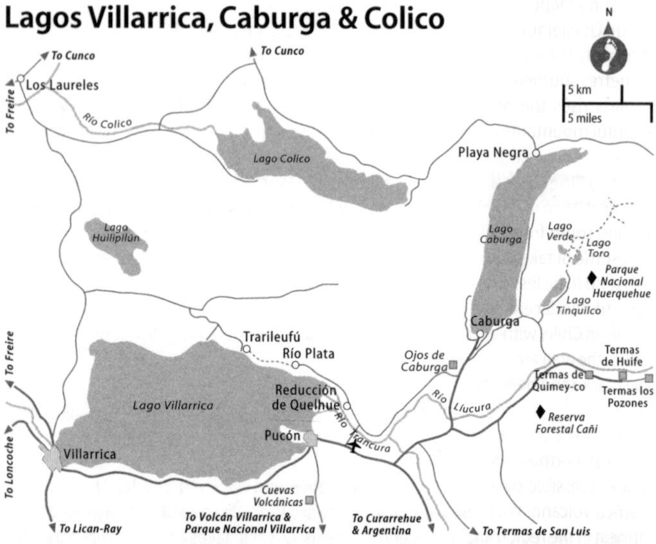

It is a three- to four-hour trek to the summit, but you can skip the first 400 m by taking the ski lift (US$10). At the summit look down into the crater and with the right conditions you can see bubbling molten lava, but beware of the sulphur fumes; take a cloth mask moistened with lemon juice. On clear days you can see six or more other volcanoes. Conditions permitting, groups may carry ski or snowboard equipment for the descent; otherwise just slide down toboggan style – great fun.

Towards Paso Mamuil Malal

From Pucón a road runs southeast along the southern bank of the valley of the Río Trancura to the Argentine border at Paso Mumuil Malal/Tromen (see page 103) and on through Parque Nacional Lanín to Junín de los Andes. Unless the pass is closed by snow, this is the route used by most international buses from Temuco. The road provides access en route to thermal springs and a number of hikeable waterfalls (*saltos*) in the Quetrupillán and Puesco sectors of the Villarrica national park.

At Km 18, a *ripio* road heads south 10 km to the Quetrupillán section of the park. On the edge of the park are the **Termas de Palguín** ⓘ *www.termasdepalguin.cl, US$10*, and the spectacular **Saltos del Puma** and **del León** ⓘ *US$2 for both*. From the springs a very rough dirt road, great for horse riding, runs south across the national park to Coñaripe. Palguín is also the starting point for a three-day hike to Puesco, with vistas over the Villarrica and Lanín volcanoes.

Back on the Curarrehue road, at Km 23, a turning leads north to the indoor and outdoor pools at **Termas de San Luis** ⓘ *www.termasdesanluis.cl, US$9*, from where it is 30 minutes' walk to **Lago del León**. At Km 35 another turning leads north for 15 km to the **Termas de Panqui** ⓘ *US$10*, where there are three pools beautifully situated in the mountains. » *See also box, page 257.*

Beyond the small town of **Curarrehue**, 36 km east of Pucón, where there is a small but interesting Mapuche museum, the road continues unpaved, climbing south past Puesco to Lago Quellelhue, a beautiful area for trekking, tranquil and with well-marked trails. This is probably the easiest area to see araucaria forest close-up from the comfort of a car. Six kilometres southeast is the border at **Paso Mamuil Malal** (Paso Tromen). To the south of the pass rises the graceful cone of **Volcán Lanín** (3747 m), one of the world's most beautiful mountains (see page 103).

Seven Lakes » *pp254-265. Colour map 1, A3.*

Heading south from Villarrica, you can rejoin the Pan-American highway towards Valdivia and Osorno or take a more leisurely route southeast to Lican Ray and the 'Siete Lagos'. These lakes tend to be less developed than the resorts to the north and south. They form a picture-postcard necklace of water, with a backdrop of thick woods and distant snows. Six of the lakes lie in Chile, with the seventh, Lago Lacar, in Argentina. After the final peace settlement of 1882 the area around these lakes was reserved for Mapuche settlements. Most of the lakes have black-sand beaches, although as the water level rises in spring, these all but disappear.

Lago Calafquén and around → *Colour map 1, A3.*

The most northerly of the seven lakes, Lago Calafquén is a popular tourist destination, readily accessible by a paved road from Villarrica, along which there are fine views of the Villarrica volcano. Wooded and dotted with small islands, the lake is reputedly one of the warmest in the region and is good for swimming. A partly paved road runs around the lake.

The major resort on the lake is **Lican Ray**, named after a legendary Mapuche woman (see box, page 253). It is 30 km south of Villarrica on the north shore and, although crowded in summer, most facilities close by April. There are two beaches, one on each side of the peninsula. Boats can be hired (US$5 an hour) and there are catamaran trips (US$7 per hour or US$23 to the islands). Some 6 km to the east is the river of lava formed when the Villarrica volcano erupted in 1971. There is a **tourist office** ⓘ *on the plaza, daily in summer, Mon-Fri in winter*.

Coñaripe, lies 21 km southeast of Lican Ray with a black-sand beach surrounded by mountains. The **tourist office** ⓘ *on the plaza, mid-Nov to mid-Apr daily; late Apr to early Nov Sat and Sun only*, can arrange excursions to local thermal springs. From Coñaripe a road (mostly *ripio*) around the lake's southern shore leads to **Lago Panguipulli**, 38 km west, with views over Volcán Villarrica.

Northeast, a decent *ripio* road heads towards the Quetrupillán sector of the Parque Nacional Villarrica. At Km 17 are the **Termas Geométricas** ⓘ *T02-2141214, www.termasgeometricas.cl, US$22*, 17 architecturally designed pools of different sizes and geometrical shapes. There's a café. After the *termas* the road continues, in a deteriorating state, passable in summer only by 4WD before arriving at the Termas de Palguín (see pages 251 and 257).

Another poor route heads southeast towards the Argentine border at **Paso Carirriñe** (see page 254). As it crosses the steep Cuesta Los Añiques, there are views of **Lago Pellaifa**, a tiny lake with rocky surroundings and a small beach. The **Termas de Coñaripe** ⓘ *Km 15, 2 km from the lakeshore, T063-431407, www.termasdeconaripe.cl*, has four pools,

The Seven Lakes

The legend of Lican Ray

At the height of the wars between the Spanish and the Mapuche a young Spanish soldier was lost and strayed into the forests near Lago Calafquén. He came across a beautiful young Mapuche woman drying her hair in the sun and singing. He began to sing along and as they exchanged glances, they fell in love. She called him Allumanche, which means white man in Mapuche, and, indicated that her name was Lican Rayan, meaning the flower of magic stone. They began to live together near the lake.

Lican Rayan's father, Curtilef, a powerful and fearsome chief, feared she might be dead. One day a boy came to him and said: "Lican Rayan is alive. I have seen her near the lake with a white man but she is not a prisoner: it is clear they are in love".

Lican Rayan saw the warriors coming to look for her. They escaped by riding on logs to one of the islands where they hid for several days. The north wind blew and it rained heavily. Unable to bear the cold and thinking that the warriors would have given up the search, they lit a fire. The smoke was spotted by Curtilef's men, so Lican Rayan and the solider fled to another island further away but again they were discovered and had to escape. This happened so many times that, although they were never caught, they were never seen again.

In the town of Lican Ray, it is said that on spring afternoons it is sometimes possible to see a distant column of smoke from one of the islands, where Lican Rayan and the soldier are still enjoying their love after over 400 years.

Abridged and translated from *Lengua Y Costumbres Mapuches* by Orietta Appelt Martin, Imprenta Austral, Temuco, 1995.

accommodation, restaurant, cycles and horses for hire. They can organize transport from the town of Coñaripe. Further south are the **Termas de Liquiñe** ⓘ *Km 32, T063-317377, US$6-10 per person*, with eight thermal springs and accommodation (but little other infrastructure), surrounded by a small native forest. About 8 km north of Liquiñe is a road going southwest (20 km) along the southeast shore of **Lago Neltume** to meet the Choshuenco–Puerto Fuy road.

Lagos Panguipulli and Pirehueico → *Colour map 1, A3.*

Covering 116 sq km, Lago Panguipulli, the largest of the seven lakes, is reached by paved road from Lanco or Los Lagos on the Pan-American Highway or by *ripio* roads from Lago Calafquén. A road leads along the beautiful northern shore, which is wooded with sandy beaches and cliffs.

The site of a Mapuche settlement, **Panguipulli**, meaning 'hill of pumas', is situated on a hillside at the northwest corner of the lake and is the largest town in the area. On Plaza Prat is the Iglesia San Sebastián, built in Swiss style, with three bells from Germany. The plaza also has a tourist office (open December to February only). In summer, catamaran trips are offered on the lake and excursions can be made to Lagos Calafquén, Neltume, Pirehueico and Riñihue.

Choshuenco lies 45 km east of Panguipulli on the Río Llanquahue, at the eastern tip of the lake and can only be reached by road from Panguipulli or Puerto Fuy. To the south is the **Reserva Nacional Mocho Choshuenco** (7536 ha), which has two volcanoes: Choshuenco (2415 m) and Mocha (2422 m). On the slopes of Choshuenco the **Club Andino de Valdivia** runs a small ski resort and three *refugios*. From Choshuenco a road leads east towards Neltume and Lago Pirehueico, via the impressive waterfalls of **Huilo**

Border crossing

Paso Carirriñe

Paso Carirriñe across the Argentine border is open between 15 October and 31 August, and is reached by a bad unpaved road about 15 km from the Termas de Liquiñe. On the Argentine side the road continues through the Parque Nacional Lanín to Junín de los Andes (see page 103).

Chilean immigration and customs Daily 0800-2000.

Argentine immigration and customs Daily 0800-2000.

Huilo. The falls are three hours' walk from Choshuenco, or take the Puerto Fuy bus and get off at **Alojamiento Huilo Huilo.**

Lago Pirehueico is a 36-km-long, narrow and deep glacial lake surrounded by virgin lingue forest. It is beautiful and largely unspoilt, although there are plans to build a huge tourist complex in Puerto Pirehueico. There are two ports on the lake: **Puerto Fuy** at the northern end and **Puerto Pirehueico** at the southern end. The ports are linked by a ferry service (the crossing is beautiful) and can also be reached by the road that runs east from Neltume to the Argentine border crossing at **Paso Hua Hum** (see page 106). The road south from Puerto Fuy, however, is privately owned and closed to traffic.

Northern lakes listings

For Sleeping and Eating price codes and other relevant information, see pages 41-44.

Sleeping

Temuco *p244, map p246*

Many cheaper *residenciales* and *pensiones* can be found in the market area.

L-AL Terraverde, Prat 0220, T045-239999, www.panamericanahoteles.cl. This is the best hotel in town, although it is starting to show its age a little and probably does not justify its 5-star status.

AL Apart Hotel Aragón, España 446, T045-262769, www.aparthotelaragon.cl. Fully furbished and comfortable apartments in a nice area just west of the centre.

A Bayern, Prat 146, T045-276000, www.hotelbayern.cl. Standard 3-star. Small rooms, clean, helpful, buffet breakfast, parking. Cheaper if paying in US dollars.

A Holiday Inn express, Av R Ortega 01800, T045-223300, www.holidayinnexpress.cl. Chileanized version of this International chain. Good value with heating, a/c, internet, pool. Out of town but convenient for bus terminal and worth considering if driving.

B-C Chapelco, Cruz 401, T045-749393 www.hotelchapelco.cl. Rooms with bath and cable TV. Breakfast, internet in lobby, comfortable, good service, recommended.

B-C La Casa de Juanita, Carrera 735, T045-213203, juany362@hotmail.com. Quiet B&B. Hot water, laundry, heating, parking. Cheaper without bath. Similar places on Bello, west of the plaza.

C Hospedaje Maggi Alvarado, Recreo 209, off Av Alemania, T045-409804, cppacl@gmail.com. **E** singles. Small rooms, but very clean, friendly, helpful, in a pleasant part of town. Also has a good-value *cabaña* sleeping 4.

C-D Hospedaje Aldunate, Aldunate 187, T045-270057, cristorresvalenzuela@hotmail.com. **E** singles. Friendly, cooking facilities. Some rooms with TV and bath.

Villarrica *p247*

Off-season is 30-40% cheaper.

LL Villarrica Park Lake, Km 13 on road to Pucón, T045-450000, www.vplh.cl. 5-star. Rooms are spacious and all have balconies overlooking the lake. Conference rooms, banquet halls, spa with pools, sauna, solarium, tours. Helpful staff. Recommended, but only if you have your own transport.

AL El Ciervo, Koerner 241, T045-411215, www.hotelelciervo.cl. 4-star. Comfortable rooms with heating, in pleasant grounds. German-style breakfasts. German and some English spoken, pool, terrace, Wi-Fi. Probably the best hotel in the town centre. Recommended.

AL Parque Natural Dos Ríos, 13 km west of Villarrica, T09-94198064, www.dosrios.de. With full board. Tranquil 40-ha nature park with *cabañas* on the banks of the Río Toltén (white-sand beach), horse riding, birdwatching, child-friendly. German, English spoken.

AL-A Hostería de la Colina, Las Colinas 115, overlooking town, T045-411503, www.hosteria delacolina.com. Large gardens, breakfast and restaurant (the owner makes fresh ice cream every day), Wi-Fi, fine views, especially from the spacious suites. English spoken, very attentive friendly service. Highly recommended.

AL-A Hotel y Cabañas El Parque, 3 km east on Pucón road, T045-411120, www.hotelel parque.cl. Lakeside with beach, tennis courts, breakfast, good restaurant with set meals. Highly recommended.

B Hostería Bilbao, Henríquez 43, T045-411186, www.interpatagonia.com/bilbao. Clean rooms, pretty patio, good restaurant.

B Hotel-Yachting Kiel, Koerner 153, T045-411631, www.yachtingkiel.cl. Small 6-room hotel, 3 with views across the lake to the volcano. The others are smaller and much cheaper. Spacious bathrooms, cable TV and heating. Clean, friendly, German and some English spoken. Good restaurant.

C La Torre Suiza, Bilbao 969, T045-411213, www.torresuiza.com. **E** pp in dorms. Some rooms with bath. Great breakfast, kitchen and laundry, camping, bike rental, book exchange. German/English spoken. Recommended.

C Villa Linda, Pedro de Valdivia 678, T045-411392, www.villalinda.tk. **E** singles. Slightly tacky charmless interior. Hot water, clean, basic, cheap, food available.
C-D Hospedaje Nicolás, Anfión Muñoz 477, T045-410232. **F** singles. Basic rooms with cable TV and bath. With breakfast. Good value, although the walls are thin.

Camping

Many sites east of town on Pucón road, but these are expensive and open in season only. It may be cheaper to stay in a *hospedaje*; nearest to town is **El Edén**, 1 km southeast of centre, T045-412772, US$6 pp. Recommended.

Pucón *p247, map p248*

Price codes are based on high-season rates; off season prices can be 20-40% lower and it's often possible to negotiate.
LL Antumalal, Km 2 west of Pucón on the Villarrica Highway, T045-441011, www.antumalal.com. Very small, picturesque Bauhaus chalet-style, set in 2 ha of parkland, magnificent views of the lake, lovely gardens, pool, hot tub, sauna, open year round.
LL-L Gran Hotel Pucón, Holzapfel 190, T045-913300, www.granhotelpucon.cl. Once Pucón's best, this hotel has seen better days. It has recently been taken over by the casino, however, and improvements are promised. Rooms at the back have beautiful lake views.
AL Malalhue, Camino Internacional 1615, T045-443130, www.malalhue.cl. One of the better hotels in town, about 15 mins walk from the centre. Staff are generally helpful and most speak English. Rooms at the back are quieter and have views of the volcano.
AL-A Gudenschwager, Pedro de Valdivia 12, T045-442025, www.hogu.cl. Refurbished 1920s hotel. 20 simple centrally heated rooms (thin walls), some with lake and volcano view. Cheaper rooms with exterior bathroom. Reasonable rates off season. Living room with big screen TV and Wi-Fi area. English spoken.
A La Posada Plaza-Pucón, Valdivia 191, T045-441088, www.hotelplazapucon.cl. Simple, somewhat dated rooms with bath, restaurant, also spacious cabins, gardens and a pool. Cheaper when paying in dollars. Great location but could do with a refit.
A-B Hostal Gerónimo, Alderete 665, T045-443762, www.geronimo.cl. Recently refurbished. Rooms with bath and cable TV. Comfortable, friendly, quiet, with restaurant, bar and terrace. Recommended, but avoid the pokey rooms on the ground floor.
B-C Hostal Willy, Arauco 565, T045-444578, www.hostalyturismowilly.com. **D** singles. Pleasant carpeted and heated rooms with cable TV and spacious bathrooms. Breakfast available, internet, use of kitchen. Friendly, good value, recommended. The annex across the street is not nearly as good.
B-C Hostería Ecole, Urrutia 592, T045-441675, www.ecole.cl. **F** pp in dorms without breakfast, rooms on the small side, some with bath, good vegetarian and fish restaurant, ecological shop, forest treks, rafting, biking, information, language classes, massage. Staff are a mixed bag, some are friendly and very helpful, others are disinterested.
B-C La Tetera, Urrutia 580, T045-441462, www.tetera.cl. Rooms with and without bath. Good breakfast with real coffee, friendly, English spoken, good Spanish classes, book swap, lots of information. Recommended, book in advance.
C Donde Germán, Brasil 640, T045-442444, www.dondegerman.cl. **F**pp in dorms. Comfortable hostel relocated in a new building. Good beds, nice common areas, clean, kitchen facilities. Friendly, tours arranged. Recommended.
C Hospedaje M@yra, Colo Colo 485, T045-442745, www.myhostelpucon.com. **E** singles. Good backpackers' hostel. Some rooms with bath and cable TV. Kitchen, internet, laundry, parking, tours offered.
C Hospedaje Víctor, Palguín 705, T045-443525, www.pucon.com/victor. **E-F** pp in 4-bed dorms. Some rooms with bath. Kitchen facilities, TV, laundry. Friendly. A decent choice.

... and relax

More than a third of all the thermal spas in Chile are in the Lake District, thanks to the high level of volcanic activity in this area. There are several east of Pucón, ranging from luxurious hotel complexes with extensive spa treatments to rustic bathtubs in the forest and natural pools or rivers. Easing your aching muscles in thermal water is the perfect way to recover after an arduous volcano trek.

The most upmarket are the **Termas de Huife**, Km 33, T045-1975666, www.termashuife.cl, US$18, reached via a turning off the Pucón–Caburga road. The complex has three modern pools on the banks of the river Liucura. Overnight guests at Hostería Termas de Huife (**AL**) stay in cabins on site and can indulge in various treatments.

Closer to Pucón and slightly more low key are the recently refitted **Termas de Quimey-Co**, Km 29, T045-441903, US$12, with a hotel (**B**), campsite and two cabins.

Further on are the **Termas los Pozones**, Km 35, US$7 per day, US$9 at night, which have six natural rock pools but little infrastructure and are popular with backpackers.

Termas de Palguín, T045-441968, www.termasdepalguin.cl, US$9, are in a beautiful spot in the Quetrupillán section of the Villarrica national park, close to the spectacular Saltos del Puma and del León. There's a pool, private baths and cabins.

Termas de San Luis, T045-443965, www.sanluis.pucon.com, US$11, are reached north off the Curarrehue road at Km 23. There's an indoor and outdoor pool, a sauna and *cabañas* (**A**), plus a pick-up service for overnight guests from Pucón.

At Km 35, another turning leads north for 15 km to the **Termas de Pangui**, US$12, where there are three pools beautifully situated in the mountains. Accommodation is in a lodge (**D-E**) or in 3-person teepees right next to the hot pools. There are also camping facilities, good vegetarian meals, trekking and aromatherapy; contact O'Higgins 555, of 2, Pucón, T045-442039, ingeluz@yahoo.com.

C Hostal Backpackers, Palguín 695, T045-441373 www.backpackerspucon.com. Kitchen facilities, internet, cycle hire, information, also run their own excursions.
C The Tree House Hostel, Urrutia 660, T045-444679, www.treehousechile.cl. **E** pp in dorms. Fun and lively English-run hostel, good matresses but mostly bunk beds. Breakfast extra. Lots of info. Kitchen facilities and large patio. Good reports.
C-D Hospedaje Graciela, Pasaje Rolando Matus 521 (off Av Brasil). **F** singles. Comfortable rooms, good food.
C-D Hospedaje Lucía, Lincoyán 565, T045-441721. **E** singles. Some rooms with bath. Friendly, quiet, garden, cooking facilities.
C-D Hospedaje Sonia, Lincoyán 485, T045-441269, www.pucon.com/sonia. **F** singles. Basic but clean rooms, some with bath. Use of kitchen, noisy and somewhat crowded, friendly. Basic English spoken.

Camping

La Poza, Costanera Geis 769, T045-441435. Hot showers, clean, quiet, good kitchen facilities, open all year. Recommended.
L'étoile, Km 2 towards Volcán Villarrica, T045-442188. Attractive forest site.
Millaray, Km 7 west of Pucón, T045-212336. Lakeside campsite.
Saint John, Km 7 west of Pucón, T045-441165, Casilla 154. Beside the lake.

Lago Caburga and around *p249*
AL-A Landhaus San Sebastián, east of Lago Caburga, T045-1972360, www.landhaus-chile.com. With bath and breakfast, tasty meals, laundry facilities, good walking base, English and German spoken, Spanish classes.
AL-A Trailanqui, 20 km west of Lago Colico (35 km north of Villarrica), T045-578218, www.trailanqui.com. Luxurious hotel on the riverbank, with suites, *cabañas*, a campsite, restaurant, horse riding and golf course.

Camping
The southern end of Lago Caburga is lined with campsites; there are a couple of basic shops, open summer only. There are several campsites near the park entrance, US$10. Inside the park, camping is allowed at *El refugio*.

There are also 2 sites about halfway along north shore of Lago Colico: **Quichelmalleu**, Km 22 from Cunco, T045-573187. **Ensenada**, Km 26, T045-221441.

Parque Nacional Villarrica *p250*
There is a **CONAF** campsite at Puesco and one near Lago Tromen, free, but no facilities.

Towards Paso Mamuil Malal *p251*
See box, page 257, for Hotel **Termas de Panqui**.
A-F Cabañas La Tranquera, Puesco. Cabins for 6, also dorms, restaurant, campsite.
C Kila Leufu, Km 20, Pucón–Curarrehue road, T09-91337657, www.kilaleufu.cl. **F** pp in shared rooms. Rooms on the Martínez family farm. The owners are Mapuche and staying here will offer an insight into their way of life. Full board available including spit-roast lamb in the *ruca* and other home-grown food. Recommended.
C Rancho de Caballos, 36 km southeast of Pucón on the dirt road to Coñaripe, T09-83461764 (limited signal), www.rancho-de-caballos.com. Restaurant with vegetarian dishes, laundry and kitchen facilities; also *cabañas* and camping, self-guided trails, horse-riding excursions US$70 per day, English and German spoken, recommended.
C Ruca Rayen, T09-97118064. Idyllic spot on the banks of the Río Palguín, 15 mins' walk from the main road (regular buses to Pucón). Some rooms with bath. Good breakfast included. Friendly English-speaking Austrian/Mapuche hosts (Margot's parents own Kila Leufu, above). The perfect choice if you want to avoid the hustle and bustle of Pucón. Meals served, horse-riding trips. Also offers trekking information and mountain bike hire, camping possible. Highly recommended.

Camping
There is a **CONAF** campsite at Puesco, free, no facilities.

Lago Calafquén and around *p251*
There are plenty of options along the north shore of Lago Calafquén towards Coñaripe.
A pp **Termas de Liquiñe**, Km 32 , T/F063-317377. Full board, cabins, restaurant, tours. Also accommodation in private houses.
C Cabañas Cacique Vitacura, Urrutia 825, Playa Grande, Lican Ray, T02-2355302, tradesic@intermedia.cl. For 2, also larger cabins with kitchen.
C Cabañas Los Nietos, Manquel 125, Lican Ray, T045-431078. Self-catering cabins.
C Hostería Inaltulafquen, Casilla 681, Playa Grande, Lican Ray, T045-431115, www.hotel-refugio.com.With breakfast and bath, English spoken, trips to thermal springs.
C-D Residencial Temuco, G Mistral 515, Playa Grande, Lican Ray, T045-431130. **F** singles, with breakfast. Clean, good.

Camping
There are also 6 sites just west of Lican Ray. **Forestal**, 500 m east of town, T045-211954. Sites for up to 6 people.
Isla Llancahue, 5 km east, T063-317360. Campsite with *cabañas* on an island in Río Llancahue. More campsites on the north and south sides of the lake, US$15 per site.
Prado Verde, 1 km east of town, T045-431161.

Lagos Panguipulli and Pirehueico *p253*
Beds are available in private houses around Lago Pirehueico and free camping is possible on the beach.
B Hostal España, O'Higgins 790, Panguipulli, T063-311166, www.hostalespana.cl.kz. Rooms with breakfast.
B-C Hostería Rayen Trai, María Alvarado y O'Higgins. **D-E** singles. Former yacht club serving good food, open all year.
C Hospedaje Familiar, Los Ulmos 62, Panguipulli, T063-311483. **F** singles. Kitchen facilities, helpful, good breakfast.
C Hotel Central, Valdivia 115, Panguipulli, T063-311331. Clean rooms, with breakfast.

Eating

Temuco *p244, map p246*
Those on a very strict budget should make for the **Mercado Municipal**, Aldunate y Portales, where there are several restaurants and fierce touting for business, or the rural bus terminal, where countless restaurants serve very cheap set meals at lunch. *Humitas* are on sale in the street in summer/autumn.
₸₸ La Caleta, Mercado Municipal, Aldunate y Portales. One of the better choices in the covered market serving fish and seafood.
₸₸ La Cumbre del Cerro Ñielol, Cerro Ñielol. Food and dancing on top of the hill, not always open.
₸₸ La Parrilla de Miguel, Montt 1095, T045-275182. Good for large servings of meat and wine. One of the best in the town centre.
₸₸ Las Tranqueras, Alemania 0888, T045-385044. One of several good mid-priced restaurants on Av Alemania (take bus 1). Meat specialists, great grills, but vegetarian options also available.
₸ El Ceache, Cruz 231. Typical Chilean food. Good-value set lunch.
₸ Rapa Nui, Aldunate 415. For take-away lunches and snacks. Recommended.
₸ Restaurante Temedors, San Martín 827. Good-value lunch.

Cafés
Good coffee can be found at **Café Marriet**, Prat 451; for ice cream try **Il Gelato**, Bulnes 420.

Villarrica *p247*
₸₸₸ El Tabor, Epulef 1187, T045-411901. Fish and seafood specialities. Long-standing reputation. Elegant, but quality perhaps not as good as in the past. Somewhat overpriced.
₸₸₸ La Cava del Roble, Valentín Letelier 658, 2nd floor, T045-416446. Excellent grill. Specializes in exotic meat and game accompanied by unusual ingredients such as pine nuts from local araucaria trees. Extensive wine list. Recommended.
₸₸ La Vecchia Cucina, Pedro de Valdivia 1011, T045-411798. Surprisingly good Italian serving the usual range of pizza and pasta.
₸₸ The Travellers, Letelier 753, T045-413617. Varied menu including vegetarian and Asian food, bar, English spoken.
₸₸-₸ Juanito, Vicente Reyes 678. Good and cheap end of the range, closed Sun.
₸ Casa Vieja, Letelier y Muñoz. Good-value set lunch. Family-run, friendly.
₸ El Marítimo, Alderete 769, T045-412034. Unpretentious restaurant serving traditional fish and seafood. Generally first rate.
₸ El Turismo, Epulef 1201 y Rodríguez. Normal range of Chilean dishes. No frills just good food. Best of the cheapies. Recommended.

Cafés
Café 2001, Henríquez 379. Best coffee in town. Also good cakes and friendly service at a reasonable price. For ice cream try the stall next door.

Pucón *p247, map p248*
Vegetarians should check out the deli at O'Higgins y Fresia. Boutique restaurants can be found on Fresia; there are several cheap restaurants around Urrutia y Ansorena.
₸₸₸ Puerto Pucón, Fresia 251. One of Pucón's older restaurants. Spanish, stylish.

ŸŸŸ-ŸŸ La Maga, Alderete 276 y Fresia, T045-444277. Uruguayan Parillada serving possibly the best steak in Chile. So good that several imitations have opened up nearby to take the overspill.
ŸŸŸ-ŸŸ Senzo, Fresia 284, T045-449005. Fresh pasta and risotto prepared by a Swiss chef.
ŸŸ Arabian, Fresia 354-B, T045-443469. Arab specialities – stuffed vine leaves, falafel, etc.
ŸŸ Ecole, Urrutia 592, T045-441675. The best option in town for vegetarians.
ŸŸ il Baretto, Fresia 124, T045-443515. Stone-baked pizzas. Much better value than **Buonatesta** across the road.
Ÿ Rap Hamburguesa, O'Higgins 625. Freshly made hamburgers and Chilean fast food.

Cafés

Café de la P, O'Higgins y Lincoyán. Real coffee.
Cassis, Fresia 223. Chocolates, ice creams, pancakes and snacks.

Lago Calafquén and around *p251*

ŸŸ-Ÿ Café Ñaños, Urrutia 105, Lican Ray. Very good, reasonable prices, helpful owner.
ŸŸ-Ÿ Restaurant-Bar Guido's, Urrutia 405, Lican Ray. Good value.

Lago Panguipulli *p253*

There are cheap restaurants in Panguipulli on O'Higgins 700 block.
ŸŸ Didáctico El Gourmet, Ramón Freire s/n. Restaurant linked to a professional hotel school. Excellent food and wine, mid-price but high quality, open in school terms only.
ŸŸ-Ÿ Café Central, M de Rozas 750. Good cheap lunches, expensive evening meals.
ŸŸ-Ÿ El Chapulín, M de Rozas 639. Good food, good value, friendly.

Bars and clubs

Pucón *p247, map p248*

At weekends in summer, there are discos 2-3 km east of town, near the airport: **Kamikaze** and **La Playa**. There are several more discotheques in the same area.
Mamas and Tapas, O'Higgins y Arauco. Drink and snacks. Several others also on O'Higgins.

Entertainment

Pucón *p247, map p248*

There are regular concerts in summer.

Festivals and events

Villarrica *p247*

Jan-Feb Many events are organized, including music, regattas, rodeo and the **Festival Cultural Mapuche**, with a market, based around the **Muestra Cultural Mapuche**, usually in 2nd week of Feb.

Pucón *p247, map p248*

Feb Pucón is home to an **international triathlon competition** every year as well as mountain bike races and other sporting events.

Shopping

Temuco *p244, map p246*

Crafts

Mapuche crafts and textiles are sold inside and around the **Mercado Municipal**, Aldunate y Portales, and also in the **Casa de la Mujer Mapuche** (see page 246).

Food

Temuco feria, Lautaro y Aníbal Pinto. This is one of the most fascinating markets in Chile. People from the surrounding countryside come to sell their wares. You will find excellent cheap fruit and vegetables, local spices like *merquén* (made from smoked chillies), fish, grains, cheese and honey; there are many inexpensive bars and restaurants nearby.

Pucón *p247, map p248*
There is a large handicraft market just south of O'Higgins on Ansorena. The local specialities are painted wooden flowers. Camping equipment is available at **Eltit Supermarket**, O'Higgins y Fresia, and from **Outdoors and** Travel, Lincoyán 361. **Pucón Express**, O'Higgins y Colo Colo, is a 24-hr supermarket. There is a larger Eltit supermarket on the Camino Internacional on the eastern outskirts of town.

Activities and tours

Tours to **Volcán Villarrica** will not run if the weather is bad; some travellers have had difficulties getting a refund. Establish in advance what terms apply in the event of cancellation and be prepared to wait a few days. For information on individual guides, all with equipment, ask at the tourist offices; prices, schedules and operators can change very quickly in this popular tourist area.

There are plenty of tour operators in Temuco, but it is far better to book with a company in Villarrica or Pucón.

Villarrica *p247*

Tour operators

Prices are fairly standard: to Parque Nacional Villarrica, US$25; to climb Volcán Villarrica, US$70-85; to Termas de Coñaripe US$40. (**Trancura**, Camilo Henríquez y Reyes, www.trancura.com, is best avoided.)
Karina Tour, Letelier 825, T045-412048.
Novena Región, Parque Ecológico 3 Esteros, 20 km south of Villarrica towards Panguipulli, T09-89012574, www.novena-region.com. Mushing and husky trekking on the winter snow with Siberian huskies. Also igloo building. A unique experience in Chile.
Politur, Henríquez 475, T045-414547, www.politur.cl. Recommended.
Ríos Family, T045-412408. Birdwatching and fishing trips.
Rodrigo Puelma, T09-96251345. Recommended private guide, speaks basic English.
Turismo Coñaripe, P Montt 525, T045-411111.

Pucón *p247, map p248*

Canopy

Several agencies offer canopy tours – ziplining from treetop to treetop in native forests.
Bosque Aventura, Arauco y O'Higgins, T045-444030, www.canopypucon.cl. Has one of the longest runs as well as being the most responsible safety-wise.

Climbing

Sierra Nevada, O'Higgins 524-A, T045-444210, www.sierranevadapucon.cl. The only company currently offering Vía Ferrata, a kind of climbing up sheer rock faces for beginners using metal hand and footholds imbedded in the rock.

Fishing

Pucón and Villarrica are celebrated as bases for fishing on Lago Villarrica and on the beautiful Liucura, Trancura and Toltén rivers. The local tourist office will supply details on licences and open seasons, etc. Prices are much more reasonable than further south.
Mario's Fishing Zone, O'Higgins 580, T045-444259, www.flyfishingpucon.com. Expensive, but good fishing guide.
Off Limits, O'Higgins 560, T045-442681, www.offlimits.cl. Fishing specialists, English and Italian spoken, offer fly-fishing excursions and courses between half and 3 days. Birdwatching trips also offered as well as cycle hire.

Horse riding

Horse hire is about US$30 half day, US$50 full day with guide.
Campo Antilco near Quelhue, T09-9713 9758, www.antilco.com. Small groups, excursions ranging from half-day to 12-day trips to Argentina.
Centro de Turismo Ecuestre Huepil-Malal, T09-96432673, www.huepil-malal.cl. Similar.
Ruca Rayen, see page 258, offer good day rides east of Pucón.

Skiing

Pucón resort, 35 mins from Pucón on the slopes of the Volcán Villarrica, T045-441901, www.skipucon.cl. The resort is owned by **Enjoy**, who own the casino and Gran Hotel. and can provide information on snow, ski lifts and, perhaps, transport; otherwise consult the tourist office in Pucón. There are 8 lifts (day ticket US$28-40, depending on the season, US$11 to the restaurant only), though rarely do more than 2 or 3 work and piste preparation is mediocre. The snow is generally soft and good for beginners, though more advanced skiers can try the steeper areas. The season runs from early Jul to late Sep (longer during exceptionally good years) and randonée skiing is usually possible until Dec. The ski centre offers equipment rental (US$23 per day, US$120 per week), ski instruction, first aid, and has a restaurant and bar with wonderful views from the terrace. Some tour operators in town offer ski hire and transport to slopes for around US$30 pp.

Sky diving

Skydive Pucón, at the airport, T09-98200194, www.skydivepucon.cl. Flights over Volcán Villarrica and tandem skydives as well as skydiving courses.

Thermal springs

There are dozens of thermal springs to the south and east of Pucón ranging from the rustic Termas los Pozones to the hip Termas Geométricas and upmarket Termas de Huife. Most operators arrange tours to a variety of termas.

Travel agent

Travel Aid, Ansorena 425, local 4, T045-444040, www.travelaid.cl. Helpful general travel agency selling trekking maps, guidebooks, GPS routes with waypoints, lots of other information, can organize transport to trailheads and are agents for **Navimag** and other boat trips. English and German spoken.

Whitewater rafting and Volcán Villarrica trek

Most operators can arrange a variety of trips, including climbing Villarrica, 12 hrs, US$65-85 including park entry, equipment provided. Whitewater rafting, Trancura bajo (basic, Grade II-III) US$30, Trancura alto (advanced, Grade III-IV) US$45. Shop around, prices vary, as well as the quality of guides and equipment. Unfortunately, while several agencies offer acceptable levels of service, none is exceptional. To reach the falls, lakes and *termas*it is cheaper for groups to flag down a taxi and negotiate a price.

Aguaventura, Palguín 336, T045-444246, www.aguaventura.com. Long-standing reputable French-run agency specializing in kayaking and rafting, but offer other activities as well. Ski equipment available for rent.

Enjoy Tour, in the Gran Hotel, T045-442303, www.enjoytour.cl. Owned by the casino. Prices are slightly above average, but equipment is generally first rate.

Kayak Chile, O'Higgins, T09-88373253, www.kayakchile.net. Day trips and classes for all levels on kayaks and duckies. All guides are UK or US trained. Maximum 2 students per instructor. Responsible. Recommended. Also sell used equipment.

Mountain Life Adventure, Palguín 360, T045-444564, www.mountainlife-adventure.com. Villarrica hike plus treks and climbs up other volcanos in the region.

Paredón, T045-444663, www.paredon expeditions.com. Specialize in small group excursions to Villarrica volcano. English spoken. Good equipment. Recommended.

Politur, O'Higgins 635, T045-441373, www.politur.com. Good for volcano trek and rafting. A little more expensive than most, but generally responsible.

Ronco Track, O'Higgins 615, esq Arauco, T045-449597, www.roncotrack.cl. Small group quadbike excursions from 1½ hrs to 1½ days. Good fun. Also hires out good-quality bicycles and offers a wide range of other tours.

Sol y Nieve O'Higgins, esq Lincoyán, T/F045-441070, www.solynieve.cl. Generally decent long-standing operator. Most guides speak English. Equipment generally good.
Sur Expediciones, O'Higgins 615, www.surexpediciones.com. One of the better agencies for the volcano trip.
Trancura, O'Higgins 211, T045-443436, www.trancura.com. The biggest agency in Pucón with several branches. Very competitive prices, but safety-wise they range from lax to dangerously irresponsible, with more than their fair share of accidents. Do not consider any sort of adventure tourism with this company if you value your personal safety.

Watersports

Equipment for waterskiing (US$16 for 15 mins), dinghy sailing (lasers US$16 per hr), jet-skis and windsurfing (sailboards US$16 per hr) can be hired in summer at Playa Grande, the beach by the **Gran Hotel**. Rowing boats can also be hired for US$8 per hr. The outlets on La Poza beach are more expensive and not recommended.

Parque Nacional Villarrica *p250*

Tours to climb the volcano from Pucón cost US$65-85, including park entry, guide, transport to park entrance and hire of equipment (no reduction for those with their own equipment). Bargain for group rates. Travel agencies will not start out if the weather is bad and some travellers have experienced difficulties in obtaining a refund; establish in advance what terms apply in the event of cancellation and be prepared to wait a few days. For information on individual guides, all with equipment, ask for recommendations at the tourist office.

Lagos Panguipulli and Pirehueico *p253*

Fishing

The following fishing trips on Lago Panguipulli are recommended: **Puntilla Los Cipreses** at the mouth of the Río Huanehue, 11 km east of Panguipulli, 30 mins by boat; the mouth of the **Río Niltre**, on east side of lake. Boat hire US$5, licences available from the **Municipalidad**, Librería Colón, O'Higgins 528, or from **Club de Pesca**.

Whitewater rafting

Good rafting opportunities on the **Río Fuy**, Grade IV-V; **Río San Pedro**, varying grades, and on the **Río Llanquihue** near Choshuenco.

Transport

Temuco *p244, map p246*

Air

LanChile and Sky fly to Manquehue airport (Temuco) from **Santiago**, 1¼ hrs, **Osorno**, 40 mins, and **Puerto Montt**, 45 mins.

Airline offices LanChile, Bulnes 687, on Plaza, T600-5262000, www.lan.com; **Sky Airline**, T600-600 2828, www.skyairline.cl.

Bus

Local Services to neighbouring towns leave from **Terminal Rural**, Pinto y Balmaceda or from bus company offices nearby: **Erbuc**, Miraflores y Bulnes; **JAC**, **NarBus** and **Igi Llaima**, Balmaceda y Aldunate; **TurBus**, Lagos 549.

JAC runs buses to **Villarrica** and **Pucón**, many daily 0705-2045, 1½ hrs, US$6, and to **Coñaripe**, 3 hrs, and **Lican Ray**, 2 hrs. To **Panguipulli**, Power and **Pangui Sur**, 2½ hrs, US$5. **Pangui Sur** also has services to **Loncoche**, US$3 and **Los Lagos**, US$4.

Long distance The terminal is north of city at Pérez Rosales y Caupolicán; to get there, take buses 2, 7 or 10 from the centre. To **Santiago**, several companies, 9 hrs, most overnight, US$18-48; to **Valdivia**, 2½hrs, US$5; to **Osorno** 4hrs, US$6; to **Puerto Montt**, 10 daily, 5½ hrs, US$10-18; to **Castro** (Chiloé), **Cruz del Sur**, 3 daily; also buses to cities further north.

To Argentina To **Neuquén** via Pucón, Paso Mamuil Malal/Tromen and Junín de los Andes, **Buses San Martín**, 3 a week, US$30. To **Neuquén** via Curacautín, Lonquimay and the Paso Pino Hachado, **Igi Llaima**, **Buses Caraza** and **Buses El Valle**, daily between them, US$30; see page 99 for onward services from Neuquén. To **Bariloche** via Osorno, Tas Choapa, daily, US$30; see page 135 for onward services.

Car hire

Budget, Lynch 471, T045-214911; Euro, MacKenna 426, T045-210311, helpful, good value; **Full Famas**, at airport and in centre T045-215420, recommended. Several others.

Train

The **station** is at Barros Arana y Lautaro Navarro, T045-233416, www.efe.cl. At the time of writing services north to Santiago and south to Puerto Montt have been suspended.

Villarrica *p247*

Bus

The main terminal is at Pedro de Valdivia y Muñoz; JAC has 2 terminals, at Muñoz y Bilbao (long-distance) and opposite for Pucón and Lican Ray (local). Other services leave from the **Terminal Rural**, Matta y Vicente Reyes.

Buses to **Santiago**, 10 hrs, US$18-55, several companies; to **Pucón**, both **Vipu-Ray** (main terminal) and **JAC**, every 15 mins in summer, 40-min journey, US$1; to **Puerto Montt**, US$11; to **Valdivia**, JAC, 5 a day, 2½ hrs, US$6; to **Lican Ray** services in summer, **JAC** and **Vipu-Ray**, US$2; to **Coñaripe**, US$2.50, and **Liquiñe** at 1600 Mon-Sat, 1000 Sun; to **Temuco**, JAC, every 30 mins in summer, US$5; to **Loncoche** (Route 5 junction for hitching), US$3. There are also occasional direct buses to **Panguipulli**, via Lican Ray.

To Argentina Buses from Temuco to Junín de los Andes stop in Villarrica en route to Paso Mamuil Malal/Tromen; fares are the same as from Temuco, see page 263.

Car and bicycle hire

Car hire Castillo Propiedades, Anfión Muñoz 417, good value.
Bike hire Mora Bicicletas, Körner 760, helpful.

Pucón *p247, map p248*

Air

Lan and Sky fly to **Santiago**, twice weekly each in summer.

Bus

There is no municipal terminal; each company has its own, mostly dotted around Uruguay and Palguín, with some international services departing from Colo Colo. The **Turbus** terminal is 1 km east of the centre on the Camino Internacional.

To **Villarrica**, JAC, every 15 mins, US$1; to **Valdivia**, JAC, 5 daily, US$7; to **Temuco** hourly, 2 hrs, US$5, or *rápido*, 1½ hrs, US$6; to **Puerto Montt**, 6 hrs, US$12, daily with JAC, or change at Valdivia. To **Santiago**, morning and evening, 11 hrs, US$20-60.

To Argentina Buses from Temuco to **Junín de los Andes** arrive in Pucón at 1000; for fares, see Temuco, page 263.

Car and bicycle hire

Avis, Arauco 302, T045-465328, www.avischile.cl; **Hertz**, in the **Gran Hotel**, T045-441664; Kilometro Libre, Alderete 480, T045-444399, www.rentacarkilometrolibre.com

Bicycles cost US$2 per hr or US$7 for 5 hrs from several travel agencies, many on O'Higgins; shop around as quality varies. Bike repairs at El Pelao, Colo Colo 430.

Taxi

Taxis are useful for out-of-town trips: Araucaria, T045-442323.

Lago Caburga and around *p249*

Bus

Buses Caburgua run minibuses every 30 mins from Pucón to **Caburga**, US$1.50. To **Parque Nacional Huerquehue**, Buses Caburgua from Pucón, 3 daily, 1½ hrs, US$3. Tour agencies can arrange transport for groups, US$12 pp. Taxis cost US$40 return.

Towards Paso Mamuil Malal *p251*

Bus

Several minibuses daily to **Curarrehue** from Pucón. 3 buses weekly from Pucón to Puesco.

Lago Calafquén and around *p251*

Bus

From Lican Ray, buses leave from offices around the plaza to **Villarrica**, JAC, frequent, 1 hr, US$2; to **Santiago**, TurBus (summer only) and JAC, 11 hrs, US$20-50; to **Temuco**, JAC 2½ hrs, US$7; to **Coñaripe**, 4-7 daily.

From Coñaripe, buses run to **Panguipulli**, 7 daily (4 off season), US$2; to **Villarrica**, 16 daily, US$2.50; to **Lican Ray**, 45 mins, US$1. Also a nightly bus direct to **Santiago** run by TurBus (summer only) and JAC, 11½ hrs, US$20-50.

Lagos Panguipulli and Pirehueico *p253*

Bus

The bus terminal in Panguipulli is at Gabriela Mistral y Portales. To **Santiago** daily, US$21-50; to **Valdivia**, Mon-Sat, 4 only on Sun, several companies, 2 hrs, US$7; to **Temuco**, frequent, Power and Pangui Sur, US$6; to **Puerto Montt**, US$10; to **Calafquén**, 3 daily at 1200, 1545 and 1600; to **Choshuenco**, **Neltume** and **Puerto Fuy** (3 hrs), 3 daily, US$5; to **Coñaripe**, for Lican Ray and Villarrica, 4-7 daily.

Ferry

The *Hua Hum* ferry sails across Lago Pirehueico from **Puerto Fuy** to **Puerto Pirehueico**, twice daily in summer, twice a week, other times, 2-3 hrs, foot passengers US$2.50, cars US$30. For reservations and information see www.sietelagos.cl. This is a recommended journey and compares with the famous lakes crossing from Puerto Montt to Bariloche but at a fraction of the price. The ferry connects with buses to **San Martín de los Andes** (Argentina), via Paso Hua Hum, daily in summer, weekly in winter (out Sat 0930, return Sun 1330).

Directory

Temuco *p244, map p246*

Banks and currency exchange ATMs at several banks on or around Plaza A Pinto also at the new JAC bus terminal. There are many *cambios* around the plaza; all deal in dollars and Argentine pesos. **Honorary consulate** Netherlands, España 494, honorary consul, Germán Nicklas, is friendly and helpful. **Internet and telephone** Gral MacKenna 445; several others around the centre. **Laundry** Alba, Zeneto 480, opposite the church, and at Aldunate 324 and Aldunate 842; Marva, M Montt 415 and 1099, Mon-Sat 0900-2030. **Post office** Portales 839.

Villarrica *p247*

Banks and currency exchange There are ATMs at the major banks. Rates at *casas de cambio* are generally poor. Exceptions are: Central de Repuestos, Muñoz 415, and Cristopher, Valdivia 1061, for TCs. **Internet and telephone** Several in and around the town centre. **Laundry** Lavacenter, Alderete 770; Lavandería y Lavaseco Villarrica, Andrés Bello 348. **Post office** Muñoz y Urrutia, Mon-Fri 0900-1300, 1430-1800, Sat 0900-1300.

Pucón *p247, map p248*

Banks and currency exchange
There are 3 or 4 banks with ATMs on O'Higgins. Several *casas de cambio* on O'Higgins, although rates are universally poor. Much better to change money in Temuco. **Internet and telephone** Several on O'Higgins. **Laundry** Urrutia 520; Palguín 460; Fresia 224; Colo-Colo 475 and 478, several others. **Post office** Fresia 183.

Southern lakes

The southern lakes are the real gateway to Patagonia. The virgin forest becomes thicker, the volcanoes more remarkable, the settlements fewer. In spite of the fact that tourism is booming on Llanquihue and Todos Los Santos, there are numerous spots where you can still escape to the old heart of Patagonia. And with activities from windsurfing and horse trekking to ice climbing, this region will keep even the most active traveller happily occupied. » *For listings, see pages 274-283.*

Ins and outs

Getting there Osorno is a key crossroads for bus routes in southern Chile and to the Argentine Lake District. Passengers heading overland to Bariloche, Neuquén, Coyhaique or Punta Arenas will pass through here before making for the Puyehue Pass into Argentina. There are hourly local services to Puerto Montt and frequent services north to Temuco and Valdivia. Puerto Varas is the main centre on Lago Llanquihue and is served by shuttle buses from Puerto Montt every few minutes; there are connections north to Osorno, Valdivia, Temuco and Santiago and east across Lago Todos Los Santos to Bariloche. A taxi to Puerto Varas from Puerto Montt airport costs US$28.

Getting around There are local bus services around most of Lago Llanquihue but the eastern shore is difficult to visit without your own transport. South of Las Cascadas, the road is narrow with lots of blind corners, necessitating speeds of 20-30 kph at best in places. There is no public transport between Las Cascadas and Ensenada and hitching is very difficult. Minibuses run along the southern shore of the lake to Ensenada for access to the Parque Nacional Vicente Pérez Rosales. » *For further details, see Transport, page 282.*

Tourist information Information is available form the regional government office of **Sernatur** ⓘ *Av Décima Región 480, Puerto Montt, T065-254580, infoloslagos@sernatur.cl, Mon-Fri only* and from **CONAF** ⓘ *Rosas 430, Osorno, T064-234393*. Puerto Varas has a not particularly helpful **tourist office** ⓘ *Municipalidad, San Francisco 413, T065-321330*. Other places in town also claim to offer information, but may only give information about their paying members' services. There is no general information centre for Lago Llanquihue, but each town has its own municipal tourist office.

Osorno and around » *pp274-283.*

Situated at the confluence of the ríos Rahue and Damas, Osorno is grey and nondescript and has little to attract tourists, but as a major transport hub, you may stop here. Founded in 1553, the city was abandoned in 1604 and was refounded by Ambrosio O'Higgins and Juan MacKenna O'Reilly in 1796. It later became a centre of German immigration to Chile. The **municipal tourist office** ⓘ *in the bus terminal and in a kiosk on Plaza de Armas, both open Dec-Feb*, offers free **city tours** ⓘ *Mon-Fri 1500 and 1700, Jan-Feb only, book in advance.*

Sights → *Colour map 1, B2.*

On the large **Plaza de Armas** stands the modern, concrete and glass cathedral, with many arches and a tower that is itself an open, latticed arch with a cross superimposed. West of the centre on a bend overlooking the river is the **Fuerte María Luisa**, built in 1793 and restored in 1977; only the riverfront walls and end turrets are still standing. East of the main plaza along Calle MacKenna are a number of late 19th-century wooden mansions built by German immigrants, now preserved as national monuments. Two blocks south of the Plaza is the **Museo Histórico Municipal** ⓘ *Matta 809, summer daily 1100-1900; winter Mon-Fri 0930-1730, Sat 1500-1800, US$1.50*, which has displays on natural history, Mapuche culture, the refounding of the city and German colonization. Three blocks southwest of the plaza, in the former train station, is the **Museo Interactivo de Osorno** (**MIO**) ⓘ *T064-212996, www.municipalidadosorno.cl, Mon-Thu 0815-1300, 1445-1815, Fri 0815-1300, 1445-1745, Sat 1415-1745, an interaactive science museum designed for both children and adults.*

East of Los Lagos

The southernmost of the Seven Lakes, **Lago Riñihue**, is most easily reached from Los Lagos on the Pan American Highway. **Riñihue**, a beautiful but small and isolated village at its western end, is worth visiting but the road around the southern edge of the lake from Riñihue to Enco is closed and there is no road around the northern edge of the lake.

South of Lago Riñihue is **Lago Ranco**, one of the largest lakes in the region, covering 41,000 ha. It has a rough road round its edge, characterized by lots of mud and animals, including oxcarts. However it is worth taking the opportunity to witness an older lifestyle and to see the beautiful lake, starred with islands, and the sun setting on the distant volcanoes. There is excellent fishing on the southern shore around the ugly town of Lago Ranco and to the west around **Puerto Nuevo**; several hotels organize fishing expeditions. The main town on the northern shore is **Futrono**, which has a daily boat service to **Huapi**, the island in the middle of the lake. On the eastern shore is **Llifén**, Km 22, a picturesque place, from where it is possible visit **Lago Maihue**, 33 km further east. From Llifén the road around Lago Ranco continues via the Salto de Nilahue (Km 14) to **Riñinahue**, Km 23, with access to beaches.

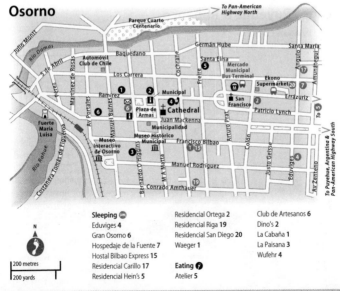

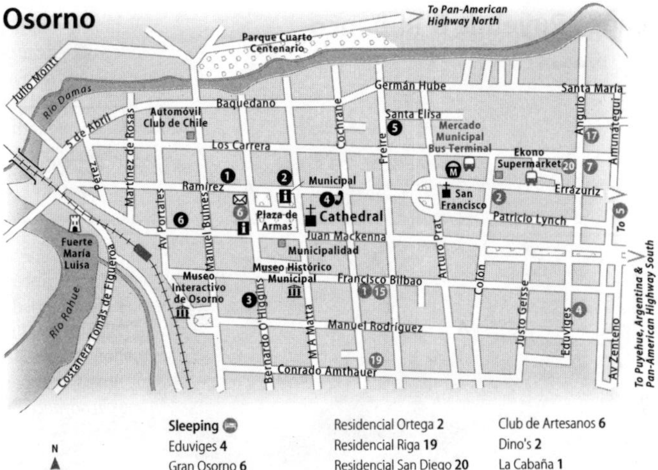

Sleeping
Eduviges 4
Gran Osorno 6
Hospedaje de la Fuente 7
Hostal Bilbao Express 15
Residencial Carillo 17
Residencial Hein's 5
Residencial Ortega 2
Residencial Riga 19
Residencial San Diego 20
Waeger 1

Eating
Atelier 5
Club de Artesanos 6
Dino's 2
La Cabaña 1
La Paisana 3
Wufehr 4

Lago Puyehue and around → *Colour map 1, B3.*

Surrounded by relatively flat countryside, 47 km east of Osorno, Lago Puyehue extends over 15,700 ha. The southern shore is much more developed than the northern shore, which is accessible only by unpaved road from **Entre Lagos** at the western end. On the opposite side of the lake are the **Termas de Puyehue** ⓘ *www.puyehue.cl, daily 0900-2000*, an upmarket spa resort with extensive facilities, US$50-60 for day visitors, including meals, drinks and access to all facilities (see page 275). From the *termas*, Route 215 heads northeast to the Anticura sector of Parque Nacional Puyehue and on towards the border, while another road leads southeast to the Aguas Calientes and Antillanca sectors of the park.

Parque Nacional Puyehue → *Colour map 1, B3.*

Parque Nacional Puyehue covers 107,000 ha, much of it in the valley of the Río Golgol. On the eastern side are several lakes, including Lago Constancia and Lago Gris. There are two volcanic peaks: **Volcán Puyehue** (2240 m) in the north (access via a private track US$10) and **Volcán Casablanca** (also called Antillanca, 1900 m). Leaflets on walks are available from the park administration at Aguas Calientes and from the ranger station at Anticura.

Four kilometres southeast of the Termas de Puyehue, in a thickly forested valley beside the Río Chanleufú, is **Aguas Calientes** ⓘ *Mon-Fri 0830-1230, 1400-1800 in summer only; Sat, Sun and holidays 0830-2030 all year; outdoor pool US$5; indoor pool US$12*, where you'll find the park administration and a dirty, open-air pool with very hot thermal water. From Aguas Calientes the road continues 18 km past three small lakes and through forests to the ski resort at **Antillanca** (www.skiantillanca.cl), on the slopes of Volcán Casablanca. In winter (and sometimes summer, depending on the weather) a one-way traffic system operates on the last 8 km of the narrow and icy road: ascending traffic

Lagos Puyehue & Rupanco

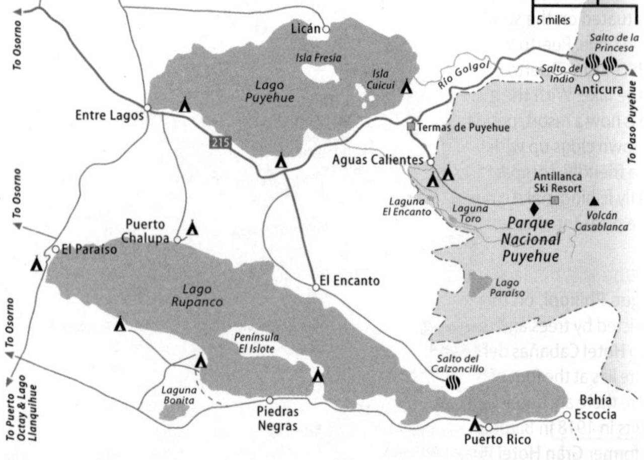

0800-1200 and 1400-1730; descending traffic from 1200-1400 and after 1730. This is a particularly beautiful area of the park, especially at sunrise, with views over Lago Puyehue to the north and Lagos Rupanco and Llanquihue to the south, as well as the snow-clad peaks of Calbuco, Osorno, Puntiagudo, Puyehue and Tronador forming a semicircle. From Antillanca it is possible to climb Casablanca for even better views; there's no path and the hike takes about seven hours there and back; information from **Club Andino** in Osorno.

The paved Route 215, meanwhile, heads northeast from the Termas de Puyehue to **Anticura.** In this section of the park are three waterfalls, including the spectacular 40-m wide **Salto del Indio**. Legend has it that an Indian, enslaved by the Spanish, was able to escape by hiding behind the falls. Situated just off the road, the falls are on a marked path through dense forest that includes a 800-year-old Coihue tree known as 'El Abuelo'. The **Argentine border** at Paso Puyehue is reached 26 km east of Anticura (see page 116).

Lago Rupanco → *Colour map 1, B2/B3.*

Lying south of Lago Puyehue and considerably larger, this lake covers 23,000 ha and is far less accessible and less developed for tourism than most of the other larger lakes. Access from the northern shore is via two unpaved roads that branch off Route 215. **El Paraíso** (aka Marina Rupanco), at the western tip of the lake, can be reached by an unpaved road south from Entre Lagos. A 40-km dirt road runs along the southern shore, via **Laguna Bonita**, a small lake surrounded by forest, and **Piedras Negras** to **Bahía Escocia** at the eastern end. From the south, access is from two turnings off the road between Osorno and Las Cascadas.

Puerto Varas and Lago Llanquihue ▸▸ *pp274-283. Colour map 1, B2.*

The second largest lake in Chile and the third largest natural lake in South America, Lago Llanquihue is one of the highlights of the Lake District. Three snow-capped volcanoes can be seen across the vast expanse of water: the perfect cone of Osorno (2680 m), the shattered cone of Calbuco (2015 m) and the spike of Puntiagudo (2480 m), as well as, when the air is clear, the distant Tronador (3460 m). On a cloudless night with a full moon, the snows reflect eerily in the lake and the peace and stillness are hard to match.

Situated on the southwestern corner of the lake, and recently voted the best place to live in Chile, Puerto Varas is the commercial and tourist centre of Lago Llanquihue. In the 19th century, Puerto Chico (on the eastern outskirts) was the southern port for shipping on the lake. With the arrival of the railway the settlement moved to its current location and is now a resort, popular with Chilean as well as foreign tourists; in February especially, the town clogs up with oversized jeeps from Santiago. Despite the numbers of visitors, it has a friendly, compact feel and its location near centres for trekking, rafting, canyoning and fly fishing make it one of the best bases for exploring the southern Lake District. It is a more pleasant alternative to Puerto Montt as a base for catching the Navimag ferry.

Around town

Parque Philippi, on top of a hill, is a pleasant place to visit, although the views are a bit restricted by trees and the metal cross at the top is unattractive. To reach the summit walk up to **Hotel Cabañas del Lago** on Klenner, cross the railway and the gate is on the right. The centre lies at the foot of the hill, but the town stretches east along the lake to **Puerto Chico**, where there are hotels and restaurants. The imposing **Catholic church** was built by German Jesuits in 1918 in Baroque style as a copy of a church in the Black Forest. North and east of the former **Gran Hotel Puerto Varas** (1934) are a number of German-style mansions.

The southern shore

Puerto Varas is a good base for trips around the lake. A paved road runs along the south shore to Ensenada on the southwestern corner of the lake. Two of the best beaches are **Playa Hermosa**, Km 7 and **Playa Niklitschek**, Km 8, where an entry fee is charged. At Km 16 narrow channels overhung with vegetation lead south from Lago Llanquihue to the little lake of **La Poza**. There are boat trips (US$5) to the beautiful **Isla Loreley**, on the lake, and a channel leads from La Poza to yet another lake, the **Laguna Encantada**. At Km 21 there is a watermill and a restaurant run by the Club Alemán.

Frutillar and the western shore → *Colour map 1, B2.*

Lying about halfway along the western side of the lake, Frutillar is in fact two towns: **Frutillar Alto**, just off the main highway, and **Frutillar Bajo**, beautifully situated on the lakeside, 4 km away. The latter is possibly the most attractive and expensive town on the lake, with superb views from the *costanera* over the water with volcanoes Osorno and Tronador in the background. The town's atmosphere is very German and somewhat snobbish, but the **tourist office** ⓘ *on the lakeside, T065-420198, summer only*, is helpful. In the square opposite is an open-air chess board and the **Club Alemán** restaurant. After eight years of construction work

Puerto Varas

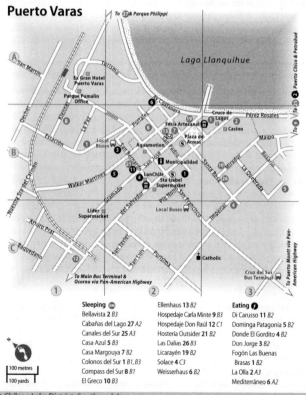

Sleeping
Bellavista **2** *B3*
Cabañas del Lago **27** *A2*
Canales del Sur **25** *A3*
Casa Azul **5** *B3*
Casa Margouya **7** *B2*
Colonos del Sur **1** *B1, B3*
Compass del Sur **8** *B1*
El Greco **10** *B3*
Ellenhaus **13** *B2*
Hospedaje Carla Minte **9** *B3*
Hospedaje Don Raúl **12** *C1*
Hostería Outsider **21** *B2*
Las Dalias **26** *B3*
Licarayén **19** *B2*
Solace **4** *C3*
Weisserhaus **6** *B2*

Eating
Di Carusso **11** *B2*
Dominga Patagonia **5** *B2*
Donde El Gordito **4** *B2*
Don Jorge **3** *B2*
Fogón Las Buenas Brasas **1** *B2*
La Olla **2** *A3*
Mediterráneo **6** *A2*

the new concert hall on the lakeside is now complete. It plays host to the town's prestigious music festival in late January (see Festivals and events, page 280).

Away from the waterfront, the appealing **Museo Colonial Alemán** ⓘ *Vicente Pérez Rosales s/n, T065-421142, museofrutillar@uach.cl, summer 1000-1930 daily; winter 1000-1730 daily, US$3.50*, is set in spacious gardens, with a watermill, replicas of two German colonial houses with furnishings and utensils of the period and a blacksmith's shop selling personally engraved horseshoes for US$9. It also has a *campanario*, a circular barn with agricultural machinery and carriages inside, as well as a handicraft shop. At the northern end of the town is the **Reserva Forestal Edmundo Winckler**, run by the Universidad de Chile and extending over 33 ha, with a guided trail through native woods. Named after one of the early German settlers, it includes a good collection of native flora as well as plants introduced from Europe.

Frutillar Bajo

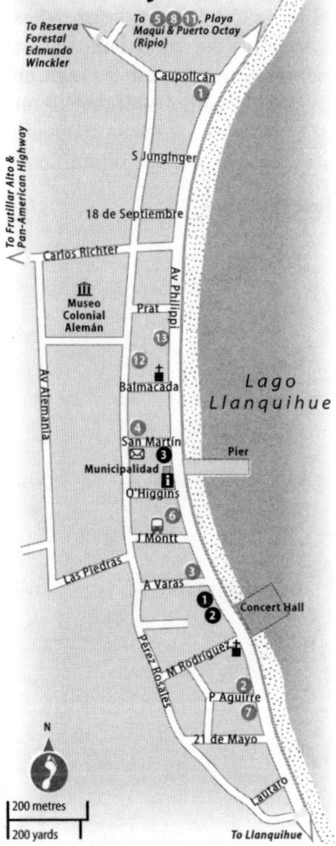

Sleeping
Apart Hotel Frutillar **2**
Ayacara **7**
Casona del 32 **1**
Hospedaje Angélica **12**
Hospedaje Tía Clarita **4**
Hospedaje Vivaldi **6**
Hostal Cinco Robles **5**
Hostería El Arroyo **3**
Lagune Club **8**
Residenz am See **13**
Salzburg **11**

Eating
Andes **1**
Casino de Bomberos **2**
Club Alemán **3**

Llanquihue, some 20 km south of Frutillar, lies at the source of the Río Maullín, which drains the lake. The site of a large dairy processing factory, this is the least touristy town on the lake, and makes a cheaper alternative to Puerto Varas and Frutillar. It has uncrowded beaches and hosts a German-style beer festival at the end of January. North of town is Colonos brewery which has a restaurant and can be visited.

Puerto Octay → *Colour map 1, B2.*

Puerto Octay is a small town at the north tip of the lake. It's 56 km southeast of Osorno, set amid rolling hills, hedgerows and German-style farmhouses with views over the Osorno volcano. Founded by German settlers in 1852, the town enjoyed a boom period in the late 19th century when it was the northern port for steamships on the lake: a few buildings survive from that period, notably the church and the enormous German-style former convent. Since the arrival of railways and the building of roads, the town has declined. Much less busy than Frutillar or Puerto Varas, Puerto Octay offers an escape for those seeking peace and quiet.

Museo el Colono ⓘ *Independencia 591, www.museopuertooctay.cl, Tue-Sun 1000-1300, 1500-1900, Dec-Feb only*, has displays on German colonization. Another part of the museum, housing agricultural implements and machinery for making *chicha*, is just outside town on the road towards **Centinela**. This peninsula, about 3 km south (taxi US$3 one way) along an unpaved road has accommodation, camping, a launch dock, bathing beaches and watersports. It is a very popular spot in good weather, especially for picnics, with fine views of the Osorno, Calbuco and Puntiagudo volcanoes.

Eastern shore

The eastern lakeside, with the Osorno volcano on your left is very beautiful. From Puerto Octay two roads run towards Ensenada, one *ripio* along the shore, and one paved. (They join up after 20 km.) At Km 10 along the lakeside route is **Playa Maitén**, a lovely beach, often deserted, with a great view of Volcán Osorno. Continue for another 24 km past **Puerto Fonck**, which has fine 19th-century mansions, and you'll reach **Las Cascadas**, surrounded by picturesque agricultural land, old houses and German cemeteries. To reach the waterfalls that give the village its name turn east at the school along a *ripio* road to a car park, continue along a footpath over two or three log bridges over a stream before arriving at an impressive jungle-like 40-m-high natural cauldron, with the falls in the middle. The round trip takes about 1½ hours.

Parque Nacional Pérez Rosales & the lakes route to Argentina

Volcán Osorno → *Colour map 1, B3.*

The most lasting image of Lago Llanquihue is the near-perfect cone of Volcán Osorno, situated north of Ensenada on the eastern edge of the lake. Although the peak is on the edge of the Parque Nacional Pérez Rosales (see below), it is climbed from the western side, which lies outside the park. Access is via two roads that branch off the Ensenada–Puerto Octay road along the eastern edge of Lago Llanquihue. The northern one is at Puerto Klocker, 20 km southeast of Puerto Octay and only suitable for 4WDs, while the main entrance is 2 km north of Ensenada along a good paved road.

Guided ascents of the volcano – with transport from Puerto Montt or Puerto Varas, food and equipment – are organized by agencies in Puerto Varas, weather permitting. They start from the *refugio* at **La Burbuja**, where there is a small ski centre in winter and pleasant short walks in summer to a couple of craters and with great views of the lake and across to Puerto Montt. From here it is six hours to the summit. Those climbing from La Burbuja must register with **CONAF** and show they have suitable equipment. The volcano can also be climbed from the north (La Picada); this route is easier and may be attempted without a guide, although only experienced climbers should attempt the summit as ice-climbing equipment is essential and there are many craters hidden below thin crusts of ice. » *See Activities and tours, page 280.*

Ensenada → *Colour map 1, B3.*

Despite its lack of a recognizable centre, Ensenada is beautifully situated at the southeast corner of Lago Llanquihue, almost beneath the snows of Volcán Osorno. A good half-day trip from Ensenada is to **Laguna Verde**, about 30 minutes from **Hotel Ensenada**, along a beautiful circular trail behind the lake (take first fork to the right behind the information board), and down the road to a secluded campsite at Puerto Oscuro on Lago Llanquihue.

Parque Nacional Vicente Pérez Rosales » *pp274-283.*

ⓘ *CONAF administration, Petrohué; guardaparque office, Peulla. Hourly minibuses in summer from Puerto Montt, Puerto Varas and Ensenada to Petrohué; no public transport out of season.*

Established in 1926, this is the oldest national park in Chile, stretching east from Lago Llanquihue to the Argentine frontier. The park is covered in woodland and contains the large Lago Todos Los Santos, plus three major volcanic peaks: Osorno, Puntiagudo and Tronador. Other peaks are visible, notably Casablanca to the north and Calbuco to the south. Near the lake are the Saltos de Petrohué, waterfalls on the Río Petrohué. A memorable journey by road and water takes you through the park from Puerto Montt to Bariloche in Argentina (see pages 124 and 293). A combination of walking and hitching rides in locals' boats is the best way to explore the park. No maps are available in the park; buy them from a tour operator in Puerto Varas (see page 281). In wet weather many treks are impossible.

Lago Todos Los Santos → *Colour map 1, B3.*

The most beautiful of all the lakes in southern Chile, Lago Todos Los Santos is a long, irregularly shaped sheet of emerald-green water, surrounded by a deeply wooded shoreline and punctuated by several small islands that rise from its surface. Beyond the hilly shores to the east are several graceful snow-capped mountains, with the mighty Tronador in the distance. To the north is the sharp point of **Cerro Puntiagudo**, and at the northeastern end **Cerro Techado** rises cliff-like out of the water. The lake is fed by several rivers, including the Río Peulla to the east, the ríos Techado and Negro to the north, and the Río Blanco to the south. At its western end the lake is drained by the Río Petrohué. The lake is warm and sheltered from the winds, and is a popular location for watersports, swimming and for trout and salmon fishing. The only scheduled vessel on the lake is the **Cruce de Lagos** service between Petrohué and Peulla, with connections to Puerto Montt and Bariloche. There are no roads round Lago Todos Los Santos and only those with houses on the lakeshore are allowed access by boat, but private launches can be hired for trips.

Petrohué and around → *Colour map 1, B3.*

At the western end of the lake, 16 km northwest of Ensenada, **Petrohué** is a good base for walking tours with several trails around the foot of Volcán Osorno, or to the *miradores* that look over it, such as **Cerro Picada**. The Petrohué office of **CONAF** incorporates a visitor centre, small museum and three-dimensional model of the national park.

Near the Ensenada–Petrohué road, 6 km west of Petrohué, is the impressive **Salto de Petrohué** ⓘ *US$2*, which was formed by a relatively recent lava flow. Near the falls are a snack bar and two short trails, the Sendero de los Enamorados and the Sendero Carileufú. In Petrohué boats can be hired (US$100) to visit the **Termas de Callao** (actually two large alerce wood tubs in a cabin) north of the lake. The boat will drop you at the uninhabited **El Rincón** (arrange for it to wait or collect you later), from where it's a 3½-hour walk to the baths through forest beside the Río Sin Nombre. The path crosses the river twice by rickety hanging bridges. Just before the baths is a house, doubling as a comfortable *refugio*, where you collect the keys and pay. From the *termas* there's a two-day trail north to Lago Rupanco.

Peulla and around → *Colour map 1, B3.*

Peulla, at the eastern end of the lake, is a good starting point for hikes in the mountains. The **Cascadas Los Novios**, signposted above the **Hotel Peulla**, are a steep walk away, but are stunning once you reach them. There is also a good walk to **Laguna Margarita**, which takes four hours. Peulla is also the location of Chilean immigration and customs for those crossing into Argentina via the **Paso Pérez Rosales**, see page 127.

Cayutué and around → *Colour map 1, B3.*

On the south shore of Lago Todos Los Santos is the little village of Cayutué, reached by hiring a boat from Petrohué, US$50. From Cayutué (no camping on the beach but there are private sites) it is a three-hour walk to **Laguna Cayutué**, a jewel set between mountains and surrounded by forest, where you can camp and swim. From the laguna it is a five-hour hike south to **Ralún** on the Reloncaví estuary (see page 287): the last half of this route is along a *ripio* road built for extracting timber and is part of the old route used by missionaries in the colonial period to travel between Nahuel Huapi in Argentina and the island of Chiloé.

Southern lakes listings

For Sleeping and Eating price codes and other relevant information, see pages 41-44.

Sleeping

Osorno *p266, map p267*

AL-A Waeger, Cochrane 816, T064-233721, www.hotelwaeger.cl. Probably the best in town. Room sizes vary from spacious to tiny, and rooms facing the street can be noisy.

A-B Gran Hotel Osorno, O'Higgins 615, T064-232171, granhotelosorno@entel chile.net. Cable TV, well-furnished, comfortable but ageing 3-star.

B Eduviges, Eduviges 856, T064-235023, www.hoteleduviges.cl. Cheaper rooms without bath. Spacious, clean, quiet, attractive, gardens, also *cabañas* and restaurant. Laundry and internet facilities. Recommended.

C Hostal Bilbao Express, Bilbao 1019, T064-262200, pazla@telsur.cl. With bath and breakfast, parking, restaurant. Also **Residencial Bilbao II**, MacKenna 1205, T064-264444.

C Residencial Hein's, Errázuriz 1757, T064-234116. **E** singles. Some rooms with bath. Old-fashioned, spacious, family atmosphere.

C Residencial Riga, Amthauer 1058, T064-232945, resriga@telsur.cl. Clean, pleasant. Internet. Recommended, but book ahead.

There are lots of cheap options (**D** or **F** singles) near the bus terminal, including the following: **Hospedaje de la Fuente**, Los Carrera 1587; **Residencial Ortega**, Colón 602; **Residencial San Diego**, Los Carrera 1551; **Residencial Carillo**, Angulo 454.

Camping

Municipal site off Pan-American Highway near southern entrance to city, open Jan-Feb only, poor facilities, US$9 per site.

East of Los Lagos *p267*

AL Hostería Huinca Quinay, 3 km east of Riñihue, Lago Riñihue, T063-1971811, gcristi@hotmail.com. 4-star *cabañas* with restaurant and lots of facilities.

AL-A Hostería Chollinco, 3 km out of Llifén, on the road towards Lago Maihue in the Lago Ranco area, T063-1971979, www.hosteriachollinco.cl. Remote country lodge with swimming pool, trekking, horse riding, fishing, hunting and other activities.

AL-A Riñimapu, northwest edge of Lago Riñihue, T063-311388, www.rinimapu.cl. Comfortable rooms and suites with views over the lake, excellent food.

A Huequecura, Llifén, T09-96535450. Includes meals and fishing, good restaurant.

C Hospedaje Futronhue, Balmaceda 90, Futrono, T063-481265. Good breakfast.

Camping

There are campsites all around Lago Ranco and several on Lago Maihue, though many are open in summer only and prices are high.

Lago Puyehue and around *p268*

A private house close to the *termas* provides cheap lodging, with full board available.

LL Hotel Termas de Puyehue, Termas de Puyehue, T064-232157, www.puyehue.cl. Large resort containing 2 thermal swimming pools (one indoors, very clean), theatre, conference centre, well maintained, meals expensive, beautiful scenery, heavily booked Jan-Feb (cheaper May to mid-Dec).

A Cabañas Ñilque, on the southern lakeshore, T064-371218, www.turismonilque.cl. Cabins (half-price May-Oct), fishing trips, watersports, car hire.

B Hospedaje Millaray, Ramírez 333, Entre Lagos, T064-371251. **F** singles. With breakfast, excellent, clean, friendly.

B-C Hostal y Cabañas Miraflores, Ramírez 480, Entre Lagos, T064-371275, olivia.hostalmiraflores@gmail.com. Pleasant rooms and cabins.

B-C Hostería Entre Lagos, Ramírez 65, Entre Lagos, T064-371225. Rooms with lake view.

D Ruta 215 Gasthaus, Osvaldo Muñoz 148, Entre Lagos, T064-371357. **F** singles with bath and good breakfast. Clean, friendly, German spoken. Good value.

Parque Nacional Puyehue *p268*

A-B Hotel Antillanca, at foot of Volcán Casablanca, T064-235114, www.skiantillanca.com. Attached to the antillanca ski resort, decent restaurant/café, pool, sauna, friendly atmosphere, also a *refugio*.

Camping

Camping No Me Olvides, Km 56, on southern lakeshore. US$15, also *cabañas*.

Chanleufu, Aguas Calientes, T064-236988. US$20 per site with hot water, also *cabañas*, an expensive café and a small shop.

Los Derrumbes, 1 km from Aguas Calientes. No electricity, US$25 per site.

Playa Los Copihues, Km 56.5, on the southern lakeshore. Hot showers, good.

There is also a **CONAF** *refugio* on Volcán Puyehue (check with CONAF in Anticura whether it is open) and a campsite beside the Río Chanleufú (US$5 pp).

Lago Rupanco *p269*

There is no accommodation on the northern shore of the lake.

AL Puntiagudo Lodge, Bahía Escocia, T064-1974731, www.puntiagudolodge.cl. With breakfast, very comfortable, good restaurant, fly-fishing, horse riding, boat excursions. Advance bookings only.

B Refugio Club de Pesca y Caza, Sector Islote, 7 km east of Piedras Negras, T064-232056, cpc.osorno@entelchile.net. Basic *refugio* with breakfast and bath.

Camping

There are several campsites on the southern shore, including at Puerto Rico.

Desague del Rupanco, just south of El Paraíso. No facilities.

Puerto Chalupa, on northern shore, T064-232680. US$32 per site.

Puerto Varas *p269, map 270*

There are many hotels all along the lake front, but in high season can be tourist traps.

L Bellavista, Pérez Rosales 060, T065-232011, www.hotelbellavista.cl. 4 star with good views over the lake, reasonably spacious rooms with king-size beds, restaurant and bar, sauna, parking. Unfortunately the rooms with a view also face the main street which can be noisy.

L Cabañas del Lago, Klenner 195, T065-232291, www.cabanasdellago.cl. Recently rebuilt 4-star hotel on Philippi hill overlooking lake. Superb views. Heating, sauna, swimming pool, games room, bar and restaurant. Often full up with package groups.

L Colonos del Sur, Del Salvador 24, T065-235555, www.colonosdelsur.cl. Recently refurbished good-quality 4 star on the lakeside. Owns another hotel at Estación 505, overlooking the town, which has seen better days.

L-AL Licarayén, San José 114, T065-232305, www.hotelicarayen.cl. Most rooms are a good size. Superior rooms have lake view. Cosy, comfortable, clean, gym and sauna.

L-AL Solace, Imperial 0211, T065-364100, www.solacehotel.cl. One of several new upmarket hotels in town, this is probably the best. Spacious rooms, clean, attentive staff. Recommended.

AL-A El Greco, Mirador 134, T065-233880, www.hotelelgreco.cl. Recently refurbished German-style mansion with wooden interior and full of artworks. Simple rooms with bath and cable TV. A good choice.

A Weisserhaus, San Pedro 252, T065-346479, www.weisserhaus.cl. Cosy family-run 10-room hotel right in the town centre. Heated rooms, good breakfast, Wi-Fi. A good choice.

A-B Hostería Outsider, San Bernardo 318, T065-232910, www.turout.com. With bath, breakfast with real coffee, meals, friendly, comfortable. German and English spoken, book in advance.

B Canales del Sur, Pérez Rosales 1631A, 1 km east of town, T065-717618, www.canalesdelsur.cl. Pleasantly set on the lakeside. Very friendly and helpful family-run guesthouse, tours arranged. Good breakfast, garden, laundry, internet and car hire service. Recommended.

B-C Casa Azul, Manzanal 66 y Rosario, T065-232904, www.casaazul.net. **E** pp in shared rooms. Some rooms with bath. German/Chilean owners, good buffet breakfast with home-made muesli (US$5 extra), large kitchen, good beds with duvets, central heating, internet, book exchange, comfortable common area, tours organized. Highly recommended, although some reports that service can be terse.

B-C Compass del Sur, Klenner 467, T065-232044, www.compassdelsur.cl. **E** pp in shared rooms. Good kitchen facilities, internet, cable TV in comfortable lounge, good breakfast, friendly, helpful, lots of information, tours, English spoken, highly recommended. Also camping, car hire.

C Casa Margouya, Santa Rosa 318, T065-237640, www.margouya.com. **E** pp in shared rooms. Bright and colourful fun hostel in the town centre with breakfast and kitchen facilities. Friendly, lots of info, though slightly cramped. French-run, English spoken. Spanish classes offered.

C Ellenhaus, Walker Martínez 239, T065-233577, www.ellenhaus.cl. Some

rooms with bath. **F** pp in dorms. Kitchen and laundry facilities, luggage stored, lounge, tours offered. German and English spoken.
C Hospedaje Carla Minte, Maipo 1010, T065-232880, www.interpatagonia.com/carlaminte. **E** singles. Rooms with bath and breakfast in a family home. Cable TV, Wi-Fi, very comfortable.
C Las Dalias, Santa Rosa 707, T065-233277, las_dalias@hotmail.com. **F** singles. Some rooms with bath. Family home, peaceful , clean, good breakfast, real coffee, parking, German spoken.
D Hospedaje Don Raúl, Salvador 928, T065-310897, hospedajedonraul@ hotmail.com. **F** singles. Laundry and cooking facilities, very friendly, garden with hammock, clean. Recommended. Camping by main road.

Camping

Los Troncos, 10 km east of Puerto Varas, T09-9206869. US$15 per site, no beach access.
Playa Hermosa, 7 km east of Puerto Varas. Fancy ground, US$22 per site, bargain off season. Recommended. Take own supplies.
Playa Niklitschek, 8 km east of Puerto Varas, T065-338352. Full facilities.
CasaTronador, Tronador y Manzanal, T09-907 89631. Expensive but central (in Puerto Varas).

Frutillar and around *p270, map p271*

During the music festival (see page 280) book rooms well in advance; alternatively stay in Frutillar Alto or Puerto Varas. In most cases on Av Philippi you are paying a premium for the view. If you are staying here, try and ensure your room has one. There are several cheap options along Carlos Richter (main street) in Frutillar Alto.
AL Casona del 32, Caupolicán 28, Frutillar Bajo, T065-421369. Comfortable old house, central heating, With breakfast. Groups-only off season. Recommended.
AL Salzburg, on the road to Playa Maqui, 1 km north of Frutillar Bajo, T065-421589, www.salzburg.cl. Excellent restaurant (open to public), plus sauna, swimming pool, mountain bikes, tours and fishing.
AL-A Ayacara, Philippi y Pedro Aguirre Cerda, T065-421550, www.hotelayacara.cl. Typical German-style wooden construction on the lakefront. 8 airy rooms, 6 with views. A good choice.
AL-A Hostal Cinco Robles, 1 km north of Frutillar Bajo, T065-421351, www.cinco-robles.com. Small hotel in pleasant large grounds with views and access to a private beach. Rooms with wooden interiors. With breakfast, restaurant, parking, Wi-Fi.
A Residenz am See, Philippi 539, Frutillar Bajo, T065-421539, www.hotelamsee.cl. Good breakfast and views. Café downstairs serving German specialities.
A-B Lagune Club, 3 km north of Frutillar Bajo, T065-330033, www.interpatagonia.com/laguneclub. In an old country house in 16 ha of land by the lake (private beach), fishing trips, free pickup from terminal. Disabled friendly. Also *cabañas*. Good value in dollars.
B Apart Hotel Frutillar, Philippi 1175, Frutillar Bajo, T065-421388, www.aparthotelfrutillar.cl. Also cabins, good breakfasts, meals available.
B Hospedaje Vivaldi, Philippi 851, Frutillar Bajo, T065-421382. **D**singles. Quiet, comfortable, excellent breakfast and lodging, also family accommodation. Recommended.
B Hostería El Arroyo, Philippi 989, Frutillar Bajo, T065-421560, alarroyo@surnet.cl. With breakfast. Recommended.
C Hospedaje Tía Clarita, Pérez Rosales 743, Frutillar Bajo, T065-421806. **E** singles, kitchen facilities, very friendly, good value.
C Hospedaje Angélica, Pérez Rosales 590, Frutillar Bajo. *Cabañas* and excellent breakfast.
C-D Hospedaje Juana Paredes, Aníbal Pinto y Winkler, Frutillar Alto, T065-421407. **F** singles. Recommended, also *cabañas* for up to 5 and parking.

Camping

Los Ciruelillos, 2 km south of Frutillar Bajo, T065-339123. Most services.
Playa Maqui, 7 km north of Frutillar, T065-339139. Fancy, expensive site.

Puerto Octay *p271*

Several farms on the road around the north and east side of the lake offer rooms. Camping is also possible.

L-AL Hotel Centinela, T064-391326, www.hotelcentinela.cl. Built in 1914 as a summer mansion, this hotel has been recently restored. It is idyllically situated and has superb views, 12 rooms, also *cabañas*, restaurant with grand minstrels' gallery and bar, open all year. Edward VIII once stayed here.

B-C Zapato Amarillo, 35 mins' walk north of town, T064-210787, www.zapatoamarillo.cl. **G** pp in shared rooms. Excellent hostel, use of spotless kitchen, great breakfasts with home-made bread, very friendly, German and English spoken. Lots of information, mountain-bike rental, tours, canoes and sailing boat, luggage storage, phone for free pickup from town. Main house has a grass roof or there are mini *cabañas* and the roundhouse next door with restaurant. Highly recommended.

C-D Hostería La Baja, Centinela, T064-391269, irisbravo1@hotmail.com. **F** singles, with breakfast and bath. Beautifully situated at the neck of the peninsula. Good value.

D Hostería Irma, on lake, 2 km south of Las Cascadas, T064-396227, julietatrivino @yahoo.es. **G** singles. Attractive former residence, good food, very pleasant.

Camping

Camping Municipal, on lakeside, T09-91717819. US$18 per site.

El Molino, by lake, T064-391375. US$20 for up to 5 people, clean, friendly. Recommended.

Volcán Osorno *p273*

E There are 2 *refugios*, both south of the summit and reached from the southern access road: La Burbuja, the former ski-club centre, 14 km north of Ensenada at 1250 m) and **Refugio Teski Ski Club**, www.teskiclub.cl, just below the snow line. Price per person, meals served. **Refugio La Picada** marked on the northern slopes on many trekking maps burned down several years ago.

Ensenada *p273*

LL Yan Kee Way Lodge, T065-212030, www.southernchilexp.com. Understated resort specializing in fly-fishing expeditions. Excellent restaurant.

L-AL Ensenada, T065-212028, www.hotelensenada.cl. With bath, old-world style, lots of antiques, good food, good view of lake and Volcán Osorno, runs tours, hires mountain bikes (guests only). Closed in winter. Also much cheaper *hostal* in the grounds with cooking facilities.

AL-B Cabañas Brisas del Lago, Km 42, T065-212012, www.brisasdellago.cl. On beach, rooms and cabins sleeping 2-6, good restaurant nearby. Recommended.

B Hospedaje Ensenada, Km 43, T065-212050, www.hospedajensenada.blogspot.com. **F** singles. Most rooms with bath. Very clean, excellent breakfast.

B-C Casa Ko, Km 37, 3 km north of main road, T09-77036477, www.casako.com. Best of the hostels around Ensenada. Good meals served, lots of info, English and French spoken. Call for pick-up from main road. Good-value camping.

Camping

Montaña, centre of town. Charges per site, good beach space.

Playa Larga, 1 km east of **Hotel Ensenada**, US$15 per site.

Puerto Oscuro, 2 km north of Ensenada, US$12 per site.

Trauco, 4 km west of Ensenada, T065-212033. Large site with shops, fully equipped, US$5-10 pp.

Petrohué *p274*

The CONAF office in Petrohué can help find cheaper family accommodation. Camping wild and picknicking is forbidden.

LL Hotel Petrohué, T065-212025, www.petrohue.com. Half board available. Magnificent views, log fires, cosy. Sauna and heated swimming pool. Hiking, fishing and other activities arranged.

Camping

In Petrohué, there's a campsite beside the lake, US$9 per site, no services (local fishermen will ferry you across for US$3). Camping wild and picnicking is forbidden at Petrohué; car parking US$5 per day.

Peulla *p274*

L Hotel Natura, T065-367094, www.hotelnatura.cl. Recenty opened luxury hotel, contrasts with traditional Hotel Peulla (see below) under the same ownership.

AL Hotel Peulla, T065-367094, www.hotelpeulla.cl. Price includes dinner and breakfast, cheaper out of season. Beautiful setting by the lake and mountains, restaurant and bar, poor meals, cold in winter, often full of tour groups, showing its age.

D Residencial Palomita, 50 m west of Hotel Peulla. Price pp for half board, lunches available. Family-run, comfortable but not spacious, separate shower, book ahead in season.

Camping

The campsite in **Peulla** is opposite the CONAF office, US$7 per site. There's also a good campsite 1¾ hrs' walk east of the village, or ask at the *carabineros* station if you can camp on the beach; no facilities.

Eating

Osorno *p266, map p267*

The bakery at Ramírez 977 sells good wholemeal bread.

TT Atelier, Freire 468, T064-213735. Fresh pasta and other Italian delights.

TT Dino's, Ramírez 898, on the plaza. Good restaurant upstairs, bar/cafeteria downstairs.

TT La Paisana, O'Higgins 827, piso 2. Arab specialities including vegetarian options.

TT Wufehr, Ramírez 959, local 2. Local raw meat specialities as well as filling sandwiches. Popular with locals.

TT-T Club de Artesanos, MacKenna 634. Hearty traditional Chilean fare.

T La Cabaña, Ramírez 774, T064-272479. Wide variety of cheap lunches ranging from Chinese to home-cooked Chilean. Excellent value.

Cafés

Café Lierario Hojas del Sur, MacKenna 1011 yy Cochrane, more like a living room than a café. Cosy, friendly. Wi-Fi.

Puerto Varas *p269, map p270*

TTT-TT Mediterráneo, Santa Rosa 068, T065-237268. On the lakefront, varied and interesting menu with a Mediterranean influence, often full. Quality has not kept up with recent price increases.

TT Di Carusso, San Bernardo 318, T065-233478. Italian tratoria. Good fresh pasta dishes on Fri. Recommended.

TT Dominga Patagonia, Walker Martínez 551, T065-238981. Interesting fusion cuisine with Peruvian elements. Tapas and also main dishes. Cosy atmosphere, generous pisco sours. Reasonably priced. Recommended.

TT Fogón Las Buenas Brasas, San Pedro 543, T065-214553. Popular Argentinian-style *parrillada*. Decent when uncrowded but service a bit of a disaster when full.

TT La Olla, Puerto Chico, 4 km east of centre along the lakefront, T065-233540. Seafood and traditional Chilean cuisine. Recommended.

TT-T Donde El Gordito, downstairs in market. Large portions, good range of meat dishes.

T Don Jorge, San Bernardo 240. Sandwiches and good-value lunches.

Cafés

Café Danés, Del Salvador 441. Good coffee and cakes.

El Molino, on road to Ensenada, 22 km east. Café next to an old water mill.

Punto Café, Del Salvador 348. Café with internet and art gallery.

Frutillar and around *p270, map p271*

TT Andes, Philippi 1057, Frutillar Bajo. Good set menus and à la carte.

TT Club Alemán, Av Philippi 747. Good but not cheap, hostile to backpackers.

T Casino de Bomberos, Philippi 1060, Frutillar Bajo. Upstairs bar/restaurant, open all year, memorable painting caricaturing firemen in action. Great value but service can be poor.

Cafés

There are several German-style cafés on C Philippi, including **Salón de Té Frutillar** at No 775 and **Guten Apetit** at No 1285.

Puerto Octay *p271*

🍴🍴 **El Rancho del Espanta-Pajaros**, 6 km south on the road to Frutillar, T065-330049. In a converted barn with wonderful views over the lake, serves all kind of spit-roasted meat. All you can eat, with salad bar and drinks included, for US$14. Also arranges horse-riding trips. Recommended.

🍴🍴 **Fogón de Anita**, 1 km out of town, T064-391455. Mid-priced grill. Also German cakes and pastries.

🍴 **Restaurante Baviera**, Germán Wulf 582. Cheap and good. Salmon and *cazuelas*.

Ensenada *p273*

🍴🍴🍴 **Latitude 42**, Yan Kee Way resort, T065-212030. Expensive, excellent and varied cuisine, very good-quality wine list. Views over the lake.

🍴 **Canta Rana**. Recommended for bread and *küchen*.

🍴 **Donde Juanito**, west of Ensenada. Excellent-value cheap set lunch.

Festivals and events

Frutillar and the western shore
p270, map p271

Jan/early Feb A highly regarded classical music festival is held in the town; tickets must be booked well in advance from the Municipalidad, T065-421290.

Llanquihue

End Jan A German-style **beer festival** with oom-pah music is held here.

Shopping

Osorno *p266, map p267*

There is a mall on C Freire 542 with 3 internet cafés and a bookshop, **CM Books**, which sells some English titles.

Alta Artesanía, MacKenna 1069. Excellent handicrafts, not cheap.

Ekono, Colón y Errázuriz. Supermarket.

Puerto Varas *p269, map p270*

Lider, Gramado 565. Supermarket with a good selection, reasonably priced.

Mamusia, San José 316. Chocolates.

Santa Isabel, Salvador 451. Supermarket.

Frutillar *p270, map p271*

Services and shops are generally much better in Frutillar Alto, although in Frutillar Bajo, seek out **Der Volkladen**, O'Higgins y Philippi, for natural products, including chocolates, cakes and cosmetics.

Ensenada *p273*

There are several shop selling basic supplies. Most places are closed off season, other than a few pricey shops, so take your own provisions.

Activities and tours

Most tours operate in season only (Sep-May).

Osorno *p266, map p267*

Skiing

Club Andino, O'Higgins 1073, T064-235114. Information and advice on skiing in the area.

Hotel Antillanca, see Sleeping, is attached to one of Chile's smaller ski resorts; 17 pistes are served by 3 lifts, ski instruction and first aid available. Piste preparation is unreliable. Skiing is not difficult but quality depends on the weather: though rain is common it often does not turn to snow. See www.skiantillanca.cl for information on the state of the pistes.

Trekking up Volcán Osorno

Weather permitting, agencies in Puerto Varas organize climbing expeditions with a local guide, transport from Puerto Montt or Puerto Varas, food and equipment, US$200 pp, payment in advance (mini mum group 2, maximum 6 with 3 guides). Weather conditions are checked the day before. A full refund is given if the trip is cancelled, and a 50% refund is available if the trip is abandoned due to weather before the real climbing begins. Those climbing from La Burbuja must register with **CONAF** at La Burbuja, and show they have suitable equipment. Those climbing from the north (La Picada) are not subject to any checks.

Also based at La Burbuja is a small skiing centre, with 11 pistes and 5 ski lifts, usually open Jun-Sep. Ski ticket US$30, equipment rental US$30, ski school. See www.volcanosorno.com for current conditions.

Lago Rupanco *p269*

Fishing

Lago Rupanco is very popular for fishing. **Bahía Escocia Fly Fishing**, offers excursions from the Puntiagudo Lodge (see Sleeping, above); advance booking required. In Osorno, fishing tackle is available from **Climet**, Angulo 603, and **The Lodge**, Los Carrera 1291, local 5.

Puerto Varas *p269, map p270*

Fishing

The area around Puerto Varas is popular for fishing. A licence (obligatory) is obtainable from the Municipalidad. Fishing expeditions are organized by many tour operators (see below). The Río Pescado (25 km east of Puerto Varas) is a good easy alternative for those who do not want to hire a guide.

Horse riding

Campo Aventura, San Bernardo 318, T065-232910, www.campo-aventura.com. English and German spoken, offers 1- to 10-day trips on horseback.

Quinta del Lago, Km 25, T065-330193, www.quinta del Lago. Generally recommended day rides. Good views.

Mountain biking

Bikes available from many tour operators, see below, for around US$14 per day; check equipment carefully.

Scuba diving

Diving Sur, Blanco Encalada 1160, Puerto Chico, T065-284399, www.divingsur.cl. Guided diving trips including night diving in Lago Llanquihue.

Tour operators

Al Sur, Aconcagua y Imperial, T065-232300, www.alsurexpeditions.com. Rafting on Rió Petrohué. Official tour operator to the Parque Pumalín. Sells trekking maps.
Cruce de Lagos, Del Salvador 72, T065-232811, www.crucedelagos.com. Operates 'lakes' trip to Bariloche, Argentina via Lago Todos Los Santos, Peulla, Cerro Tronador, plus other types of excursions.
Aqua Motion, San Francisco 328, T065-232747, www.aquamotion.cl. Rafting, trekking, mountain biking, fishing, birdwatching.
Kokayak, Km 40, T09-93105272, www.kokayak.com, French/Chilean-run, offers bike hire, white-water rafting and sea kayaking. Good day trips.
Miralejos Chile Adventure, San Pedro 311, T065-234892, www.miralejos.travel. Runs a variety of small-group and bespoke tours around the Cochamó area from 1 to 10 days,

including horse riding, sea-kayaking and treks across the border to El Bolsón in Argentina.

Yak Expediciones, T065-234409, www.seakayakpatagonia.com. Repeatedly recommended for multi-day sea-kayak trips around the Seno de Reloncaví and the Gulf of Ancud.

Transport

Osorno *p266, map p267*

Air

LanChile, E Ramírez 802, T600-5262000, flies daily to **Santiago** via Temuco.

Bus

Main terminal 4 blocks from Plaza de Armas at Errázuriz 1400, bus from centre, US$0.70. Left luggage open 0730-2030.

Local Some local services leave from the Mercado Municipal terminal, 1 block west of the main terminal. To **Entre Lagos**, frequent in summer, reduced service off-season, Expreso Lago Puyehue, T064-234919, and Buses Puyehue, 45 mins, US$2; buses by both companies also continue to **Aguas Calientes**, off-season according to demand, 2 hrs, US$4. To **Puyehue**, 4-5 daily, 1½ hrs, US$3.50, but the buses don't stop by the lakeside (unless you want to get off at Hotel Termas de Puyehue and clamber down).

Bus from Osorno to **Piedras Negras** from the main terminal, leaves Mon-Fri 1230, Sat 1630, returns from Piedras Negras early morning.

Long distance To **Santiago**, frequent, 11½ hrs, US$20-55; to **Temuco**, US$10; to **Panguipulli**, Buses Pirehueico, 4 a day; to **Pucón** and **Villarrica**, TurBus, frequent, US$13; to **Valdivia**, frequent, 2 hrs, several companies, US$5; to **Frutillar**, US$3, **Llanquihue**, **Puerto Varas** and **Puerto Montt**, every 30 mins, US$4; to **Puerto Octay**, Vía Octay, every 30 mins, US$3; to **Lago Ranco** (town), 6 a day, Empresa Ruta 5, 2 hrs, US$4; to **Punta Arenas**, several each week, US$65; to **Anticura**, 2 or 3 buses daily, 3 hrs, US$8.

To Argentina Several buses run daily services from Puerto Montt via Osorno to **Bariloche** via Paso Puyehue (see page 292).

Car hire

Salfa Sur, Av Fuschlocher, T064-240124, www.salfasur.cl. Also at airport. Good value, recommended.

Lago Rupanco *p269*

Buses from Valdivia to **Llifén** via Futrono, Cordillera Sur, 4 daily, US$3; to **Riñihue** via Paillaco and Los Lagos, frequent. To **Osorno**, Empresa Ruta 5, 6 daily.

Parque Nacional Puyehue *p268*

Expreso Lago Puyehue, T064-23499, and Buses Puyehue, run from Osorno to **Aguas Calientes**, according to demand, 2 hrs, US$4. Note that buses from Osorno to Entre Lagos and Aguas Calientes do not stop at the lakeside (unless you want to get off at Hotel Termas de Puyehue and clamber down). There is no public transport from Aguas Calientes to **Antillanca**; hitching is always difficult, but it is not a hard walk. Buses run from Osorno to **Anticura**, daily at 1620, 3 hrs.

Puerto Varas *p269, map p270*

Minibuses to **Ensenada** and **Petrohué** leave from San Bernardo y Martínez; long-distance buses leave from the new terminal on the northern edge of town.

To **Santiago**, Turbus, Pullman, Cruz del Sur and several others, US$30-75. Thaebus, Full Express and others have services to **Puerto Montt**, every 15 mins, 30 mins, US$1.20; same companies, same frequency to **Frutillar**, 30 mins, US$1.50, and **Osorno**, 1 hr, US$4. Same companies hourly to **Petrohué**, US$3. To **Valdivia**, 3 hrs, US$7; to **Temuco**, US$10; to **Cochamó** via Ensenada, 5 a day, US$5. Services from Puerto Montt to **Bariloche** (Argentina) also stop here. For the **Cruce de Lagos** lakes route via Lago Todos Los Santos, see page 293.

Car and bicycle hire
Adriazola Expediciones, Santa Rosa 340, T065-233477, www.adriazolaflyfishing.com; **Hunter**, San José 130, T065-237950; **Turismo Nieve**, Gramado 560, T065-346115. Bicycle hire is available from many tour operators, see above, for around US$18 per day; check equipment carefully.

Train
Train station at Klenner 350. Train services to Temuco and Puerto Montt are currently suspended.

Frutillar and around *p270, map p271*
Colectivos run between the 2 towns, 5 mins, US$0.60. Most buses to other destinations leave from Alessandri y Richter in Frutillar Alto. **Thaebus** and others have frequent services to **Puerto Varas**, US$1.50, and **Puerto Montt**, US$1.80. To **Osorno**, Turismosur, 1¼ hrs, US$3; to **Puerto Octay**, Thaebus, 5 a day.

Train
Train staion at Alessandri s/n. Train services to Temuco and Puerto Montt are currently suspended.

Puerto Octay *p271*
Buses to **Osorno**, every 30 mins, US$3; to **Las Cascadas** Mon-Fri 1730, return next day 0700. **Thaebus** runs 5 daily services to **Frutillar**,1 hr, US$1.50, **Puerto Varas**, 2 hrs, and **Puerto Montt**, 2¼ hrs, US$3.

Lago Todos Los Santos *p273*
Boat
The **Cruce de Lagos** catamaran sails between **Petrohué** and **Peulla**, departing Petrohué Mon-Sat 1030, departing Peulla Mon-Sat 1500, 2 hrs, US$50 pp one way, bicycles free (book in advance); most seating indoors, no cars carried, commentaries in Spanish and English, expensive refreshments. This is the only public service across the lake and it connects with the **Cruce de Lagos** tour bus between Puerto Montt and Bariloche (see page 293). Local fishermen also make the trip across the lake and for a group this can be cheaper than the public service, allow 3½ hrs.

Bus
Minibuses from **Puerto Varas** to **Ensenada** continue to **Petrohué** in summer; last return bus from Petrohué to Puerto Varas, 1800. Note that apart from the **Cruce de Lagos** service from Puerto Montt, there is no transport from Peulla to the border at Paso Pérez Rosales.

Ensenada *p273*
Frequent minibuses run from **Puerto Varas** in summer. Buses from Puerto Montt via Puerto Varas to **Cochamó** also stop here. Hitching from Puerto Varas is difficult.

Directory

Osorno *p266, map p267*
Banks and currency exchange Several banks and *casas de cambio* in the centre. **Internet and telephone** Several in and around the town centre. **Laundry** Prat 678, allow at least a day. **Post office** O'Higgins 645.

Puerto Varas *p269, map p270*
Banks Good exchange rates at **Banco Osorno**, Del Salvador 399. Also numerous *casas de cambio*. **Internet and telephone** Several in the centre, although if you want coffee while you browse try **Punt Café**, Del Salvador 348. **Laundry** Gramado 1090; **Lavanderia Delfin**, Martínez 323, expensive. **Medical emergencies** Clínica **Alemana**, Otto Bader 810, T065-232336, emergencies T065-232274, usually has English-speaking doctors. **Post office** San José y San Pedro; Del Salvador y Santa Rosa.

Puerto Montt and around

The capital of Región X (Los Lagos), Puerto Montt lies on the northern shore of the Seno de Reloncaví 1016 km south of Santiago. The jumping-off point for journeys south to Chiloé and southern Patagonia, it is a busy, modern and often windy city, flourishing with the salmon-farming boom. As the fastest-growing city in Chile, it sometimes seems as if it is buckling under the pressure, with infrastructure struggling to keep up with population growth. It was founded in 1853, as part of the German colonization of the area, on the site of a Mapuche community known as Melipulli, meaning four hills. There are good views over the city and bay from outside the Intendencia Regional on Avenida X Región. There is a wide range of accommodation here, but you might prefer to stay in Puerto Varas, which is more picturesque and only 25 minutes away by bus. ▸▸ *For listings, see pages 289-294.*

Ins and outs ➔ *Colour map 1, B2.*

Getting there **El Tepual airport** ⓘ *13 km northwest of town*, served by **ETM** buses from the **bus terminal** ⓘ *T065-294292, 1½ hrs before departure, US$3*; there's also a minibus service to/from hotels, US$7 per person. There are several daily flights north to Santiago and Temuco, and south to Coyhaique and Punta Arenas. Ferries serve Chaitén (four times

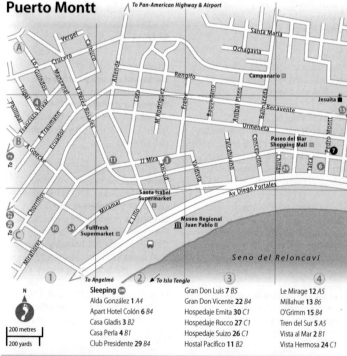

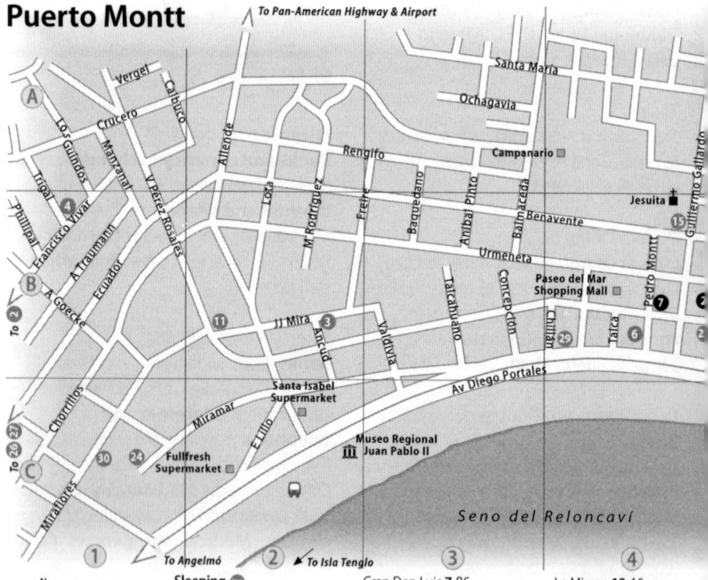

Sleeping
Alda González **1** *A4*
Apart Hotel Colón **6** *B4*
Casa Gladis **3** *B2*
Casa Perla **4** *B1*
Club Presidente **29** *B4*
Gran Don Luis **7** *B5*
Gran Don Vicente **22** *B4*
Hospedaje Emita **30** *C1*
Hospedaje Rocco **27** *C1*
Hospedaje Suizo **26** *C1*
Hostal Pacífico **11** *B2*
Le Mirage **12** *A5*
Millahue **13** *B6*
O'Grimm **15** *B4*
Tren del Sur **5** *A5*
Vista al Mar **2** *B1*
Vista Hermosa **24** *C1*

weekly) and Puerto Chacabuco (twice weekly); there's also a weekly service south to Puerto Natales. Puerto Montt is the departure point for bus services south to Coyhaique and Punta Arenas, and for buses north to Santiago and all the intermediate cities. *See also Transport, page 292.*

Tourist information **Sernatur regional tourist office** ⓘ *Av X Región 480, Casilla 297, T065-254580, infoloslagos@sernatur.cl, Mon-Fri only*, is in the Intendencia Regional. There's an **information kiosk** ⓘ *Plaza de Armas, Sat till 1800*, run by the municipality, which has town maps and poor information. **CONAF** ⓘ *Ochogavia 458*, cannot supply details of conditions in the national parks.

Sights

The **Plaza de Armas** lies at the foot of steep hills, one block north of Av Diego Portales, which runs east-west parallel to the shore. The **Teatro Municipal Diego Rivera** ⓘ *Quillota 116, off the Plaza de Armas, T065-261817*, hosts temporary exhibitions, concerts and plays. Two blocks west of the square is the **Iglesia de los Jesuitas** on Calle Gallardo, dating from 1872, which has a fine blue-domed ceiling; behind it on a hill is the **campanario** (clock tower). Further west, near the bus terminal, is the **Museo Regional Juan Pablo II** ⓘ *Diego Portales 997, daily 1030-1800, US$1*, documenting local history. It has a fine collection of historic photos of the city and memorabilia of the Pope's visit in 1988. Next to the museum is a small park with an old crane and a couple of rusting steam engines. *For Parque Nacional Alerce Andino, see page 299.*

Eating
Café Central **2** *B4*
Café Haussman **1** *B5*
Café Real **2** *B4*
Centro Español **3** *B5*
Club Alemán **4** *B5*
Club de Yates **8** *C6*
Cotele **5** *C6*
Dino **7** *B4*
Pazos **6** *C6*

Angelmó

The little fishing port of Angelmó, 2 km west along Avenida Diego Portales (a pleasant 30-minute walk) has become a tourist centre thanks to its dozens of seafood restaurants and handicraft shops. Launches depart from Angelmó for the wooded **Isla Tenglo**, a favourite place for picnics, with views from the summit. The island is famous for its *curanto*, served by restaurants in summer. Boat trips round the island from Angelmó last for 30 minutes, US$9. A longer boat trip (two hours) will take you to **Isla Huar**.

Towards Chiloé

Monumento Nacional Lahuen Ñadi (US$3) lies between Puerto Montt and the airport, along a *ripio* road going north signed "Lagunillas" branching off the main road 5 km before the airport. There is a pleasant, short and easy (30-minute) trail

Going further ... Valdivia

For a complete contrast to the rural communities around the lakes, visit the lively student city of Valdivia to the west. It's a good place to rest after arduous treks in the mountains.

Founded in 1552 by Pedro de Valdivia, the city was abandoned as a result of the Mapuche insurrection of 1599 and was not refounded until 1645 when it became the only Spanish mainland settlement south of the Río Biobío. The Spanish fortified the area throughout the 1600s but the defences proved of little avail during the Wars of Independence, when the Chilean naval squadron under Lord Cochrane seized control of Valdivia's forts in two days. Until the 1880s Valdivia remained an outpost of Chilean rule, reached only by sea or by a coastal route. In 1960, a devastating earthquake and tidal wave caused the land around Valdivia to drop by 3 m, creating new lagunas to the north of the city.

Ins and outs

There are daily flights to the airport, 29 km north of the city from Santiago, as well as numerous buses from Santiago, Puerto Montt and Temuco. Access from the Panamericana is via Loncoche (toll US$2.50), Paillaco or by ripio road from Los Lagos. Tourist information is available from Prat 555, T063-342300, infovaldivia@sernatur.cl.

Don't miss ...

→ **Cervecería Kunstmann**, T063-292969, www.cerveza-kunstmann.cl. Tour the working brewery and museum before tucking into German food and five types of beer.

→ **Plaza de la República** The heart of the city and the site of the cathedral museum, for four centuries of Christian history.
→ **Isla Teja** This island is home to the university, the botanical gardens and two good museums.
→ **Santuario de la Naturaleza Río Cruces** Boat trips from the city dock run north to this flooded nature reserve, which now attracts many bird species.
→ **Niebla and Corral** Take a boat downstream to visit two of the most important 17th-century Spanish forts. The boat also stops midstream at Isla Mancera, a small island dominated by the Castillo de San Pedro de Alcántara, the earliest of the Spanish forts.
→ **Semana Valdiviana** This festival in mid-February, culminates in Noche Valdiviana, when a procession of elaborately decorated boats sail past the Muelle Fluvial.

Sleeping and eating

AL Naguilán, General Lagos 1927, T063-212851, www.hotelnaguilan.com. Pleasant 4-star, south of the city centre along the river. Clean, quiet, nice views, outdoor pool, good restaurant.
C pp Aires Buenos Central, García Reyes 550, T063-222202. Small doubles or dorms. Good HI-affiliated hostel. Friendly English-speaking staff, Wi-Fi, book exchange, kitchen facilities, pleasant garden with pet duck! Lots of info. Recommended.
♔♔♔ **Restaurante Camino de Luna**, Prat s/n. A floating restaurant next to the costanera, unique in Chile.

through mixed native forest. This is perhaps the most easily accessible place in Chile to see alerce forests, although they are nowhere near as old or impressive as in other parts. Note that it is easy to get lost on the way back to the main road from the park.

The road west from Puerto Montt is very beautiful. **Chinquihue** (the name means 'place of skunks'), beyond Angelmó, has many seafood restaurants, oysters being a speciality. Further south is **Calbuco**, scenic centre of the fishing industry. It is on an island linked to the mainland by a causeway and can be visited direct by boat or road. West of here is the Río Maullín, which drains Lago Llanquihue, and has some waterfalls and good salmon fishing. At its mouth is the fishing village of **Maullín**, founded in 1602. On the coast to the southeast is **Carelmapu**, with an excellent beach and *cabañas* at Playa Brava, about 3 km away. At the southern tip of the mainland, **Pargua** is the departure point for car ferries to Chiloé (see box, page 288).

Seno de Reloncaví » *pp289-294.*

The Seno de Reloncaví, east of Puerto Montt and south of the Parque Nacional Pérez Rosales, is the northernmost of Chile's glacial inlets. It is a quiet and beautiful estuary, often shrouded in mist, but stunning nonetheless, and recommended for its wildlife, including sea lions and dolphins, and for its peaceful atmosphere. It is relatively easily reached by a road that runs along the wooded lower Petrohué valley south from Ensenada and then follows the eastern shore of the estuary for almost 100 km to join the Carretera Austral.

Ralún and around → *Colour map 1, B3.*

A small village situated at the northern end of the estuary, Ralún is 31 km southeast from Ensenada by a poorly paved road. There is a village shop and post office, and on the outskirts are **thermal baths** ⓘ *US$2, reached by boat, US$2.50 across the Río Petrohué*. Ralún is the departure point for a five-hour walk north to **Laguna Cayutué** in the Parque Nacional Vicente Pérez Rosales. From Ralún you can either travel along the eastern shore of the estuary to Cochamó or take the road that branches off and follows the western side of the estuary south, 36 km to Lago Chapo and the Parque Nacional Alerce Andino (see page 299).

Cochamó and further south → *Colour map 1, B3.*

Some 17 km south of Ralún along a poor *ripio* road is the pretty village of Cochamó. It's situated in a striking setting, on the east shore of the estuary with the volcano behind, and has a small, frequently deserted waterfront, where benches allow you to sit and admire the view. Cochamó's fine wooden church dates from 1900 and is similar to those on Chiloé. It has a clock with wooden hands and an unusual black statue of Christ.

Further south, on the south bank of the Río Puelo (crossed by a new bridge) is **Puelo**, a most peaceful place. From here the road continues 36 km further southwest to Puelche on the Carretera Austral (see page 300). The Gaucho Trail east from Cochamó to **Paso León** on the Argentine frontier was used in the colonial period by the indigenous population, Jesuit priests and later by *gauchos*. It runs along Río Cochamó to La Junta, then along the north side of Lago Vidal, passing waterfalls and the oldest surviving alerce trees in Chile at **El Arco**. The route takes three to four days by horse, five to six days on foot.

Sea routes south of Puerto Montt » *pp289-294.*

Puerto Montt is the departure point for several popular voyages along the coast of southern Chile. All sailings are from Angelmó; timetables should be checked carefully in advance as schedules change frequently.

To Puerto Natales

One of the highlights of many journeys to Chile is the 1460-km voyage between Puerto Montt and the southern port of Puerto Natales, made by the *M/N Evangelistas*; it is quicker

Going further ... Chiloé

The mysterious archipelago of Chiloé is one of the most fascinating areas of Chile. Isolated from mainstream Spanish development for 200 years, Chiloé is different to the mainland and retains many unique traditions, including the belief in witchcraft and local mythical figures such as 'El Trauco', an ugly, smelly creature who is said to seduce virgins and the 'La Fiura', who attracts men with her colourful clothes before putting them to sleep with her foul breath.

Chiloé consists of one main island, La Isla Grande de Chiloé (180 km long), and numerous islets. There are two main towns, Ancud and Castro, in which most of the island's 120,000 people live, and a number of small villages. The Parque Nacional de Chiloé covers extensive areas of uninhabited temperate rainforest on the wild western and southern sides of the island. At Cucao, an immense 20-km-long beach is battered by thundering Pacific surf. The more sheltered east coast and offshore islands are covered with wheat fields and dark green plots of potatoes and the roads are lined with wild flowers in summer. There are often dolphins playing in the bay and, on a clear day, views across to Corcovado volcano on the mainland. The Humboldt Current ensures a wide variety of fresh shellfish is available all year; try *curanto* (a stew, traditionally cooked in a hole in the earth). Chiloé is famous for its painted churches, now designated UNESCO World Heritage Sites. The earliest example from 1730 is in Achao on the island of Quinchao.

Ferry services connect the island with Chaitén and the Carretera Austral (see page 300), but the main sea link is the frequent vehicle ferry service between Pargua on the mainland (55 km south-west of Puerto Montt) across the Chacao straits to Chacao (30 minutes, cars US$16 one way, foot passengers US$1). Frequent bus services meet the ferries, linking Ancud and Castro with Puerto Montt and beyond. Local services, however, can be crowded and slow. Mountain bikes and horses are ideal for travelling through the more remote parts of Chiloé; there are also limited opportunities for hiking.

Sleeping **B-C Mundo Nuevo**, Costanera 748, Ancud, T065-628383, www.newworld.cl. **C-D** singles, **F** per person in dorms. Some rooms with bath. Breakfast included, comfortable, great views over the bay, lots of info, heating, good showers, Wi-Fi, kitchen facilities, bike rental, car hire, one room has a boat-bed. Tours offered. English and German spoken. Recommended.

and cheaper to fly or go by bus via Argentina but the voyage by boat is spectacular, given a little luck with the weather. The route south from Puerto Montt crosses the Seno de Reloncaví and the Golfo de Ancud, then continues south through the Canal Moraleda and the Canal Errázuriz, which separate the mainland from the outlying islands. It then heads west through the Canal Chacabuco to Bahía Anna Pink and across the open sea and the infamous Golfo de Penas (Gulf of Sorrows) – where sea-sickness pills come in more than handy – to reach a series of channels, which provide one of the narrowest routes for large shipping in the world, before making a short detour to the massive Pío XI (southbound) or Amalia (northbound) glacier. There are spectacular views of the wooded fjords, weather permitting, particularly at sunrise and sunset, and a sense of desolate peace pervades everything except the ship, which is filled with people having a good time.

The only regular stop on this route is the fishing village of **Puerto Edén** on Isla Wellington, one hour south of the Angostura Inglesa. It has three shops, one off-licence, one café, and a *hospedaje* (open intermittently) for up to 20 people. The population of 250 includes a few remaining native Alacaluf people. **Isla Wellington** is largely untouched, with stunning mountains. If you do stop here, take all food; maps (not very accurate) are available in Santiago. The onward fare to Puerto Natales is US$150.

This is a cargo ferry rather than a cruise liner; standards of service and comfort vary, depending on the number of passengers and weather conditions. Economy class is basic but comfortable, in 22-berth dormitories. The food is variable though served in abundant portions, and, apart from videos and a few talks, organized entertainment is limited. There is a bar on board, but you are welcome to bring your own drinks.

To Puerto Chacabuco and Laguna San Rafael

A once- or twice-weekly ferry service sails between Puerto Montt and **Puerto Chacabuco**, 80 km west of Coyhaique. This beautiful voyage passes forested cliffs, seemingly within touching distance, and offers glimpses of distant snows. However, taking this route south means that travellers miss out on the attractions of the Carretera Austral. The **Navimag** ferry continues (September to April only) from Puerto Chacabuco to visit **Laguna San Rafael** (see page 308). However, the cabins are on the expensive side and be sure to double check departure times. A better option is to take a catamaran service direct to the Laguna from Puerto Chacabuco (see page 308) or to charter a small plane (in good weather only) from Coyhaique (see page 315). A luxury alternative is to board *Skorpios II* for a cruise to Chiloé and Laguna San Rafael. Generally service is excellent, the food superb and, at the laguna, you chip ice off the face of the glacier for your whisky. After San Rafael the ship visits **Quitralco fjord**, where there are thermal pools and boat trips. There are also four- to six-day tours from Puerto Montt with **Patagonia Connection**, which visit Puerto Chacabuco, Laguna San Rafael and the Termas de Puyuhuapi (see page 305).

To Chaitén

The sea route to Chaitén (see page 301) through the Golfo de Ancud is quicker and more reliable than the Carretera Austral but you'll miss much of the spectacular scenery encountered along the way. However, if you are pushed for time, **Naviera Austral** both offer two to four ferry services weekly. The journey normally takes 10 hours.

Puerto Montt and around listings

For Sleeping and Eating price codes and other relevant information, see pages 41-44.

Sleeping

Puerto Montt *p284, map p284*
Accommodation is expensive in season, much cheaper off season. There are lots of *cabañas* on the outskirts of the city and in Pelluco.

L Gran Hotel Don Vicente, Varas 447, T065-432900, www.granhoteldonvicente.cl. Business-class hotel. Some rooms noisy, restaurant serving seafood, fine views.

AL Club Presidente, Portales 664, T065-251666, www.presidente.cl. Comfortable 4-star with breakfast. Large rooms or suites, many with views. English spoken. Recommended.

AL Gran Hotel Don Luis, Quillota 146, T065-259001, www.hoteldonluis.cl. Another comfortable 4-star hotel and decent restaurant as well as a gym and sauna.

AL O'Grimm, Gallardo 211, T065-252845, www.ogrimm.com. Pleasant, spacious slightly dated rooms with lounge area, cosy restaurant with occasional live music, central.

A Apart Hotel Colón, Pedro Montt 65, T065-264290, www.aparthotelcolon.cl. Fully furbished studio apartments, good value, especially when paying in dollars.

A-B Le Mirage, Rancagua 350, T065-255125, www.hotellemirage.cl. A basic business-class hotel with breakfast, small rooms, clean.

A-B Tren del Sur, Santa Teresa 643, T065-343939, www.trendelsur.cl. Self-styled boutique hostel. Pleasant spacious lobby and cosy common areas, decorated with objects recycled from the old railway, but rooms a tad overpriced, especially those with no windows. Very helpful English-speaking owner.

B Hostal Pacífico, J J Mira 1088, T065-256229, www.hostalpacifico.cl. With bath, some rooms a little cramped, breakfast, cable TV, parking, comfortable.

B Millahue, Copiapó 64, T065-253829, www.hotelmillahue.cl. With breakfast and bath, slightly run-down, restaurant, also apartments at Benavente 959, T/F065-254592.

B-C Hospedaje Suizo, Independencia 231, T/F065-252640, rossyoelckers@yahoo.es. **F** singles, with breakfast. Some rooms with bath. Attractive house near the bus terminal, clean, German and Italian spoken, painting and Spanish classes. Convenient for Navimag. Recommended.

C Alda González, Gallardo 552, T065-253334. **F** singles. Some rooms with bath, breakfast included, cooking facilities, English and German spoken, good value, near the Plaza de Armas.

C Hospedaje Emita, Miraflores 1281, T065-250725, hospedaje_emita@hotmail.com. **E** singles with breakfast, including home-made bread. Some rooms with bath. Clean, friendly, safe, near the bus terminal.

C Hospedaje Rocco, Pudeto 233, T/065-272897, www.hospedajerocco.cl. **D-E** pp in shared rooms. All rooms with shared bath. Impeccably clean but with no frills. Excellent breakfast included, real coffee, English and Italian spoken, friendly atmosphere, laundry. Quiet residential area, convenient for Navimag. A little overpriced but still recommended.

C Vista al Mar, Vivar 1337, T065-255625, www.hospedajevistaalmar.unlugar.com . **E** singles. Friendly, helpful, welcoming, good breakfast. Phone for lift from bus terminal.

C-D Casa Perla, Trigal 312, T065-262104, www.casaperla.com. **F** pp in shared rooms. With breakfast. Slightly ramshackle house uphill from the bus terminal, helpful, friendly, meals, laundry, internet, pleasant garden, English spoken, Spanish classes offered, good meeting place. Recommended.

D Casa Gladis, Ancud y Mira. Some double rooms. **F** pp for dormitory beds, kitchen and laundry facilities, near bus terminal.

D Vista Hermosa, Miramar 1486, T/F065-268001, vistahermosa@mixmail.com. **F** singles without bath, 10 mins' walk from bus terminal. Peaceful area. Room at the front has the best views, although somewhat compromised by the new high-rise in front.

Camping

Wild camping is possible along the sea front. Several official sites west of Puerto Montt.

Anderson, 11 km west. American-run, hot showers, private beach, home-grown fruit, vegetables and milk products.

El Ciervo, 3 km west. Good site.

Municipal, Chinquihue, 10 km west. Open Oct-Apr, fully equipped with tables, seats, barbecue, toilets and showers, small shop, no kerosene, bus service from town.

Towards Chiloé *p285*

B Cabañas El Pangal, 5 km from Maullin, T065-451244, m_essedin@hotmail.com. Campsite and cabins on the beach.

B Hotel Colonial, Calbuco, T065-461546, www.hotelcolonial@hotmail.com. One of several decent hotels.

C Huelmo, un destino no turístico, T09-8314 2656. **E** Singles. Simple cabins near Huelmo, a small seafront village completely off the beaten track. English spoken. Recommended.

Seno de Reloncaví *p287*

Accommodation in Puelo is also available with local families.

LL Río Puelo Lodge, Puelo, T02-2298533, www.rio-puelo-lodge.cl. Plush lodge recently refurbished, offering all-in fly-fishing packages.
A Campo Aventura, 4 km south of Cochamó, T065-232910, www.campo-aventura.com. For details of riding and trekking expeditions, see below. Accommodation is offered at the base camp (signpost on road) with great breakfast, kitchen, sauna. Camping is also possible. Very fresh milk from Campo Aventura's cow, herb garden, expensive but good food using local produce, vegetarian also available, book exchange. There's another base in a renovated mountain house in the valley of La Junta. Office at San Bernardo 318, Puerto Varas.
C-D Cochamó, T065-216212. **F** singles. Basic but clean, friendly, often full with salmon farm workers, good meals. Recommended.
C-D Mercado Particular Sabin, Catedral 20, Cochamó. One of several *pensiones*, next to Hotel Cochamó.
C-D Navarrito, Ralún. **F** singles in basic accommodation. Also restaurant.
D Hospedaje Edicar, Cochamó. **F-G** singles. Breakfast available. Without bath, spacious. Recommended.
D Hospedaje Maura, JJ Molina 12, Cochamó. **F-G** singles. Some rooms with bath. Beautifully situated, good food.
D Posada Campesino, Ralún. **F-G** singles. Without breakfast, very friendly, simple, clean.

Camping

Los Castaños, Cochamó, T065-216212.

Eating

Puerto Montt *p284, map p284*

Angelmó, the old fishing port past the fish market, has many small, very popular seafood restaurants serving excellent lunches only (fierce touting for business). Look out for local specialities such as *curanto* and *picoroco al vapor*, a giant barnacle whose flesh tastes like crab, and ask for *té blanco* (white wine; the stalls are not licensed to serve wine). The city centre is full of cheap unpretentious places; most upmarket restaurants are around Pelluco along the coast on Puerto Montt's southeastern outskirts (10 mins from the centre by *colectivo*).

𝍣𝍣𝍣 **Club de Yates**, Juan Soler s/n. Fancy restaurant on a pier serving expensive seafood with pretty much the best view in town.
𝍣𝍣𝍣-𝍣𝍣 **Club Alemán**, Varas 264, T065-252551. Old fashioned, good food and wine.
𝍣𝍣𝍣-𝍣𝍣 **Cotele**, Juan Soler s/n, Pelluco, T065-278000. Only serves one thing – beef, but serves it as well as anywhere in southern Chile. Recommended. Reservations advised.
𝍣𝍣 **Café Haussman**, San Martín y Urmeneta. German-style cakes, beer and *crudos* (raw meat).
𝍣𝍣 **Centro Español**, O'Higgins 233, T065-343753. Decent traditional Chilean and Spanish food. Vegetarian options.
𝍣𝍣 **Dino**, Varas 550, T065-252785. Restaurant upstairs, snacks downstairs (try the lemon juice). Often has an all-you-can-eat buffet.
𝍣𝍣 **Pazos**, Pelluco, T065-252552. Serves the best *curanto* in the Puerto Montt area.
𝍣 **Café Central**, Rancagua 117, T065-482888. Spartan decor, generous portions (sandwiches and *pichangas*). Giant TV screen for football enthusiasts.
𝍣 **Café Real**, Rancagua 137, T065-253750. For *empanadas*, *pichangas*, *congrío frito* and cheap lunches.
𝍣 **Restaurant de las Antiqüedades**, Av Angelmó. Attractive and unusual decor, real coffee, interesting menu.

Cafés

Asturias, Angelmó 2448. Limited menu but often recommended.
Café Alemana, Rancagua 117. Good coffee.

Towards Chiloé *p285*

𝍣𝍣 **Kiel**, Chinquihué, T065-255010. Good meat and seafood dishes.

Seno de Reloncaví *p287*

Eateries in Cochamó include **Donde Payi**, opposite the church, and **Reloncaví**, on the road to the waterfront. On the seafront there's a cheap fish/seafood restaurant, which also hires out canoes, US$2 for 30 mins.

Bars and clubs

Puerto Montt *p284, map p284*
Several of the 'bars' near the port and along Pérez Rosales are very sleezy.
Star, RN 5 north of the city. Disco. Several more in Pelluco, east of Puerto Montt.

Shopping

Puerto Montt *p284, map p284*
Woollen goods and Mapuche-designed rugs can be bought at roadside stalls in Angelmó and on Diego Portales opposite the bus terminal. Prices are much the same as on Chiloé, but quality is often lower.
Santa Isabel, opposite bus terminal. Supermarket open daily 0900-2200.
Sotavento, Diego Portales 570. Bookshop with a small selection of English novels, also maps and local interest books.
Paseo del Mar, Talca y Antonio Varas. Large modern shopping mall. There is also a new mall, the **Paseo Costanera** on the seafront which also has a multi-screen cinema.

Activities and tours

Puerto Montt *p284, map p284*
Most agencies offer 1-day excursions to **Chiloé** (US$45) and to **Puerto Varas, Isla Loreley, Laguna Verde** and the **Petrohué Falls**: these are cheaper from kiosks inside the bus terminal. Some companies offer 2-day excursions along the Carretera Austral to **Hornopirén**, US$120, with food and accommodation.
Andina del Sud, Varas 437, close to central tourist kiosk, T065-257797. Sells a variety of tours, and offers the lakes trip to Bariloche through its subsidiary **Cruce de Lagos** , www.crucedealgos.com.
Ecosub, Panamericana 510, T065-263939, www.ecosub.cl. Scuba diving excursions.
Eureka Turismo, Gallardo 65, T065-250412, www.chile-travel.com/eureka.htm. Helpful, German and English spoken.
Kayaking Austral, T09-96980951, or book through **Casa Perla**. Guided sea kayaking.
Travellers, General Bulnes 1009, 22 de Mayo, T065-262099, www.travellers.cl. Booking office for **Navimag** ferry to Puerto Natales, bespoke excursions, also sells imported camping equipment and runs computerized tourist information service, good book swap, map display, TV, real coffee, English-run.

Seno de Reloncaví *p287*
Horse riding/trekking
Campo Aventura, 4 km south of Cochamó, T065-232910, www.campo-aventura.com. Specializes in all-inclusive riding and trekking expeditions with packhorses along the Gaucho trail between the Reloncaví Estuary and the Argentine border, 2-10 days, roughly US$100 pp, per day; good guides, spectacular scenery, English, French and German spoken, highly recommended. It also organizes other activities including combined sea kayaking-horse-riding trips with **Kokayak** in Puerto Varas.
Miralejos, San Pedro 311, Puerto Varas, T065-234892, www.miralejos.cl. Runs a variety of small group and bespoke tours around the Cochamó area from 1 to 10 days, including horse riding, sea-kayaking, and treks across the border to El Bolsón in Argentina.
Sebastián Contreras, C Morales, Cochamó, T065-216220. An independent guide who offers tours on horseback and hires out horses. Recommended.

Transport

Puerto Montt *p284, map p284*
Air
LanChile and **Sky** have several flights daily to **Santiago**, from US$95 return (best one-way prices with **Sky**); to **Balmaceda** for Coyhaique, from US$75 return; to **Punta Arenas**, from US$100 return. Jan-Mar flights get booked up; however, cancellations are sometimes available from the airport. To **Port Stanley** (Falkland Islands/Islas Malvinas), from Santiago via Punta Arenas, **LanChile**, Sat, US$700 return.

Airline offices Aerotaxis del Sur, A Varas 70 , T065-731315, www.aerotaxisdelsur.cl; **Cielomar Austral**, Quillota 245, local 1, T065-264010; **LanChile**, O'Higgins 167, T600-5262000, www.lan.com; **Sky**, T600-600 2828, www.skyairline.cl.

Bus

The very crowded terminal on the seafront at Diego Portales y Lota has telephones, restaurants, a casa de cambio and left luggage (US$2.50 per item for 24 hrs). Theft is a common problem in the terminal sokeep a tight hold of your baggage.

Expreso Puerto Varas, Thaebus and Full Express run minibuses every few mins to **Puerto Varas**, US$1.20, **Llanquihue** and **Frutillar**, US$2, and to **Osorno**, US$3. Buses and *colectivos* Nos 2, 3 and 20 ply the route to **Anglemó**, US$0.60 each way.

To **Ensenada** and **Petrohué**, several companies, hourly; to **Ralún**, **Cochamó** and **Puelo**, Buses Fierro and Buses Bohle, 5 daily via Puerto Varas and Ensenada, US$6; to **Pucón**, JAC, several daily, 6 hrs, US$12; to **Santiago**, several companies, 13 hrs, US$30-75; to **Temuco**, US$10; to **Valdivia**, US$8. For services to Chiloé, see box, page 288.

To **Punta Arenas**, Pacheco and Queilén Bus, 1-3 weekly, 32-38 hrs, approximately US$80 (bus goes through Argentina via Bariloche; take US$ cash to pay for meals, etc in Argentina); book well in advance in Jan-Feb and check if you need a multiple-entry Chilean visa; also book any return journey before setting out. To **Coyhaique** via Bariloche, 2 weekly, Turibus, US$55.

International Buy tickets for international buses from the bus terminal, not through an agency. Andes Mar has through-services to Buenos Aires, Neuquén and Bahía Blanca; less in winter.

To **Bariloche** via Osorno and the Puyehue pass, daily, 7 hrs, Andes Mar, Río de la Plata and Tas Choapa, US$23. Cruce de Lagos (see page 292) runs a mixed bus and boat service to **Bariloche** via Lago Todos Los Santos and Paso Pérez Rosales, depart company offices in Puerto Montt daily at 0800, US$230 one way (plus US$110 May-Aug for overnight stay in the **Hotel Peulla**; for a cheaper alternative see page 279). The trip may be cancelled if the weather is poor; there are reports of difficulty in obtaining a refund. If you have time but are short of money, you can buy tickets for the boat in Puerto Montt or Puerto Varas and do the rest of the trip independently, but bear in mind that there is no transport from Peulla to the border, 26 km.

Car hire

Autovald, Sector Cardenal, Pasaje San Andrés 60, T065-256043, www.autovald.cl, cheap rates; **Avis**, Benavente 670, T065-367840, and at airport; **Budget**, Antonio Varas 162, T065-286277, www.budget.cl, and at airport; **Egartur**, Benavente 575, local 3, T065-257336, www.egartur.cl, good service, recommended, will deliver your car to your hotel for free; **First**, Antonio Varas 447, T065-252036; **Full Famas**, Diego Portales 506, T065-258060, F065-259840, and airport, T065-263750, friendly, helpful, good value, has vehicles that can be taken to Argentina; **Hertz**, At the airport, T065-268944, www.autorentas.cl; **Salfa Sur**, Pilpilco 800, also at Airport, T065-290224, www.salfasur.cl. Good value.

Ferry

Shipping offices **Catamaranes del Sur**, Diego Portales 510, T065-267533, www.catamaranesdelsur.cl; **Navimag**, Terminal Transbordadores, Av Angelmó 2187, T065-253318, www.navimag.com; **Skorpios**, Angelmó 1660 y Miraflores (Castilla 588), T065-252619, www.skorpios.cl; **Naviera Austral**, Terminal Transbordadores, Angelmó 2187, T065-270400, www.navieraustral.cl. **Transmarchilay**, Terminal Transbordadores, Angelmó 2187, T065-270000, www.transmarchilay.cl.

Train

The station is 2 km north of the city centre at Cuarta Terraza s/n, La Paloma, T600-

5855000, www.efe.cl. At the time of writing all services have been suspended.

Seno de Reloncaví *p287*

Bus

Buses **Fierro** and **Bohle** from Puerto Montt via Puerto Varas and Ensenada, to **Ralún**, **Cochamó** and **Puelo**, 5 daily all year.

Boat

In summer boats sail up the estuary from **Angelmó**. Get a group of people together and convince one of the fishermen to take you. For information on (irregular) scheduled trips, contact the regional Sernatur office in Puerto Montt.

Sea routes south of Puerto Montt *p287*

To Puerto Natales

Navimag ferry the *Evangelistas* sail once a week, Nov-Apr, departing Puerto Montt Mon 1600, returning Fri 0400 (although departures are frequently delayed so double check departure times), 3½ days, economy from US$555 pp, private cabin with view US$1720 (double US$1750), all prices include meals, 10% discount for ISIC holders in cabin class only, fares 10-20% lower Apr-Oct. Book well in advance for cabin-class departures Dec-Mar (at least a month in advance in Feb), especially for the voyage south; Puerto Natales to Puerto Montt is less heavily booked; it is worth putting your name on the waiting list for cancellations at busy periods. Tickets can be bought in advance from **Navimag** offices in Puerto Montt, Puerto Natales and Punta Areńas, from travel agencies throughout the country, or online at www.navimag.com (occasional internet only offers off-season).

To Puerto Chacabuco and Laguna San Rafael

Navimag sails to Puerto Chacabuco throughout the year, usually once a week, 24 hrs, accommodation US$60-210, cars US$230, motorcycles US$100, cycles US$50. In the summer (Sep-Apr) the ferry continues once a week (usually at the weekend) from Puerto Chacabuco to **Laguna San Rafael**, 21-24 hrs, return fare Puerto Montt–Laguna San Rafael US$400-800; better offers are available from from Puerto Chacabuco to Laguna San Rafael (see page 308).

Skorpios Cruises luxury ship *Skorpios 2* leaves Puerto Montt Sat 1100 for a 6-day cruise to **Laguna San Rafael**, returning to Puerto Montt Fri, double cabin from US$1300 pp. For further details (and information about routes sailed by *Skorpios II*, consult www.skorpios.cl).

Other sea routes

To **Chaitén**, **Naviera Austral**, 2-4 ferries weekly, 10 hrs, passengers reclining seat US$35, bunk US$50, cars US$150, bicycles US$15.

Directory

Puerto Montt *p284, map p284*

Banks ATMs at several banks and supermarkets in the centre and in both malls; commission charges for TCs vary widely. **Consulates** **Argentina**, Cauquenes 94, piso 2, T065-253996, quick visa service; **Germany**, Antonio Varas y Gallardo, piso 3, Oficina 306, Tue-Wed 0930-1200; **Netherlands**, Chorillos 1582, T065-253003; **Spain**, Rancagua 113, T065-252557. **Internet and telephone** Several in the centre and on Av Angelmó. **Laundry** **Center**, Antonio Varas 700; **Lavatodo**, O'Higgins 231; **Narly**, San Martín 187, local 6, high prices, US$7 for 3 kg; **Nautilus**, Av Angelmó 1564, cheaper, good; **Unic**, Chillán 149; **Yessil't**, Edif Caracol, Urmeneta 300, service washes. **Medical services** Seminario s/n, T065-261134. **Post office** Rancagua 126, open Mon-Fri 0830-1830, Sat 0830-1200.

Carretera Austral

Contents

Footprint features

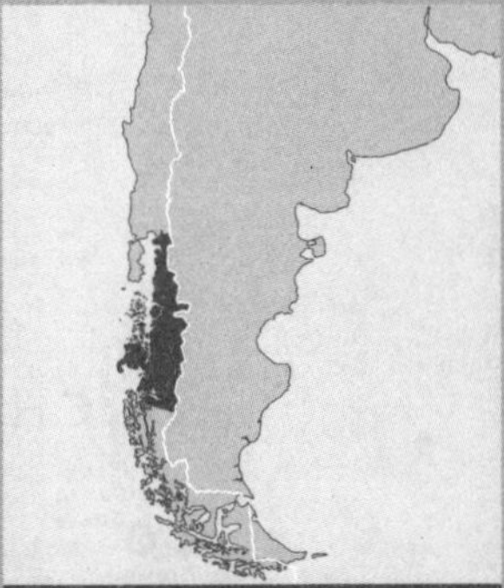

At a glance

Getting around Boat, minibus, air taxi, pickup or, ideally, mountain bike. You will need a lot of patience.

Time required At least a week and twice as much as you think.

Weather Cold in winter, wet on the coast but surprisingly pleasant in summer.

When not to go Winter is unforgiving, while the road is liable to flooding in spring and autumn.

★ Don't miss ...

1. Cycling along the Carretera Austral, page 298.
2. Parque Pumalín, page 300.
3. Whitewater rafting at Futaleufú, pages 304 and 314.
4. Cruising to the San Rafael glacier, page 308.
5. Trekking around Cerro Castillo, page 318.

Travelling along the Carretera Austral is one of the greatest journeys South America has to offer. The Carretera is a largely unpaved *ripio* road stretching almost 1200 km through spectacular ever-changing scenery and with a similar length of branch roads heading either to the fjords or the mountains and Argentine Patagonia beyond. Before the opening of the road, this part of Chile was largely inaccessible; it remains breathtaking. The journey will take you past trees growing out of vertical cliffs; impenetrably thick millennial forests and burned pastures dotted with glacial debris; innumerable waterfalls rushing right down to the road's edge, while spiralling volcanoes and sparkling glaciers feed turquoise lakes and fast-flowing rivers, all rich with southern Chile's unique flora.

The only town of any size, Coyhaique, lies in the valley of the Río Simpson. South of Coyhaique are Lago General Carrera, the largest lake in Chile, and the Río Baker, one of the country's longest rivers. Further south still is Villa O'Higgins and the icefields of the Campo de Hielo Sur, which feed several magnificent glaciers and prevent further road building, although a route (by boat and on foot or mountain bike) exists to El Chaltén in Argentina. Coyhaique enjoys good air connections with Puerto Montt and Santiago, while nearby Puerto Chacabuco can be reached by ferry from Puerto Montt, Chaitén and Chiloé. The most appealing parts of this region, however, can only be visited by travelling along the Carretera Austral.

The recent eruptions of Volcán Chaitén (see below) have caused considerable damage to the town of Chaitén, which has been almost entirely evacuated save for the ferry terminal, and to the southern section of the Parque Pumalín which remains closed at the time of writing. With further eruptions a possibility it is hard to say when normal services will resume. See the relevant text for more detail.

Ins and outs

Travelling the length of the Carretera Austral can be quite a challenge. The first and most important piece of advice is to take enough cash. While there are Cirrus and MasterCard ATMs in Futaleufú and Cochrane, Coyhaique is the only place between Puerto Montt and Villa O'Higgins with Visa ATMs. After heavy rain, parts of the Carretera are liable to flood, so check the weather carefully and be prepared to be stuck in one place for a few days while conditions improve. Off season much of the northern section of the Carretera is inaccessible when the Arena–Puelche and Hornopirén–Caleta Gonzalo ferries are suspended. You will have to go to Chaitén directly from Puerto Montt or Chiloé instead.

Getting around

The road can be divided into three sections: **Puerto Montt to Chaitén** (242 km), including two or three ferry crossings; **Chaitén to Coyhaique** (435 km); and **Coyhaique to Villa O'Higgins** (582 km), including one ferry crossing. There is also a branch that runs along the southern shore of **Lago General Carrera** from Puerto Guadal to Chile Chico. The Puerto Montt–Chaitén section can only be travelled in summer, when the ferries are operating, but an alternative route, through Chiloé to Chaitén, exists year round (see page 288). The road is paved around Coyhaique from Mañihuales and Puerto Chacabuco to Villa Cerro Castillo and Puerto Ibáñez.

Bus Most of the buses that ply the Carretera Austral are minibuses (or converted transit vans) operated by small companies and often driven by their owners. Services are less reliable than elsewhere in Chile and timetables change frequently. Booking your ticket in advance means that if your bus does not leave for whatever reason, the company is liable to pay for your accommodation until the bus is ready to depart. Complaints should be directed to **SERNAC**, the government consumer rights department, in Coyhaique.

Driving Some sections of the road can be difficult or even impossible after heavy rain or snowfall; check the weather carefully and be prepared to be stuck in one place for a few days while conditions improve. Take a pick-up or 4WD and fill your tank whenever possible. Although tourist infrastructure is growing rapidly and unleaded fuel is available all the way to Villa O'Higgins, you should protect windscreens and headlamps and carry adequate spare fuel and parts, especially if you are intending to detour from the main route.

Hitching Popular in summer, but extremely difficult out of season, particularly south of Cochrane. Watching the cloak of dust thrown up by the wheels from the back of a pick-up, while taking in the lakes, forests, mountains and waterfalls, is an unforgettable experience, but be prepared for long delays, carry a tent and plenty of food and allow at least three days from Chaitén to Coyhaique.

Cycling The Carretera Austral is highly recommended for cycling as long as you have enough time and are reasonably fit. A good mountain bike is essential and a tent is an advantage. Most buses will take bicycles for a small charge.

Best time to visit

January and February are probably the best months. April to September it is bitterly cold inland; roads are subject to snowfall or flooding, and some ferry services are suspended.

Puerto Montt to Chaitén

This 242-km section of the Carretera Austral is the most inaccessible and secluded stretch along the entire route, passing through two national parks and the private Parque Pumalín. Beautiful old trees close in on all sides, the rivers and streams sparkle and, on (admittedly rare) clear days, there are beautiful views across the Golfo de Ancud to Chiloé. ▸▸ *For listings, see pages 301-303.*

Parque Nacional Alerce Andino → *Colour map 1, B3.*

ⓘ *Entrances 2.5 km from Correntoso (35 km east of Puerto Montt) and 7 km east of Lenca (40 km south of Puerto Montt), US$8.*

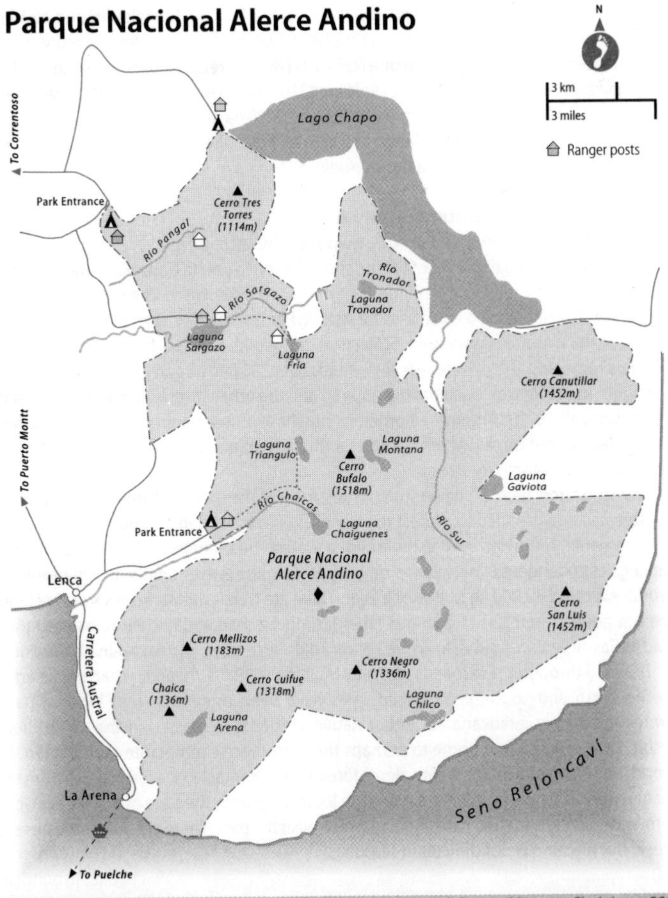

This national park covers 39,255 ha of steep forested valleys between the beautiful Seno de Reloncaví (see page 287) and Lago Chapo, and contains ancient alerce trees, some over 1000 years old (the oldest are estimated to be 4200 years old). There are also some 50 small lakes and many waterfalls in the park. Wildlife includes pudú, pumas, vizcachas, condors and black woodpeckers. There are ranger posts at Río Chaicas, Lago Chapo, Laguna Sargazo and at the north entrance, and a map is available from **CONAF** in Puerto Montt.

Hornopirén and around → *Colour map 1, B3.*

Some 46 km south of Puerto Montt (allow one hour), **La Arena** is the site of the first ferry, across the Reloncaví estuary to **Puelche**. From Puelche there is an unpaved road north to Puelo but the Carretera Austral continues 58 km south to **Hornopirén**, also called Río Negro, which lies at the northern end of a fjord. At the mouth of the fjord is **Isla Llancahué**, a small island with a hotel and thermal springs. The island is reached by **boat** ⓘ *T09-96424857, US$60 one way shared between group*, look out for dolphins and fur seals on the crossing. From Hornopirén, excursions can be made to the Hornopirén volcano (1572 m), Lago Cabrera and the **Parque Nacional Hornopirén**. The park lies 16 km east by *ripio* road and encompasses the Yates volcano (2187 m) as well as the basins of two rivers, the Blanco and the Negro. The park protects some 9000 ha of alerce forest as well as areas of mixed native forest including lenga and coigue. From the entrance a path leads 8 km east up along the Río Blanco to a basic *refugio*.

Parque Pumalín and around → *Colour map 1, B3.*

ⓘ *Klenner 299, Puerto Varas, T065-250079, www.pumalinpark.org, free.*

Hornopirén is the departure point for the second ferry, to Caleta Gonzalo, situated on the southern edge of the Fiordo Reñihue (or direct to Chaitén when Caleta Gonzalo is not accessible). Caleta Gonzalo is the base for visiting Parque Pumalín, seen by many as one of the most important conservation projects in the world. Created by the US billionaire Douglas Tompkins, this private reserve extends over 280,000 ha and is in two sectors, one just south of the Parque Nacional Hornopirén and the other stretching south and east of Caleta Gonzalo to the Argentine border. Its purchase aroused controversy, especially in the Chilean armed forces, which saw it as a threat to national sovereignty, but now the park has nature sanctuary status.

Covering large areas of the western Andes, most of the park is occupied by temperate rainforest and is intended to protect the lifestyles of its inhabitants as well as the physical environment. Tompkins has established a native tree nursery, producing 100,000 saplings of endangered species, and developed apiculture; the Pumalin bee stations can produce around 30,000 kg of honey a year. There are treks ranging from short trails into the temperate rainforest to arduous hikes lasting for several days. Three marked trails lead to Cascadas Escondidas; to an area of very old alerce trees; and to Laguna Tronador.

The road through these forests was only built in the 1980s, meaning that, unlike areas to the north and south, endangered trees have been protected from logging (laws protecting alerces, araucaria and other native species were passed in the 1970s). As a result, Parque Pumalín is home to perhaps the most diverse temperate rainforest in the world, and is the only place where alerce forests remain intact just a few metres from the main road. It is a truly humbling experience looking up from the base of a 3000-year-old, 3-m-wide alerce, and this, in itself, is a reason to visit the park. There are only three buses a week, but hitching is not difficult in season.

Much of the this section of the park was covered in ash after recent eruptions of Volcán Chaitén and at the time of writing the southern half of the park, between Caleta Gonzalo and Chaitén, is closed. Repair work is under way and the hope is that the park will open again in the not too distant future. However, this is dependent on the volcano calming down.

The Carretera Austral runs through the park, climbing steeply before reaching two lakes, Lago Río Negro and Lago Río Blanco. The coast is reached at Santa Bárbara, 48 km south, where there is a black-sand beach. Towards sunset dolphins often swim right up to the beach. You can join them, although the water is very cold.

Chaitén → *Colour map 1, C2.*

Chaitén lies in a beautiful spot, with a forest-covered hill rising behind it, and a quiet inlet leading out into the Patagonian channels. In many ways it is a cultural crossroads. Until relatively recently, the town had more contact with Argentina than the central Chilean mainland, while a Chilote influence is clear in the town's architecture. Indeed, until the construction of the Carretera this area was known as Chiloé Continental and was governed as part of the island opposite.

In May 2008, Volcán Chaitén, previously thought to be extinct, erupted, spewing a 20-cm layer of ash over the surrounding countryside and causing the Río Blanco to shift its banks and flood most of the town of Chaitén, destroying many buildings and covering much of the town with a thick layer of volcnic mud. A further eruption followed in February 2009. The govenment decided to abandon the town, making plans to rebuild Chaitén 10 km to the north, at Santa Bárbara. The population was evacuated to Puerto Montt and Chiloé, and most have stayed away either for fear of a future eruption, or because they have no work to return to. The seat of provincial government has been moved to Futaleufú taking with it the bank, and an important source of local employment.

Out of an original population of over 4000, about 80 diehard locals remain in the remnants of the town, mostly in the northwestern sector that survived relatively unscathed. At the time of writing the ferry terminal is still in use, with connecting bus services to Futaleufú and the south. Despite having to use generators for electricity, there are basic amenities such as food and lodging. Whether Chaitén has a future on its present site is ultimately dependent on the future activity of its eponymous volcano. In the meantime construction work on the new town is well underway at Santa Bárbara.

Chaitén remains important as a port for ferries to Puerto Montt and to Chiloé (see Transport, below), and when the new town is rebuilt will once again be a growing centre for adventure tourism. There is excellent fishing nearby, especially to the south in the ríos Yelcho and Futaleufú and in lagos Espolón and Yelcho.

Puerto Montt to Chaitén listings

For Sleeping and Eating price codes and other relevant information, see pages 41-44.

Sleeping

Parque Nacional Alerce Andino *p299*
There are basic *refugios* at Río Pangal, Laguna Sargazo and Laguna Fría, and campsites at Río Chaicas and at the northern entrance; no camping is permitted within the park.

Hornopirén and around *p300*
Lots of *cabañas* and *residenciales* here.
AL-A Termas de Llancahue, Isla Llancahue, T009-96424857, www.termasdellancahue.cl. **B** singles. Full board, good food, access to thermal springs.

C-D Holiday Country, O'Higgins 637, T065-217220. Restaurant, also *cabañas*.
C-D Hostería Catalina, Ingenieros Militares s/n, T065-217359, www.hosteriacatalina.cl. Simple, spacious rooms with breakfast and bath. Recommended.
D Hornopirén, Carrera Pinto 388, T065-217256. Rooms with shared bathrooms. Recommended, also *cabañas*.

Camping
There's a good site on Ingenieros Militares, US$14 per site, and 4 more sites south of Hornopirén on the road to Pichanco.

Parque Pumalin and around *p300*
There's a restaurant, *cabañas* and a campsite in Caleta Gonzalo, as well as a visitors' centre (not always open) and demonstrations of agricultural techniques in the region. Camping is available in the park at several well-run sites from US$8 per tent. Accommodation in the park suspended at the time of press.

Chaitén *p301*
At the time of writing, accommodation is being offered in Chaitén in 3 or 4 basic *hostales* which also offer food.

Activities and tours

Chaitén *p301*
Chaitur, O'Higgins 67, T09-74685608, www.chaitur.com. Travel agent selling bus and boat tickets. Also trekking, horse riding, fishing and trips to Parque Pumalín, Termas de Amarillo and Yelcho Glacier. Highly recommended. Most buses leave from here.

Transport

Before setting out, check when the ferries are running and, if driving, make a reservation for your vehicle: do this at **Naviera Austral**, in Puerto Montt (see page 293).

Parque Nacional Alerce Andino *p299*
To reach the northern entrance, take **Fierro** or **Río Pato** bus from Puerto Montt to **Correntoso** (or **Lago Chapo** bus which passes through Correntoso), several daily except Sun, then walk. To reach the southern entrance, take any **Fierro** bus to Chaicas, La Arena, Contau and Hornopirén, US$1.50, get off at **Lenca** sawmill, then walk (signposted).

A ferry makes the 30-min crossing, from La Arena to **Puelche**, 10 daily Dec-Mar, reduced service off season. Arrive 30 mins early for a place; buses have priority, cars US$17, bicycles US$5.

Hornopirén and around *p300*
Bus
Fierro 2 buses daily from Puerto Montt. No buses south from Hornopirén.

Ferry
In Jan and Feb only, the **Naviera Austral** ferry *Mailen* sails from Hornopirén to **Caleta Gonzalo**, 1600 daily, 6 hrs, return departures 0900 daily, cars US$110 one way, foot passengers US$18, bicycles US$11. Advance booking required: there can be a 2-day wait. **Chaitur** organizes connecting transport between the ferry port in Caleta Gonzalo and Chaitén (see Activities and tours). At time of press the Hornopirén ferry is bypassing Caleta Gonzalo and sailing direct to Chaitén via Ayacara. Fares 20% more than to Caleta Gonzalo.

Chaitén *p301*
Bus
Terminal at **Chaitur** office, O'Higgins 67. Recent disruptions mean that there is no permanent schedule for buses from Chaitén. However, minibuses are running along the Carretera Austral to **Coyhaique**, 3 weekly, direct in summer, 2 a week with overnight stop in La Junta or Puyuhuapi in winter, departures usually 0800-0900. Minibuses usually travel full, so can't pick up passengers en route. **Chaitur** acts as an agent for all these services (see Activities and tours). To **Futaleufú**, 3 weekly, 4 hrs, US$12.

Sea

The ferry port is about 1 km north of town. Schedules change frequently and are infrequent off season. To **Chiloé**, **Naviera Austral**, Corcovado 266, T065-731272, www.navieraustral.cl, operates ferry services to **Castro** or **Quellón**, 4 per week Dec-Mar, reduced service off season, 5 hrs, US$32 one way, US$132 cars, US$12 bikes.

To **Puerto Montt**, Naviera Austral, 4 weekly, 10 hrs, US$35, US$50 with bunk, car US$141, bike US$16.

Chaitén to Coyhaique

This section of the Carretera Austral, 422 km long, runs through long stretches of virgin rainforest, passing small villages, the still, white waters of Lago Yelcho and the Parque Nacional Queulat, with its glaciers and waterfalls. Roads branch off east to the Argentine border and west to Puerto Cisnes and Puerto Aisén. Near Coyhaique, the road passes huge tracts of land destroyed by logging, where only tree-stumps remain as testament to the depredations of the early colonists. Founded in 1929, Coyhaique is the administrative and commercial centre of Región XI and is the only settlement of any real size on the Carretera Austral. A lively city, it provides a good base for excursions in the area. ▸▸ *For listings see pages 309-317.*

Ins and outs

Getting there Coyhaique is the transport hub for Región XI. There are two airports in the area: **Teniente Vidal** ⓘ *5 km southwest of Coyhaique, taxi US$7*, which handles only smaller aircraft, and **Balmaceda** ⓘ *56 km southeast of Coyhaique, 1 hr*, near the Argentine border at Paso Huemules. Flying to Balmaceda is the most direct way to reach Coyhaique, with three or four flights daily from Santiago and Puerto Montt and three flights weekly to/from Punta Arenas. Minibuses, known as 'transfers', run between Balmaceda and Coyhaique, collecting/delivering to hotels; contact **Transfer & Turismo** ⓘ *Cochrane 387, T067-256000* or **Transfer Valencia** ⓘ *Lautaro 828, T067-233030, US$7 per person*.

There are long-distance buses (several weekly) from Puerto Montt to Coyhaique but they do not travel along the Carretera Austral, using instead the long and expensive route via Argentina. Another enjoyable way to reach this part of the country is to take the boat from Puerto Montt to Puerto Chacabuco (see page 294). ▸▸ *For further details, see Transport, page 315.*

Lago Yelcho and the border → *Colour map 1, C3.*

Surrounded by forest, 45 km south of Chaitén, **Puerto Cárdenas** lies on the northern tip of **Lago Yelcho**, a beautiful glacial lake on the Río Futaleufú surrounded by hills and the beautiful Yelcho glacier. The lake is frequented by anglers. Further south, at Km 60, a path leads to the **Yelcho glacier**, a two-hour walk each way (there is a viewing station halfway up), US$3.50. The Argentine border is reached at Futaleufú and Palena, along a road that branches off the Carretera Austral at **Villa Santa Lucía** (Km 81). The road to the border is *ripio*, of variable standard, best with a high-clearance vehicle. At **Puerto Ramírez**, at the southern end of **Lago Yelcho**, the road divides: the north branch runs along the valley of the Río Futaleufú to Futaleufú, while the southern one continues to Palena. The border is 8 km east of both Futaleufú and Palena. Both crossings lead to the Welsh settlement of Trevelin (45 km east of Futaleufú, 95 km east of Palena; see page 142) and Esquel (23 km northeast; see page 140). ▸▸ *For full details, see page 144.*

Futaleufú → *Colour map 1, C3.*

Futaleufú (big river in the Mapuche language) has now established itself as the centre for the finest whitewater rafting in the southern hemisphere. Every year, hundreds of fanatics travel to spend the southern summer here and there is no shortage of operators offering trips. The river is an incredible deep blue colour and offers everything from easy Grade II-III sections downstream to the extremely challenging Grade V Cañón del Infierno (Hell Canyon), surrounded by spectacular mountain scenery.

The village, hemmed in by mountains and the Río Espolón, is peaceful, with wide streets and Chilote-style houses. There is a **tourist office** ⓘ *on the plaza, T065-721241, daily in summer 0900-2100, www.futaleufu.cl* which also sells fishing licences. **Lago Espolón**, west of Futaleufú, is reached by a turning 41 km northeast of Puerto Ramírez. The beautiful lake enjoys a warm microclimate, regularly reaching 30°C in the day in summer. If you take a quick dip, beware of the currents.

La Junta and around → *Colour map 1, C3.*

From Villa Santa Lucía, the Carretera Austral follows the Río Frío and then the Río Palena to **La Junta**, a tranquil, nondescript village at the confluence of Río Rosselot and Río Palena, 151 km south of Chaitén. Fuel is available here. There's a **tourist office** ⓘ *on the plaza, Mon-Fri 1000-2100 summer only.*

From La Junta a new road heads northwest, past some rustic thermal springs (not always open), across the broad expanse of the Río Palena (4 ferry crossings daily) and on to **Puerto Raúl Marín Balmaceda** on the coast, a tranquil fishing village with more than its share of rainfall. Different species of dolphin (and if you are lucky, blue whales) can be seen and when it is clear there are wonderful views of Volcán Melimoyu from the beach, and in early summer you can pick the wild strawberries that grow on the dunes. Accommodation is available and camping is possible.

Some 9 km east of La Junta is **Lago Rosselot**, surrounded by forest and situated at the heart of a *reserva nacional* (12,725 ha). From Lago Rosselot the road continues for 74 km to a **border crossing** ⓘ *summer 0730-2200; winter 0800-2000*, at **Lago Verde** towards Las Pampas and Gobernador Costa in Argentina.

Puyuhuapi and around → *Colour map 2, A2.*

The Carretera Austral continues south from La Junta, along the western side of Lago Risopatrón, past several waterfalls, to **Puyuhuapi** (also spelt Puyuguapi). Located in a beautiful spot at the northern end of a fjord, the village is a tranquil stopping place between Chaitén and Coyhaique. It was founded by four Sudeten German

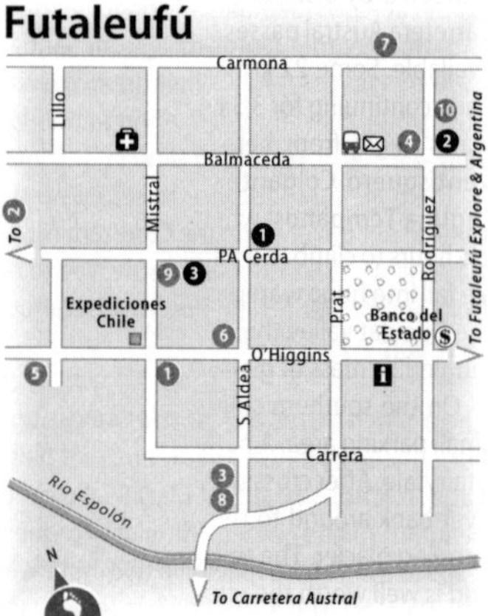

100 metres
100 yards

Sleeping
Adolfo B&B **1**
Cabañas la Escondida **10**
Cabañas Río Espolón **2**
Cabañas Veranada **3**
Continental **4**
El Barranco **5**
Hostería Río Grande **6**
Los Troncos **7**
Posada la Gringa **8**
Sur Andes **9**

Eating
Futaleufú **1**
Martín Pescador **2**
Sur Andes **3**

Termas de Puyuhuapi

Situated on the western edge of the fjord, 18 km southwest of Puyuhuapi, are the Termas de Puyuhuapi, T067-325103, US$15 per person, under-12s US$10. This resort, accessible only by boat (US$5 each way, 10-minute crossing), has several 40°C springs filling three pools near the beach. Accommodation at the resort (L) includes use of the pools and the boat transfer. Price depends on the season and type of room. The hotel restaurant is good; full board US$50 extra. The resort can be visited on a four- or six-day tour with **Patagonia Connection** (see page 314). Transport to the hotel can be arranged via hydroplane from Puerto Montt.

families in 1935 and its economy is based around fishing, tourism and the factory where Puyuhuapi's famous handmade carpets are produced and which can be visited. **Alfombras de Puyuhuapi** ⓘ *T067-325131, www.puyuhuapi.com, daily in summer 0830-1930, closed lunch, English spoken.* From Puyuhuapi, the road follows the eastern edge of the fjord along one of the most beautiful sections of the Carretera Austral, past the **Termas del Ventisquero** ⓘ *www.termasventisqueropuyuhuapi.cl,* and with views of the **Termas de Puyuhuapi** on the other side (see box, above).

Covering 154,093 ha of attractive forest around Puyuhuapi, the **Parque Nacional Queulat** ⓘ *administration at the CONAF office in La Junta, T067-314128,* is, supposedly, the former location of the legendary Ciudad de los Césares. According to myth, the city was protected by a shroud of fog and hence was impossible for strangers to discover. The Carretera Austral passes through the park, close to **Lago Risopatrón**, where boat trips are available. Some 22 km south of Puyuhuapi, a road turns off to the main entrance of the park, continuing for 3.5 km past the *guardaparques*' hut to a campsite and carpark. Three walks begin from here: a short stroll through the woodland to a viewpoint of the **Ventisquero Colgante** hanging glacier; or cross the river where the path begins to **Laguna Témpanos,** where boats cross the lake in summer; the third trail, 3.25 km, takes 2½ hours to climb to a panoramic viewpoint of the Ventisquero, where you can watch the ice fall into huge waterfalls like sifted sugar. From here the Carretera Austral climbs out of the Queulat valley through a series of hairpin bends surrounded by an impressive dense jungle-like mass of giant Nalcas. There are fine views of several glaciers.

On the southern side of the pass there is a sign labelled **Bosque Encantado** with a small parking area. A path leads west through a forest of arrayanes, like something out of a fairytale. After crossing a series of small bridges the path runs out at the river. Follow the river bank around to the right to get to a beautiful *laguna* with floating icebergs and a hanging glacier. The trek to the *laguna* and back should not take more than three hours and is well worth the effort.

Río Cisnes → *Colour map 2, A2.*

Stretching 160 km from the Argentine border to the coast at Puerto Cisnes, the Río Cisnes is recommended for rafting or canoeing, with grand scenery and modest rapids – except for the horrendous drop at Piedra del Gato, about 60 km east of Puerto Cisnes. Good camping is available in the forest. Possibly the wettest town in Chile, **Puerto Cisnes** is reached along a 33-km winding road that branches west off the Carretera Austral about 59 km south of Puyuhuapi. The **Argentine border** is reached via a road that follows the Río Cisnes east for 104 km, via La Tapera. In Argentina, the road continues via Río Frías to meet up with Route 40, the north-south road at the foot of the Andes. **Chilean immigration** ⓘ *12 km west of the border, daylight hours only.*

Towards Coyhaique

Heading south again on the main spine of the Carretera the paved section of the road begins at Km 77. The **Reserva Nacional Lago Las Torres** is 98 km south of Puyuhuapi and covers 16,516 ha. There are no trails, but it includes the wonderful Lago Las Torres, which offers good fishing and a small *hospedaje* and campsite. Further south, at Km 125, a road branches east to El Toqui where zinc is mined.

Coyhaique and around » *pp309-317. Colour map 2, A2.*

Located 420 km south of Chaitén, Coyhaique (also spelt Coihaique) lies in the broad green valley of the Río Simpson. The city is encircled by a crown of mountains and, for a few hours after it has rained, the mountainsides are covered in a fine layer of frost – a spectacular sight. Although there are many more attractions outside Coyhaique, it is a pleasant, friendly place, perfect for relaxing for a couple of days or as a base for day trips. The town is centred around an unusual pentagonal plaza, built in 1945, on which stand the cathedral, the Intendencia and a handicraft market. Further north on Baquedano is a display of old military machinery outside the local regimental headquarters. In the Casa de Cultura the **Museo Regional de la Patagonia Central** ⓘ *Lillo23, Tue-Sun 0900-2000 (summer), 0830-1730 (winter), US$1*, has sections on history, mineralogy, zoology and archaeology, as well as photos of the construction of the Carretera Austral. The very helpful **Sernatur office** ⓘ *Bulnes 35, T067-231752, infoaisen@sernatur.cl, Mon-Fri 0830-1700*, has up to date bus timetables. **CONAF** ⓘ *Ogana 1060, T067-212125, Mon-Fri 0830-1730.* Maps (photocopies of 1:50,000 IGM maps) are available from **Dirección de Vialidad** on the plaza.

From Coyhaique there are two routes into Argentina: via Coyhaique Alto and Paso Huemules (see page 187). The former route takes you past the **Monumento Natural Dos Lagunas** ⓘ *25 km east of Coyhaique, US$2, camping US$15 per site*, a small park that encompasses Lagos El Toro and Escondido. The latter route passes Balmaceda airport.

Around Coyhaique

There are two national reserves close to Coyhaique: 5 km northwest off the Carretera Austral is **Reserva Nacional Coyhaique**, which covers 2150 ha of forest (mainly introduced species) and has a number of well marked trails of between 20 minutes and five hours, while west of Coyhaique (take any bus to Puerto Aisén) is the **Reserva Nacional Río Simpson**, covering 40,827 ha of steep forested valleys and curiously rounded hills rising to 1878 m. There are beautiful waterfalls, lovely views of the river and very good fly fishing here. The southeastern sector of the reserve is designated as the **Reserva Nacional Río Clara** and is one of the best places to see the native huemul (see pages 19 and 397), although visitors must be accompanied by a warden. Other wildlife includes pudú and pumas, and a variety of birds ranging from condors to several species of duck. Administration is 32 km west of Coyhaique, just off the road.

Puerto Aisén and Puerto Chacabuco → *Colour map 2, A2.*

Puerto Aisén lies at the confluence of the rivers Aisén and Palos. First developed in the 1920s, the town grew as the major port of the region until the silting up of the Río Aisén forced the port to move 15 km further downriver to Puerto Chacabuco. There is a helpful **tourist office** ⓘ *Prat y Sgto Aldea, Dec-Feb only*, in the Municipalidad.

The town is linked to the south bank of the Río Aisén by the Puente Presidente Ibáñez, once the longest suspension bridge in Chile. From the far bank a paved road leads to **Puerto Chacabuco**, from where ferry services depart for Puerto Montt and **Laguna San Rafael** (see page 308).

Coyhaique

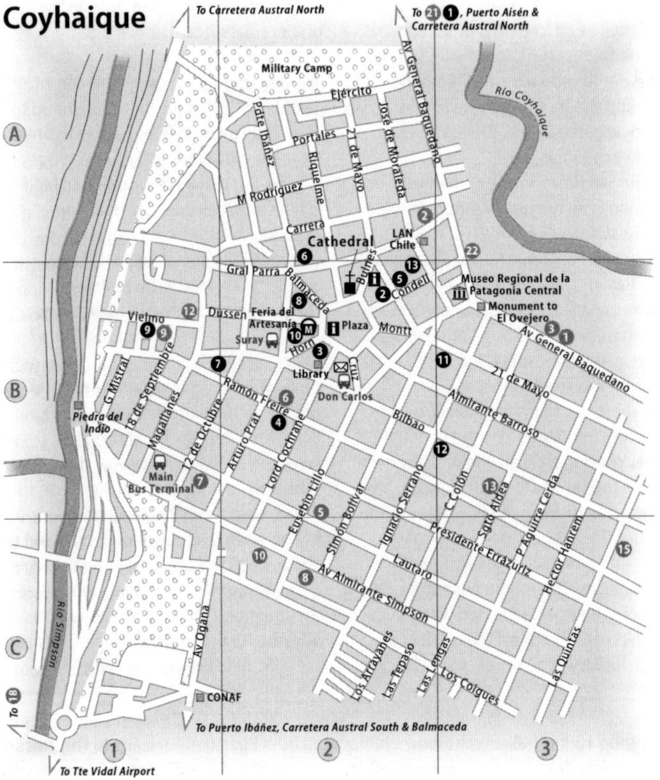

200 metres
200 yards

Sleeping
Albergue Las Salamandras **18** *C1*
Cabañas Mirador **1** *B3*
El Reloj **3** *B3*
Hospedaje Gladys **2** *A2*
Hospedaje Lautaro 269 **7** *B1*
Hospedaje María Ester **5** *B2*
Hospedaje Mondaca **8** *C2*
Hospedaje Natti **10** *C2*
Hospedaje Patricio y Gedra Guzmán **21** *A3*
Hospedaje Pochi **6** *B2*
Hostal Araucarias **9** *B1*
Hostal Español **13** *B3*
Hostal Las Quintas **15** *C3*
Hostería Coyhaique **12** *B1*
San Sebastián **22** *A3*

Eating
Café Alemana **5** *B2*
Café Oriente **2** *B2*
Café Ricer **3** *B2*
Casino de Bomberos **6** *A2*
Cipres **1** *A3*
Club Sandwich **13** *B2*
Donde Ramiro **4** *B2*
El Mastique **7** *B2*
Histórico Ricer **3** *B2*
La Casona **9** *B1*
La Fiorentina **10** *B2*
La Olla **8** *B2*
Las Piedras **11** *B3*
Yangtse **12** *B3*

Going further ... Glaciar San Rafael

Situated some 200 km south of Puerto Chacabuco, the San Rafael glacier is one of the highlights for many travellers to Chile. About 45 km in length and towering 30 m above water level, the deep blue glacier groans and cracks as it carves off icebergs, which are carried across the Laguna San Rafael and out to sea via the Río Tempano. Around the shores of the laguna is thick vegetation and above are snowy mountain peaks.

The San Rafael is one of many glaciers flowing from the giant Campo de Hielo Norte, which covers much of the 1,740,000-ha Parque Nacional Laguna San Rafael (entry fee US$6). In the national park are puma, pudú, foxes, dolphins, occasional sea-lions and sea otters, and many species of bird.

There is a small ranger station on the shore of Laguna San Rafael, which provides information on the national park. Walking trails are limited (about 10 km in all) but a lookout platform has been constructed, with fine views of the glacier. The rangers are willing to row you out to the glacier in calm weather: an awesome three-hour adventure, past icebergs and swells created when huge chunks of ice break off the glacier and crash into the laguna.

The glacier is rapidly disintegrating and is likely to have become a hanging glacier by 2013. It is thought that waves created by motorized tourist boats are adding to the problem. Visitors should insist that their boats do not go too close to the glacier creating further damage.

Getting there Don Carlos provide air taxis from Coyhaique, US$1000 for up to five; some pilots in Puerto Aisén will also fly to the glacier for around US$150 per person, but many are unwilling to land on the rough airstrip. Other air-tour options available from Coyhaique, see page 315. The aircraft are small and should be avoided if the weather is rough. Boats from Puerto Montt Slow service with Navimag (via Puerto Chacabuco); official cruises by Skorpios; tours with Patagonia Connection; also private yacht charters. See page 289. Boats from Puerto Chacabuco Slow service with Navimag; one- or three-day trips with Catamaranes del Sur. Local fishing boats from Puerto Chacabuco/ Puerto Aisén (enquire at the port) take about 18-20 hours each way and charge the same as the tourist boats. Note that they might not have adequate facilities or a licence for the trip. Out of season, trips are difficult to arrange. See page 317.

A good 10-km walk north along a minor road from Puerto Aisén leads to **Laguna Los Palos**, calm, deserted and surrounded by forested hills. **Lago Riesco**, 30 km south of Puerto Aisén, can be reached by an unpaved road that follows the Río Blanco. In season, the *Apulcheu* sails regularly to **Termas de Chiconal** ⓘ *US$50*, about one hour west of Puerto Chacabuco on the northern shore of the Seno Aisén, offering a good way to see the fjord.

Chaitén to Coyhaique listings

For Sleeping and Eating price codes and other relevant information, see pages 41-44.

Sleeping

Lago Yelcho and the border *p303*

AL-A Cabañas Yelcho en La Patagonia, Lago Yelcho, 7 km south of Puerto Cárdenas, T065-576005, www.yelcho.cl. Cabins and rooms on the lakeshore. Also expensive campsite and café.

B Termas de Amarillo, Termas de Amarillo, T065-731326. Also camping and *cabañas*.

D Residencial Yelcho, Puerto Cárdenas, T065-264429. Clean, full board available.

E Residencial Marcela, Amarillo, T065-264442. Also *cabañas* and camping.

Futaleufú *p304, map p304*

L-AL El Barranco, O'Higgins 172, T065-721314, www.elbarrancochile.cl. Probably the best rooms in town, but still a little overpriced. There is a bar, restaurant, outdoor swimming pool, Wi-Fi and free bicycles for the guests. Disabled access. Fishing trips organized.

AL Hostería Río Grande, O'Higgins 397, T065-721320, www.pachile.com. Overpriced though comfortable, en suite bathrooms, friendly, bar, good restaurant.

A Posada la Gringa, Sargento Aldea 498, T065-721260, www.lagringa.home stead.com/h.html. Elegant and charming guesthouse set in large gardens and with the best view in town. Price includes a large brunch. English spoken. Recommended.

B Cabañas Río Espolón, PA Cerda s/n, 5 mins' walk west of centre, Futaleufú, T065-721216, rioespolon@yahoo.es. Secluded cabins with bar and restaurant overlooking the river, the sound of which is a constant in the background. Book ahead as it often fills up with rafting groups.

B Cabañas Veranada, Sargento Aldea 480, T065-721266, www.turismofutaleufu.cl. Well-equipped cabins with excellent beds and good kitchens. Most have wood-burning stoves. Friendly owners. Recommended.

B-C Cabañas la Escondida, Rodríguez 57, T065-721219. Decent no-frills cabins with good beds. Sleep 4.

B-C Sur Andes, Cerda 308, T065-721405. Rustic but tasteful apartment, fully equipped and with Wi-Fi, but with no kitchen.

C-D Adolfo B&B, O'Higgins 302, T065-721256, lodeva@surnet.cl. **F** singles. Well-kept and friendly family home. With breakfast and kitchen facilities.

C-D Los Troncos, Carmona 541, T065-721269. **F** singles. Basic clean *hospedaje* on the northern edge of town. With breakfast and kitchen facilities.

E-F Continental, Balmaceda 595, T065-721222. **G** singles. Pokey rooms, creaky floors, squeaky beds and no toilet paper provided, but clean and you can't ask for more at this price.

Camping

There is a decent, if basic, campsite on the west edge of town next to Laguna Espejo, US$5 pp with hot water.

Aldea Puerto Espolón, Sector La Puntilla, 400m from town, T09-94477448, www.aldeapuertoespolon.blogspot.com. Accommodation in pre-erected tepees and dome-tents.

Los Copihues, T065-721413, is on the river, 500 m from Futaleufú. Horse-riding trips.

La Junta and around *p304*

AL Espacio y Tiempo, La Junta, T067-314141, www.espacioytiempo.cl. Attractive garden, friendly, English spoken, good restaurant, internet, fishing expeditions and other tours.

C Residencial Copihue, Varas 611, T09-95018874. **E** singles. Some rooms with bath, with breakfast, good meals, changes money at very poor rates.

C-D Hostería Valdera, Varas s/n, T067-314105, luslagos@hotmail.com. **E-F** singles. Breakfast and bath, meals served. Excellent value.

D-E Residencial Patagonia, Lynch 331, T09-77028181. **C-D** singles. Good meals, small rooms, limited bathrooms.

Puyuhuapi and around *p304*

There's a CONAF campsite at Lago Risopatrón.

LL-L Fiordo Queulat Ecolodge, Seno Queulat, Parque Nacional Queulat, T067-233302, www.aisen.cl. Half board. Has a good reputation, offers hikes and fishing trips. Campsite nearby.

LL-L Puyuhuapi Lodge and Spa, T067-325103, www.patagonia-connection.com. For reservations contact **Patagonia Connection**, Fidel Oteíza 1921, oficina 1006, Santiago. Price depends on season and type of room but always includes use of baths and the boat transfer to/from the hotel. Good restaurant; full board extra. Recommended. Boat schedule from jetty, 2 hrs' walk from town, frequent in season, US$5 each way, 10-min crossing. Transport to the hotel may be arranged independently via hydroplane from Puerto Montt. See also Activities and tours, page 314.

L Cabañas El Pangue, north end of Lago Risopatrón, Carretera Austral Norte, Km 240, Parque Nacional Queulat, T067-325128, www.elpangue.com. Cabins sleep 4, private bathrooms, hot water, heating, telephone, parking, swimming pool, fishing trips, horse riding, mountain bikes. Recommended.

B Aonikenk, Hamburgo 16, T067-325208, aonikenkturismo@yahoo.com. Pleasant newly built, heated cabañas. Good beds, friendly service, good information, bike hire. Noise insulation non-existent within each cabin.

B Casa Ludwig, Av Otto Uebel s/n, on the southern edge of town, T067-325220, www.casaludwig.cl. English and German spoken. Recommended.

B-C Hostería Alemana, Av Otto Uebel 450, T067-325118. A large, comfortable, wooden house on the main road, owned by Señora Ursula Flack Kroschewski. Highly recommended, closed in winter.

D-E Sra Leontina Fuentes, Llantureo y Circunvalación. **F-G** singles. Clean, hot water, good breakfast for US$3.

Camping

CONAF, reservations T067-212125, runs a basic campsite (cold water) 12 km north of Puyuhuapi on the shores of Lago Risopatrón, and another near the Ventisquero Colgante. There is also a dirty campsite by the fjord behind the general store in Puyuhuapi.

Río Cisnes *p305*

B Cabañas Río Cisnes, Costanera 101, Puerto Cisnes, T067-346404. Cabins sleep 4-8. Owner, Juan Suazo, has a boat and offers good sea trout/salmon fishing.

C Hostería El Gaucho, Holmberg 140, Puerto Cisnes, T067-346514. With breakfast, dinner available, hot water.

F Residencia Bienvenido, Ibar 248, Villa Mañihuales. Clean, friendly, with a restaurant.

F Villa Mañihuales, E Ibar 200, Villa Mañihuales, T067-234803. Friendly, with breakfast.

Coyhaique and around *p306, map p307*

The tourist office has a list of all accommodation, but look out for notices in windows since any place with fewer than 6 beds does not have to register with the authorities.

L-AL El Reloj, Baquedano 828, T067-231108, www.elrelojhotel.cl. Small boutique hotel in a former saw mill. Good restaurant, nice lounge, conference room, some rooms have wonderful views. English spoken. Best hotel in town. Not the bargain it once was but still highly recommended.

AL Hostería Coyhaique, Magallanes 131, T067-231137, www.hotelcoyhaique.cl. Bills itself as Coyhaique's premier hotel although it is now showing its age. Set in spacious gardens, once decent rooms are now careworn, doubles have full bathtub.

A Cabañas Mirador, Baquedano 848, T067-233191, www.miradorcoyhaique.blogspot.com. Fully equipped cabins sleeping 2-4. The end cabin has tremendous views.

Advance booking essential in season (deposit required). Long-term lets off season.

A Hostal Español, Sargento Aldea 343, T067-242580, www.hostalcoyhaique.cl. New, small family-run hotel. 7 rooms all with views, carpets, bathrooms and cable TV. Spacious living room downstairs. Recommended though reports that reservations are not always honoured.

A San Sebastián, Baquedano 496, T067-233427, www.sansebastianhotel.cl. Small hotel with spacious rooms, all with view, good breakfast, recommended, though could do with a refit.

B Cabañas Río Simpson, 3 km north of town, T067-232183, www.cabanasrio simpson.cl. Fully equipped cabins for 2-6 people plus one luxury cabin, **L** sleeping 7. Horse riding, fishing and tours. Several tame alpacas in the grounds.

B Hostal Araucarias, Vielmo 71, T067-232707. Spacious, creaky rooms with bath and TV, pleasant lounge with good view, quiet.

B Hospedaje Gladys, Parra 65, T067-251076. **D** singles. Clean and well-kept rooms with cable TV. Some with bathrooms. Breakfast extra. Doubles as a beauty salon. A little dark and somewhat overpriced.

C Albergue Las Salamandras, 2 km south of town, T067-211865, www.salamandras.cl. Double rooms, dorm beds **E-F**, *cabañas* **B** and camping in attractive forest location. With breakfast. Kitchen facilities, winter sports, trekking and tours. Maps, including good trekking maps, and cycling information provided. Wood fired hot tub. English spoken. Informative website. Highly recommended.

C Hospedaje Patricio y Gedra Guzmán, Baquedano 20, T067-232520, www.balasch.cl/cabanas. Small but comfortable self-contained cabins on the edge of town with extensive views. English spoken. Good value. Range in quality from excellent to tatty. Recommended. Preference given to those taking Spanish classes.

C Hostal Las Quintas, Bilbao 1208, T067-231173. **D** singles. Spartan, but clean and extremely spacious rooms with bath and breakfast. Some of the rooms are architecturally among the most bizarre of any hostel in Chile.

C-D Hospedaje Natti, Av Simpson 417, T067-231047. **F** singles. Clean, kitchen facilities, breakfast US$2 extra. Also good-value camping including access to hot showers.

C-D Hospedaje Pochi, Freire 342, T067-256968. **F** singles. Rooms in a family home with bath and cable TV. Breakfast included. Cluttered garden. Very pleasant owners. English spoken by the daughter. Good value. Recommended.

D Hospedaje Lautaro 269, T067-237184. **F** singles. Large old wooden house with creaky floors. With parking, internet access and kitchen facilities. Camping available in the front garden.

D Hospedaje María Ester, Lautaro 544, T067-233023. **F** singles. Some rooms with bath and TV. Friendly, local information given, laundry facilities, good value but breakfast is extra and kitchen use charged for.

D Hospedaje Mondaca, Av Simpson 571, T067-254676. **F** singles. Small (only 3 rooms) but spotless family home. Friendly, breakfast extra, will heat up pre-prepared food.

Campsites

Sernatur in Coyhaique (see page 306) has a full list of all sites in Región XI. Also see **Albergue Las Salamandras**, **Hospedaje Natti** and **Hospedaje Lautaro 269**, above. There are several other campsites in Coyhaique and on the road to Puerto Aisén.

In the Reserva Nacional Coyhaique, there are basic campsites, US$7, at **Laguna Verde** and at **Casa Bruja**, 4 km and 2 km respectively from the entrance, and a *refugio*, US$2, 3 km from the entrance. There's also a campsite near the turning to Santuario San Sebastián, US$7, in the **Reserva Nacional Río Simpson**.

Puerto Aisén and Puerto Chacabuco *p306*

Accommodation can be hard to find, most is geared towards workers in the fishing industry in both Puerto Aisén and Puerto Chacabuco. There's no campsite but free camping is easy.

LL-L Parque Turístico Loberías de Aisén, Carrera 50, Puerto Chacabuco, T067-351112, www.loberiasdelsur.cl. Recently rebuilt 5-star complex, the best hotel serving the best food in this area. Climb up the steps direct from the port for a drink or a meal overlooking boats and mountains before boarding your ferry. Car hire available.

A Patagonia Green, 400 m from bridge (on Puerto Chacabuco side), T067-336796, www.patagonia green.cl. Nice cabins for up to 5, kitchen, heating, TV, gardens, arranges tours to Laguna San Rafael, fishing, mountain biking, riding, trekking, etc, English spoken.

A-B Hotel Caicahues, Michimalonco 660, Puerto Aisén, T067-336633. With bath, heating, telephone and internet; book in advance. Recommended.

C Mar Clara, Carrera 970, Puerto Aisén, T067-330030. **F** singles. More expensive with bath. Basic, clean, thin walls, looks nicer from outside than within.

D Moraleda, O'Higgins 82, Puerto Chacabuco, T067-351155. **F** singles. Basic. Full board available.

Eating

Futaleufú *p304, map p304*

Martín Pescador, Balmaceda y Rodríguez, T065-721279. Decent meat and fish.

Futaleufú, Cerda 407, T065-721295. All the normal Chilean fare plus, of course, trout.

Sur Andes, Cerda 308, T065-721405. Pleasant little café serving real coffee as well as a variety of cakes, sweets, snacks and light meals. Local handicrafts also sold.

Puyuhuapi and around *p304*

Café Rossbach, Costanera, Puyuhuapi. Limited menu, including excellent salmon; also good for tea and *küchen*; building is in the style of a German Black Forest inn.

K-Cos Café Restaurante, Prat 270, Puerto Cisnes. Good snacks.

Restaurante Marili, Otto Übel s/n, Puyuhuapi. Cheaper option.

Coyhaique and around *p306, map p307*

Restaurant Histórico Ricer, Horn 48 y 40, 2nd floor, T067-232920. Regional specialities, historical exhibits, somewhat overpriced and a bit of a tourist trap.

Cipres, Baquedano 022, T067-25183. Bizarre entrance through someone's house leading to a restaurant with as breathtaking a view as any in Coyhaique. Aims for rustic elegance, occasionally at odds with the music they play. Patagonian-Mediterranean cuisine. Abundant portions. Decent food. Wine sold by the glass.

El Reloj, Baquedano 444, T067-231108 (see Sleeping, above). Unusual dishes using all local ingredients. Good service, recommended.

La Casona, Obispo Vielmo 77, T067-238894. Good lamb and fish dishes, long-standing reputation, popular with locals, considered by many to be the best in town. Recommended.

La Olla, Gral Prat 176, T067-242588. Spanish, excellent cuisine, not cheap but there are good-value lunches. Recommended.

Las Piedras, 21 de Mayo 655, T067-233243. Slightly upmarket but with good-value set lunches. Dishes include venison and emu. Fills up at weekends. Recommended.

Yangtse, Bilbao 715, T067-242173. Better-than-average (in Chilean terms) Chinese. You can hear your food being stir-fried fresh to order. Reasonable prices but the quantity of MSG leaves you almost happy to fork out for the exorbitantly expensive drinks.

Casino de Bomberos, Gral Parra 365, T067-231437. Wide range, large portions, very good value. Slow service, especially if full.

Donde Ramiro, Freire 319, T067-256885. Decent basic set lunches. Big screen TV. A good place to watch football matches.

La Fiorentina, Prat 230, T067-238899. Good value pizza and pasta.

Club Sandwich, Moraleda 433. 24-hr fast food.

El Mastique, Bilbao 141. Cheap but good pasta and Chilean food.

Cafés

Café Alemana, Condell 119. Excellent cakes, coffee, vegetarian dishes. Recommended.

Café Oriente, Condell 201 y 21 de Mayo. Good bakery, serves tea.

Café Ricer, Horn 48. Also serves light food.

Puerto Aisén and Puerto Chacabuco *p306*

Café Restaurante Ensenada, O'Higgins 302, Puerto Chacabuco. Basic grub.

Restaurante La Cascada, Km 32 between Coyhaique and Puerto Aisén. Waterfalls nearby. Recommended for meat and fish.

There are cheap places on Aldea in Puerto Aisén, between Municipal and Dougnac.

Bars and clubs

Coyhaique *p306, map p307*

Bar West, Bilbao y 12 de Octubre. Western-style bar.

El Boliche, Moraleda 380. Bar for the beer-drinking crowd. Many other bars on the same street.

Pepe le Pub, Parra 72. Good cocktails and snacks, relaxed ambience, live music at weekends.

Piel Roja, Moraleda y Condell. Friendly, laid-back atmosphere, meals served, not cheap.

Festivals and events

Futaleufú *p304, map p304*

Late Feb **Futa Festival**, rafting and kayaking races on the river Futaleufú. www.futafest.org.

Puerto Aisén and around *p306*

2nd week of Nov Local festival of folklore is held in Puerto Aisén.

Shopping

Coyhaique *p306, map p307*

For *artesanía* try the **Feria de Artesanía**, on the plaza, or **Manos Azules**, Riquelme 435. **Kaienk**, Plaza 219-A, T067-2245216, www.telaresdelapatagonia.cl, sells good-quality locally produced knitware.

Decent camping equipment can be obtained from **Condor Explorer**, Dussen 357, T067-670349.

Food, especially fruit and vegetables, is more expensive here than in Santiago.

El Rincón del Poeta, Moraleda y Parra has a good selection of local interest books as well as a small selection of second hand books in English. **Fly Fishing Suray**, Prat 231, for fly fishing equipment.

There are large supermarkets at Prat y Lautaro and Lautaro y Cochrane. Good sheep's cheese is occasionally available from a kiosk by the plaza.

Activities and tours

Lago Yelcho and the border *p303*

Fishing

Isla Monita Lodge, near Puerto Cárdenas, www.islamonita.cl, offers packages for anglers and non-anglers on a private island on Lago Yelcho, as well as fishing in many nearby locations.

Kayaking

Patagonian Waters, main road in Puyuhuapi, T09-97771820, www.patagonianwaters.com, offers canoeing and sea kayak trips in the fjord, as well as trekking and horse riding. There is also an office in La Junta.

Río Cisnes *p305*

Fishing

There are good opportunities for fishing on Río Futaleufú and Lago Espolón (see page 304; ask for the Valebote family's motorboat on the lake) and in the area around Puerto

Angling for a catch

The rivers around Coyhaique provide the greatest fishing in Chile; each year the international fishing fraternity converge on the town for the season, which runs from 15 November to 15 April. Rivers range from the typically English slow chalk stream to fast-flowing Andean snowmelt torrents, requiring diverse angling techniques.

On the outskirts of Coyhaique, the spectacular **Río Simpson** teems with rainbow and brown trout. It is renowned for its evening hatches (sedge and mayfly), which take place throughout the season. Catches in excess of five pounds are frequent and rainbow trout weighing over 12 pounds have been landed.

Near the Argentine border, a scenic one-hour drive from Coyhaique, **Río Nirehuao** is a fly-fisher's dream as brown trout feed voraciously on grasshoppers and dragonfly. The easy wading and moderate casting distances make this river a favourite.

South of Coyhaique, the **Río Baker** offers a unique fishing experience in its turquoise blue water. The Baker is huge and intimidating, as are its fish: rainbows up to 12 pounds lurk here and anglers regularly take fish of seven pound. The **Río Cochrane,** a gin-clear tributary of the Baker, also holds large rainbows. The Cochrane is mainly a 'sight-fishing' river, which requires skill, patience and an experienced guide.

Cisnes (see page 305). For the latter, contact **German Hipp**, Costanera 51, Puerto Cisnes, T067-346587, or **Cabañas Río Cisnes** (see above). For further information contact **Turismo Lago Las Torres**, 130 km Carretera Austral Norte, T067-234242.

Futaleufú *p304, map p304*

Tour operators in Futaleufú can arrange whitewater rafting. Prices start at US$75 pp. There are several local fishing guides who can be contacted in the village.

Earth River, www.earthriver.com. Excellent choice for river rafting and kayaking trips, book in advance.

Expediciones Chile, Mistral 296, T065-721386, www.exchile.com. Offers the best multi-day trips. Book in advance. Day trips can be booked on site. Also offer trekking and horse riding.

Futaleufú Expediciones, O'Higgins 397, Futaleufú, T/F065-258634. Organizes rafting, canyoning, trekking and horse-riding expeditions around Futaleufú.

Futaleufú Explore, O'Higgins 772, Futaleufú T065-721411, www.futaleufuexplore.com. Another respected rafting company.

Puyuhuapi and around *p304*

Patagonia Connection, Fidel Oteíza 1921, oficina 1006, Providencia, Santiago, T02-2256489. Operates a 3-night catamaran tour to Laguna San Rafael via **Puyuhuapi Lodge and Spa** (see page 310) on board the *Patagonia Express*. Also offers special fly-fishing programmes and other excursions.

Coyhaique *p306, map p307*

A full list of specialist tours and fishing guides is available from **Sernatur**, see page 306. Excursions and good trekking information is available from **Albergue Las Salamandras** (see Sleeping, page 311). There is also an association of independent local guides who offer (as a rule) good-value and well-informed excursions within the region. See www.escueladeguias.cl for more detailed information. The **Casa del Turismo Rural**, Dussen 357-B, T067-214031, www.casaturismorural.cl, Mon-Fri 1000-1330, 1530-2000 (also weekends in high season), is an association of 40 or so familes, mostly rural, who offer activities such as horse riding and fishing. Many of these people do not have telephones or internet so reservations should be made here.

Fishing

There are excellent opportunities for fishing in the Coyhaique area, especially southwest at Lagos Atrevesado (20 km) and Elizalde (also yachting and camping), and southeast at lagos Frío, Castor and Pollux. In addition to those listed below, most of the general tour operators offer specialist fishing trips.

General tours

Andes Patagónicos, Horn 48 y 40, local 11, T067-216711, www.ap.cl. Trips to local lakes as well as Tortel, historically based tours and bespoke trips all year round. Good, but not cheap. Provides general tourist information.
Aysen Tour, Gral Parra 97, T067-237070, www.aysentour.cl. Typical range of tours along the Carretera Austral.
Cabot, Lautaro 339, T067-230101, www.cabot.cl. Horse-riding excursions to Cerro Castillo and other tours.
Camello Patagón, Moraleda 463, T067-244327, www.camellopatagon.cl. Trips to Capilla de Marmol in Río Tranquilo.
Condor Explorer, Dussen 357, T067-573634, www.condorexplorer.com. Good small-scale agency who specialize in trekking but also do general Carretera tours. English spoken. Recommended.
Expediciones Coyhaique, Portales 195, T067-231783, www.coyhaiqueflyfishing.com. Fly-fishing experts.
Geo Turismo, Balmaceda 334, T067-573460, www.geoturismopatagonia.cl. Offers wide range of tours throughout the region, English spoken, professional, recommended.
Turismo Prado de la Patagonia, 21 de Mayo 417, T067-231271, www.turismoprado.cl. Tours of local lakes and other sights, Laguna San Rafael trips and historical tours. Also offers general tourist information.

Skiing

El Fraile, office in Coyhaique at Dussen y Plaza de Armas 376, T067-231690. Near Lago Frío, 29 km southeast of Coyhaique, this ski resort has 5 pistes, 2 lifts, a basic café and equipment hire (season Jun-Sep).

Puerto Aisén and Puerto Chacabuco *p306*

Turismo Rucaray, on the plaza, Puerto Aisén, rucaray@entelchile.net. Recommended for local tours. Internet access.

Transport

Lago Yelcho and the border *p303*

Transporte Patagonia Norte, T065-741257, runs a weekly bus from Palena to **Puerto Montt** via Argentina, Mon 0630, 13 hrs, US$33.

Futaleufú *p304, map p304*

Bus

To **Chaitén**, 3 weekly, 5 hrs, US$9; to **La Junta** 3 weekly, 6 hrs, US$13; to **Coyhaique** 3 weekly, 12 hrs, US$34; to **Palena** 3 weekly, 3 hrs, US$7; to **Puerto Montt** via Argentina, Tue and Fri, US$37; to the **Argentine border** Mon and Fri 0900 and 1800 from Balmaceda 419, 30 mins, US$4; on the Argentine side there are connecting services to **Trevelin** and **Esquel**.

La Junta and around *p304*

There is no bus terminal in La Junta. All minibuses should be booked in advance. There are daily buses to **Coyhaique**, 8 hrs, US$16; 2 weekly services to **Puerto Cisnes**, US$10, 3 weekly to **Chaitén**, 4 hrs, US$10.

Puyuhuapi and around *p304*

3 buses weekly from Puyuhuapi north to **Chaitén**. Daily service south to **Coyhaique**, plus 2 weekly to **Lago Verde**.

Río Cisnes *p305*

Transportes Terra Austral, T067-346757, runs services from Puerto Cisnes to **Coyhaique**, Mon-Sat 0600, US$9; **Buses Norte**, T067-346 440 offers the same route once a week, US$8.

Coyhaique *p306, map p307*

Air

Airline offices **Sky**, Prat 203, T067-240827, local calls 600-6002828; **LanChile**, Moraleda

402, T067-231188, local calls 600-5262000; Don Carlos, Subteniente Cruz 63, T067-231981.

Teniente Vidal airport Don Carlos flies to **Chile Chico**, Mon-Sat, US$50; to **Cochrane**, Mon and Thu, 45 mins, US$75, and to **Villa O'Higgins**, Mon and Thu, US$100, recommended only for those who have strong stomachs, or are in a hurry. There are also flights to **Tortel**, Wed, US$35, but these are subsidized for residents of the village.

Balmaceda airport LanChile and Sky to **Santiago**, several daily, US$90-270 return plus tax; to **Puerto Montt**, daily in summer, US$55-215 return plus tax. Sky also flies to **Punta Arenas**, 3 flights weekly, US$85-170 return plus tax. The best 1-way fares are generally with Sky. For transport to/from the airport, see page 303. For flights to Laguna San Rafael, see page 308.

Bicycle

Bike hire from: Manuel Iduarte, Parra y Bulnes, check condition first; Bilbao 500 block, poor supply of spares but good repair service; Motortech, Baquedano 131; Tomás Enrique, Madrid Urrea, Pje Foitzick y Libertad, T067-252132.

Bicycle spares repair services are also available from several shops on Simpson.

Bus

The main terminal is at Lautaro y Magallanes. In the terminal there is a left-luggage store as well as: Bus São Paulo, T067-255726; Bus Sur, T067-211460, www.bus-sur.cl; Don Oscar, T067-254335, Giobbi, T067-232607; Interlagos, T067-240840, www.patagonia interlagos.cl; Queilen Bus, T067-240760; Trans Austral, T067-232067; Transportes Terra Austral, T067-254335; Via Bariloche, T067-253841. Other companies are Bus Bronco, Lautaro 728; Buses Becker, Parra 335, T067-2321670; Buses Daniela, Baquedano 1122, T067-231701; Buses Queulat, Parra 329, T067-242626;Don Carlos, Subteniente Cruz 63, T067-232981; Suray, Prat 265, T067-238387.

Carretera Austral north Suray and São Paulo minibuses run to **Puerto Aisén** every 15 mins between them, 1 hr, US$2, with connections for Puerto Chacabuco. There are also a few buses daily to **Mañihuales**. To **Chaitén** via Puyuhuapi and La Junta, Buses Queulat and Buses Becker, 3 weekly between them, US$34. To **Futaleufú** via La Junta, Buses Becker, Buses Queulat and Buses Daniela, US$34. To **Lago Verde** via La Junta, Gerardo Valenzuela, T09-81978793, US$18; also Bus Bronco, Wed, Fri, Sat. To **Puerto Cisnes**, Transportes Terra Austral and Don Oscar, each Mon-Sat, US$9.

Carretera Austral south To **Cochrane**, Sao Paulo, and Don Carlos, and Acuario 13, US$19. Buses to Cochrane stop at **Cerro Castillo**, US$6, **Bahía Murta**, US$10, **Puerto Río Tranquilo**, US$13, and outside **Puerto Bertrand** , US$15. To **Tortel**, direct services on Wed and Sat.

Colectivos to **Puerto Ibáñez** on Lago General Carrera will pick you up at 0700 from your hotel to connect with *El Pilchero* ferry to Chile Chico, 2 hrs, book the day before, US$7; operators include Dario Figueroa, T067-233286; Bus Freddy, T09-6503593; Miguel Acuña, T067-251579 Bus Carolina, T067-219009.

Long distance To **Puerto Montt**, via Bariloche ond Osorno, all year, Trans Austral, Tue and Fri 1645, US$50; Queilen Bus, Mon, Wed, Fri, Sat, US$50, with connections to Valdivia, Temuco, Santiago and Castro, often heavily booked. To **Punta Arenas** via Coyhaique Alto and Comodoro Rivadavia, Bus Sur, Tue, US$55. To **Bariloche** (Argentina), Vía Bariloche, Daily, 0730, US$21. To **Comodoro Rivadavia** (Argentina), Trans Austral, Mon, Fri, 0800, 12 hrs, US$35.

Car hire

Hire from: AGS, Av Ogana 1298, T067-253225; Automotriz Varona, Carrera 330, T067-216673, www.varona.cl; Automundo AVR, Bilbao 510, T067-231621; Sur Nativo

Renta Car; Baquedano 457, T067-231648; **Turismo Prado**, 21 de Mayo 417, T067-231271, www.turismoprado.cl. Mechanic at **Automotores Santiago**, Los Ñires 811, T067-238330, T099-6406896, speaks English, can obtain spare parts quickly.

Ferry

Shipping offices are at **Navimag**, Horn 47-D, T067-233306, www. navimag.com.

Taxi

Hailing a taxi on the street is expensive and fares are 50% extra after 2100. It is cheaper to call a radio taxi, T067-242424, any journey within the city limits US$2. *Colectivos* congregate at Prat y Bilbao, fare US$0.70.

Puerto Aisén and Puerto Chacabuco *p306*

Bus

Suray runs buses between the 2 ports every 20 mins, US$0.75. **Interlagos** and **Suray** have frequent services to **Coyhaique**, 1 hr, US$2 (see above).

Ferry

Shipping offices are at **Catamaranes del Sur**, Carrera 50, Puerto Chacabuco, T067-351112, www.catamaranes delsur.cl; **Naviera Austral**, Terminal de Transbordadores, Puerto Chacabuco, T067-351493, www.navieraustral.cl; **Navimag**, Terminal de Transbordadores, Puerto Chacabuco, T067-351111, www. navimag.cl.
Navimag have year-round ferry services from Puerto Chacabuco to **Puerto Montt** via the Canal Moraleda once or twice a week in summer, irregular off season, 24 hrs, from US$55, cars US$235. **Naviera Austral** have a service services from Puerto Chacabuco to **Quellón** via Puerto Cisnes, Raúl Marín Balmaceda and Melinka, irregular off season, from US$55, cars US$220.

To Laguna San Rafael It is best to make reservations for this trip at the ferry's offices in Puerto Montt, Coyhaique or Santiago. **Catamaranes del Sur**, Carrera 50, T067-351112, www.catamaranesdelsur.cl, 1-3 weekly Sep-Apr, 1-day trips US$299, 3-day trips from US$550. **Navimag**. Official services, all year, reduced service off season, 24 hrs, from US$259.

❶ Directory

Futaleufú *p304, map p304*

Banks Banco del Estado, ATM accepts MasterCard but not Visa. Changing foreign currency is difficult, but US dollars and Argentine pesos are accepted in many places. **Hospital** Balmaceda y Aldea, T065-721231.

Coyhaique *p306, map p307*

Bank Several with Redbanc ATMs in centre, for dollars, TCs and Argentine pesos. Both the following *casas de cambio* are recommended: **Casa de Cambio Emperador**, Bilbao 222, and **Lucía Saldivia**, Baquedano 285. **Hospital** C Hospital 068, T067-233172. **Internet** **Ciber Patagonia**, 21 de Mayo 525, best value; several others. **Language schools** **Baquedano Language School**, Baquedano 20, T067-232520, www.balasch.cl. US$400 per week, including 4 hrs one-to-one tuition daily, lodging and all meals, other activities organized at discount rates, friendly, informative, highly recommended. **Laundry** **Lavandería**, Simpson 417-A; **QL**, Bilbao 160. **Post office** Cochrane 202, Mon-Fri 0900-1230, 1430-1800, Sat 0830-1200. **Telephone** Several call centres; shop around as prices are relatively expensive.

Puerto Aisén *p306*

Banks **BCI**, Prat, for Visa; **Banco de Chile**, Plaza de Armas, only changes cash, not TCs. There's a Redbanc ATM machine in Puerto Chacabuco. **Post office** South side of bridge. **Telephone** Plaza de Armas, next to Turismo Rucuray; **ENTEL**, Libertad 408, internet access.

Lago General Carrera and beyond

The section of the Carretera Austral around the north and western sides of Lago General Carrera is reckoned by many to be the most spectacular stretch of all. Straddling the border with Argentina, the lake is the largest in South America after Lake Titicaca and is believed to be the deepest on the continent, with a maximum depth of 590 m. The southern side of the lake has 300 days of sunshine a year and rainfall is low. In general, the climate here has more in common with Argentine Patagonia than with the rest of the Carretera Austral. South from Cochrane, the scenery becomes increasingly remote and dramatic. The final stretch of the Carretera Austral leads to the small town of Villa O'Higgins at the end of the road. ▸▸ *For listings, see pages 324-328.*

Ins and outs → *Colour map 2, B3.*

Getting there and around There are direct buses and flights to Cochrane from Coyhaique. Minibuses also run along the Carretera Austral in summer to Puerto Ibáñez (five weekly), from where a ferry connects with Chile Chico. Overland routes between Coyhaique and Chile Chico are much longer, passing either through Argentina via Los Antiguos, or along the Carretera Austral and west around the lake. Public transport is scarce: air taxis link the small towns but there are only five weekly buses from Chile Chico to Cochrane and two from Cochrane to Villa O'Higgins. A 4WD makes getting around much easier. ▸▸ *See Transport page 327.*

Reserva Nacional Cerro Castillo and around→ *Colour map 2, B3.*

Beyond Coyhaique, the Carretera Austral runs through slightly wilder, more rugged land, with the occasional cow or wild horse feeding by the side of the road. Forty kilometres south of Coyhaique the Carretera enters the Reserva Nacional Cerro Castillo, which extends over 179,550 ha. The park is named after the fabulous **Cerro Castillo** (2675 m), which resembles a fairy-tale castle with rock pinnacles jutting out from a covering of snow. It also includes Cerro Bandera (2040 m) just west of Balmaceda and several other peaks in the northern wall of the valley of the Río Ibáñez. The park offers a number of excellent day treks and some of the best self-contained multi-day trekking in Patagonia. There is a *guardería* at the northeastern end of the park near Laguna Chinguay. At Km 83 the road crosses the **Portezuelo Ibáñez** (1120 m) and drops through the **Cuesta del Diablo**, a series of bends with fine views over the Río Ibáñez.

The principal port on the Chilean section of the lake, **Puerto Ibáñez** is reached by taking a paved branch road, 31 km long, from La Bajada, 97 km south of Coyhaique. You will probably just pass through to reach the ferry. It is, however, a centre for distinctive pottery, leather production and vegetable growing (you can visit potters and buy salad from greenhouses). Local archaeology includes rock art and the largest Tehuelche cemetery in Patagonia. There are some fine waterfalls, including the **Salto Río Ibáñez**, 6 km north.

From the turning to Puerto Ibáñez the Carretera Austral goes through **Villa Cerro Castillo** (Km 8), a quiet village in a spectacular setting beneath the striking, jagged peaks of Cerro Castillo, overlooking the broad valley below. There's a petrol station, public phone, several food shops and a tiny tourist information kiosk by the road side (January-February only), with details of guides offering horse rides and trekking to the Cerro.

The village is a good place to stop for a few days with two appealing attractions. There's a truly spectacular four-day trek around the fairy-tale castle peaks of Cerro Castillo, in the Reserva Nacional Cerro Castillo, whose entrance is 64 km south of Coyhaique. The walk

The long road south

Although the first town in this area, Balmaceda, was founded in 1917, followed by Puerto Aisén in 1924, the first road, between Puerto Aisén and Coyhaique, was not built until 1936. It was not until the 1960s, when new roads were built and airstrips were opened, that this region began to be integrated with the rest of the country.

The Carretera Austral has helped transform the lives of many people in this part of Chile, but the motivation behind its construction was mainly geopolitical. Ever since Independence, Chilean military and political leaders have stressed the importance of occupying the southern regions of the Pacific coast and preventing any incursion by Argentina. Building the Carretera Austral was seen by General Pinochet as a means of achieving this task: a way of occupying and securing territory.

Begun in 1976, the central section of the Carretera Austral, from Chaitén to Coyhaique, was opened in 1983. Five years later, the northern section, linking Chaitén with Puerto Montt, and the southern section, between Coyhaique and Cochrane, were officially inaugurated. Since then, the Carretera has been extended south of Cochrane to Puerto Yungay and Villa O'Higgins. Work is continuing, building branch roads and paving the most important sections.

starts at Las Horquetas Grandes, a bend in the Río Ibáñez, 8 km south of the park entrance, where any bus driver will let you off. It follows Río La Lima to the gorgeous Laguna Cerro Castillo, then animal trails around the peak itself, returning to the village (accommodation or bus back to Coyhaique). This is a challenging walk; attempt it only if fit, and ideally, take a guide, as trails are poorly marked (IGM map essential, purchase in advance in Coyhaique). The *guardería* is on the Senda Ibáñez, 50 m to the left of the main road (as you head south), opposite Laguna Chinguay to the right, with access to walks and a campsite (beware the CONAF dog that bites; camping US$5, November to March, take equipment – there are no *refugios*). The picnic ground is open summer 0830-2100, winter to 1830. A new, equally if not more spectacular five-day trekking route around Monreal has recently been opened up. Ask in Villa Cerro Castillo for details.

A few kilometres south of the village is the **Monumento Nacional Manos de Cerro Castillo** ⓘ *US$1 charged Dec-Apr*. In a shallow cave, a few handprints have been made on the side of vertical rocks high above the Río Ibáñez. There's no clue to their significance, but they're in a beautiful place with panoramic views. This makes a delightful two-hour walk. The site is accessible all year, signposted clearly from the road. There is also a small local **museum** ⓘ *open Dec-Mar 0900-1200*, 2 km south of Villa Cerro Castillo.

From Villa Cerro Castillo the road climbs out of the valley, passing the emerald-green **Laguna Verde** and the Portezuelo Cofré, before descending to the boggy Manso valley.

Lago General Carrera » *pp324-328.*

Known as General Carrera in Chile and as Buenos Aires in Argentina, this lake is a beautiful azure blue, surrounded at its Chilean end by predominantly Alpine terrain and at the Argentine end by dry pampa. The eruption of Volcán Hudson in 1991 (northwest of the lake) polluted parts of Lago General Carrera and many rivers and, although the waters are now clear, the effects can still be seen in some places.

The western shore

Some 5 km from the Carretera Austral, at Km 203, **Bahía Murta** is situated on the northern tip of the central 'arm' of Lago General Carrera. This sleepy, almost forgotten village dates from the 1930s, when it exported timber to Argentina via Chile Chico. There is a tiny **tourist information hut** ⓘ *summer 1000-1430, 1500-1930 (in theory)*. Back on the Carretera, the road follows the lake's western shore. At Km 207 from Coyhaique is a small privately owned forest of ancient and gnarled arrayanes, worth a visit, US$3.50. Twenty kilometres further south is **Río Tranquilo**, where the buses stop for lunch and fuel is available. The lake reflects the mountains that surround it and the clouds above. Close to Río Tranquilo is the unusual **Catedral de Mármol**, a peninsula made of marble, with fascinating caves that can be visited by boat. The whole tour takes two hours (US$45 to hire a boat with guide), and be prepared to get wet. The best time to go is early in the morning when the lake is calmer. The village also has an unusual cemetery made up of mausolea in the form of miniature Chilote-style houses. A new branch of the Carretera Austral heads northwest from Río Tranquilo to **Puerto Grosse** on the coast at Bahía Exploradores. At Km 52 on this road is a refugio from which a well-maintained path (US$5 entry) leads to a lookout opposite the Exploradores

Lago General Carrera

glacier. Guided hikes are available to the glacier, US$45 per person, six hours including two to three hours on the glacier. Crampons provided. The hike can be treacherous in bad weather. Book though **El Puesto** in Río Tranquilo.

The southern shore

At the southwestern tip of Lago General Carrera, at Km 279, is **El Maitén**, from where a road branches off east along the south shore of the lake towards Chile Chico. Ten kilometres east of El Maitén, **Puerto Guadal** is a friendly, picturesque town that is a centre for fishing. It also has shops, accommodation, restaurants, a post office, petrol and a lovely stretch of lakeside beach. Further east, just past the nondescript village of **Mallin Grande**, Km 40, the road runs through the **Paso de las Llaves**, a 30-km stretch carved out of the rock-face on the edge of the lake. The south side of the lake is much drier than the rest of the Carretera but there are still gorges and waterfalls dotted along the route. The landscape is more open as there is less of an influence from the icefields. The road climbs and drops, narrow and poor in places, offering wonderful views across the lake and the icefields to the west. At Km 74, a turning runs to **Fachinal**. A further 5 km east is the Garganta del Diablo, an impressive narrow gorge of 120 m with a fast-flowing stream below. A little further on, there is an opencast mine, which produces gold and other precious metals.

Chile Chico and around → *Colour map 2, B3.*

Chile Chico is a quiet, friendly but dusty town situated on the lake shore 122 km east of El Maitén, close to the Argentine border. The town dates from 1909 when settlers crossed from Argentina and occupied the land, leading to conflict with cattle ranchers who had been given settlement rights by the Chilean government. In the showdown that followed (known as the war of Chile Chico) the ranchers were driven out by the settlers, and it was not until 1931 that the Chilean government recognized the town's existence.

Now the centre of a fruit-growing region, it has an annual festival at the end of January and a small museum open in summer; outside is a boat that carried cargo on the lake before the opening of the new road along the southern shore. There are fine views from the **Cerro de las Banderas** at the western end of town. The **tourist office** ⓘ *Municipalidad, O'Higgins 333, www.chilechico.cl*, can help in arranging tours. From Chile Chico a road runs 2 km east to the border and on for 5 km to **Los Antiguos** (see page 186).

The country to the south and west of Chile Chico provides good walking terrain, through weird rock formations and dry brush scrub. The northern and higher peak of **Cerro Pico del Sur** (2168 m) can be climbed by the agile from Los Cipres (beware dogs in the farmyard). You will need a long summer's day and the 1:50,000 map. From the summit you'll enjoy indescribable views of the lake and the Andes. Twenty kilometres south of Chile Chico towards Lago Jeinimeni is the **Cueva de las Manos**, a cave full of Tehuelche paintings, the most famous of which are the *manos azules* (blue hands). The path is difficult and partly hidden, so you're recommended to take a guide.

Reserva Nacional Lago Jeinemeni → *Colour map 2, B3.*

ⓘ *53 km south of Chile Chico, open all year but access limited between Apr and Oct due to high river levels, US$4, camping US$8.*

This park covers 160,000 ha and includes two lakes, **Lago Jeinemeni** and **Lago Verde**, which lie surrounded by forests in the narrow valley of the Río Jeinemeni. Impressive cliffs, waterfalls and small glaciers provide habitat for huemul deer, pumas and condors. Activities include fishing for salmon and rainbow trout, trekking and rowing. Access is via an unpaved road, which branches south off the road to Los Antiguos and crosses five rivers. At Km 42, there is a small lake, **Laguna de los Flamencos**, where large numbers of flamingos can be seen. The park entrance is at Km 53; just beyond is a ranger station, a campsite and fishing area at the eastern end of Lago Jeinemeni. Take all supplies, including a good map.

Towards Cochrane ➡ *pp324-328.*

South of El Maitén, the Carretera Austral becomes steeper and more winding; in winter this stretch is icy and dangerous. The picturesque tranquil village of **Puerto Bertrand**, 5 km away, is a good place for fishing and the best base in the region for whitewater rafting and kayaking. Day hikes (guided or unguided) are possible along decent trails. Beyond Puerto Bertrand, the road climbs up to high moorland, passing the confluence of the rivers Neff and Baker, before winding south along the east bank of the gleaming turquoise Río Baker to Cochrane. The road is rough but not treacherous and the scenery is splendid. Watch out for cattle and hares on the road (and the occasional huemul) and take blind corners slowly.

Cochrane and around → *Colour map 2, B2.*

Sitting in a hollow on the northern banks of the Río Cochrane, 343 km south of Coyhaique, Cochrane is a simple, somewhat godforsaken place. However, with its pleasant summer climate it is a good base for walking and fishing. **Tourist information** ⓘ *in the museum, San Valentín 555, summer Mon-Fri 0830-2000, Sat-Sun 1100-2000, off season Mon-Fri 0830-1730, www.cochranepatagonia.cl.* Four kilometres northeast of Cochrane is the entrance to the **Reserva Nacional Tamango** ⓘ *Dec-Mar 0830-2100, Apr-Nov 0830-1830, US$5, guided visits to see the huemul, Tue, Thu, Sat, US$80 for a group of 6.* The reserve covers 6925 ha of lenga forest and is home to one of the largest colonies of the rare huemul as well as guanaco, foxes and lots of birds, including woodpeckers and hummingbirds. There are marked paths for walks between 45 minutes and five hours, up to Cerro Tamango (1722 m) and Cerro Temanguito (1485 m). Take water and food, and windproof clothing if climbing the *cerros*. The views from the reserve are superb, over the town, the nearby lakes and to the Campo de Hielo Norte to the west. Tourist facilities, however, are rudimentary. Excursions can be made from the town to **Lago Cochrane**, which covers over 17,500 ha, straddling the frontier with Argentina (the Argentine section is called Lago Puerredón).

Some 17 km north of Cochrane, a road runs east for 78 km through Villa Chacabuco to the border at **Paso Roballos**. On the Argentine side the road continues to **Bajo Caracoles**, an isolated settlement on Ruta 40 (see page 187). There is no public transport along this route and the road is generally in a poor state, often flooded in spring. ➡ *Border crossing, page 187.*

South of Cochrane ➡ *pp324-328.*

Travelling by bus on the final 224-km stretch of the Carretera Austral from Cochrane to Villa O'Higgins can be frustrating, as you will want to stop every 15 minutes to marvel at the views. This is a beautiful trip through thick forest, with vistas of snow-capped mountains and waterfalls.

Tortel → *Colour map 2, B2.*

Built on a hill at the mouth of the river, 135 km from Cochrane, Tortel has no streets, the village being connected by 7 km of stairs and walkways made of cypress wood. There are a couple of beaches and two plazas built on stilts, roofed for protection from the almost constant drizzle. Its main industries are wood, for trade with Punta Arenas, shellfish, and now tourism. The village became famous in October 2000 as the place where Prince William spent time working for **Operation Raleigh**; it is also where Rosie Swale ended her epic horseback journey through Chile, as recorded in *Back to Cape Horn* (see page 399). At the entrance to the village is a small tourist information office with information on the dozen or so *residenciales* and a useful map. A branch of the Carretera Austral, beginning 2 km south of Vagabundo and reaching south 23 km to Tortel, was completed in early 2003, so the village is now accessible by road, and the effect on its character has been enormous. From Tortel, you can hire a boat to visit two spectacular glaciers: **Ventisquero Jorge Montt**, five hours southwest by boat, or **Ventisquero Steffens**, north on the edge of the Parque Nacional San Rafael, 2½ hours by boat and then a three-hour trek on a very wet but well-signed trail including a river crossing by rowing boat to a viewing point from which the glacier can be seen across the lake. Trips can also be made to the nearby **Isla de los Muertos**, where some 100 Chilote workers died in mysterious circumstances early in the 20th century.

The main spine of the Carretera continues southwards to **Puerto Yungay** (allow 1¼ hours by car from Tortel under normal conditions), a tiny village with a military post and a pretty church. This section of the road is hilly and in places very bad; it is not advisable to drive along here at night. From Puerto Yungay, there is a **ferry crossing to Río Bravo** ⓘ *45 mins, free, southbound 1000, 1200 and 1800, northbound 1100, 1300, 1900 (check off-season timetables locally)*, run by the army. If you miss the last boat the *carabineros* will help you find accommodation. Beyond the ferry crossing, the road continues south. After 9 km there is a turn-off marked 'Ventisquero Montt'. This road is still under construction and at the time of writing is a dead end. Carry on through more spectacular scenery – lakes, moors, dense forest, swamps, rivers and waterfalls, often shrouded in mist – before arriving at the Carretera's final destination.

Villa O'Higgins and across the lake to Argentina → *Colour map 2, C2.*

Situated at the southernmost end of the Carretera Austral, Villa O'Higgins has the atmosphere of a frontier town. It lies 2 km from a northerly 'arm' of **Lago O'Higgins**, which straddles the Argentine border as Lago San Martín. The lake is dotted with numerous icebergs that have split off the Campo de Hielo Sur to the west. **Tourist information** ⓘ *T067-211849, www.voh.cl*, is available in the plaza in summer or from the Municipalidad, which can also provide guides and information on trekking. Behind the town, a mirador affords spectacular views of nearby mountains, lakes and glaciers.

From Villa O'Higgins, the road continues 7 km south to **Bahía Bahamóndez** on the shores of Lago O'Higgins, US$3 transfer, connecting with a boat that departs to Chilean immigration at Candelario Mancila, November to April, frequency varies between once a fortnight and three a week depending on the season (contact the Municipalidad in Villa O'Higgins for details). After docking at Calendario Mancilla, the boat makes a return trip to the face of the spectacular glaciar O'Higgins before heading back to Villa O'Higgins in the evening.

From Calendario Mansilla, it is 23 km to the Argentinian control post at the northern end of Lago del Desierto. Horses may be hired for US$26 to carry your packs during this leg of the journey – usually one horse can carry two or three peoples' equipment. Approximate journey times: five hours on foot (without packs), 3½ hours by bike (unladen) and seven hours by bike (fully laden). Note that the last 2 km are treacherous and you may well have to carry your bike for part of the way. From Argentine immigration there is a boat service across to the southern side of Lago del Desierto programmed to tie in with the arrivals from

Chile, 45 minutes, US$30. The lake can also be skirted on foot (five hours) but not by bike. On the south side of the lake there is a bus service along a *ripio* road for the remaining 37 km to **El Chaltén**, one hour, US$28. In theory if you take both boats and the bus, you should arrive in El Chaltén at 2100 on the same day you set off from Villa O'Higgins. Add an extra day if you want to visit the glacier. With the opening of this route, it is now possible to travel along the whole of the Carretera Austral and on to Torres del Paine without having to double back on yourself. The journey is much easier to coordinate from north to south as there are regular last-minute disruptions to the Catamaran schedule due to inclement weather.

Lago General Carrera and beyond listings

For Sleeping and Eating price codes and other relevant information, see pages 41-44.

Sleeping

Reserva Nacional Cerro Castillo and around *p318*

B Cabañas Shehen Aike, Risopatrón 55, Puerto Ibáñez, T067-423284, www. aike.cl. Child-friendly *cabaña* complex run by a Swiss-Chilean family. Lots of local information as well as horse riding and fishing trips. English, German, French spoken. Recommended.

C Residencial Villarrica, O'Higgins 59, Villa Cerro Castillo, T067-419500. **F** singles. Basic good-value accommodation, good mid-price meals and a grocery store. Also cabins (**A-B**) sleeping 5-7.

D Cabañas Don Niba, Los Pioneros 872, Villa Cerro Castillo, T067-419920. **F** singles. Another friendly but basic *hospedaje*. Good value. Recommended.

D Residencial Ibáñez, Bertrán Dixon 31, Puerto Ibáñez, T067-423227. **F** singles. Clean, warm, hot water. Similar next door at No 29.

D Vientos del Sur, Bertrán Dixon 283, Puerto Ibáñez, T067-423208. **F** singles. Cheap meals available, good.

Camping

Municipal campsite, Puerto Ibáñez, T067-423234. Open Dec-Mar, US$10 per site.

The western shore *p320*

In Feb there is often a lack of accommodation in Río Tranquilo.

AL Hostal el Puesto, Pedro Lagos 258, Río Tranquilo, T02-1964555, www.elpuesto.cl. Without a doubt the most comfortable place in Río Tranquilo. The owners can organize tours.

A Hostal Los Pinos, Godoy 51, T067-411576, Río Tranquilo. Family-run, well-maintained, basic rooms with bath. Overpriced, but better standard than most. Mid-price meals served (check price first).

B Campo Alacaluf, Km 44 on the Río Tranquilo–Bahía Exploradores side road. Wonderful guesthouse hidden away from civilization and run by a very friendly eccentric German family. Good-value camping. Meals served, boxed lunches available. Recommended.

C Cabañas Jacricalor, Carretera Austral 245, Río Tranquilo, T067-419500 (public phone). **F** singles. Tent-sized *cabañas*.

C Hostería Carretera Austral, 1 Sur 223, Río Tranquilo, T067-419500 (public phone), lopezpinuer@yahoo.es. Serves meals.

C-D Hospedaje y Cabañas Silvana, Godoy 197, Río Tranquilo. Basic accommodation. Clean and good value.

E Hostería Lago General Carrera, Av 5 de Abril 647 y Colombia, Bahía Murta, T067-419600 (public). **F-G** singles. Cheap meals.

E Residencial Patagonia, Pasaje España 64, Bahía Murta, T067-419600 (public). **F-G** singles. Very basic, without bath.

Free camping is possible by the lake in Bahía Murta, with good views of Cerro Castillo.

Camping Pudú, 1 km south of Río Tranquilo, www.puduexpediciones.cl.

Chile Chico and around *p321*

C Hostería de la Patagonia, Camino Internacional s/n, T067-411337. **D** singles; full board available. Clean, excellent food,

English, French, Italian spoken, trekking, horse riding and whitewater rafting, also camping.
C Ventura, Carrera 290, T067-411311.
E singles. Unprepossessing rooms with bath.
C-D Casa Quinta No Me Olvides, Camino Internacional s/n, Sector Chacra. **E-F** singles. Without bath. Clean, cooking facilities. Also camping. Tours arranged to Lago Jeinimeni and Cueva de las Manos.
C-D Plaza, Balmaceda 102 y O'Higgins, T067-411215. Basic, clean.
E Hospedaje Don Luis, Balmaceda 175, T067-411384. **F-G** singles. Clean, meals available.

Camping

Free campsite at **Bahía Jarra**, 5 km from Chile Chico, then 12 km north. **Camping del Sol** at the eastern end of the town.

Towards Cochrane *p322*

LL Mallín Colorado, 2 km west of El Maitén, T02-2741807, www.mallincolorado.cl. *Cabañas*, adventure activities, horse riding, rafting, fishing, English and German spoken.
L Hacienda Tres Lagos, 2 km west of Cruce El Maitén, Puerto Guadal, T02-3334122, www.haciendatreslagos.com. Set in spacious grounds on the lakeshore. This boutique resort with capacity for only 34 guests, is an unexpected piece of luxury in the middle of Patagonia. The bungalows and suites are much nicer than the standard cabins. Good restaurant, games room, wide range of excursions, sauna, jacuzzi. Good service. English spoken. Recommended.
AL Patagonia Baker Lodge, Orillas del Río Baker, 3 km north of Puerto Bertrand, T067-411903, www.pbl.cl. Fishing lodge. Advance booking only.
A Río Baker Lodge, Costanera s/n, Puerto Bertrand, T067-411499, riobaker@hotmail.com. Fly-fishing lodge.
C Hostería Puerto Bertrand, Sector Costanera, Puerto Bertrand, T067-419900 (public). **E** singles. Also meals, *cabañas*, and activities.
D Doña Ester, Casa 8, Puerto Bertrand. Rooms in a pink house. **F** singles. Full board available. Good.Camping is available in Puerto Bertrand, basic but with access to hot water.

Cochrane *p322*

In summer it's best to book rooms in advance. The quality is generally mediocre.
A Cabañas Rogeri, Tte Merino 502, T067-522264. Small but decent cabins sleep 4, with kitchen facilities. Bigger cabins opposite. Same owners. Also good.
A Hotel Wellmann, Las Golondrinas 36, T067-522171. Good-sized rooms, comfortable, warm, meals served. Recommended.
A Ultimo Paraíso, Lago Brown 455, T067-522361. Regarded as the best place to stay. Not always open. Also arranges fishing trips.
C Hostal Latitud 47 sur, Lago Brown 564, T067-522280. **E** singles. Friendly, family-run residencial. Simple rooms but pleasant atmosphere. Internet, tours offered.
C Residencial Cero a Cero, Lago Brown 464, T067-522158, ceroacero@ze.cl. **E** singles, with decent breakfast, cheaper without bath, avoid downstairs rooms, those on upper floor are much better, though floorboards are creaky.
C Residencial Sur Austral, Prat 334, T067-522150. **E** singles, with breakfast and hot water. Some rooms with bath. Often full as it doubles as the Don Carlos bus terminal.
C-D Hospedaje Ana Luz, Los Ñadis 569, T09-77874011. **F** singles. Neat but basic cabins sleeping 2-3. Also basic rooms in the main house. Friendly. Recommended.
D Hospedaje Cochrane, Dr Steffens 451, T067-522377. **F** singles. Good meals, also camping (popular).
D Hospedaje Paola, Lago Brown 150, T067-522215. **F** singles. Run-down. Also camping.

Camping

In the Reserva Nacional Tamango, there are campsites and *cabañas* at **Los Correntadas**, US$14 per site, and **Los Coigües**, US$18 per site. Details and booking through **CONAF**, Av Ogana 1060, T067-212125.

South of Cochrane *p322*

AL Entre Hielos lodge, Sector Centro, Tortel. T02-1960271, www.entrehielostortel.cl. Newly built, the only upmarket place in town.

B El Mosco, at the northern entrance to Villa O'Higgins, T067-431819, patagoniaelmosco@yahoo.es, **E-F** pp in dorms. Spanish-run, kitchen facilities, games, laundry facilities, trekking maps and information. Can help with bike repairs. Overpriced singles. Camping available. English spoken. More expensive than the rest, but nothing else competes in terms of infrastructure. Recommended.

C Cabañas San Gabriel, Lago O'Higgins 310, Villa O'Higgins. Nice cabins, a good choice for small groups.

C Estilo, Sector Centro, Tortel, tortelhospedajeestilo@yahoo.es. Warm, comfortable, good food, very friendly, funny and talkative host (if your Spanish is up to it). Recommended.

C Hospedaje Costanera, Sector Centro, Tortel, T067-211876 (public). Price includes breakfast (also open to non-residents). Clean, warm, with attractive garden. The end room has good views.

D La Sureña, Sector Playa Ancha, Tortel. **F** singles. One guest comments: "Expect fresh mutton meals and if you are squeamish ... don't look out of the window when they butcher the 2 lambs a day on the front porch."

D Residencial Campanario, Lago O'Higgins 72, opposite El Mosco, Villa O'Higgins. Friendly, kitchen facilities, camping.

E Los Ñirres, Lago O'Higgins 72, Villa O'Higgins. **F** singles. Basic accommodation. Goods meals served. Several other similar places in town. There are about 6-8 beds available in local houses in **Calendario Mancilla**.

Camping

Camping Río Ñadis, 9 km west of the Carretera (turn-off at Puente Barrancoso, 45 km south of Cochrane), lillischindele@yahoo.de, or contact through Casa Turismo Rural in Coyhaique. Camping also available at several *hospedajes* (see above). There is a camping area in **Tortel** at the far end of town (sector Junquillo). There are very basic camping areas at either end of **Lago del Desierto**.

Eating

Chile Chico and around *p321*

🍴🍴 **Café Holiday**, C González. Good coffee, friendly service.

🍴🍴 **Cafetería Loly y Elizabeth**, González 25, on plaza. Serves coffee, ice cream and cakes.

Pub El Minero, Carrera 205. Recommended for a drink.

Cochrane *p322*

There are a couple of mid-range options on Teniente Merino and San Valentín too.

🍴 **Café Tamango**, Esmeralda 464, on the Plaza. Good fresh juices, quiches and cakes. Avoid the coffee.

🍴 **El Fogón**, San Valentín 653, T067-522240. One of few eating places in town. Basic southern Chilean fare.

Tortel *p322*

🍴 **Café Celes Salom**, Tortel. Basic cheap meals and disco on Sat with occasional bands.

Villa O'Higgins and across the lake to Argentina *p323*

🍴🍴 **Entre Patagones**, northern entrance to the town, T067-431810, The only restaurant in town with any sort of style.

Festivals and events

Chile Chico and around *p321*

Last week of Jan The town hosts the Festival Internacional de la Voz.

Towards Cochrane *p322*

3rd weekend of Feb Semana de Bertrand. 3 days of drunken revelry.

Activities and tours

Lago General Carrera *p320*

El Puesto Expediciones, Lagos 258, Río Tranquilo, T02-1964555, www.elpuesto.cl.

Fishing trips, ice-hiking, kayaking and other excursions.

The southern shore *p321*

Pascual Díaz, Puerto Guadal, cabalgasur@hotmail.com, leads trips to nearby fossil fields.

Towards Cochrane *p322*

Patagonia Adventure Expeditions, T067-411330, www.adventurepatagonia.com. Professional outfit running exclusive fully supported treks to the Campo de Hielo Norte and the eastern side of Parque Nacional Laguna San Rafael. Expensive but a unique experience and recommended. Also rafting on the Río Baker and general help organizing tours, treks and expeditions.

Horse riding, fishing guides and white-water rafting in the Río Baker (generally easy with a few Grade III rapids) can all be arranged at the tourist information office, T067-419900 (public phone). Advance booking helpful. **Hacienda Tres Lagos** (see under Sleeping) run a series of canopy zip lines, US$30.

Cochrane *p322*

Fishing

Lago Cochrane offers excellent fishing all-year round; boats can be hired for US$15 pp.

Tour operators

Casa del Turismo Rural, Dussen 357-B, Coyhaique, T067-524929, www.casaturismorural.cl, has many members in this area.

Expediciones San Lorenzo, Fundo San Lorenzo, 60 km southeast of Cochrane. T067-522326, or contact through the Casa del Turismo Rural in Coyaique, offer the best horse-riding trips in the area.

Tortel *p322*

Charter boats can easily be arranged. Prices to **Ventisquero Jorge Montt**, US$275 for upto 8 people. To **Ventisquero Steffens**, US$225 for upto 8 people. To **Isla de los Muertos** US$85 for upto 8 people. The condition of the boats varies. Check first. In theory the harbourmaster will only allow boats out in good conditions, however the weather can change very quickly and occasionally boats will have to turn back mid-trip. Make sure you agree beforehand with your guide whether you get any sort of refund if this happens.

Villa O'Higgins and across the lake to Argentina *p323*

Nelson Henríquez, Lago Cisnes 5, T067-431820. Fishing trips on Lagos Ciervo, Cisnes and El Tigre.

Alberto Guinao, Horse-riding guide. Horse rides from ½ a day to a week can be arranged, but note that the quality of horses in Villa O'Higgins is not the best.

Transport

Reserva Nacional Cerro Castillo and around *p318*

Minibuses and jeeps meet the ferry in Puerto Ibáñez for connections to **Coyhaique**, 2 hrs, US$7. There is also a road from Puerto Ibáñez to **Perito Moreno** in Argentina. It is poor-quality *ripio*, suitable for 4WD only and there is no public transport. **Tomás Urreta**, T09-99500276, provides transport from Villa Cerro Castillo to **Coyhaique**, US$6.

Ferry

The car ferry, *El Pilchero*, sails from Puerto Ibáñez to **Chile Chico**, Tue 1000, Wed 1000, Fri 1000, Sat 1100, Sun 1500, return departures Mon 0800, Tue 1500, Thu 1300, Fri 1500, Sun 1200, 2½ hrs, cars US$47, passengers US$8, motorbikes US$9 and bicycles US$4.The number of passengers is limited to 75 plus 5 cars; arrive 30 mins before departure. Reserve at least 2 days in advance through **Mar del Sur**, Baquedano 146, Coyhaique, T067-231255 (southbound) or at the Terminal de Transbordadores, Chile Chico, 067-411864 (northbound). This is a very cold crossing, even in summer; take warm clothing.

Chile Chico and around *p321*

Air

Don Carlos flies to **Coyhaique** (Tte Vidal airport), 5 weekly, US$50, from an airstrip just outside Chile Chico.

Bus

5 minibuses a week along south side of the lake to **Puerto Guadal**, US$12, and **Cochrane**, US$20. Minibuses from Chile Chico to **Los Antiguos** (Argentina), 45 mins including formalities, US$4 (Chilean pesos only), are run by **Arcotrans**, T067-411841, and **Transportes Padilla**, T067-411904. Buses depart when they are full – usually about 5 times daily each. For onward transport, see page 190.

Ferry

For services to **Puerto Ibáñez**, see above. Tickets should be reserved in advance from the terminal in Chile Chico.

Towards Cochrane *p322*

Buses do not enter Purto Bertrand, stopping instead 1 km away on the main Carretera.

Cochrane *p322*

Air

Don Carlos flies to **Coyhaique**, Mon, Thu, US$75, from an airstrip just north of town.

Bus

To **Coyhaique**, Sao Paulo, Don Carlos and **Acuario 13**, 6 days a week between them, US$19. To **Chile Chico**, **Buses Ali**, Thu, Sun, US$15. To **Tortel**, Gabriel Becerra and Buses Aldeas, daily, US$10. To **Villa O'Higgins**, Don Carlos, 2 weekly, Tue, Fri, 0800, US$19.

Tortel *p322*

Air

Don Carlos to **Coyhaique** (Tte Vidal), Mon and Wed, US$35 (subsidized price for residents of the village; other travellers must buy a standby ticket and should expect to pay much more.

Bus

To **Cochrane**, daily, US$10.

Villa O'Higgins and across the lake to Argentina *p323*

Air

Don Carlos air taxi flies to Villa O'Higgins from **Coyhaique**, via Cochrane, Mon, Thu, US$100.

Boat

Hielo Sur, www.hielosur.com, contact Hans Silva. Catamaran to **Calendario Mancilla** 2½ hrs, US$45; with glaciar visit 8½ hrs, US$70; return to Villa O'Higgins via Glaciar 11½ hrs, US$90. Tickets for the connecting boat and bus in Argentina can be paid here or directly in Argentina.

Bus

Bus terminal at Res Cordillera, Lago Salto 302 T067-431829. If you have a return bus ticket northwards reconfirm on arrival at Villa O'Higgins. There are 1 or 2 buses weekly to **Cochrane**, US$19 as well as a local fortnightly bus to **Lago Cristi**, US$16 return.

❶ Directory

Chile Chico and around *p321*

Banks Generally it's best to change money in Coyhaique or Argentina, but dollars and Argentine pesos can be changed here in small amounts (at poor rates) at shops and cafés, including **Cafetería Loly y Elizabeth**. **Hospital** Lautaro s/n, T067-411334.

Cochrane *p322*

Banks Banco del Estado, on the plaza, changes dollars. ATM accepts MasterCard and Cirrus but not Visa. **Internet** On the western side of the plaza.

Tortel *p322*

Banks There is no bank in Tortel but a mobile bank comes twice a month. **Medical services** Medical centre staffed by doctors, nurses and dentists visits Tortel monthly. **Post office** Mon-Fri 0830-1330, post leaves Tortel weekly by air.

Far South

Contents

Footprint features

At a glance

Getting around Good bus links between the 2 main cities and to Torres del Paine. Hiring a 4WD will give you a little more freedom, but mostly you will be travelling on foot.

Time required A couple of days for a whistlestop tour, 5 or 6 to make the most of your trip, and more if you want to hike the circuit.

Weather Unpredictability is the watchword. Can range from gorgeous sun to bitingly cold frozen rain in a few hours. Winter is calmer but cold.

When not to go Winter is beautiful here, but trekking is complicated due to the short days and snowfall that closes many (but not all) trekking routes in Torres del Paine.

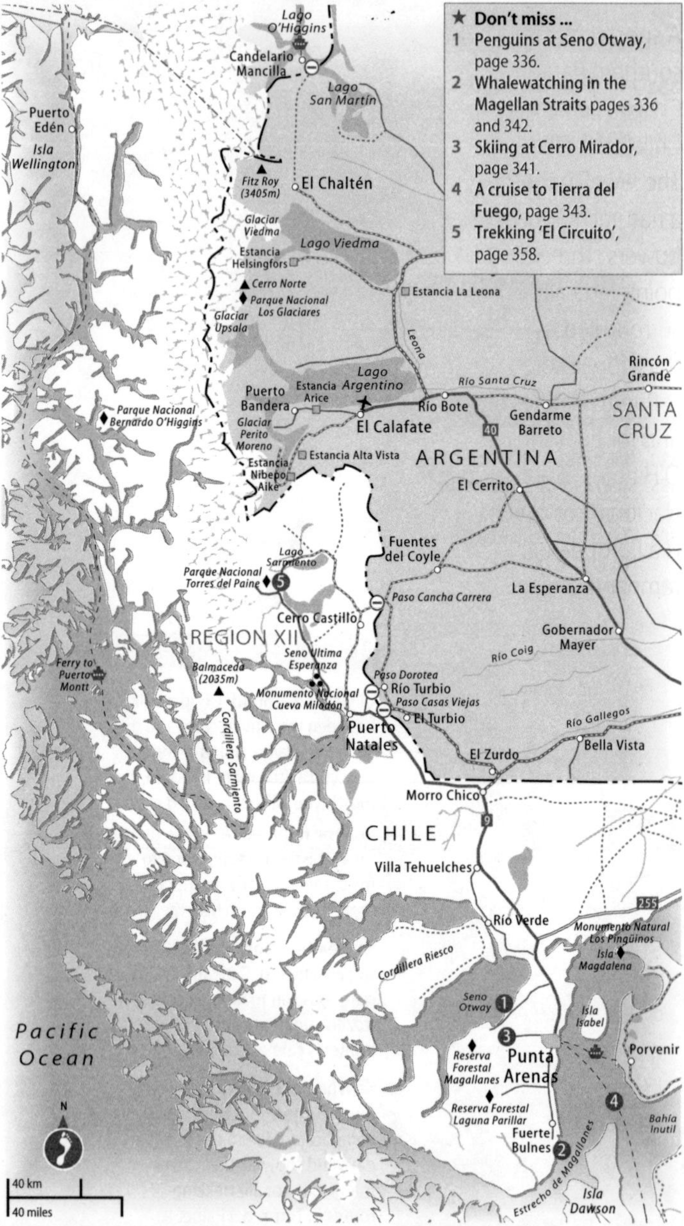
★ Don't miss ...
1 Penguins at Seno Otway, page 336.
2 Whalewatching in the Magellan Straits pages 336 and 342.
3 Skiing at Cerro Mirador, page 341.
4 A cruise to Tierra del Fuego, page 343.
5 Trekking 'El Circuito', page 358.
Lago O'Higgins
Candelario Mancilla
Lago San Martín
Puerto Edén
Isla Wellington
Fitz Roy (3405m)
El Chaltén
Glaciar Viedma
Lago Viedma
Estancia Helsingfors
Cerro Norte
Parque Nacional Los Glaciares
Glaciar Upsala
Estancia La Leona
Leona
Lago Argentino
Puerto Bandera
Estancia Arice
Río Santa Cruz
Rincón Grande
Río Bote
Gendarme Barreto
SANTA CRUZ
Parque Nacional Bernardo O'Higgins
Glaciar Perito Moreno
El Calafate
40
Estancia Alta Vista
ARGENTINA
Estancia Nibepo Aike
El Cerrito
Fuentes del Coyle
Lago Sarmiento
Parque Nacional Torres del Paine
Paso Cancha Carrera
La Esperanza
Cerro Castillo
REGION XII
Gobernador Mayer
Río Coig
Seno Ultima Esperanza
Ferry to Puerto Montt
Balmaceda (2035m)
Paso Dorotea
Río Turbio
Monumento Nacional Cueva Milodón
Paso Casas Viejas
El Turbio
Cordillera Sarmiento
Puerto Natales
Río Gallegos
Bella Vista
El Zurdo
Morro Chico
9
CHILE
Villa Tehuelches
255
Río Verde
Monumento Natural Los Pingüinos
Isla Magdalena
Cordillera Riesco
Seno Otway
Isla Isabel
Pacific Ocean
Reserva Forestal Magallanes
Punta Arenas
Porvenir
Reserva Forestal Laguna Parillar
Bahía Inutil
Fuerte Bulnes
N
40 km
40 miles
Estrecho de Magallanes
Isla Dawson

A spectacular land of fragmenting glaciers and teetering icy peaks, southern Patagonia feels like nowhere else on earth. Although Chileans posted here will often say that they are a "long way from Chile", this is the country's most popular destination for visitors. The jewel in the crown is the Parque Nacional Torres del Paine, a natural magnet for travellers from all over the world. The 'towers', three distinctive columns after which the park is named, point vertically upwards from the Paine massif like fingers, surrounded by imposing glaciers, turquoise-coloured lakes and thick forests of native trees.

Puerto Natales is the base for exploration of Torres del Paine and for boat trips to the glaciers in the Parque Nacional Bernardo O'Higgins. It also provides access to El Calafate and the Parque Nacional Los Glaciares in Argentina. Further south, Punta Arenas is a European-style city with a lively Chilote community and remnants of earlier English and Croatian influences.

Punta Arenas and around

Capital of Región XII, Punta Arenas lies 2140 km due south of Santiago. The city was originally named 'Sandy Point' by the English, but adopted the Hispanic equivalent under Chilean colonization. A centre for natural gas production, sheep farming and the fishing industry as well as an important military base, it is also the home of Polar Austral, one of the most southerly breweries in the world. Although Punta Arenas has expanded rapidly, it remains a tranquil and pleasant city. The climate and architecture give it a distinctively northern European atmosphere, quite unlike anywhere else in Chile. ▸▸ *For listings, see pages 338-344.*

Ins and outs

Getting there

Punta Arenas is cut off from the rest of Chile. Puerto Natales aside, the only road connections are via the Argentinian towns of Comodoro Rivadavia and Río Gallegos to Coyhaique and the Carretera Austral, or via Bariloche to Puerto Montt. It is quicker, and often cheaper, to take one of the many daily flights to/from Puerto Montt or Santiago instead. There are also direct flights to Porvenir, Puerto Williams and Ushuaia. **Carlos Ibáñez del Campo airport** is 20 km north of town. Buses from Puerto Natales to Punta Arenas will only stop at the airport if they are scheduled to drop passengers there. There are minibuses operated by **Transfer Austral** ⓘ *Lautaro Navarro 975, T061-615100, www.transferaustral.com, US$5,* which will drop you anywhere near the city centre. A taxi ordered at the airport costs US$13, while a radio taxi ordered in advance from the city is a little cheaper. For ferry routes to Tierra del Fuego, see page 366. ▸▸ *See Transport, page 342.*

Tourist information

The municipal **tourist office** on the plaza is good, T061-200610, or try **Sernatur** ⓘ *Lautaro Navarro 999 (temporary offices; location of permanent office yet to be decided), T061-225385, www.patagonia-chile.com, 0830-1845, closed weekends in winter*, and **CONAF** ⓘ *Bulnes 0309, opposite the shepherd monument, between the racetrack and cemetery, T061-238544, Mon-Fri.* To contact the **Falkland Islands Tourist Board** ⓘ *Old Philomel Store, PO Box 618, Stanley, FIQQ 1ZZ, T+500 22215/27019, www.visitorfalklands.com.* See also box, page 337.

Background

After its foundation in 1848, Punta Arenas became a penal colony modelled on Australia. In 1867, it was opened to foreign settlers and given free port status. From the 1880s, it prospered as a refuelling and provisioning centre for steam ships and whaling vessels. It also became a centre for the new sheep estancias since it afforded the best harbour facilities. The city's importance was reduced overnight by the opening of the Panama Canal in 1914. Although immigrants from Britain and Croatia were central in the growth of Punta Arenas (their influence can be seen to this day), most of those who came to work in the estancias were from Chiloé; many people in the city have relatives in Chiloé and feel an affinity with the island (the *barrios* on either side of the upper reaches of Independencia are known as Chilote areas); the Chilotes who returned north took Patagonian customs with them, hence the number of *mate* drinkers on Chiloé.

Punta Arenas

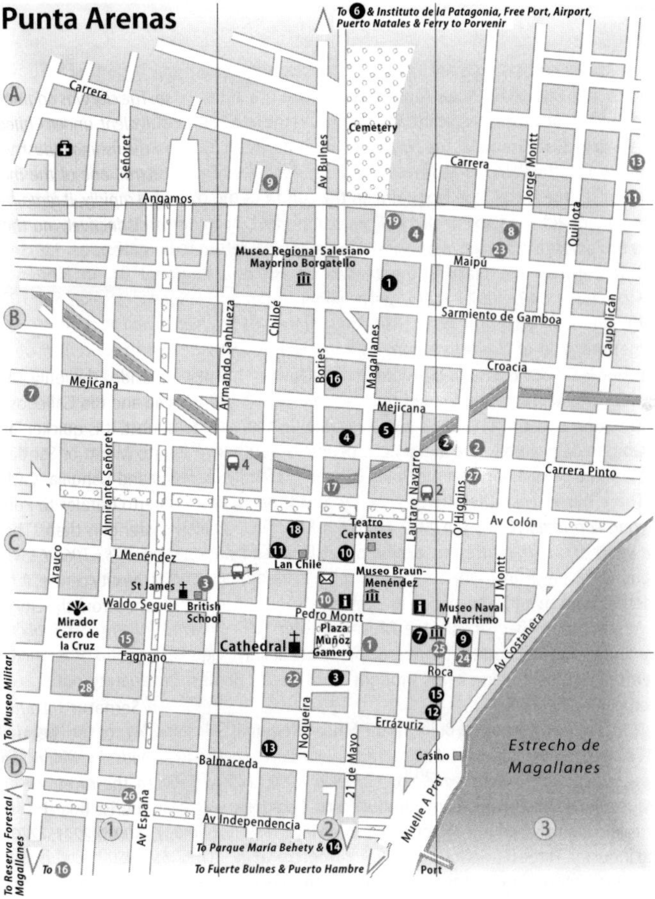

N

300 metres

300 yards

Sleeping
Backpackers Paradise **2** *C3*
Cabo de Hornos **1** *C2*
Chalet Chapital **3** *C1*
Hospedaje Miramar **28** *D1*
Hostal Ainil **4** *B2*
Hostal al Fin del Mundo **25** *C3*
Hostal del Sur **7** *B1*
Hostal Dinka's House **11** *A3*
Hostal El Conventillo **24** *D3*
Hostal Independencia **26** *D1*
Hostal Keoken **19** *B2*
Hostal La Estancia **27** *C3*
Hostal Parediso **8** *B3*
Hostal Quo Vadis **16** *D1*
Hostal Sonia Kuscevic **9** *A2*
Hostal Taty's House **23** *B3*
José Nogueira (Palacio Sara Braun) **10** *C2*
Oro Fueguino **15** *C1*
Pink House **13** *A3*
Plaza **22** *D2*
Tierra del Fuego **17** *C2*

Eating
Carioca **11** *C2*
Damiana Elena **1** *B2*
Dino's Pizza **16** *B2*
El Asador Patagónico **2** *C3*
El Estribo **4** *C2*
El Quijote **7** *C2*
La Luna **9** *C3*
La Marmite **5** *C2*
La Tasca **3** *D2*
Lomit's **10** *C2*
Parrilla Los Ganaderos **6** *A2*
Puerto Viejo **12** *D2*
Remezón **14** *D2*
Sabores de Chiloé **13** *D2*
Santino **18** *C2*
Sotitos **15** *D3*

Buses
Fernández **4** *C2*
Pacheco **2** *C2*
Sur **1** *C2*

Sights

Punta Arenas is not a huge city and walking about is a pleasant way of getting to know it. Around the attractive **Plaza Muñoz Gamero** are a number of mansions that once belonged to the great sheep-ranching families of the late 19th century. A good example is the **Palacio Sara Braun** ⓘ *Tue-Sun, US$2*, built between 1894 and 1905 with materials from Europe; the Palacio has several elegantly decorated rooms open to the public and also houses the **Hotel José Nogueira**. In the centre of the plaza is a statue of Magellan with a mermaid and two Fuegian *indígenas* at his feet. According to local wisdom, those who rub or kiss the big toe of one of the Fuegians will return to Punta Arenas.

Just north of the plaza is the **Museo de Historia Regional Braun Menéndez** ⓘ *Magallanes 949, T061-244216, www.dibam.cl/sdm_mr_magallanes, Mon-Sat 1030-1700, Sun 1030-1400 (summer) or 1030-1300 (winter), US$2, children half price*, the opulent former mansion of Mauricio Braun, built in 1905. A visit is recommended. Part of the museum is set out as a room-by-room regional history; the rest of the house has been left with its original furniture. Guided tours are in Spanish only but a somewhat confusing information sheet in English is also available. In the basement there is a permanent exhibition dedicated to the indigenous people of southern Patagonia, somewhat ironic considering the leading part the Braun-Menéndez family played in their demise.

Three blocks east, the **Museo Naval y Marítimo** ⓘ *Pedro Montt 981, T061-205479, terzona@armarda.cl, Tue-Sun 0930-1700 (Jan-Feb); Tue-Sun 0930-1230, 1400-1700 (rest of the year), US$1.50*, houses an exhibition of local and national maritime history, with sections on naval instruments, cartography, meteorology and shipwrecks. There is a video in Spanish and information in English.

At Zenteno y Balmaceda, the **Museo Militar** ⓘ *Regimiento Pudeto, T061-247133, Tue-Sun 0900-1300, 1500-1700, free*, displays lots of knives, guns, flags and other military memorabilia, plus many items brought from Fuerte Bulnes. Explanatory notes are in excruciating English.

North of the centre along Bulnes is the **Museo Regional Salesiano Mayorino Borgatello** ⓘ *Colegio Salesiano, Av Bulnes 336, entrance next to church, T061-221001, www.museomaggiorinoborgatello.cl, Tue-Sun 1000-1230, 1500-1800, hours change frequently, US$3.50*, an excellent introduction to Patagonia with a large collection of stuffed birds and animals from the region, exhibits on local history, geology, athropology, aviation and industry. Three blocks further on, the **cemetery** ⓘ *Av Bulnes, daily 0800-1800*, is one of the most interesting places in the city, with cypress avenues, gravestones in many languages bearing testimony to the cosmopolitan provenance of Patagonian pioneers, and many mausolea and memorials to pioneer families and victims of shipping disasters. Look out for the statue of *Indicito*, the little Indian, on the northwest side, which is now an object of reverence, bedecked with flowers. Further north still, the Instituto de la Patagonia houses the **Museo del Recuerdo** ⓘ *Av Bulnes 1890, Km 4 north (opposite the zona franca), T061-207056, Mon-Fri 0830-1130, 1430-1815, Sat 0830-1300, US$2, children free*, an open-air museum with artefacts used by the early settlers, pioneer homes and botanical gardens.

On 21 de Mayo, south of Independencia, is a small ornate Hindu temple, while further along the same street, on the southern outskirts of the city, the wooded **Parque María Behety**, features a scale model of Fuerte Bulnes, a campsite and children's playground, popular for Sunday picnics. In winter, there is an ice rink here.

Shackleton and the rescue from Elephant Island

Shackleton's 1914-1916 Antarctic expedition is one of the epics of polar exploration. Shackleton's vessel, *Endurance*, which left England in August 1914 with 28 men aboard, became trapped in pack-ice in January 1915. After drifting northwards with the ice for eight months, the ship was crushed by the floes and sank. With three boats, supplies and the dogs, the group camped on an ice floe which continued to drift north for eight months. In April 1916, after surviving on a diet of seals and penguins, the party took to the boats as the ice broke up. After seven days at sea they reached Elephant Island. From there Shackleton and five other men sailed 1300 km in 17 days to South Georgia, where there were whaling stations. On reaching the south shore of South Georgia, Shackleton and two men crossed the island (the first such crossing) to find help. Shackleton, from whom nothing had been heard by the outside world since leaving the island 18 months before, was not recognized at first.

The British government sent a rescue vessel to Elephant Island, but the delays involved led Shackleton to seek help locally. After ice had prevented three rescue attempts – the first from South Georgia, the second from the Falkland Islands/Islas Malvinas and the third from Punta Arenas – Shackleton persuaded the Chilean authorities to permit a fourth attempt using the tug *Yelcho*. Leaving Punta Arenas on 25 August 1916, the vessel encountered thick fog but, unusually for the time of year, little ice and it quickly reached Elephant Island where the men, who had endured an Antarctic winter under upturned boats, were down to four days of supplies.

Although the expedition failed to cross Antarctica, Shackleton's achievement was outstanding: despite the loss of *Endurance*, the party had survived two Antarctic winters without loss of life. Shackleton returned in 1921 to lead another expedition but, in January 1922, aged 47, he suffered a fatal heart attack in South Georgia.

Around Punta Arenas pp338-344.

Reserva Forestal Magallanes → *Colour map 3, B3.*

ⓘ *7 km west of town, US$5.*

Known locally as the Parque Japonés, this forest reserve extends over 13,500 ha and rises to 600 m. Although getting there by taxi is the easiest option, it can also be reached on foot or by bike: follow Independencia up the hill and take a right turning for Río de las Minas, about 3 km from the edge of town; the entrance to the reserve is 2 km beyond. Here you will find a self-guided nature trail through lenga and coigue trees. The road continues through the woods for 14 km passing several picnic sites. From the top end of the road a short path leads to a lookout over the **Garganta del Diablo** (Devil's Throat), a gorge with views over Punta Arenas and Tierra del Fuego. From here a slippery path leads down to the Río de las Minas Valley and then back to Punta Arenas. Also within the reserve, **Cerro Mirador** is one of the few places in the world where you can ski with a sea view (see page 341). There's also a good two-hour hike here in summer; the trail is clearly marked and flora is labelled.

Fuerte Bulnes and south → *Colour map 3, B3.*

About 25 km south of Punta Arenas, a fork to the right leads to the very peaceful **Reserva Forestal Laguna Parrillar**, surrounded by snow-capped hills. It has older forest than the

Magallanes Reserve and sphagnum bogs, and offers excellent salmon trout fishing. There is a three-hour walk to the tree-line along poorly marked, boggy paths, and fine views from the Mirador. Camping is forbidden but there are sites for cooking on gas stoves. There is no public transport to the reserve; a radio taxi will cost about US$50.

Some 56 km south of Punta Arenas, **Fuerte Bulnes** is a replica of the wooden fort erected in 1843 by the crew of the Chilean vessel *Ancud*. Built in the 1940s and originally designed to house a museum, nearly all the interesting exhibits and artefacts were moved to museums in Punta Arenas and Santiago in 1986 and now only the empty shells of the various buildings remain.

Nearby is **Puerto Hambre** (see box, page 391), where there are ruins of the church built in 1584 by a group of ill-fated Spanish colonists led by Sarmiento de Gamboa. Disaster struck the fledgling colony when their only remaining ship, with Sarmiento on board, was blown into the Atlantic, leaving many men stranded on land. Sarmiento organized two rescue missions, but was captured by the English and imprisoned. When the English corsair Thomas Cavendish sailed through the straits in 1587 he found only 18 survivors. Only one of them trusted Cavendish enough to set sail with him; the rest of the men were left to die and Cavendish named the place Port Famine as a reminder of their grisly fate. This is a very beautiful area with views towards the towering ice mountains near Pico Sarmiento; it was of Puerto Hambre that Darwin wrote: "looking due southward ... the distant channels between the mountains appeared from their gloominess to lead beyond the confines of this world".

At the intersection of the roads to Puerto Hambre and Fuerte Bulnes, 51 km south of Punta Arenas, is a small monolith marking the **Centro Geográfico de Chile**, the midway point between Arica and the South Pole. Bypassing Fuerte Bulnes, the road continues past a memorial to Captain Pringle Stokes, Captain of the Beagle, who committed suicide here in 1829, being replaced as captain by Fitz Roy. The road carries on, past San Juan to the lighthouse at San Isidro. The last part of this journey can only be done in a high-clearance vehicle and at low tide and in summer, as it involves crossing an estuary at the mouth of the Río San Pedro. Alternatively leave your vehicle on the north side of the estuary, ford the river (at low tide) and walk 2½ hours to San Isidro. From here, it is a day hike to **Cape Froward**, the southernmost point of the continent of South America, marked by a 24-m-high cross. There is no path, and a guide is essential (this can be arranged by the *hostería* at San Isidro with advance notice). Some 70 km west of Cape Froward along the Magellan Straits is Isla Carlos III, a popular base for humpback whale watching.

North of Punta Arenas

Seventy kilometres north of Punta Arenas, **Seno Otway** is the site of a colony of Magellanic penguins, which can be visited ⓘ *Oct-mid Mar, US$5*. There are beautiful views across the sound to the mountains to the north and rheas, skunks and foxes can also be seen. Several agencies offer trips to the colony (five hours, US$15 plus entry fees at peak season); if you wish to visit independently, a taxi from Punta Arenas will cost US$40 return. Note that access to the colony is via a private road where a toll of US$1.75 per person is charged.

A small island, 30 km northeast, **Isla Magdalena** is the location of the **Monumento Natural Los Pingüinos**, a colony of 150,000 penguins, administered by **CONAF**. Deserted apart from during the breeding season from November to early February, Magdalena is one of a group of three islands visited by Drake (the others are Marta and Isabel), whose men killed 3000 penguins for food. Boat trips to the island are run by **Comapa** ⓘ *Tue, Thu,*

Going further: Falkland Islands/Las Malvinas

These remote southern outposts, where there are more penguins than people, are the only part of South America where UK sterling is the currency and the British monarch's head appears on the stamps. Windswept they may be, but the islands are a haven for wildlife and for those who wish to see it: albatross nest in the tussac, sea lions breed on the beaches and orca whales cruise off the coast.

About 640 km east of the South American mainland, the Falkland Islands/Islas Malvinas are made up of two large islands and hundreds of smaller ones. The capital, Stanley, is a small modern town with reminders of its seafaring past in the wrecks of sailing ships in the bay. Its residents live mostly in brightly painted houses, many of which have corrugated-iron roofs. Surrounded by rolling moorland, Stanley resembles parts of the Scottish Hebrides. To visit the Camp, as the land outside Stanley is known, 4WD vehicles make tours, or you can fly to farming outposts for warm hospitality, huge skies and unparalleled nature watching. In the southeast, Sea Lion Island is a delightful place to explore and relax; and it's worth taking the one-hour flight to West Falkland or one of the smaller islands for the stunning scenery.

Ins and outs The best time to visit is October to March. The climate is cool and oceanic and the weather is very unpredictable. Average temperatures are 15°C in January, and 4°C in June.

Stanley has two small hotels, three guesthouses and a growing number of B&Bs. Elsewhere are tourist lodges offering comfortable full-board, cottages to rent, and the opportunity to share in the life and work of a farm.

All visitors must have a full passport. Citizens of Britain, USA, Chile and most Commonwealth or EU countries do not need a visa. Visitors are issued a one-month visitor permit on arrival upon presentation of a return ticket. Visitors should book accommodation in advance and have sufficient funds. There are ATMs on the islands. Visa and MasterCard are widely accepted.

Flights from Santiago, via Puerto Montt and Punta Arenas with **LAN** every Saturday. Return fares: Santiago £530, Punta Arenas £285. Once a month, the flight calls at Río Gallegos, Argentina. Trips can be arranged through **International Tours and Travel**, see page 342. For further information contact the **Falkland Islands Tourist Board**, Old Philomel Store, PO Box 618, Stanley, FIQQ 1ZZ, T+500 22215/27019, www.visitorfalklands.com.

Sat, 1600 (Dec-Feb), 2 hrs each way, with 2 hrs on the island, US$34, subject to cancellation if windy; full refund given. Tours are also organized by several operators in Punta Arenas. Take a hat, coat and gloves.

Beyond, Route 255 heads northeast past Kimiriaike (from where a road branches south towards Tierra del Fuego) to Punta Delgada. From here there is a turn-off north along a *ripio* road for 26 km to **Parque Nacional Pali Aike**, a fantastic volcanic landscape dotted with small cones and craters. There are five easy, marked trails, all of which can be done in a day. From Punta Delgada Route 255 continues to the Argentine border and then along Route 3 to Río Gallegos. For routes to El Calafate, see page 347.

Punta Arenas and around listings

For Sleeping and Eating price codes and other relevant information, see pages 41-44.

Sleeping

Punta Arenas *p332, map p333*
Hotel prices are substantially lower during winter months (Apr/May-Sep). Most hotels include breakfast in the room price. Accommodation is also available in many private houses; ask at the tourist office. There are no campsites in or near the city.

LL Cabo de Hornos, Muñoz Gamero 1039 on the plaza, T061-715000, www.hoteles-australis.com. 4-star, newly refurbished and comfortable. Bright and spacious rooms. Good views from the 4th floor up, either of the Magellan Straits or the plaza.

LL-L José Nogueira, Bories 959, in former Palacio Sara Braun, T061-711000, www.hotelnogueira.com. Beautiful *loggia*. Small rooms, but high ceilings. The rooms on the 2nd floor are best. Good suites, lovely dining room, parking. Probably the nicest hotel in town. Recommended.

L Tierra del Fuego, Colón 716, T061-226200, www.puntaarenas.com. Good breakfast, parking. Decent-sized rooms, some rooms with kitchenette. **Café 1900** is downstairs.

AL Plaza, Nogueira 1116, piso 2, T061-241300, www.hotelplaza.cl. Historic building on the corner of the main plaza with high ceilings and old-fashioned charm, redone recently. English spoken. Limited parking and no elevators. Recommended.

A Chalet Chapital , Sanhueza 974, T061-730100, www.hotelchaletchapital.cl. Small well-run hotel. Rooms are on the small side (although there is a common lounge area) and the stairs are a bit creaky, but the staff are friendly and helpful. A good choice in this price range. Recommended.

A Oro Fueguino, Fagnano 356, T061-249401, www.orofueguino.cl. Recently refurbished, TV and phone. Some rooms with no windows. Good breakfast. Often fills up with groups so book ahead. Cheaper in US dollars than pesos.

A-B La Casa Escondida , Parcela 26A, Sector Ojo Bueno, T061-223003, www.lacasaescondida.cl. Cosy rustic guest-house hidden in the woods 15 km north of Punta Arenas towards the airport. Free pickup from town/airport. Very friendly and helpful owners, sauna, meals served. English spoken. Recommended.

B Hostal del Sur, Mejicana 151, T061-227249, hostaldelsur@hotmail.com. Homely and impeccably kept late 19th-century house. The living room is top-of-the-range 1960s, but the rooms are modern. Excellent breakfast with cereal and cakes. Not central, but in a peaceful neighbourhood. Advance booking advised in summer. Good value. Recommended.

B Hostal Sonia Kuscevic, Pasaje Darwin 175, T061-248543, www.hostalsk.50megs.com. One of the oldest guesthouses in Punta Arenas. Impeccably kept rooms with TV and bath. Very quiet. Good breakfast including omelette. Good value off-season.

B-C Hostal Ainil, Lautaro Navarro 230, T061-220962, www.hostalainil.com. Comfy bed and breakfast with smallish rooms. The ones at the front of the house are brightest. At the back are two lovely cabins, **A-B**, sleeping 3-4 people and good value.

B-C Hostal La Estancia, O'Higgins 765, T061-249130, www.estancia.cl. Simple but comfortable rooms, some with bath. Heating in passageways but not in rooms. Very good kitchen facilities, internet, lots of information, friendly. English spoken. Excellent breakfast with real coffee. Recommended.

B-C The Pink House, Caupolicán 99, T061-222436, www.chileanpatagonia.com/pinkhouse. **D-E** singles. Impeccable rooms with or without bath, breakfast included. Pickup from bus station. English spoken, internet.

C Hostal al Fin del Mundo, O'Higgins 1026, T061-710185, www.alfindelmundo.cl. **E** singles, **F** pp in dorms. With breakfast. Bright, cosy and friendly. Shared baths, central, helpful, laundry service, book exchange, internet, cooking facilities, English spoken, helpful, recommended.

C Hostal Dinka's House, Caupolicán 169, T061-244292, www.dinkashouse.cl. Heated rooms with bath, breakfast, use of kitchen, laundry.

C Hostal Keoken, Magallanes 209, T061-244086, www.hostalkeoken.cl. **D-E** singles. Bizarre construction on 3 floors, each with its own entrance up rickety outside staircases. With breakfast. Some rooms with bath, kitchen facilities, Wi-Fi. Good value, friendly. Some local info. Top-floor rooms with shared bathroom have paper thin walls.

C Hostal Paredíso, Angamos 1073, T061-224212, hostalparediso@hotmail.com. **C-E** singles. Decent rooms with cable TV and heating, with or without bath (some cheaper rooms have no window). Good breakfast, parking, use of kitchen. Friendly, basic information given, some English spoken. Recommended.

C Hostal Quo Vadis, Paraguaya 150, T061-247687, www.hostalquovadis.cl. **E** singles. Motorcycle parking, meals, safe, quiet. Recommended.

C Hostal Taty's House, Maipú 1070, T061-241525, www.hostaltatyshouse.cl. Decent rooms with bath and cable TV. Good beds, decent value, a good choice in this price bracket. Basic English spoken.

C-D Hostal El Conventillo, Pasaje Korner 1034, T061-242311, www.hostalelconventillo.com. New 'hip' hostel. Rooms for 2-6 with shared bath, none with outside windows. Cheerful, good value, free internet. Good location.

D Backpackers Paradise, Carrera Pinto 1022, T061-240104, backpackersparadise@hotmail.com. **G** pp in basic dormitories. Fun cheap backpackers' with cooking facilities, limited bathroom facilities, lots of info, good meeting place, luggage store, internet, laundry service, little privacy, book exchange. Expensive bike rental. Recommended.

E Hospedaje Miramar, Almirante Señoret 1190, T061-215446. **G** pp in dorms. Slightly exotic location on the edge of the red-light district. Friendly staff, good views over the bay. Breakfast extra.

F Hostal Independencia, Independencia 374, T061-227572, www.chileaustral.com/independencia. **G** pp in shared rooms. Friendly, small basic rooms. Breakfast extra, kitchen facilities, laundry service, internet, bike rental and cheap camping. Also *cabañas* away from the centre. Good value. Recommended.

Fuerte Bulnes and south *p335*

L Hostería Faro San Isidro, 75 km south of Punta Arenas, booking office Lautaro Navarro 1163, Punta Arenas, T061-710511, hosteriafarosanisidro.cl. The southernmost lodging on the American continent and within striking distance of Cape Froward. Excursions offered.

Eating

Punta Arenas *p332, map p333*

TTT Remezón, 21 de Mayo 1469, T061-241029, www.patagoniasalvaje.net. Regional specialities such as krill. Very good, and so it should be given the exorbitant prices.

TTT-TT Damiana Elena, Magallanes 341, T061-222818. Stylish restaurant serving Mediterranean food with a Patagonian touch. Menu changes on a daily basis. Popular with locals. Advance booking essential at weekends. Recommended.

TTT-TT El Asador Patagónico, O'Higgins 694, T061-222463. A new branch of the well-regarded Natales restaurant specializing in spit-roast lamb.

TTT-TT El Estribo, Carrera Pinto 762, T061-244714. Specializes in local and exotic dishes such as guanaco. Something of a tourist trap.

Fishy business

Visitors to Punta Arenas and the surrounding region should be especially wary of eating shellfish. In recent years, the nearby waters have been affected by a *marea roja* (red tide) of poisonous algae. Infected molluscs can kill humans almost instantly, so never pick up mussels along the shore of Punta Arenas. However, all shellfish sold in restaurants have been inspected and so are theoretically safe. There are seasonal bans on *centolla* (king crab) fishing to protect dwindling stocks; do not purchase *centolla* out of season.

TTT-TT José Nogueira (see Sleeping). The hotel has one of the best restaurants in town.

TTT-TT La Tasca, Centro Español, Plaza Muñoz Gamero 771. Large helpings, limited selection, quite expensive. Decent lunch menu.

TTT-TT Puerto Viejo, O'Higgins 1167, T061-225296. By the port. Once the most traditional of the seafood restaurants, now relocated and more upscale. Service could be a lot better.

TTT-TT Sotitos, O'Higgins 1138. Good service and old-fashioned elegance. Recommended.

TT La Luna, O'Higgins 1017, T061-228555. Fish and shellfish including local specialities, huge pisco sours, lively atmosphere.

TT La Marmite, Plaza Sampaio. Intimate restaurant decorated in desert pastel colours. Self-styled 'mestizo' restaurant – regional food with an international touch. Friendly service. Good value for Punta Arenas.

TT Parrilla Los Ganaderos, Bulnes 0977, T061-222818. Best place for spit-roast lamb. It's a long walk past the hippodrome from the town centre. Take a taxi or a *colectivo* going towards the Zona Franca.

TT Santino, Colón 657, T061-220511. Good pizzas, large bar, good service.

T Carioca, Menéndez 600 y Chiloé. Cheap lunches, snacks and beer, good service.

T Cocinerías, Lautaro Navarro, south of the port entrance. Stalls serving cheap fish meals.

T Dino's Pizza, Bories 557. Good pizzas, huge sandwiches. For something different, try the rhubarb juice. Recommended.

T El Quijote, Lautaro Navarro 1087, T061-241225. Good burgers, sandwiches and fish dishes. Good-value set lunch. Recommended.

T Lomit's, Menéndez 722. A Punta Arenas fast-food institution serving cheap snacks and drinks, open when the others are closed, always busy. Recommended.

T Sabores de Chiloé, Chiloé esq Balmaceda. Chilote food as the name implies.

Cafés

Café Montt, Pedro Montt 976. With Wi-Fi.

Chocolatta, Bories 852. Probably the best coffee in town.

Coffeenet, Waldo Seguel 670. Proper internet café serving espresso.

Entre Fierros, Roca 875, T061-223436. Small diner, colloquially known as the 'kiosko Roca', that by all accounts has remained unchanged since the 1950s. It is famous for its banana milkshakes and tiny *choripan* (spicy sausage-meat sandwiches).

Bars and clubs

Punta Arenas *p332, map p333*

Be aware that anywhere that calls itself a 'nightclub' is in fact a brothel.

La Taberna del Club de la Unión, Plaza Muñoz Gamero y Seguel. Atmospheric pub in the basement of the **Nogueira hotel**, smoky.

Olijoe, Errázuriz 970. Reasonably plush British-style pub, leather interior. Recommended.

Pub 1900, Av Colón esq Bories. Friendly, relaxed atmosphere.
Santino, Colón 657, T061-220511, www.santino.cl. Pizzeria that doubles as a popular bar at night.

Entertainment

Punta Arenas *p332, map p333*

Casino The new casino is on O'Higgins just north of the port.
Cinema There is a single-screen cinema at Mejicana 777.

Festivals and events

Punta Arenas *p332, map p333*

Late Jan/early Feb Muestra custumbrista de Chiloé, when the Chilote community celebrates its culture.
21 Jun Carnaval de invierno is the winter solstice marked by a carnival on the weekend closest to 21 Jun.

Shopping

Punta Arenas *p332, map p333*

Zona Franca, 3.5 km north of the centre, on the right-hand side of the road to the airport, take bus E or A from Plaza Muñoz Gamero or a *colectivo*. Punta Arenas has certain free-port facilities. Cheap electrical goods are especially worth seeking out, as is camping equipment. The quality of most other goods is low and the prices little better than elsewhere. Open Mon-Sat 1000-1230, 1500-2000. There is a new mall, the **Espacio Urbano,** 2 km to the west of the town centre. Take *colectivo* 300, 777 or 800.

Camping equipment

Alfgal, Errazuriz y Lautaro Navarro, camping gear.
Andes gear, Espacio Urbano mall, the best store for outdoor equipment.
Sports Nativa, Colón 614. Camping and skiing equipment.
The North Face, Bories 887. Outdoor gear.

Handicrafts and local products

Punta Arenas is famous for the quality of its handmade **chocolate**, sold at several shops on Calle Bories.
Chile Típico, Carrera Pinto 1015, T061-225827. Chilean souvenirs.
Chocolates Norweisser, Carrera 663. Good chocolate factory.
Pingüi, Bories 404. Crafts and books on Tierra del Fuego, Patagonia and Antarctica.
The Wool House Patagonia, Fagnano 675, by the plaza. Good-quality, reasonably priced woollen clothes.

Activities and tours

Punta Arenas *p332, map p333*

Skiing

Cerro Mirador, 9 km west of Punta Arenas in the Reserva Nacional Magallanes, is one of the few places in the world where you can ski with a sea view. Season Jun to Sep, weather permitting. Daily lift-ticket, US$11; equipment rental, US$9 per adult. There's a mid-way lodge with food, drink and equipment. For cross-country skiing facilities, contact the **Club Andino**, T061-241479, www.clubandino.tierra.cl. However, the ski centre is often closed due to lack of snow. There's also a good 2-hr hike here in summer; the trail is clearly marked and flora is labelled. Skiing is also available at **Tres Morros**.

Tour operators

Most organize tours to Fuerte Bulnes, the *pingüineras* on Otway sound and Torres del Paine. Note that a 1-day tour to the latter involves leaving at 0500 and returning around 2300. Several also offer bespoke tours: shop around as prices vary. Specify in advance if you want a tour in English. There are many more tour operators than these listed. For more information ask at the Sernatur office.

Arka Patagonia, Señoret 1597, T061-248167, www.arkapatagonia.com. General agent offering all types of tours, rafting, fishing, etc.
International Tours & Travel, 1 Dean St, Stanley, T+500-22041, www.falkland islands.travel. **LanChile** agents on the Falkland Islands, offer tailor-made and special-interest tours, handle inbound tourist bookings and book FIGAS flights.
Pali Alke, Lautaro Navarro 1125, T061-223301/229388, www.turismopaliaike.com. Wide range of tours including horse riding trips.
Solo Expediciones , Nogueira 1255, T061-710219, www.soloexpediciones.com. Bespoke and off-the-beaten-track excursions on and around the Magellan Straits.
Turismo Aonikenk, Magallanes 619, T061-221982, www.aonikenk.com. Expensive but very good bespoke excursions. Recommended.
Turismo Aventour, Patagonia 779, T061-241197, www.aventourpatagonia.com. General excursions and multi-day tours.
Turismo Comapa, Magallanes 990, T061-200200, www.comapa.com. Tours to Torres del Paine, Tierra del Fuego and Isla Magdalena, also agents for trips to the Falklands/Malvinas, Ushuaia and Cape Horn.
Turismo Ruta Club Internacional, Carrera Pinto 1142, T061-229000, www.turismo rutaclub.cl. General travel agent also offering local tours. Cycle hire, US$2 per hr.
Turismo Viento Sur, Fagnano 585, T061-226930, www.vientosur.com. For camping equipment, fishing excursions, sea kayaking, cycle hire, English spoken, good tours.
Whale Sound, Lautaro Navarro 1163, T061-710511, www.whalesound.com. Whale-watching trips in the Magellan Straits.

Transport

Punta Arenas *p332, map p333*
Transport is heavily booked from late Dec-Mar; advance booking is advised.

Air

Airline offices Aerovías DAP, O'Higgins 891, T061-616100, www.dap.cl, 0900-1230, 1430-1930; **LanChile**, Bories 884, T600-5262000, www.lan.com; **Sky Airline**, Roca 933, T600-6002828, www.skyairline.cl.

Long-distance To **Ushuaia** (Argentina), **LanChile**, 3 weekly in summer, 1 hr, from US$200 one way; reserve in advance from mid-Dec to Feb. To **Falkland Islands/Islas Malvinas**, LanChile, Sat, US$600 return. **International Tours & Travel**, T+500-22041, www.falklands travel.com, serve as LanChile agents on the Falkland Islands.

Local To **Balmaceda** (for Coyhaique), with **LanChile** (LanExpress), daily in summer and **Sky Airline**, 3 weekly all year. To **Puerto**

Montt, with **LanChile** (**LanExpress**) and **Sky Airline**, 10 daily from US$120 return. Cheapest one-way tickets with Sky. To **Santiago**, **LanChile** (**LanExpress**) and **Sky Airline** several daily, from US$200 return, via Puerto Montt (sit on the right for views). To **Porvenir**, **Aerovías DAP**, 3 daily Mon-Sat, US$34 one way, plus other irregular flights, with Twin-Otter and Cessna aircraft, 10kg baggage allowance. To **Puerto Williams**, **Aerovías DAP**, daily in summer (book well in advance), US$95 one way, 10 kg baggage allowance.

Bus

Buses depart from the company offices as follows: **Bus Sur**, Menéndez 552 T061-227145, www.bus-sur.cl; **Cruz del Sur**, **Pingüino** and **Fernández**, Sanhueza 745, T061-242313, www.busesfernandez.com; **Gesell**, Menéndez 556, T061-222896; **Ghisoni**, **Queilen Bus** and **Tecniaustral**, Lautaro Navarro 971, T061-222078, www.ghisoni.terra.cl; **Pacheco**, Colón 900, T061-242174, www.busespacheco.com; **Turbus**, Errázuriz 932, T061-225315.

Services and frequencies change every year, so check on arrival at the helpful Sernatur office. Timetables are also printed daily in El Austral. The services detailed below are for high season only.

Note that there is a project to build a new bus terminal north of town by the Zona Franca to be shared by all bus companies.

Fernández, **Buses Pacheco** (best buses) and **Bus Sur** (cheapest), all run several services each day to **Puerto Natales**, 3 hrs, last departure 2000, US$9 one way, US$16 return (although this means you have to return with the same company). Buses will pick up at the airport with advance booking and payment.

To **Coyhaique**, 24 hrs, **Buses Sur**, 1 per week via Argentina, US$55, meals not included. **Pacheco** (*semi-cama* and *salón-cama*), **Queilen Bus** and Cruz del Sur have services through Argentina to **Osorno**, **Puerto Montt** and **Castro**, several weekly, 36 hrs to Castro, US$50-75.

To Argentina To **Río Gallegos**, **Pingüino**, **Ghisoni** and **Pacheco**, 2 or 3 daily between them. All cost US$12 and take about 5 hrs. For services to **Buenos Aires** it is cheaper to go to Río Gallegos and buy an onward ticket from there. **Pacheco** and **Tecni Austral** have buses most days to **Río Grande** via Punta Delgada, 8 hrs, US$33, heavily booked. To **Ushuaia** via Punta Delgada, US$50, 12-14 hrs, book any return at same time, **Tecni Austral** and **Pacheco**, Mon-Sat between them.

Car

Bargain if you want to hire a car for several days. **Budget**, O'Higgins 964, T061-202720, www.budgetpatagonia.com; **Econorent**, Waldo Seguel 443, T600-2000000, www.econorent.cl; **EMSA**, Roca 1044, and at the airport, T061-2229049, www.emsarentacar.cl. Avis agents; **Hertz**, O'Higgins 931, T061-613087, www.autorentas.cl; **Lubag**, Colón 975, T061-242023, www.lubag.cl; **Magallanes Rent a Car**, O'Higgins 949, T061-220780, www.magallanesrentacar.cl ; **Payne Rent a Car**, Menéndez 631, T061-240852, www.payne.cl, try bargaining, friendly.

Ferry

For ferry services to **Tierra del Fuego**, see page 366. All tickets on ships must be booked in advance for Jan and Feb. **Transbordadores Austral Broom**, Bulnes 05075, T061-218100, www.tabsa.cl, has a weekly ferry service to **Puerto Williams**, leaves Wed, 34 hrs, US$175 in a reclining seat, US$210 in a bunk.

Cruceros Australis, see page 233, operate a pair of luxury cruise ships, sailing twice weekly from Punta Arenas to Ushuaia via Cape Horn and Puerto Williams. The trip lasts 4 days with daily excursions and, weather permitting, fantastic views of glaciers and wildlife; details from **Comapa**

in Punta Arenas (or direct from **Cruceros Australis** SA, El Bosque Norte 0440, piso 11, T02- 442 3115, www.australis.com). Advance booking advised.

Most **cruise ships** to **Antarctica** (see page 386) leave from Ushuaia. However, there are a few operators based in Punta Arenas, for example **Antarctica XXI**, Lautaro Navarro 987, piso 2, T061-228783, www.antarcticaxxi.com, who offer a mixed flight/cruise package.

Shipping offices Comapa (Compañía Marítima de Punta Arenas), Magallanes 990, T061-200200, www.compapa.com; **Navimag**, Magallanes 990, T061-244400, www.navimag.com.

Taxis

Ordinary taxis have yellow roofs. Reliable service is available from **Radio Alce vip**, T061-710999, and **Taxi Austral**, T061-247710/244409. *Colectivos* (all black) run on fixed routes within the city, US$0.60-70 for anywhere on the route.

Directory

Punta Arenas *p332, map p333*

Banks and currency exchange

Several banks around Plaza Muñoz Gamero, all have ATMs. Argentine pesos can be bought at **Cambio Gasic**, Roca 915, oficina 8, T061-242396. **Consulates** Argentina, 21 de Mayo 1878, T061-261912, Mon-Fri 1000-1530, visas take 24 hrs; **UK**, Catarates de Niaguara 01325, T061-211535, helpful, information on Falkland Islands. For others, ask the tourist office. **Hospitals** Hospital Regional Lautaro Navarro, Angamos 180, T061-244040; **Clínica Magallanes**, Bulnes 01448, T061-211527, private clinic; minimum US$45 per visit. A list of English-speaking doctors is available from Sernatur. **Internet** Lots of places offer access, including at Magallanes y Menéndez, and below Hostal Calafate on Magallanes, ½ block north of plaza. Prices are generally US$1 per hr. **Laundry** Lavasol, O'Higgins 969, the only self-service laundry, Mon-Sat 0900-2030, Sun 1000-1800, US$6 per machine, wash and dry, good but busy. **Post office** Bories 911 y Menéndez, Mon-Fri 0830-1930, Sat 0900-1400. **Telephone** There are several call centres in the centre (shop around as prices vary).

Puerto Natales and around

From Punta Arenas a good paved road runs 247 km north to Puerto Natales through forests of southern beech and prime pastureland; this is the best sheep-raising area in Chile. Ñandúes and guanacos can often be seen en route. Founded in 1911, the town grew as an industrial centre and, until recent years, its prosperity was based upon employment in the coal mines of Río Turbio, Argentina. Today, Puerto Natales is the starting point for trips to the magnificent Bernardo O'Higgins and Torres del Paine national parks and also provides access across the border to the Parque Nacional Los Glaciares. Unsurprisingly, tourism is the mainstay of the town's economy.
▸▸ *For listings, see pages 347-353.*

Ins and outs

Getting there Puerto Natales is easily reached by daily buses from Punta Arenas and from El Calafate via Río Turbio or Cerro Castillo (both roads part *ripio*). There are also two buses weekly from Río Gallegos. Note that buses from Argentina invariably arrive late. In theory buses from Punta Arenas to Puerto Natales will pick passengers up at Punta Arenas airport as long as reservations have been made with advance payment through an agency in Puerto Natales. In practice, though, they are often unreliable. In summer there are flights from Santiago via Puerto Montt. The town is the terminus of the *Evangelistas* ship from Puerto Montt (see page 353). If driving between Punta Arenas and Puerto Natales make sure you have enough fuel.

Tourist information There is a **Sernatur kiosk** ⓘ *Av Pedro Montt y Philippi, T061-412125,* on the waterfront. Information is also available from the **Municipalidad** ⓘ *Bulnes 285, T061-411263*, and from **CONAF** ⓘ *O'Higgins 584*.

Sights

The **Museo Histórico Municipal** ⓘ *Bulnes 285, T061-411263, museonat@123mail.cl, Mon-Fri 0800-1900, Sat 1000-1300, 1500-1900, closed Sat off season, US$21*, houses a small collection of archaeological and native artefacts as well as exhibits on late 19th-century European colonization. Reasonable descriptions in English.

South of the town centre past the end of calle Baquedano is the **Museo de Fauna Patagónica** ⓘ *Colegio Salesiano, Padre Rossa 1456, T061-411258, museo@fagnano.cl, Mon-Sat 0900-1315, 1430-1930 in summer, US$1.50*. It houses a collection of around 350 stuffed animals from the region.

The colourful old steam train in the main square was once used to take workers to the the meat-packing factory at **Puerto Bories**, 5 km north of town. It is a pleasant hour-long walk along the shore to Bories (US$4 by taxi), with fine views across the sound to the Península Antonio Varas and the jagged peaks and receding glaciers of the Parque Nacional Bernardo O'Higgins beyond. In its heyday the plant was the biggest of its kind in Chile with a capacity for 250,000 sheep. Bankrupted in the early 1990s, much of the plant was dismantled in 1993. Belatedly the plant was given National Monument status and is slowly being restored. The remaining buildings and machine rooms can be visited. **Museo Frigorífico Puerto Bories** ⓘ *T061-414328, www.museopuertobories.cl, Mon-Sun 1000-1900 in summer, US$6 with an audioguide in several languages.*

The slab-like **Cerro Dorotea** dominates the town, with superb views of the whole Seno Ultima Esperanza. It can be reached on foot or by any Río Turbio bus or taxi (recommended, as the hill is further off than it seems). The trail entrance is marked by a sign marked 'Mirador Cerro Dorotea'. Expect to be charged US$5-8 in one of the local houses, where you will be given a broomstick handle which makes a surprisingly good walking stick. It is a 1½-hour trek up to the 600-m lookout along a well-marked trail. In

Puerto Natales

N

200 metres

200 yards

Sleeping
Altiplanico Sur 2 *A2*
Aquaterra 17 *B2*
Casa Cecilia 3 *A2*
Casa Teresa 23 *B2*
Charles Darwin 21 *B1*
Costaustralis 5 *B1*
Glaciares 19 *B1*
Hospedaje Chila 6 *C2*
Hospedaje Nancy 24 *C3*
Hostal Dos Lagunas 18 *B2*
Hostal Las Carretas 16 *C3*
Hostal Sir Francis Drake 25 *A2*
Hostel Natales 26 *B1*
Indigo Patagonia 4 *B1*
Keoken 13 *A2*
Lady Florence Dixie 7 *B3*
Los Inmigrantes 9 *C2*
Martín Gusinde 10 *A2*
Natalino 20 *B2*
Patagonia Adventure 11 *B2*
Remota 30 *A2*
Residencial Dickson 12 *B2*
Residencial El Mundial 31 *B2*
Residencial Gabriela 14 *B2*
Residencial Niko's 15 *C3*
Residencial Niko's II 28 *A2*
Weskar Patagonian Lodge 29 *A2*

Eating
Afrigonia 4 *B2*
Andrés 1 *B1*
Angelicas 3 *B2*
Cormorán de las Rocas 15 *A2*
El Asador Patagónico 9 *B2*
El Living 6 *B2*
El Marítimo 7 *B3*
El Rincón de Don Chicho 8 *C2*
La Casa de Pepe 2 *B2*
La Mesita Grande 11 *B2*
La Oveja Negra 2 *B2*
La Picada de Carlitos 14 *B3*
La Repizza 12 *B3*
La Ultima Esperanza 10 *B2*
Masay 5 *B2*
Parrilla Don Jorge 13 *A2*

theory you can continue along the top of the hill to get better views to the north, but the incredibly strong winds often make this dangerous.

Monumento Nacional Cueva Milodón → *Colour map 3, A2.*

ⓘ *25 km north of Puerto Natales, US$6. Buses JB US$8, taxi US$30 return.*

The cave, a massive 70 m wide, 220 m deep and 30 m high, contains a plastic model of the prehistoric ground sloth whose remains were found there in 1895. The remains are now in London, although there is talk of returning them to the site. Evidence has also been found of occupation by Patagonians some 11,000 years ago. Nearby, there is a visitor centre, with summaries in English. There's also a good restaurant and handicraft store. Most day tours to Torres del Paine stop at the cave.

Parque Nacional Bernardo O'Higgins → *Colour map 3, A2.*

Often referred to as the **Parque Nacional Monte Balmaceda**, this park covers much of the Campo de Hielo Sur, plus the fjords and offshore islands further west. A three-hour boat trip from Puerto Natales up the Seno de Ultima Esperanza takes you to the southernmost section, passing the **Glaciar Balmaceda**, which drops from the eastern slopes of Monte Balmaceda (2035 m). The glacier is retreating; in 1986 its foot was at sea level. The boat docks one hour further north at **Puerto Toro**, from where it is a 1-km walk to the base of the **Glaciar Serrano** on the north slope of Monte Balmaceda. On the trip, dolphins, sea-lions (in season), black-necked swans, flightless steamer ducks and cormorants can often be seen. Take warm clothes, including a hat and gloves.

There is a route from Puerto Toro on the eastern side of the Río Serrano for 35 km to the Torres del Paine administration centre (see page 354); guided tours are available on foot or on horseback. It is also possible to travel to the Paine administration centre along the river by boat or zodiac (five hours, US$85), details from tour agencies in Puerto Natales.

Towards Argentina

From Puerto Natales, the Argentine border can be crossed at three points: Paso Casas Viejas, Paso Dorotea and Paso Cancha Carrera (see page 196). They all eventually meet Route 40, which runs north to El Calafate and east to Río Gallegos. All buses use the Río Turbio crossing, but if you're driving to El Calafate, the Cerro Castillo crossing is a shorter route. » *For onward routes from the border to El Calafate, see page 209.*

Puerto Natales and around listings

For Sleeping and Eating price codes and other relevant information, see pages 41-44.

Sleeping

Puerto Natales *p345, map p346*

Most prices include breakfast. Hotels in the countryside are open only in the summer months; specific dates vary. In season, cheaper accommodation fills up quickly after the arrival of the **Navimag** ferry from Puerto Montt. Most of the more expensive hotels are much of a muchness give or take the view. Occasionally one of these will have a special offer. Call round for quotes.

LL Altiplanico Sur, Huerto 282, T061-412525, www.altiplanico.cl. Minimalist hotel with a unique design built into the hillside 1 km north of town and with views across the sound.

LL Costaustralis, Pedro Montt 262, T061-412000, www.hoteles-australis.com. The most expensive hotel in the town centre. No better than the other big hotels. In effect you are paying for the view, which, to be fair, is the best there is. The rooms facing inland are an expensive waste.

LL Indigo Patagonia Hotel & Spa, Ladrilleros 105, T061-413620, www.indigopatagonia.com. Old 3-storey house on the waterfront with fantastic views, recently expanded and converted into a boutique hotel, together with restaurant (open to the public) and roof-top spa.

LL Remota, Huerto 279, 1km north of town along the coast, T061-412727, www.remotahotel.com. Expensive all-inclusive packages of 3 days or more with a wide range of activities inside and outside Torres del Paine. Rooms are spacious with extensive views.

L Weskar Patagonian Lodge, Km 1, road to Bories, T061-414168, www.weskar.cl. Quiet lodge overlooking the bay, understated wooden interior. Rooms are simple but most have extensive views. There is a good but expensive restaurant for guests and bike rental. Helpful staff. A good out-of-town place to relax.

L-AL Charles Darwin, Bulnes 90, T061-412478, www.hotelcharlesdarwin.com. Newly refurbished comfortable 3-star standard. Some rooms with partial views. Permanently empty restaurant downstairs. Good rates off-season.

L-AL Martín Gusinde, Bories 278, T061-412770, www.hotelmartingusinde.com. Comfy 3-star, although the carpets could do with a change and rooms do not have a view. Good-value rates off season.

AL Aquaterra, Bulnes 299, T061-412239, www.aquaterrapatagonia.com. Understated design. No frills but thought and effort have gone into it. Not cheap, but unlike many other places in the same price bracket you get the feeling that the staff are there to help and are able to answer any question you might have. Living room upstairs and a resto-bar downstairs. Alternative therapies also offered. Thin walls a drawback.

AL Glaciares, Eberhard 104, T061-411452, www.hotelglaciares.com. A standard 3-star. Comfortable enough and some rooms have a partial view. Good day tours to Torres del Paine.

AL-A Lady Florence Dixie, Bulnes 655, T061-411158, www.hotelflorencedixie.cl. 3-star. Helpful staff. The standard rooms are a bit cramped and cold, but the superior rooms are bigger, carpeted and good value.

A Hostal Sir Francis Drake, Philippi 383, T061-411553, www.hostalfrancisdrake.com. Simple, smallish but comfortable rooms with bath and cable TV. There is a pleasant living room on the upper floor with views. Wi-Fi, French spoken. Recommended.

A Keoken, Señoret 267, T061-413670, www.keokenpatagonia.com. New homely upmarket bed and breakfast. Spacious living room. Some rooms with views. All rooms have their own bathroom but note that not all are en suite. Some English spoken.

A-B Hostel Natales, Ladrilleros 209, T061-411081, www.hostelnatales.cl. **D-E** pp in dorms. All rooms with bath. Formerly a decent hotel converted into a luxury hostel. The place has been fully refurbished and is very comfortable, even if the dorm beds are a little overpriced.

B-C Casa Cecilia, Tomás Rogers 60, T061-613560, www.casaceciliahostal.com. **D** singles. With good breakfast, some rooms with bath, clean, cooking facilities, Wi-Fi, English, French and German spoken, heating, luggage store, camping equipment rental, information on Torres del Paine, tours organized, bus tickets sold, credit cards accepted. Better value in US dollars. Warmly recommended.

B-C Hostal Las Carretas, Galvarino 745, T061-414584, www.lascarretashostal.com. Tastefully decorated and impeccably clean bed and breakfast. Comfortable rooms, some with bath, good beds, kitchen facilities, Wi-Fi, friendly staff. Some English spoken. Recommended. The downside is that it is a 15-min walk to the centre – not nice in bad weather.

C Hospedaje Nancy, E Ramírez 540, T061-4510022, www.nataleslodge.cl. **F** singles. Some rooms with bath. Cooking facilities, internet access, laundry service, helpful, tours and lots of information. Good budget option. Recommended.

C Hostal Dos Lagunas, Barros Arana 104, T061-415733, doslagunas@hotmail.com. **D** singles. Simple clean unpretentious residencial. All rooms with shared bathrooms. Very friendly English-speaking owner eager to help with travellers' needs. Good breakfast including real coffee. Recommended.

C Patagonia Adventure, Tomás Rogers 179, T061-411028, www.apatagonia.com. **E-F** pp in dorms. Shared bathrooms. Friendly, clean, English spoken, camping equipment for hire, luggage store, book exchange. Good bike and kayak tours offered. Also a general agent selling trips to Torres del Paine. Breakfast is served in the café annex.

C-D Residencial Dickson, Bulnes 307, T061-411871, patagoniadickson@hotmail.com. **F** singles. Some rooms with bath. Good breakfast, clean, helpful, cooking and laundry facilities, internet.

C-D Residencial Niko's, Ramírez 669, T061-412810, nikoresidencial@hotmail.com. **E-F** singles. With breakfast, basic rooms, some rooms with bath, good meals, also dormitory accommodation. Recommended.

C-D Residencial Niko's II, Philippi 528, T061-411500, www.nikostwoadventure.com. With good breakfast. Some rooms with bath and cable TV, English spoken, tours, tent hire, book exchange, free internet if you can get the owners' children off the PC. Recommended.

D Los Inmigrantes, Carrera Pinto 480, T061-413482, losinmigrantes@hotmail.com. **F** singles. Good breakfast, clean, kitchen facilities, equipment rental, luggage store.

D Natalino, Eberhard 371, T061-411968. Clean and very friendly. Rooms with bath and breakfast, parking.

D Residencial Gabriela, Bulnes 317, T061-411061. **F** singles. Clean, good breakfast, helpful, luggage store, heating. Recommended.

E Casa Teresa, Esmeralda 463, T061-410472, freepatagonia@hotmail.com. **G** singles. Good value, warm, cheap meals, quiet, friendly. Tours to Torres del Paine arranged. Recommended.

E Hospedaje Chila, Carrera Pinto 442, T061-412328. **G** singles. Use of kitchen, welcoming, laundry facilities, luggage store, bakes bread. Recommended.

Camping There is a campsite in town on Esmeralda y Prat with hot water and tent hire.

Road from Punta Arenas

AL Hostal Río Penitente, Km 138, T061-331694. In an old *estancia*.

A Hostería Río Verde, Km 90, east off the highway on Seno Skyring, T061-311122. Private bath, heating.

B Hostería Llanuras de Diana, Km 215 (30 km south of Puerto Natales), T061-410661. Hidden from road, beautifully situated. Recommended.

C Hotel Rubens, Km 183, T061-226916. Popular for fishing.

North of Puerto Natales

AL-A Cisne de Cuello Negro, 6 km from town, Km 275 near Puerto Bories, for bookings contact Av Colón 782, Punta Arenas, T061-244506, pehoe1@ctcinternet.cl. Clean, decent food. Recommended.

A Estancia Tres Pasos, 40 km north, T061-221930, www.trespasos.cl. Simple and beautiful lodge between Puerto Natales and Torres del Paine. Horse-riding trips offered.

B Cabañas Kotenk Aike, 2 km north of town, T061-412581. Sleeps 4, modern, very comfortable, great location.

Parque Nacional Bernardo O'Higgins *p347*

AL Hostería Monte Balmaceda, T061-220174. Although the park is uninhabited, guest accommodation is available here.

Eating

Puerto Natales *p345, map p346*

TTT Afrigonia , Eberhard 343, T061-412232, afrigonia@hotmail.com. A totally unexpected mixture, Patagonia meets East Africa in this new Kenyan/Chilean-owned fusion restaurant, considered by many to be the best, and certainly the most innovative in town.

TTT-TT Angélicas, Bulnes 501, T061-410365, angelicas@rest.cl. A sign of how Puerto Natales has turned into a boutique town. Elegant Mediterranean-style restaurant originally from Santiago. Quality ingredients well prepared. Pricey but more than reasonable for Natales, and customers invariably leave satisfied. Staff can be a little flustered when the restaurant is full. Recommended.

TTT-TT Cormoran de las Rocas, Miguel Sánchez 72, T061-413723, www.cormoran delas rocas.com. Patagonian specialities with an innovative twist. Wide variety of well-prepared dishes. First-rate *pisco sours*. Good service and attention to detail and incomarable views. Recommended.

TTT-TT El Asador Patagónico, Prat 158 on plaza. Specializes in spit-roast lamb. Book in advance as spaces are limited. Recommended.

TTT-TT Parrilla Don Jorge, Bories 430 on plaza, T061-410999. Another restaurant specializing in *cordero al palo*, but also serving fish, etc. The open plan leaves you feeling a little exposed when the restaurant is not full. Decent service.

TT El Marítimo, Baquedano 379. One of the best places in town to eat fish and seafood.

TT El Rincón de Don Chicho, Luis Cruz Martínez 206, T061-414339. All-you-can-eat *parrillada*. Vegetarian options on request. 15 mins' walk from town centre. Recommended.

TT La Casa de Pepe, Tomas Rogers 131 on the plaza. For those who want to sample the traditional food of central Chile – *pernil, pastel de choclo*, etc. Uncomfortable seats.

TT La Mesita Grande, Prat 196 on the plaza, T061-411571, www.mesitagrande.cl. First-rate pizzas made in a wood-burning clay oven. Also pasta, salads and good desserts. Not much atmosphere, but there's a fantastic antique till.

TT La Oveja Negra, Tomas Rogers 169, on the plaza. Typical Chilean dishes, book swap. Ownership of this restaurant seems to change every year.

TT La Ultima Esperanza, Eberhard 354. Recommended for salmon, seafood, huge portions, not cheap but worth it.

TT-T La Picada de Carlitos, Blanco Encalada y Esmeralda. Good, cheap tradicional Chilean food. Often full of locals at lunchtime. Service can be slow when full.

T Andrés, Ladrilleros 381. Excellent, good fish dishes, good service.

T La Repizza, Blanco Encalada 294, T061-410361. Good-value sarnies and light meals.

T Masay, Bulnes 429. Cheap sandwiches.

Cafés

Aquaterra, Bulnes 299. Cosy, good, also a shiatsu and reiki centre.

Café & Books, Blanco Encalada 224. Cosy café with an extensive 2-for-1 book exchange.

Cerritos , Miguel Sánchez 11. Tiny hidden café with friendly owners and a fantastic view.

El Living, on the plaza. Cosy, British-run, with English newspapers and magazines. Wide

variety of cakes, good tea and coffee, wine and vegetarian food. Book exchange.
Emporio de la Pampa, Eberhard 302, T061-413279. Small café/delicatessen selling wine and local gourmet products.
Patagonia Adventure, Tomás Rogers 179 on the plaza. Opens at 0630 for early risers.
Patagonia Dulce, Barros Arana 233, T061-415285, www.patagoniadulce.cl. For the best hot chocolate in town.

Bars and clubs

Puerto Natales *p345, map p346*
There are a couple of discos on Blanco Encalada.
Casino, Bories 314, T061-411834. Daily 1300-0400. Modest, tables open from 2100.
El Bar de Ruperto, Bulnes 371. Good, English-run pub with a lively mix of locals and tourists. For a kick, try the chile vodka.
Iguana, Magallanes y Eberhard. There is invariably a bar here, but it seems to change name and ownership each year.
Kaweshkar, Eberhard 161. European-style lounge bar.
Murciélagos, Murciélagos, Bulnes 731. Popular bar with late night music and dancing.
Toore, Eberhard 169. Another popular bar.

Shopping

Puerto Natales *p345, map p346*

Camping equipment

Camping gas is available in hardware stores, eg at Baquedano y O'Higgins. Wares tend to be more expensive than the Zona Franca in Punta Arenas.
Alfgal, Barros Arana 299, T061-413622.
Balfer, Bulnes 660.
La Maddera, Prat 297, T061-41331. Outdoor clothing.

Casa Cecilia and Patagonia Adventure (see Sleeping, above) have a reputation for hiring out good-quality gear, but there are an increasing number of alternatives mostly with tour agencies and hostels. Shop around and check all equipment and prices carefully. Average charges, per day: tent US$8; sleeping bag US$4-6; mat US$2; raincoat US$1; also cooking gear US$2. Deposits sometimes required: tent US$200; sleeping bag US$100. Note that it is often difficult to hire walking boots.

Food

Food prices are variable so shop around, although everything tends to be more expensive than in Punta Arenas. The biggest supermarket is **Abu Gosch** at Bulnes y Ramírez. Also **Don Bosco**, Baquedano 358. The town markets are also good.

Handicrafts

El Toque Campero , Eberhard 148. Good quality and reasonably priced leather and woolen handicrafts as well as locally produced cakes, jams, etc sold from a characterful old shepherd's wagon. Friendly owners.
Ñandu, Eberhard 586 y Magallanes. Popular craft store. Another branch at the Milodon Cave.
Pueblo Artisanal Etherh Aike, Philippi y Valdivia. Covered market with many handicraft stalls.

Activities and tours

Puerto Natales *p345, map p346*
Reports of the reliability of agencies, especially for their trips to Parque Naciónal Torres del Paine, are very mixed. It is better to book tours in Puerto Natales than through agents in Punta Arenas or Santiago, where huge commissions may be charged. While most tours can be booked direct with the operators there are several agencies in Puerto Natales who can make bookings with all of the operators below as well as transport and accommodation within the park.

Some agencies offer 1-day tours to the Perito Moreno glacier in Argentina (see page 186), 14-hr trip, 2 hrs at the glacier, US$65 excluding food and park entry fee; take US dollars cash or Argentine pesos as

Chilean pesos are not accepted. However, if you have more time it is better to break the trip by staying in Calafate, and organizing a tour from there.

As most organized activities within Torres del Paine such as horse riding and ice trekking are operated by exclusive licence holders, many other agencies are concentrating on the area to the south of the park around the Río Serrano and the route between Puerto Natales and the park.

Antares, Barros Arana 111, T061-414611, www.antarespatagonia.com. Kayaking and trekking.

Baguales Group, Galvarino 661, T061-412654, www.bagualesgroup.com. Specialists in the route from the park back to Puerto Natales. Tailor-made multi-activity tours that can incorporate zodiacs, horse riding, kayaking and trekking, mostly off the beaten track. A real experience. Recommended.

Bella Patagonia, Barros Arana 160, T061-412489, www.bellapatagonia.com. Belgian-run operator specializing in kayak trips and trekking.

Chile Nativo, Eberhard 320, Casilla 42, Región XII, T061-411835, T1800-649 8776 (toll free in USA and Canada), www.chile nativo.travel. Specializes in tailor-made tours of Torres del Paine and surroundings.

Comapa, Eberhard 555, T061-414300, www.comapa.com. Large regional operator offering decent day tours to the park.

Criollo Expediciones, Huerto 157-B, T09-85284225, www.criolloexpediciones.com. Guided horse rides around Natales and Last Hope Sound as well as the edge of Parque Nacional Torres del Paine and multi-day trips to the wild Sierra Baguales. US/Chilean-run. Friendly attentive guides. Well-kept horses. Recommended.

Erratic Rock, Baquedano 719, T061-410355, www.erraticrock.com. Trekking experts offering interesting and alternative expeditions from ½ a day to 2 weeks. Also hire out good-quality equipment.

Estancia Travel, Casa 13B, Puerto Bories (5 km north of Puerto Natales), T061-412221, www.estanciatravel.com. English/Chilean operator offering horse riding around Puerto Natales. Bilingual guides and well-kept horses. Good ½-day trips to the Cueva del Milodón. Prices start from US$35 for 2 hrs. Multi-day trips only for the well off. Book direct or through agencies in Natales.

Indomita, Bories 206, T061-414525, www.indomitapatagonia.com. Kayak trips ranging from 3 hrs to 12 days.

Punta Alta, Punta Alta, Blanco Encalada 244, T061-411015, www.puntaalta.cl. Runs trips along the same route as 21 de Mayo but in a faster boat and then a zodiac to the Pueblito Serrano at the park's southern edge. There is an option to return to Natales on the same day by minibus along the southern access road thus avoiding park entry fees.

Rutas Patagonia, Blanco Encalada 353, T061-613874, www.rutaspatagonia.com. The concession holders for ice hiking on

the Grey Glacier and kayaking on Lago Grey. Book direct or through an agency.
Sendero Aventura, Hostal Patagonia Adventure, Tomás Rogers 179, T061-415636, sendero_aventura@terra.cl. Trekking in Torres del Paine, cycle and kayak trips to the park, boats to Parque Nacional Bernado O'Higgins, camping equipment and bike hire.
Serrano Aventura, Prat 379, T061-410100, www.serranoaventura.cl. Ice hiking and kayaking on and around Glaciar Serrano.
Skorpios, www.skorpios.cl. 2-3 day cruises up the southern fjords to Puerto Edén and the Pío XI Glacier. No office in Puerto Natales. Book online or through an agency.
Tour Express, Bulnes 769, T061-410734, www.tourexpress.cl. Day trips to Torres del Paine.
Turismo 21 de Mayo, Eberhard 554, T061-411476, www.turismo21demayo.cl. Runs boat trips to Parque Nacional Bernado O'Higgins and Glaciar Serrano and on to the southern entrance of Torres del Paine national park in motor zodiac. This can be combined in a very long day with a trip to the park returning by public bus. US$125 one way including food but excluding park entry.
Tu Travesía, Bulnes 37, T061-415747, www.tutravesia.com. Kayaking and jetski trips around last hope sound and Península Varas.

Transport

Puerto Natales *p345, map p346*

Air

Airline offices Sky Airline, Bulnes 684, T600-6002828, www.skyairline.cl.
Flights arrive at the tiny **Teniente Julio Gallardo Airport**, 7 km north of town.
To **Santiago** via **Puerto Montt**, Sky Airline, 3 weekly in summer.

Bus

There are buses to **Punta Arenas** by **Bus Fernández**, Eberhard 555, T061-411111; **Bus Sur**, Baquedano 668 (poor buses) T061-411325; and **Bus Pacheco**, Baquedano 500 (best buses); several daily, 3 hrs, US$49, book in advance. **Bus Sur** runs to **Coyhaique**, Mon, 24 hrs, US$50. For details of buses to **Torres del Paine**, see page 362.

To Argentina Bus Sur has 3 weekly direct services to **Río Gallegos**, US$18. **Lagoper** (Baquedano y Valdivia), **Turisur**, **Bus Sur** and **Cootra** run hourly services to **Río Turbio**, 2 hrs (depending on customs), US$5. To **El Calafate**, **Bus Sur** and **Bus Zaahj**, 4½ hrs, US$19, daily; **Cootra** also runs a service via Río Turbio, 7 hrs, reserve at least 1 day ahead.

Car hire

Avis, Bulnes 632, T061-410775; **Motor Cars**, Blanco 330, T061-413593, www.motorcars.cl; **Punta Alta**, Blanco 244, T061-410115, www.puntaalta.cl, good reports; **Ultima Esperanza**, Blanco Encalada 206, T061-410461.

Hire agents can arrange permission to drive into Argentina, but this is expensive and takes 24 hrs to arrange.

Ferry

The **Navimag** ferry *Evangelistas* sails every Fri in summer to **Puerto Montt**, less often off season (see page 287); confirmation of reservations is advised.

Shipping offices Navimag, Pedro Montt 262, Local B, Terminal Marítimo, T061-411421, www.navimag.com.

Directory

Puerto Natales *p345, map p346*

Banks Some *casas* offer very poor rates (much better to change money in Punta Arenas). **Banco Santiago**, Bulnes y Blanco Encalada, MasterCard and Visa, ATM; **Enio América**, Blanco Encalada 266, Argentine pesos can be changed here. Others on Bulnes and Prat. **Hospital** Ignacio Carrera Pinto 537, T061-411583. **Internet** Several places in the centre. **Laundry** Servilaundry, Prat 337, express service. **Post office** Eberhard 417, open Mon-Fri 0830-1230, 1430-1745, Sat 0900-1230.

Parque Nacional Torres del Paine

Covering 242,242 ha, 145 km northwest of Puerto Natales, this Chilean national park is a UNESCO Biosphere Reserve and a must-visit thanks to its diverse wildlife and spectacular surroundings. Taking its name from the Tehuelche word Paine, meaning 'blue', the park encompasses some truly stunning scenery, with constantly changing panoramas of peaks, glaciers and icebergs, vividly coloured lakes of turquoise, ultramarine and grey, and quiet green valleys filled with wild flowers. In the centre of the park is one of the most impressive mountain areas on earth, a granite massif from which rise oddly shaped peaks of over 2600 m, known as the Torres (towers) and Cuernos (horns) of Paine.

In total, there are 15 peaks above 2000 m, of which the highest is Cerro Paine Grande (3050 m); few places can compare to its steep forested talus slopes topped by 1000-m vertical shafts of basalt with conical caps. These are the remains of frozen magma in ancient volcanic throats, everything else having been eroded. On the western edge of the park is the enormous Campo de Hielo Sur icefield; four main glaciers – Grey, Dickson, Zapata and Tyndall – branch off it, their meltwater forming a complex of lakes and streams, which lead into Pacific fjords. Two other glaciers, Francés and Los Perros, descend on the western side of the central massif.
▸▸ *For listings, see pages 360-362.*

Ins and outs

Getting there The most practical way to get to Torres del Paine is with one of the many bus or tour companies that leave Puerto Natales daily. If you want to drive, hiring a pickup from Punta Arenas or Puerto Natales is an economical proposition for a group, US$400 for four days. There are two *ripio* roads to the park from Puerto Natales; it takes about 3½ hours along the old road to the administration via Cerro Castillo and Lago Sarmiento. This is the route taken by public buses. The new road links Natales to the south side of the park via the pueblito Serrano. While it is a more direct route (total journey time to the administration is around 1½ hours), the road is narrow, with lots of blind corners and sudden gusts of wind, and can be rough in patches. ▸▸ *See Transport, page 362.*

Getting around Allow a week or 10 days to see the park properly. Most visitors will find that they get around on foot, however, there are minibuses between the **CONAF** administration and Guardería Laguna Amarga, as well as boats across Lago Pehoé. Roads inside the park are narrow and bendy with blind corners. In theory, rangers keep a check on the whereabouts of all visitors; you are required to register and show your passport when entering the park or setting off on any hike.

Tourist information Entrances at Laguna Amarga, Lago Sarmiento and Laguna Azul and the Puente Serrano, foreigners US$25 payable in Chilean pesos only (proceeds are shared between all Chilean national parks). If you are based outside the park and plan on entering and leaving several times explain this when paying your entrance; your ticket will be given a multiple-entry stamp. Otherwise you will have to pay each time you enter the park. **CONAF** ⓘ *administration centre at the northern end of Lago del Toro near the head of the Río Serrano, T061-691931, daily 0830-2000 in summer, 0830-1230, 1400-1830 off season.* Interesting videos and information on request. There are nine ranger stations (*guarderías*) in the park staffed by *guardaparques*, who give advice. The outlying *guarderías* are open October to April only. A basic map is provided with your park entrance ticket; other maps (US$4) are obtainable at

Tourists del Paine

→ The park has become increasingly popular, receiving over 100,000 visitors a year. Despite efforts to manage the ever-growing numbers, the impact of such a large influx is starting to show.
→ Litter has become a problem, especially around *refugios* and camping areas; please take all your rubbish out of the park, including all toilet paper; human waste should be buried.
→ Bring all necessary equipment and your own food from Puerto Natales; don't rely on the shops within the park, which are expensive and have a limited selection.
→ The wind tends to increase in the evening so, if you're camping, it is a good idea to pitch tents by 1600.
→ Rats and mice can be a problem around campsites and *refugios*, so don't leave food in your pack, instead, hang food in a bag on a wire.
→ Forest fires are a serious hazard; you are not allowed to build fires in the park. Bring a stove if camping.

CONAF offices in Punta Arenas or Puerto Natales but most are unreliable. The map produced by **Patagonia Interactiva** has been recommended as more accurate. There are a limited number of lockers availailable for storing luggage at the Hostería Las Torres.

Best time to visit The weather in the park can change in a few minutes. The warmest months are December to March, although it can be wet and windy at this time of year. Most visitors come to the park during January and February, which, if possible, should be avoided due to overcrowding and the unpredictability of the weather. Many parts of the park are now open all year round, although after mid-March, there is less public transport and trucks are irregular. October and November are recommended for wild flowers, and visiting in winter is increasingly popular as there is little wind. Snow may prevent access but well-equipped hikers can do some good walking, when conditions are stable. Rain and snowfall are heavier the further west you go and bad weather sweeps off the Campo de Hielo Sur without warning. For information in Spanish on weather conditions, phone the administration centre.

Wildlife

The park enjoys a microclimate especially favourable to plants and wildlife. Over 200 species of plant have been identified and, although few trees reach great size, several valleys are thickly forested and little light penetrates. There are 105 species of bird in the park, including 18 species of waterfowl and 11 birds of prey. Particularly noteworthy are condors, black-necked swans, kelp geese, ibis, flamingos and austral parakeets. The park is also one of the best places for viewing rheas and guanacos. Other mammals include hares, foxes, skunks, huemules (see pages 19 and 397) and pumas (the last two only very rarely).

Trekking

Torres del Paine has become increasingly popular with foreigners and Chileans alike, receiving well over a hundred thousand visitors a year. Efforts to manage the ever-growing number of visitors have been poor and the impact of such a large influx is showing. Litter is a serious problem, especially around *refugios* and camping areas on the 'W'; please take all your rubbish out of the park and remember that this also includes toilet paper. Most importantly, if you are using your own cooking stove, only cook in designated

Parque Nacional Torres del Paine

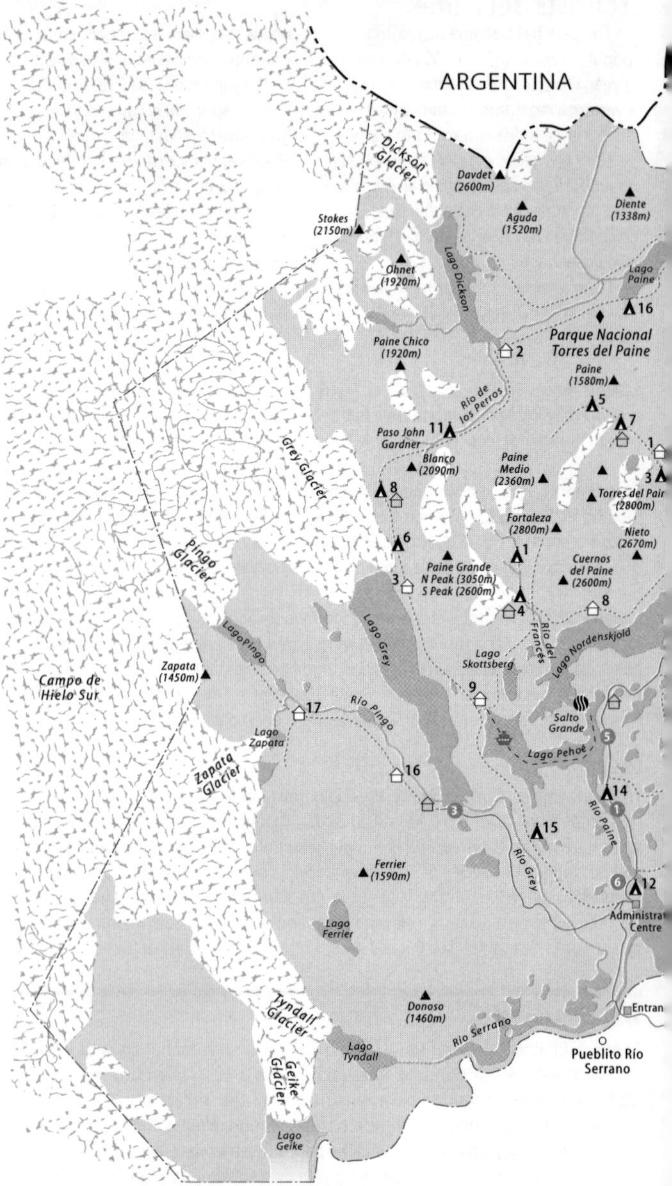
ARGENTINA
Dickson Glacier
Davdet (2600m)
Aguda (1520m)
Diente (1338m)
Stokes (2150m)
Ohnet (1920m)
Lago Dickson
Lago Paine
16
Parque Nacional Torres del Paine
Paine Chico (1920m)
2
Paine (1580m)
5
7
1
3
Río de los Perros
Paso John Gardner
11
Blanco (2090m)
Paine Medio (2360m)
Torres del Pair (2800m)
Grey Glacier
8
Fortaleza (2800m)
Nieto (2670m)
6
1
Cuernos del Paine (2600m)
Pingo Glacier
3
Paine Grande N Peak (3050m) S Peak (2600m)
4
8
Lago Grey
Río del Francés
Lago Nordenskjold
Lago Pingo
Lago Skottsberg
Zapata (1450m)
Campo de Hielo Sur
9
Salto Grande
17
Río Pingo
Lago Zapata
5
Lago Pehoe
Zapata Glacier
16
14
3
1
Río Paine
15
Río Grey
Ferrier (1590m)
6
12
Administra Centre
Lago Ferrier
Entran
Donoso (1460m)
Tyndall Glacier
Río Serrano
Lago Tyndall
Pueblito Río Serrano
Geike Glacier
Lago Geike

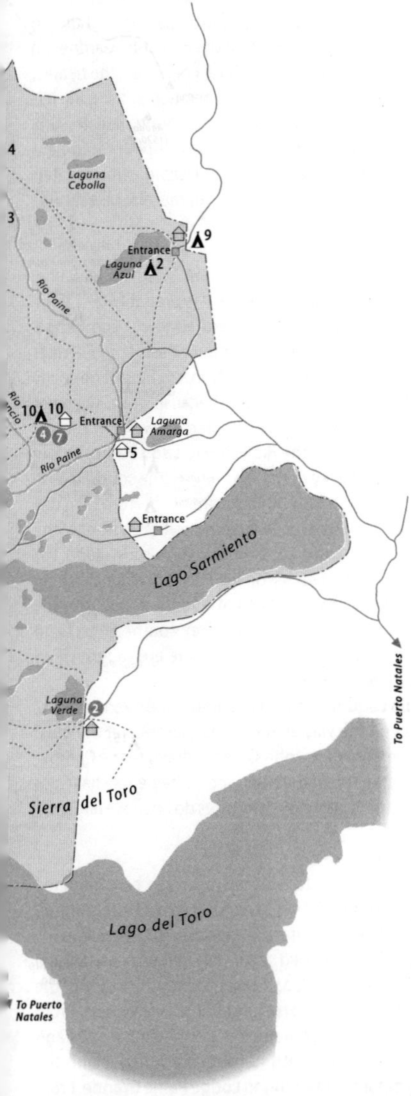

Sleeping
Explora **1**
Hostería Lago Grey **3**
Hostería Las Torres **4**
Hostería Mirador del Payne **2**
Hostería Pehoé **5**
Patagonia Ecocamp **7**
Posada Río Serrano **6**

Refugios
Chileno (Fantástico Sur) **1**
Grey (Vertice) **3**
Lago Dickson (Vertice) **2**
Lago Paine **4**
Laguna Amarga **5**
Las Torres (Fantástico Sur) **10**
Lodge Paine Grande (Vertice) **9**
Los Cuernos (Fantástico Sur) **8**
Pingo **16**
Zapata **17**

Camping
Campamento Británico **1**
Campamento Cairon **16**
Campamento Chileno **3**
Campamento Italiano **4**
Campamento Japonés **5**
Campamento Lago Paine **2**
Campamento Las Carretas **15**
Campamento Las Guardas **6**
Campamento Las Torres **7**
Campamento Paso **8**
Lago Pehoé **14**
Laguna Azul **9**
Las Torres **10**
Los Perros **11**
Río Serrano **12**
Serón **13**

Ranger stations (*guarderías*)

N
4 km
4 miles

areas. The negligence of one backpacker caused around 14,000 ha of forest to burn down in the northeastern sector of the park in 2005.

There are about 250 km of well-marked trails. Visitors must keep to the trails: cross-country trekking is not permitted. It is vital not to underestimate the unpredictability of the weather, nor the arduousness of some stretches on the long hikes. Some paths are confusingly marked and it is all too easy to end up on precipices with glaciers or churning rivers awaiting below; be particularly careful to follow the path at the Paso John Gardner on 'El Circuito' (see below). The only means of rescue are on horseback or by boat; the nearest helicopter is in Punta Arenas and high winds usually prevent its operation in the park. It is essential to be properly equipped against cold, wind and rain. A strong, streamlined, waterproof tent is essential if doing El Circuito (although you can hire camping equipment for a single night at most *refugios*). Also essential are protective clothing, strong waterproof footwear, sunscreen, compass, good sleeping bag and mat. In summer also take shorts.

El Circuito

The park's most emblematic trek is a circuit round the Torres and Cuernos del Paine. Although most people start at the *guardería* at **Laguna Amarga**, it is probably best done anticlockwise starting from **Lodge Paine Grande** at the western edge of Lago Pehoe. Some walkers advise doing the route clockwise so that you climb to Paso John Gardner with the wind behind you. While some people complete the route in less time, it normally takes five days to a week. The circuit is often closed in winter because of snow; major rivers are crossed by footbridges, but these are occasionally washed away. From Laguna Amarga the route is north along the western side of the Río Paine to **Lago Paine**, before turning west to follow the lush pastures of the valley of the Río Paine to the southern end of **Lago Dickson** (it is possible to add a journey to the *campamento* by the Torres on day one of this route); the *refugio* at Lago Dickson lies in a breathtaking position in front of the icy white lake with mountains beyond. From Lago Dickson the path runs along the wooded valley of the **Río de los Perros**, past the Glaciar de los Perros, before climbing through bogs and up scree to **Paso John Gardner** (1241 m, the highest point on the route), then dropping steeply through forest to follow Glaciar Grey southeast to **Lago Grey**, continuing to **Lago Pehoé** and the administration centre. There are superb views en route, particularly from the top of Paso John Gardner.

The longest stretch is between **Refugio Laguna Amarga** and **Refugio Dickson** (30 km, 10 hours in good weather; two campsites on the way at Serón and Cairon), but the most difficult section is the steep, slippery slope from Paso John Gardner down to the **Campamento Paso**; the path is not well signed at the top of the pass, and some people have got dangerously lost. Camping gear must be carried, as many campsites do not have *refugios*.

The W

A more popular alternative to El Circuito, this four- to five-day route can be completed without camping equipment as there is accommodation in *refugios* en route. In summer this route is very crowded and far from being the solitary Patagonian experience many people expect. It combines several of the hikes described separately below. From Refugio Laguna Amarga the first stage runs west via **Hostería Las Torres** and up the valley of the **Río Ascensio** via Refugio Chileno to the base of the **Torres del Paine** (see below). From here return to the Hostería Las Torres and then walk along the northern shore of **Lago Nordenskjold** via Refugio Los Cuernos to Campamento Italiano. From here climb the Valley of the **Río del Francés** (see below) before continuing to **Lodge Paine Grande**. From here you can complete the third part of the 'W' by walking west along the northern shore of **Lago Grey** to Refugio Grey and the Grey Glacier before returning to Lodge Paine Grande and the boat back across the lake to the **Refugio Pudeto**.

To the base of the Torres del Paine

From Refugio Laguna Amarga, this six-hour route follows the road west to **Hostería Las Torres** (1½ hours), before climbing along the western side of the **Río Ascensio** via Refugio Chileno (two hours) and Campamento Chileno to Campamento Las Torres (two hours), close to the base of the **Torres del Paine** (be careful when crossing the suspension bridge over the Río Ascensio near Hostería Las Torres, as the path is poorly marked and you can end up on the wrong side of the ravine). The path alongside the Río Ascensio is well marked, and the Campamento Las Torres is in an attractive wood (no *refugio*). A further 30 minutes up the morraine takes you to a lake at the base of the towers themselves; they seem so close that you almost feel you could touch them. To see the Torres lit by sunrise (spectacular but you must have good weather), it's well worth carrying your camping gear up to Campamento Torres and spending the night. One hour beyond Campamento Torres is Campamento Japonés, another good campsite.

Valley of the Río del Francés

From Lodge Paine Grande this route leads north across undulating country along the western edge of **Lago Skottberg** to Campamento Italiano and then follows the valley of the Río del Francés, which climbs between Cerro Paine Grande and the Ventisquero del Francés (to the west) and the Cuernos del Paine (to the east) to Campamento Británico; the views from the mirador a 30-minute walk above Campamento Británico are superb. Allow 2½ hours from Lodge Paine Grande to Campamento Italiano, 2½ hours further to Campamento Británico.

Treks from Guardería Grey

Guardería Grey, 18 km west by road from the administration centre, is the starting point for a five-hour trek to Lago Pingo. From the *guardería* follow the **Río Pingo**, via Refugio Pingo and Refugio Zapata (four hours), with views south over Ventisquero Zapata (look out for plenty of wildlife and for icebergs in the lake) to reach the lake. **Ventisquero Pingo** can be seen 3 km away over the lake. Two short signposted walks from Guardería Grey have also been suggested: one is a steep climb up the hill behind the ranger post to **Mirador Ferrier**, from where there are fine views; the other is via a suspension bridge across the Río Pingo to the peninsula at the southern end of **Lago Grey**, from where there are good views of the icebergs on the lakes.

To Laguna Verde

From the administration centre follow the road north 2 km, before taking the path east over the **Sierra del Toro** and then along the southern side of Laguna Verde to the Guardería Laguna Verde. Allow four hours. This is one of the easiest walks in the park and may be a good first hike.

To Laguna Azul and Lago Paine

This route runs north from Laguna Amarga to the western tip of **Laguna Azul**, from where it continues across the sheltered **Río Paine** valley past Laguna Cebolla to the Refugio Lago Paine at the western end of the lake. Allow 8½ hours.

Parque Nacional Torres del Paine listings

For Sleeping and Eating price codes and other relevant information, see pages 41-44.

Sleeping

Parque Nacional Torres del Paine

p354, map p356

Accommodation is available on several levels inside the park itself: there are hotels (all are expensive, some feel overpriced); 6 privately run refugios, well equipped, staffed, offering meals and free hot water for tea, soup, etc; 3 free very basic *refugios*, 10 campsites with amenities, some of which have pre-pitched tents available, and 10 basic *campamentos*. All options fill up quickly in peak summer months, Jan-Feb, so plan your trip and book hotels and *refugios* in advance. Paying in US dollars (you must show your passport) means you will save 19% tax, but check prices in pesos as well as they may be cheaper.

As accommodation space is limited within the park and prices are exorbitent, there is an increasing amount of better-value accommodation springing up around the park limits especially to the south at the Pueblito Río Serrano.

Inside the park

LL Explora, Salto Chico on edge of Lago Pehoé, T061-411247, www.explora.com. Ugly building but the most luxurious hotel in the park, offering all-inclusive packages, spectacular views, pool, gym, tours and transfer from Punta Arenas.

LL Hostería Lago Grey, reservations T061-712100, www.turismolagogrey.com. Small rooms on edge of Lago Grey with views of the Grey Glacier, decent restaurant.

LL Hostería Las Torres, T061-360364, reservations T061-363636, www.lastorres.com. Probably the best of the *hosterías* in the park. Recently expanded. Nice rooms, although strangely none has a particularly good view, good restaurant, disabled access, English spoken, horse riding, transport from Laguna Amarga ranger station. There is a limited number of standard rooms which are considerably cheaper.

LL Patagonia Ecocamp, reservations T02-232 9878, www.ecocamp.travel. Luxury all-inclusive tented camp with geodesic design and powered by renewable energy. Offers 4- to 10-day walking and wildlife-watching packages.

LL-AL Hostería Pehoé, 5 km south of Pehoé ranger station, 11 km north of park administration, T061-411390, www.pehoe.com. On an island with spectacular view across the lake to Cerro Paine Grande and Cuernos del Paine, this place does not make the most of its stunning location, run-down, overpriced.

AL Posada Río Serrano, reservations advisable; book through Baqueano Zamora, Baquedano 534B, Puerto Natales, T061-412911, www.baqueanozamora.com. An old estancia, much improved recently, some rooms with bath, some with shared facilities, breakfast extra, near park administration, with expensive but good restaurant and a shop.

Private refugios

2 companies between them run the 6 private *refugios* in the park, providing dormitory space only (bring your own sleeping bag or hire one for US$8). Prices are around US$40 pp with full board about US$35 extra. *Refugios* have kitchen facilities, hot showers and space for camping. Most will hire out tents for around US$12 per night. In high season accommodation and meals in the non-CONAF *refugios* should be booked in advance in Puerto Natales, or by asking staff in 1 *refugio* to radio another. In winter most of the *refugios* close, although 1 or 2 may stay open depending on the weather.

Fantástico Sur refugios, book in agencies in Puerto Natales or direct on T061-710050, www.wcircuit.com. It runs:

Refugio Las Torres, next to the Hostería Las Torres (see above). There are 2 refugios here, the **Torre Norte** and the newer, more comfortable and slightly more expensive Torre Central.

Refugio Los Cuernos, on the northern shore of Lago Nordenskjold, which also has a few small 2-person cabins.

Refugio Chileno, valley of the Río Ascensio at the foot of the Torres.

Vertice refugios, book through agencies in Puerto Natales or via www.verticepatagonia.cl. It runs:

Lodge Paine Grande, new and large on the northwestern edge of Lago Pehoe. In theory the most comfortable of all, but in practice has had teething troubles and several complaints regarding customer service.

Refugio Grey, on the eastern shore of Lago Grey.

Refugio Lago Dickson, on the northern part of the circuit.

Campsites

The wind tends to increase in the evening so it is a good idea to pitch tents early (by 1600). Open fires are not allowed. These restrictions should be observed as forest fires are a serious hazard. Use camping stoves. *Guardaparques* also require campers to have a trowel to bury their waste. Equipment can be hired in Puerto Natales (see Shopping, page 351).

In addition to sites at the private *refugios*, there are the following sites:

Lago Pehoé, www.campingpehoe.com, US$7 pp, hot showers, shop, restaurant.

Laguna Azul, hot showers.

Las Torres, run by **Fantástico Sur**, US$7, hot showers.

Los Perros, run by **Vértice**, with shop and hot showers.

Serón, run by **Fantástico Sur** , US$7, hot showers.

Free camping is permitted in 10 other locations in the park; these sites are known as *campamentos* and have the most basic of facilities.

East of the park

L Hostería Mirador del Payne (Estancia Lazo), reservations at Fagnano 585, Punta Arenas, T061-226930, www.miradordel payne.com. Beautifully situated on Laguna Verde with spectacular views and good fishing, restaurant. Recommended but an inconvenient base for visiting the park; own transport essential, or you can trek to it from within the park.

At the Pueblito Río Serrano

LL Cabañas del Paine, T061-243354, www.cabanasdelpaine.cl. Lodge-style cabins on the edge of the Río Serrano. Decent restaurant.

LL Río Serrano, T061-240528, www.hotel rioserrano.cl. Monstrous construction. The new wing has blocked the view for many neighbours. Decent rooms, many with great views. Poor, canteen-style restaurant. Mixed reports on service. All-inclusive packages available.

LL-L Hostería Lago Toro, www.lagodel toro.com. Decent rooms and rustic cabins with kitchen facilities. Some of the view has been blocked by the expansion of the hotel in front. Friendly staff and reasonable food. Good value given the alternatives.

Campsites

Camping Río Serrano, www.camping chile.com. Peaceful campsite with fine views. With advance notice owners can prepare spit-roasted lamb dinners. Good-value cabin accommodation also available as well as horse riding and transport within the park. Recommended.

Activities and tours

Parque Nacional Torres del Paine
p354, map p356

Before booking a tour check all the details carefully and get a copy in writing, as there have been increasingly mixed reports of the quality of some tours. Many companies who claim to visit the Grey Glacier, for example, only visit Lago Grey (you see the glacier in the distance). After mid-Mar there is less public transport and trucks are irregular.

Agencies in Puerto Natales offer 1-day minibus tours, US$35 plus park entry; these give a good impression of the lower parts of the park, but you spend most of the day in the vehicle. Ideally you need to stay several days, or at least overnight, to appreciate it fully. Recommended agencies include **Comapa, Los Glaciares** and **Tur Express**. Cheaper tours are also available, but both guide and vehicle may not be as good. There are many more operators based in Puerto Natales offering trekking, kayaking, ice-hiking and boat trips (see page 351). The following do not have offices in Puerto Natales.

Cascada Expediciones, T02-232 9878, www.cascada-travel. Based in Santiago and Puerto Natales. 5- to 7-day all-inclusive treks to Torres del Paine, Los Glaciares and Cerro Fitz Roy. Also 4-day wildlife-watching trips.

Experience Chile, T07977-223326, www.experiencechile.org. UK company that arranges itineraries and accommodation.

Hostería Lago Grey, see Sleeping, above, provides excursions by boat to the face of the Grey Glacier at 0900 and 1500 daily, 3½ hrs, US$70 pp. Book direct or through agencies in Puerto Natales.

Transport

Parque Nacional Torres del Paine
p354, map p356

Bus

From early Nov to mid-Apr daily bus services run from Puerto Natales to the park administration via Laguna Amarga, leaving between 0630 and 0800, and again at around 1430, 2½ hrs to Laguna Amarga, 3½ hrs to Refugio Pudeto and 4½ hrs to the administration centre, US$15 one way, US$24 open return (return tickets are not interchangeable between different companies); return departures are usually around 1300 and 1800. The buses also stop at **Refugio Pudeto** to connect with the boats to/from Reufgio Lago Pehoé. Travel between 2 points within the park (eg Pudeto–Laguna Amarga), US$6. Services are provided by **Bus Gómez** , Prat 234, T061-411971; **JB**, Prat 258, T061-410242; and **Trans Vía Paine** , Bulnes 518, T061-413672. In season there are also minibuses from Laguna Amarga to **Hostería Los Torres**, US$46, and from the administration centre to **Hostería Lago Grey** US$15.

At other times, services by travel agencies are subject to demand; arrange your return date with the driver and try to coincide with other groups to keep costs down; **Luis Díaz** has been recommended, about US$17, minimum 3 persons.

In season, there is a direct bus service from Torres del Paine to **El Calafate** (Argentina), with **Chaltén Travel**, US$60. At other times you must either return to Puerto Natales and catch a bus, or get a ride from the park to Villa Cerro Castillo and try to link with the Natales–El Calafate bus schedule.

Boat

A boat service runs across Lago Pehoé from Refuglo Lago Pehoé to Refugio Pudeto, 30 mins, US$19 one-way with one piece of baggage free, US$6 per bag thereafter, tickets available on board. Daily departures from Paine Grande 1000, 1230, 1830; from Pudeto 0930, 1200, 1800. Reduced service off season, no service May-Oct.

Tierra del Fuego

Contents

Footprint features

At a glance

Getting around Local buses will take you to the local attractions, but not much further afield.

Time required 3-4 days will allow you to visit Ushuaia and surrounds; double if you plan to trek on Isla Navarino.

Weather Mar-Nov brings harsh winds and cold temperatures culminating in snow in Jun and Jul.

When not to go The height of winter (May-Jul) can be unpleasantly cold, unless you want to ski.

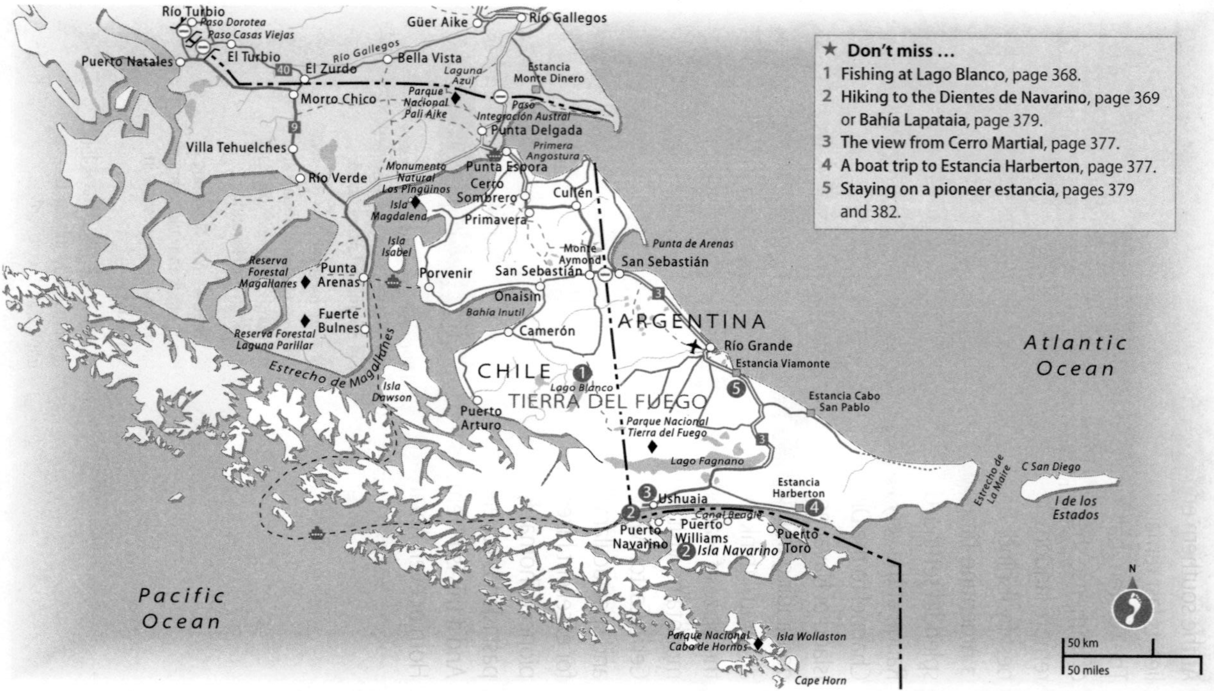
★ Don't miss ...
1 Fishing at Lago Blanco, page 368.
2 Hiking to the Dientes de Navarino, page 369 or Bahía Lapataia, page 379.
3 The view from Cerro Martial, page 377.
4 A boat trip to Estancia Harberton, page 377.
5 Staying on a pioneer estancia, pages 379 and 382.
Río Turbio
Paso Dorotea
Paso Casas Viejas
El Turbio
Puerto Natales
Güer Aike
Río Gallegos
Río Gallegos
Bella Vista
El Zurdo
40
Laguna Azul
Estancia Monte Dinero
Morro Chico
Parque Nacional Pali Aike
Paso Integración Austral
Punta Delgada
9
Villa Tehuelches
Primera Angostura
Monumento Natural Los Pingüinos
Punta Espora
Río Verde
Cerro Sombrero
Cullén
Isla Magdalena
Primavera
Monte Aymond
Punta de Arenas
San Sebastián
Isla Isabel
Reserva Forestal Magallanes
Punta Arenas
Porvenir
San Sebastián
Onaisin
3
Bahía Inutil
Fuerte Bulnes
Reserva Forestal Laguna Parillar
Camerón
ARGENTINA
Río Grande
Estancia Viamonte
Estrecho de Magallanes
CHILE
Lago Blanco
Isla Dawson
TIERRA DEL FUEGO
Puerto Arturo
Estancia Cabo San Pablo
Parque Nacional Tierra del Fuego
3
Lago Fagnano
Estancia Harberton
Ushuaia
Canal Beagle
Puerto Navarino
Puerto Williams
Puerto Toro
Isla Navarino
Estrecho de La Maire
C San Diego
I de los Estados
Atlantic Ocean
Pacific Ocean
Parque Nacional Cabo de Hornos
Isla Wollaston
Cape Horn
N
50 km
50 miles

At the southern end of Patagonia and at the very end of the world lies its last remaining wilderness, the island of Tierra del Fuego. The western half belongs to Chile, an almost untamed expanse of immense sheep farms and virgin mountains, dotted with remote lagoons, including Lago Blanco, which offers the world's best fly fishing. The only settlement is the tiny town of Porvenir.

Argentine Tierra del Fuego boasts a welcoming city with a splendid setting: Ushuaia nestles below the mighty Darwin Range at the very tail of the Andes and looks out over the Beagle Channel to the Dientes de Navarino mountains on the Chilean island of Navarino opposite, with some of Patagonia's most demanding trekking routes. Visit in autumn (March to May), and you'll think the island's name, 'Land of Fire', derives from the blaze of scarlet and orange beech forest covering the mountains; visit in winter (June to August), and the slopes of Cerro Castor (www.cerrocastor.com) offer good powder snow and spectacular views. Head to Parque Nacional Tierra del Fuego for excellent hikes for every ability or be inspired by original pioneer Thomas Bridges to sail forth along the Beagle Channel, past islands covered with basking fur seals, to Estancia Harberton. And if this isn't remote enough, take a boat from Ushuaia to Cape Horn or even Antarctica.

Ins and outs

Getting there

There are frequent flights into Porvenir, Puerto Williams, Río Grande and Ushuaia, but all land access to Tierra del Fuego is via the Chilean side of the island. Transport to the island is heavily booked in summer, especially in January, and even the buses fill quickly, so this part of your journey requires some careful forward planning.

Air There are flights to **Río Grande** and **Ushuaia** in Argentine Tierra del Fuego, from Buenos Aires and El Calafate, and from many other towns in Patagonia with the army airline **LADE**. There are daily flights from Punta Arenas to **Porvenir** in Chilean Tierra del Fuego and five to six a week to **Puerto Williams** on Isla Navarino. Ushuaia is the best entry point for most visitors, with hiking, boat trips and winter sports all nearby; Río Grande provides access to some fantastic estancias, while Porvenir is better for exploration of the remote Chilean plains and lakes.

Ferry There are no road/ferry crossings between the Argentine mainland and Argentine Tierra del Fuego. You have to go through Chilean territory. It's essential to book ahead November to March. From Río Gallegos, Ruta 3 reaches the Chilean border at Monte Aymond (67 km; open summer 24 hours, April-October 0900-2300), passing Laguna Azul. For bus passengers the border crossing is easy, although you have about a 30-minute wait at each border post as luggage is checked and documents are stamped (it's two more hours to Punta Arenas). Hire cars need a document for permission to cross the border.

Some 30 km into Chile is Kamiri Aike, with a dock 16 km east at Punta Delgada for the 20-minute Magellan Strait ferry crossing over the Primera Angostura (First Narrows) to Bahía Azul. At Punta Delgada is **Hostería El Faro** for food and drinks. There are two boats working continuously, *Pionero* and *Fueguino*. On board is a café, lounge, toilets and decks for getting splashed. Buses can wait up to 90 minutes to board. Boats run 0700-0100 (April-October 0830-2345), US$24 per vehicle, foot passengers US$2.80, www.tabsa.cl.

The road is paved to Cerro Sombrero, from where *ripio* roads run southeast to Chilean San Sebastián (130-140 km from ferry, depending on route). Chilean San Sebastián is just a few houses with **Hostería La Frontera** 500 m from the border. It's 15 km east, across the border (24 hours) to Argentine San Sebastián, not much bigger, with a seven-room ACA *hostería* (**C**), T02964-425542; service station open 0700-2300. From here the road is paved to Río Grande (see below) and Ushuaia.

The second main ferry crossing is Punta Arenas–Porvenir. The ferry dock is 5 km north of Punta Arenas centre, at Tres Puentes. The ferry crosses to Bahía Chilota, 5 km west of Porvenir, Tuesday-Sunday, two hours 20 minutes, US$54 per vehicle (reservations essential), bike US$12, foot passengers US$8.65. From Porvenir a 234-km *ripio* road runs east to Río Grande (six hours, no public transport) via San Sebastián.

There is also a weekly ferry service from Punta Arenas–Puerto Williams on Isla Navarino, 36 hours, no creature comforts, US$175 for a reclining seat, US$210 for a bunk, meals included, while **Crucero Australis** luxury cruises run between Punta Arenas and Ushuaia, stopping at Navarino. Fruit and meat may not be taken between Argentina and Chile.

Note Transportadora Austral Broom, Bulnes 05075, Punta Arenas, T061-218100 (T061-580089 in Porvenir),www.tabsa.cl, publishes timetables a month in advance. These are dependent on tides and subject to change; check in advance. Crossings can be rough and cold; watch for dolphins. Reservations are essential especially in summer (at least 24 hours in advance for cars); obtainable from Transbordadora Austral Broom.

Making the most of Tierra del Fuego

→ Avoid visiting in January. Beds and buses are full, and Tierra del Fuego is not at its most tranquil. March and April are blissful.

→ To save time and avoid disappointment, arrange hiking trips before you arrive, with a reputable adventure tourism company, like **Compañía de Guías de Patagonia** or **Canal**. See page 387.

→ Tolhuin has a fabulous bakery that's open 24 hours. It's worth a detour to see the tranquil lakeside, too. See page 375.

→ Agency tours will only allow you two hours at Estancia Harberton. For a fuller experience of pioneer life and the chance to walk around the beautiful coastline, hire a car and drive. See page 377.

→ Boat trips from Ushuaia along the Beagle Channel are much more pleasant on board the charming old *Barracuda* than on the modern catamarans, and the commentary is better too. See page 384.

→ Parque Nacional Tierra del Fuego is best in the late afternoon when the tour buses have gone, particularly Lago Roca and Bahía Lapataia. But make sure you allow enough daylight to get back! See page 378.

Getting around

The only legal crossing between the Chilean and Argentine parts of Tierra del Fuego is 142 km east of Porvenir. There are two settlements called **San Sebastián**, one on each side of the border, but they are 14 km apart and taxis are not allowed to cross the frontier, which means you must travel on one of the scheduled buses or with your own transport. **Chilean immigration and customs** ⓘ *San Sebastián (Chile), 0800-2200.* **Argentine immigration and customs** ⓘ *San Sebastián (Argentina), 24 hrs daily.* From Argentine San Sebastián, Route 3 heads east to Río Grande and then south to Ushuaia. This is the main route through the Argentine half of the island and is surfaced apart from a 50-km section between Ushuaia and Tolhuin. Other roads on Tierra del Fuego are narrow and gravelled. Fuel is available in Porvenir, Cerro Sombrero and Camerón (Chile) and Río Grande, Ushuaia and San Sebastián (Argentina). There are scheduled buses linking Punta Arenas with Río Grande and Ushuaia. However, there is no guaranteed public transport along the *ripio* roads either south of Camerón or east of Ushuaia to Harberton and Estancia Moat on the south coast.

Tourist information

Information on Chilean Tierra del Fuego is best sought from tour operators in Punta Arenas (see page 341) or from **Sernatur** (www.sernatur.com), although there is a small information desk in Porvenir's museum. The tourist office in Ushuaia (see page 375) is a good source for information on the Argentine side of the island. See also www.tierradelfuego.org.ar.

Best time to visit

Summer (December to February) is best for trekking, when daytime temperatures hover around 15°C. Try to avoid Ushuaia in January, however, when it is swamped with tourists. There are very stiff winds at this time of year, particularly further north, around Río Grande, where they can gust up to 200 kph. Ushuaia is at its most beautiful in autumn (March to May), when the dense forests turn rich red and yellow, and there are many bright clear days. The ski season is from mid-June to October, when temperatures hover around zero, but the wind drops.

Chilean Tierra del Fuego

Chilean Tierra del Fuego forms part of Región XII (Magallanes), of which the capital is Punta Arenas. It is a wild spot, less populated than the Argentine side of the island, and is characterized by a mixture of thick forests, wide rolling pampas and imposing glaciers. There are peaks of well over 2000 m and numerous lakes and rivers, rich in trout and salmon. To the south of Tierra del Fuego, across the Beagle Channel, Isla Navarino is even more remote and inaccessible. » *For listings, see pages 371-373.*

Ins and outs

Visitors to Chilean Tierra del Fuego arrive either by air to Porvenir or by ferry to Porvenir or Punta Espora. The ferry is recommended for occasional sightings of porpoises following the ships, though arriving by air gives a memorable view of the island. From the Porvenir ferry, minivans (US$2) and taxis (US$5.50) run to the town centre, from where local buses depart for Camerón and Cerro Sombrero two to three times a week. There is no local bus service to or from Punta Espora. Isla Navarino can be reached by air or ferry from Punta Arenas, or by zodiac from Ushuaia accross the straits.

Porvenir → *Colour map 3, A4.*

Chilean Tierra del Fuego has a population of 7500, most of whom live in Porvenir. Founded in 1894 as a port serving the sheep estancias of the island, this is the only town on the Chilean side of the island. It is quiet and pleasant, with painted zinc houses and tall trees lining the main avenue. Many inhabitants are descended from Croatian goldminers who came to seek their fortune during the gold boom of the 1890s; the signpost at the port marks the distance to Croatia. There is a small but interesting museum, **Museo Fernando Cordero Rusque** ⓘ *Zavattaro 402, on the plaza, T061-580098, US$1*, with archaeological and photographic displays on the Selk'nam (Onas) and a good collection of Selk'nam ceremonial masks as well as good displays on natural history and the early gold diggers and sheep farmers. A fair bit of information is in English.

Although it's small and not geared up for tourism, Porvenir is the base for exploring the wonderful virgin territory of western Tierra del Fuego and for fly fishing for brown trout, sea run brook trout and steelheads in the island's richly stocked lakes and rivers.

Beyond Porvenir

About 90 km east of Porvenir, roads head north to San Sebastián and south to **Camerón**. This large farm settlement is the only other community of any size on the Chilean part of the island and lies 149 km southeast of Porvenir on the opposite shore of windswept Bahía Inútil. Nearing Camerón, the southern mountains loom ahead and the road passes secluded canyons and bays, interspersed with a few farms.

From Camerón a road runs southeast for a further 40 km before splitting north to San Sebastián and south to **Sección Río Grande** (7 km from the junction) – there is very little traffic here. The road south climbs into the hills, through woods where guanacos hoot and run off into glades and the banks are covered with red and purple moss. The north shores of **Lago Blanco** can be reached by cutting through the woods from Sección Río Grande, with superb views of the mountains surrounding the lake and the snows in the south. In the centre of the lake is Isla Victoria, which has accommodation (see Sleeping below). The lake area can be very cold, even in mid-summer, when biting winds sweep in from the south, so wrap up warmly.

Isla Navarino and Cape Horn » pp371-373.

Situated on the southern shore of the Beagle Channel, Isla Navarino is unspoilt and beautiful, and encompasses great geographical diversity: the **Dientes de Navarino** range has peaks over 1000 m, covered with southern beech forest up to 500 m, while to the south stretch great plains covered with peat bogs and lagoons abundant in flora. Wildlife is prolific: guanacos and condors can be seen inland, as well as large numbers of beavers, which were introduced to the island and have done a lot of damage. The island was the centre of the indigenous Yámana culture, and has 500 archaeological sites, dating back 3000 years. The flight from Punta Arenas is beautiful, with superb views of Tierra del Fuego, the Cordillera Darwin and the islands stretching south to Cape Horn.

Puerto Williams → *Colour map 3, C4.*

The only settlement of any size on the island is Puerto Williams, a Chilean naval base situated about 50 km east of Ushuaia (Argentina). Puerto Williams is the southernmost permanently inhabited town in the world; Puerto Toro, 50 km east-south-east, is the world's southernmost permanently inhabited settlement. Due to the long-running border dispute with Argentina here, Puerto Williams is controlled by the Chilean Navy. Outside the naval headquarters, you can see the bow section of the *Yelcho*, the tug chartered by Shackleton to rescue men stranded on Elephant Island (see box, page 335).

Museo Martín Gusinde ⓘ *Mon-Thu 1000-1300, 1500-1800, Sat and Sun, US$1*, known as the Museo del Fin del Mundo ('End of the World Museum') is full of information about vanished indigenous tribes, local wildlife and famous voyages by Charles Darwin and Fitzroy of the *Beagle*. A visit is highly recommended. There is a **tourist office** ⓘ *Municipalidad de Cabos de Hornos, Presidente Ibáñez 130, T061-621011, closed in winter*, near the museum, which can provide maps and information on hiking. A kilometre west of the town is the yacht club (one of Puerto Williams' two nightspots), whose wharf is made from a sunken 1930s Chilean warship. The last of the Yámana people live at **Villa Ukika**, 2 km east, where there are beaver dams and waterfalls.

Exploring the island

For superb views, climb **Cerro Bandera**, which is reached by a path from the dam 4 km west of the town (a steep three- to four-hour round trip). A challenging 53-km circuit of the **Dientes de Navarino** begins here. This is the southernmost trail in the world and passes through impressive mountain landscapes, frozen lagoons and snowy peaks. It takes four to five days and is possible only between December and March; ask at the Puerto Williams tourist office for further information. At the southernmost point of the walk, there are views of Cape Horn in clear weather, but conditions change quickly and it can snow on the hills, even in high summer, so take warm clothes.

Beyond Cerro Bandera, a road leads 56 km west of Puerto Williams towards Puerto Navarino. There is little or no traffic on this route and it is very beautiful, with forests of *lengas* stretching right down to the water's edge. At **Mejillones**, 32 km from Puerto Williams, is a graveyard and memorial to the Yámana people. At **Puerto Navarino** there are a handful of marines and an abandoned police post, where you may be allowed to sleep. There are beautiful views across to Ushuaia and west to icebound Hoste Island and the Darwin Massif. A path continues to a cliff above the Murray Narrows: blue, tranquil and utterly calm.

The people of Tierra del Fuego

Human habitation on Tierra del Fuego dates back some 10,000 years; four indigenous groups inhabited the island until the early 20th century. The most numerous, the **Ona** (also known as the Selk'nam), were hunter-gatherers in the north, living mainly on guanaco and several species of rodents. The south eastern corner of the island was inhabited by hunter-gatherers known as the Haus or **Hausch**, while the Yaganes or **Yámanas** lived along the Beagle Channel and on the islands further south. A seafaring people who survived mainly on seafood, fish and seabirds, they developed strong upper bodies for rowing long distances. The fourth group, the **Alacalufe**, lived in the west of Tierra del Fuego as well as on the Chonos Archipelago, surviving by fishing and hunting seals.

The first Europeans to visit the island came with the Portuguese navigator **Fernão Magalhães** (Magellan), who, in 1520, sailed through the channel that would bear his name. He saw fires lit on shore and so named the island 'Tierra del Fuego' ('the land of fire'). However, numerous maritime disasters meant that the indigenous population were left undisturbed for three centuries.

Robert Fitzroy and Charles Darwin visited in 1832 and 1833 and several disastrous attempts to convert the indigenous groups followed but it wasn't until 1869 that the first successful mission was established. In 1884, the **Reverend Thomas Bridges** (see page 374) founded a mission at Ushuaia and soon many Yámana had settled nearby. Bridges learnt the Yámana language and compiled a Yámana-English dictionary to ease the conversion process. Darwin had written that the Yámana language "barely deserves to be called articulate" but, in fact, it turned out to have an extraordinarily rich vocabulary: the dictionary had 32,000 words and was not complete at the time of Bridges' death in 1898.

The work of the missionaries was disturbed by the discovery of gold in 1887 and the growth of sheep farming. The gold rush began when Julio Popper, a German settler, founded the successful El Paramó mine at San Sebastián. He was followed by treasure seekers from North America and Europe, including many Croatians, whose descendents still live on the island. Sheep farms were created as the Argentine and Chilean governments attempted to populate the island following a border settlement in 1883. The Ona hunted the 'white guanacos' and the colonists responded by offering two sheep for each Ona that was killed (proof was provided by a pair of Ona ears). The indigenous groups were further ravaged by epidemics of European diseases. Despite the efforts of Salesian missionaries in the early 20th century, the Ona went into terminal decline; the last Ona died in 1999. The Hausch have also died out. One old Yámana lady survives near Puerto Williams and there is a handful of Alacalufe at Puerto Edén, in the Chonos Archipelago.

Cape Horn → *Colour map 3, C5.*

It is possible to catch a boat south from Isla Navarino to Cape Horn (the most southerly piece of land on earth apart from Antarctica). There is one pebbly beach on the north side of the island; boats anchor in the bay and passengers are taken ashore by motorized dinghy. A rotting stairway climbs the cliff above the beach, up to the building where three marines run the naval post. A path leads from here to the impressive monument of an albatross overlooking the wild, churning waters of the Drake Passage below. ▸▸ *See Transport, page 373.*

Chilean Tierra del Fuego listings

For Sleeping and Eating price codes and other relevant information, see pages 41-44.

Sleeping

Porvenir *p368*

B-C España, Croacia 698, T061-580160. **C** singles. The largest hotel in town, decent standard, recently refitted and with spacious rooms. Slightly aloof service.

B-C Rosas, Philippi 296, T061-580088, hotelrosas@chile.com. With bath, hot water, heating, restaurant and bar, internet, laundry facilities.

C Hostel Kawi, Pedro Silva 144, T061-581638, hostalkawi@yahoo.com. **D** singles. A comfor table hostal, with rooms for 3, all with bath, and offering fly-fishing trips on the island.

E Residencial Dalmacia, Croacia 469, T061-580008, angelacardenas1945@hotmail.com. **F-G** singles. Basic residencial.

Beyond Porvenir *p368*

If you get stuck in the wilds, it is usually possible to camp in a barn at an estancia.

B-E Hostería de la Frontera, San Sebastián, T061-696004, escabini@tie.cl. Rooms with bath and a decent restaurant. Avoid the more basic accommodation in an annexe.

C-F Hostería Tunkelen, Prat 101, Cerro Sombrero, 46 km south of Primera Angostura, T061-212757, hosteria_tunkelen@hotmail.com. Rooms and dorms. Recommended.

D Posada Las Flores, Km 127 on the Porvenir–San Sebastián road. Reservations via **Hostal de la Patagonia** in Punta Arenas.

E Pensión del Señor Alarcón, Cerro Sombrero, 46 km south of Primera Angostura. Good, friendly.

E Refugio Lago Blanco, Lago Blanco, T061-241197. The only accommodation on the lake.

Puerto Williams *p369*

LL Lodge Lakutaia, on the edge of Lauta bay, 2 km out of town, T061-621733, www.lakutaia.cl. The only upmarket place on the island. Simple, attractive rooms. Lovely views from spacious common areas. Splendid walks in the area. A range of activities offered.

A Bella Vista Hostal, Teniente Muñoz 118, T061-621010, www.victory-cruises.com/bella_vista_hostal.html. **B-C** singles. Some rooms with views. English spoken Sailing trips offered. Also camping, US$10.

B Hostal Yagan, Piloto Pardo 260, T061-621334, hostalyagan@hotmail.com. **D** singles. Good meals available. Clean and comfortable, friendly, tours offered.

B-C Hostal Akainij, Austral 22, T061-621173, www.turismoakainij.cl. Smallish but comfortable rooms with bath. Very friendly hosts. Excellent, filling meals served. Kitchen facilities. Basic English spoken. Tours offered. Recommended.

B-C Hostal Coirón, Maragaño 168, T061-621 227, hostalcoiron@hotmail.com. Some rooms with bath, kitchen and laundry facilities, also organizes sailing trips, treks and other activities.

C Hostal Camblor, Capedeville 41, T061-621 033, hostalcamblor@hotmail.com. Full board available. Gets very booked up. Good value.

C Hostal Pusaki, Piloto Pardo 222, T061-621116, pattypusaky@yahoo.es. **D-E** singles. Friendly, good meals served.

C Residencial Onashaga, Uspashun 15, T061-621564, run by Señor Ortiz – everyone knows him. Accommodation is basic, but the welcome is warm. Good meals, helpful, full board available.

Eating

Porvenir *p368*

₶ Club Croata, Senoret y Philippi. On waterfront, good food, lively.

₶-₸ El Chispa, Señoret 202, T061-580 054. Seafood and other hearty home-cooked fare. Friendly service. Good value.

Puerto Williams *p369*

There are several grocery stores; prices are high because of the remoteness. Most hostels will serve food.

Activities and tours

Porvenir *p368*

For adventure tourism and trekking, tour operators in Punta Arenas are the best bet: **Turismo Cordillera de Darwin**, Señoret 511, T061-580450, jebr_darwin@hotmail.com. Day tours of the area around Porvenir.

Puerto Williams *p369*

Sea, Ice and Mountains, Ricardo Maragaño 168, T061-621150, www.simltd.com. Sailing trips, trekking tours and many other adventure activities, including kayaking and wildlife spotting.

Shila, O'Higgins 322 (hut at entrance to Centro Comercial), T061-621366, www.turismoshila.com. Luis Tiznado Gonzáles is an adventure guide, trekking and fishing, equipment hire: bike US$10 per day, tent US$4-8, sleeping bag US$10, stove US$10, and more. Lots of trekking information, US$1.60 for photocopied maps.

Turismo Akainij, see Sleeping, above. Adventure expeditions and transfers.

Sailing

Captain Ben Garrett, www.victory-cruises.com, offers recommended adventure sailing in his schooner *Victory* in Dec and Jan, including special trips to Ushuaia, cruises in the canals and voyages to Cape Horn, the glaciers, Puerto Montt and Antarctica.

Crucero Australis, www.australis.com, calls at Wulaia Bay on the west side of Isla Navarino after visiting Cape Horn; you can disembark to visit the museum and take a short trek.

Transport

Porvenir *p368*

Air

Aerovías DAP, Señoret s/n, Porvenir, T061-580089, www.aeroviasdap.cl, flies from **Punta Arenas** (weather and bookings permitting), 2-3 times Mon-Sat, 15 mins, US$35 one way. Heavily booked so make sure you have your return reservation confirmed.

Bus

Buses from Punta Arenas to Ushuaia don't take on passengers in Chilean Tierra del Fuego. Local buses run to **Camerón** from Manuel Señoret, in theory Tue and Fri 1600, 2 hrs, return at 2030, US$3. There is also a service to **Cerro Sombrero**, leaving from opposite the Municipalidad, Mon, Wed, Fri 0800, 1¾ hrs, return service at 1700 or 1800, US$4.50.

Ferry

See also Ins and outs, page 368.

The *Melinka* sails from **Tres Puentes** (5 km north of Punta Arenas; catch bus A or E from Av Magallanes or *colectivo* 15, US$1; taxi US$3) to **Bahía Chilota**, 5 km west of Porvenir, Tue-Sun 0900 with an extra afternoon sailing Tue-Thu in season, 2½ hrs, pedestrians US$9, bicycles US$12, cars US$54. The boat returns from Porvenir in the afternoon Tue-Sun.

The ferry service from **Punta Delgada** on the mainland to **Punta Espora**, 80 km north of Porvenir, departs usually every 40 mins 0830-2300 (schedules vary with the tides) and takes just 15 mins, pedestrians US$4, cars US$25. This is the main route for buses and trucks between Ushuaia and mainland Argentina. Before 1000 most space is taken by trucks.

Puerto Williams *p369*

Air

Aerovías DAP, Centro Comercial s/n, T061-621051, www.aeroviasdap.cl, flies 20-seater Cessna aircraft from Punta Arenas Mon-Sat, departure time varies, 1¼ hrs, US$96 one way. Book well in advance; there are long waiting lists. Luggage allowance 10 kg (US$2 per kg extra). DAP or **Aeropetrel** will charter a plane from Puerto Williams to Cape Horn (US$2600 for 8-10 people).

Ferry

The following all depart from **Punta Arenas**: Austral Broom ferry Cruz Australis, www.tabsa.cl, once a week, 36 hrs, US$175 for a reclining seat, US$210 for a bunk, meals included; Navarino (contact Carlos Aguilera,

21 de Mayo 1460, Punta Arenas, T061-228 066), 3rd week of every month, 12 passengers, US$210 one way. Some cruises to **Ushuaia** also stop at Puerto Williams. There are also irregular services by small operators in yachts, zodiacs and small catamarans from Ushuaia to Puerto Williams, US$80-150 pp.

Cape Horn *p370*
Crucero Australis cruises from **Ushuaia** stop at Cape Horn, see page 233). In addition, the naval vessel *PSG Micalvi*, which sails once every 3 months from Punta Arenas via Puerto Williams, may take passengers to Cape Horn for US$300 (letters of recommendation required). Navy and port authorities in Puerto Williams may deny any knowledge, but everyone else knows when a boat is due; ask at the **Armada** in Punta Arenas (see page 343). Otherwise ask at the yacht club about hitching a ride to Cape Horn.

Directory

Porvenir *p368*
Banks There's a bank on the plaza, ATM accepts MasterCard but not Visa. Currency exchange available at Estrella del Sur, Santos Mardones and at Señoret 346. Poor rates.

Puerto Williams *p369*
Post office Closes 1900. **Telephone** CTC, Mon-Sat 0930-2230, Sun 1000-1300, 1600-2200.

Argentine Tierra del Fuego

Argentine Tierra del Fuego belongs to the province of Tierra del Fuego, Antártida y Las Islas del Atlántico Sur, the capital of which is the welcoming tourist centre Ushuaia. The population of the Argentine sector is around 85,000, most of whom live in the two towns of Río Grande and Ushuaia. Both bigger and more developed than the Chilean side of the island, it provides good territory for guided explorations of the wilderness. ▸▸ *For listings, see pages 379-388.*

Ins and outs

Getting there The main point of entry is **Aeropuerto Internacional Malvinas Argentinas** ⓘ *4 km from Ushuaia, on a peninsula in the Beagle Channel, T02901-423970, www.tierradelfuego.org.ar/aeropuerto/*, which receives daily **flights** from Buenos Aires (four hours), frequent flights from El Calafate and Punta Arenas, as well as weekly flights with army airline **LADE** from many towns in Patagonia. This is by far the easiest way to get to the Argentine side of the island and the view from the plane as you land over jagged mountains onto the quiet channel below is magical. From the airport, a taxi to the centre of town costs US$3. There is another airport at Río Grande with flights to/from Buenos Aires and Ushuaia. **Buses** from mainland Argentina and from Punta Arenas in Chile travel to Río Grande and Ushuaia via Punta Delgada and San Sebastián. There are also buses from Porvenir to Río Grande.

Getting around Buses from Río Grande and Ushuaia are frequent, but are heavily booked in summer. There are abundant tours from Ushuaia to suit most needs, and some great hiking adventures on offer, too. If you fly in and out of Ushuaia, you can get around fine by bus and boat for the national park and visits along the Beagle Channel, including Harberton. However, if you want to visit Lago Fagnano or more remote estancias or hike in places not visited by the many adventure tourism companies, you could consider hiring a car. ▸▸ *See Transport, page 387.*

Building bridges

The story of the first successful missionary to Tierra del Fuego, Thomas Bridges, is one of the most stirring in the whole history of pioneers in Argentina. An orphan from Bristol, Thomas Bridges was so called because he was found as a child under a bridge with a letter 'T' on his clothing. He was adopted by a reverand and, as a young man, was taken to start a Christian mission in wild, uncharted Tierra del Fuego where no white man had survived.

Until his death in 1898, Bridges lived near the Beagle Channel, first creating the settlement of Ushuaia and then Harberton. He devoted his life to working with the Yámanas (Yaghanes) and gave up converting them in favour of compiling a dictionary of their language, and protecting them from persecution. Thomas's son **Lucas** (1874-1949), one of six children, spent his early life among the Yámanas and Onas, living and hunting as one of them, learning their language, and even, almost fatally, becoming involved in their blood feuds and magic rituals. Lucas became both defender and protector of the indigenous people whose culture he loved, creating a haven for them at Harberton and Estancia Viamonte (see page 380), at a time when most sheep farmers were more interested in shooting them. His compelling memoirs, *Uttermost Part of the Earth* (1947) trace the tragic fate of the native population with whom he grew up; it is now out of print, but available from www.abebooks.co.uk.

Río Grande → *Colour map 3, B5.*

Río Grande grew rapidly in the oil boom of the 1970s and suffered when tax benefits were withdrawn in recent years, leading to increasing unemployment and emigration and leaving a rather sad, windy town today. It is a sprawling modern coastal town, and the centre for a rural sheep-farming community. The people are friendly but there's little culture, and you're most likely to visit in order to change buses. There are a couple of good places to stay, however, and two small museums: the **Museo de Ciencias Naturales e Historia** ⓘ *El Cano 225, Tue-Fri 0900-1700, Sat and Sun 1500-2000*, and the **Museo de la Ciudad** ⓘ *Alberdi 555, T02964-430414, Tue-Fri 1000-1700*, which recounts the city's history through sheep, missions, pioneers and oil. In the blue-roofed hut on the plaza is the small but helpful **tourist office** ⓘ *Rosales 350, T02964-431324, www.tierradelfuego.org.ar, Mon-Fri 0900-2100, Sat 1000-1700.*

The Salesian mission **La Candelaria** ⓘ *11 km north on Route 3, T02964-421642, Mon-Sat 1000-1230, 1500-1900, Sun 1500-1900, US$2, afternoon tea US$3*, was founded in 1893 by José Fagnano to try to protect the Ona people from gold prospectors and sheep farmers. It now houses displays of natural history and indigenous artefacts, with strawberry plantations, piglets and an aviary.

South of Río Grande

A fan of roads spreads out south and west from Río Grande to numerous estancias; these are unpaved and best attempted in a 4WD vehicle. **Estancia Viamonte**, on the coast 40 km south, is a working sheep farm with a fascinating history. Here, Lucas Bridges, son of Tierra del Fuego's first settler, built a home to protect the large tribe of indigenous Onas, who were fast dying out. The estancia is still inhabited by his descendants, who can take you riding and to see the life of the farm. Accommodation is also available. It's highly recommended for an insight into Fuegian life and a cosy place to read *Uttermost Part of the Earth*, see box, above.

The paved road south, Ruta 3, continues across wonderfully open land, more forested than the expanses of Patagonian steppe further north, and increasingly hilly as you near Ushuaia. After around 160 km, you could turn left along a track to the coast, to find **Estancia Cabo San Pablo**, 120 km from Río Grande. This simple working estancia is in a beautiful position, surrounded by native woodland for walking and riding, birdwatching and fishing. It's open all year, but reserve well in advance.

Route 3 then climbs high above **Lago Fagnano**, a large expanse of water at the heart of Tierra del Fuego, which straddles the border with Chile. In the small settlement of **Tolhuin** there's a YPF service station just off the main road and a tiny, friendly **tourist office**. Drive into the village to visit the famous bakery **La Unión**, where you can buy all kinds of bread, great *empanadas* and delicious fresh *facturas* (pastries), before heading down to the tranquil lake shore, There's a quiet stretch of beach and a couple of good places to stay.

Further along Route 3, about 50 km from Ushuaia, a road to the right swoops down to **Lago Escondido**, a long, fjord-like lake with steep green mountains descending into the water on all sides. There are *cabañas* and a couple of *hosterías*, one with a good restaurant for lunch.

Ushuaia » *pp379-388. Colour map 3, C4.*

Ushuaia's setting is spectacular. Its brightly coloured houses look like toys against the dramatic backdrop of snow-covered Cerro Martial to the north. Opposite are the forbidding peaks of Isla Navarino, and between flows the green Beagle Channel. Sailing these waters, it is easy to imagine what it was like when Darwin arrived here in 1832 and when the Bridges family first settled here in 1871. Although the town has expanded in recent years, sprawling untidily along the coast, Ushuaia still retains the feel of a pioneer town, isolated and expectant. There are lots of places to stay (which fill up entirely in January) a fine museum and some great fish restaurants. There is dramatic landscape to be explored in all directions, with good treks in the Parque Nacional Tierra del Fuego just to the west of the city and more adventurous expeditions into the wild heart of the island, trekking, climbing or riding. There's splendid cross-country skiing nearby in winter, as well as downhill skiing at **Cerro Castor** (see page 386). And to the east, along a beautiful stretch of coastline is the historic Estancia Harberton (see below), which you can reach by a boat trip along the Beagle Channel.

Tourist information ⓘ *San Martín 674, corner with Fadul, T/F02901-432000, www.tierradelfuego.org.ar, Mon-Fri 0800-2200, Sat, Sun and holidays 0900-2000.* Quite the best tourist office in Argentina. The friendly and helpful staff speak several languages and will find you somewhere to stay, even in the busiest period. They also have a great series of leaflets in English, French, German and Dutch about all the things to see and do, including bus and boat times. There's also an office at the **airport** ⓘ *T02901-423970.* **Tierra del Fuego National Park Office** ⓘ *San Martín 1395, T02901-421315*, has a useful little map of the park.

Background

Missionary Thomas Bridges first established a mission here in 1884 and the fledgling settlement soon attracted pioneers in search of gold. A penal colony, on nearby Staten Island, moved to the town in 1902, and Croatian and Spanish immigrants, together with shipwreck survivors, began to settle here. However, the town remained isolated until planes arrived in 1935. When the prison closed it was replaced by a naval base and, in the 1970s, a wave of new inhabitants arrived, many of them from Buenos Aires, attracted by reduced income taxes and cheap car prices. Now the city is capital of Argentina's most southerly province and, although fishing still plays a key role in the local economy, Ushuaia has become an important tourist centre as the departure point for voyages to Antarctica.

Sights

It's easy to walk around the town in a morning, since all its sights are close together. You'll find banks, restaurants, hotels and shops along calle San Martín, which runs parallel to the shore, a block north of the coast road, Maipú. Boat trips leave from the **Muelle Turístico** (tourist pier) by a small plaza, 25 de Mayo, on the seafront. There are several museums worth looking at if bad weather forces you indoors. The most fascinating is **Museo del Fin del Mundo** ⓘ *on the seafront at Maipú and Rivadavia, T02901-421863, www.tierradelfuego.org.ar/museo, Nov-Apr daily 0900-1900, May-Oct Mon-Sat 1200-1900, US$4*, in the 1912 bank building, which tells the history of the town through a small collection of carefully chosen exhibits on the indigenous groups, missionaries, pioneers and shipwrecks. There's also a stuffed collection of Tierra del Fuego's birdlife and an extensive reference library. Further east, the old prison, Presidio, at the Naval Base, houses the **Museo Marítimo** ⓘ *Yaganes and Gob Paz, www.museomaritimo.com, daily 1000-2000, US$8*, which has models and artefacts from seafaring days, and, in the cells, the **Museo Penitenciario**, which details the history of the prison. **Museo Yámana** ⓘ *Rivadavia 56, T02901-422874, www.tierradelfuego.org.ar/mundoyamana, daily 1000-2000 (winter 1200-1900), US$2*, has interesting scale models of everyday indigenous life.

Sleeping
Albergue Cruz del Sur **1**
Antárctica **2**
B&B Nahuel **5**
Canal Beagle **7**
Cap Polonio **8**
Familia Velásquez **11**
Freestyle **4**
Galeazzi-Basily **12**
Hostal Malvinas **13**
Hostería Posada Fin del Mundo **14**
La Casa de Tere **6**
Lennox **16**
Los Troncos **17**
Mil810 **9**
Posada del Duende **10**
Tzion **15**
Yakush **3**

Eating
137 Pizzas & Pastas **12**
Bodegón Fueguino **9**
Café Bar Banana **6**
Café de la Esquina **1**
Café Tante Sara **2**
El Turco **4**

200 metres
200 yards

For exhilarating views along the Beagle Channel and to Isla Navarinho beyond, don't miss a trip on the chair lift up to **Cerro Martial** ⓘ *daily 1000-1800 (winter 1030-1630), US$8.50*, about 7 km behind the town. From the top of the lift, you can walk for 90 minutes through *lenga* forest to Glaciar Martial, where there's limited skiing in winter. There's also a splendid tea shop, *refugio* and *cabañas* at the Cerro. Several companies run minibuses from the corner of Maipú and Roca to the bottom of the chairlift, hourly in summer, US$4 return, last buses return at 1900 and 2100. Otherwise it's a 1½-hour walk from town via Magallanes.

The **Tren del Fin del Mundo** ⓘ *station 8 km west of Ushuaia (bus US$2 from Maipú and Roca, taxi US$3), T02901-431600, www.trendelfindelmundo.com.ar, 50 mins, 2 departures daily in summer, 1 in winter, US$23 return, plus US$8 park entrance*, is the world's southernmost steam train, running new locomotives and carriages on track first laid by prisoners to carry wood to Ushuaia. It travels into the Tierra del Fuego National Park (see page 378) and is an unashamedly touristy experience with relentless commentary in English and Spanish. However, it might be fun for children and is one way of getting into the national park to start a walk. Sit on the left on the outbound journey for the best views. Tickets are available at the station or from travel agencies in town.

Estancia Harberton

ⓘ *85 km east of Ushuaia (2 hrs' drive), T02901-422742, www.acatushun.org, 15 Oct-15 Apr daily except holidays. Tour of the estancia US$5, museum entrance US$2.*

In a land of extremes and superlatives, Harberton still stands out as special. The oldest estancia in Tierra del Fuego was built in 1886 on a narrow peninsula overlooking the Beagle Channel by the missionary Thomas Bridges (see box, page 374). He was granted the land by President Roca for his work with the indigenous people and for rescuing victims of shipwrecks in the channels. Harberton is named after the Devonshire village where Thomas's wife Mary was born; the farmhouse was pre-fabricated by her father in England and assembled on a spot chosen by the Yámana. The English connection is evident in the neat garden of lawns, shrubs and trees between the jetty and the farmhouse; behind the buildings is a large vegetable garden, a real rarity on the island.

Still operating as a working farm, Harberton is run by Thomas Goodall, great-grandson of the founder. Visitors receive an excellent guided walk (bilingual guides) through protected forest around the estancia, where there are reconstructions of the Yámana dwellings, plus a tour of the impressive **Museo Acatushun**, founded by Thomas' wife, Natalie Goodall. The museum

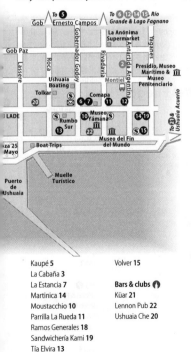

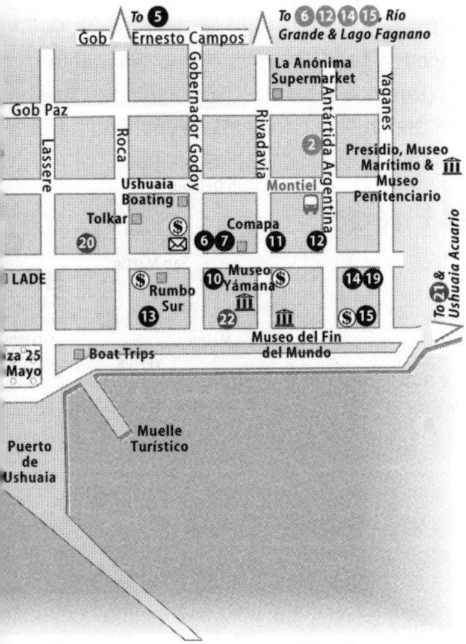

Kaupé **5**
La Cabaña **3**
La Estancia **7**
Martinica **14**
Moustacchio **10**
Parrilla La Rueda **11**
Ramos Generales **18**
Sandwichería Kami **19**
Tía Elvira **13**
Volver **15**

Bars & clubs
Küar **21**
Lennon Pub **22**
Ushuaia Che **20**

is the result of 23 years' scientific investigation into the area's rich marine life and contains the complete skeletons of dolphins, whales and seals. Tea or lunch (if you reserve ahead) are served in the room overlooking the bay. You can camp free, with permission from the owners, or rent one of the two simple cottages on the shore. There are wonderful walks along the coast, and noticeably more wildlife here than in the Tierra del Fuego National Park, probably owing to the estancia's remoteness. »» *See Transport, page 388.*

Beagle Channel → *Colour map 3, C4.*

A sea trip along the Beagle Channel can be rough but is highly recommended. Excursions leave from the Muelle Turístico in Ushuaia. Destinations include the sea lion colony at **Isla de los Lobos, Isla de los Pájaros, Les Eclaireurs lighthouse** and the penguin colony at **Isla Martillo**. You can visit Estancia Harberton by boat but always check that your tour actually includes the estancia and not just Harberton Bay. »» *See Activities and tours, page 384.*

Parque Nacional Tierra del Fuego »» *pp379-388.*

ⓘ *Park administration: San Martín 1395, Ushuaia, T02901-421315, www.parquesnacionales.gov.ar, US$7. Park entrance 11 km west of Ushuaia. Note there are no legal crossing points into Chile from the national park.*

Covering 63,000 ha of mountains, lakes, rivers and deep valleys, this small but beautiful park stretches west to the Chilean border and north from Bahía Lapataia on the Beagle Channel to beyond Lago Fagnano. Large areas are closed to tourists to protect the environment, but there are marvellous walks for every level of fitness. Lower parts of the park are forested with lenga, ñirre and coihue and are rich in birdlife, including geese, the beautiful torrent duck, Magellanic woodpeckers and austral parakeets. Even if you have just a couple of hours to spare, take a bus or taxi to Lago Roca or Bahía Lapataia.

Parque Nacional Tierra del Fuego

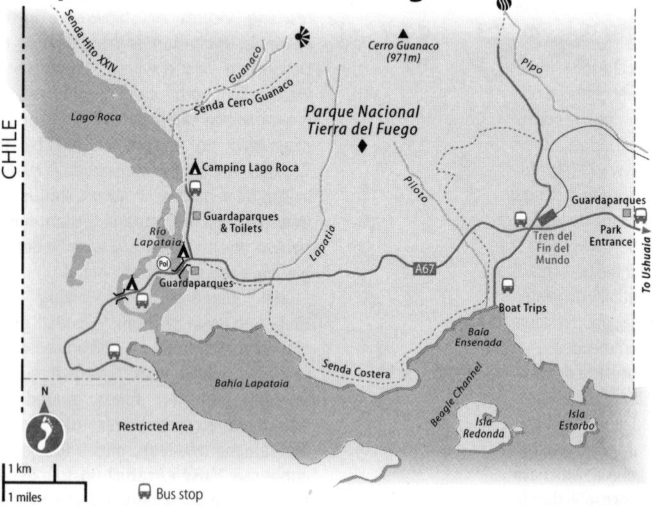

Walking in the park

Senda Costera (6.5 km, three hours each way) This lovely easy walk along the shore of the Beagle Channel gives you the essence of the park: its rocky coastline, edged with a rich forest of beech trees and glorious views of the low islands and steep mountains. Start at **Bahía Ensenada** (where the bus can drop you off and where boats leave for trips to Bahía Lapataia, daily 1000-1700, two hours, US$20, reservation essential). Walk along a well-marked path along the shoreline and then rejoin the road briefly to cross Río Lapataia (ignoring signs to Lago Roca to your right). After crossing the broad green river and a second stretch of water (where there's a small camping spot and the *gendarmería*), it's a pleasant stroll inland to the beautifully tranquil **Bahía Lapataia**, an idyllic spot, with views across the sound.

Lago Roca or Sendo Hito XXIV (4 km, 1½ hours one way). Another easy walk, this time alongside peaceful Lago Roca, where there's a very helpful *guardaparque*, plus camping and a *confitería*. It takes in lovely pebble beaches and dense forest, with lots of bird life and is especially recommended in the evening, when most visitors have left. Get off the bus at the junction for Lago Roca, turn right along the road to the car park (passing the *guardaparque*'s house) and follow the lake side.

Cerro Guanaco (4 km, four hours one way). Starting at the car park for Lago Roca, this is a challenging, steep hike up through forest to a mirador with splendid views over Lago Roca, the Beagle Channel and far-off mountains. The ground is slippery after rain: take care and don't rush. Allow plenty of time to return in daylight, especially in winter.

Argentine Tierra del Fuego listings

For Sleeping and Eating price codes and other relevant information, see pages 41-44.

Sleeping

Río Grande *p374*

Book ahead, as there are few decent choices. Several estancias offer full board and some, mainly on the northern rivers, have expensive fishing lodges, others offer horse riding: see www.tierradelfuego.org.ar and www.estanciasfueguinas.com.

A Posada de los Sauces, Elcano 839, T02964-432868, www.posadadelossauces.com.ar. By far the best choice. Breakfast included, beautifully decorated and comfortable rooms, good restaurant and cosy bar. Recommended.

B Hotel Isla del Mar, Güemes 963, T02964-422883, www.hotelguia.com/hoteles/isladelmar. Right on the sea shore, looks very bleak in bad weather and is frankly run-down, but cheap, with bathrooms and breakfast included, and the staff are welcoming.

B Villa, Av San Martín 281, T02964-424998, hotelvillarg@hotmail.com. Central, modern, restaurant/confitería, internet, TV, parking, discount given for cash.

C pp **Hotel Argentina**, San Martín 64, T02964-422546, hotelargentino@yahoo.com. Quite the best cheap place to stay. Set in a beautifully renovated 1920s building close to the sea with kitchen facilities, a bright sunny dining room and welcoming owner, Graciela, who knows all about the local area. Highly recommended. Parking, Wi-Fi and book exchange.

Estancias around Río Grande

LL Estancia María Behety, 15 km from Río Grande. Established in 1897 on a 40-km stretch of river that has become legendary for brown trout fishing. 18 comfortable rooms and good food. At US$5350 per week, this is one of the country's priciest fishing lodges, apparently deservedly so. Reservations through **Fly shop**, www.maribety.com.ar.

L Estancia Rivadvia, 100 km from Río Grande, on route H, www.estanciariva

davia.com, T02901-492186. A 10,000-ha sheep farm, owned by descendants of the original Croatian pioneer who built the place. Luxurious accommodation in a splendid house near the mountains and lakes at the heart of Tierra del Fuego, where you can enjoy a trip around the *estancia* to see wild horses and guanacos, good food, and trekking to the trout lake of Chepelmut and Yehuin.
L Estancia Viamonte, some 40 km southeast on the coast, T02964-430861, www.estancia viamonte.com. For a really authentic experience of Tierra del Fuego. Built in 1902 by pioneer Lucas Bridges, this working estancia is run by his descendants. You'll be warmly welcomed as their guest, in traditional, beautifully furnished rooms, with comfortable bathrooms, and delicious meals (extra cost). Also a spacious cottage for 7, US$310. Join in the farm activities, read the famous book by blazing fires, ride horses over the estate and completely relax. Warmly recommended. Reserve a week ahead.

Camping

Club Náutico Ioshlelk-Oten, Montilla 1047, 2 km from town on river. Clean, cooking facilities, camping in heated building in cold weather. YPF petrol station has hot showers.

South of Río Grande *p374*

AL-A Cabañas Khami , T02964-15611243, www.cabaniaskhami.com.ar. Isolated in a lovely spot at the head of the lake. Very comfortable and well-equipped *cabañas*, nicely decorated and with great views of the lake. Good value at US$40 per day for 6. Recommended.
A Hostería Petrel, RN 3, Km 3186, Lago Escondido, T02901-433569, hosteria.petrel@ hotmail.com. The only place to stay in this secluded forest position on a tranquil beach of the lake. Decent rooms with bath, and a good restaurant overlooking the lake which serves delicious lamb, open to non-residents. Also has tiny *cabañas* right on the water.
D Parador Kawi Shiken, off the main road on the way to Ushuaia, 4 km south of Tolhuin on RN 3, Km 2940, T02964-424380 . Rustic, with 3 rooms, shared bathrooms, *casa de té* and restaurant. Phone ahead to arrange a *cordero al asador* (barbecued lamb). Horse riding.
D Terrazas del Lago, RN 3, Km 2938, T02964-432300, terrazas@uol.com.ar. A little way from the shore, smart wooden *cabañas*, well decorated, and also a *confitería* and *parrilla*.
F pp **Refugio Solar del Bosque**, 18 km from Ushuaia, RN 3, Km 3020, Lago Escondido, T02901-421228 , solardelbosque@tierradel fuego.org.ar. Further along the road is this basic hostel for walkers, with shared bathrooms in dorms for 4, breakfast included.

Camping

Camping Hain del Lago, T02964-425951, T02964-15603606, robertoberbel@hot mail.com. Lovely views, fireplaces, hot showers, and a *quincho* for when it rains.
Camping La Correntina, T156-05020, 17 km from Tolhuin. In woodland, with bathrooms, and horses for hire.

Ushuaia *p375, map p376*

The tourist office has lists of all accommodation, and can help find you somewhere to stay, but in Jan you must reserve ahead.

Outside the city

LL Cabañas del Beagle, Las Aljabas 375, T02901-432785/1551 1323, www.cabaniasdel beagle.com. 3 rustic-style cabins 1.3 km above the city, fully equipped with kitchen, hydromassage, fireplace, heating, phone, self-service breakfast, very comfortable, personal attention.
LL Finisterris Lodge Relax, Monte Susana, Ladera Este, 7 km from city, T02901- 1561 2121 (mob), Buenos Aires T011-5917 8288, www.finisterris.com. In 17 ha of forest, 5-star luxury in individual cabins, with top-of-the-range fittings, hydromassage and private spa, rustic style but spacious, 'home-from-home' atmosphere, 24-hr attention from owner, given mobile phone on arrival. Meals can be ordered in, or private chef and sommelier can be booked for you.
LL Las Hayas, Martial 1650 (road to Glaciar Martial), T02901-430710, www.lashayas.com.ar. A 5-star hotel, in a spectacular setting, high

up on the mountainside with outstanding views over the Beagle Channel. Light, tasteful, impeccable rooms. Breakfast included and use of pool, sauna, gym, squash court, 9-hole golf course, shuttle from town in high season, and transfer from airport. A lovely calm atmosphere, friendly staff, recommended.

LL Los Cauquenes, at Bahía Cauquen, C Reinamora 3462, T02901-441300, www.loscauquenes.com. High-quality 5-star hotel overlooking Beagle Channel, room price depends on room size and view, with spa, very tastefully decorated, prize-winning restaurant with US$13 lunch menu, regional food on dinner menu.

LL Los Yámanas, Costa de los Yámanas 2850, western suburbs, T02901-445960, www.hotelyamanas.com.ar. In the same group as Canoero tour operator, all rooms with Channel view, spacious, well-decorated with DirectTV, Wi-Fi, hydromassage, fitness centre, spa and conference centre in wooded grounds, shuttle to town. Very pleasant.

LL-L Cumbres del Martial, Luis F Martial 3560 (7km from town), T02901-424779, www.cumbresdelmartial.com.ar. A charming cottage by a mountain stream in the forested slopes of Martial range with comfortable rooms and balconies looking out to the Beagle Channel. Homely, relaxed and in a secluded location, there are also 4 *cabañas* with fireplace and big windows opening on to the woods. Superb fondues are served.

L Tierra de Leyendas, Tierra de Vientos 2448, T02901-443565, www.tierradeleyendas.com.ar. Western suburbs. 5 comfortable rooms with views of the Beagle Channel, or the mountains at the back, 1 room with jacuzzi, others with shower, excellent restaurant serving regional specialities, open only for guests for breakfast and dinner. Free internet, no cable TV, but DVDs, living room with games, library, deck overlooking Río Pipo's outflow. Only for non-smokers. Recommended. In **Rusticae** chain.

In town

L Canal Beagle, Maipú y 25 de Mayo, T02901-432303, www.hotelcanalbeagle.com.ar. ACA hotel (discounts for members), comfortable and well attended, with a small pool, gym, sauna and clear views over the channel from some rooms (others see the container dock), good restaurant.

L Lennox, San Martín 776, T02901-436430, www.lennoxhotel.com.ar. Boutique hotel on the main street, with breakfast, services include internet, hydromassage, TV, frigobar, restaurant and *confitería* on 4th floor.

L Mil810, 25 de Mayo 245, T02901-437710, www.hotel1810.com. City hotel with 30 standard rooms, 1 with disabled access, no restaurant but breakfast and *confitería*, all rooms with flat-screen TV, minibar, safe, quite small but cosy, calm colours, good views, business centre and multiple-use room where you can hang out while waiting for flight.

AL Cap Polonio, San Martín 746, T02901-422140, www.hotelcappolonio.com.ar. A smart central modern city hotel with very comfortable minimalist rooms, all with bath, phone, TV, Wi-Fi; some have views of the canal. There's a chic restaurant downstairs.

B Hostal Malvinas, Gob Deloqui 615, T/F02901-422626, www.hostal malvinas.net. Neat, comfortable if rather small rooms with excellent bathrooms, and good views, in this central and well-run town house hotel. A basic breakfast is included, and all-day tea and coffee. Recommended.

B Hostería Posada Fin del Mundo, Gob Valdez 281, T02901-437345, www.posadafindelmundo.com.ar. A relaxed family atmosphere in a quiet residential area close to centre, homely rooms and friendly staff. Good value.

C pp **La Casa de Tere**, Rivadavia 620, T02901-422312, www.lacasadetere.com.ar. Shared bath, with breakfast, home-made bread and cake, use of kitchen, some rooms get lots of sun, singles, doubles and triples, hot water, helpful owner.

C Tzion, Gob Valdez 468, T02901-432290, tzion_byb@hotmail.com. B&B with 3 rooms, 1 with bath (**B**), high above town, 10 mins' walk from centre, nice family atmosphere (contact Daniel Pirruccio at Tolkar Turismo), cheaper in low season, laundry service, English and French spoken.

D B&B Nahuel, 25 de Mayo 440, T02901-423068. byb_nahuel@yahoo.com.ar. A family house, views over channel, with brightly painted and tastefully decorated rooms, and a lovely welcome from the charming and talkative owner. Great value. Recommended.

Hostels

D-E pp **Antárctica**, Antártida Argentina 270, T02901-435774, www.antarcticahostel.com. Welcoming and central hostel with a spacious chill-out room and an excellent bar open till late. Dorms are rather basic and cramped, with larger private doubles (**C**). Cooking facilities, breakfast and the use of internet are included. Bikes for hire (US$8.50 per day).

E pp **Freestyle**, Gob Paz 866, T02901-432874, www.ushuaiafreestyle.com. Very busy, good, central hostel, with laundry (US$3), TV room, DVDs and pool table. Also has doubles with bath (**B**), TV and kitchenette, which will move to new Alto Andino hotel, which is being built in front.

E-F pp **Yakush**, Piedrabuena and San Martín, T02901-435807, www.hostelyakush.com.ar. A very well-run hostel with spacious rooms to share and a few private ones, a light kitchen and dining room, and a steep garden with views.

F pp **Albergue Cruz del Sur**, Deloqui 636, T02901-434099, www.xdelsur.com.ar. Relaxed Italian-owned *hostal* with a very friendly atmosphere, cosy dorms, use of kitchen and a lovely quiet library. Recommended.

F pp **Posada del Duende**, Deloqui 1482, T432562, posadadelduende@hotmail.com. Also has doubles with bath (**C**), kitchen, email, hot water and heating, laundry service.

Private homes

C Galeazzi-Basily, Gob Valdez 323, T02901-423213, www.avesdelsur.com.ar. The best option by far. A cosy, stylish family home, with welcoming owners who speak excellent English, in a pleasant residential area 5 blocks from the centre. Delicious breakfast included. There are also excellent-value *cabañas* (**A**) in the garden. Highly recommended.

C-D Familia Velásquez, Juana Fadul 361, T02901-421719, almayo@arnet.com.ar. Basic rooms with breakfast in cosy cheerful pioneer family home, where the kind owners look after you.

D Los Troncos, Gob Paz 1344, T02901-421895, lostroncos@speedy.com.ar. A welcoming house run by charming Mrs Clarisa Ulloa, with simple rooms, breakfast, TV and free internet.

Estancias

L Estancia Rolito, Route 21 (ex 'A'), Km 14, T02901-437351, www.tierradelfuego.org.ar/rolito. A magical place on the wooded heart of the island, with cosy accommodation in traditionally built houses, and friendly hosts Annie and Pepe, booked through **Turismo de Campo**, www.turismodecampo.com. Also day visits with recommended walks or horse rides in mature southern beech forest.

A-B Harberton, T02901-422742, estancia harberton@tierradelfuego.org.ar. 2 impeccably restored historical buildings on the tranquil lakeside, giving space and privacy from the main house. Simple accommodation, but wonderful views, and beautiful walks on the *estancia*'s coastline. 90 km east of Ushuaia, along RN 3 and 33, a spectacular drive. Open mid-Oct to mid-Apr.

Camping

Camping del Solar del Bosque, RN 3, Km 19, heading to Río Grande, T02901-435276. US$3 pp. At a small ski resort that in summer offers plenty of activities. Hot showers, and also a large dorm with good facilities.

Camping Haruwen, Haruwen Winter Sports complex (Km 36), en route to Río Grande, T02901-431099. US$4 per tent, electricity, shop, bar, restaurant in a winter sports centre, open also in summer for outdoor activities.

Parque Nacional Tierra del Fuego *p378, map p378*

Camping

Camping Lago Roca, T02901-433313 (entry fee to park US$13), 21 km from Ushuaia. By the forested shore of tranquil Lago Roc, this beautiful site with good facilities, is reached by bus Jan-Feb, expensive small shop, *cafetería*, US$4 pp. Tents/sleeping bags for hire.

There are also various sites with no facilities: **Bahía Ensenada Camping**, 14 km from Ushuaia; **Río Pipo**, 16 km from Ushuaia, and **Camping Las Bandurrias**, Cauquenes and **Camping Laguna Verde**, 20 km from Ushuaia.

Eating

Río Grande *p374*

¥¥ El Rincón de Julio, next to Posada de los Sauces, Elcano 800 block. For excellent *parrilla*.

¥ La Nueva Colonial, Av Belgrano and Lasserre. Half a block from the plaza, next to **Casino Club**, where the locals go for delicious pasta in a warm family atmosphere.

¥ La Nueva Piamontesa, Belgrano y Mackinlay, T02964-426332, to the side of the charming 24-hr grocery store. Cheap set menus and also delivers food.

¥ La Rueda, Islas Malvinas 998, 1st floor. Excellent *parrilla* in a welcoming place. Has another branch on O'Higgins 200 block.

Cafés

El Roca (sic), Espora entre Av San Martín y Rosales, ½ block from Plaza. *Confitería* and bar in historic premises (the original cinema), good and popular.

Tío Willy, Alberdi entre Espora y 9 de Julio. Serves *cerveza artesanal* (microbrewery).

South of Río Grande *p375*

La Unión bakery, Tolhuin. Famous bakery, open 24 hrs, daily except Mon 2400- Tue 0600. On the same block there are pizzas at **Pizzería Amistad**, and more of a range at **La Posada de los Ramírez**, a cosy restaurant and *rotisería*, weekends only, lunch and dinner.

Ushuaia *p375, map p376*

¥¥¥ Bodegón Fueguino, San Martín 859, T02901-431972. In a stylishly renovated 1896 house in the main street, this stands out from the crowd by serving *picadas* with delicious and imaginative dips, good roast lamb, and unusual *cazuelas*, *picadas* and dips. A buzzy atmosphere and welcoming staff.

¥¥¥ Kaupé, Roca 470 y Magallanes, T02901-437396. The best restaurant in town, with exquisite food. King crab and meat dishes all beautifully served in a lovely environment – a great treat.

¥¥¥ La Cabaña, Luis F Martial 3560, T02901-434699. The cosy restaurant and tea room of **Cumbres del Martial** hotel serves several excellent types of fondue for dinner, that may be preceded at teatime by a rich list of cakes, scones and brownies. Open every day.

¥¥¥ Tía Elvira, Maipú 349, T02901-424725. Retains its reputation for excellent seafood, with a good choice of fresh fish and views over the channel. Open every day.

¥¥¥ Volver, Maipú 37, T02901-423977. In an atmospheric old 1898 house, with ancient newspaper all over the walls (read intriguing fragments while you eat). Cosy stoves and an intimate atmosphere. Delicious salmon and *arroz con mariscos*.

¥¥¥-¥¥ La Estancia, San Martín 253, T02901-432700. Cheery and good-value *parrilla tenedor libre*. Packed in high season.

¥¥¥-¥¥ Parrilla La Rueda, San Martín and Rivadavia, T02901-436540. A good *tenedor libre* for beef, lamb and a great range of salads. US$13 pp with dessert.

¥¥ 137 Pizzas and Pastas, San Martín 137. A brightly lit functional place with tasty filling food. Also take-away empanadas and pizzas.

¥¥ Moustacchio, San Martín 272 and Gob Godoy, T02901-423308. Long-established, good for seafood in a cosy atmosphere. Next door is a cheaper all-you-can-eat sister restaurant.

¥¥-¥ Martinica, San Martín entre Antártida Argentina and Yaganes. Cheap, small, busy, sit at the bar facing the *parrilla* and point to your favourite beef cut. Takeaway (T02901- 432134) and good meals of the day, also pizzas and empanadas. Open 1130-1500, 2030-0000.

¥ El Turco, San Martín 1410. One of few good and cheap places, popular with locals, serves generous *milanesas*, pastas, steaks and pizzas.

Cafés

Café Bar Banana, San Martín 273, T02901-424021. Quite small, always busy, with a pool table at the back, offers good fast food, such as burgers, small pizzas, puddings, breakfasts and an all-day *menú* for US$7.50.

Café de la Esquina, San Martín y 25 de Mayo. Lots of lunch choices, specials, sandwiches, tortas, *picadas*, *lomitos*, café and bar. Open for 15 years, used by locals and tourists alike.

Café Tante Sara, Fadul and San Martín. The most appealing of the cafés on San Martín. Smart and modern with an airy feel, serving good coffee and tasty sandwiches.

Ramos Generales, Maipú 749, T02901-424317, www.ramosgeneralesushuaia.com. An old warehouse, with wooden floor and shelves and a collection of historic objects and dusty ledgers. Sells breads, pastries, wines and drinks, also cold cuts, sandwiches, salads, ice cream and coffee. Dish of the day or soup for lunch, breakfasts till 1300, teas 1300-2000. Not cheap but atmospheric. Recommended.

Sandwichería Kami, San Martín 54. Open 0800-2130. Friendly, simple sandwich shop, selling rolls, baguettes and *pan de miga*.

Bars and clubs

Ushuaia *p375, map p376*

Küar, Av Perito Moreno 2232, east of town. Great setting by the sea, restaurant, bar and brewery open from 1800.

Lennon Pub, Maipú 263. A lively friendly atmosphere and live music.

For a bit of Irish loving try **Galway Irish Pub**, Lasserre 108, or **Dublin Bar Irlandés**, 9 de Julio. Both are favourites of locals and tourists alike.

Ushuaia Che, San Martín 452. A lively place with Mexican and Brazilian food.

Festivals and events

Río Grande *p374*

Jan The **sheep-shearing festival** is definitely worth seeing, if you're in the area.

2nd week of Feb Rural exhibition with handicrafts.

1st week of Mar Shepherd's day, with impressive sheepdog display.

20-21 Jun Winter solstice, the longest night, has fireworks and ice-skating contests, though this is a very inhospitable time of year.

Activities and tours

Río Grande *p374*

Tour operators

Mariani Travel Rosales 259, T02964-426010, mariani@netcombbs.com.ar.

Tecni Austral, Moyano 516, T02964-432885. Bus tickets to Ushuaia.

Ushuaia *p375, map p376*

Fishing

The lakes and rivers of Tierra del Fuego offer great fishing for brown and rainbow trout and stream trout in Lago Fagnano. Both fly-casting and spinning are allowed, and permits must be bought. The trout season is 1 Nov-Apr (though this varies slightly every year), licences US$10 per day (an extra fee is charged for some rivers and lakes). Contact Asociación de Caza y Pesca, Maipú 822, cazapescush@infovia.com.ar. Mon, Wed, Fri 1700-2100 and they sell licences and are very helpful.

Boat trips and cruises

All short boat trips leave from the Muelle Turístico. Take your time to choose the size and style of boat you want. Representatives from the offices are polite and helpful. All have a morning and afternoon sailing and include Isla de los Lobos, Isla de los Pájaros and Les Eclaireurs lighthouse, with guides and some form of refreshment. Note that weather conditions may affect sailings, prices can change and that port tax is not included.

Barracuda, T02901-437233, barracuda@speedy.com.ar. On a lovely old motor yacht, the first tourist boat in Ushuaia, US$32; their other boat, Lanín, includes Isla Bridges, US$36; all trips include a discount at the Acuario.

Canoero, T02901-433893, losyamanas@arnet.com.ar. Catamarans for 60-100 passengers, 2½-hr trips to the 3 main sites and Isla Bridges, US$36. Thay also have a 5-hr trip almost daily to the Pingüinera on Isla Martillo near Estancia Harberton (Oct-Mar only), boats stay for 1 hr, but you cannot land on Martillo. Passengers can return to Ushuaia by bus: US$65 without stops on bus ride, US$76 with stops.
Paludine, T02901-434865, navegandoelfindelmundo@gmail.com, fast boats with 12 passengers, US$40. Also has all-day trips on a sailing boat, 1000-1700 with lunch, prepared during a trek on Bridges, US$56 all inclusive.
Patagonia Adventure Explorer, T02901-1546 5842, www.patagoniaadvent.com.ar. Has a sailing boat and motor boats for the standard trip, plus Isla Bridges: US$50 sailing, US$40 motoring. Good guides.
Pira-Tour, T02901-1560 4646, piratour@gmail.com. Runs 2-3 buses a day to Harberton, from where a boat goes to the Pingüinera on Isla Martillo: 15 people allowed to land (maximum 45 per day – the only company licensed to do this). US$85 for a morning tour, including lunch at Harberton and entry to Acatushún museum; US$70 for afternoon tour.
Tres Marías, T02901-421987, www.tresmariasweb.com. The only company licensed to visit Isla H, which has archaeological sites, cormorants, other birds and plants. Also has sailing boat, no more than 10 passengers; specialist guide, café on board, US$40 on Tres Marías, US$50 on sailing boat.

Also **Rumbo Sur** and **Tolkeyen**; see Tour operators, below.

Sea trips and Antartica

Ushuaia is the starting point, or the last stop, en route to Antarctica for several cruises from Oct-Mar that usually sail for 9-21 days along the western shores of the Antarctic peninsula and the South Shetland Islands. Other trips include stops at **Falkland/ Malvinas** archipelago and at South Georgia. Go to Oficina Antártica for advice (see page 386). Agencies sell 'last-minute tickets', but the price is entirely dependent on demand (available 1 week before sailing). Coordinator for trips is **Turismo Ushuaia**, Gob Paz 865, T02901-436003, www.ushuaiaturismoevt.com.ar, which operates with IAATO members only. End-2007 prices: 1-day flight, US$3000, 8 passengers from Punta Arenas, 2-day plane and ship from Punta Arenas, US$9000, all-ship tours from about US$4000.
To **Chile** **Cruceros Australis**, www.australis.com, see page 233, operates 2 luxury cruise ships between Ushuaia and Punta Arenas, with a visit to Cabo de Hornos, frequently recommended. Full details are given under Punta Arenas, Tour operators, page 344.

Ushuaia Boating, Deloqui 302 y Godoy, T436153 (or at the Muelle Turístico), T02901-436193, ushuaiaboating@argentina.com.ar. Operates all year round a channel crossing to **Puerto Navarino** (Isla Navarino), 20-90 mins depending on weather, and then bus to **Puerto Williams**, 1 hr, US$100 one way, not including US$6.60 taxes. At Muelle AFASYN, near the old airport, T02901-435805, ask about possible crossings with a club member to Puerto Williams, about 4 hrs, or if any foreign sailing boat is going to Cabo de Hornos or Antarctica. From Puerto Williams a ferry goes once a week to Punta Arenas.

Hiking and climbing

Club Andino, Fadul 50, T02901-422335, www.clubandinoushuaia.com.ar. For advice, Mon-Fri 1000-1200, 1400-2030. Sells maps and trekking guidebooks; free guided walks once in a month in summer; also offers classes, eg yoga, dancing, karate-do and has excercise bikes. The winter sports resorts along Ruta 3 (see below) are an excellent base for summer trekking and many arrange excursions.
Nunatak, 25 de Mayo 296, T02901-430329, www.nunatakadventure.com. Organizes treks, canoeing, mountain biking and 4WD trips to lagos Escondido and Fagnano.

Horse riding

Centro Hípico, Ruta 3, Km 3021, T02901-443996, 1556 9099 (mob), www.centrohipicoushuaia.com.ar. Rides through woods, on

Going further ... Antarctica

Ushuaia is the starting point for a number of excellent expeditions to Antarctica. These usually run from mid-November to mid-March and last between eight and 11 days, taking in the Antarctic peninsula and the Wedell sea. Some offer extra activities, such as camping and kayaking. Its not exactly a luxury cruise: trips are usually made in non-tourist boats used for scientific exploration, so the accommodation is informal and simple and the food is reasonable but not excessive. The expedition leader organizes lectures during the three-day journey to reach the Antarctic, with at least two disembarkations a day in a zodiac to see icebergs and penguins. When selecting your trip, bear in mind that there's most ice in November and December, more baby penguins in January and February, and whales in March. The landscape, however, is always impressive.

A longer trip of 18 to 19 days, combines the Antarctic with the Malvinas/Falklands and South Georgia islands. There are weekly departures in season. It's worth turning up in Ushuaia and asking the major tour operators for availability; there's a 30% discount if you book last minute in Ushuaia.

For further information and bookings contact **Rumbo Sur**, **Turismo de Campo** and **All Patagonia**, see Activities and tours, below. Seats can also sometimes be purchased on Chilean Naval supply vessels heading for Antarctica, though this requires patience and a long period of waiting in Punta Arenas, see Transport, page 343, for further details.

Monte Susana, along coast and through river, 2 hrs, US$35; 4-hr ride with light lunch, US$70; 7-hr ride with *asado*, US$105. Gentle well-cared-for horses all guides have first-aid training. Very friendly and helpful. All rides include transfer from town and insurance. Hats provided for children; works with disabled children. They can arrange long-distance rides of several days, eg on Península Mitre.

Winter sports

Ushuaia is becoming popular as a winter resort with 11 centres for skiing, snowboarding and husky sledging.

Cerro Castor complex, Ruta 3, Km 27, T02901-499301, www.cerro castor.com, is the only centre for alpine skiing, with 24 km of pistes, powder snow and an 800-m vertical drop. Attractive centre with complete equipment rental, also for snowboarding and snowshoeing.

The other centres along Ruta 3 at Km 18-36 east of Ushuaia offer excellent cross country skiing (and alternative activities in summer).

Kawi Shiken at Las Cotorras, Ruta 3, Km 26, T02901-444152, T02901-1551 9497 (mob), www.tierradelfuego.org.ar/hugoflores, specializes in sled dogs, with 100 Alaskan and Siberian huskies: 2-km ride on snow US$20, 2-hr trips with meal US$56. In summer offers 2-km rides in a dog cart, US$13.50.

Tierra Mayor, 20 km from town, T02901-423240, or T02901-155 13463, is the largest and recommended. In a beautiful wide valley between steep-sided mountains, offering half- and full-day excursions on sledges with huskies, as well as cross-country skiing and snow-shoeing. Equipment hire and restaurant.

Tour operators

All agencies charge the same fees for excursions; ask tourist office for a complete list: Tierra del Fuego National Park, 4 hrs, US$30 (entry fee US$6.65 extra); Lagos Escondido and Fagnano, 7 hrs, US$45 without lunch. With 3 or 4 people it might be worth hiring a *remise* taxi.

All Patagonia, Juana Fadul 40, T02901-433622, www.allpatagonia.com. Trekking, ice climbing, and tours; trips to Cabo de Hornos and Antarctica.

Canal, 9 de Julio 118, local 1, T02901-437395, www.canalfun.com. Huge range of activities, trekking, canoeing, riding, 4WD excursions. Recommended.

Comapa, San Martín 245, T02901-430727, www.comapa.com. Conventional tours and adventure tourism, bus tickets to Punta Arenas and Puerto Natales, trips to Antarctica, agents for **Curceros Australis** and **Navimag** ferries for Puerto Natales–Puerto Montt (10% ISIC discount for Navimag). **Hertz** also here.

Compañía de Guías de Patagonia, San Martín 628, T02901-437753, T1549 3288 (mob), www.companiadeguias.com.ar. The best agency for walking guides, expeditions for all levels, rock and ice climbing (training provided), also diving, sailing, riding, 7-day crossing of Tierra del Fuego on foot and conventional tours. Recommended.

Límite Vertical, T02901-1560 0868, www.limiteverticaltdf.com.ar. 4WD adventures off-road to the shores of lagos Escondido and Fagnano, taking logging trails and *ripio* roads, seeing beaver damage in the forests, etc. Lunch is an *asado* at an old saw mill; similar tours by other companies stop for lunch on shore of Fagnano. Good fun.

Rumbo Sur, San Martín 350, T02901-422275, www.rumbosur.com.ar. Flights, buses, conventional tours on land and sea, plus Antarctic expeditions, mid-Nov to mid-Mar, English spoken.

Tolkar, Roca 157, T02901-431412, www.tolkar turismo.com.ar. Flights, bus tickets to Argentina and Chile, conventional and adventure tourism, canoeing and mountain biking to Lago Fagnano.

Tolkeyen, San Martín 1267, T02901-437073, www.tolkeyenpatagonia.com. Bus and flight tickets, catamaran trips (50-300 passengers), including to Harberton (Mon, Wed, Fri, US$65) and Parque Nacional, large company.

Travel Lab, San Martín 1444, T02901-436555, travellabush@speedy.com.ar. Conventional and unconventional tours, mountain biking, trekking, etc, English and French spoken, helpful.

Turismo de Campo, Fuegia Basket 414, T/F02901-437351, www.turismodecampo.com. Adventure tourism, English- and French-speaking guides, boat and trekking trips in the national park, birdwatching, sailing and trips to Antarctica.

Transport

Book ahead in summer, as flights fill up fast. In winter, poor weather often causes delays. Passport needed to buy tickets. See also Getting there, page 366.

Río Grande *p374*

Air

The airport is 4 km west of town, T02964-420600. A taxi to the centre costs US$2. To **Buenos Aires**, Aerolíneas Argentinas, San Martín 607, T02901-424467, daily, 3½ hrs direct. LADE flies to **Ushuaia**, once a week and to other Patagonian towns.

Bus

Buses leave from the terminal Elcano and Güemes, T02964-420997, or from the office of **Tecni Austral**, Moyano 516, T02964-430610. To **Porvenir** (Chile), 5 hrs, **Gesell**, Wed and Sun 0800, US$10, passport and luggage control at San Sebastián. To **Punta Arenas** (Chile), via Punta Delgada, 10 hrs, **Pacheco**, Tue, Thu, Sat 0730, US$16. To **Río Gallegos** for connections to **El Calafate**, Tecni Austral, 3 times a week, US$15. To **Ushuaia**, **Tecni Austral**, 3-4 hrs, 2 daily (heavily booked in summer), US$14; also **Tolkeyen**, US$8.

Ushuaia *p375, map p376*

Air

Schedules change from season to season, so call airline offices for times and prices: **Aerolíneas** Argentinas, Roca 116, T02901-422267, www.aerolineas.com.ar; **Aerovías DAP**, 25 de Mayo 64, T02901-431110; **LADE**, Lasserre 445, T02901-422968 www.lade.com.ar.

Aerolíneas and LADE fly to **Buenos Aires**, 3½-5 hrs depending on whether service is direct, and **El Calafate**, 1¼ hrs. Also flights to **Río Gallegos**, 1 hr, and **Río**

Grande, 1 hr, but check with agents. To **Punta Arenas** (Chile), Aerovías DAP, 1 hr.

Bus

Long distance Buses arrive at offices around town: **Tecni Austral/Tolkar**, Roca 157, T02901-431412; **Líder**, Gob Paz 921, T02901-436421; **Tolkeyen**, Maipú 237, T02901-437073. To **Buenos Aires**, 36 hrs, US$72, **TAC, Don Otto, El Pingüino** and **Transportadora Patagónica**. To **Río Grande**, 4 hrs, **Tecni Austral** and **Líder**, both US$10, 2 daily; **Tolkeyen**, US$11. No through services from Ushuaia to **Río Gallegos**; instead, go to Río Grande, and change (total 8-10 hrs); book a ticket for the journey with **Tolkar** in Ushuaia, US$18.

To **Punta Arenas** (Chile), via Punta Delgada (15-min ferry crossing), 12 hrs, **Tecni Austral**, Mon, Wed, Fri 0600, US$30; **Tolkeyen/Pacheco**, Tue, Thu, Sat, 0630, US$36; also less frequent via **Porvenir**, 12 hrs (2½-hr ferry crossing), US$52.

Local Ebenezer and Bella Vista, daily to **Lago Escondido**, US$10 return, and **Lago Fagnano**, US$13. In summer, various companies, hourly to **Lago Roca**, US$3 return, and **Bahía Lapataia**, US$9, from the tourist pier; last return 2000/2100. Ebenezer and Gonzalo to the **Fin del Mundo station** (see page 377) 0800, 0900, 1400; return 1700, US$4. For services to Harberton, see below.

Urban buses from west to east across town, most stops along Maipú, US$0.45. Tourist office provides a list of minibus companies that run daily from town (stops along Maipú) to nearby attractions. To the national park: in summer buses and minibuses leave from the bus stop on Maipú at the bottom of Fadul. Pasarella, 9 a day from 0800, last back 1900, US$11.50 return, US$13.30 to Lapataia; **Ebenezer** 8 a day from 0830, last back 2000. From same bus stop, many other *colectivos* go to the Tren del Fin del Mundo, Lago Escondido, Lago Fagnano and Glaciar Martial, leave when full. For Harberton, check the notice boards at the station at Maipú y Fadul.

Car hire

Most companies charge US$50 per day including insurance and 150 km per day. **Europcar**, Av Belgrano 423, T02901-430365, www.europcar.com. Localiza, San Martín 642, T02901-430191.

Sea

For cruises to Cape Horn and Punta Arenas, see page 15. For trips to Antarctica, see box, page 386.

Taxi

Remise Carlitos, T02901-422222; **Tienda Leon**, San Martín 995, T02901-422222.

Estancia Harberton *p377*

Access by car is along a good unpaved road which branches off Route 3, 40 km east of Ushuaia. Marvellous views en route but no petrol beyond Ushuaia. **Boat** trips twice weekly in summer from the Muelle Turístico, US$25 for a day trip. Daily **minibuses**, Bella Vista and **Lautaro**, from Maipú and Juana Fadul, US$16 return. **Tours**, US$42 plus entrance.

Directory

Río Grande *p374*

Banks and currency exchange 4 banks with ATMs on San Martín between 100 and 300. **Post office** Piedrabuena y Ameghino. **Telephone** *Centro de llamada* at San Martín 170 and 458.

Ushuaia *p375, map p376*

Banks and currency exchange ATMs are plentiful along San Martín. Changing TCs is difficult but possible at **Banco de Tierra del Fuego**, San Martín 396. **Consulate** Chile, Malvinas Argentinas and Jainen, Casilla 21, T02901-421279. **Internet and telephone** Cyber cafés and *centros de llamada* along San Martín. **Post office** San Martín, Mon-Fri 0900-1300, 1700-1900, Sat 0830-1200.

Background

Contents

Footprint features

A sprint through history

Early days

50,000 years ago, the first people cross the temporary land bridge between Asia and America at the Bering Straits and begin a long migration southwards, reaching Tierra del Fuego 12,000 years ago. Hunters and foragers, they follow in the path of huge herds of animals such as mammoths, giant sloths, mastodons and wild horses, adapting to fishing along the coasts. The area remains sparsely populated and many Patagonian peoples remain nomadic until the encroachment of European settlers in the 19th century.

15-16th centuries

The Incas expand their empire into central Chile. They are stopped by hostile forest tribes at the Río Maule, near present-day Talca. Due to its topography, Patagonia is not touched by Inca incursions.

1516

Juan de Solis arrives in the Plata estuary. He and his men are killed by the indigenous Querandí. Other Europeans follow, including Portuguese explorer Ferdinand Magellan who ventures south into the Pacific via the straits north of Tierra del Fuego. The straits become an important trade route until the building of the Panama Canal in 1914.

1541

Following the overthrow of the Incas by a tiny force of Spaniards led by Francisco Pizarro, Pedro de Valdivia is given the task of conquering Chile. He reaches the fertile Mapocho valley and founds Santiago. The settlements of Concepción, Valdivia and Villarica follow.

1580s

Buenos Aires is established, but the discovery of precious metals in Peru and Bolivia, focuses colonial attention elsewhere, and it remains a backwater for 200 years. Meanwhile, a group of settlers led by Pedro de Sarmiento seeks to found a colony on the north banks of the Magellan Straits. The colony is a disaster and only two people survive. This is the end of attempts at European settlement in southern Patagonia for centuries.

1598

A rebellion by the Mapuche in the Chilean Lake District (see page 245) drives the Spanish back to the north of the Rio Biobío, leaving isolated groups of settlers in Valdivia and on Chiloé, and ensuring that European influence in Patagonia will remain marginal.

17th century

In 1616, a Dutch navigator names the southernmost tip of Argentina Cape Horn after his hometown, Hoorn. Meanwhile, the indigenous groups and the Spanish authorities are in a state of permanent war. The Spanish want to enslave the natives into a system of *encomiendas* – a feudal regime that has been successful in Peru. The colonizers have more sophisticated weapons, but the indigenous peoples use guerilla warfare and fight using spears, bows and arrows. The Spanish are unable to defeat the Mapuche and there is something of a stand-off. During this period a generation of *criollos* (Spaniards born in the colonies) develops and intermarriage takes place resulting in *mestizo* populations. The

Port Famine (Puerto Hambre)

In 1582, Felipe II of Spain, alarmed by Drake's passage through the Straits of Magellan, decided to establish a Spanish presence on the Straits. A fleet of 15 ships and 4000 men, commanded by Pedro Sarmiento de Gamboa, was despatched in 1584. However, before they had even left the Bay of Biscay a storm scattered the fleet, sinking seven ships and killing 800 people. Further depleted by disease, the remaining three ships arrived at the Straits with just 300 men on board. This small force founded two cities: Nombre de Jesús on Punta Dungeness at the eastern entrance to the Straits and Rey Don Felipe near Puerto Hambre.

Disaster struck again when their only remaining vessel broke its anchorage; the ship, with Sarmiento on board, was blown into the Atlantic, leaving many of his men stranded on land. After attempts to re-enter the Straits, he set sail for Rio de Janeiro and organized two rescue missions: the first ended in shipwreck, the second in mutiny. Captured by the English, Sarmiento was taken to England and imprisoned. Until his death in 1608, Sarmiento besieged Felipe II with letters urging him to rescue the stranded men.

When the English corsair Thomas Cavendish sailed through the Straits in 1587 he found only 18 survivors. With the English and Spanish at war, only one man – Tomé Hernández – trusted Cavendish. They set sail, leaving the rest of the men to die. He named the place Port Famine as a reminder of their grisly fate.

indigenous people are gradually weakened due to famine, lack of resistence to diseases such as small pox and the production of alcohol. However, It is not until 1881 that the treaty ending Mapuche Independence from Chile is signed.

1776

Buenos Aires is made the capital of the new Viceroyalty of the Río de la Plata and becomes an important trade route for European goods and contraband. Estancias are formed to farm and export cattle in the area around Buenos Aires.

1808-1816

Napoleon invades Spain and deposes King Ferdinand VII. Argentine independence from Spain is declared on 9 July 1816 by José de San Martín, who goes on to lead armies of freedom fighters into Chile with Simón Bolívar. But independence brings neither stability nor unity in Argentina, with fighting by federalist groups.

1827

The royalist citizens of Carmen de Patagones – an outpost at the gateway to Patagonia – are reluctant to accept the *criollo* government and, in 1827, soldiers, gauchos, slaves and pirates are sent to stamp the new government's authority on the region.

1832-1833

General Rosas, dictator of Argentina and military supremo, leads a campaign against the indigenous Pampas people, destroying their independence and their way of life. This is the beginning of the incursion of European forces into Patagonia. Charles Darwin wrote that he doubted any indigenous Pampas people would be left within a generation.

1843

Alarmed by widespread naval activity in the region, the Chilean navy sends a cutter to the Magellan Strait and erects a fort at Fuerte Bulnes, to claim the straits for Chile – the rest of Patagonia between here and the mainland now falls under Chilean jurisdiction.

1845-1880

The Chilean government encourages settlement around Lago Llanquihue, provoking extensive immigration to the area by German colonists. Legacy of this settlement can be seen in the German-looking buildings around Puerto Octay, Frutillar and Puerto Varas.

In 1848, Chile founds Punta Arenas, making Chile's claim of the Strait of Magellan permanent. It becomes a penal colony modelled on Australia, and in 1867 is opened to foreigners and given free port status. The town prospers as a refuelling and provisioning centre for steam ships until the opening of the Panama Canal in 1914.

1853

Juan de Rosas, a powerful governor of Buenos Aires, brings order, gaining support by seizing lands from indigenous peoples and handing them to friends in the 'Campaign of the Desert'. This is followed by a new era of growth and prosperity.

1865

Welsh immigrants arrive in Puerto Madryn on the Atlantic coast and settle inland along the Chubut Valley. Their aim is to free themselves of their English oppressors and to find a haven in which to practise their religion in their own language. They learn from the indigenous Tehuelche people and successfully irrigate the valley for agriculture. In 1889 a railway connects Puerto Madryn with Trelew, enabling the Welsh to export their produce.

1879

Expansion in the south becomes more aggressive with increasing confrontation with indigenous populations. President Julio Roca's 'Conquest of the Wilderness' sends a force against the indigenous peoples of Patagonia, exterminating many of them and herding the rest into settlements. The government pushes the frontier, and the railway, south, paving the way for further European settlement.

Late 19th century

Large swathes of land are divided up and settlers are allocated 40 ha apiece. Argentina is transformed by a stable economy based on cattle farming, foreign investment and European immigration. Thomas Bridges founds a mission in Tierra del Fuego (see page 374).

Early 20th century

Rural poverty in both countries leads to urbanization and high unemployment, wealth is concentrated in the hands of the very few. The wool boom encourages the creation of large farms for sheep-raising in Patagonia. Many migrants come from the island of Chiloé to work at farms in Argentine Patagonia and on Chilean Tierra del Fuego.

1940s-1950s

Following a military coup in 1943, Juan Perón wins the presidency in 1946 and 1952. An authoritarian and charismatic leader, he institutes stringent reforms against the economic elite and in favour of the workers. In 1955 he is ousted and exiled to Spain, but remains popular with the people, making a brief return to power in 1973.

1960s-1970s

Chile's politics become increasingly polarized. The Marxist coalition led by Salvador Allende, introduces sweeping reforms, such as redistribution of income and the takeover of many private enterprises. The country is plunged into economic chaos.

11 September 1973

General Pinochet seizes power in a bloody coup. Allende allegedly commits suicide and thousands of his supporters are murdered. During the dictatorship which follows, an estimated 80,000 are tortured, murdered or exiled; one of the early detention centres is on Isla Dawson in the Magellan Straits.

1976-1983

In Chile, the building of the Carretera Austral begins. The new military government in Argentina institutes a reign of terror known as the 'Dirty War'. Any vaguely left-wing thinking, opposition or criticism of the military is met with violent torture and elimination by death squads. Up to 30,000 people 'disappear'. Internal conflict ends with the war against Britain over the disputed Malvinas (Falkland Islands). Democracy of a kind returns, when Alfonsín becomes president in 1983.

1978

Argentina and Chile nearly go to war over a territorial dispute over three islands – Lennox, Nueva and Picton – in the Beagle Channel. The Pope has to intervene, and the islands are awarded to Chile.

1973-1990

Pinochet dissolves Congress in Chile, bans leftist parties and suspends all opposition. His economic policies bring relative prosperity, but a referendum in 1988 sees him rejected by a majority of 12%. Democracy returns and Christian democrat, Patricio Aylwin is elected President in 1990.

1990s

In Argentina, Peronist president Carlos Menem institutes major economic reforms, selling off nationalized industries, and opening the economy to foreign investment. The country falls heavily into debt. In 1999 President Fernando de la Rua of the UCR centre-left Alliance, promises a crackdown on corruption and tough measures to balance Argentina's budget.

2001

In December, nationwide demonstrations erupt when access to bank accounts is restricted in the 'corralito'. Argentina is plunged into serious economic and political crisis. Rioting, looting and widespread civil chaos result in the death of 27 people.

January 2002

Eduardo Duhalde becomes Argentina's fifth president in two weeks. He is forced to devalue the peso in order to borrow money from the International Monetary Fund. The middle class is devastated, many losing their life savings. Widespread poverty becomes a reality, with child malnutrition, and unemployment over 20%.

2003

Argentine elections threaten to return Menem to power, even though he bankrupted the nation by selling off national industries. Kirchner wins by a narrow lead, promising to reduce corruption and lessen the burden of government employees. The country recovers some stability. Tourism flourishes – both from foreigners enjoying low prices, and Argentines realizing that holidaying in their own country is more magnificent than in Miami, which had become the aspirant norm under Menem.

2005

After years of political battles, Parque Pumalín is given official Nature Sancuary status.

2006

Plans to build a huge aluminium plant in Chilean Patagonia are scrapped, but there is now a project to dam some of Aisén's most important rivers to generate hydroelectric power. Michelle Bachelet is voted in as Chile's first woman president. In December 2006 General Augusto Pinochet dies, aged 91.

Today

Patagonia remains very much an extremity of both Argentina and Chile. Historically absent from the national boundaries until the 19th century, it still feels very different to the rest of the countries. Some long for the utopia of a united Patagonia, free of the internal wranglings of the power bases of Buenos Aires and Santiago.

Arts and crafts

Indigenous crafts

Present-day handicrafts represent either the transformation of utilitarian objects into works of art, or the continued manufacture of pieces that retain symbolic value. A number of factors threaten these traditions: the loss of types of wood and plant fibres through the destruction of forests; the mechanization of farm labour; and migration from the countryside to the city. However, city dwellers and tourists have created a demand for 'traditional' crafts so their future is to some degree assured.

Knitwear and textiles

Chiloé is famous for its woollen goods, hand knitted and coloured with natural dyes. Sweaters, knitted caps, *mantas*, socks are very popular. Rugs, blankets and patch dolls are all sold locally and in Puerto Montt. The Mapuche are also weavers of sheep's wool, making ponchos, *mantas*, sashes (*fajas*), reversible rugs (*lamas*) with geometric designs and bedspreads (*pontros*). The colours come from natural dyes.

Silverware

Although silverware is one of the traditional crafts of the Mapuche, its production is in decline owing to the cost of the metal. Traditional women's jewellery includes earrings, headbands, necklaces, brooches and *tupus* (pins for fastening the *manta* or shawl). Nowadays, the most common items are *chawai* (earrings), but these are smaller than those traditionally worn by Mapuche women. It is not known whether Mapuche silversmiths had perfected their skills before the arrival of the Spaniards; certainly the circulation of silver coins in the 18th century gave great impetus to this form of metalwork.

Specialist crafts

The Mapuche make musical instruments: the *trutruca*, a horn 1.5 to 4 m long; *pifilka* (or *pifüllka*), a wooden whistle; the *kultrún* drum; *cascahuilla*, a string of bells; and *trompe*, similar to a Jew's harp. The village of Rari, near the Termas de Panimávida, some 25 km northeast of Linares (Región VII), specializes in beautiful, delicate items made from dyed horsehair: bangles and brooches in the shape of butterflies, little hats, flowers, etc.

Glacial landscapes

Patagonia provides some of the best examples of glacial landscapes on earth. One common sign of the region's glacial past is the U-shaped valleys. Perhaps one of the best examples is the Río Simpson between Coyhaique and Puerto Aisén. High above these valleys, sharp mountain ridges can be seen; these have been caused by the eroding action of the ice on two or more sides. In some places, the resulting debris or 'moraine' formed a dam, blocking the valley and creating a lake, as in the Lake District at Lagos Calafquén, Panguipulli and Riñihue.

The drowned coastline south of Puerto Montt also owes its origin to glaciation. The ice that once covered the southern Andes was so heavy that it depressed the relatively narrow tip of South America. When the ice melted and the sea level rose, water broke through, leaving the western Andes as islands and creating the Chilean fjords, glaciated valleys carved out by the ice and now drowned.

Land and environment

Landscape

Patagonia stretches roughly from Rio Colorado (39°) to the Magellan Straits and covers some 780,000 sq km. Shaped by tectonic pressures, volcanic activity and the ice age, it is made up of three main geographical features: mountain, steppe and coast.

Mountain

The Andes, which form a natural frontier between Chile and Argentina, diminish in size south of Santiago (eroded by glacial action), but become increasingly volcanic in nature. Geographical faults associated with the mountains, lead to frequent volcanic eruptions and earthquakes. In the Lake District, the mountain passes are low enough in places for crossing. However, further south the increase in precipitation and latitude lead to larger snowfalls and more glaciation. The U-shaped valleys that can be seen throughout the south are typical of a glacial landscape. Though of modest height, Cerro Fitz Roy and other peaks on the fringes of the Patagonian ice cap are among the most dramatic on the continent.

Some of Patagonia's richest national parks are to be found in mountain areas. As the glaciers melted, lakes were left in the foothills on both sides of the Andes. Frequent rainfall and fertile soil has led to large expanses of southern beech forest, with some areas of magnificent virgin Valdivian rainforest. Here you will see coihues (evergreen beeches) over 450 years old and alerces over 1500 years old, with the ancient species of bamboo cane (*caña colihue*) growing everywhere. The rivers and lakes have abundant trout and salmon.

Steppe

Lying in the eastern shadow of the Andes and sheltered from the rain, this area is characterized by an arid, wind-swept plateau with terraces, which drop in altitude from west to east. The surface of the ancient rocks has been subjected to endless erosion; the dry conditions and strong winds strip the surface of cover, and fill the air with dust. Only where rivers have scored deep valleys in the rock base can soil accumulate. Overgrazing by sheep has produced serious desertification in many parts of the steppe, creating a dramatic and desolate landscape. Plant life in the steppe has had to adapt to the severe climatic conditions. The northwest of this area is covered by bushy scrublands, such as the coiron grasses and calafete (*Berberis buxifolia*). All have deep roots to access the water deep below, and many have small leaves or spines. Nearer the mountains where the climate is less severe and the soil more fertile, there is a herbaceous steppe which includes coiron blanco and shrubs such as the neneo.

Coast

In the far south of Patagonia the coastline has been dissected by Ice Age glaciers into a maze of islands and channels. The ice that once covered the southern Andes was so heavy that it depressed the relatively narrow tip of South America. When the ice melted and the sea level rose, water broke through leaving the western Andes as islands and creating the Chilean fjords, glaciated valleys carved out by the ice and now drowned. Much of the coastal area and the archipelagic islands are covered with lichen, moss and fern, as well as wild flowers including orchids, and trees such as the antarctic beech (*Nothofagus moorei*).

Climate

Patagonia is generally thought of as a temperate climate with cool summers and mild winters, but it is well known for its unpredictable weather. Two factors have a major effect the weather: the Andes and the Humbolt current. Cold air that accompanies the current sweeps in from the Antarctic and meets with warmer air over the land, creating rainfall in Chile, but very little of the moisture reaches the Argentinian side of the mountains. Further south, coastal temperatures are moderated by the ocean; there is no real summer, but the winters are rarely severe, although there are frequent storms.

Wildlife

The varied geography of Patagonia has created a number of different ecosystems, so it's no surprise that the wildlife is extremely varied, as animals and plants have been forced to adapt to the severe climatic conditions. Chile in particular is an ecological island: fauna that is commonplace in neighbouring countries has not been able to migrate here because of the Andes, the desert, the ice and the sea, and the country's isolation has contributed to a range of endemic wildlife. Specialist wildlife and birdwatching tours led by experts are available in most areas and are detailed throughout the guide.

Land mammals

Typical of Patagonia, is the **guanaco** – a coffee-coloured, cousin of the llama, with a long neck and small head. Standing at 1.5 m tall and weighing 55 kg, they are very agile and fast runners. Both grazers and browsers, they live in deserts, shrub land, savannah and occasionally on forest fringes. An estimated 20,000 now survive. Two species of deer found in Patagonia are the **huemul** and the **pudú**. The huemul appears on Chile's coat of arms, along with the condor. Both the huemul and the pudú are very rare and difficult to spot, see page 19. A large, reddish-brown species of **puma** can still be found in the mountain valleys, although it's a solitary, nocturnal creature and understandably shy of humans. Other land mammals typical of Patagonia include a small hairless vole called the **tucotuco**, unique to Tierra del Fuego; a type of chinchilla called a **vizcacha**; a rodent called a **mara**; as well as the **otter**, **cougar**, **armadillo**, **skunk** and several species of **fox**.

Marine mammals

Numerous colonies of **seal** (including the elephant seal which can weigh up to three tonnes) and **sea lion** live all along the Patagonian coast and come ashore to mate in December and January. Five species of **dolphin**, including the Fitzroy, Commerson and Peale, can be spotted, frequently off the coast of Chiloé. Types of **whale** include the southern right whale, which comes to breed off the coast of Península Valdés and can be spotted from June to December; and the killer whale, which arrives to feed on the young seal pups from March to April.

Birds

The **choique**, known as 'Darwin's rhea', is a large, flightless, ostrich-like bird, which roams the Patagonian steppes. Once hunted for its feathers, it is now farmed for meat and protected in the wild. Another long-legged bird is the **southern** flamingo, most commonly seen around lake shores, it also inhabits coastal areas on the Península Valdés and the Isla de los Pájaros. From the coast to the mountains, **geese** can be seen flying in pairs; other species to look out for are the **black-necked swan**, the **Andean duck**, the **Austral parakeet** and the **Magellanic woodpecker**. Birds of prey include the **condor**, with a wingspan of more than four metres; and various species of **eagle**, **hawk** and **buzzard**. Two regional birds of prey, the **jote** and the **tiuque**, are also common. Half the world's species of **penguin** can be found along the coast of Chile, including the Humbolt, Magellanic and King species. They live in the sea for most of the year, but colonize Patagonia and Tierra del Fuego by the thousand, as they come onto land from October to March in order to breed. Other coastal birds include the **petrel**, **oystercatcher**, **cormorant**, **heron** and **albatross**.

Books

Argentina

Reference/travel

Bigongiari, Diego (ed) *Pirelli Guide*, including map for cultural, historical and nature information, highly recommended.
Hudson, W H *Far Away and Long Ago* and *Idle Days in Patagonia*, deal with this English writer's early life in the countryside.
Kirbus, Federico B *Guía de Aventuras y Turismo de la Argentina* (with comprehensive English index – 1989); and *La Argentina, país de maravillas*, Manrique Zago ediciones (1993), a beautiful book of photographs with text in Spanish and English; *Patagonia* (with **Jorge Schulte**) and *Ruta Cuarenta*, both fine photographic records with text (both Capuz Varela). Also by Kirbus, *Mágica Ruta 40* and *Quebrada de Humahuaca*; see www.magicaruta40.com.ar and www.kirbus.com.ar.
Lucas Bridges, E *Uttermost Part of the Earth*, about the early colonization of Tierra del Fuego.

Literature

Borges, Jorge Luis (1899-1986) Argentina's most famous writer, and at the forefront of avant-garde experimental and urban themes. He is best known for his teasing, revolutionary and poetic short stories, as seen in *Ficciones* (1944) and *El Aleph* (1949).
Cortázar, Julio (1914-1984) The leading Argentine representative of the 1960s 'boom'. His novel *Rayuela* (Hopscotch, 1963) typifies the philosophy and freedom of the period.
Güiraldes, Ricardo (1886-1927) *Don Segundo Sombra*, a second great gaucho work (see Hernández, below), further cementing the figure of the gaucho as national hero.
Hernández, José *El gaucho Martín Fierro* (1872), an epic poem about the disruption of local communities by the march of progress; the eponymous hero and dispossessed outlaw came to symbolize Argentine nationhood.
Martínez, Tomás Eloy (1934-) Two highly acclaimed novels on Argentina's enduring 20th-century figures, *Santa Evita* (1995) and *La novela de Perón* (The Perón Novel, 1985).
Puig, Manuel (1932-1990) A writer fascinated by mass culture, gender roles and the banal as art, who expressed these ideas in novels such as *El beso de la Mujer Araña* (The Kiss of the Spider Woman, 1976 – made into a renowned film).
Sábato, Ernesto (1911-) Important 1960s writer whose most famous novel is *Sobre héroes y tumbas* (On Heroes and Tombs, 1961) and who also wrote the preface to *Nunca más* (Never again, 1984), the report of the commission into the disappearances in the 1970s 'dirty war'.
Soriano, Osvaldo (1943-1998) Another writer dealing with dictatorship and the 'dirty war' in *No habrá más penas ni olvido* (A Funny, Dirty Little War, 1982).

Chile

Reference/travel

Green, Toby *Saddled with Darwin* (Phoenix, 2000).
Keenan, Brian and **McCarthy, John** *Between Extremes* (Transworld, 1999).
Swale, Rosie *Back to Cape Horn* (Fontana, 1988) desribes her epic horse ride through Chile.
Wheeler, Sara *Travels in a Thin Country* (Little, Brown and Co, 1994).

Poetry

Huidobro, Vicente (1893-1948) Among many books, see *Altazor* (1931).
Mistral, Gabriela (1889-1957; Nobel Prize 1945). *Desolación* (1923). *Tala* (1938), *Lagar* (1954).
Neruda, Pablo (1904-1973; Nobel Prize 1971) Of Neruda's many collections, see *Veinte poemas de amor y una canción deseperada* (1924), *Tercer residencia* (1947), *Canto general* (1950) and his memoirs *Confieso que he vivido* (1974). See also **Feinstein, Adam**, *Pablo Neruda, a passion for life* (Bloomsbury, 2004).
Nicanor Parra (1914-) Brother of the singer and artist Violeta, *Poemas y antipoemas* (1954).

20th-century prose

Allende, Isabel (born 1942) Novels such as *The House of the Spirits*, *Of Love and Shadows* and *Eva Luna* are world famous.

Bolaño, Roberto *By Night in Chile* (Harvill, 2002).

Bombal, María Luisa (1910-80) *La última niebla* (1935).

Brunet, Marta (1901-1967) *Montaña adentro* 1923, *María Nadie* (1957).

Donoso, José (1924-1996) *El obsceno pájaro de la noche*.

Dorfman, Ariel (born 1942) *La muerte y la doncella* (Death and the Maiden), *La última canción de Manuel Sendero* (The Last Song of Manuel Sendero).

Eltit, Damiela (born 1949) *Vaca sagrada* (1991), *El cuarto mundo* (1988).

Skármeta, Antonio (born 1940) Best known for *Ardiente paciencia*, retitled *El cartero de Neruda* and filmed as *Il Postino* (The Postman).

Valenzuela, Luisa (1938-) Cola de lagartija (The Lizard's Tail, 1983).

Contents

Footnotes

Basic Spanish for travellers

Learning Spanish is a useful part of the preparation for a trip to Latin America and no volumes of dictionaries, phrase books or word lists will provide the same enjoyment as being able to communicate directly with the people of the country you are visiting. It is a good idea to make an effort to grasp the basics before you go. As you travel you will pick up more of the language and the more you know, the more you will benefit from your stay.

General pronunciation

Whether you have been taught the 'Castilian' pronounciation (*z* and *c* followed by *i* or *e* are pronounced as the *th* in think) or the 'American' pronounciation (they are pronounced as *s*), you will encounter little difficulty in understanding either. Regional accents and usages vary, but the basic language is essentially the same everywhere. In Argentina, the accent is distinctly different to the rest of Latin America in one crucial area. The letters *ll* in all other Spanish-speaking countries are pronounced like the *y* in yellow, in Argentina they are pronounced similar to the *sh* in she. The letter *y* in Argentina is also pronounced like the *sh* in she, instead of the *ee* in feet. Another change is that Argentines tend to use *vos* instead of *tú*.

Vowels

a	as in English *cat*
e	as in English *best*
i	as the *ee* in English *feet*
o	as in English *shop*
u	as the *oo* in English *food*
ai	as the *i* in English *ride*
ei	as *ey* in English *they*
oi	as *oy* in English *toy*

Consonants

Most consonants can be pronounced more or less as they are in English. The exceptions are:

g	before *e* or *i* is the same as *j*
h	is always silent (except in *ch* as in *chair*)
j	as the *ch* in Scottish *loch*
ll	as the *y* in *yellow*
ñ	as the *ni* in English *onion*
rr	trilled much more than in English
x	*x*, *s*, *sh* or *j* (depending on its position)

Spanish words and phrases

Greetings, courtesies

hello	*hola*
good morning	*buenos días*
good afternoon/ evening/night	*buenas tardes/noches*
goodbye	*adiós/chao*
pleased to meet you	*mucho gusto*
see you later	*hasta luego*
how are you?	*¿cómo está?¿cómo estás?*
I'm fine, thanks	*estoy muy bien, gracias*
I'm called...	*me llamo...*
what is your name?	*¿cómo se llama? ¿cómo te llamas?*
yes/no	*sí/no*
please	*por favor*
thank you (very much)	*(muchas) gracias*
I speak Spanish	*hablo español*
I don't speak Spanish	*no hablo español*
do you speak English?	*¿habla inglés?*
I don't understand	*no entiendo/ no comprendo*
please speak slowly	*hable despacio por favor*
I am very sorry	*lo siento mucho/ disculpe*
what do you want?	*¿qué quiere? ¿qué quieres?*
I want	*quiero*
I don't want it	*no lo quiero*
leave me alone	*déjeme en paz/ no me moleste*
good/bad	*bueno/malo*

Questions and requests

Have you got a room for two people?
¿Tiene una habitación para dos personas?
How do I get to_? *¿Cómo llego a_?*
How much does it cost?
¿Cuánto cuesta? ¿cuánto es?
I'd like to make a long-distance phone call
Quisiera hacer una llamada de larga distancia
Is service included?*¿Está incluido el servicio?*
Is tax included? *¿Están incluidos los impuestos?*
When does the bus leave (arrive)?
¿A qué hora sale (llega) el autobús?
When? *¿cuándo?*
Where is_? *¿dónde está_?*
Where can I buy tickets?
¿Dónde puedo comprar boletos?
Where is the nearest petrol station?
¿Dónde está la gasolinera más cercana?
Why?*¿por qué?*

Basics

bank	*el banco*
bathroom/toilet	*el baño*
bill	*la factura/la cuenta*
cash	*el efectivo*
cheap	*barato/a*
credit card	*la tarjeta de crédito*
exchange house	*la casa de cambio*
exchange rate	*el tipo de cambio*
expensive	*caro/a*
market	*el mercado*
note/coin	*le billete/la moneda*
police (policeman)	*la policía (el policía)*
post office	*el correo*
public telephone	*el teléfono público*
supermarket	*el supermercado*
ticket office	*la taquilla*
traveller's cheques	*los cheques de viajero/ los travelers*

Getting around

aeroplane	*el avión*
airport	*el aeropuerto*
arrival/departure	*la llegada/salida*
avenue	*la avenida*
block	*la cuadra*
border	*la frontera*
bus station	*la terminal de autobuses/camiones*
bus	*el bus/el autobús/ el camión*
collective/ fixed-route taxi	*el colectivo*
corner	*la esquina*
customs	*la aduana*
first/second class	*primera/segunda clase*
left/right	*izquierda/derecha*
ticket	*el boleto*
empty/full	*vacío/lleno*
highway, main road	*la carretera*
immigration	*la inmigración*
insurance	*el seguro*
insured person	*el/la asegurado/a*
to insure yourself against	*asegurarse contra*
luggage	*el equipaje*
motorway, freeway	*el autopista/la carretera*
north, south, west, east	*norte, sur, oeste (occidente), este (oriente)*
oil	*el aceite*
to park	*estacionarse*
passport	*el pasaporte*
petrol/gasoline	*la gasolina*
puncture	*el pinchazo/ la ponchadura*
street	*la calle*
that way	*por allí/por allá*
this way	*por aquí/por acá*
tourist card/visa	*la tarjeta de turista*
tyre	*la llanta*
unleaded	*sin plomo*
to walk	*caminar/andar*

Accommodation

air conditioning	*el aire acondicionado*	power cut	*el apagón/corte*
all-inclusive	*todo incluido*	restaurant	*el restaurante*
bathroom, private	*el baño privado*	room/bedroom	*el cuarto/la habitación*
bed, double/single	*la cama matrimonial/ sencilla*	sheets	*las sábanas*
		shower	*la ducha/regadera*
blankets	*las cobijas/mantas*	soap	*el jabón*
to clean	*limpiar*	toilet	*el sanitario/excusado*
dining room	*el comedor*	toilet paper	*el papel higiénico*
guesthouse	*la casa de huéspedes*	towels, clean/dirty	*las toallas limpias/ sucias*
hotel	*el hotel*		
noisy	*ruidoso*	water, hot/cold	*el agua caliente/fría*
pillows	*las almohadas*		

Health

aspirin	*la aspirina*	diarrhoea	*la diarrea*
blood	*la sangre*	doctor	*el médico*
chemist	*la farmacia*	fever/sweat	*la fiebre/el sudor*
condoms	*los preservativos, los condones*	pain	*el dolor*
		head	*la cabeza*
contact lenses	*los lentes de contacto*	period/sanitary towels	*la regla/ las toallas femeninas*
contraceptives	*los anticonceptivos*		
contraceptive pill	*la píldora anti- conceptiva*	stomach	*el estómago*
		altitude sickness	*el soroche*

Family

family	*la familia*	boyfriend/girlfriend	*el novio/la novia*
brother/sister	*el hermano/la hermana*	friend	*el amigo/la amiga*
daughter/son	*la hija/el hijo*	married	*casado/a*
father/mother	*el padre/la madre*	single/unmarried	*soltero/a*
husband/wife	*el esposo (marido)/ la esposa*		

Months, days and time

January	*enero*	Tuesday	*martes*
February	*febrero*	Wednesday	*miércoles*
March	*marzo*	Thursday	*jueves*
April	*abril*	Friday	*viernes*
May	*mayo*	Saturday	*sábado*
June	*junio*	Sunday	*domingo*
July	*julio*		
August	*agosto*	at one o'clock	*a la una*
September	*septiembre*	at half past two	*a las dos y media*
October	*octubre*	at a quarter to three	*a cuarto para las tres/ a las tres menos quince*
November	*noviembre*		
December	*diciembre*	it's one o'clock	*es la una*
Monday	*lunes*	it's seven o'clock	*son las siete*

it's six twenty	*son las seis y veinte*
it's five to nine	*son las nueve menos cinco*
in ten minutes	*en diez minutos*
five hours	*cinco horas*
does it take long?	*¿tarda mucho?*

Numbers

one	*uno/una*
two	*dos*
three	*tres*
Four	*cuatro*
five	*cinco*
six	*seis*
seven	*siete*
eight	*ocho*
nine	*nueve*
ten	*diez*
eleven	*once*
twelve	*doce*
thirteen	*trece*
fourteen	*catorce*
fifteen	*quince*
sixteen	*dieciséis*
seventeen	*diecisiete*
eighteen	*dieciocho*
nineteen	*diecinueve*
twenty	*veinte*
twenty-one	*veintiuno*
thirty	*treinta*
forty	*cuarenta*
fifty	*cincuenta*
sixty	*sesenta*
seventy	*setenta*
eighty	*ochenta*
ninety	*noventa*
hundred	*cien/ciento*
thousand	*mil*

Food

avocado	*la palta*
baked	*al horno*
bakery	*la panadería*
banana	*la banana*
beans	*los frijoles/ las habichuelas*
beef	*la carne de res*
beef steak	*el lomo*
boiled rice	*el arroz blanco*
bread	*el pan*
breakfast	*el desayuno*
butter	*la manteca*
cake	*la torta*
chewing gum	*el chicle*
chicken	*el pollo*
chilli or green pepper	*el ají/pimiento*
clear soup, stock	*el caldo*
cooked	*cocido*
dining room	*el comedor*
egg	*el huevo*
fish	*el pescado*
fork	*el tenedor*
fried	*frito*
garlic	*el ajo*
goat	*el chivo*
grapefruit	*la toronja/el pomelo*
grill	*la parrilla*
grilled/griddled	*a la plancha*
guava	*la guayaba*
ham	*el jamón*
hamburger	*la hamburguesa*
hot, spicy	*picante*
ice cream	*el helado*
jam	*la mermelada*
knife	*el cuchillo*
lemon	*el limón*
lobster	*la langosta*
lunch	*el almuerzo/la comida*
meal	*la comida*
meat	*la carne*
minced meat	*la carne picada*
onion	*la cebolla*
orange	*la naranja*
pepper	*el pimiento*
pasty, turnover	*la empanada/ el pastelito*
pork	*el cerdo*
potato	*la papa*
prawns	*los camarones*
raw	*crudo*

restaurant	*el restaurante*
salad	*la ensalada*
salt	*la sal*
sandwich	*el bocadillo*
sauce	*la salsa*
sausage	*la longaniza/el chorizo*
scrambled eggs	*los huevos revueltos*
seafood	*los mariscos*
soup	*la sopa*
spoon	*la cuchara*
squash	*la calabaza*
squid	*los calamares*
supper	*la cena*
sweet	*dulce*
to eat	*comer*
toasted	*tostado*
turkey	*el pavo*
vegetables	*los legumbres/vegetales*
without meat	*sin carne*
yam	*el camote*

Drink

beer	*la cerveza*
boiled	*hervido/a*
bottled	*en botella*
camomile tea	*la manzanilla*
canned	*en lata*
coffee	*el café*
coffee, white	*el café con leche*
cold	*frío*
cup	*la taza*
drink	*la bebida*
drunk	*borracho/a*
firewater	*el aguardiente*
fruit milkshake	*el batido/licuado*
glass	*el vaso*
hot	*caliente*
ice/without ice	*el hielo/sin hielo*
juice	*el jugo*
lemonade	*la limonada*
milk	*la leche*
mint	*la menta*
rum	*el ron*
soft drink	*el refresco*
sugar	*el azúcar*
tea	*el té*
to drink	*beber/tomar*
water	*el agua*
water, carbonated	*el agua mineral con gas*
water, still mineral	*el agua mineral sin gas*
wine, red	*el vino tinto*
wine, white	*el vino blanco*

Key verbs

to go	**ir**
I go	*voy*
you go (familiar)	*vas*
he, she, it goes, you (formal) go	*va*
we go	*vamos*
they, you (plural) go	*van*
to have (possess)	**tener**
I have	*tengo*
you (familiar) have	*tienes*
he, she, it, you (formal) have	*tiene*
we have	*tenemos*
they, you (plural) have	*tienen*

there is/are	*hay*	
there isn't/aren't	*no hay*	
to be	**ser**	**estar**
I am	soy	estoy
you are	eres	estás
he, she, it is, you (formal) are	es	está
we are	somos	estamos
they, you (plural) are	son	están

This section has been assembled on the basis of glossaries compiled by André de Mendonça and David Gilmour of South American Experience, London, and the Latin American Travel Advisor, No 9, March 1996.

Index → *Entries in bold refer to maps*

Advertisers' index

About the authors

Janak Jani

Janak Jani was born in London. Travelling is in his genes and he has lived and worked in several countries in four continents. He arrived in Chile eight years ago and, enchanted by the magic of Valparaíso, he decided to settle down, following in the family tradition of westward migration. He now owns and runs a guesthouse with his wife, Lorena, and spends his spare time breaking down in his car on gravel roads in the middle of nowhere and getting lost with his dog in the Andes.

Lucy E Cousins

Australian-born Lucy E Cousins started travelling at the age of 18 months when she crawled across the road in front of her house – much to her mother's horror. Since then she hasn't stopped. She has visited more than 30 countries from Jordan to Venezuela, travelled by bus, bicycle, canoe, Amazon ferry and on foot, and has lived in London, Bolivia and Argentina. In 2004, while backpacking around South America, she fell in love with Buenos Aires. Two years later she moved there to start her own English-language newspaper called *The Argentimes*. She has since worked as the editor of the Buenos Aires pages of www.ontheroadtravel.com and the *South American Explorers Magazine* and has spent two years as director of the Buenos Aires office of the South American Explorers. She has previously written for *Condé Nast Traveller*, *Timeout*, *The Independent* and several other publications. Lucy fell in love for a second time when she met her Argentine husband Gabriel, and they currently live in Buenos Aires, speaking a mixture of Spanish and English, eating *dulce de leche* and spending time relaxing in the Delta.

Acknowledgements

Janak Jani

As always, numerous people have helped in making this book as precise and relevant as possible. Wholehearted thanks go to the regional SERNATUR offices throughout Southern Chile as well as to CONAF and municipal tourist offices who gave their time, expertise and local knowledge to ensure that the information on their area was thorough and complete.

Special thanks go to the following for providing help and information: Hans in Pucón, a mine of local information as always. Peter and Margot for good company in one of my favourite places in the Lake District. Mauro and Mallín for five days of home life during a hectic journey and a couple of unexpected day trips; Armin for rescuing me and my clapped out car and Nadia for nursing me through the flu; Nico for keeping me up to speed on the disaster-zone around Chaitén; Jorge and Conzuelo for being talked into a road trip down the Carretera Austral; Juan Pablo for a fine day on horseback and teaching me how to splay and spit-roast a lamb. Thanks also to Ben Box, editor of the South American Handbook, for help and advice, Felicity, Sarah, Kassia and all at Footprint for working tirelessly and to a very tight schedule on the production of this book and to the countless readers whose letters and emails have helped to make this guide as up-to-date as possible. Finally, thanks to Juan Carlos, Vero, Rubén and the rest of the team for holding the fort at Luna Sonrisa these past months, and to my wife, Lorena for her help, support and company.

Lucy E Cousins

I would like to thank the many people who help me along the way to finishing this book. As always I would like to thank Alan for offering me this amazing opportunity. I also owe a lot to Felicity Laughton, Sarah Sorensen and the team at Footprint. I must also thank my co-author Janak Jani; it was a pleasure to work with him.

Wonderful people to thank are Ron from www.travellersguru.com for all his time and wisdom about Bariloche and surrounds, Will Massa for his research on the Argentine film industry, and Layne Mosler for her help invaluable help in the Buenos Aires food section.

Throughout Argentina there have been many helpful people who also deserve a thank you: the wonderful Romina and Virginia from Las Balsas, Irina Schugurensky from one of the best on-the-ground guides, María from Hostels del Glaciar, María from Albergue Rukalhue, Facundo from El Gualicho Hostel, and the guys from Below 40 in Bariloche.

I pledge my undying gratitude to my parents, mother-in-law and sister for their constant encouragement. And finally I would like to thank my fantastic husband Gabriel García Isola for his endless patience, support, invaluable advice and the many cups of tea, delicious dinners and yummy lunches he made me while I was neck high in research.

Credits

Footprint credits
Editor: Felicity Laughton
Map editor: Sarah Sorensen
Colour section: Kassia Gawronski

Managing Director: Andy Riddle
Commercial Director: Patrick Dawson
Publisher: Alan Murphy
Editorial: Nicola Gibbs, Sara Chare, Ria Gane, Jen Haddington, Jo Williams, Alice Jell

Cartography: Robert Lunn, Kevin Feeney, Emma Bryers
Cover design: Robert Lunn
Design: Mytton Williams
Marketing: Liz Harper, Hannah Bonnell
Sales: Jeremy Parr
Advertising: Renu Sibal
Finance and administration: Elizabeth Taylor

Photography credits
Front cover: Parque Nacional Los Glaciares, Gareth McCormack/Alamy
Back cover: Rockhopper penguin, Johnathan Esper/Shutterstock

Manufactured in India by Nutech Print Services, Delhi
Pulp from sustainable forests

Footprint feedback
We try as hard as we can to make each Footprint guide as up to date as possible but, of course, things always change. If you want to let us know about your experiences – good, bad or ugly – then don't delay, go to **www.footprintbooks.com** and send in your comments.

Publishing information
Footprint Patagonia
3rd edition

ISBN: 978 1 906098 73 5
CIP DATA: A catalogue record for this book is available from the British Library

Published by Footprint
6 Riverside Court
Lower Bristol Road
Bath BA2 3DZ, UK
T +44 (0)1225 469141
F +44 (0)1225 469461
www.footprintbooks.com

Distributed in the USA by Globe Pequot Press, Guilford, Connecticut

Footprint Mini Atlas
Patagonia

1
Victoria
Temuco
Villarrica
Pucón
Neuquén
Valdivia
Parque Nacional Lanin
San Martín De Los Andes
Osorno
Parque Nacional Nahuel Huapi
Puerto Montt
Bariloche
Parque Nacional Alerce Andino
Chiloé
Parque Nacional Los Alerces
Chaitén
Esquel
2
Coyhaique
Lago General Carrera
Lago Buenos Aires
Comodoro Rivadavia
Golfo San Jorge
CHILE
ARGENTINA
Puerto Deseado
Villa O'Higgins
Fitz Roy (3405m)
El Chaltén
Lago Viedma
Parque Nacional Los Glaciares
Lago Argentino
3
El Calafate
Parque Nacional Torres del Paine
Puerto Natales
Río Gallegos
Punta Arenas
Tierra del Fuego
Parque Nacional Tierra del Fuego
Ushuaia
Pacific Ocean
4
Bahía Blanca
Viedma
Golfo San Matías
Puerto Madryn
Península Valdés
Trelew
Altitude in metres
2000
1000
500
200
0
Highway paved
Highway unpaved
Primary road paved
Primary road unpaved
Secondary road paved
Secondary road unpaved
Track
Path
Stanley
West Falkland/ Gran Malvina
East Falkland/ Isla Soledad
N
200 km
200 miles

Map 1

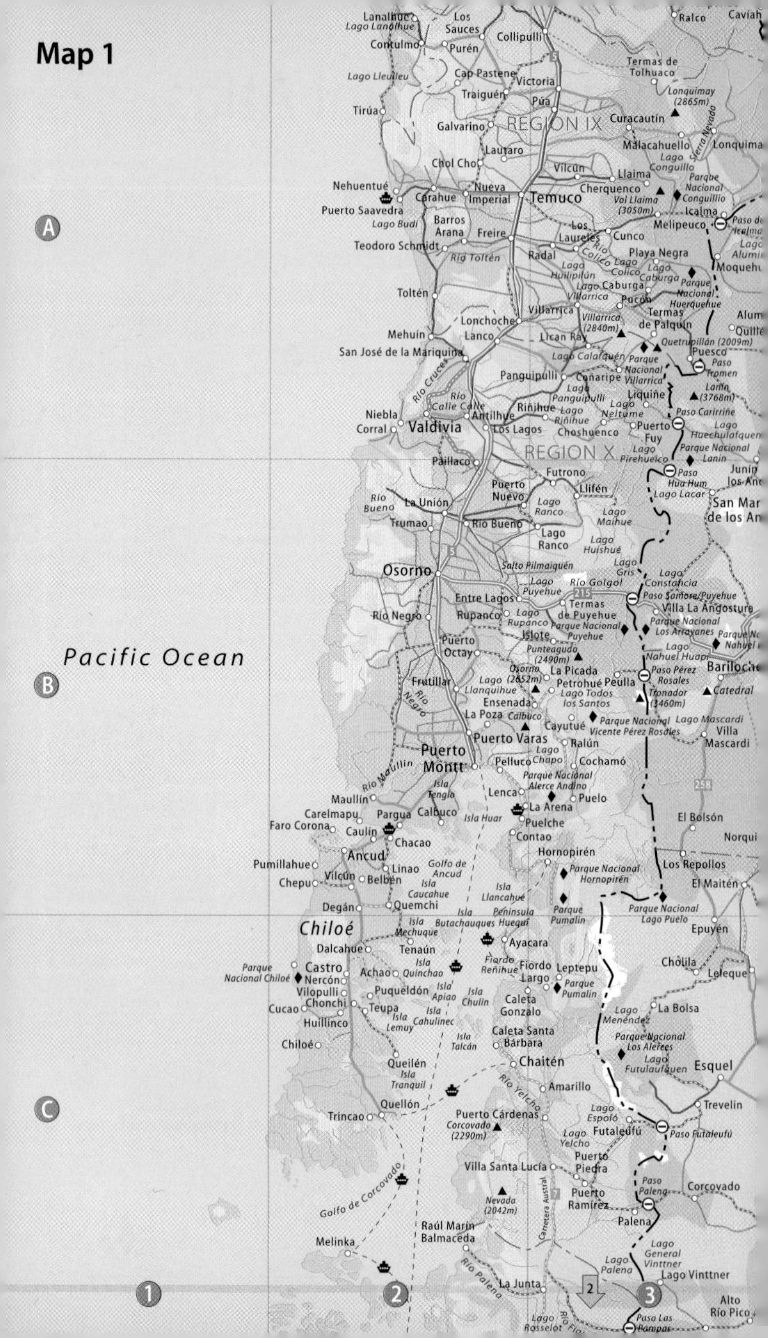

Lanalhue
Lago Lanalhue
Los Sauces
Ralco
Caviahue
Contulmo
Purén
Collipulli
Termas de Tolhuaco
Lago Lleulleu
Cap Pastene
Victoria
Traiguén
Lonquimay (2865m)
Púa
Tirúa
Sierra Nevada
Galvarino
REGION IX
Curacautín
Malacahuello
Lonquimay
Lautaro
Lago Conguillío
Chol Chol
Vilcún
Llaima
Parque Nacional Conguillío
Nehuentué
Nueva Imperial
Temuco
Cherquenco
Carahue
Vol Llaima (3050m)
Puerto Saavedra
Icalma
Paso de Icalma
Lago Budi
Barros Arana
Los Laureles
Melipeuco
Freire
Cunco
Lago Aluminé
Teodoro Schmidt
Río Toltén
Radal
Río Colico
Playa Negra
Lago Colico
Lago Huilipilún
Lago Caburga
Moquehue
Toltén
Caburga
Parque Nacional Huerquehue
Villarrica
Lago Villarrica
Pucón
Termas de Palquín
Aluminé
Lonchoche
Villarrica (2840m)
Quillén
Mehuín
Lanco
Lican Ray
Quetrupillán (2009m)
Puesco
San José de la Mariquina
Lago Calafquén
Parque Nacional Villarrica
Paso Tromen
Río Cruces
Panguipulli
Coñaripe
Lago Panguipulli
Liquiñe
Lanín (3768m)
Río Calle Calle
Riñihue
Lago Riñihue
Lago Neltume
Paso Carirriñe
Niebla
Antilhue
Puerto Fuy
Lago Huechulafquen
Corral
Valdivia
Los Lagos
Choshuenco
Lago Pirehueico
Parque Nacional Lanín
REGION X
Paillaco
Futrono
Paso Hua Hum
Junín de los Andes
Puerto Nuevo
Llifén
Lago Lacar
Río Bueno
La Unión
Lago Ranco
San Martín de los Andes
Lago Maihue
Trumao
Río Bueno
Lago Ranco
Lago Huishué
Osorno
Salto Pilmaiquén
Lago Gris
Lago Constancia
Lago Puyehue
Río Golgol
Entre Lagos
Termas de Puyehue
Paso Samoré/Puyehue
Villa La Angostura
Río Negro
Rupanco
Lago Rupanco
Parque Nacional Puyehue
Parque Nacional Los Arrayanes
Parque Nacional Nahuel Huapi
Islote
Puerto Octay
Punteagudo (2490m)
Lago Nahuel Huapi
Pacific Ocean
Osorno (2652m)
La Picada
Paso Pérez Rosales
Bariloche
Frutillar
Lago Llanquihue
Petrohué
Peulla
Río Negro
Lago Todos los Santos
Catedral
Ensenada
Tronador (3460m)
La Poza
Calbuco
Parque Nacional Vicente Pérez Rosales
Lago Mascardi
Cayutué
Villa Mascardi
Puerto Varas
Ralún
Puerto Montt
Lago Chapo
Pelluco
Cochamó
Río Maullín
Isla Tenglo
Parque Nacional Alerce Andino
Maullín
Lenca
Puelo
La Arena
Carelmapu
Pargua
Calbuco
Isla Huar
El Bolsón
Faro Corona
Caulín
Puelche
Chacao
Contao
Norquinco
Ancud
Hornopirén
Pumillahue
Linao
Golfo de Ancud
Los Repollos
Parque Nacional Hornopirén
Chepu
Vilcún
Belbén
Isla Caucahue
El Maitén
Isla Llancahue
Degán
Quemchi
Isla Butachauques
Península Huequi
Parque Pumalín
Parque Nacional Lago Puelo
Chiloé
Isla Mechuque
Epuyén
Ayacara
Dalcahue
Tenaún
Fiordo Reñihue
Parque Nacional Chiloé
Castro
Isla Quinchao
Fiordo Largo
Leptepu
Cholila
Nercón
Achao
Leleque
Vilopulli
Isla Apiao
Parque Pumalín
Chonchi
Puqueldón
Isla Chulin
Caleta Gonzalo
Cucao
Teupa
Isla Lemuy
Isla Cahulinec
Lago Menéndez
La Bolsa
Huillinco
Caleta Santa Bárbara
Parque Nacional Los Alerces
Chiloé
Isla Talcán
Lago Futulaufquen
Queilén
Chaitén
Esquel
Isla Tranquil
Río Yelcho
Amarillo
Quellón
Trevelin
Trincao
Puerto Cárdenas
Lago Espolón
Futaleufú
Paso Futaleufú
Corcovado (2290m)
Lago Yelcho
Golfo de Corcovado
Villa Santa Lucía
Puerto Piedra
Paso Palena
Corcovado
Nevada (2042m)
Carretera Austral
Puerto Ramírez
Palena
Melinka
Raúl Marín Balmaceda
Lago General Vinttner
Lago Palena
Lago Vinttner
Río Palena
La Junta
Alto Río Pico
Lago Rosselot
Río Figueroa
Paso Las Pampas
A
B
C
1
2
3

Loncopué
40
Rio Neuquen
NEUQUÉN
Bajado
del Agro
Las Lajas
Mariano Moreno
Zapala
PN Laguna
Blanca
Plaza
Huincal
Cutral-Có
Villa El Chocón
40
Emb Ezequiel
Ramos Mexia
Picún Leufú
Piedra del
Aguila
RGENTINA
RIO NEGRO
Confluencia
Río Limay
Mencué
Aguada de Guerra
Comallo
Ingeniero
Jacobacci
Los Juncos
Bayas
40
Gastre
Paso del Sapo
Rio Chubut
CHUBUT
Colán Conhué
El Pajarito
Pampa
de Agria
Paso de Indios
José de
San Martín
Gobernador

Map 2

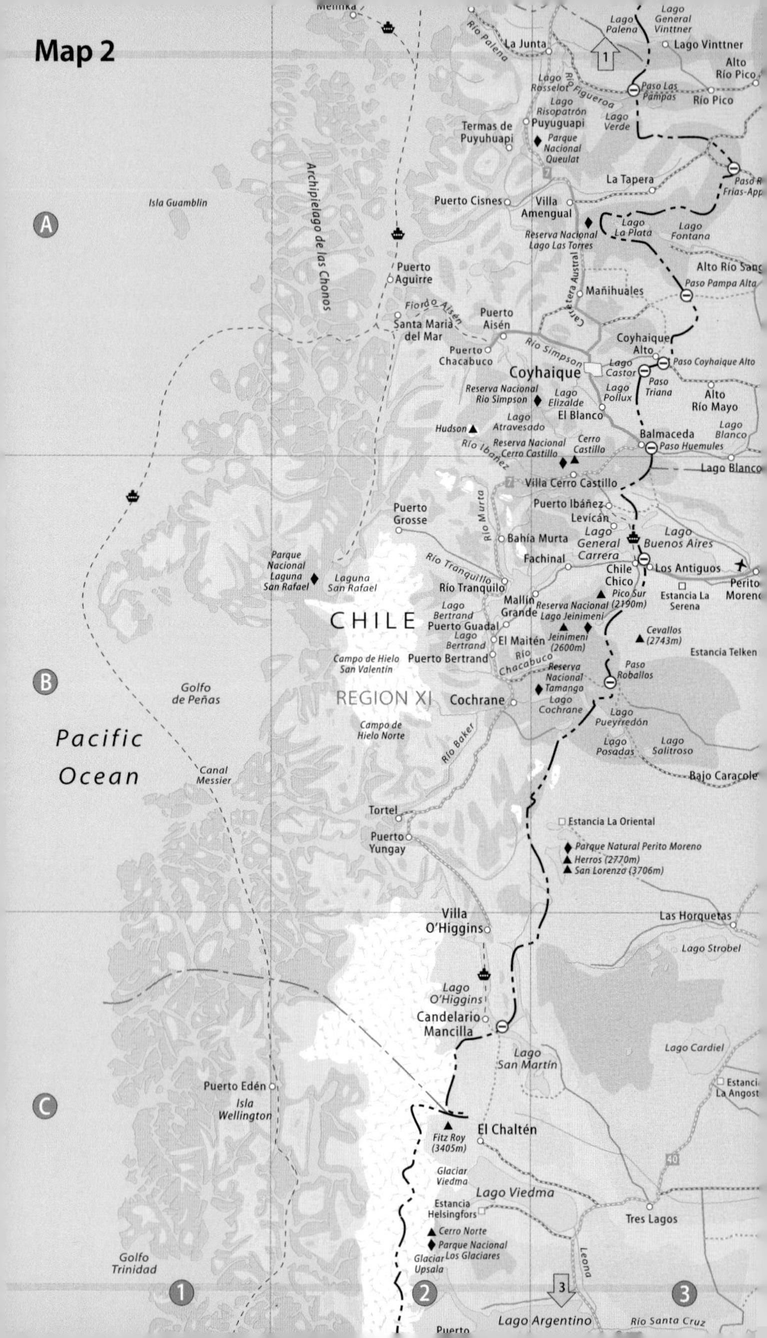

Melinka
La Junta
Río Palena
Lago Palena
Lago General Vinttner
Lago Vinttner
Alto Río Pico
1
Lago Rosselot
Río Figueroa
Paso Las Pampas
Río Pico
Lago Risopatrón
Lago Verde
Puyuguapi
Termas de Puyuhuapi
Parque Nacional Queulat
7
La Tapera
Paso Río Frías-App
Archipiélago de las Chonos
Isla Guamblin
Puerto Cisnes
Villa Amengual
Lago La Plata
Lago Fontana
Reserva Nacional Lago Las Torres
A
Puerto Aguirre
Carretera Austral
Alto Río Sang
Paso Pampa Alta
Mañihuales
Fiordo Aisén
Santa María del Mar
Puerto Aisén
Coyhaique Alto
Río Simpson
Puerto Chacabuco
Paso Coyhaique Alto
Coyhaique
Lago Castor
Paso Triana
Reserva Nacional Río Simpson
Lago Elizalde
Lago Pollux
Alto Río Mayo
El Blanco
Hudson
Lago Atravesado
Lago Blanco
Balmaceda
Río Ibáñez
Reserva Nacional Cerro Castillo
Cerro Castillo
Paso Huemules
Lago Blanco
Villa Cerro Castillo
Puerto Ibáñez
Puerto Grosse
Río Murta
Levicán
Bahía Murta
Lago General Carrera
Lago Buenos Aires
Fachinal
Parque Nacional Laguna San Rafael
Laguna San Rafael
Río Tranquilo
Chile Chico
Los Antiguos
Perito Moreno
Río Tranquilo
Pico Sur (2190m)
Estancia La Serena
Mallín Grande
Lago Bertrand
Reserva Nacional Lago Jeinimeni
CHILE
Puerto Guadal
Jeinimeni (2600m)
Cevallos (2743m)
Lago Bertrand
El Maitén
Estancia Telken
Campo de Hielo San Valentín
Puerto Bertrand
Río Chacabuco
Paso Roballos
Reserva Nacional Tamango
B
Golfo de Peñas
REGION XI
Cochrane
Lago Cochrane
Lago Pueyrredón
Pacific Ocean
Campo de Hielo Norte
Río Baker
Lago Posadas
Lago Salitroso
Canal Messier
Bajo Caracoles
Tortel
Estancia La Oriental
Puerto Yungay
Parque Natural Perito Moreno
Herros (2770m)
San Lorenzo (3706m)
Villa O'Higgins
Las Horquetas
Lago Strobel
Lago O'Higgins
Candelario Mancilla
Lago San Martín
Lago Cardiel
Puerto Edén
Isla Wellington
Estancia La Angostura
C
El Chaltén
Fitz Roy (3405m)
40
Glaciar Viedma
Lago Viedma
Estancia Helsingfors
Tres Lagos
Cerro Norte
Parque Nacional Los Glaciares
Glaciar Upsala
Leona
Golfo Trinidad
1
2
3
3
Lago Argentino
Río Santa Cruz
Puerto

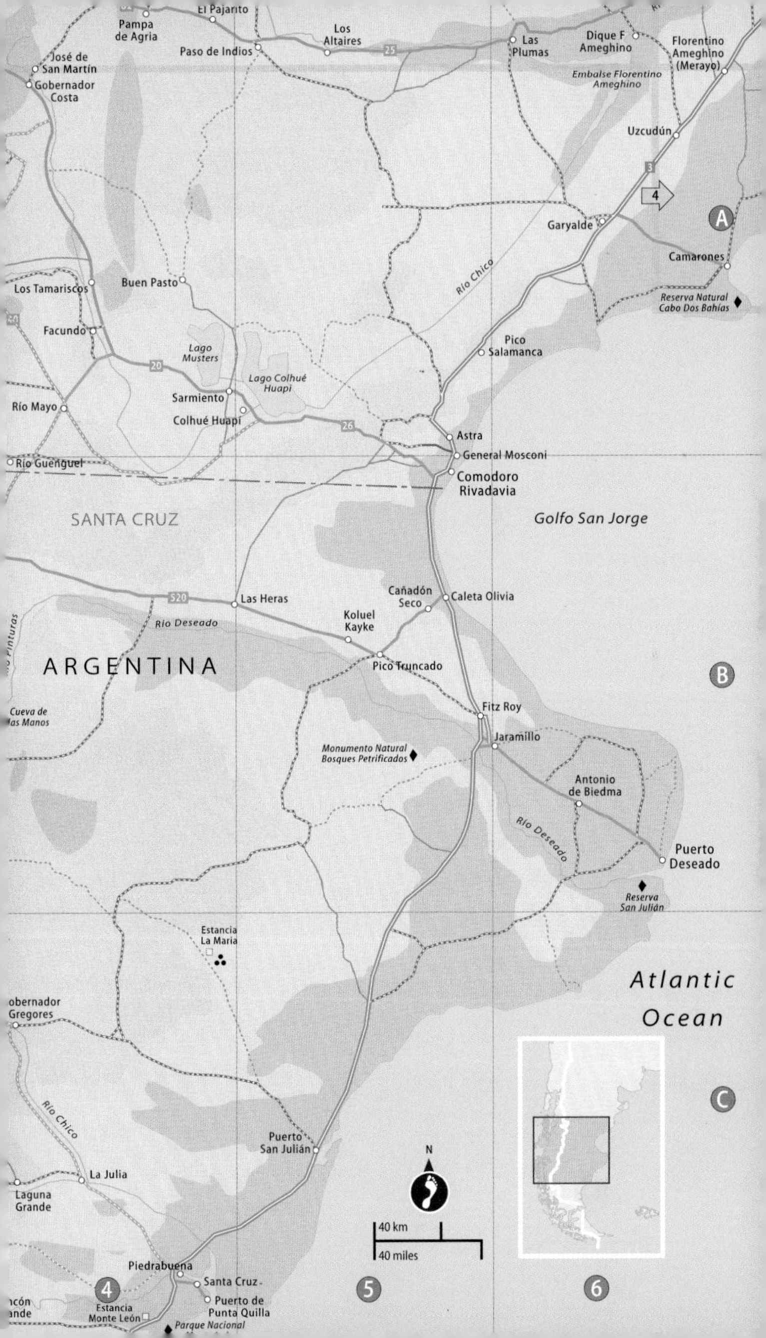

El Pajarito
Pampa de Agria
Los Altaires
Paso de Indios
25
Las Plumas
Dique F Ameghino
Florentino Ameghino (Merayo)
Embalse Florentino Ameghino
José de San Martín
Gobernador Costa
Uzcudún
3
4
Garyalde
A
Camarones
Río Chico
Reserva Natural Cabo Dos Bahías
Buen Pasto
Los Tamariscos
Facundo
Lago Musters
Lago Colhué Huapi
Pico Salamanca
20
Sarmiento
Colhué Huapí
Río Mayo
26
Astra
General Mosconi
Río Guenguel
Comodoro Rivadavia
SANTA CRUZ
Golfo San Jorge
520
Las Heras
Cañadón Seco
Caleta Olivia
Río Deseado
Koluel Kayke
ARGENTINA
Pico Truncado
B
Cueva de las Manos
Fitz Roy
Jaramillo
Monumento Natural Bosques Petrificados
Antonio de Biedma
Río Deseado
Puerto Deseado
Reserva San Julián
Estancia La María
Atlantic Ocean
Gobernador Gregores
Río Chico
C
Puerto San Julián
N
La Julia
Laguna Grande
40 km
40 miles
Piedrabuena
Santa Cruz
Puerto de Punta Quilla
Estancia Monte León
Parque Nacional
4
5
6

Map 3

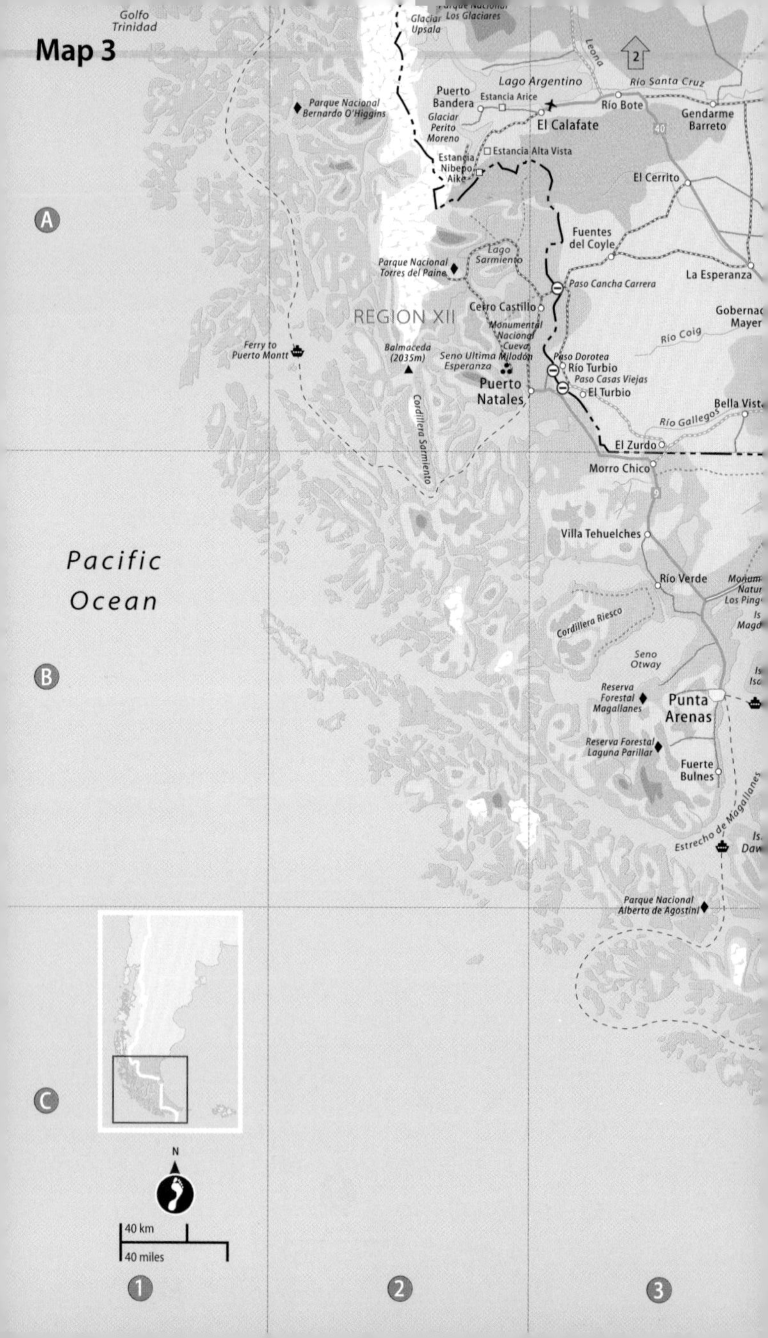
Golfo Trinidad
Glaciar Upsala
Los Glaciares
Leona
2
Lago Argentino
Río Santa Cruz
Parque Nacional Bernardo O'Higgins
Puerto Bandera
Estancia Arice
Río Bote
Gendarme Barreto
Glaciar Perito Moreno
El Calafate
40
Estancia Alta Vista
Estancia Nibepo Aike
El Cerrito
A
Fuentes del Coyle
Lago Sarmiento
Parque Nacional Torres del Paine
La Esperanza
Paso Cancha Carrera
Cerro Castillo
REGION XII
Gobernac Mayer
Monumental Nacional Cueva Milodón
Río Coig
Ferry to Puerto Montt
Balmaceda (2035m)
Seno Ultima Esperanza
Paso Dorotea
Río Turbio
Puerto Natales
Paso Casas Viejas
El Turbio
Bella Vist
Río Gallegos
Cordillera Sarmiento
El Zurdo
Morro Chico
9
Villa Tehuelches
Pacific Ocean
Río Verde
Cordillera Riesco
Seno Otway
B
Reserva Forestal Magallanes
Punta Arenas
Reserva Forestal Laguna Parillar
Fuerte Bulnes
Estrecho de Magallanes
Parque Nacional Alberto de Agostini
C
N
40 km
40 miles
1
2
3

Piedrabuena
Santa Cruz
Puerto de Punta Quilla
Estancia Monte León
Parque Nacional Monte León
ANTA CRUZ
Cañadón de las Vacas
Puerto Coig
Río Coig
Bahía Grande
Atlantic Ocean
Estancia Hill Station
Güer Aike
Río Gallegos
Laguna Azul
3
Estancia Monte Dinero
Paso Integración Austral
ta Delgada
Punta Espora
Primera Angostura
255
Segunda Angostura
Cerro Sombrero
Cullén
Primavera
Bahía San Sebastián
San Sebastián
venir
Onaisin
San Sebastián
Paso San Sebastián
Bahía Inutil
Camerón
Río Grande
Puerto Arturo
Lago Blanco
Tierra del Fuego
CHILE
TIERRA DEL FUEGO
Lago Fagnano
ARGENTINA
Lago Escondido
Parque Nacional Tierra del Fuego
Ushuaia
Estancia Harberton
Estrecho de La Maire
Isla de los Estados
Canal Beagle
Puerto Navarino
Puerto Williams
Wulara
Puerto Toro
Isla Navarino
Isla Wollaston
Parque Nacional Cabo de Hornos
Cape Horn
A
B
C
4
5
6

Map 4

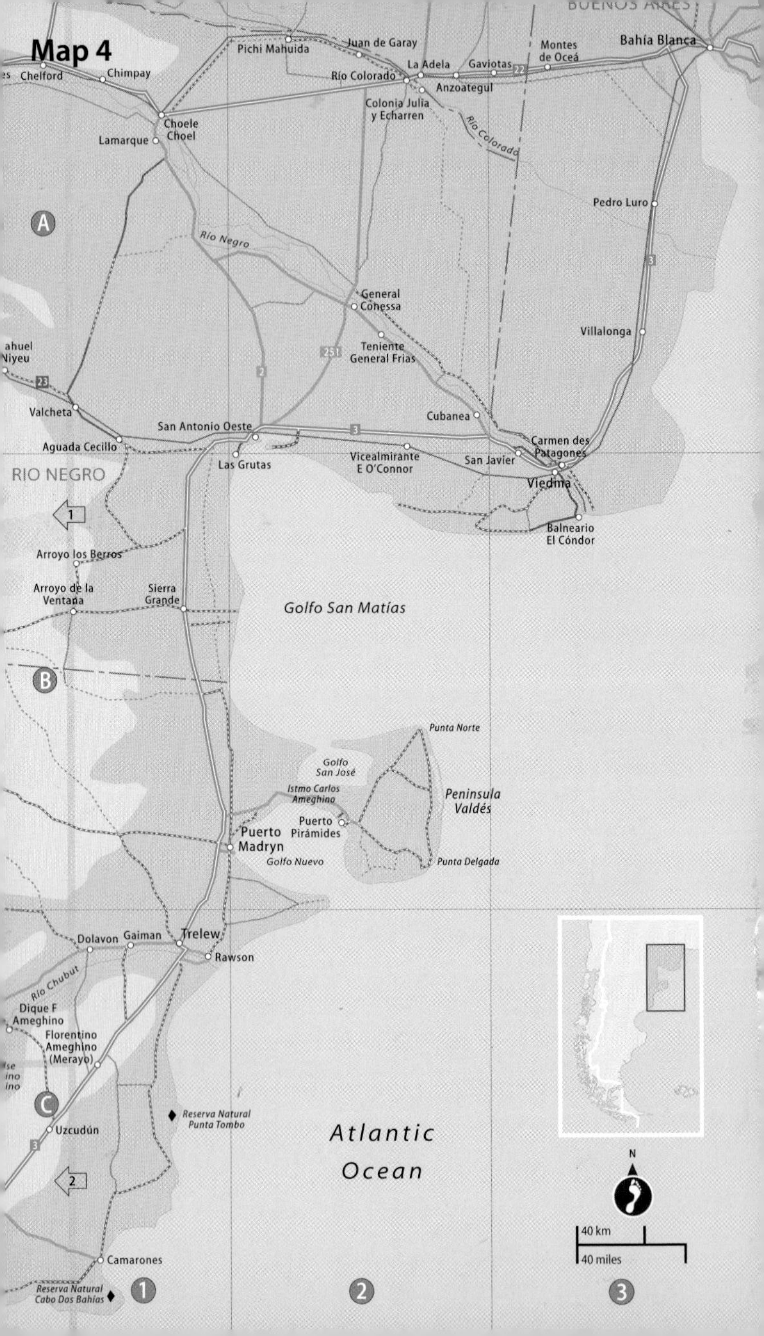

BUENOS AIRES
Pichi Mahuida
Juan de Garay
La Adela
Gaviotas
Montes de Oceá
Bahía Blanca
22
Chelford
Chimpay
Río Colorado
Anzoategui
Colonia Julia y Echarren
Río Colorado
Choele Choel
Lamarque
A
Pedro Luro
Río Negro
3
General Conessa
Villalonga
ahuel Niyeu
251
Teniente General Frias
2
23
Valcheta
Cubanea
San Antonio Oeste
3
Carmen des Patagones
Aguada Cecillo
Las Grutas
Vicealmirante E O'Connor
San Javier
Viedma
RIO NEGRO
1
Balneario El Cóndor
Arroyo los Berros
Arroyo de la Ventana
Sierra Grande
Golfo San Matías
B
Punta Norte
Golfo San José
Istmo Carlos Ameghino
Peninsula Valdés
Puerto Pirámides
Puerto Madryn
Golfo Nuevo
Punta Delgada
Dolavon
Gaiman
Trelew
Rawson
Río Chubut
Dique F Ameghino
Florentino Ameghino (Merayo)
C
Reserva Natural Punta Tombo
Uzcudún
3
Atlantic Ocean
N
2
40 km
40 miles
Camarones
Reserva Natural Cabo Dos Bahías
1
2
3

Driving distances

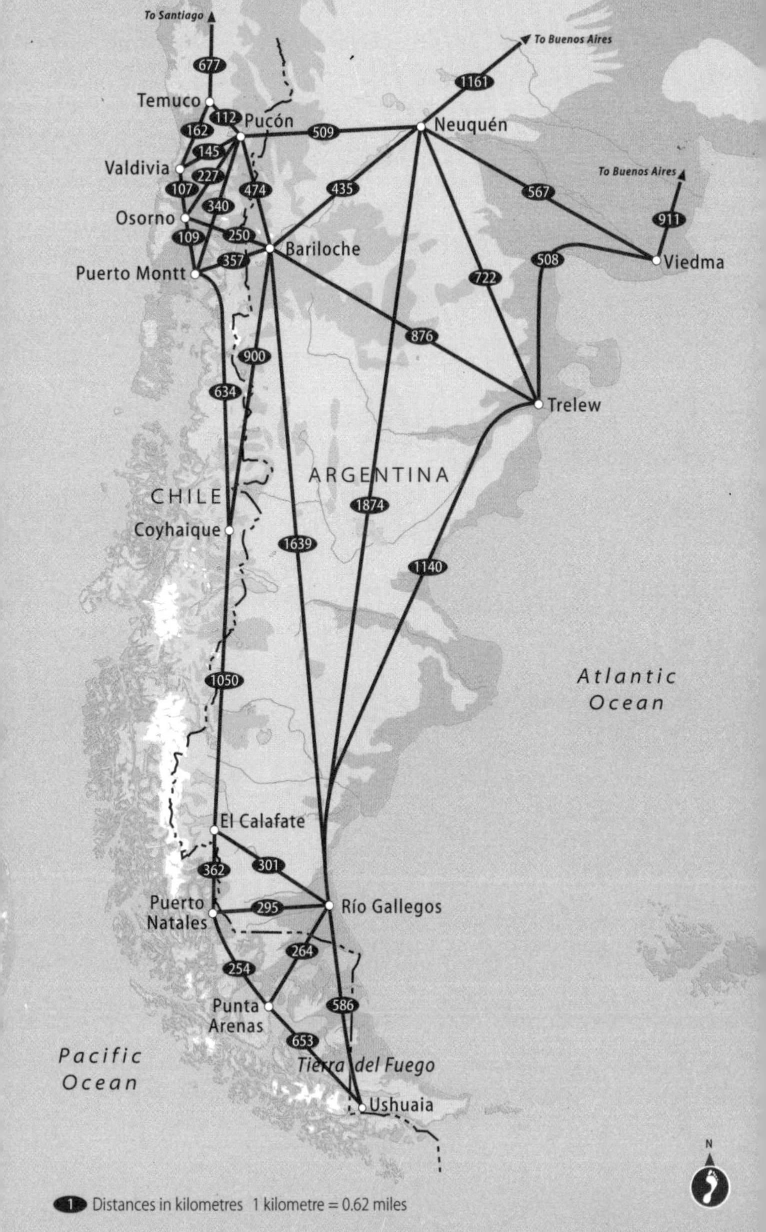

Distances in kilometres 1 kilometre = 0.62 miles

Index